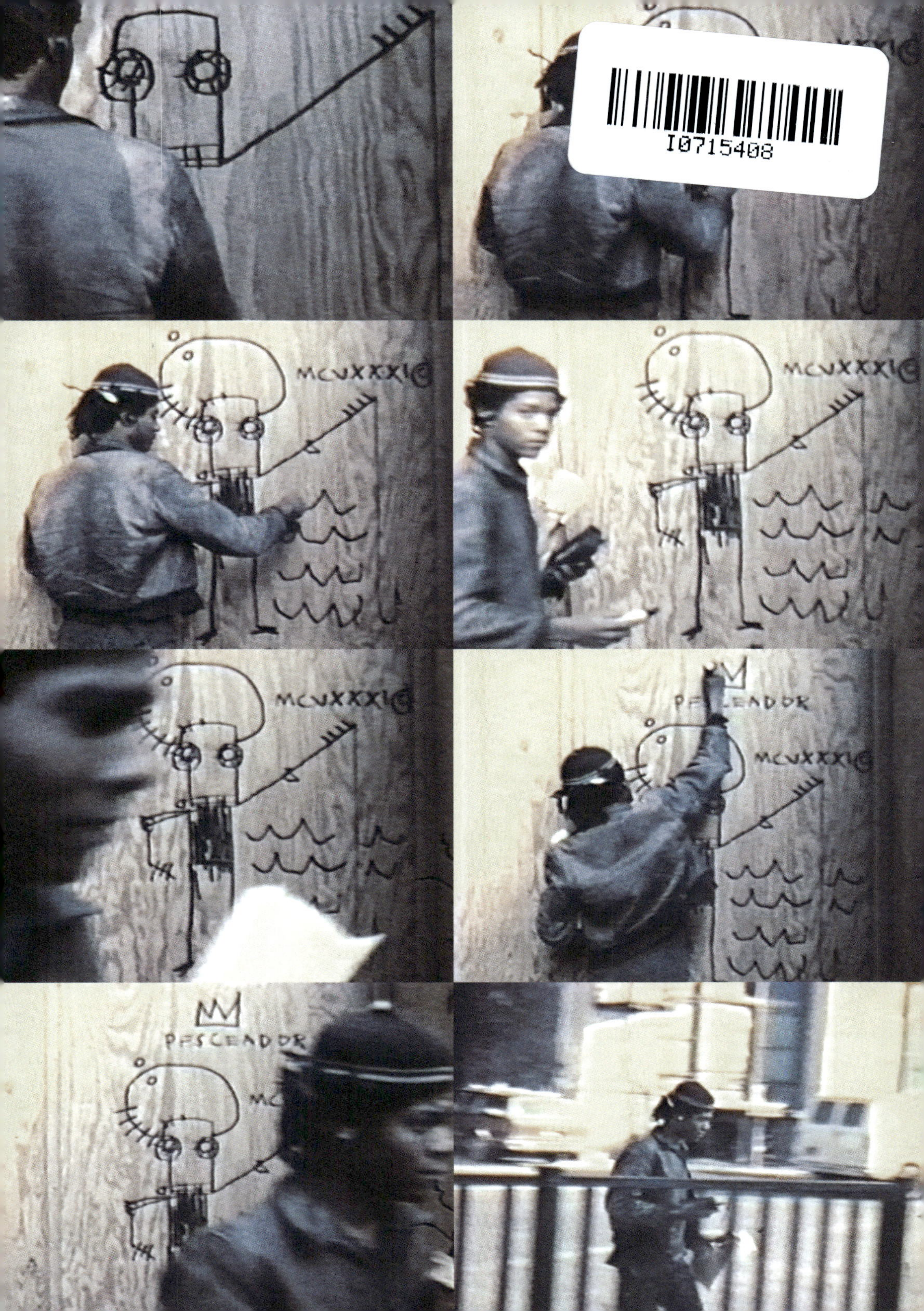

I0715408
MCVXXXI©
MCVXXXI©
MCVXXXI©
PESCEADOR
MCVXXXI©
PESCEADOR
MC

SAMO...
AS AN ALTER
NATIVE TO
BULLSHIT
FAKE HIPPY
WHACK
CHEEB....
SAM 7

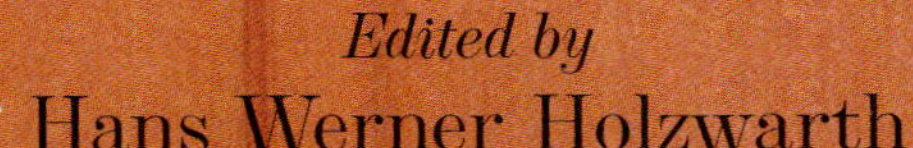

Jean-Michel BASQUIAT

and the Art of Storytelling

With an essay by
Eleanor Nairne

Directed and produced by
Benedikt Taschen

TASCHEN

Contents

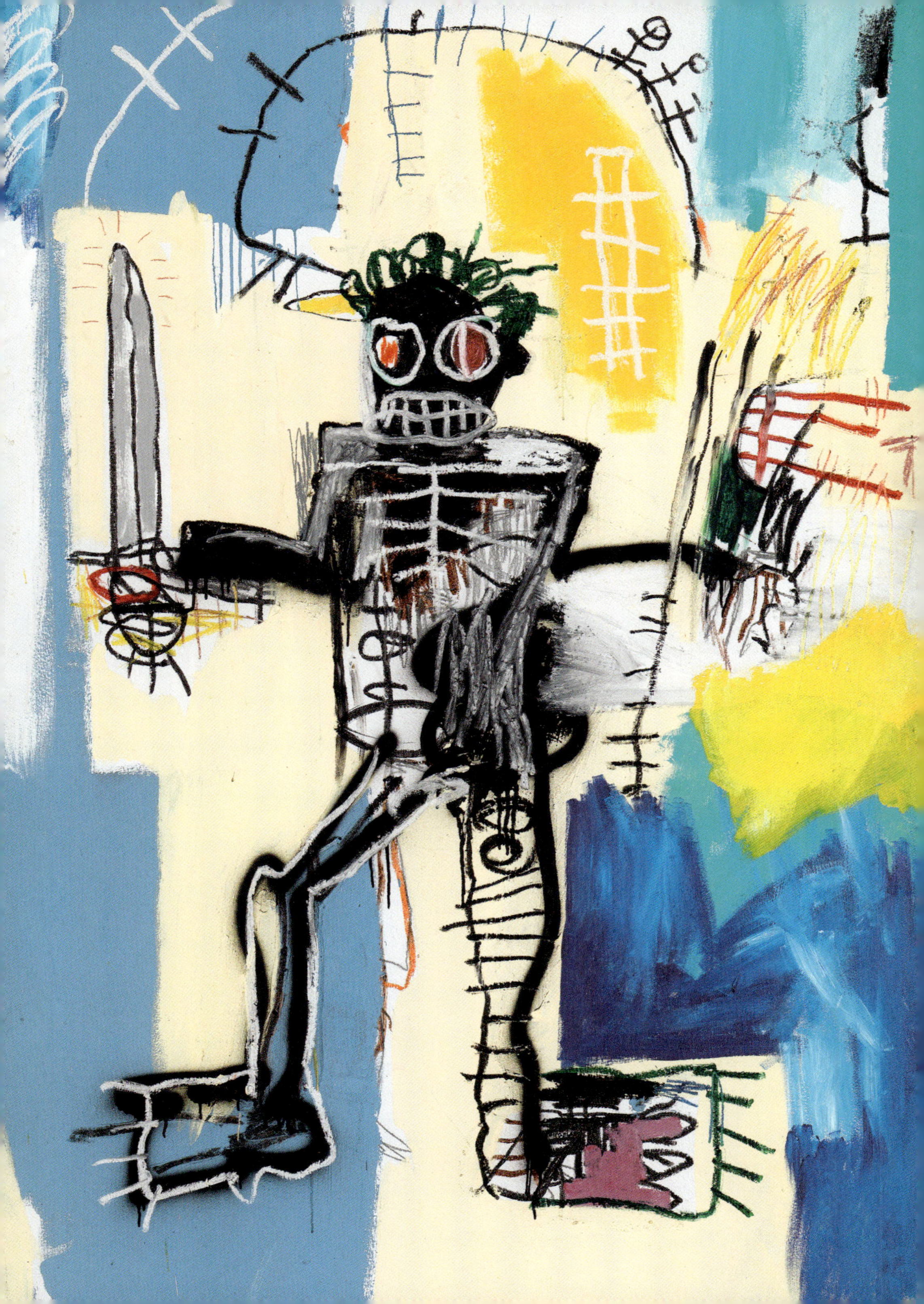

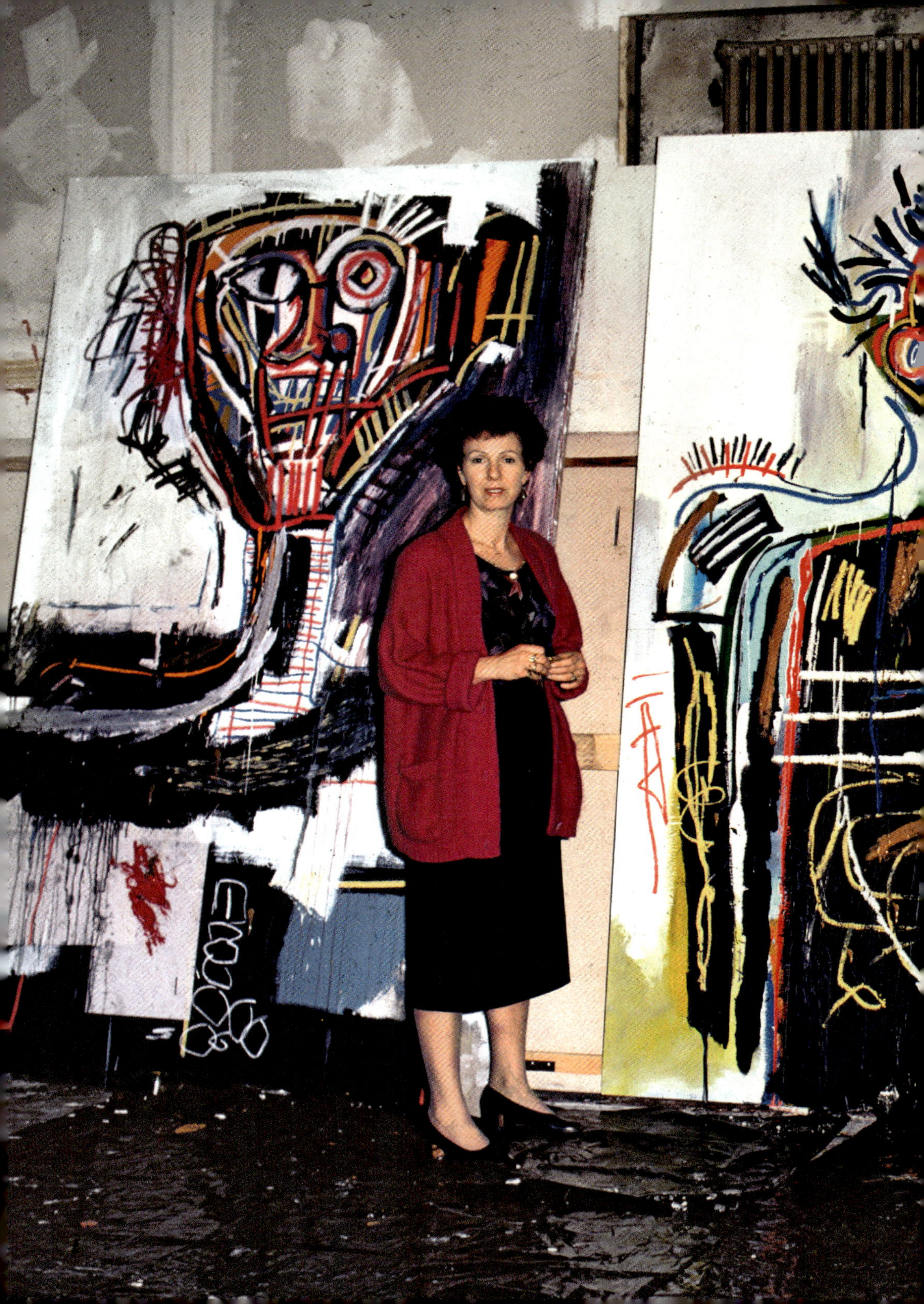

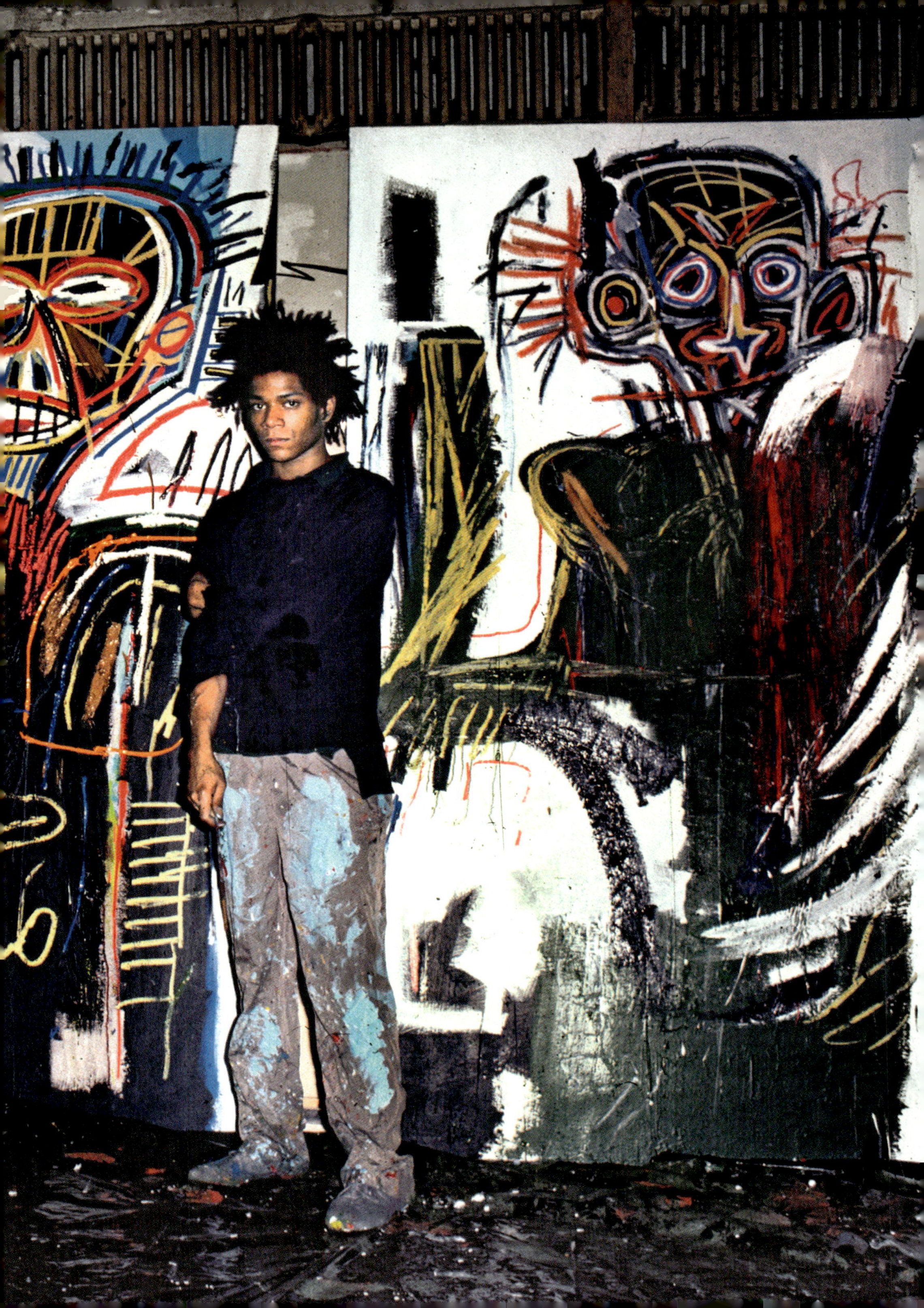

Introducing Jean-Michel Basquiat

Hans Werner Holzwarth

*"I don't think about art when I'm working.
I try to think about life."*
—JEAN-MICHEL BASQUIAT[1]

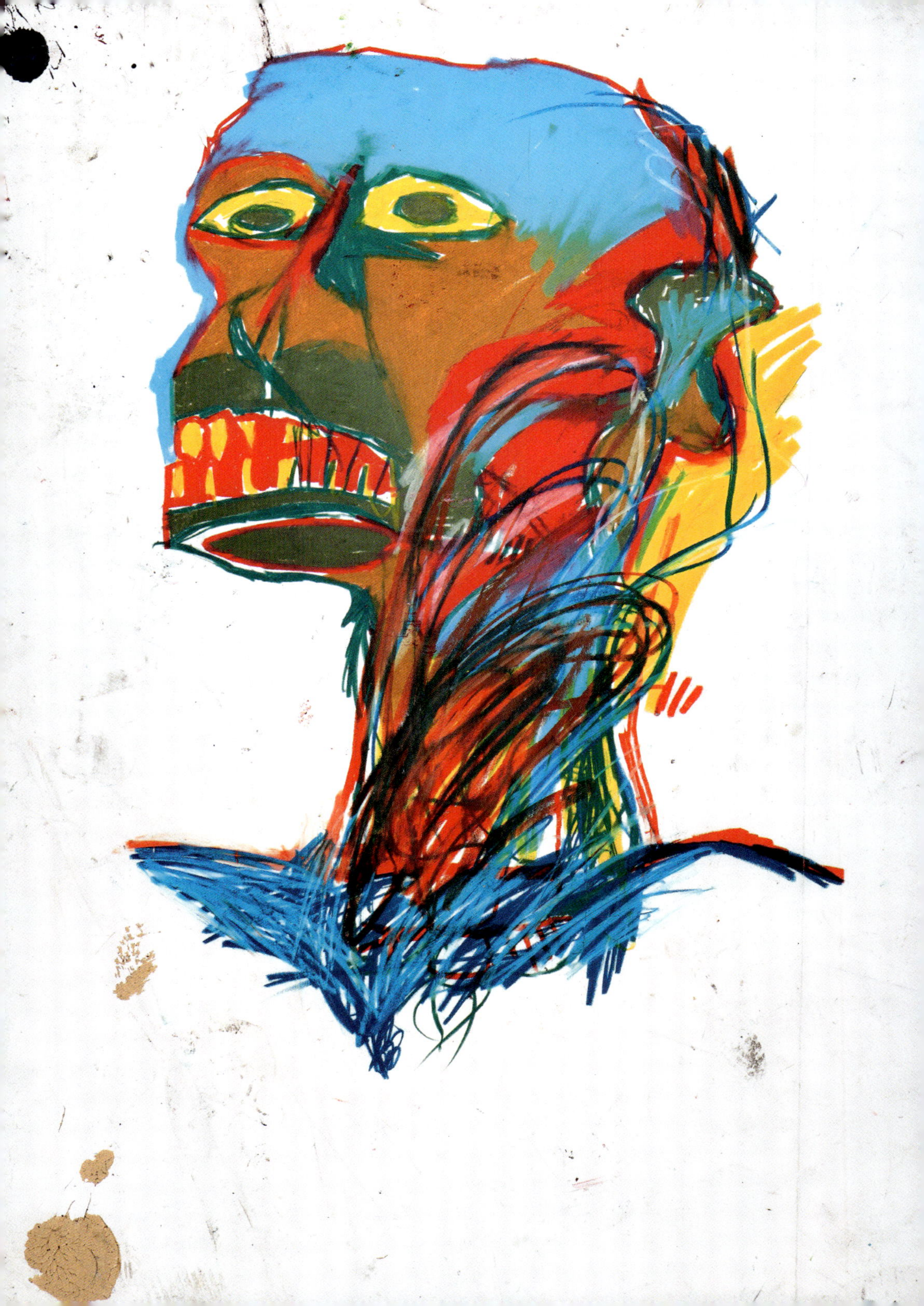

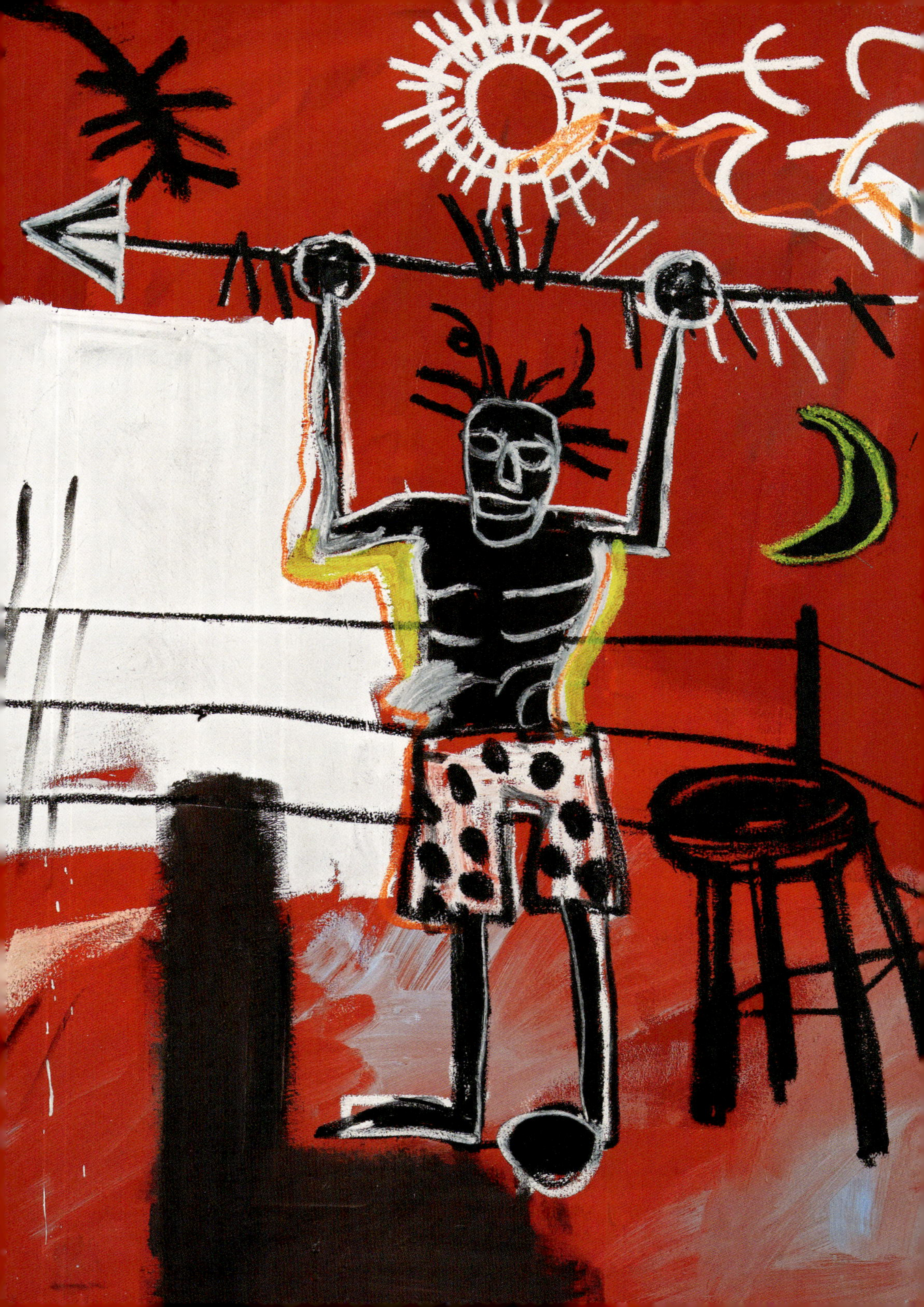

The Visual Metronome

The paintings of Jean-Michel Basquiat are full of life. His unruly oilstick line puts the same maximum amount of expression into a figure or the letters of a word. His every brushstroke has incredible energy and focus. The complete canvas bristles with youthful intensity all over, no matter if covered with complex constellations of words and figures, plastered with rows of photocopies, or smothered with thick overpaintings that let the full anecdotal detail of the ground shimmer through. White ground is marked by the painter's shoeprints, as he carelessly stepped on canvases while working them on the floor. The paintings carry very immediate traces of what was happening in the studio.

Often we encounter a figure at their center, a face-like mask, a skull covered by wiry brushstrokes like tendons, a shadowy outline of a head, or the full figure of a man occupying a kind of stage or boxing ring. Even if few of them are explicitly labeled as self portraits—see the *Self-Portrait as a Heel* (1982; p. 26), or a *Self-Portrait* (1982; pp. 220/221) on which the black outline appears like a hunter in a cave painting brandishing an arrow—they are like stand-ins for the artist (you can tell by the hair), arms lifted in a gesture between triumph and despair. Their anonymized features and battle-ready stances tell us they're at odds with the world we live in. And yet these figures have an inner life. They are as existential as Munch's *Scream.*

Basquiat painted quickly and directly, surrounding himself with sources for inspiration—he listened to music in the studio, especially to bebop and hip hop, worked with the TV running and books lying on the floor, from which he copied images, names, and incidents. Seemingly without filter, whatever grasped his attention found a way into his paintings. He even quite literally integrated the city when he used materials he found in the streets, doors and window frames to paint on, or, closer to home, the walls of a fridge (p. 101).

The city he lived in was downtown New York, which was going through a particularly precarious but creative period in the late 1970s and early 1980s. The whole city struggled to survive, but survival was easy, criminality was high but rents were cheap, so everybody with the inclination found it possible to exist as an artist. Basquiat was part of a scene that met at night spots like the Mudd Club or Club 57, his youthful posse mingling with established artists and showbiz celebrities. Inspired by the liberating DIY ethos of punk, the art was low-budget and boundary-crossing: self-organized exhibitions in off-spaces, independent films made on a shoestring budget, vaudeville-like performance events, and experimental music, something that Basquiat took part in when he played raw clarinet, guitar with a file, and prepared shopping cart in his band Gray.

The Ring, 1981
Acrylic and oilstick on canvas,
152.5 x 122 cm / 60 x 48 inches

Pages 6/7: Annina Nosei and Jean-Michel Basquiat at his studio in the basement of Nosei's Gallery, New York 1982.

Meanwhile, hip hop had broken into public consciousness, and Basquiat was friends with the avant-garde of the new rappers and graffiti artists such as Fab 5 Freddy and Rammellzee. Beside the street-smart sounds, hip hop offered another technique of incorporating the world into one's work: sampling. Basquiat's own favorite critic, Robert Farris Thompson, discussed his paintings in these terms, citing *Charles the First* (1982; p. 184) as an example: "The mnemonic and phonetic motors of the computer age, the keyboard instruments of instant retrieval, the letters, the signs, are used as another kind of brushstroke. This parallels hip hop, New York's musical revolution, at once funky and futuristic, in which certain rap recording studios have computer programmed the sounds of industrial noise, James Brown horn 'hits,' and other pulsations for instant playback on electric 'pianos.' Basquiat is not afraid of the hi-tech wolf. He sees enormous fun and potency. He sees ways of pulsing phonetic writing, literary allusion, and chromatic structure. The trick is having the beat, the visual metronome, to keep these different instruments going all at once."[2]

Because New York had been the world's art capital since the 1950s, this community-driven local scene found quick access to the big limelight. There was only a short way from the dance floor (where Basquiat practically lived for a time) to a globally distributed music video (Basquiat appeared in a cameo as DJ in the video to Blondie's "Rapture," which was on heavy MTV rotation from 1980 on). Success at an artist- organized group show could mean immediate entry into the rosters of blue-chip galleries worldwide. The painting of the time was about a new expressionism, a show of personality after the reign of conceptual art. The rising stars included Julian Schnabel, David Salle, Robert Longo, Francesco Clemente, and Basquiat's friend Keith Haring, who followed a similar career trajectory. From the older generation, it was Andy Warhol, not necessarily so much for his paintings—which despite themes from common life appeared cold and distant—but for his stardom, the way he combined art, party, and his persona into a instantly recognizable brand.

It seemed impossible that a black visual artist could achieve the same level of success. Yet while these pioneering days of the art market are often seen negatively as the start of a thoroughly commercialized era, they also created an intoxicating buzz. As Richard Marshall wrote: "Jean-Michel Basquiat first became famous for his art, then he became famous for being famous, then he became famous for being infamous."[3] Keith Haring described the same loop: "The hype of the art world of the early '80s became a constant blur. There was very little criticism that actually talked of the works themselves. Rather, the talk was about the circumstances surrounding the *success* of the work."[4] And yet the self-fulfilling hype and the unprecedented prices for contemporary art translated into very real opportunities for artists from outside any academic background. Basquiat summed up all the implications of this new, market-driven logic when he simply painted the words "5,000 Dollars" on a canvas of 1982 (p. 188), offering both a critique of the

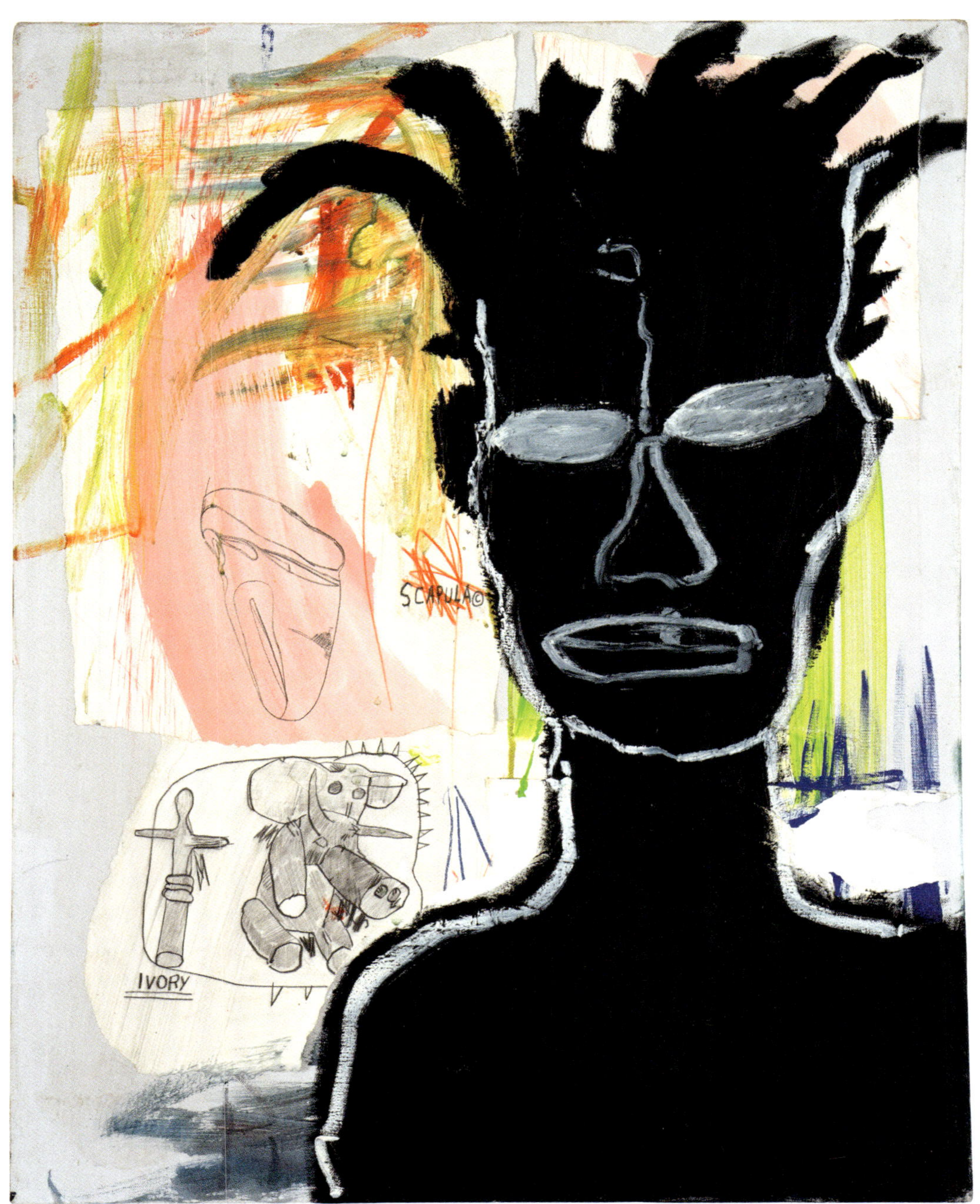

Untitled, 1984
Acrylic, oilstick, marker, graphite, and photocopy
collage on canvas, 76 x 61 cm / 30 x 24 inches

Page 9: **Untitled**, 1982
Oilstick on paper,
76 x 56 cm / 30 x 22 inches

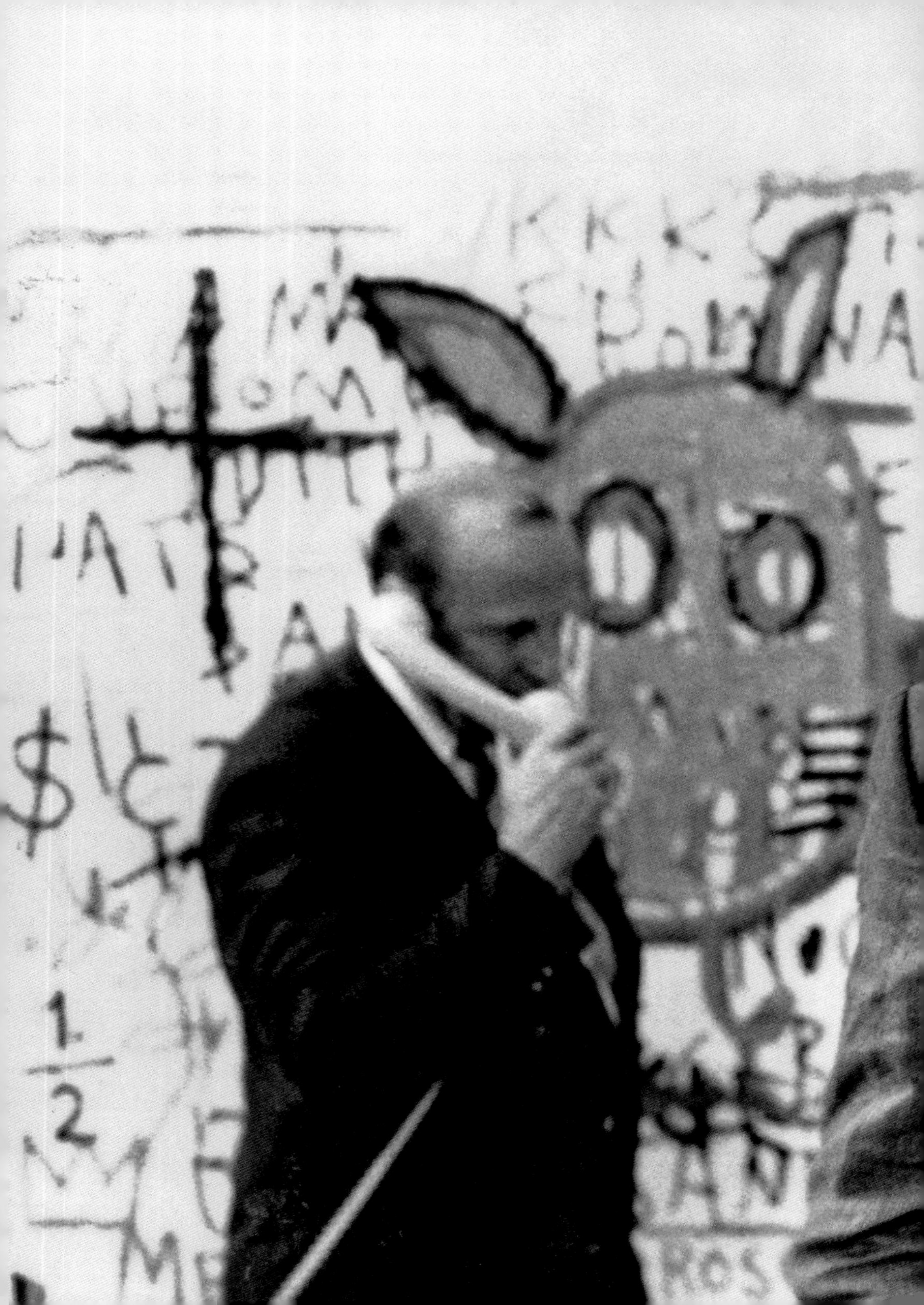

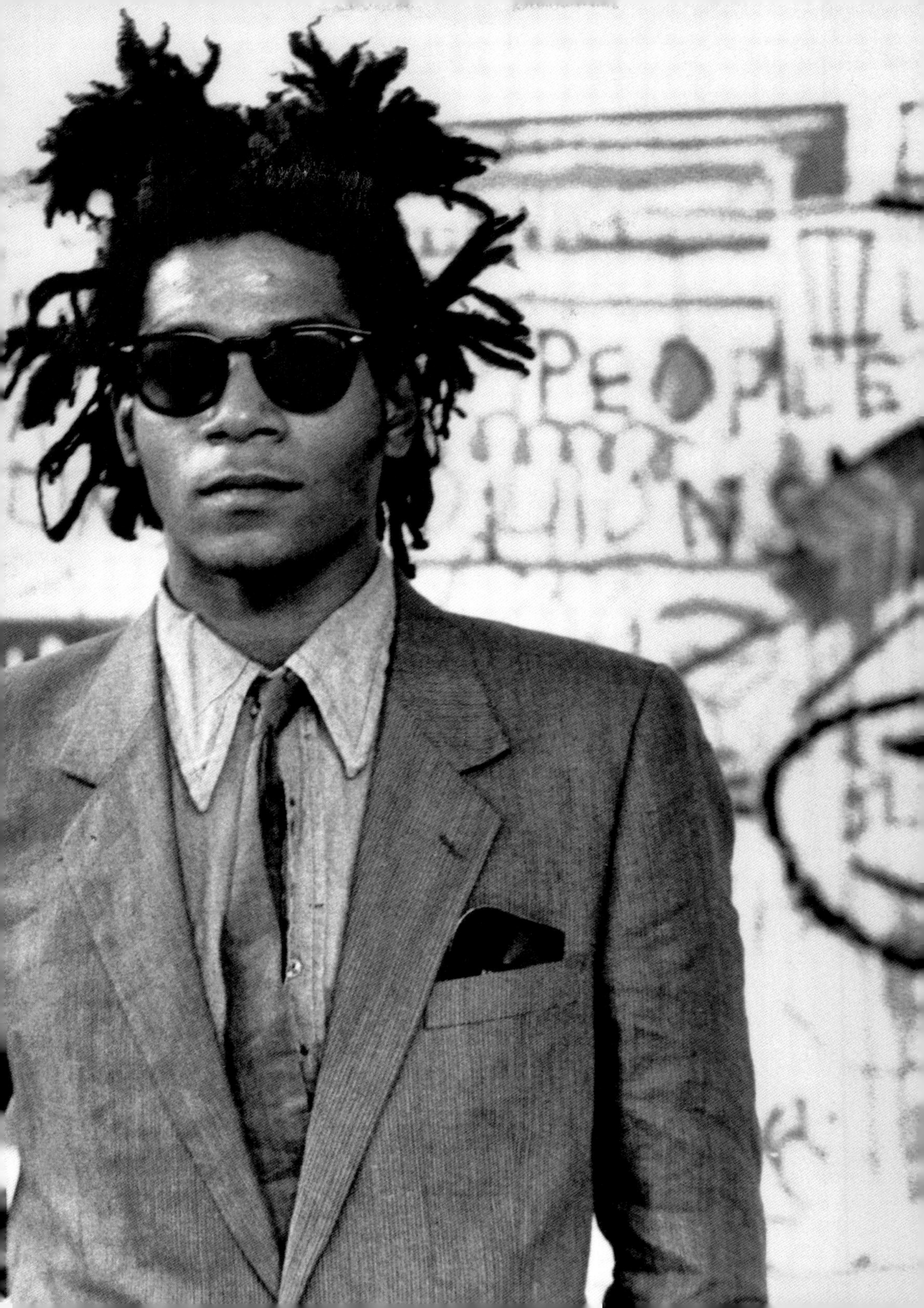
PEOPLE
DIONS

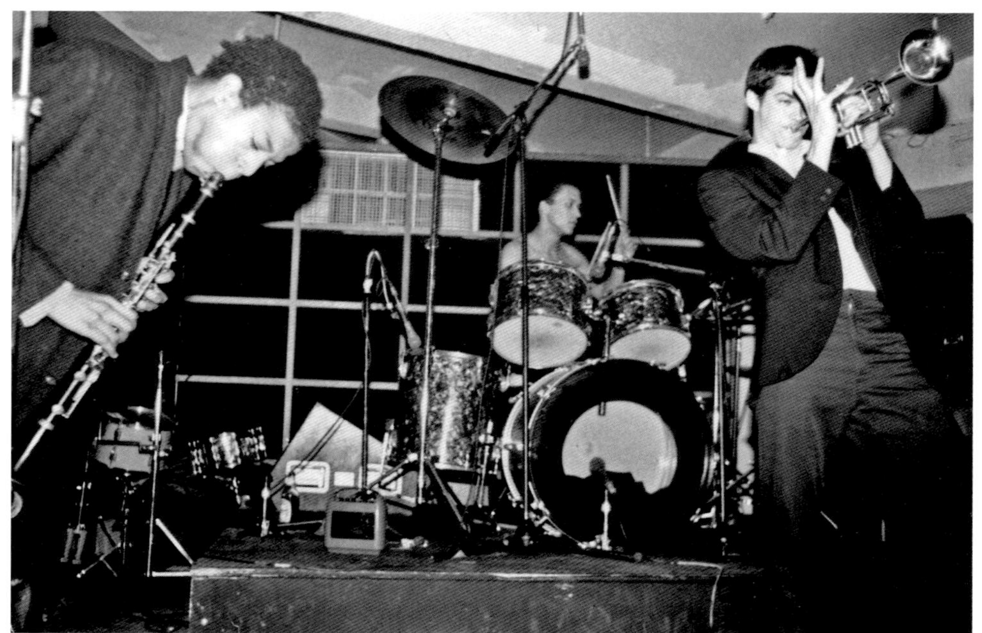

Gray at Hurrah's, New York 1979.
From left to right: Jean-Michel Basquiat, Michael
Holman, Shannon Dawson. Photo Nicholas Taylor

Pages 14/15: Bruno Bischofberger and Jean-Michel
Basquiat at Galerie Bruno Bischofberger, Zürich 1982.
Photo Beth Philipps

commodity status of the artwork and also a true miracle transformation of a few materials and gestures into an object of real value.

"Royalty, heroism, and the streets," Basquiat said when asked what his paintings were about.[5] Among the legends he painted, famous black athletes such as boxers Joe Louis or Cassius Clay, jazz musicians such as Charlie Parker and Miles Davis, as well as the graffiti writers in Basquiat's own day, culture was about legacy, about how they earned their crown and what they would be remembered for, achieving fame while still being true to the streets. Of course Basquiat had barely begun when he died so early—at the age of 27, when most artists are just coming into their own. Still, in his few years he left a legacy large enough for a complete lifetime.

A Legendary Life

Because of the youthful energy of Basquiat's paintings, his magnetic personality, and his early death, sometimes the work threatens to be overshadowed by the artist's legend. This is not due to posthumous hagiography or Julian Schnabel's star-studded biopic from 1996. Even during his life Basquiat often found himself seen as a celebrity more than as an artist: "It's a life that is documented and put out there, you know, you go to a restaurant and they write about it in *The Post* on page six."[6] Because he was black, he attracted certain stereotypes, so talk was about his upbringing in the ghettos (in reality his father was an accountant from Haiti, and his mother visited the museums with young Jean-Michel), or he was labeled a graffiti artist (which he rejected, since his graffiti had always been poetry and social commentary instead of more visually elaborate sprayed tags).

Then again, even Basquiat's true story reads like legend: here is an outcast who almost overnight becomes king among painters, but then has to pay the price—a story rich with instructive detail and peopled by a cast of colorful characters. It starts not with an anecdote of the child prodigy ("I was a really lousy artist as a kid," Basquiat says, "too abstract expressionist … really messy, I'd never win painting contests"[7]), but a severe accident: as a seven-year-old, he is run over by a car while playing in the street. Badly hurt, he is carried to the hospital, where his spleen has to be removed. His mother brings him a copy of *Gray's Anatomy* to teach him about his ailing body—and cars and street games would play a big role in Basquiat's early paintings, while body parts and their scientific names recur throughout his work, and he will name his band Gray.

Dropping in and out of high school, Basquiat leaves without a diploma, living in parks and on the sofas of friends, always finding a home in the clubs, where he cuts a conspicuous figure on the dance floor. With his friend Al Diaz he writes graffiti under the name of SAMO, placing their enigmatic sayings strategically in the gallery district: "SAMO© as an alternative 2 playing art with the 'radical chic' set on Daddy's $funds." He creates art postcards on a color photocopier and paints T-shirts, selling his wares on the streets. In one portentous meeting, he discovers Andy Warhol in a café and screws up the nerve to sell two postcards to him.

And then he plays himself as a legend before the fact, in *New York Beat*, a film scripted by Glenn O'Brien, who discovered the young artist's star potential after inviting him to his cable television show *TV Party*. In the film, Basquiat portrays an unknown artist adrift on the streets with no destination but enough charisma to win the good fairy's kiss in the end. He acts as a casual cicerone through the New York underground (unfortunately without Basquiat's true voice, since when the film is finally released in 2000 under the title *Downtown 81* the missing dialog track requires a new dub).

Basquiat's rise is meteoric: in his first group exhibition, the *Times Square Show* in 1980, he is immediately singled out by the critics as a promising talent; with his second big group exhibition, *New York/New Wave* at P.S.1 the following year, he already gains the interest of some of the world's leading gallerists such as Bruno Bischofberger and Annina Nosei. Within hardly more than a year of starting to paint his first real canvases, he already has found top representation and commands considerable prices.

Then, late in 1981, we have an emblematic scene: Basquiat in the basement studio of Nosei's gallery, churning out one large canvas after another for his growing customer base.

While for the moment this arrangement appears practical to all, still the idea makes the rounds of a black artist locked in a basement in order to paint, and bad feelings linger, also because Basquiat is disturbed by frequent unannounced visits from obtrusive buyers, and paintings seem to sell even before they are properly finished, meat for a market gone mad . . . or so the rumors suggest.

During the height of his success, in 1984, Basquiat changes to Mary Boone's gallery, at the time synonymous with the painting boom. And here suddenly the mood changes: critics start casting doubt, suspecting Basquiat of being a mere art world mascot, especially when he starts collaborating with Andy Warhol—the older artist is branded as a has-been using a young star to regain some stature, and Basquiat as an upstart using the older artist's fame for his own advancement. It goes completely unnoticed that together they create a body of work whose vibrant heterogeneity appears more relevant than ever three decades on.

While Basquiat suffers from the unwanted attentions of the press, his lifestyle is fabulous, money is spent wildly or given to those in need, though still his blackness means that taxis won't stop for him ("black taxi drivers drive past me too," he stresses[8]). And yet it is a difficult time, and Basquiat has an almost paranoiac distrust that people might use him, make money from him, that impecunious friends will sell the paintings which he has given to them as gifts.

After those difficult years with few exhibitions in New York, his last show in 1988 is an artistic and critical comeback, showing a new, more painterly approach, but also more darkly incisive themes that seem to presage his early death: especially *Riding with Death* (pp. 492/493), a black figure riding a skeleton made up of just a few telling bones. And indeed, at the tragically young age of 27, Basquiat dies of an overdose, like too many other legends of the pop age. In life, finding a balance proved difficult for Basquiat, the first black artist to conquer the white cube to become a true star. In his paintings, on the other hand, the works that make his legacy, the balancing act between the "High" tradition of Western art and the supposed "Low" of the everyday culture of a black experience, works out perfectly.

The Work

In his catalog essay for the first big Basquiat retrospective at the Whitney Museum four years after the artist's death, curator Richard Marshall divides the artist's oeuvre into three broad phases. The first lasted from 1980 to late 1982 and was characterized by "painterly gestures on canvases, most often depicting skeletal figures and masklike faces that signal his obsession with mortality, and imagery derived from his street existence, such as automobiles, buildings, police, children's sidewalk games, and graffiti."[9] This work group is anything but stable, though; Basquiat's stylistic and thematic development in the early years was incredibly rapid.

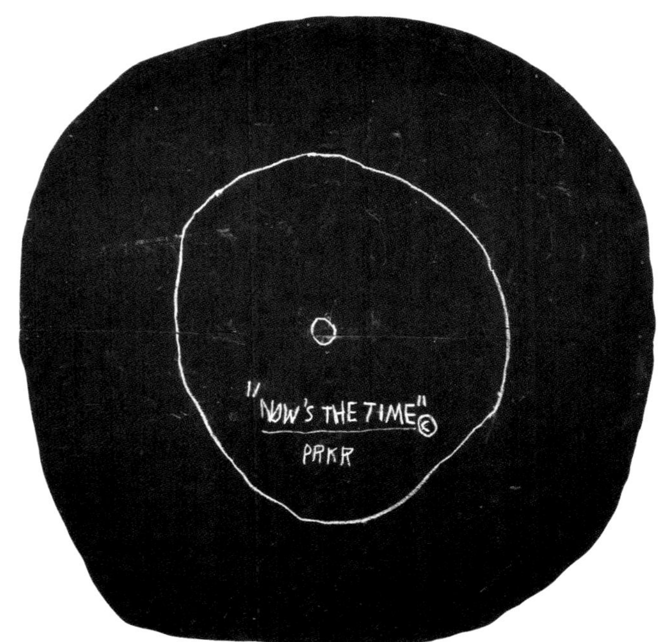

Now's the Time, 1985
Acrylic and oilstick on wood,
diameter: 235 cm / 92 ¹/₂ inches

Pages 20/21: **Acque Pericolose
(Poison Oasis)**, 1981
Acrylic, oilstick, and spray paint
on canvas, 167.5 x 244 cm /
66 x 96 inches

The first larger paintings take the rough simple message of graffiti from the streets to the canvas. The motifs are easily readable: heads *en face*, cars or airplanes in profile, a few outlines of houses forming a city block, small abstract frames within the larger frame of the picture, text fragments and lines from his SAMO poems ("Jimmy Best on his back to the suckerpunch of his childhood files") or single letters. Some canvases are like pieces of notepaper blown up to painting dimensions. Usually one or two colors dominate a painting, holding together a wealth of playful detail.

Then, within a very short time, Basquiat developed much of what would occupy him in greater depth during his later oeuvre: constellations of words, names of athletes and jazz musicians, cartoonish figures, masklike faces, backgrounds made from stacked color photocopies that he then overpainted, polyptych-like compositions. Basquiat's line is growing both more nervous and more precise, energetic but struggling against an unseen resistance, or hesitating and thoughtful in paintings that seem extensions of private thoughts from his notebooks.

Basquiat's middle period lasted from late 1982 to 1985. Here he often painted larger compositions made from several canvases or panels with interrelating themes. The amount of information on these works grows much larger, which brings them closer to contemporary media reality. The words are sometimes organized in lists, and some of them are crossed out, which visually puts them on a background level, but at the same

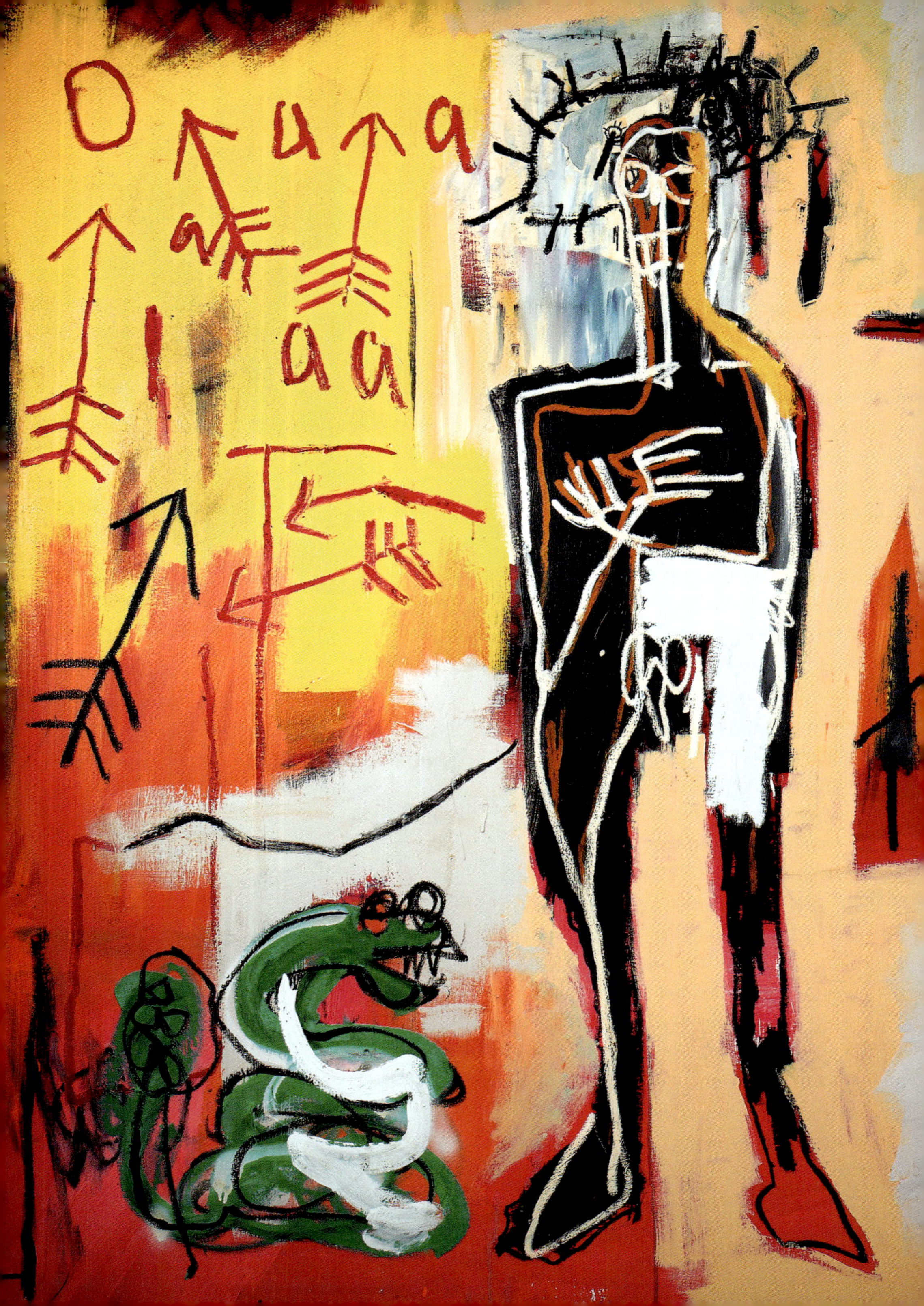

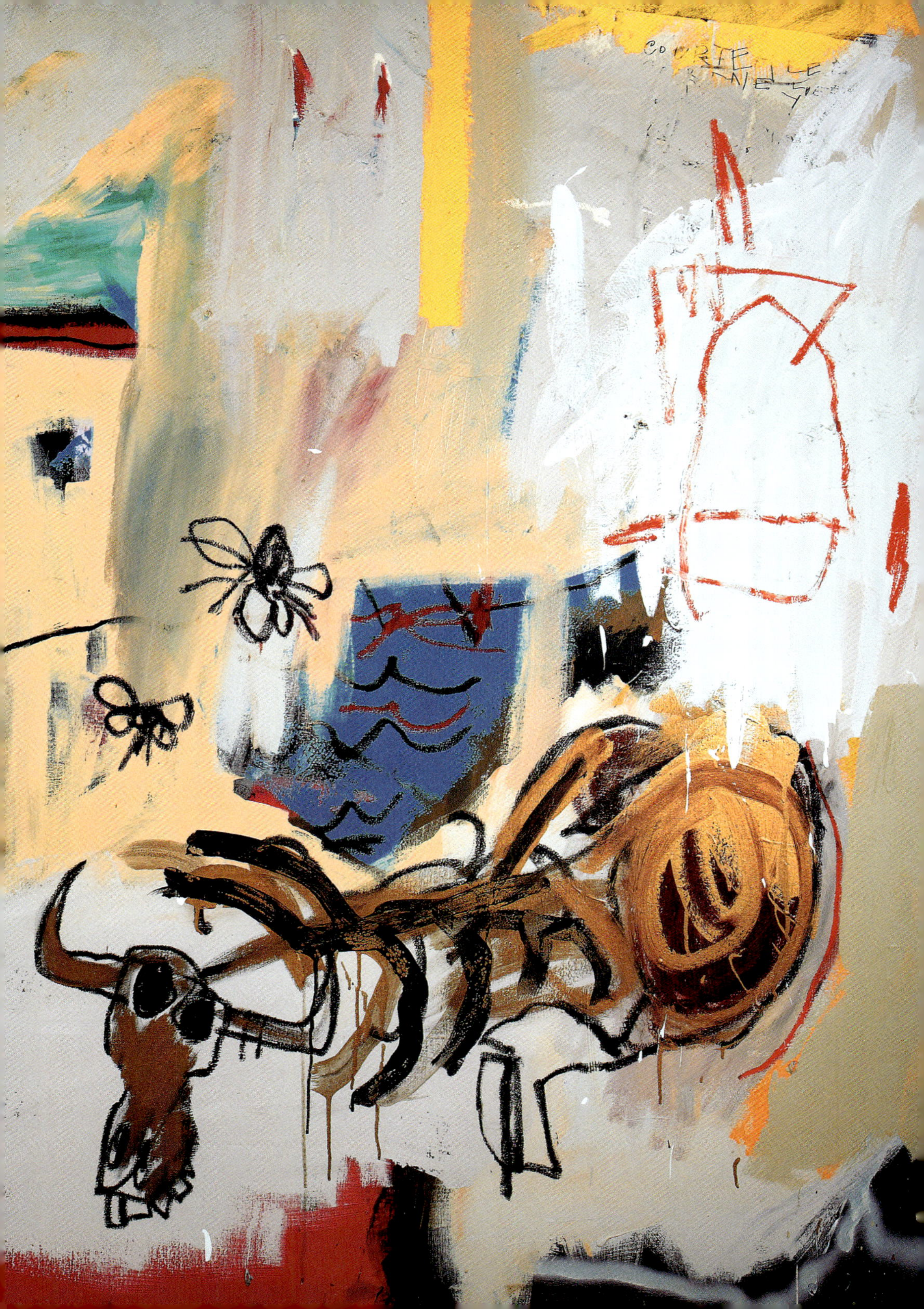

COURTE
CORNELLE
Y

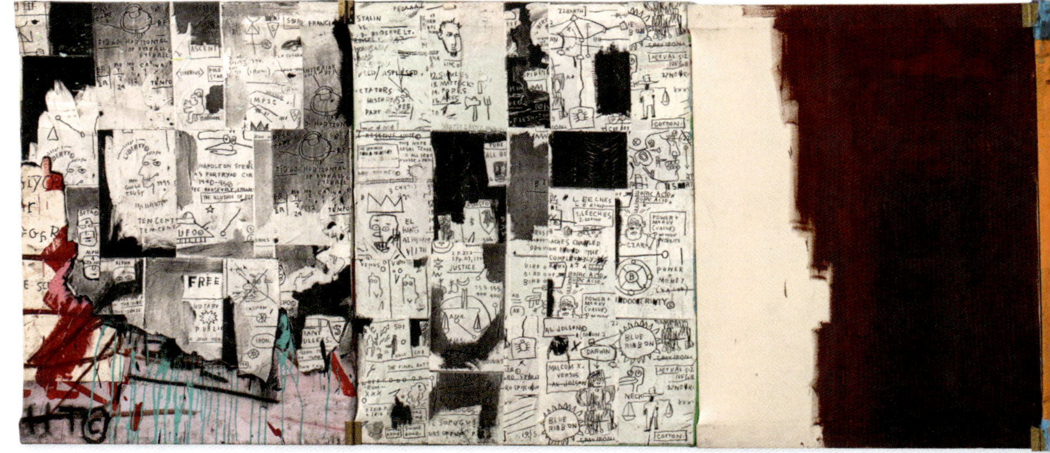

time enhances their weight, as the artist explains: "I cross out words so that you will see them more; the fact that they are obscured makes you want to read them."[10] The gesture is one of open thinking, second-guessing and discarding some of the facts. At the same time, Basquiat's writing is like texture, he uses words as "brushstrokes,"[11] as he himself said. The word becomes a motif, interacting with figures, marks, and pictograms on an equal footing.

The same strategy of crossing-out or erasing also increasingly guides Basquiat's painting, when he applies thick overpaintings that leave several earlier layers barely visible like fragments of a palimpsest—"most of the paintings have one or two paintings under them," Basquiat reveals. "I'm worried that in the future, parts might fall off and some of the heads underneath might show through."[12]

The rawness of technical means is another remarkable aspect of these works, especially in canvases where the stretcher seems so roughly put together that the laths are exposed at the corners. Of course, in reality "everything is well stretched even though it looks like it may not be," as Basquiat insisted.[13] It is a calculated aesthetic that embodies a certain cool and a street credibility which cannot be threatened by white gallery walls . . . as well as an ironic dig at the idea of a primitivist simplicity that viewers might expect from an African-American artist.

Thematically, the black experience comes to the fore: "I use the 'black' as the protagonist because I am black, and that's why I use it as the main character in all the paintings," Basquiat said.[14] Apart from a few explicitly political paintings, the approach is one of cultural identification: we find the names of heroes from ancient history and jazz greats, references to cartoon figures and classic works of art, scientific classifications and social

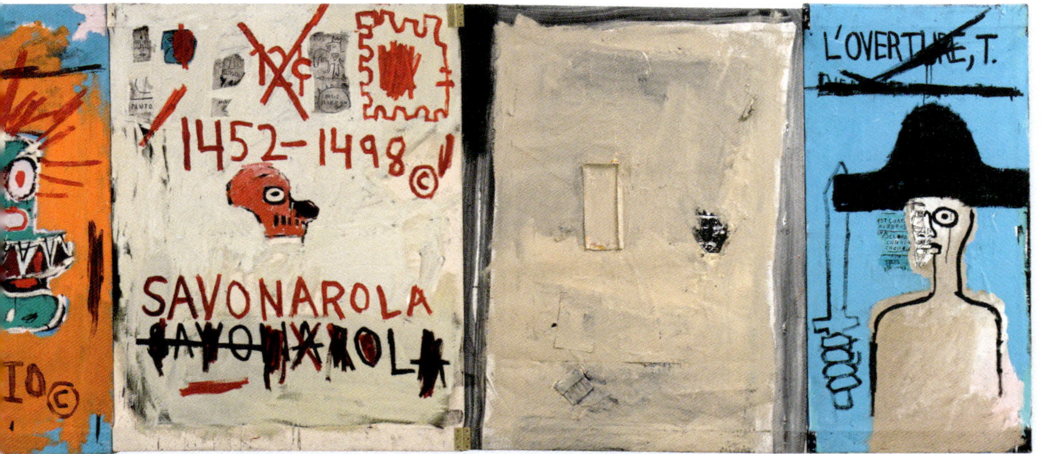

conditions. Dry facts are noted down like a pupil copying words from a blackboard, but in that process a simple list of names from ancient history comes to offer both a choice of heroic role models, and a questioning of classical education, especially its use for the black protagonist of the paintings.

In the midst of this second phase, in late 1983, Basquiat embarked on his collaboration with Andy Warhol. It proved a formative experience for the older artist as well, as Basquiat reported: "I was the one who helped Andy Warhol paint! It had been twenty years since he'd touched a brush."[15] At the same time, Basquiat learned from the pop art giant about color as decor, about the aura of the painting surface, the motif as icon—and this new, more painterly understanding would become noticeable especially in Basquiat's last years.

This last phase (again, following Marshall's timeline) began around 1986. Here the colors have become much stronger, single marks combine into an allover surface, and the surface becomes more alive: overpaintings often blanket the previous complexity under layers of paint reminiscent of colorfield painting. Then again there are other, very sparse works, with signs repeating more insistently than ever, stacked in rows like a reference to minimalist art. And in this moment of an exciting meeting of new and old elements in Basquiat's art, which offered so many possible directions and syntheses, the work's development comes to a sudden halt with the death of the artist.

A Cultural Memory

Basquiat's work draws a more or less fixed set of comparisons to earlier modernists: Jean Dubuffet is cited for the supposed primitivism, Pablo Picasso for the use of African masks and the endless ease of invention, Cy Twombly for the use of words. Basquiat's own canon of immediate forebears consisted of Twombly, Robert Rauschenberg, Franz Kline, Jasper Johns, Andy Warhol, as well as the Europeans Francesco Clemente, Enzo Cucchi, and A.R. Penck. He saw himself as part of the great Western painting tradition, going back to the old masters, especially Leonardo, and accordingly he deemed the gallery walls as the best setting for his works: "I think I like seeing them in museums more than anything else."[16] Of course, a clean white cube also emphasizes the subversiveness of Basquiat's raw, makeshift aesthetic like nothing else.

Meanwhile the black protagonist of Basquiat's paintings is always searching for an own identity: "I'm an artist who has been influenced by his New York environment," Basquiat said. "But I have a cultural memory. I don't need to look for it; it exists. It's over there, in Africa."[17] In many of his works, Basquiat engaged with black themes and culture. When we look at his drawing *Undiscovered Genius* (1982–1983; pp. 264/265), we find a slave ship along the Statue of Liberty and a blues musician holding his guitar as if waiting for some white record producer to unearth him and release his work into public existence, much as a gallerist does for the artist (the ironies run deep: many blues musicians of the 1920s saw themselves as cutting-edge artists but were sold as "authentic" race music to a white market). And especially after Basquiat had encountered the Africanist Robert Farris Thompson and his book *Flash of the Spirit* (1983), Africa itself moved into the focus, with direct quotes from tribal art and mythologies.

While Basquiat was sometimes described as a primitivist artist—or even as a "primal expressionist," which made him snap back, "like an ape?"[18]—comparisons to the artistic strategies of early modernism miss the mark: Picasso appropriated African tribal masks looking for purer forms, not for his cultural roots. Instead the raw look of Basquiat's figures serves an exploration of black status in contemporary society, as the feminist critic bell hooks pointed out: "The 'ugliness' conveyed in Basquiat's paintings is not solely the horror of colonizing whiteness; it is the tragedy of black complicity and betrayal. Works such as *Irony of Negro Policeman* (1981; p. 59) document this stance. The images are nakedly violent. They speak of dread, of terror, of being torn apart, ravished. Commodified, appropriated, made to 'serve' the interests of white masters, the black body as Basquiat shows it is incomplete, not fulfilled, never a full image. And even when he is 'calling out' the work of black stars—sports figures, entertainers—there is still the portrayal of incompleteness."[19]

That incompleteness echoes Basquiat's own status, for while his genius was discovered immediately, he still was never fully accepted, which puzzled the black cultural critic Greg Tate at the time of the Whitney retrospective in 1992: "Why do some people think Basquiat was a genius and others think he's a fraud? Why are major museums in Chicago, Los Angeles, and Washington, D.C., opposed to picking up the Whitney's Basquiat retrospective for a tour? If the criterion for entering the modern painting pantheon is an

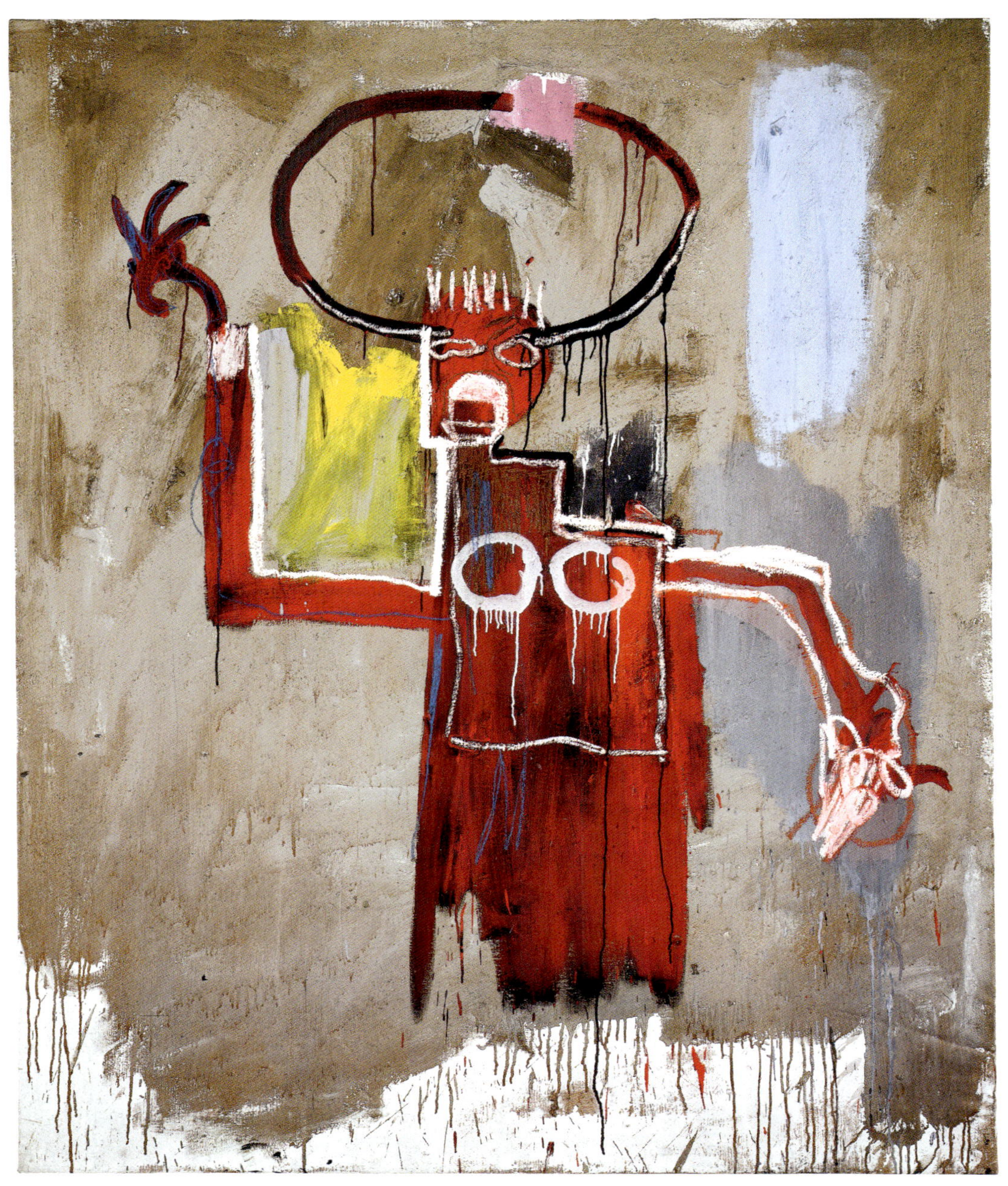

Untitled, 1981
Acrylic and oilstick on canvas,
183 x 152.5 cm / 72 x 60 inches

Pages 22/23: **Toussaint l'Overture versus Savonarola**, 1983
Acrylic, oilstick, and photocopy collage on canvas,
polyptych: 122 x 584 cm / 48 x 230 inches

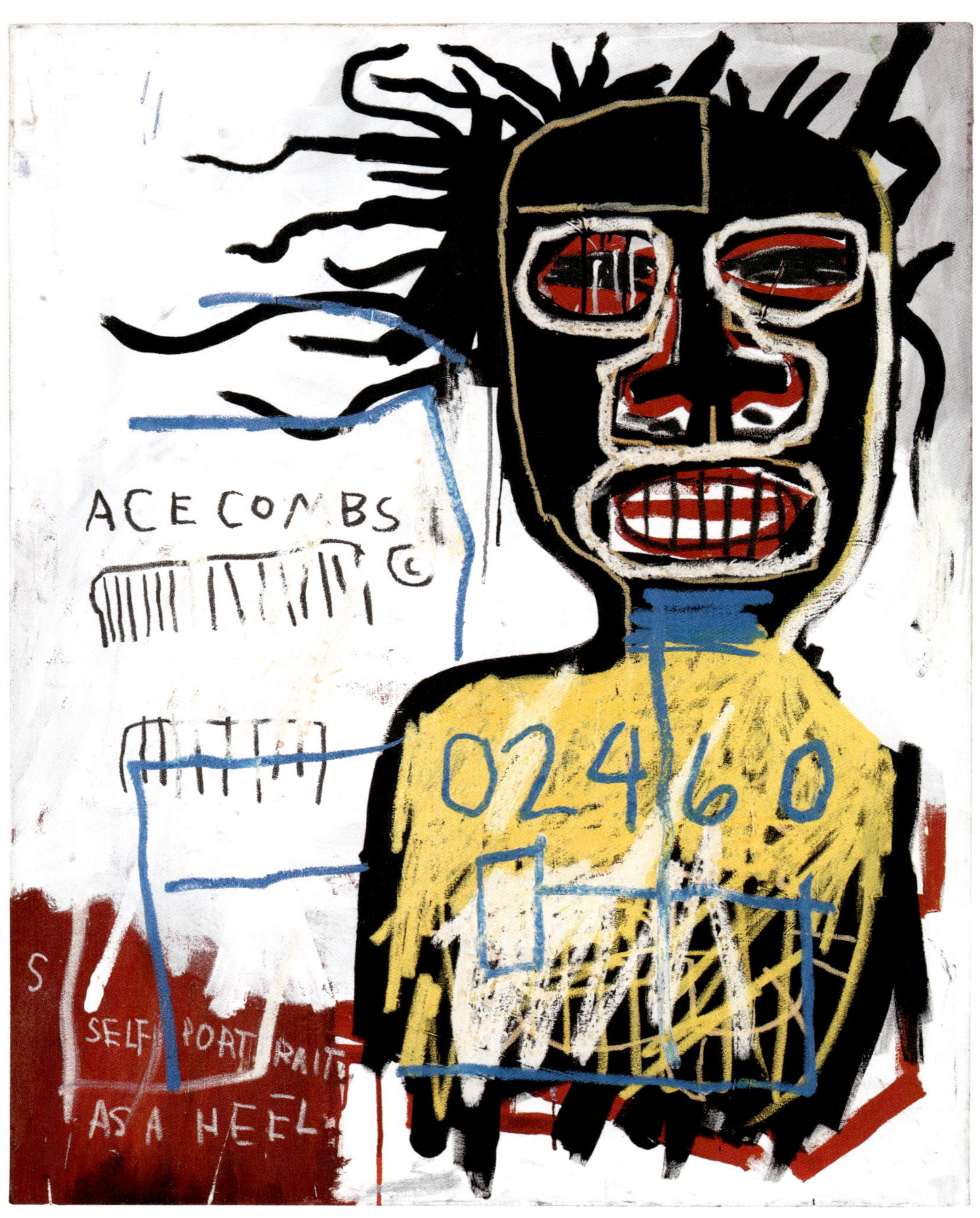

Self-Portrait as a Heel, 1982
Acrylic and oilstick on canvas,
127 x 101.5 cm / 50 x 40 inches

Pages 28/29: **Gravestone**, 1987
Acrylic and oil on wood panel,
139.5 x 175 x 56 cm / 55 x 69 x 22 inches

original voice, painterly sophistication, skills and ideas, then Basquiat more than made the grade."[20]

Part of the answer was a latent racism, probably best exemplified in Robert Hughes' notorious postmortem, "Requiem for a Featherweight," which explained the artist's meteoric rise by the fact that he was black and "the otherwise monochrome Late American Art Industry felt a need to refresh itself with a touch of the 'primitive.'"[21] More generally, Tate diagnoses a fundamental misreading if we understand the work in purely art-historical terms and ignore the cultural background of a generation "born into a world of monster movies and science fiction, comic books and cultural nationalism, parliament-funkadelic, hip hop, and punk rock. And if you're a young black person you're constantly trying to square the futurism of America with the barbarism of the place. So we live in a multiplicity of imaginative realms, the world of the technocrat and the world of the dixiecrat, savage Africa and Africa as paradise lost. We live in a world of signs and ciphers we manipulate to perform symbolic magic of our own devise. We ironically respond to language as a tool of oppression by disempowering it with crazed black wit."[22]

Telling Stories

Since then, a quarter of a century has gone, and we live in a slow-burning perpetuation of the 1980s art boom and its values. When we look at Basquiat's paintings now, they have lost none of their startling freshness and energy, which explains why they have stood the test of time (along with the huge prices they fetch at auction). More than that, Basquiat's work seems to embody the excitement of that formative era like no other; it has become synonymous with 1980s New York. This function of art was recognized by Basquiat when he said: "If I see a painting from the Middle Ages, I can see the life, I can see how people were … like seeing a sculpture from Africa, I can see the tribe, I can see the life around it … Even with things that aren't so obvious, like the abstract expressionist painters … you know it looks like New York in the '50s … they seem to be true historical documents you know, that I can get more from them than reading and other things."[23]

We have seen that Basquiat thought in terms of storytelling when he placed the black protagonist at the center of his work. Of course, he does not tell a straight yarn. In her essay for this book, Eleanor Nairne describes Basquiat's method: "He populated his work with reference points, which invite the viewer to seek out constellations of meaning. Sometimes, he would sample from his everyday environment … but he would also work from the Bible, literature, poetry, and ancient myths and he never shied away from substantial, often existential, subject matter. From his earliest experiments writing conceptual graffiti to some of his most celebrated multi-panel paintings, Basquiat understood how to create compelling visual narratives."[24] Nairne then details the development of the artist's vocabulary and shows us how to dig into his iconography and his storytelling techniques.

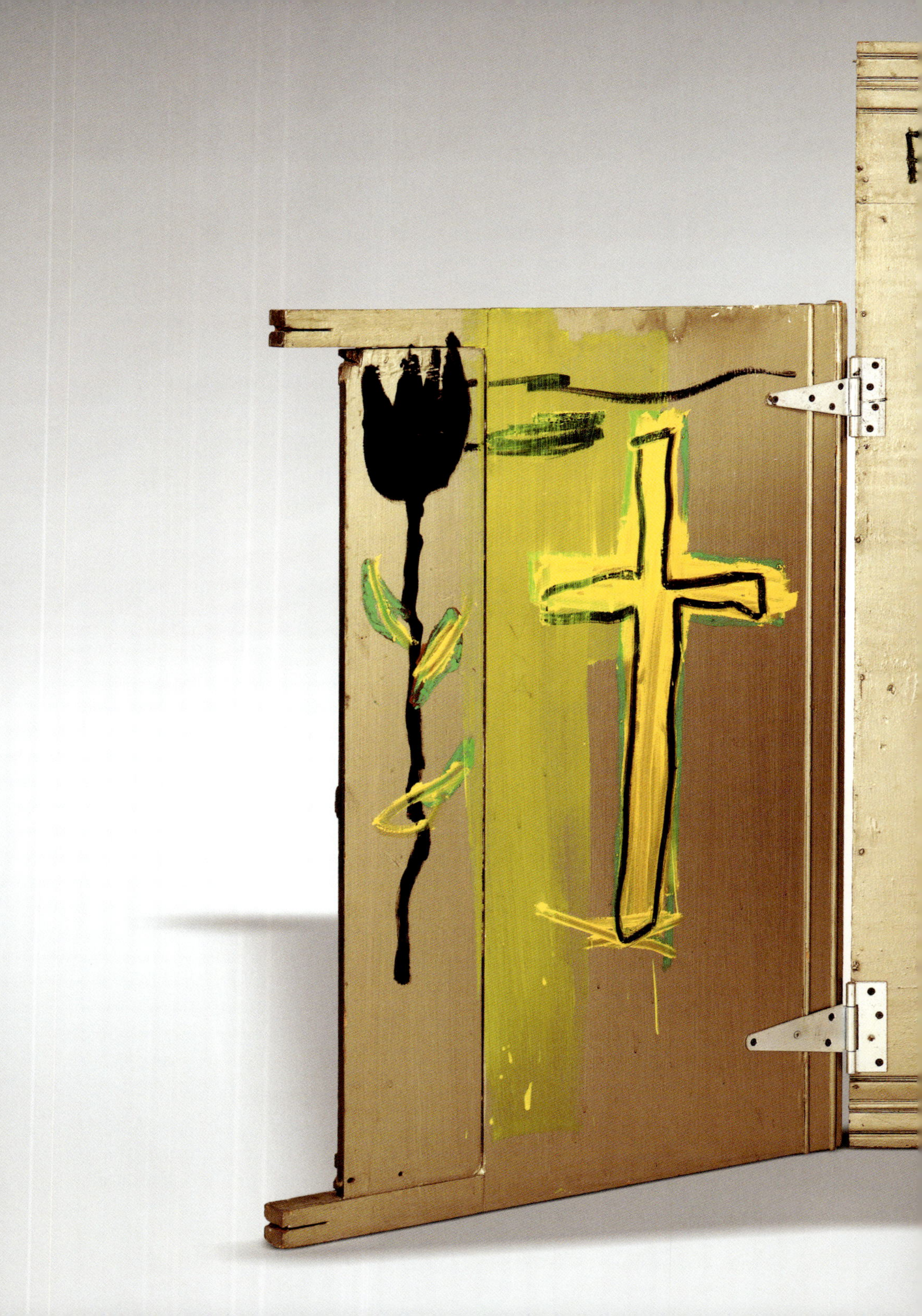

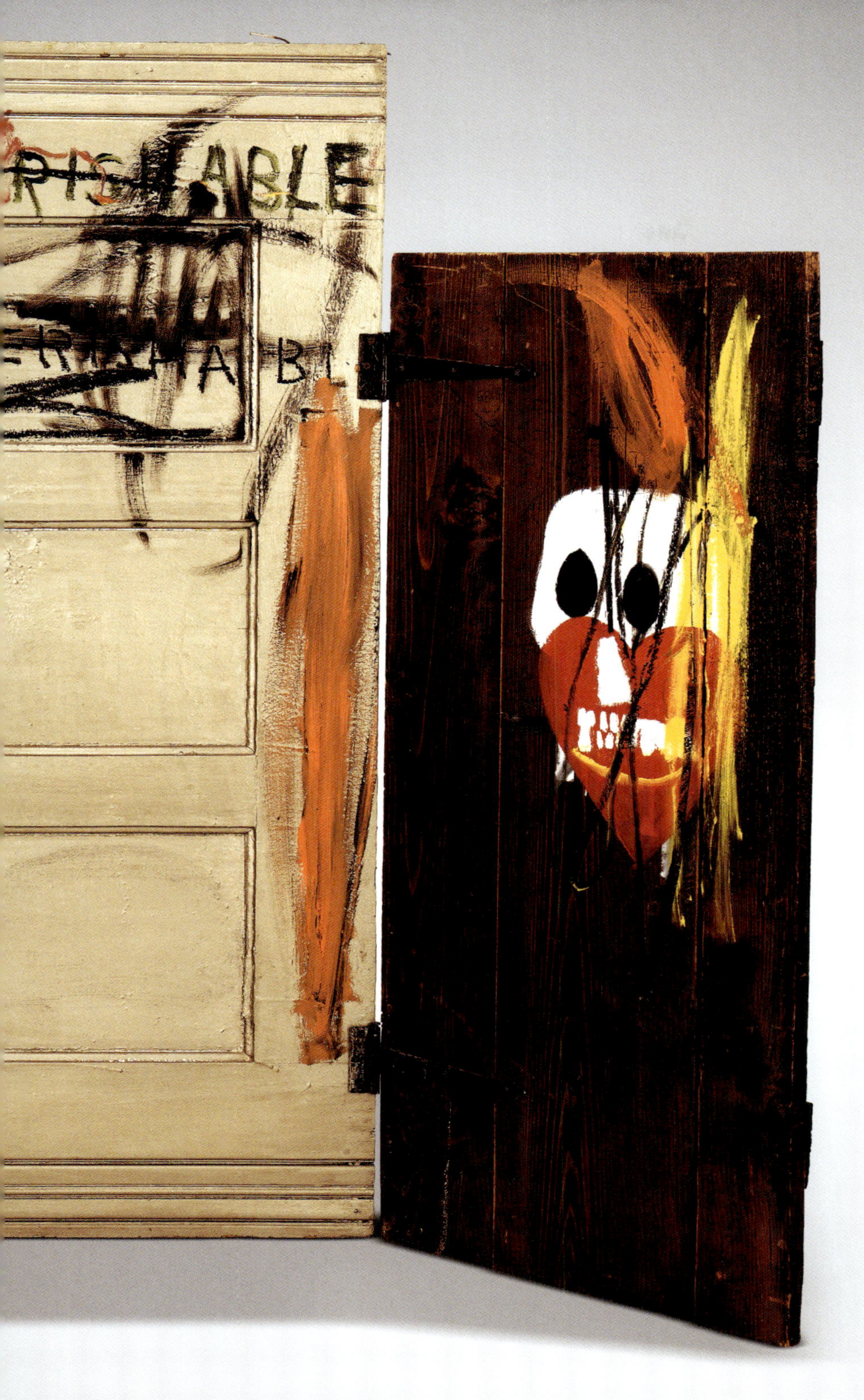
RISHABLE
RISHABL

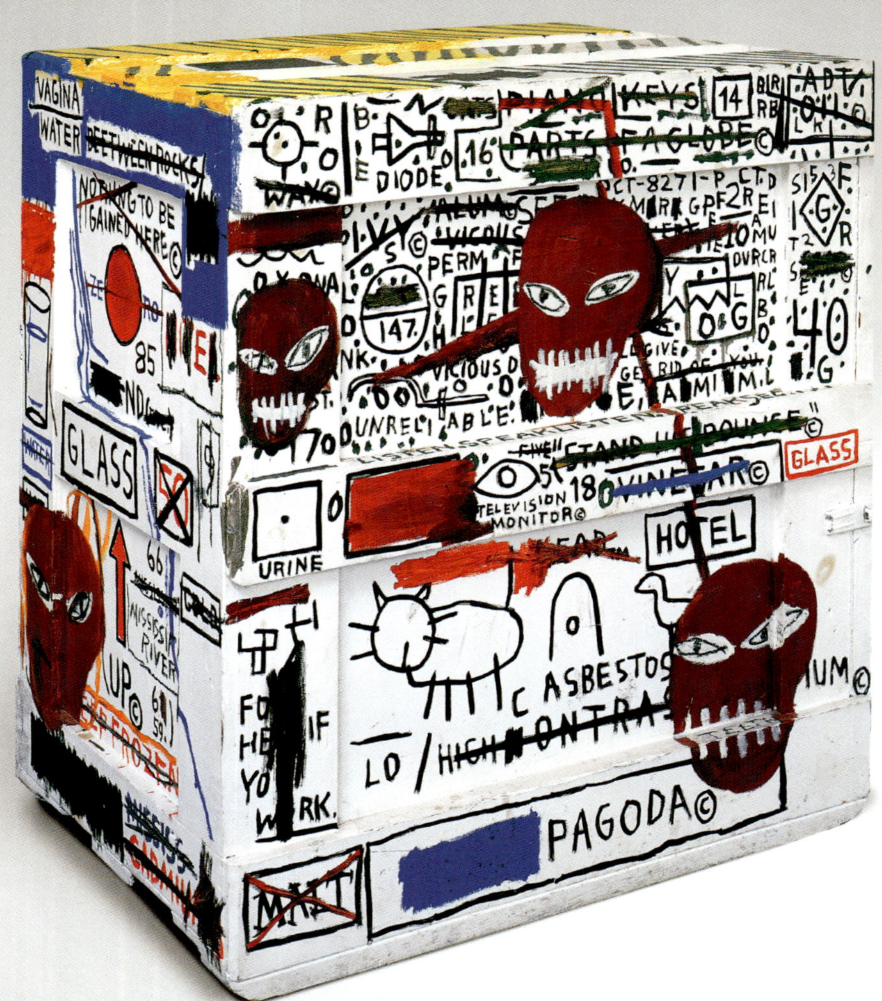

Indeed much of the joy of viewing Basquiat's paintings is to go into these particulars, to piece things together, decode allusions and references, as far as one will get. "I want clarity but I also want to have some sort of obscurity," Basquiat said, "to be sort of more cryptic."[25] Like poetry, some of it will remain opaque while it still rings beautiful and true, and an integral part of the story is to follow the artist's gestures across the canvas and re-trace the chain of decisions that guided his hand. Every repeated viewing of these paintings will offer undiscovered details and new layers of meaning, and that is what this book, with its generous selection of works, was especially created for.

[1–25] *See Endnotes on page 506.*

Untitled, 1987
Acrylic and oilstick on wood,
115.5 x 109 x 72.5 cm / 45 ¹/₂ x 43 x 28 ¹/₂ inches

Pages 32/33: Jean-Michel Basquiat in his
Great Jones Street studio, New York 1987.
Photo Tseng Kwong Chi

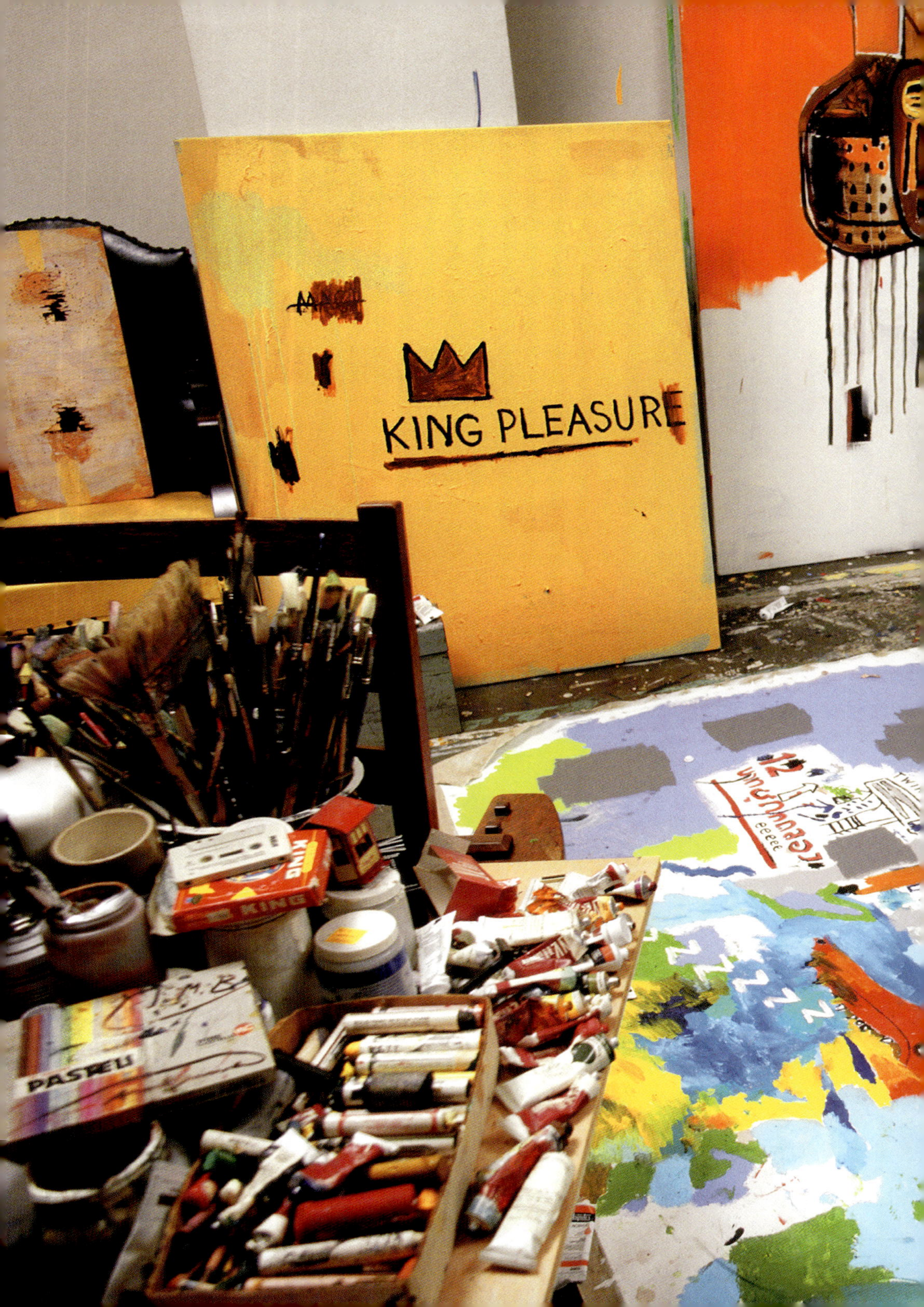

KING PLEASURE
PASTEL
KING

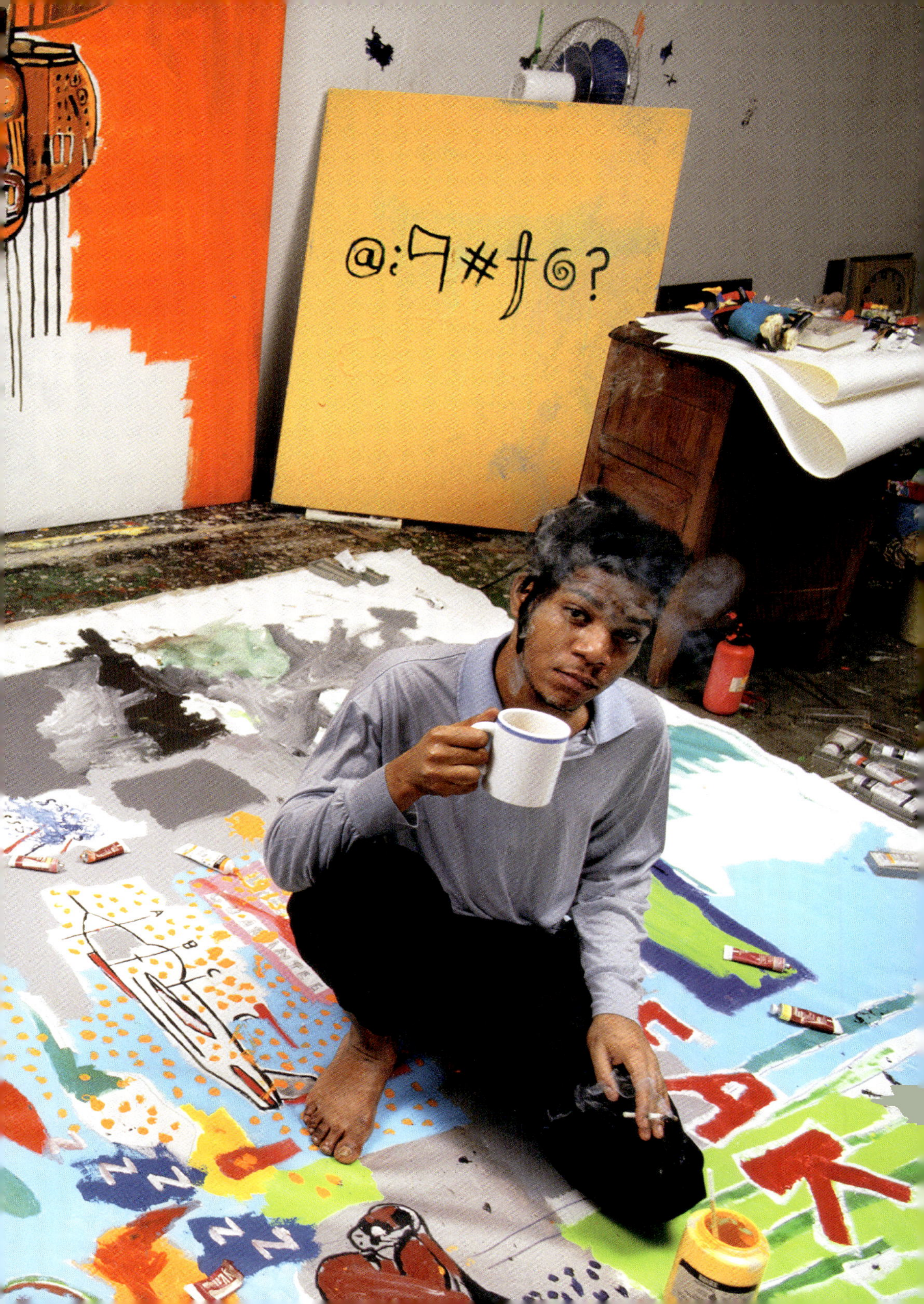

@¡7#ƒ©?

The Art of Storytelling

Eleanor Nairne

"So what defines the art look? When people say Jean-Michel looks like art, the occult significance of the comment is that it looks like our expectation of art; there is observable history in his work. His touch has spontaneous erudition that comforts one as the expected does."

—RENE RICARD, *ARTFORUM*, 1981[1]

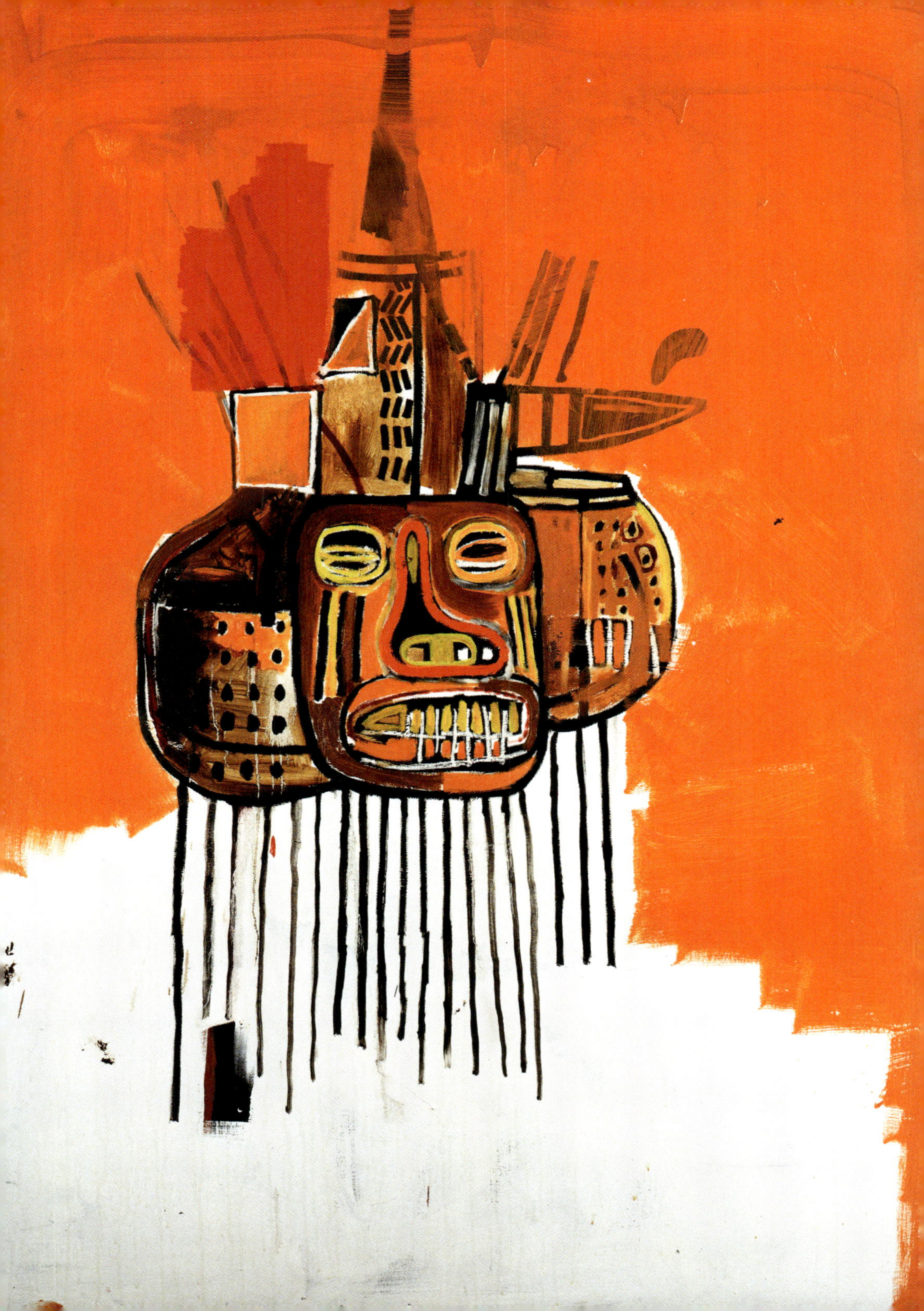

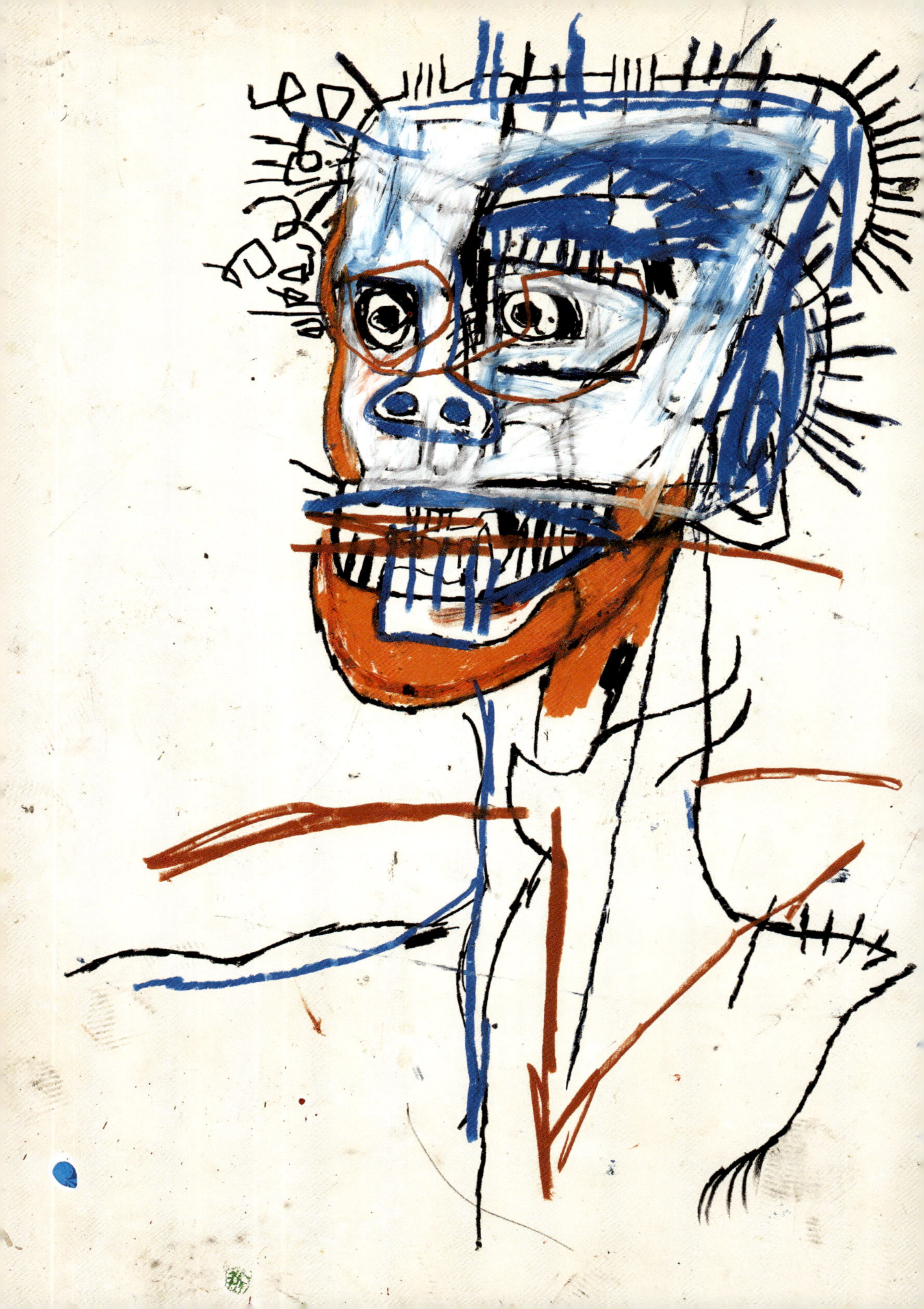

In the spring of 1987, Jean-Michel Basquiat began work on *Pegasus* (pp. 486/487), a drawing like nothing he had made before.[2] On an epic sheet of paper about 90 inches square, he intricately drew symbols and text until the entire page was covered. He mostly used black and white, perhaps to reflect his sober subject matter: life and death and their corollaries of light and dark and flight and descent. The title, for example, links both to the winged stallion of Greek mythology and to the logo of the American oil company Mobilgas.[3] "SCHWARZ," which is German for "black," connects to the refrain "SO IT WASN'T PETROL," likely taken from *The Third Man* (1949), a black-and-white film noir written by British novelist Graham Greene. The swathes of black across the upper part of the work meld with the repetition of the word "ASPHALT" to suggest sticky bitumen about to engulf the artist's whirring thoughts below.[4]

Set against this dark imagery are several mentions of "ICARUS," who famously flew too close to the sun on improvised wings; "POLARIS," commonly known as the North Star, the brightest in the constellation Ursa Minor;[5] and "DA VINCI'S HELICOPTER," which was designed by Leonardo in 1493 and is the earliest known drawing of any helicopter-like machine. "PLUTO" and the "GRIFFITH OBSER-VATORY" consolidate these celestial references, while "ANDROMEDA" relates both to a spiral galaxy and to the Ethiopian princess in Greek mythology, who is saved from death by Perseus, flying in on the winged Pegasus. Her ethnicity (and its frequent misrepresentation, as in the 1981 classic *Clash of the Titans*, where she is played by British actor Judi Bowker) draws attention to the racial significance of Basquiat's black-and-white theme, further indicated by the word "MONTICELLO," the slave plantation owned by Thomas Jefferson, third President of the United States.

The starkness of this work and its teeming range of references (many repeated in obsessive lists) give an impression of Basquiat's darkened mood at the time. Barely 26 years old, he had now lived in Manhattan for almost a decade and had weathered the mixed fortunes of being one of the youngest, most brilliant artists of his generation. Two years earlier, in February 1985, he had been emblazoned on the cover of *The New York Times Magazine*, armed with a brush and a recalcitrant stare;[6] by September of that year he was described in a review in the same newspaper as an "art world mascot."[7] On February 22 in 1987, Andy Warhol, his dear friend, mentor and collaborator, unexpectedly died, following a routine gall bladder operation. By all accounts (and despite their recent estrangement) Basquiat was devastated.[8] His former gallerist, Annina Nosei, recalls him crying over the phone, despairing that he didn't have "anybody to talk to now."[9] When Nosei visited him soon after at his Great Jones Street studio, she found him immersed in *Pegasus*, "the most beautiful drawing ever."[10]

Untitled (Head of Madman), 1982
Oilstick on paper mounted on canvas,
109 x 78.5 cm / 43 x 31 inches

Page 35: **Untitled**, 1987
Acrylic and oilstick on canvas,
218.5 x 172.5 cm / 86 x 68 inches

Warhol's death returned Basquiat to themes of vulnerability and mortality. Strewn amid other icons he drew symbols from his beloved copy of Henry Dreyfuss' *Symbol Sourcebook* (1972), working mostly from the section on "hobo signs."[11] He picked unnerving phrases such as "cowards will give to get rid of you" and "nothing to be gained here."[12] It was a source that he would return to in some of his final works, such as *Eroica II* (1988; p. 481), in which the words and symbol for "MAN DIES" are written ominously in strips like musical staves. *Pegasus* was exhibited at Tony Shafrazi Gallery in May 1987, just one year and three months before Basquiat's death, and it is hard, looking back, not to see it in this shadow. Yet he had long been interested in the idea of the memento mori and this work is as much a meditation on trajectories of fame as it is a premonition of his own demise. After all, Warhol was the so-called King of Pop and with his death came not just the loss of a friend but of a hero.

In works such as *Pegasus*, we encounter what a virtuoso storyteller Basquiat was. He populated his work with reference points, which invite the viewer to seek out constellations of meaning. Sometimes, he would sample from his everyday environment; as Leo Steinberg once said of Rauschenberg, he created pictures for "the consciousness immersed in the brain of the city."[13] But he would also work from the Bible, literature, poetry, and ancient myths and he never shied away from substantial, often existential, subject matter.

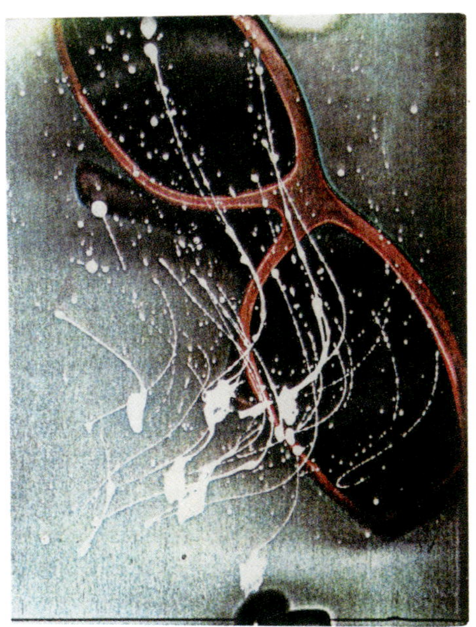

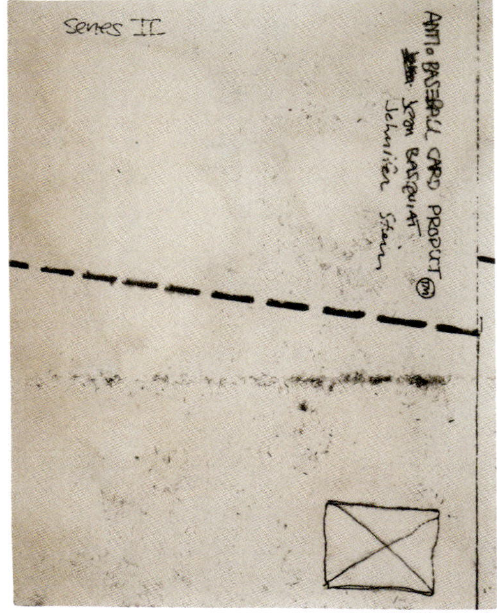

Sunglasses 2 (with Jennifer Stein), 1979
Color photocopy, 14 x 10.5 cm /
5 ¹/₂ x 4 ¹/₈ inches

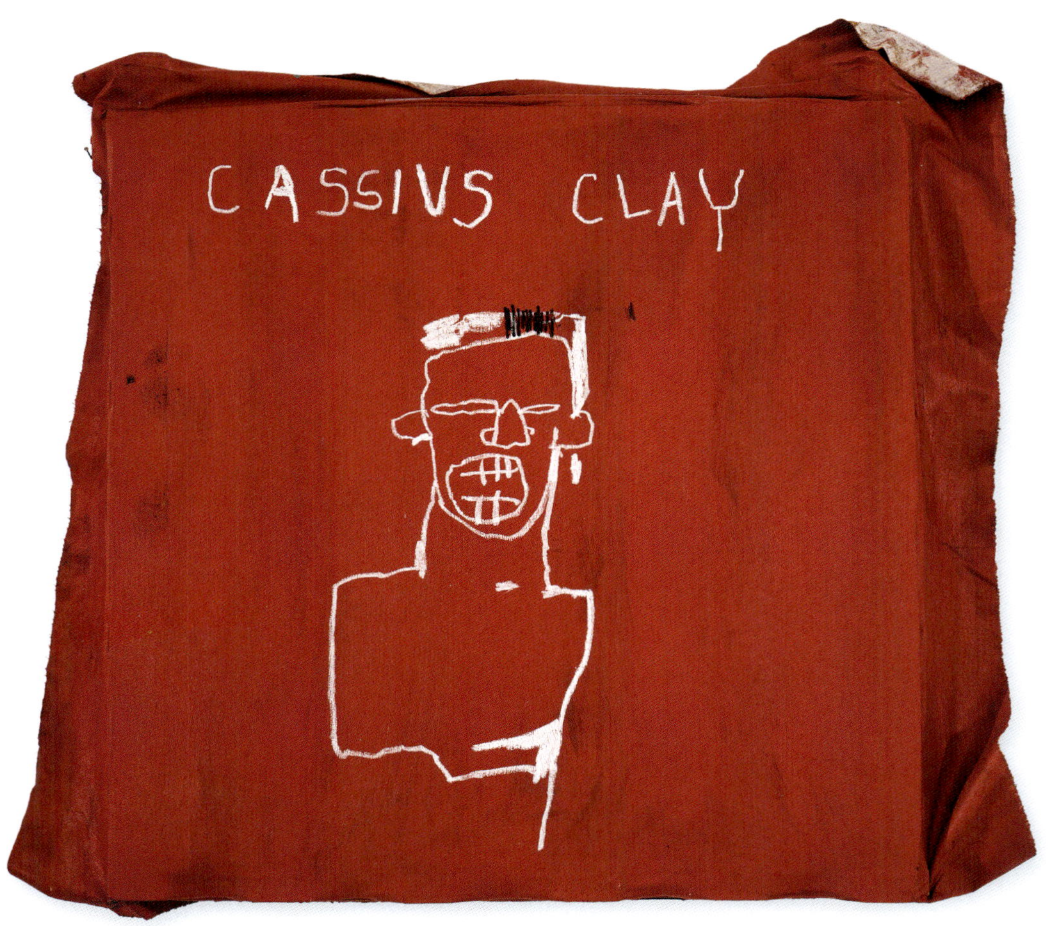

From his earliest experiments writing conceptual graffiti to some of his most celebrated multi-panel paintings, Basquiat understood how to create compelling visual narratives that would propel him into the canon of 20th century art. He cited history in part to write his own. Aesthetically and conceptually, this was also what lent his work a certain gravitas—as he balanced pop references and lofty allusions—creating works that managed to look both startlingly new and somehow familiar. As Rene Ricard identified in "The Radiant Child," the first major article on Basquiat: "The greatest thing is to come up with something so good it seems as if it's always been there, like a proverb."[14]

Cassius Clay, 1982
Acrylic and oilstick on canvas,
106.5 x 104 cm / 42 x 41 inches

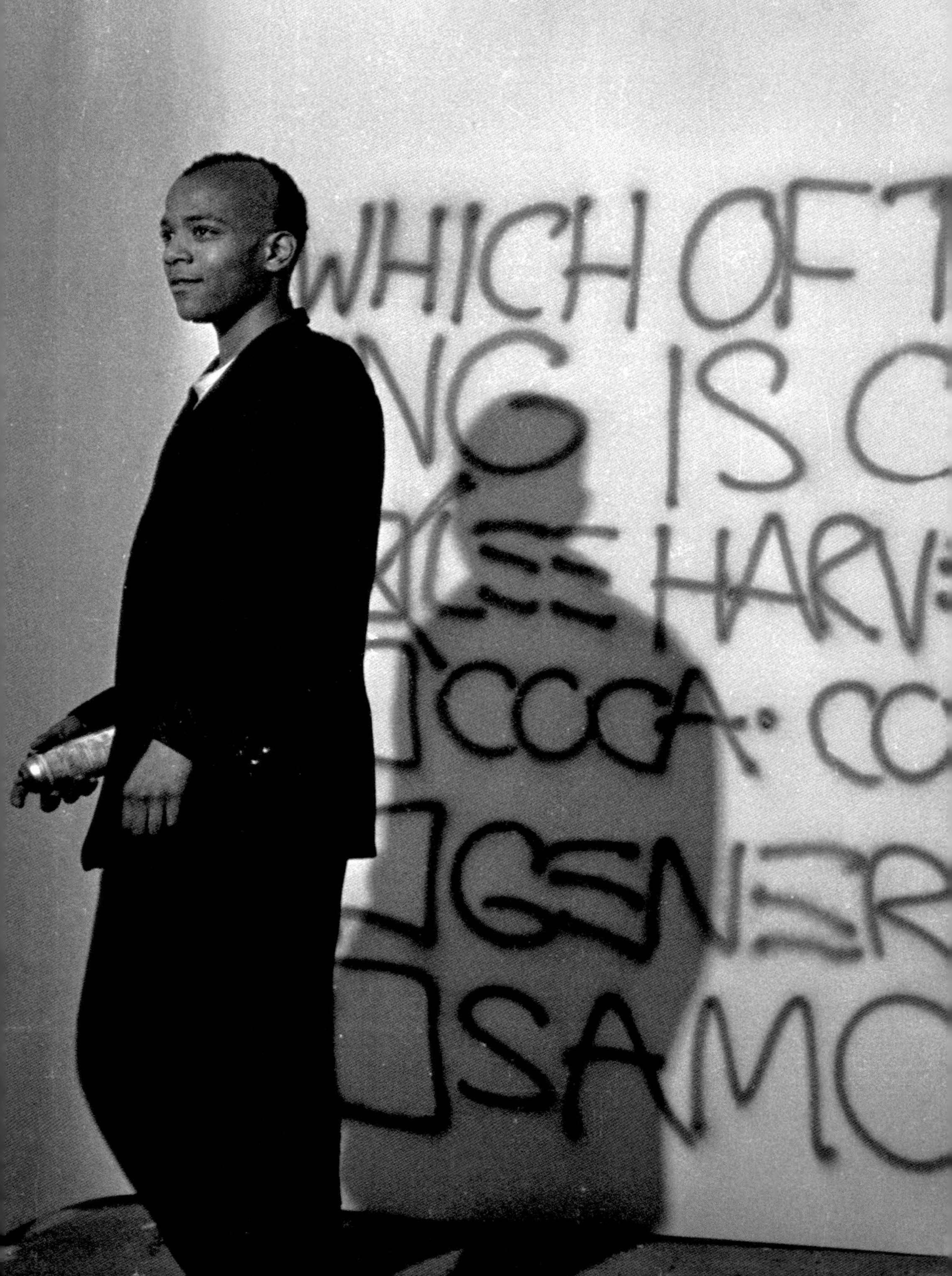

WHICH OF T
NG IS C
HARV
CCCA· CC
GENER
SAMO

HE FOLLOW·
MNIPRZNT?
Y OSWALD
A LOGO
AL MELONRY
@ILLI

The SAMO© Story

New York in 1978 offered bright prospects for young artists—in stark contrast to the state of the city, which had disintegrated to the point of financial ruin. On May 20, 1974, *New York Magazine* ran a cover article announcing SoHo to be "The Most Exciting Place to Live in the City" with a pull-out guide to the galleries and lofts in the area[15]; on October 30, 1975, *New York Daily News* ran the infamous headline "Ford to City: Drop Dead" after the President had denied Federal assistance to bail the City out from defaulting on its debt.[16] Murders, assaults, and car thefts had more than doubled in the preceding decade, while rapes had tripled and burglaries had shot up tenfold.[17] Films like Martin Scorsese's *Taxi Driver* (1976), one of Basquiat's favorites, portrayed the grime and violence that had seized the city. But as the great chronicler of downtown culture, Glenn O'Brien, wrote: "Instead of dropping dead, New York came alive. There was a viral outbreak of contagious fun and madcap genius."[18]

It was an extraordinary moment for the young Basquiat to leave his Brooklyn family home for good, as he did in June 1978, and move to Lower Manhattan. He had left the City-as-School (a pioneering alternative high school) and was now writing graffiti with Al Diaz, a former classmate. While still at school they had developed the concept of SAMO©, a play on the phrase "same old, same old shit," and had begun decorating the walls of SoHo with pseudo-philosophical statements: "SAMO© AS A CONGLOMERATE OF DORMANT GENIOUS" (sic), "SAMO© AS AN ESCAPE CLAUSE," and "SAMO© AS A NEW WAVE NEO ART FORM." Basquiat claimed to write 30 "on a good day" and soon the burgeoning art quarter was awash with their cryptic messaging.[19] Debate was fierce as to who was responsible. On September 21, the *SoHo Weekly News* published two photographs with a plea for the author to get in touch.[20] The following week, the newspaper published a collaged reply from Basquiat and Diaz: "SAMO© AS A MEANS OF DRAWING ATTENTION TO INSIGNIFICANCE … FOR FURTHER DETAILS HANG ON WE'LL CONTACT YOU."[21]

The identities of "the most ambitious—and sententious—of the new wave of Magic Marker Jeremiahs" were revealed, in the end, by the *Village Voice,* who paid them for the story.[22] That they managed to create sufficient intrigue to warrant such attention (not to mention $100, which was no mean sum in 1978) is a testament to their audacity and wit. The pair split soon after; Basquiat scrawled "SAMO© IS DEAD" on their former grounds in a nod to beat poet Ted Joans' writing of "Bird Lives" after the death of Charlie Parker, and Keith Haring delivered a eulogy at Club 57. But Basquiat was not one to relinquish the hype that he had generated. He appeared as Mr Samo on *TV Party*, with Glenn O'Brien

Pages 40/41: Jean-Michel Basquiat at the Canal Zone Party, New York 1979. Photo Anton Perich

Untitled (Maid from Olympia), 1982
Acrylic, oilstick, and paper collage on canvas mounted on wooden supports, 122.5 x 76 cm / 48 ¹/₄ x 30 inches

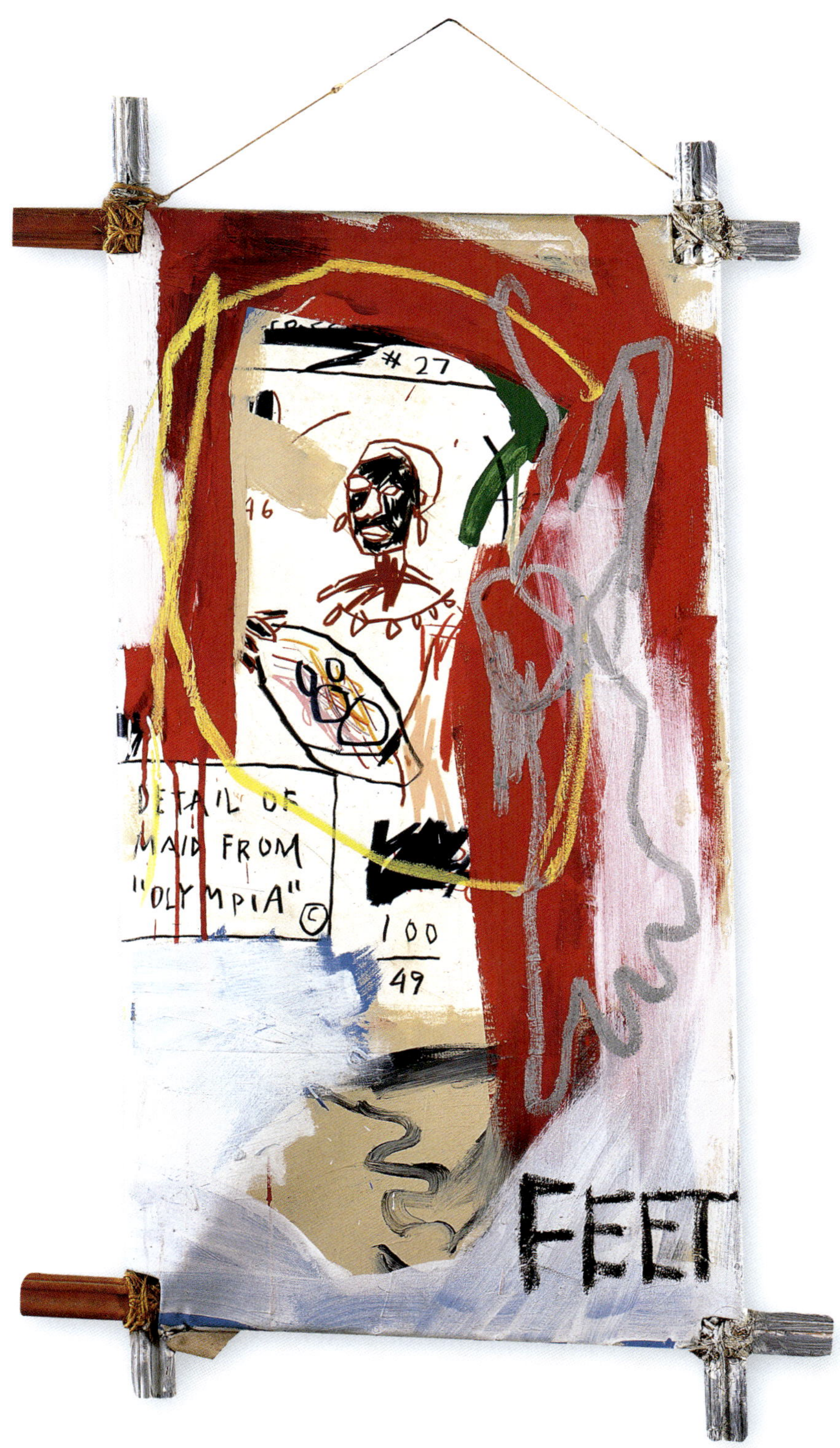

27
DETAIL OF
MAID FROM
"OLYMPIA"
©
100
49
FEET

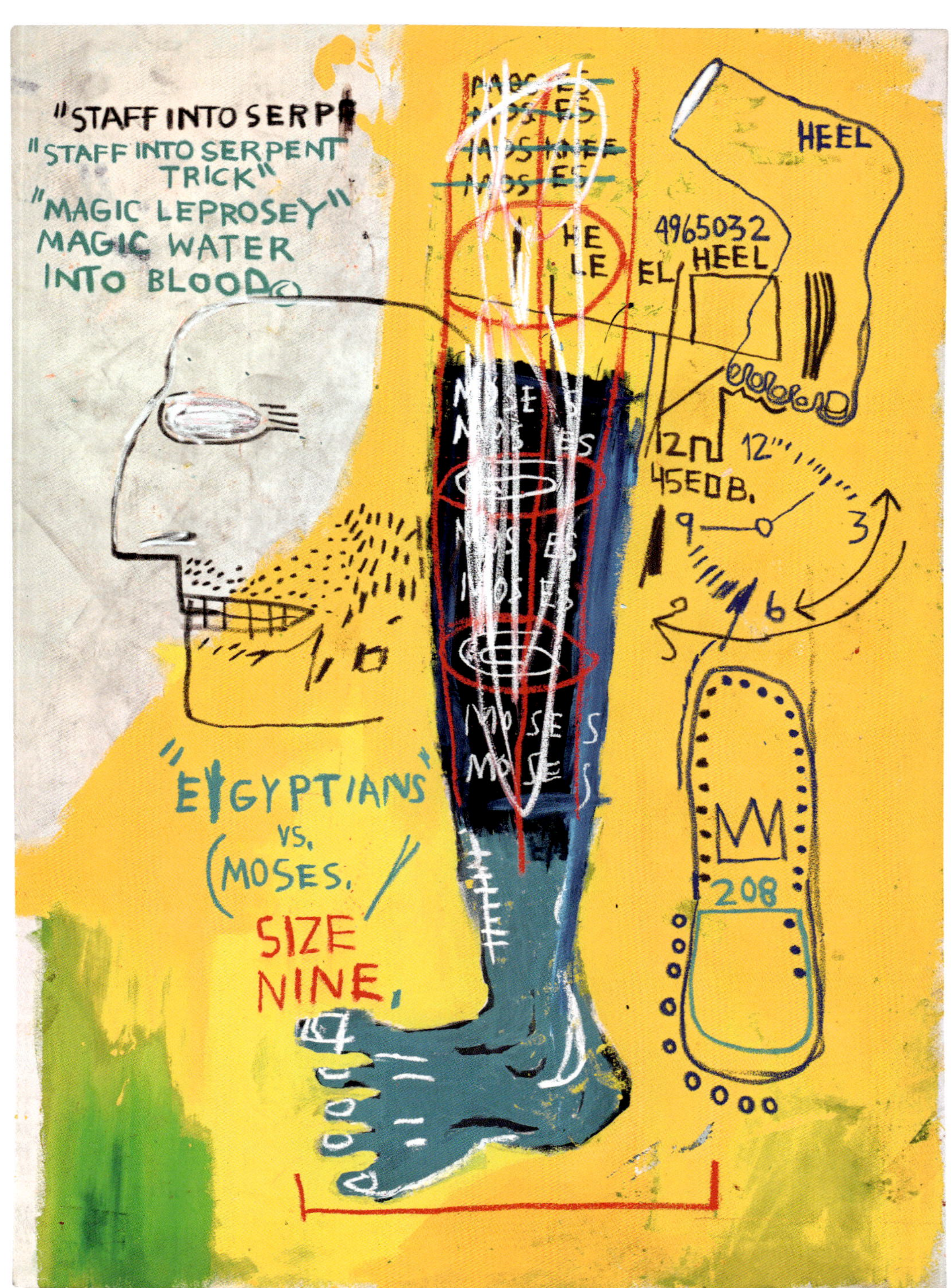

"STAFF INTO SERP
"STAFF INTO SERPENT
TRICK"
"MAGIC LEPROSEY"
MAGIC WATER
INTO BLOOD
HEEL
HE
LE
EL
4965032
HEEL
12
12'''
45EO B.
9
3
2
6
"EGYPTIANS"
VS.
(MOSES.
SIZE
NINE.
MOSES
208

introducing him as "probably the most language-oriented of all graffiti artists"[23], and just weeks later spray-painted a live SAMO© multiple-choice question at the Canal Zone Party (pp. 40/41). His SAMO© Is Dead Jazz Band performed at Arleen Schloss' loft in December and he continued to exhibit under this name right up to (and including) his first solo show at Galleria d'Arte Emilio Mazzoli in Modena, Italy, in May 1981.

The Canal Zone Party, on April 29, 1979, proved to be a particularly fateful evening. It was here that Basquiat met Michael Holman, of the glam-rock band The Tubes. They conspired to start a band of their own—which would go through several iterations (including Test Pattern and Channel 9) before being called Gray. With fellow members including Nick Taylor, Shannon Dawson, and Vincent Gallo (among others), they hoped to make music inspired by John Cage. In Basquiat's words, they were aiming to be "incomplete, abrasive, oddly beautiful"—the quintessential No Wave sound.[24] That night he also met Jennifer Stein.[25] She had already been working on a series of baseball cards, customizing each with correction fluid, when he elaborated on the idea by adding his own nicknames—"JOe" or "JERK." He showed her how they could make postcards, turning an 11 by 8 $^1/_2$-inch sheet of paper into four, creating compositions in each quadrant, color photocopying the sheet, mounting it on cardboard, and then cutting it into individual cards that could be sold for $1 each.

Color photocopying was a relatively new technology at the time—Xerox released their first electrostatic color copier machines in 1973—and it was not cheap. Stein recalls that they would use the machine at Jamie Canvas, an art supply store on Spring Street, where it would cost as much as $2.50 per sheet (and that's without any mistakes).[26] With a potential profit of 37.5 cents per postcard, this was not a lucrative venture—but it offered Basquiat a calling card as he took to the streets with his wares. On a particularly notorious occasion, he spied Andy Warhol having lunch in the WPA restaurant with the Commissioner of Cultural Affairs for New York City, Henry Geldzahler. True to his generation, Basquiat was an avid fan of *From A to B and Back Again: The Philosophy of Andy Warhol* (1975)[27] and, as he later recalled in an interview with Geldzahler, it took him "about 15 minutes to get up the nerve to go in there."[28] While Geldzahler dismissed him as "too young" ("too young for what?" he retorted in their interview), Warhol bought a sunglasses postcard (p. 38 left).[29]

Like an aspiring actor, Basquiat also created costumes for himself. He had worked for a time at the Unique Clothing Warehouse on Broadway, an enormous store selling antique clothing, military surplus, athletic gear, and work clothes (all to the blaring soundtrack of punk music), which may have been where he sourced his inspiration and materials. Lab coats, jumpsuits, T-shirts, and jumpers were daubed with acrylic paint to become like

Early Moses, 1983
Acrylic and oilstick on canvas,
198 x 141 cm / 78 x 55 $^1/_2$ inches

Pages 46/47: Jean-Michel Basquiat's
Crosby Street studio, New York 1983.
Photo Roland Hagenberg

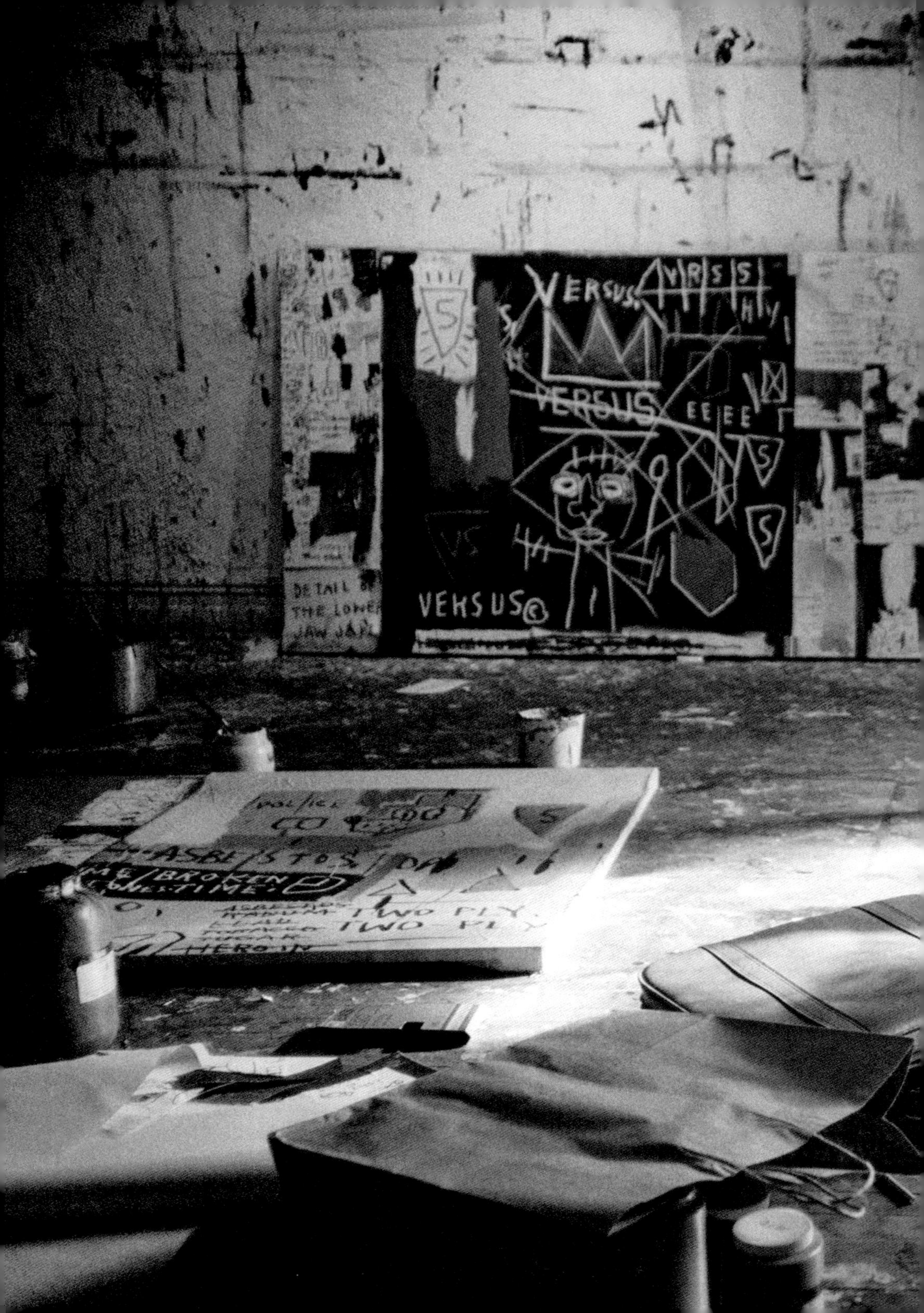

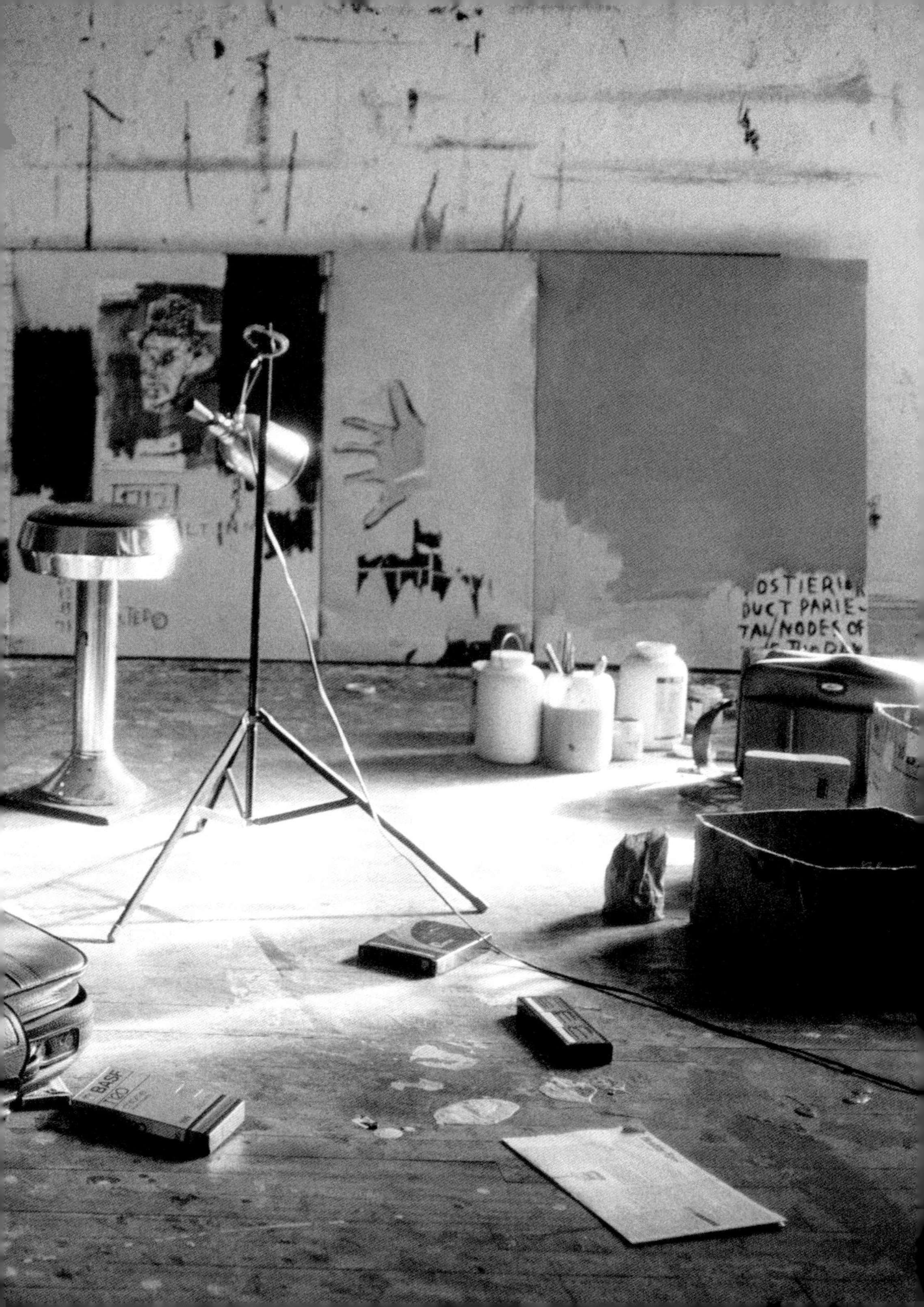
POSTIERIOR
DUCT PARIE-
TAL NODES OF
BASF

wearable Franz Klines. He sheared the sleeves off a sweatshirt and crudely wrote the letters EPZ on the front to wear while selling postcards, many of which were embellished with the cut-out letters from PEZ sweet dispensers. In 1979, the designer Patricia Field allowed him to show work in her 8th Street boutique, which Keith Haring recorded seeing in his diary. He also wrote: "SAMO … told me about the painting he had done that day. He bought a canvas at Utrecht's and … put all this paint on [it] and let cars run over it and got the paint all over himself and then got on the subway and went to an appointment at Fiorucci and got paint on EVERYTHING on the way and at Fiorucci he got paint on the rug and couch and rich ladies' furs. He was asked to leave before his appointment."[30]

These exploits brought Basquiat notoriety in the downtown art world. Even Warhol, writing later in his diary, recalled: "He's the kid who used the name 'Samo' when he used to sit on the sidewalk in Greenwich village and paint T-shirts, and I'd give him $10 here and there … He was a middle-class Brooklyn kid … and he was trying to be like that, painting in the Greenwich village."[31] Basquiat's work was already inflected with an astute awareness of precedent. The painting described by Haring, for example, sounds remarkably like a chaotic reenactment of Rauschenberg's *Automobile Tire Print* (1953), in which twenty sheets of drawing paper were glued into a 23-foot line and laid out in front of his Fulton Street studio, for John Cage to drive his Model A Ford over. Equally, when Basquiat exhibited his first work as part of the *Times Square Show* in June 1980, the Abstract Expressionist parallel that Jeffrey Deitch remarked upon in his review, calling it a "knockout combination of de Kooning and subway spray-paint scribbles," was no coincidence.[32]

In late 1980, Basquiat was cast in the starring role of *New York Beat.*[33] Directed by Edo Bertoglio, written by Glenn O'Brien, and produced by Maripol, the film was intended to be an urban fairytale, set in the post-punk subculture of Lower Manhattan. Featuring a roster of the scene's coolest characters, from Fab Five Freddy to James Chance and Debbie Harry, it was loosely based on a day in Basquiat's life as a down-and-out artist. Although it was not released until 2000, the film's success was premised on some (uncannily accurate) wishful thinking about who the lead actor would become. Now, looking back, it seems remarkable that the production office at 54 Great Jones Street, Basquiat's first make-shift studio, was directly opposite 57 Great Jones Street, which he would later rent from Warhol at the height of his career, while the materials bought for him to create props for the film became some of his earliest paintings. He even re-enacted SAMO©, scarcely two years after the original. This enabled a slew of high-quality stills to be taken, which would illustrate the story of SAMO© for years to come (p. 42).

Peel Quickly, 1984
Acrylic and oilstick
on canvas, 193 x 132 cm /
76 x 52 inches

Pages 50/51: **Hollywood Africans in front of the Chinese Theater with Footprints of Movie Stars**, 1983
Acrylic and oilstick on canvas mounted on wooden supports, 90 x 207 cm / 35 $^1/_2$ x 81 $^1/_2$ inches

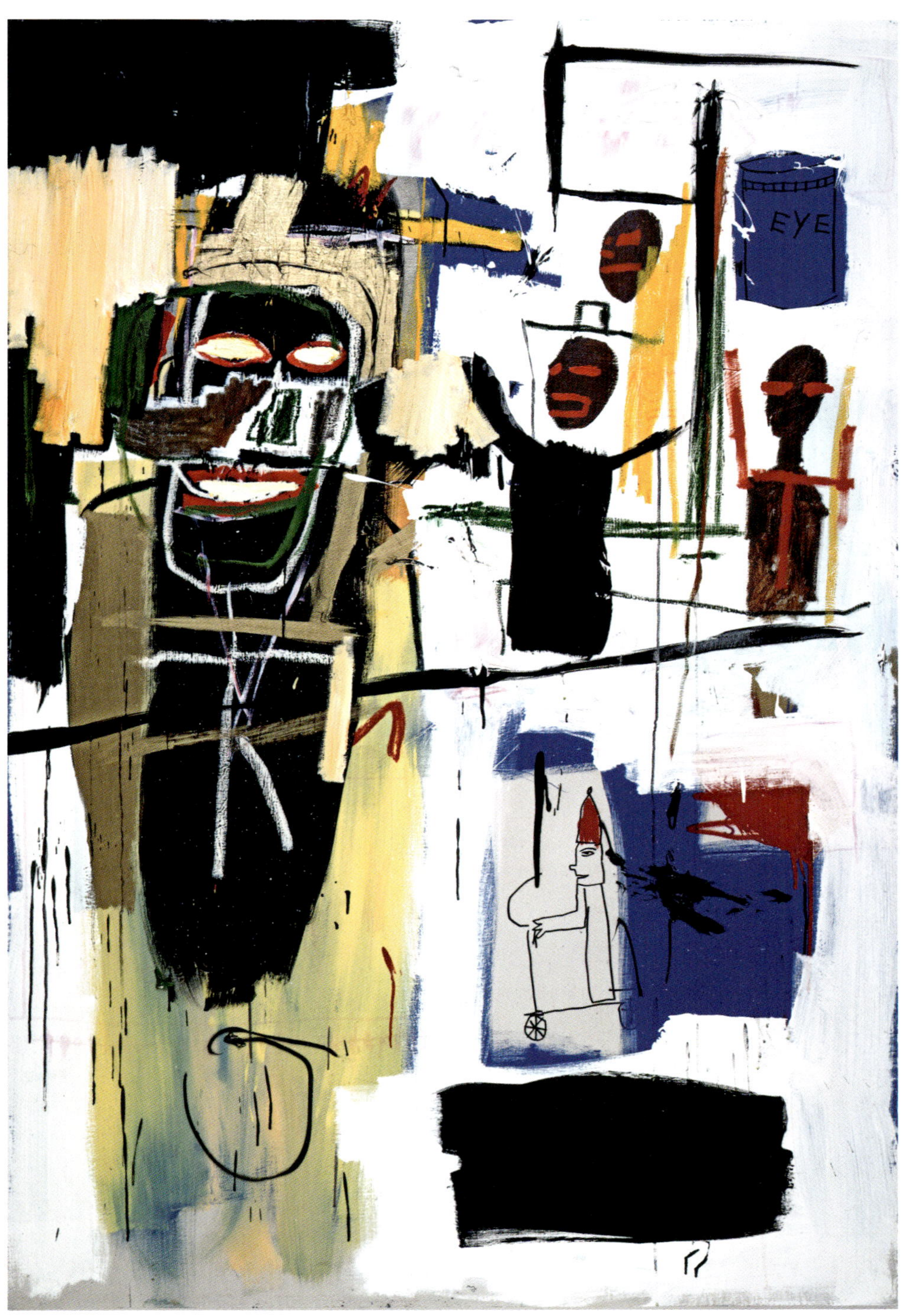
EYE

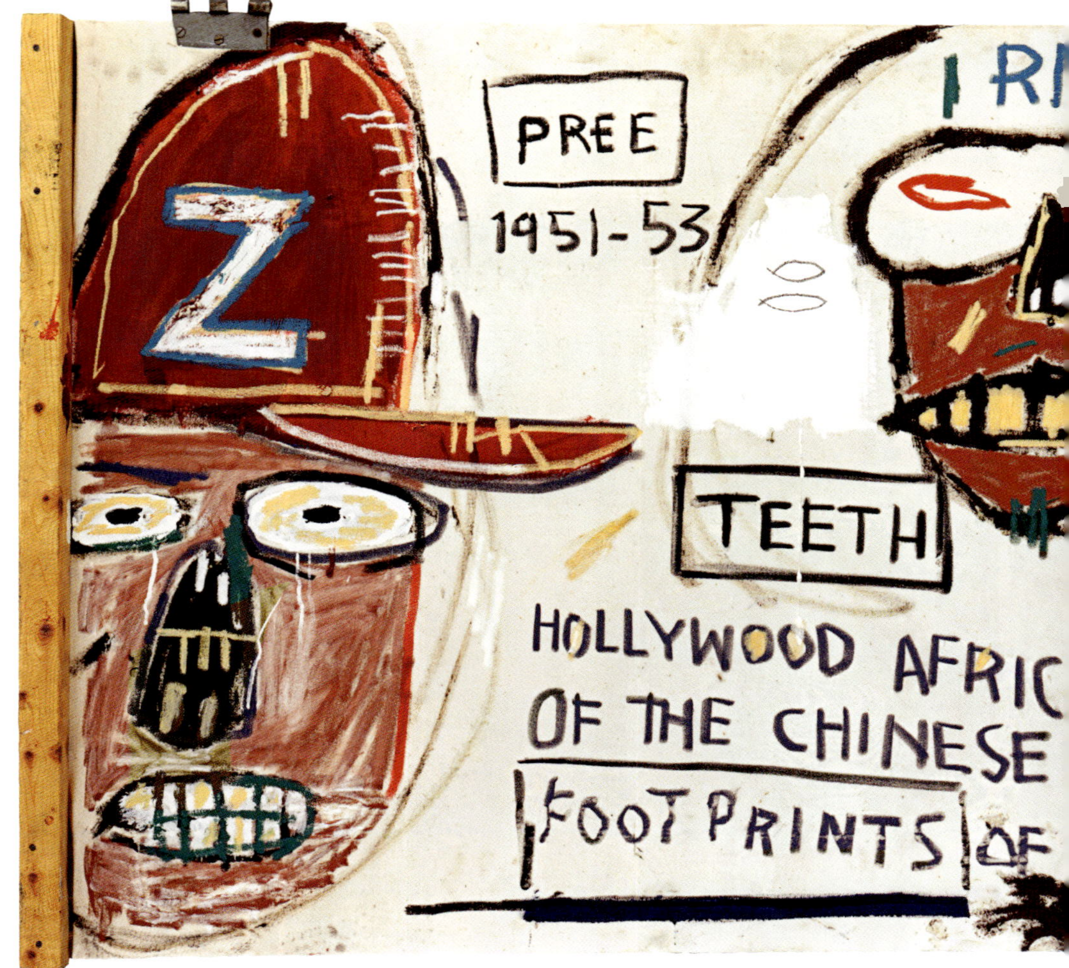

The Radiant Child

In 1981, Basquiat had his breakthrough moment. Diego Cortez, one of the founders of the Mudd Club, invited him to take part in his group show *New York/New Wave*, which opened on Valentine's Day at the P.S.1 Institute for Art and Urban Resources in Long Island City. Although Basquiat had only publically exhibited once (in the *Times Square Show* the previous June), Cortez gave him an entire wall, which together they hung salon-style with a group of 20 pieces.[34] He created them on canvas and paper and foam mattress and wood. As he explained in an interview in 1985: "I wanted to paint like the Lower East Side and what it was like to live there."[35] Using the discarded materials of the city was one way, metonymically, to do so. Both the comment and the gesture allude (again) to an older

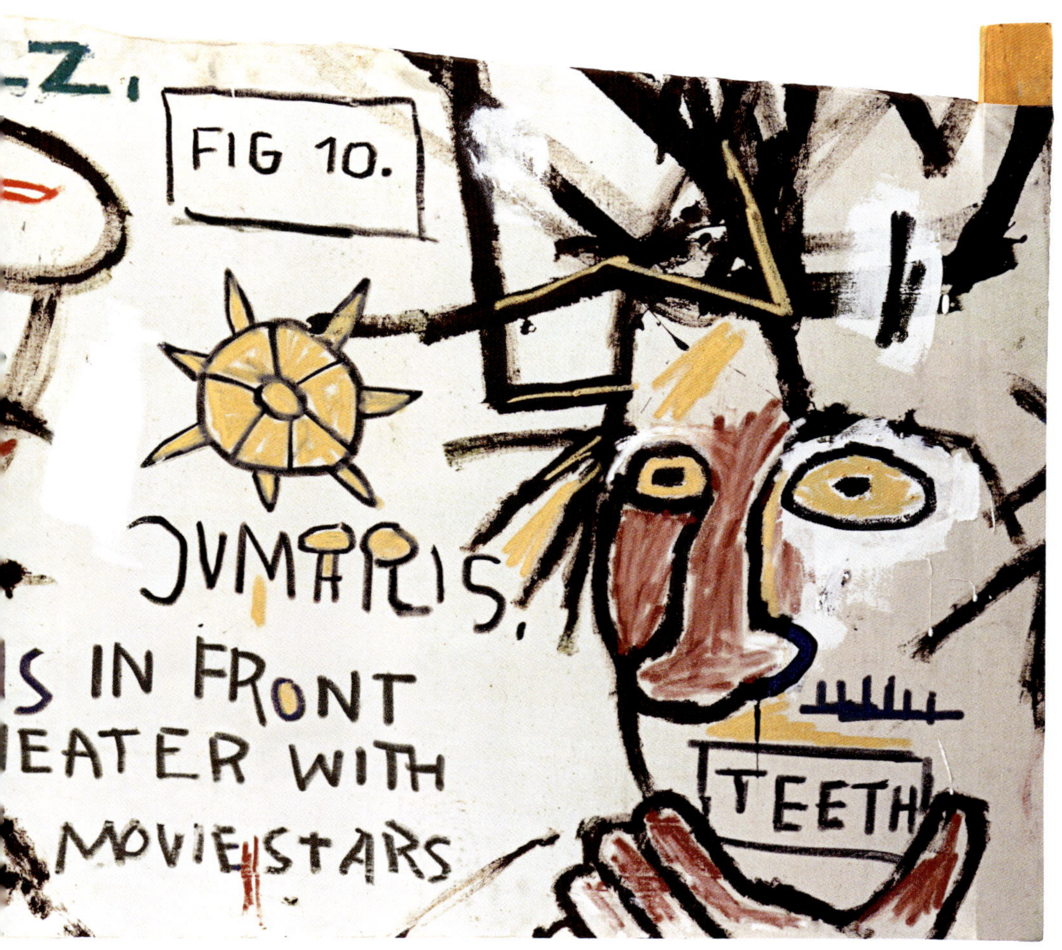

generation of New York artists, notably Rauschenberg, who developed his Combines as a means to capture his subject matter more accurately. As he put it to the critic Calvin Tomkins: "I think a picture is more like the real world when it's made out of the real world."[36]

In *New York/New Wave*, Basquiat matched the rough nature of his materials with the energy of quickly drawn elements, to conjure the noise of city life. There were four-paned windows, soaring skyscrapers, and strewn letters. The cars, often in collision, could be read in relation to the accident that he suffered as a child, which left him hospitalized with internal injuries for a month at King's County Hospital, or as a metaphor for the financial crash of the city. The airplanes give a sense of a Brooklyn childhood lived under the flight paths, but could also be read as combat aircraft, given other work that he made around the same time, such as *Gringo Pilot (Anola Gay)* (p. 53), which refers to the Boeing B-29 that dropped the first atomic bomb.[37] Present in several works is a frontal, mask-like face, with protruding ears and a cage-like grimace. These masks had first been seen in the late graffiti Basquiat did after splitting from Al Diaz and offered a point of continuity for those who knew him as SAMO©.

Basquiat had begun to elaborate a visual vocabulary for himself. Several works featured the word "AARON," for example, while others were scattered with the letters of this name. The origins of this reference could be Hank "Hammer" Aaron, the black baseball player, who in 1973–74 was the subject of a heated debate as to whether he would beat Babe Ruth's sacrosanct record for home runs. The question unleashed considerable racism; as *Sports Illustrated* wrote: "Is this to be the year in which Aaron, at the age of thirty-nine, takes a moon walk above one of the most hallowed individual records in American sport? Or will it be remembered as the season in which Aaron, the most dignified of athletes, was besieged with hate mail and trapped by the cobwebs and goblins that lurk in baseball's attic?"[38] Basquiat may well have wanted to reference these "cobwebs and goblins" (as well as the fact that Aaron did beat the record), but there are further possible allusions too—to Aaron the black antihero of Shakespeare's revenge tragedy *Titus Andronicus* and to the brother of Moses in the Old Testament, who helps free the Israelites from servitude in Egypt.

This biblical reference is endorsed by the three heads that appear in *Untitled* (1981; p. 118), a possible reference to the holy trinity, and by the strewn letters A and O, which could relate to *Revelations* 22:13: "I am Alpha and Omega, the beginning and the end." This ties into a visual allusion to Cy Twombly, who was famed for his classical imagery and often scattered his works with letters from the Greek alphabet. Basquiat likely saw Twombly's retrospective at the Whitney Museum of American Art in 1979, given that he cited *Apollo and the Artist* (1973) as one of his favorite works in his interview with Henry Geldzahler in 1983.[39] Twombly's classical citations, layered materials and scrawled lettering clearly had a powerful impact. The combination of this imagery—relating to antiquity, the Bible, New York, racial tension, Abstract Expressionism—amounts to a body of work that feels strangely anachronistic; both entirely of the moment and deeply historic.

Although now considered a watershed show, *New York/New Wave* was widely dismissed, if not derided, by critics at the time. Peter Schjeldahl described it in the *Village Voice* as "the most all-around problematic art event in recent memory . . . having been intoxicated from a distance by the vague but heady promise of the New Wave—a reinvigoration, from the bottom up, of urban culture and style—I was crashingly disappointed."[40] Given this, it is rather remarkable that a young Basquiat was picked out favorably in almost all of the reviews. Schjeldahl went on to say: "I would not have suspected from Samo's generally grotty defacements of my neighborhood the graphic and painterly talents revealed here . . . A kind

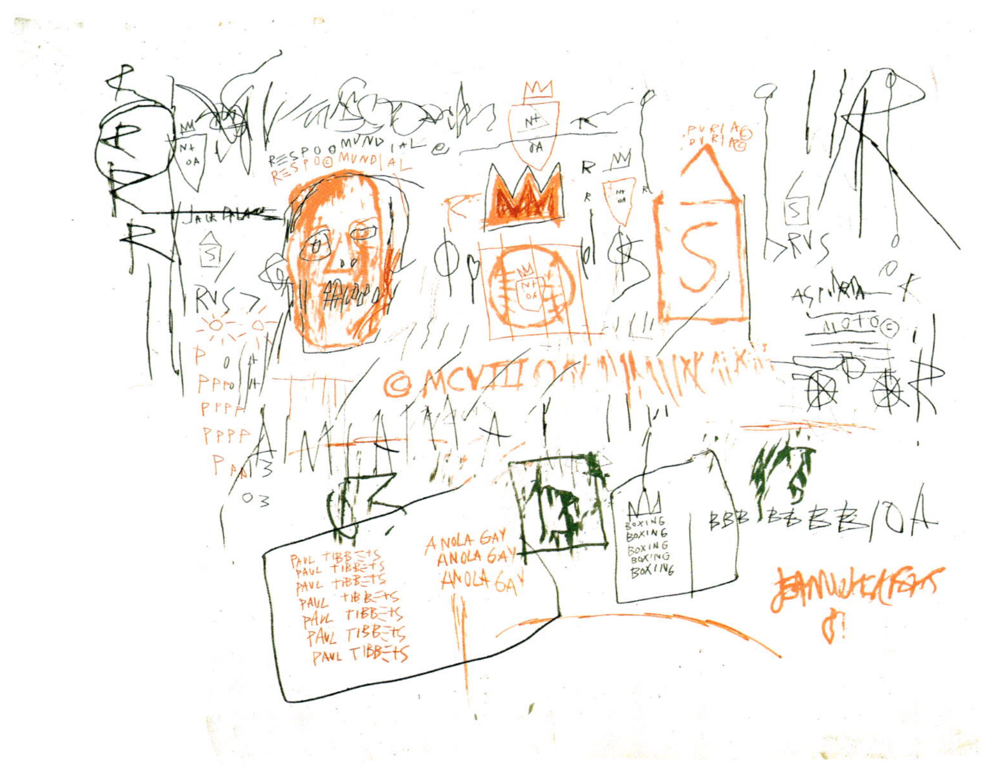

of street Dubuffet (who says he never heard of Dubuffet), he has flair, humor, and an al-most automatic abstract elegance."[41] Even photographer Robert Mapplethorpe, who (like most visitors to the show) had never encountered Basquiat's work before, picked him out as a favorite, "a little bit Cy Twombly but somehow that was interesting."[42]

Certainly, the collectors and gallerists were in no doubt, with Basquiat quickly winning the attention and admiration of Annina Nosei, Emilio Mazzoli, and Bruno Bischofberger. Mazzoli, who was known for representing Italian artists of the Transavanguardia move-ment, such as Sandro Chia and Francesco Clemente, staged Basquiat's first solo exhibition at his gallery in Modena in May 1981. Basquiat elaborated on his lexicon, adding skelly courts, a little house with the letter S, and suddenly, as if in recognition of his new-found

Gringo Pilot (Anola Gay), 1981
Acrylic, oilstick, and graphite on paper,
205.5 x 261.5 cm / 81 x 103 inches

OGO
SHIT
MOTHER
FUCKER
LINK SAUSAGE©
HALF
SMOK ES

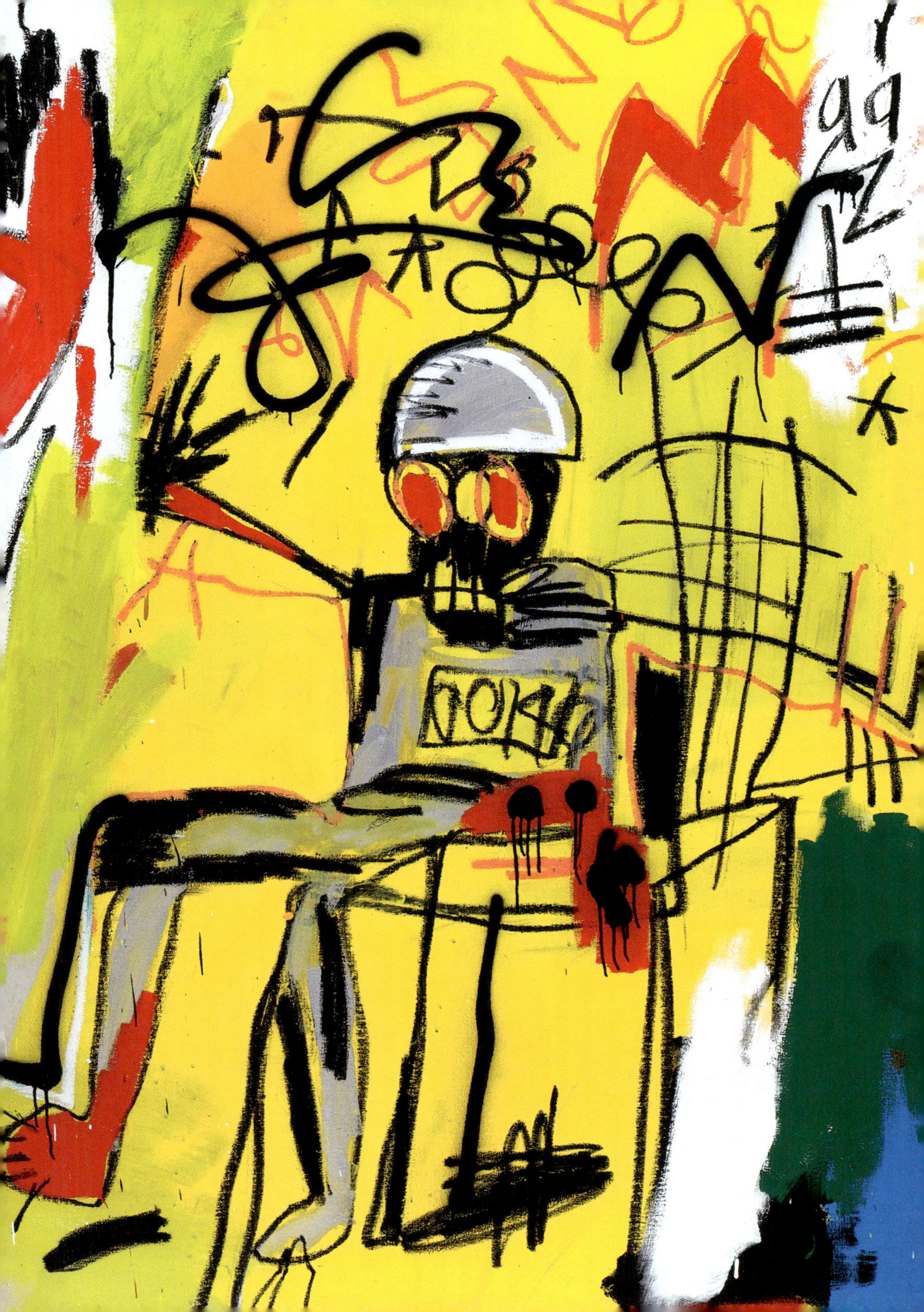

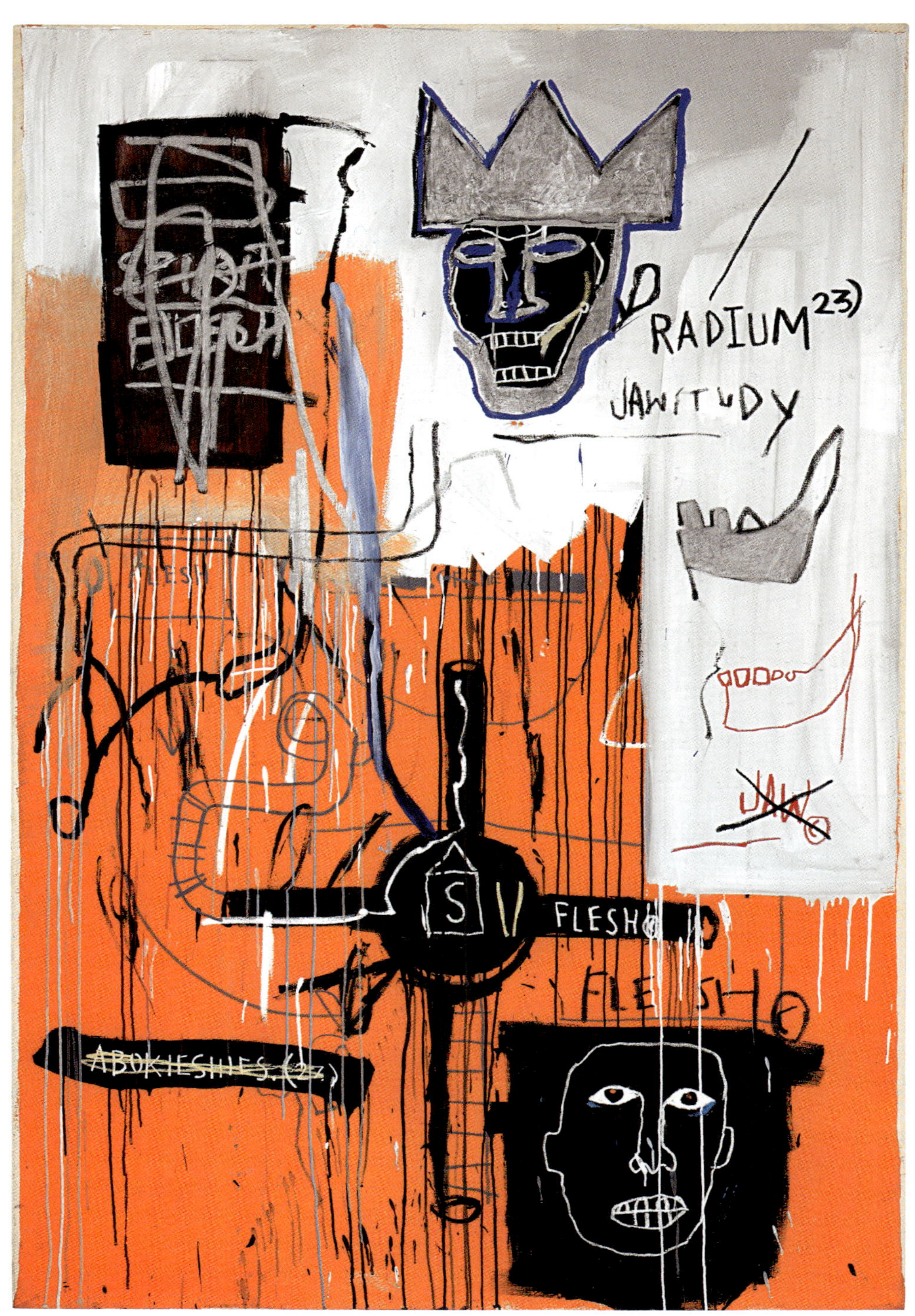

RADIUM 23)
JAWITUDY
FLESH
S V
FLESH
FLESH
ABUKIESHES.
JAW

fame, a three-pointed crown. In the autumn, Basquiat persuaded Nosei to allow him to participate in her group exhibition *Public Address*, which featured a number of artists tackling social issues, including Jenny Holzer, Barbara Kruger, and Keith Haring. Initially, she was unconvinced, thinking his work too "lyrical, personal, and intense," but he insisted that his "purpose was to address sociopolitical issues, and . . . in his opinion, was perfect for [the] show."[43]

Nosei offered Basquiat the downstairs space in her gallery as a studio in preparation for the exhibition and (given that he didn't even have a fixed address at the time) he willingly agreed. This became a fabled part of their story, as friends balked at the implications of him working in an underground lair. Fab 5 Freddy told him: "A black kid painting in the basement. It's not good man."[44] Basquiat shrugged off the implications, remarking in an interview with Marc Miller: "Oh Christ, if I was white, they would just say artist-in-residence."[45] For him, the bigger problem was the stream of interruptions from collectors. Yet he still managed to create some remarkable paintings that delivered on the political engagement promised while demonstrating a newfound maturity of style. *Irony of Negro Policeman* (1981; p. 59) confronts the viewer with a stocky figure, his eyes glowering and his lips sealed shut with menacing red stitches. The contracted title (further condensed on the work to "PLCEMN"), adds to the impression of a reviled character, an oppressed who has joined the oppressors, not deemed worthy of definite or indefinite articles. Other works included *Untitled (Skull)* (1981; p. 147), an enormous Picasso-like head wrenched between full and three-quarter profile, with a spiky mohawk, haphazard scars, and a twisted snarl of teeth.

In December 1981, Basquiat's annus mirabilis was crowned with an article in *Artforum*, which brought him to the attention of an international audience. Titled "The Radiant Child," the piece was written by Rene Ricard, a flamboyant New York poet and critic. As the writer Raymond Foye recalled, by 1981, Ricard had become a "mentor and he loved the role because it meant his vast body of arcane art historical knowledge could be channeled into contemporary works . . . [and] no one made better use of what Rene had to offer than Jean-Michel Basquiat."[46] In his profile piece, Ricard took great care to place graffiti in a historical context: "In these autographs is the inherent pathos of the archaeological site, the cry down the vast endless track of time that 'I am somebody' on a wall in Pompeii."[47] Defending the power of brevity ("Fellini manages with pasty millions a bad reproduction of what Jack Smith achieved with a sequin") he consolidated Basquiat's newly mythic status: "There is observable history in his work. His touch has spontaneous erudition that comforts one as the expected does."[48]

In January 1982, Basquiat moved into a loft at 151 Crosby Street, arranged by Annina Nosei. He had his first U.S. solo show lined up at the gallery in March and his rent was to be paid for in paintings. Works exhibited included *Per Capita* (1981; p. 130/131), twelve and a half feet in width, featuring a black silhouette of a man, in Everlast boxing shorts, with a torch held aloft in his outstretched arm and a halo above his head. The words "E PLURIBUS" are inscribed above; translating from Latin as "out of many," they come from the motto "E Pluribus Unum" (meaning out of 13 states, one country) adopted by America's Founding Fathers and written on the Great Seal. The torch, Lady Liberty's symbol of hope, is positioned at the very center of the composition, like a burning question mark around the omission of "unum." The issue of disparity is made explicit in the words "peR CAPITA" to the right and a scrawled alphabetical list of states to the left: "ALABAMA, ALASKA, ARIZONA, ARKANSAS, CALIFORNIA," accompanied by their respective per capita wealth.

As if to signal his origins to unfamiliar visitors, Basquiat also included a number of works on paper, adorned with lines of searing poetry that he had written in the aftermath of SAMO©, such as "PAY FOR SOUP / BUILD A FORT / SET THAT ON FIRE." The show was met with great acclaim from critics, including Jeffrey Deitch, who tackled directly the rumors of a "primitive prodigy": "Basquiat is likened to the wild boy raised by wolves, corralled into Annina's basement … A child of the streets gawked at by the intelligentsia. But Basquiat is hardly a primitive. He's more like a rock star, seemingly savage, but completely in control."[49] Others, meanwhile, picked up on the way in which his imagery carried epic narratives and its rich capacity to be read in many lights—"this is about as refined as poetry gets!" exclaimed Ricard.[50] As Lisa Liebmann wrote in *Art in America*, the "apemen, skulls, predatory animals, stick figures—look incorporeal because of the fleetness of their execution,and in their cryptic half-presence, they seem to take on Shaman-like characteristics."[51]

In June 1982, Basquiat was included in *documenta 7* in Kassel, the youngest artist in the history of this prestigious international exhibition, where his work was presented alongside such established figures as Joseph Beuys, Gerhard Richter, and Cy Twombly as well as fellow artists from the New York scene, including Matt Mullican, Martha Rosler, Andy Warhol, and Cindy Sherman.[52] *Acque Pericolose (Poison Oasis)* (1981; pp. 20/21) was one of three works included, an extraordinary painting made the previous year that elaborated on a more narrative style. A black figure, crowned with a thorny nimbus, stands in the center of the work, almost life-size. To the left is a coiled green snake with menacing

Irony of Negro Policeman, 1981
Acrylic and oilstick on wood,
183 x 122 cm / 72 x 48 inches

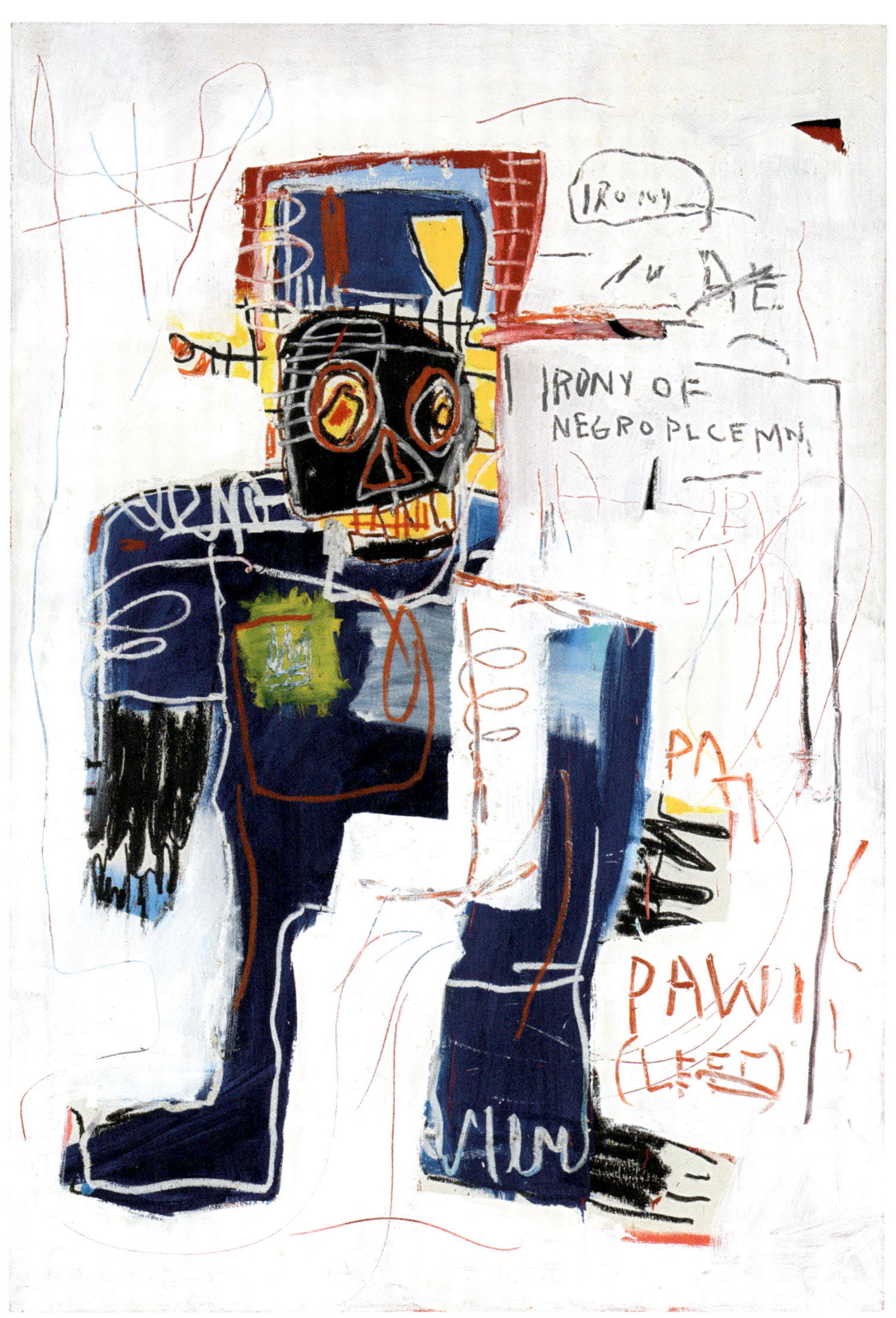
IRONY
IRONY OF
NEGRO PLCEMN,
PA
PAW
(LEFT)

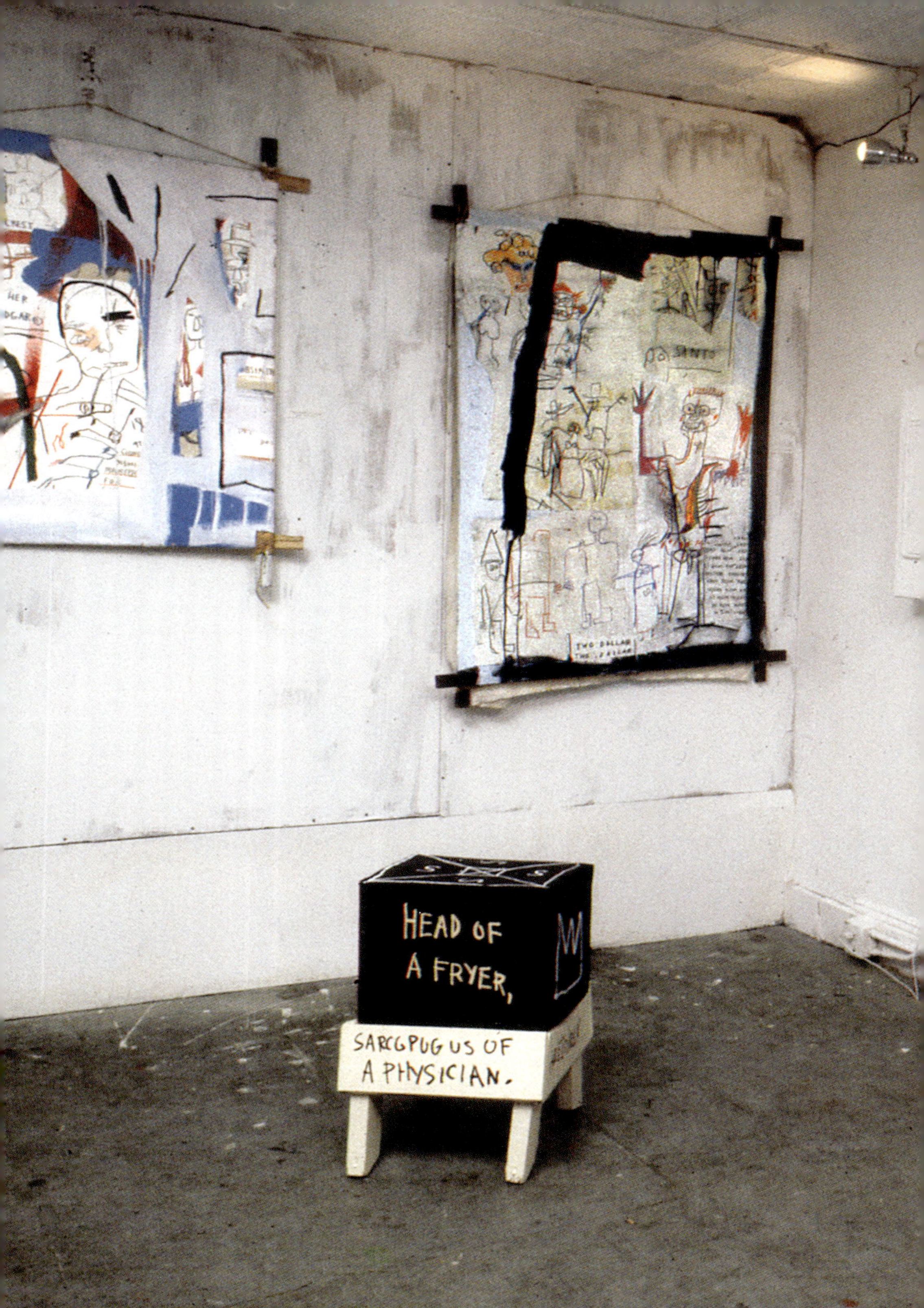
HEAD OF
A FRYER,
SARCGPUG US OF
A PHYSICIAN.

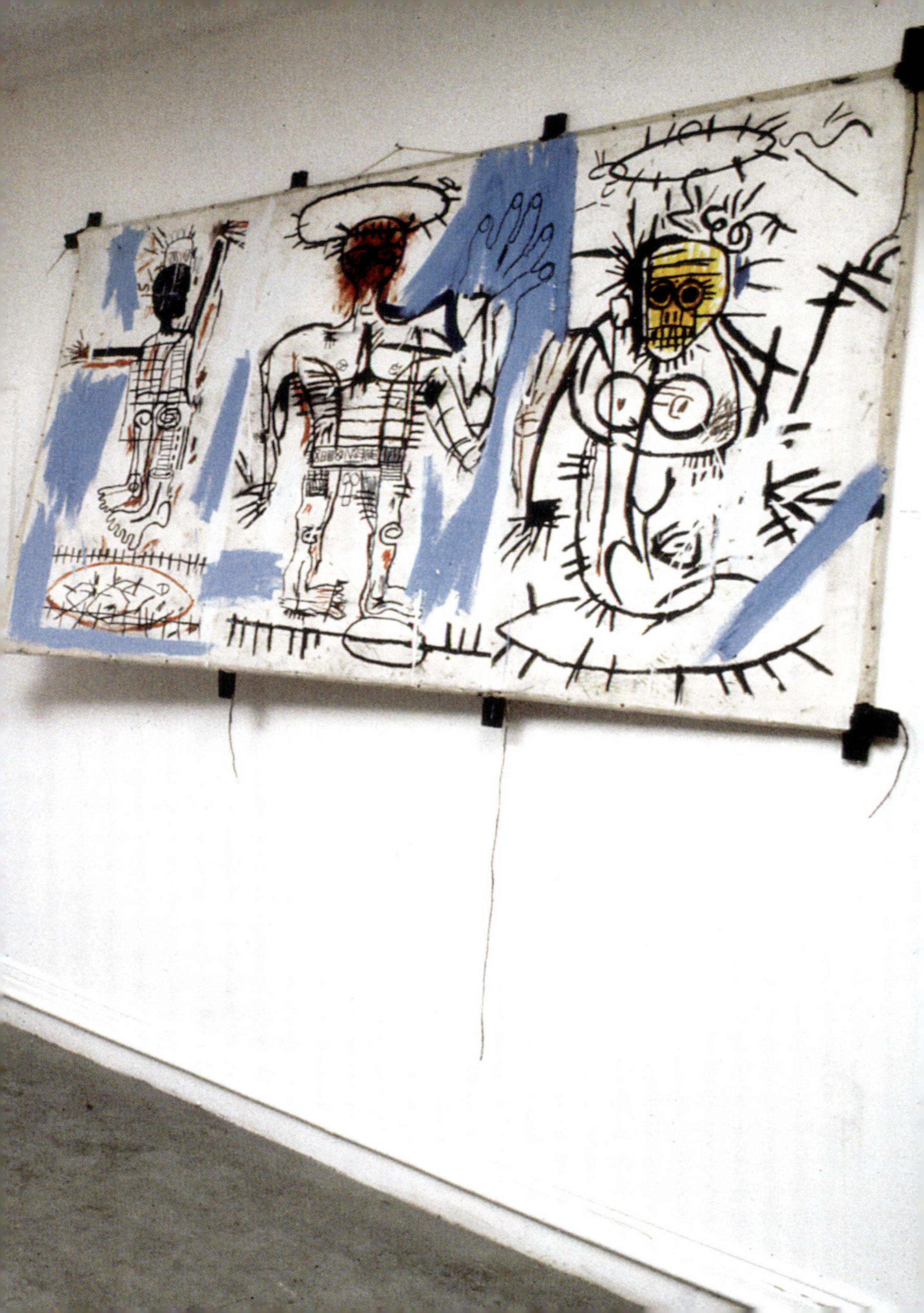

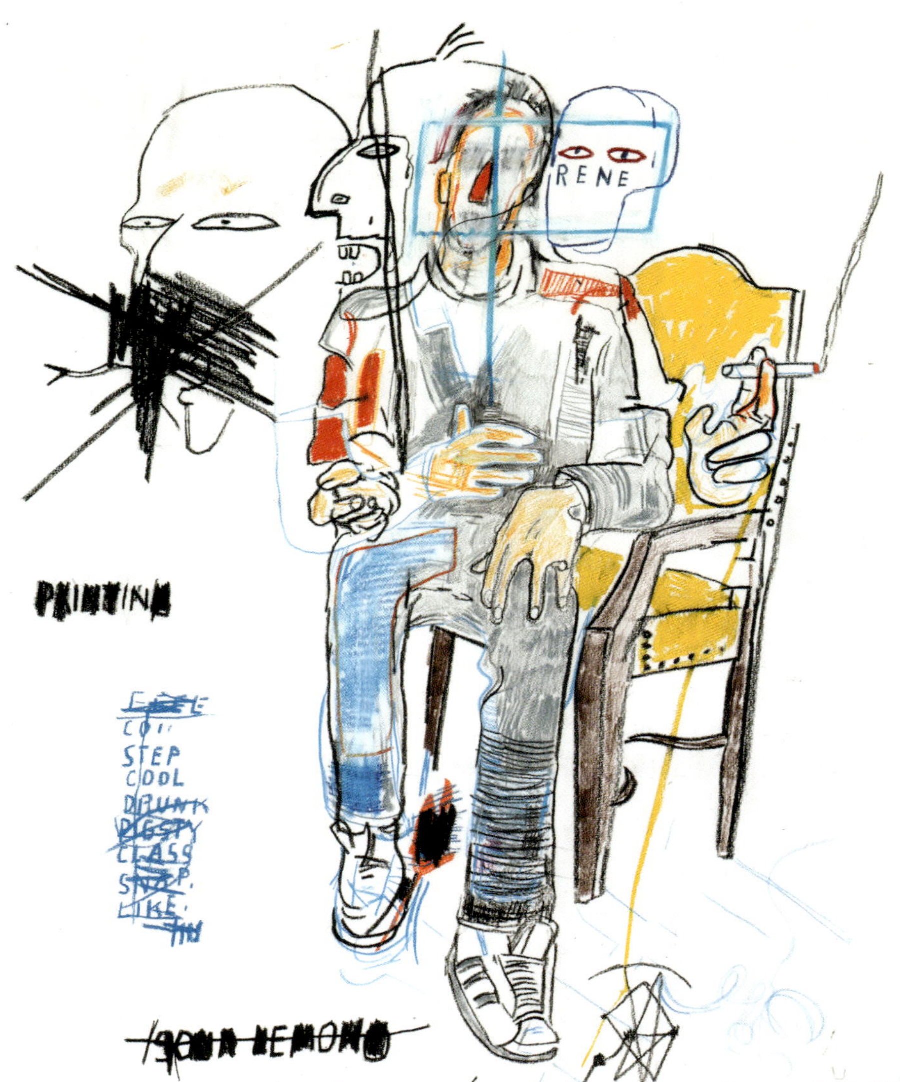

RENE

PRINTING

FEEL
COOL
STEP
COOL
DRUNK
PRETTY
CLASS
STOP.
LIKE.

JOHN LEMON

"EVERYBODY KNOWS (SIC) HAS NO/FRIENDS AND PAYS WELL FOR IT"
"GET YOUR NIGGERS OFF OF ME©"/ FRIENDS / "CHATEAU PINK©" —
HE'S ENJOYING THIS LOOK AT HIM. ◇FREINDS CHATEAU
EVERYBODY KNOWS (SIC) HAS NO/ FRIENDS AND PAYS WELL FOR IT.

"FALSE·TEETH"
L " " C "

fangs, to the right is a skeletal horned cow. The hot colors of the background and the two buzzing flies give an impression of the parched heat of the desert. The cluster of an "O" and five "a"s in the top-left corner returns us to the Alpha and Omega of *Revelation*, while the animal imagery seems to relate to *Genesis*: "And the Lord God said unto the serpent, Because thou hast done this, thou art cursed above all cattle … dust shalt thou eat all the days of thy life."[53]

Later that year, Basquiat worked feverishly on a new body of work to be presented at the Fun Gallery. As he later recalled: "I made the best paintings ever. I was completely reclusive, worked a lot, took a lot of drugs."[54] Opened by Bill Stelling and Patti Astor, the Fun Gallery was one of the first in the East Village, the gritty tenement storefront acting as a direct riposte to the slick galleries of SoHo. It was the perfect context for Basquiat to reveal a new direction, with "cross-bar" canvases made out of salvaged wood from skips and a generally more rough, energetic aesthetic. As Stelling explained in a letter to the curator Richard Marshall, Basquiat conceived of the exhibition as a "total installation" in which "the architecture reflected the rawness of the work. He designed … a couple of sheetrock walls dividing the gallery space into three areas [which] were left half finished, with exposed joint compound and metal studs."[55] He even soaped up the windows with wax to graffiti on (pp. 156/157).

Widely considered the most important show during his lifetime, the Fun Gallery exhibition was full of works that were dense with mythic stories. Even the invitation card (p. 499) featured a work with the name of the Norse god "THOR," with Basquiat's by-now trademark crown above and stars and a thunderbolt below. Works such as *Leonardo da Vinci's Greatest Hits* (1982; pp. 180/181), a playful take on Leonardo's annotated sketch-books, also featured the thunderbolt. "PROMETHEUS BOUND," written to the left, refers to the ancient Greek myth in which Prometheus defies the gods to gift fire to the people, for which he is subjected to eternal punishment; here, the thunderbolt may represent the one used by Zeus to strike him when he refuses to confess, plunging him into the abyss. Other pertinent phrases on this work include "RETURN OF THE PRODIGAL," which relates to the parable told by Jesus about a profligate son who seeks forgiveness from his father. Rembrandt depicted the story, which is said to demonstrate God's redemptive grace, in a painting from around 1665. Basquiat references this work in the kneeling leg that accompanies the inscription, which was likely taken from the illustration of it in his copy of H.W. Janson's *History of Art*.

The story of the Prodigal Son may well have been one that Basquiat identified with, given his own extravagant lifestyle. He used biblical imagery as a form of self-mythology

Pages 61/62: Jean-Michel Basquiat,
exhibition view, Fun Gallery,
New York 1982

Rene Ricard, 1984
Oilstick on paper, 76 x 56 cm /
30 x 22 inches

elsewhere too. *Portrait of the Artist as a Young Derelict* (1982; pp. 216/217), for example, is comprised of several pieces of wood, including a graffitied toilet door, hinged into a triptych. A soaring tower appears in the middle, with a coffin at the base, adorned with a simple white cross and the word "MORTE" (Italian for death). The theme of killing is continued with a crown, surrounded by a spray of white drips, rendering the image of a severed head; nearby in the exhibition, the work *Charles the First* (1982; p. 184) was inscribed with the line: "MOST ~~YOUNG~~ KINGS GET THEIR HEAD CUT OFF." To the right were the crossed-out words "~~HICE [ST] REX~~." Basquiat partially obscures his source, *Luke* 23:38, "Hic est rex luaeorum" ("This is the King of the Jews") and offers a Spanish slant: *hice* rex—"I did" or "I took" the king. *Luke* connects back to the title, given that the word "derelict" comes from the Latin, "de" (completely) and "relinquere" (forsaken); in *Matthew* 27:46, Jesus cries out "Eli, Eli, lama sabachthani?"—"My God, my God, why hast thou forsaken me?" The resulting imagery is of a homeless man, a stolen crown, and a forsaken father—which could be a dramatization of Basquiat's own experience, or a rendition of *Hamlet*.

The dizzying swarm of references in works such as this was offset by the graphic simplicity of others, such as *Untitled (Sugar Ray Robinson)* (1982; p. 202). Here a ghostly white outline demarcates a head, beneath a simple crown and name. It is as if an encyclopedic entry has been erased, because all that might be said—turned professional at 19, 91-fight unbeaten streak—is already known of the legend. *St. Joe Louis Surrounded by Snakes* (1982; p. 187), meanwhile, depicts the world heavyweight champion amidst a coterie of faces in his corner of the ring. The black surround to the work gives the impression of a television set, while the title likely refers to the "handlers" who took most of Joe Louis' profits. Prize-winning boxers were often dogged by (usually white) managers, who siphoned off the majority of their earnings. That both these fighters suffered financial ruin (as did athletes such as Jesse Owens, depicted in *Jesse*, 1983; p. 305) may have led Basquiat to foreground their names as a way to pose the question of whether a name or a title is ever enough. As Owens remarked: "You can't eat four gold medals."[56]

Few ranked higher in Basquiat's esteem than the great bebop pioneers, notably Charlie Parker, Thelonious Monk, Dizzy Gillespie, Miles Davis, and Max Roach. Basquiat had a personal connection to Roach, whose godson was Fab 5 Freddy, and he clearly felt a profound connection to the iconoclastic spirit with which this circle broke from older jazz harmonies. Basquiat was said to declare that he would "go crazy" if he could not listen to Charlie Parker every day[57] and he kept a box of copies of Ross Russell's biography *Bird Lives! The High Life and Hard Times of Charlie "Yardbird" Parker* (1973) in the studio

Brown Jaw, 1986
Acrylic, oilstick, and photocopy collage on canvas,
126 x 100 cm / 49 ¹/₂ x 39 ¹/₂ inches

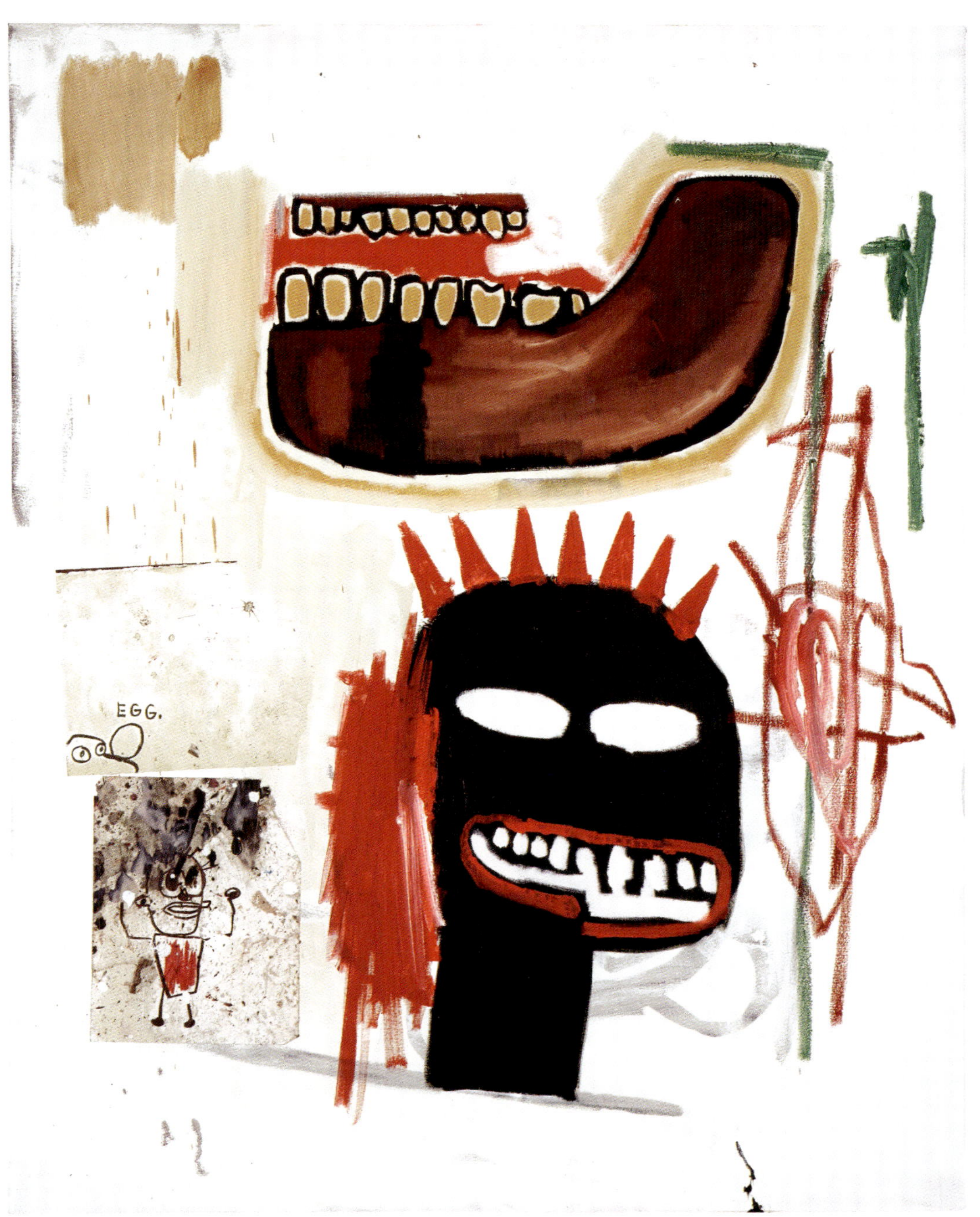

EGG.

to distribute to friends. One of his most important works at the Fun Gallery was *CPRKR* (1982; p. 67), an homage to his idol, featuring a contraction of his name; the "STANHOPE HOTEL," where he died; and the date "APRIL SECOND NINETEEN FIFTY ~~THREE~~ FIVE." By crossing out the number three, Basquiat introduces the year that Parker's daughter Pree died. By including April 2 (rather than March 12, the day Parker died), Basquiat highlights the extraordinary concert that was staged in Parker's memory at Carnegie Hall. The tea-stained hue of the painting could be an allusion to the program pages from this concert, in which Parker was described as "one of the great awakening forces in the evolution of Jazz."[58]

"YERE WOLO": Multi-Panel Mythology

In 1983, Basquiat began work on a new kind of painting. He started repurposing old pieces "that didn't work out," cutting them down and hinging them together into long polyptychs that could be concertinaed into his lift.[59] This technique (and perhaps some of the confidence from his recent critical success) enabled him to play out narratives on a grander scale. *Life Like Son of Barney Hill* (1983; pp. 242/243), for example, is comprised of six panels and is over 17 feet long. The title refers to an incident in 1961, when Barney and Betty Hill, a couple living in rural New Hampshire, claimed to have been abducted by aliens. Basquiat may have been intrigued by their supernatural story (widely disseminated in 1975 by the television film *The UFO Incident*) and to the fact that they were an interracial couple, active in the National Association for the Advancement of Colored People (NAACP). He pasted photocopied drawings in the background of several panels, as if to suggest the profusion of media coverage around these events, and overlaid images, including the red notary seal, Superman's emblem, and two circles joined by a horizontal line, which is the alchemical symbol for arsenic. The connection to death is emphasized by the appearance of Anubis, the Greek word for the Ancient Egyptian god of the afterlife, and the inscription "Lux Lucet in Tenebris," meaning light shines in the darkness.

Ancient mythology also appears in several other works of this period, such as *Ishtar* (1983; pp. 314/315), named after the goddess of fertility, sex, and war. This was a moment in which Afro-centrism was gaining momentum in New York and the history of Egypt, in particular, was being reclaimed by scholars from the Anglo-centric accounts that for centuries had misrepresented this ancient civilization as Caucasian. Basquiat's triptych is tiled with black-and-white photocopied drawings, barely legible beneath swathes of vibrant turquoise paint, which read like hieroglyphs on a wall. Amid them, in the upper

CPRKR, 1982
Acrylic, oilstick, and paper collage
on canvas mounted on wooden supports,
152.5 x 101.5 cm / 60 x 40 inches

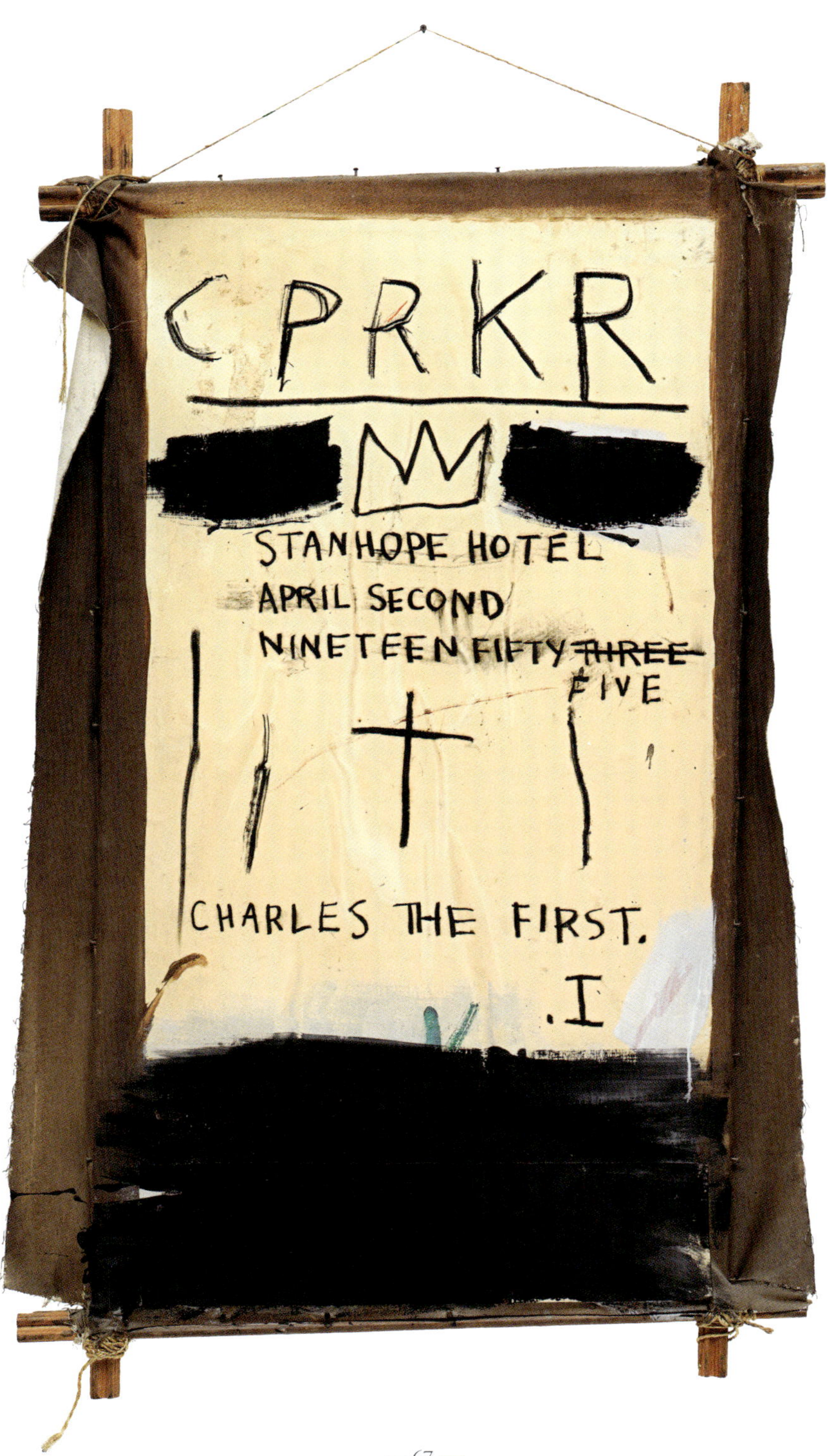
CPRKR
STANHOPE HOTEL
APRIL SECOND
NINETEEN FIFTY THREE
FIVE
CHARLES THE FIRST.
.I

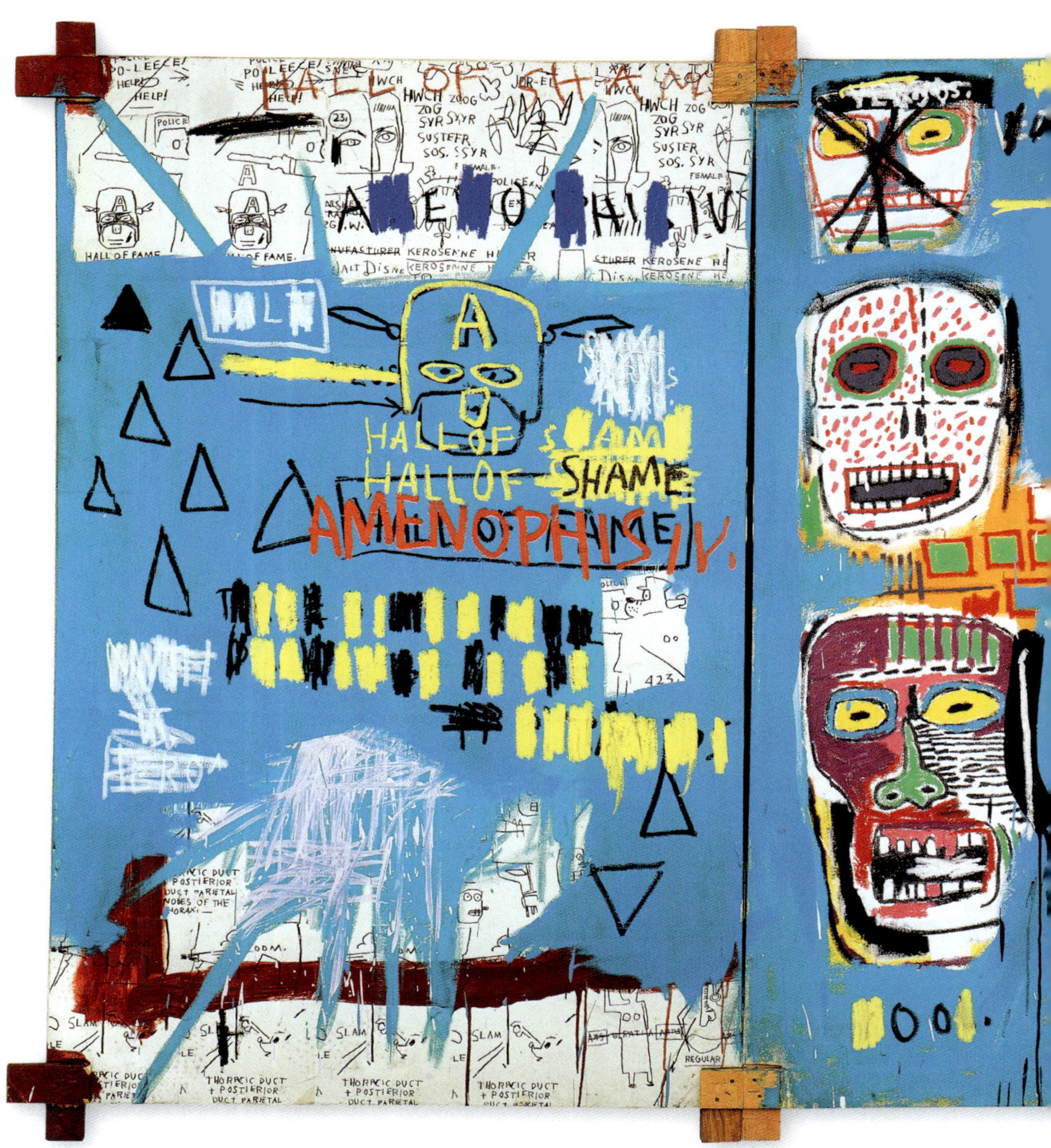

Mitchell Crew, 1983
Acrylic, oilstick, and photocopy collage on canvas
mounted on wooden supports with chain,
triptych: 181.5 x 350 cm / 71 ¹/₂ x 137 ³/₄ inches

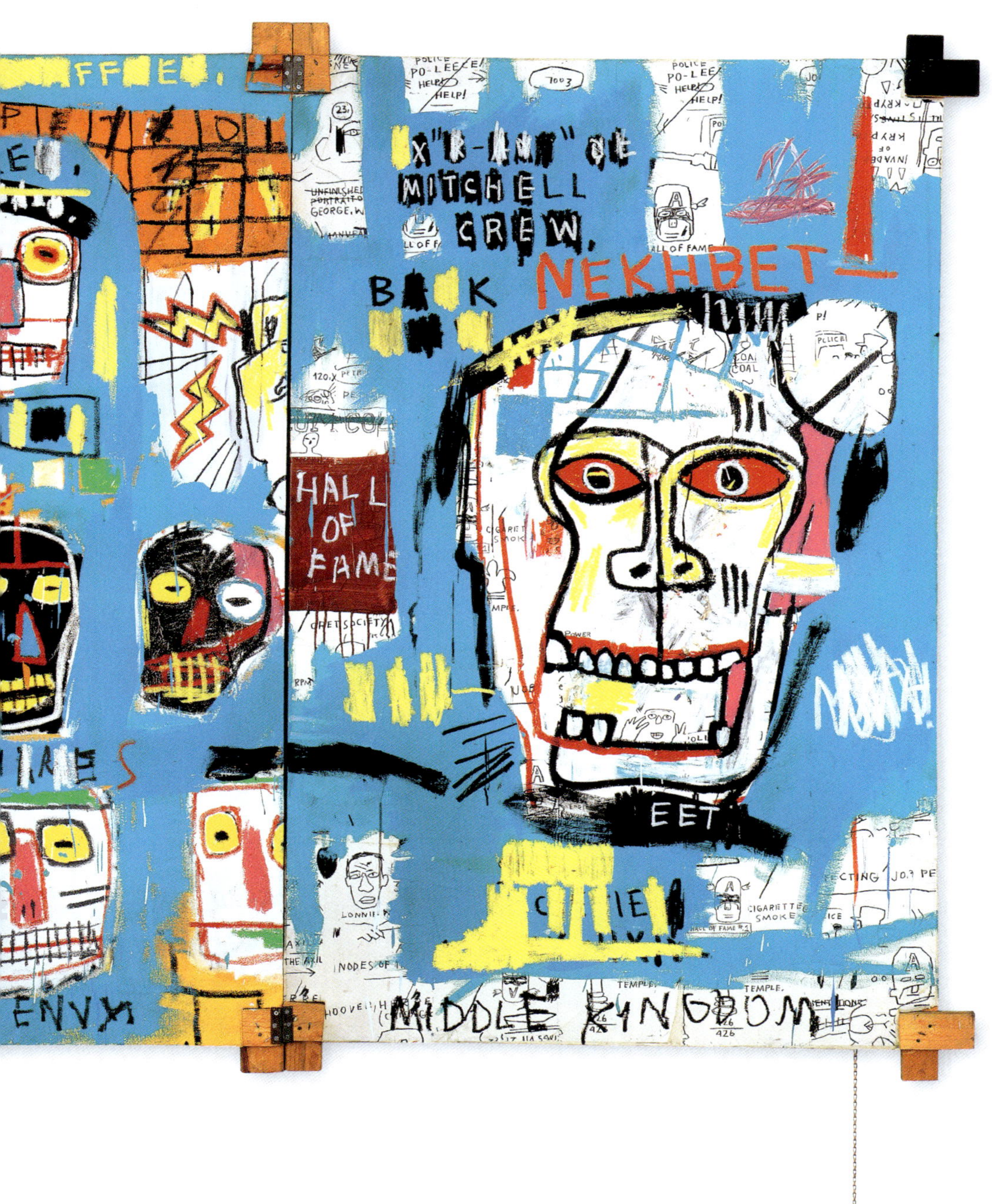

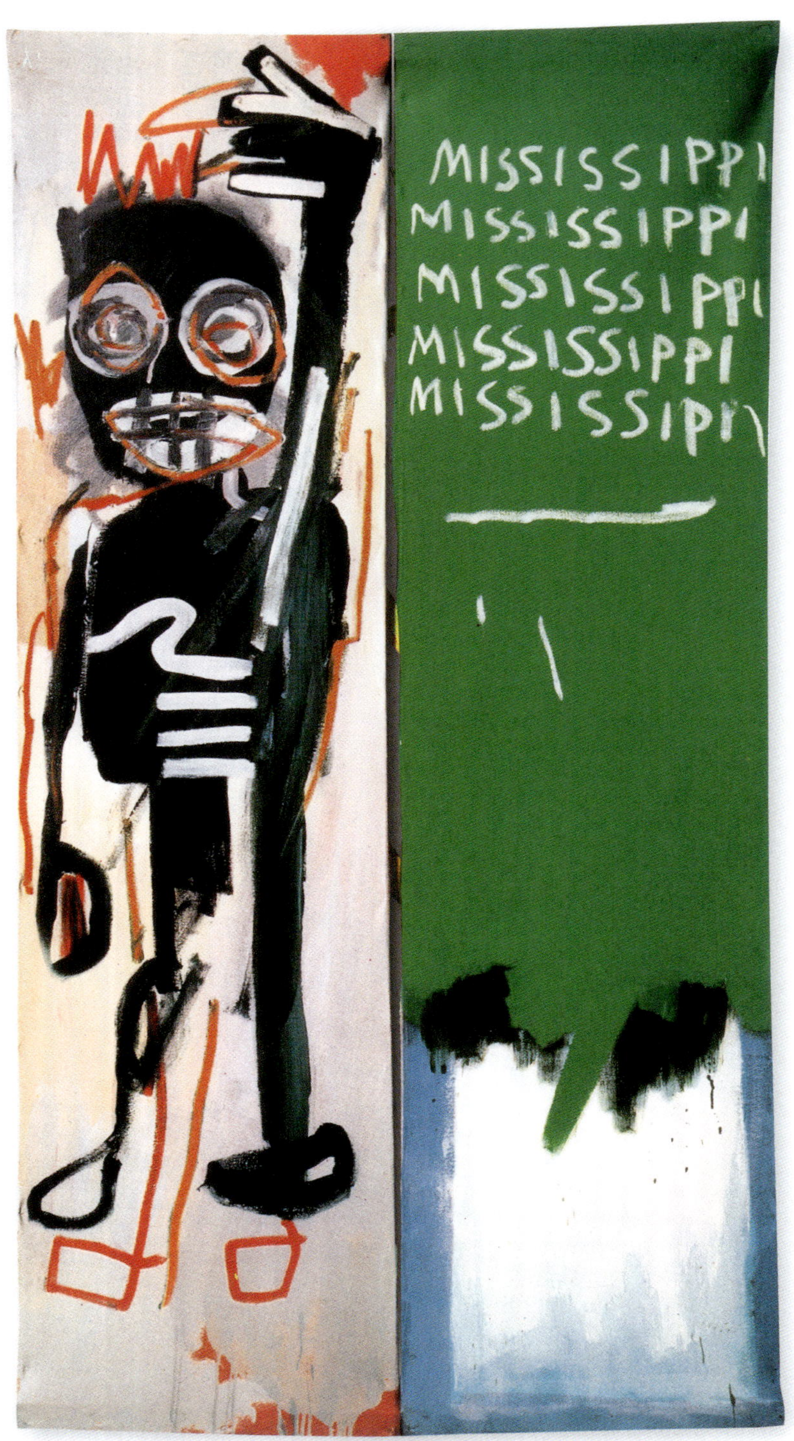

MISSISSIPPI
MISSISSIPPI
MISSISSIPPI
MISSISSIPPI
MISSISSIPPI

left, is a small drawing of a pig, beneath a seemingly incoherent list: "HWCH, ZOG, SYR, SUSTER, SOS." This detail must derive from *The Lost Language of Symbolism* (1912), in which Harold Bayley explains that "in Egypt the Sow was held sacred to Isis … Judging from the word *sus*, a sow, the female pig symbolized the SUSTAINER … The Welsh for *sow* is *hwch*, the Dutch is *zog*, and the Icelandic is *syr* … The root *sos* in Cornish, meaning *friend* and *comforter*, reappears in the name Jesus, the Ever-Existent Sos or Sus."[60] This rich line of connection between ancient Egypt and the Bible is developed elsewhere on the work. An apotropaic "LEFT EYE" appears above the word "KHNUM," the ancient river god, and to the left of the name "SEBEK," his son, who protected against the dangers of the Nile. On the left-hand panel there are biblical citations, including "KINGS VII, 21, 22," the story of Samson's "TEMPLE" (a word written above) and below "SIDE VIEW OF AN OXEN'S JAW," which likely refers to the "jawbone of an ass" with which Samson is said to have slain a thousand men.[61]

Around this time, Basquiat also began a spate of works dedicated to the stories of his personal pantheon of great jazz musicians, including *Horn Players* (1983; p. 286), *Max Roach* (1984; p. 330), *Trumpet* (1984; p. 331) and *Now's the Time* (1985; p. 19). In *Discography (One)* and *(Two)* (1983; pp. 270 and 271), he painted the background of two canvases black, and chalked up in white, like a faithful student, the details of two records from *Charlie Parker: The Complete Savoy Studio Sessions*—a box set of five LPs released in 1978. The works bear a close resemblance to Joseph Kosuth's *Art as idea as idea* (1967), a Photostat mounted on board of the dictionary definition of the word "black." Basquiat came of age against the backdrop of conceptual art and explicitly set out to create work as a counterpoint. As he explained in one interview, he was trying to differ from the "alienating" work he saw while growing up: "I wanted to make very direct paintings that most people would feel the emotion behind."[62] Alluding to Kosuth, he created a work that is both pared back and full of emotion; perhaps also wanting to indicate that there is more to the word "black" than its dictionary definition.

In the summer of 1984, with his work and reputation growing in scale, Basquiat had his first solo show in a public space at the Fruitmarket Gallery in Edinburgh. Curated by Mark Francis, the exhibition toured to the ICA in London that autumn. While installing in the Pall Mall galleries, Basquiat took the opportunity to create a new work, *Grillo* (1984; pp. 342/343), which is close to six yards in length and is as much a sculpture as a painting, with four wooden sections bristling with vertical lines of nails. In preparation, he made a series of detailed drawings, which were then photocopied to form the back-drop. Studying one of the originals (pp. 324/325) reveals the extent to which the artist

Mississippi, 1982
Acrylic and oilstick on canvas, diptych:
197 x 108 cm / 77 ¹/₂ x 42 ¹/₂ inches

engaged with being in the UK. The long lists of the phrase "HALF NELSON," like so many of Basquiat's favorite phrases, can be read in several ways. The term is generally used in wrestling to refer to the hold in which one arm is passed under the opponent's arm from behind with the palm applying pressure to the neck. "Half Nelson" was also a track recorded by Miles Davis in 1947, with Charlie Parker on tenor sax, John Lewis on piano, Max Roach on drums, and Nelson Boyd (after whom the song was named) on bass. The simple phrase is loaded with imagery of subjugation and what it might take to break free.

The key source for the drawing was the book *Flash of the Spirit* (1983) by Robert Farris Thompson.[63] "LEOPARD SKIN," for example, connects to Thompson's discussion of the "all-important male 'leopard society' [which] promulgated Ngbe values of nobility and government."[64] The figure with arrow hands in the bottom-left (who appears in a line of photocopies on *Grillo*) is taken from the "Emblems of Prowess" section and is said to mean: "All of this country belongs to me."[65] The phrase is intriguing in relation to the multiple mentions of "SUGAR" and "BRITISH WEST INDIES," referring to the British use of indentured labor in sugar cultivation in colonial territories, even after the abolition of slavery. The word "BREADFRUIT" amplifies this connection, relaying the story of Captain William Bligh, who in 1787 embarked on a six-year journey to Tahiti to seek out breadfruit as a cheap source of food for the slave population. Elsewhere on the drawing are the words "YERE WOLO," which Thompson explains is a Mande concept: "the search for simplicity … by stripping away the superficial cover, by discovering its inner and true nature."[66] The phrase literally translates as giving birth to yourself, and in Basquiat's story telling we find him doing exactly that: exploring a whole encyclopedia of subject matter in order to understand—and construct—his place in the world.

"Just real stories"

Basquiat was always remarkably confident about the celebrated artist that he would become. In January 1981, he had just finished filming for *Downtown 81* and by February he was the toast of the town for his first body of work in *New York/New Wave.* On October 4, 1982, when Bischofberger brought Basquiat to Warhol's studio to have his portrait taken, he didn't stay for lunch but dashed straight back to Crosby Street, where he painted *Dos Cabezas* (p. 199). The work captures a remarkable likeness of the two artists: Warhol with his wild wig and Basquiat with his crown of dreadlocks, unashamedly positioning himself as an equal to his hero. Basquiat had it delivered back to Warhol later that afternoon, still dripping in paint, perhaps knowing that for Warhol speed was the ultimate skill. Sure enough, within a year they would begin collaborating (first with Francesco Clemente and then on their own) on a series of joint paintings, and would develop a friendship as unexpected as it was profound.

By the time Basquiat embarked upon *Pegasus,* shortly after Warhol's death, he had racked up the curriculum vitae of a veteran, with exhibitions in countries as far-flung as

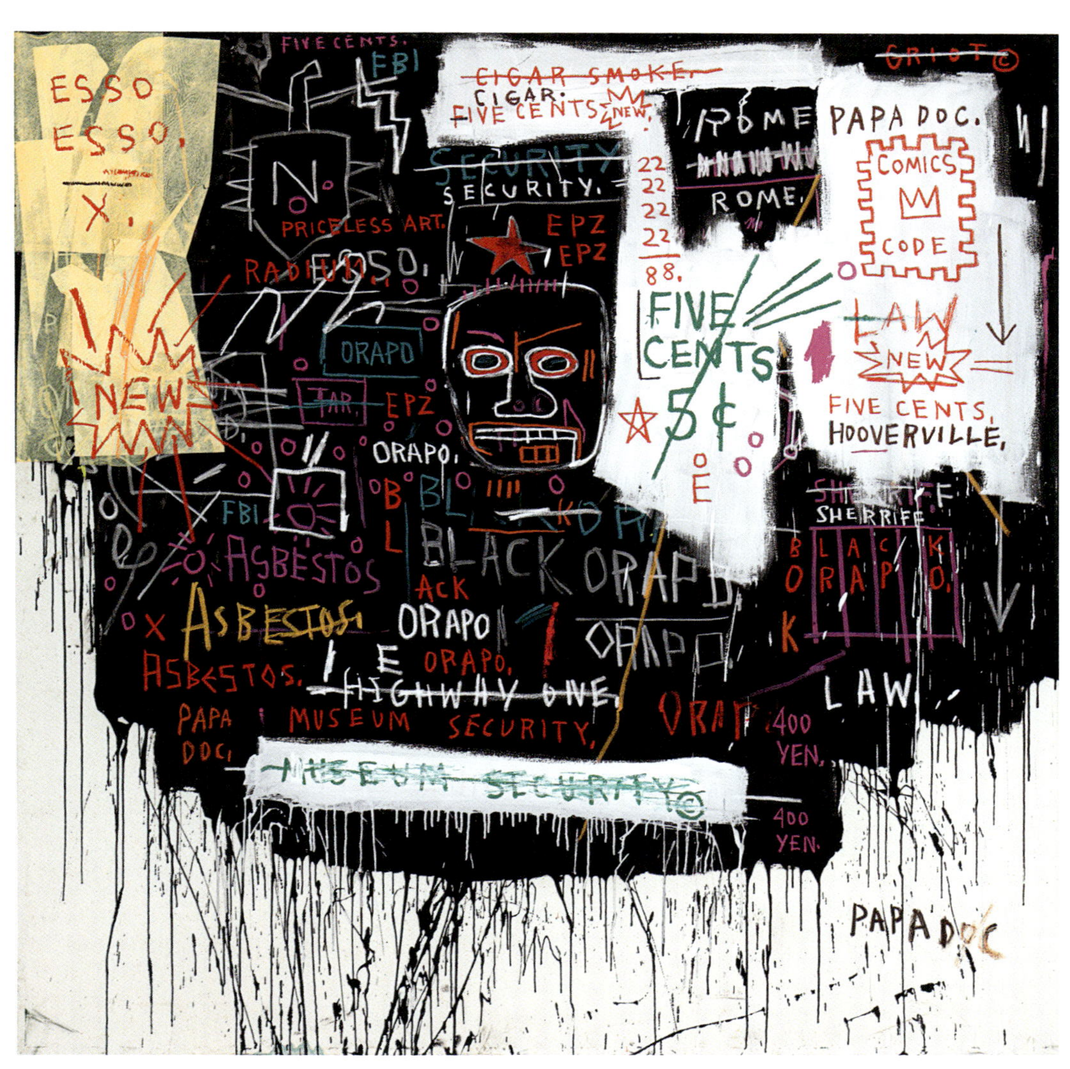

Museum Security (Broadway Meltdown), 1983
Acrylic, oilstick, and paper collage on canvas,
213 x 213 cm / 83 ³/₄ x 83 ³/₄ inches

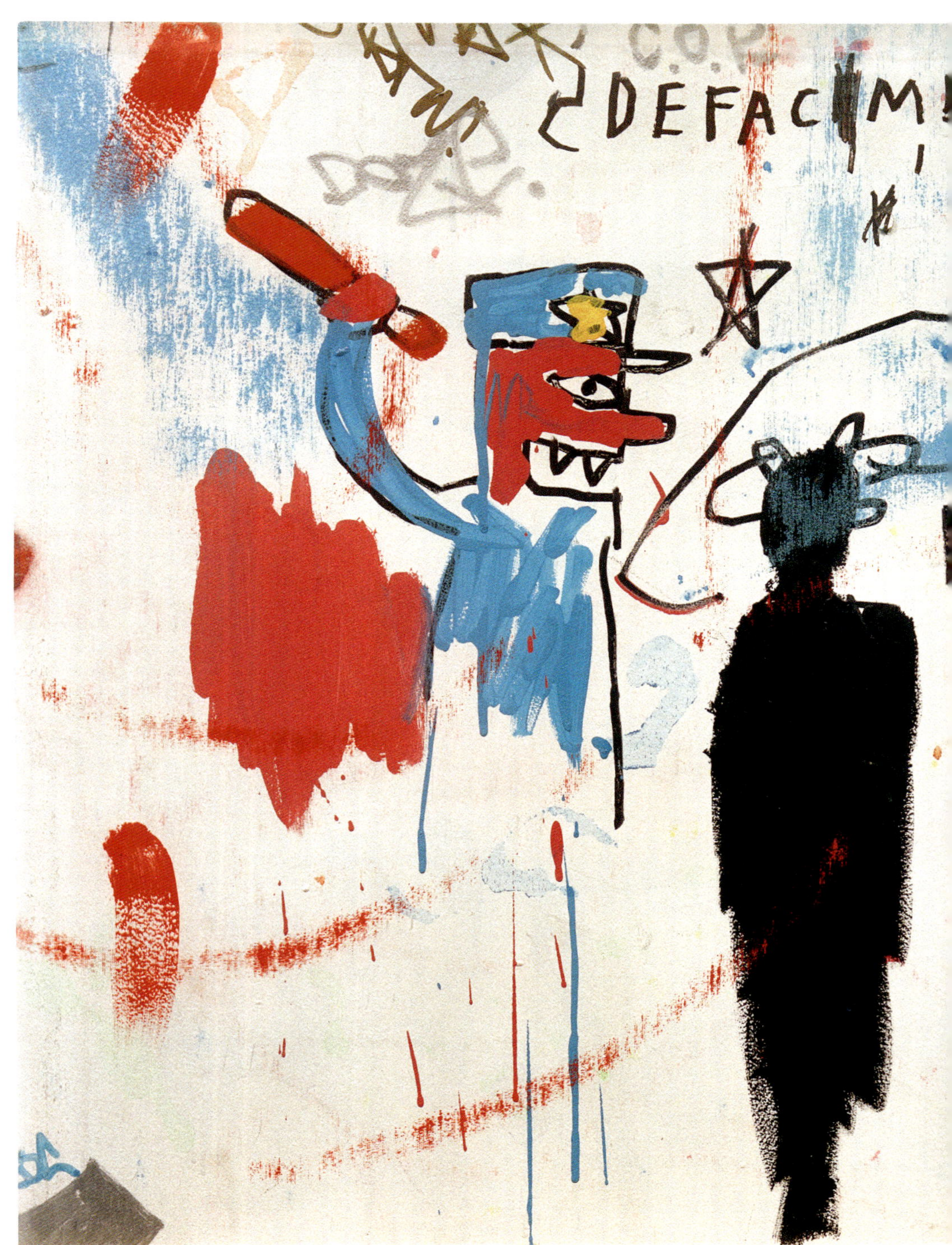
C.O.P.
DEFACM

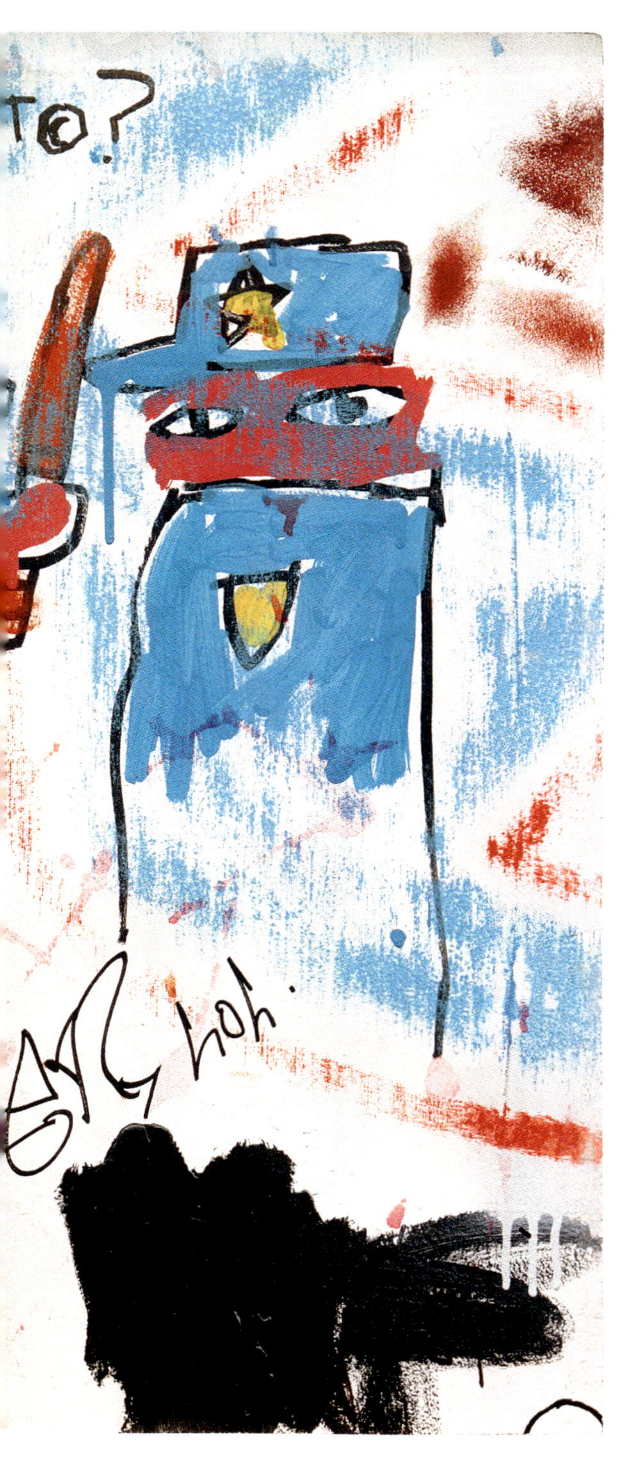

Defacement
(The Death of Michael Stewart), 1983
Acrylic and marker on board,
63.5 x 77.5 cm / 25 x 30 ¹/₂ inches

the Ivory Coast and Japan. He had been the subject of extensive media coverage, and in an interview in 1985 had explained: "I try to be a little reclusive, and not just to be out there and be brought up and down."⁶⁷ He was likely referring to the collaborations with Warhol, which had been exhibited that September to very mixed reviews, no doubt making him feel disillusioned with the media. By 1987, his appetite for the whole art world was waning (even though he would exhibit important new works in the year to come) and he had begun to contemplate alternative career paths. With his friend Kevin Bray, he dreamed of making experimental films, such as a re-staging of a Hitchcock classic but with all the parts played by real people they would seek out on a road trip.⁶⁸ Similarly, in an interview with his friends Tamra Davis and Becky Johnston, when they asked what he would be doing if he weren't painting, he replied: "Directing movies, I guess. I mean ideally."⁶⁹ When they asked what kind, he said: "Ones in which black people are portrayed as being people of the human race. And not aliens and not all negative and not all thieves and drug dealers and the whole bit. Just real stories."⁷⁰

The narratives that Basquiat constructed within his work were hardly the kitchen-sink realism implied here. Although he did often feature evidence of his everyday life—such as the shoe prints that testify to how he abused his work, walking over drawings scattered on the floor, or the phone numbers that he would write directly on a canvas if he didn't have a notebook to hand. Perhaps in reaching for extraordinary stories—of biblical figures, Ancient Egyptian kings, sporting heroes, bebop musicians—he felt he had a better chance of rebalancing the books, fighting the pejorative stereotypes of "drug dealers and the whole bit." Although not always explicitly political, Basquiat worked with a poster of the pan-African proponent Marcus Garvey on the wall of his Great Jones Street studio and we do well to recall his father's words: "He didn't have to politicize through a microphone. The works possess messages and speak for themselves."⁷¹

Those messages resound with wit and knowing charm. They have a way of reaching back into the darkest recesses of human history and forward to touch us now. When confronted with the work, it is hard to fathom the bounding intellectual curiosity that brought together such a constellation of reference points and harder still to imagine the process required to do so in a pre-digital age. Basquiat may be gone but his work stands to impel and inspire us still; the strands of ancient and modern myth converge on questions of who we were and what we have become.

¹⁻⁷¹ See Endnotes on pages 506ff.

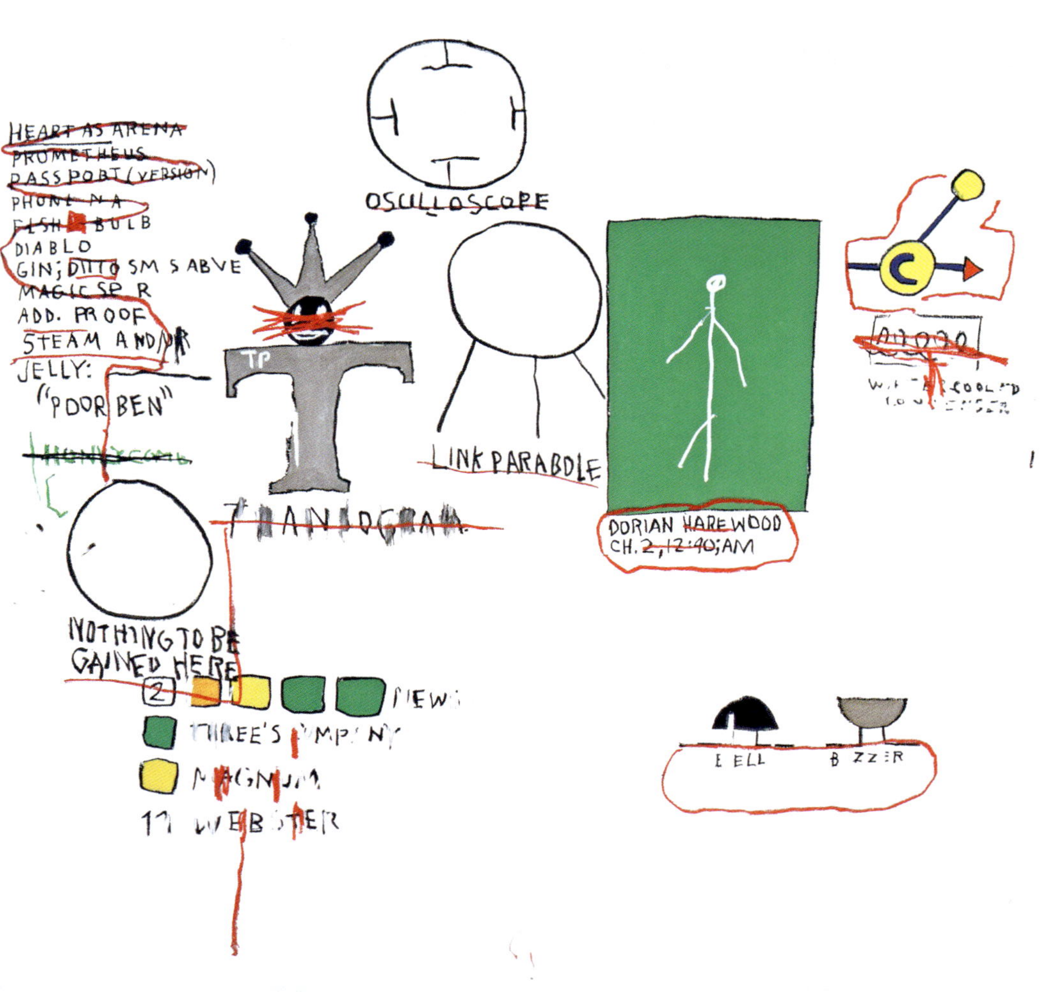

TV Star, 1988
Acrylic and oilstick on canvas,
277 x 289.5 cm / 107 x 111 inches

King Pleasure, 1987
Acrylic on canvas, 125.5 x 100.5 cm /
49 ¹/₂ x 39 ¹/₂ inches

Pages 80/81: Jean-Michel Basquiat in his
Great Jones Street studio, New York 1985.
Photo Lizzie Himmel

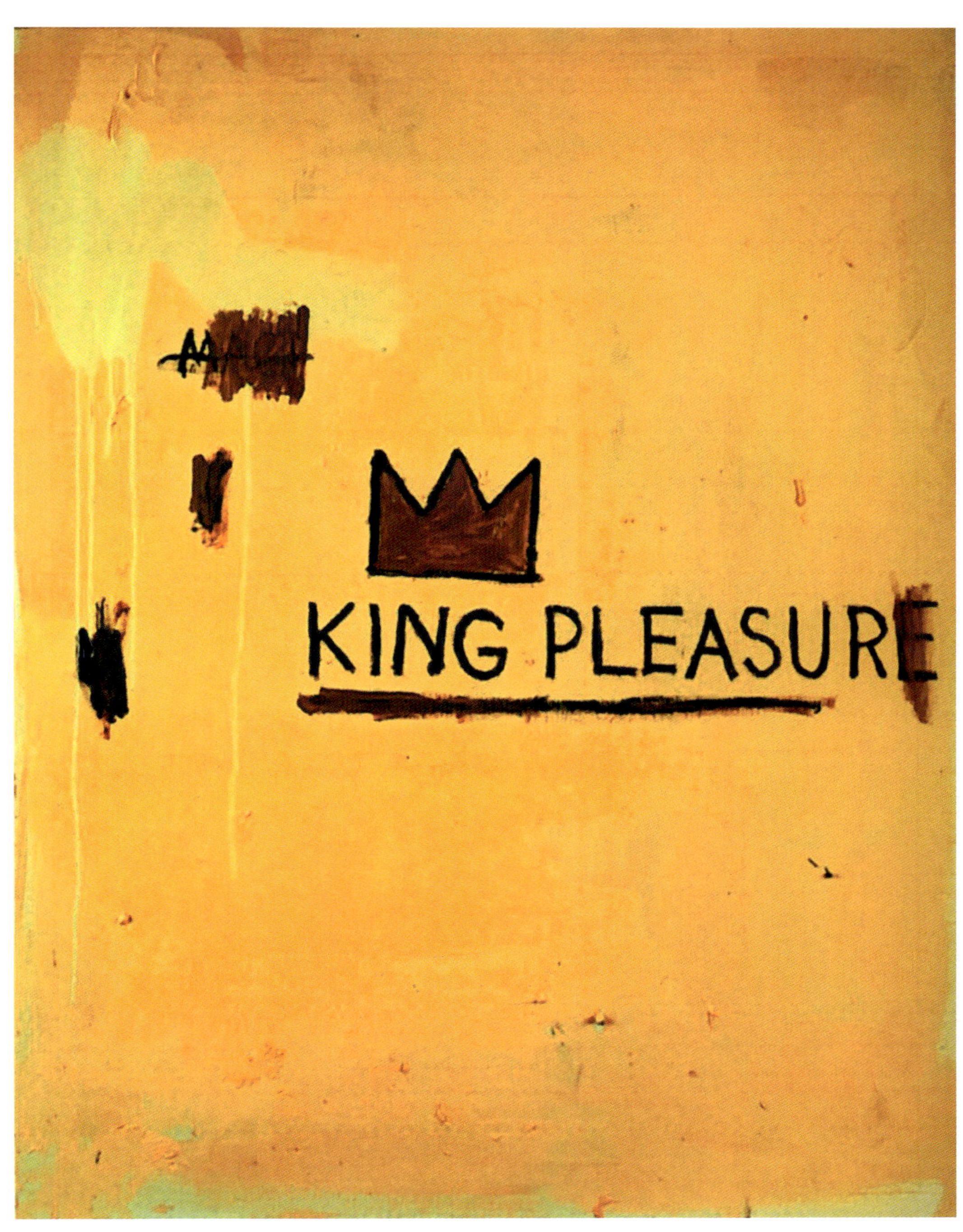

KING PLEASURE

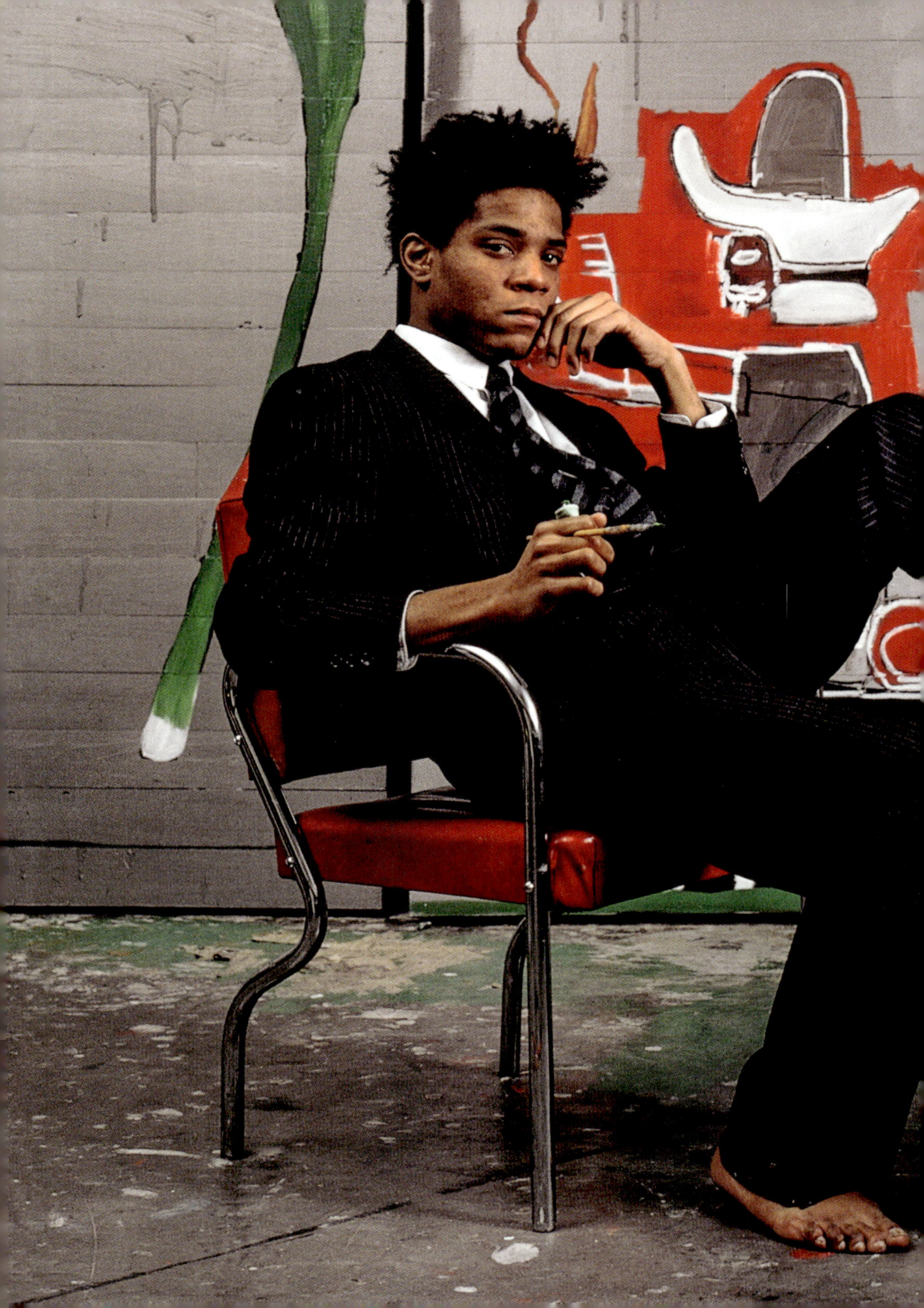

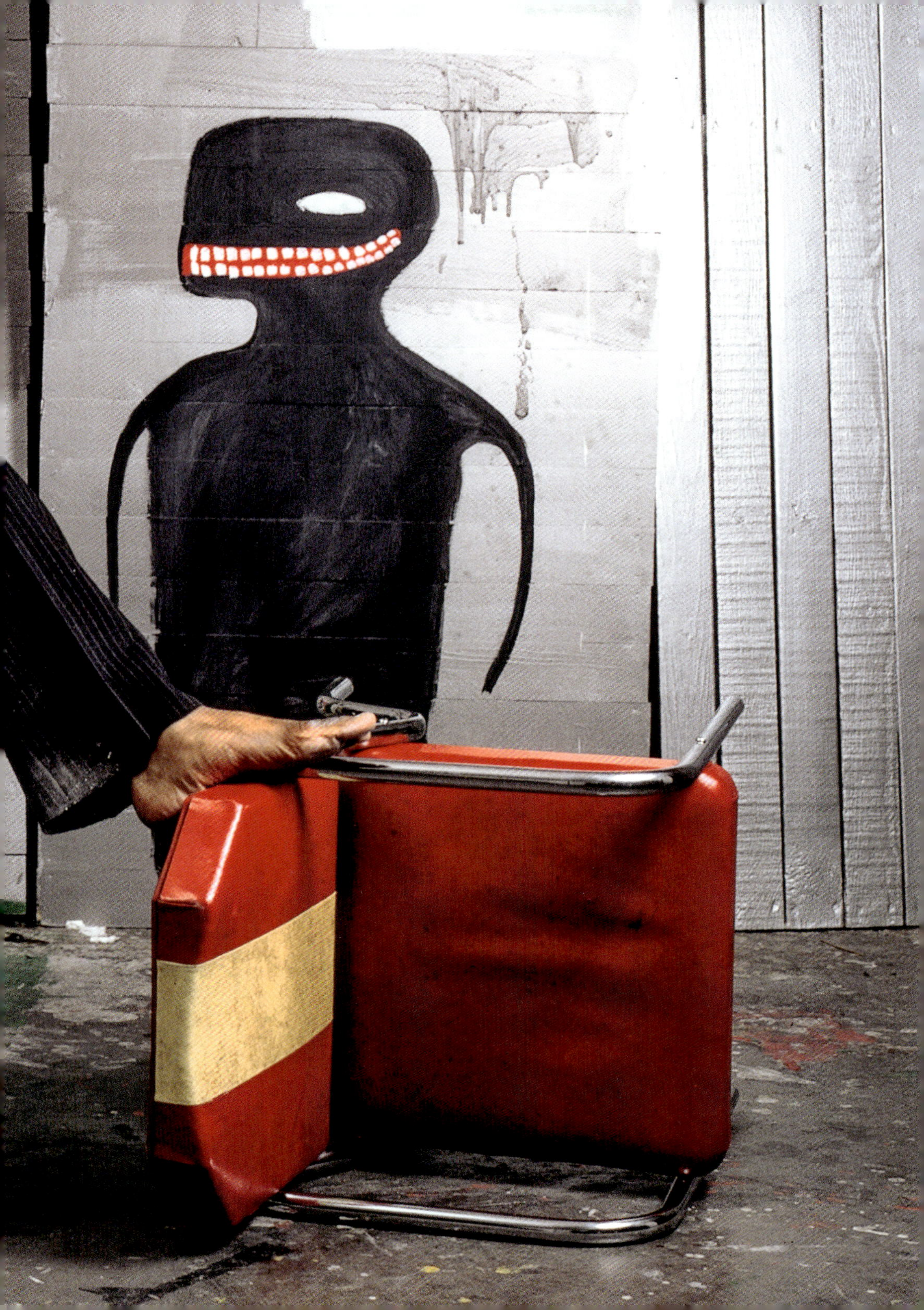

I.

1978–1980
Samo is coming

—PHILIP FAFLICK, *THE VILLAGE VOICE*, 1978[1]

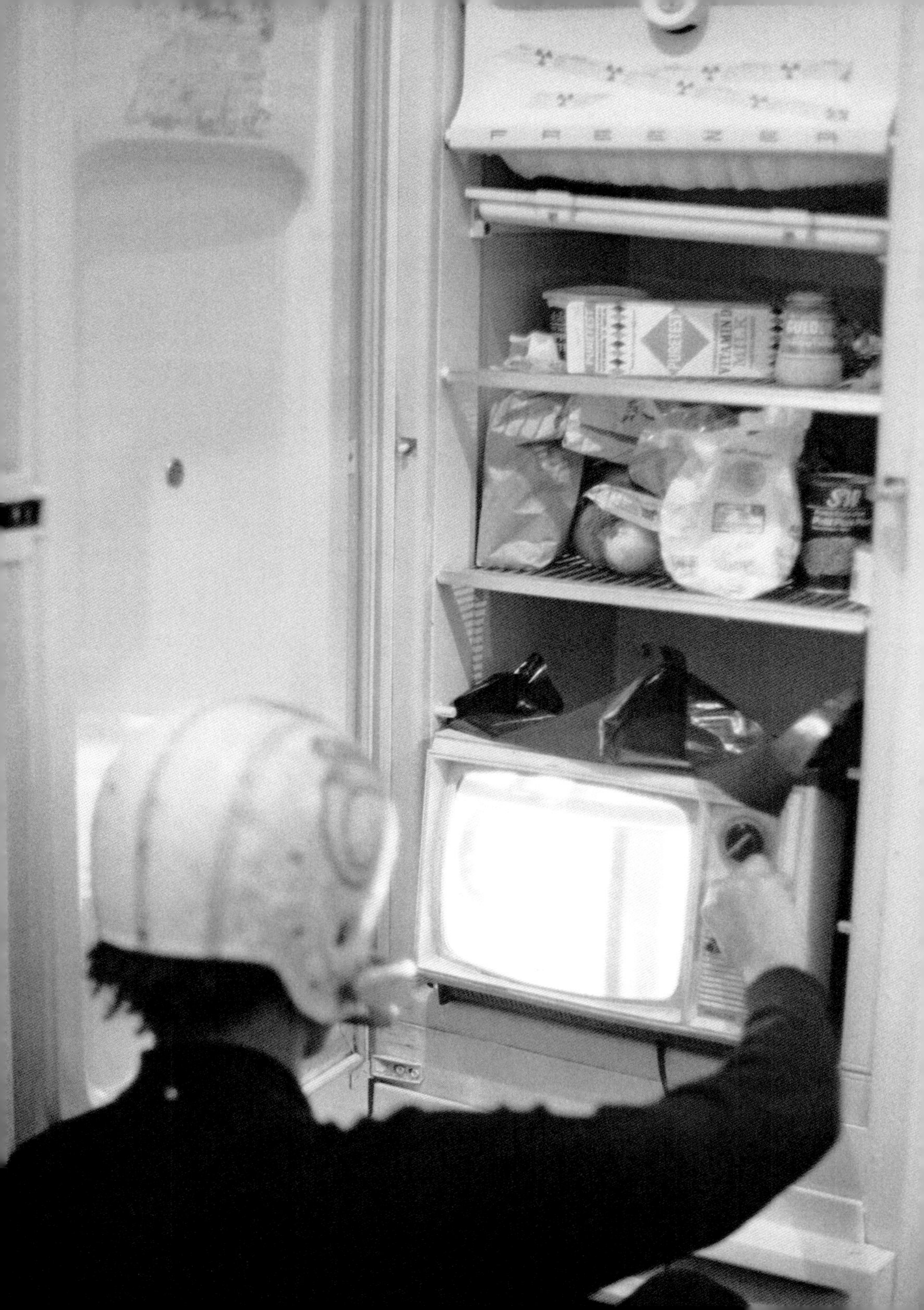

On December 11, 1978, an article in the New York weekly *Village Voice* reveals Jean-Michel Basquiat and Al Diaz as the originators of the intriguing graffiti messages that have sprung up all over the city (front papers till p. 3): "SAMO© was hatched this spring in the alternative high school in Brooklyn Heights where Jean and Al ended up ... This May, Jean and Al took SAMO© to the streets. The first, at the Corner of Church and Franklin: SAMO© IS NOW! A little way up the block: SAMO© IS COMING! On a church on West Broadway: SAMO© AS AN ALTERNATIVE TO GOD. And in the men's room of their high school: SAMO© AS AN ALTERNATIVE TO ALTERNATIVE EDUCATION. Does SAMO© in fact provide an alternative? 'No way,' Jean and Al agree. 'SAMO© is just a means of bringing it out,' Jean continues. 'A tool for mocking bogusness.'"[2] Yet soon after they have gone public, in early 1979, the words "SAMO© IS DEAD" begin appearing on the streets. These are written by Basquiat as a farewell, and the two go their different ways. Diaz will stay true to his graffiti background, while Basquiat, taking the name Samo with him, follows his ambition to become an artist.

At 19, Basquiat is very much a central actor on the New York club scene with other artists and musicians—among them Patti Astor, David Byrne, Diego Cortez, Debbie Harry, Arto Lindsay, John Lurie, and Madonna—haunting CBGBs, Club 57, and the newly opened Mudd Club. He also has friends in graffiti and rap circles such as Fab 5 Freddy, Lee Quinones, and the Afro-futurist Rammellzee. Like many of his fellow scenesters, Basquiat appears on Glenn O'Brien's newly inaugurated cable television show *TV Party* as Samo, first introduced in April 1979 by the host as "probably the most language-oriented of all graffiti artists in New York."[3] He designs his own T-shirts, makes collages, and, like many budding artists, creates and photocopies art postcards that he sells on the streets, some in collaboration with Jennifer Stein and John Sex. On one occasion approaches Andy Warhol and Henry Geldzahler inside a SoHo restaurant and manages to sell a couple of postcards to Warhol.

In May, Basquiat founds the band Gray with Michael Holman and Shannon Dawson, later joined

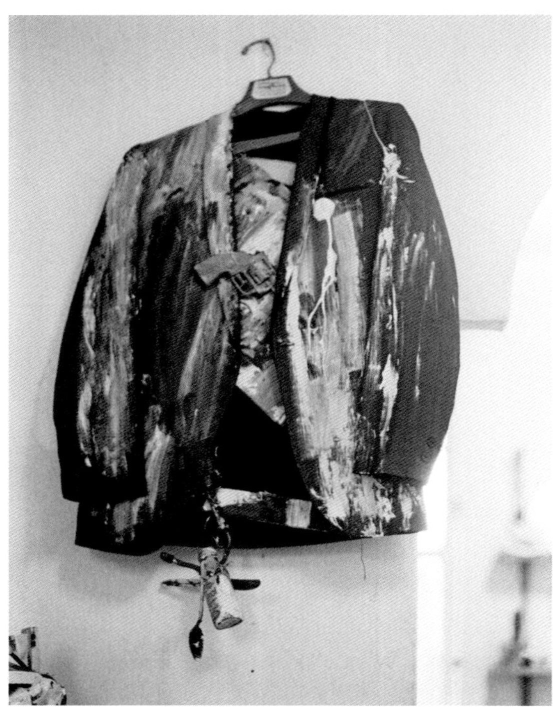

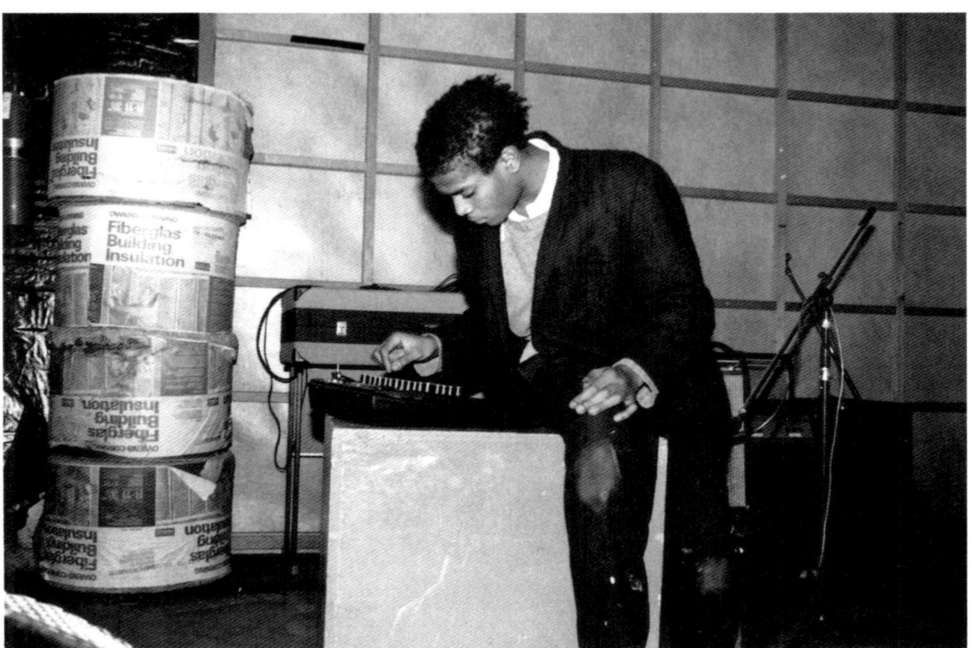

Page 83: Jean-Michel Basquiat stages a performance in his flat on 527 East 12th Street, New York 1979. Photo Alexis Adler

Jean-Michel Basquiat at Hurrah's, New York 1979. Photo Nicholas Taylor

Page 84: Artwork by Jean-Michel Basquiat, New York 1979. Photo Alexis Adler

by Wayne Clifford, Nick Taylor, and Vincent Gallo. The name is chosen after *Gray's Anatomy*, an anatomy book his mother gave him when as a seven- year-old child he spent time in a hospital after being hit by a car, and which would remain influential throughout his artistic development. The band takes an experimental approach: their freely improvised music is about discovering new sounds rather than recognizable songs; Basquiat plays un-tutored clarinet, synthesizers, or guitar with a file; and their self-consciously avant-garde performances place them within New York's noisy No Wave aesthetic.

After a time of finding shelter with any friends and acquaintances that would offer him a couch, Basquiat now lives with his girlfriend Alexis Adler in a first proper apartment on 527 East 12th Street. Without a studio to work in, he draws on floors and walls, refrigerator doors, window frames, and whatever he can find on the streets. He befriends fellow artists Keith Haring and Kenny Scharf, who make a similar transition from the streets to the gallery circuit, as well as artist and fledgling curator Diego Cortez, who starts selling some of his drawings and making connections.

In June 1980, the collaboratively organized group exhibition *Times Square Show* (pp. 88/89) opens in a vacant building on 41st Street and Seventh Avenue, presenting a proliferation of mostly still unknown artists. This is the first public showcase for Basquiat, and critics are quick to spot his work. Jeffrey Deitch in *Art in America*: "A patch of wall by SAMO, the omnipresent graffiti sloganeer, was a knock-out combination of de Kooning and subway spray-paint scribbles."[4] Lucy Lippard in *Artforum* gives us the exhibition details: "And a hand sink overflowing with grimy salt crystals, and some terrific feminist comic-strip posters, and a room of painted clothes, and SAMO's critical graffiti, and 'Take Back the Night' scrawled here and there, and a scab-picker's bathroom of peeling red paint I liked better than the work in it, and a garbage and rat fountain and the ubiquitous decorated machines and a lot of other Indescribable Things … You get the picture?"[5]

In December, Basquiat starts acting as the lead character in the film *New York Beat*, written by Glenn O'Brien—who has also cast him—and directed by Edo Bertoglio. Basquiat more or less plays himself, reenacting his days as a graffiti writer while painting raw canvases and trying to make it as an artist (until fortune kisses him in the form of Debbie Harry in a cameo role as the good fairy). During the two months of filming, Basquiat lives in the production offices, buys some proper art supplies from his fee, and also paints there. He sells his first work to Harry for $100. Among other seminal acts of the downtown music scene, the film also presents his band Gray. It remains the only record of his activities with the band, which he soon quits to completely focus on art. The film will only be released in 2000 under the title *Downtown 81*.

^{4 5} *See Endnotes on page 508.*

Untitled, 1980
Acrylic and oilstick on sheet metal,
244 x 122 cm / 96 x 48 inches

Pages 88/89: Exterior view of the
Times Square Show, New York 1980.
Photo Terise Slotkin

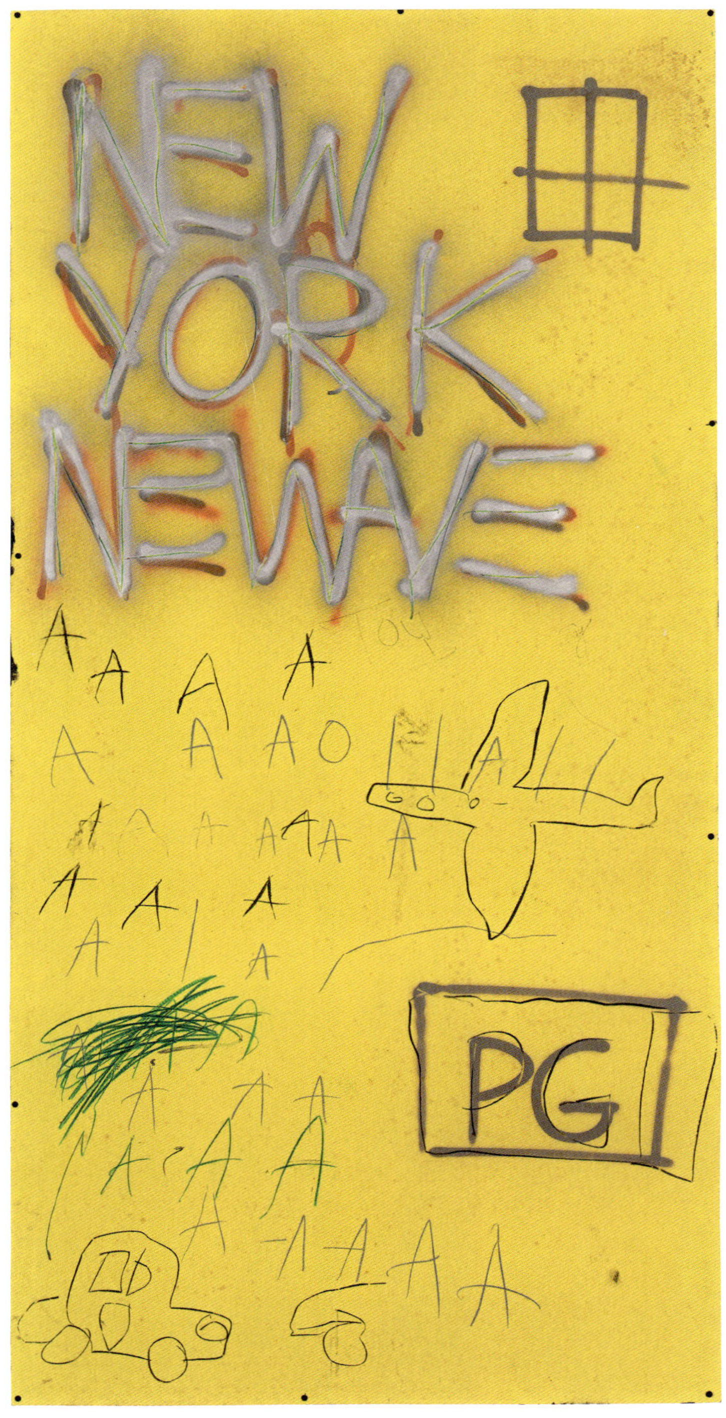
NEW
YORK
NEW WAVE
PG

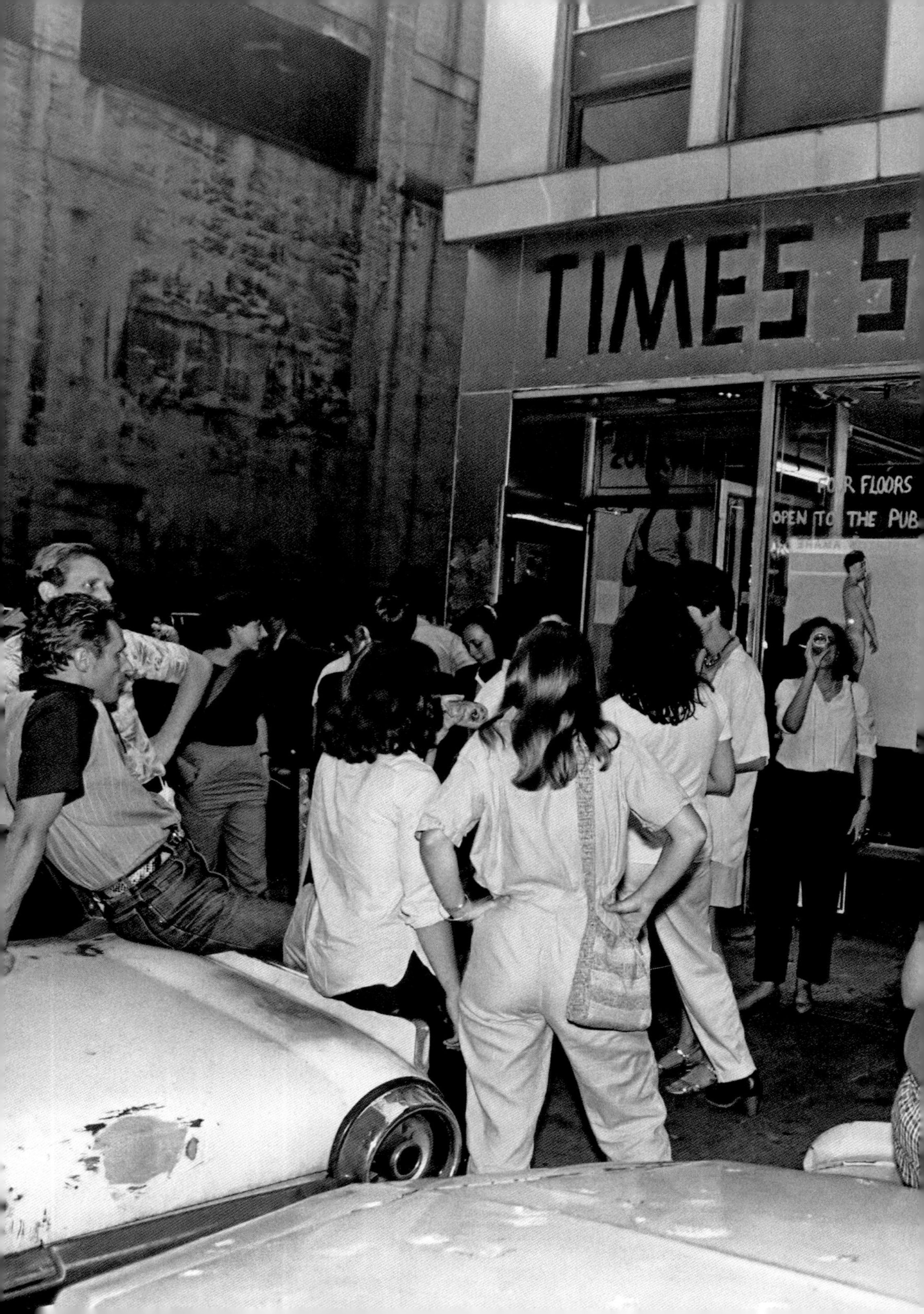

TIMES S
FOUR FLOORS
OPEN TO THE PUB

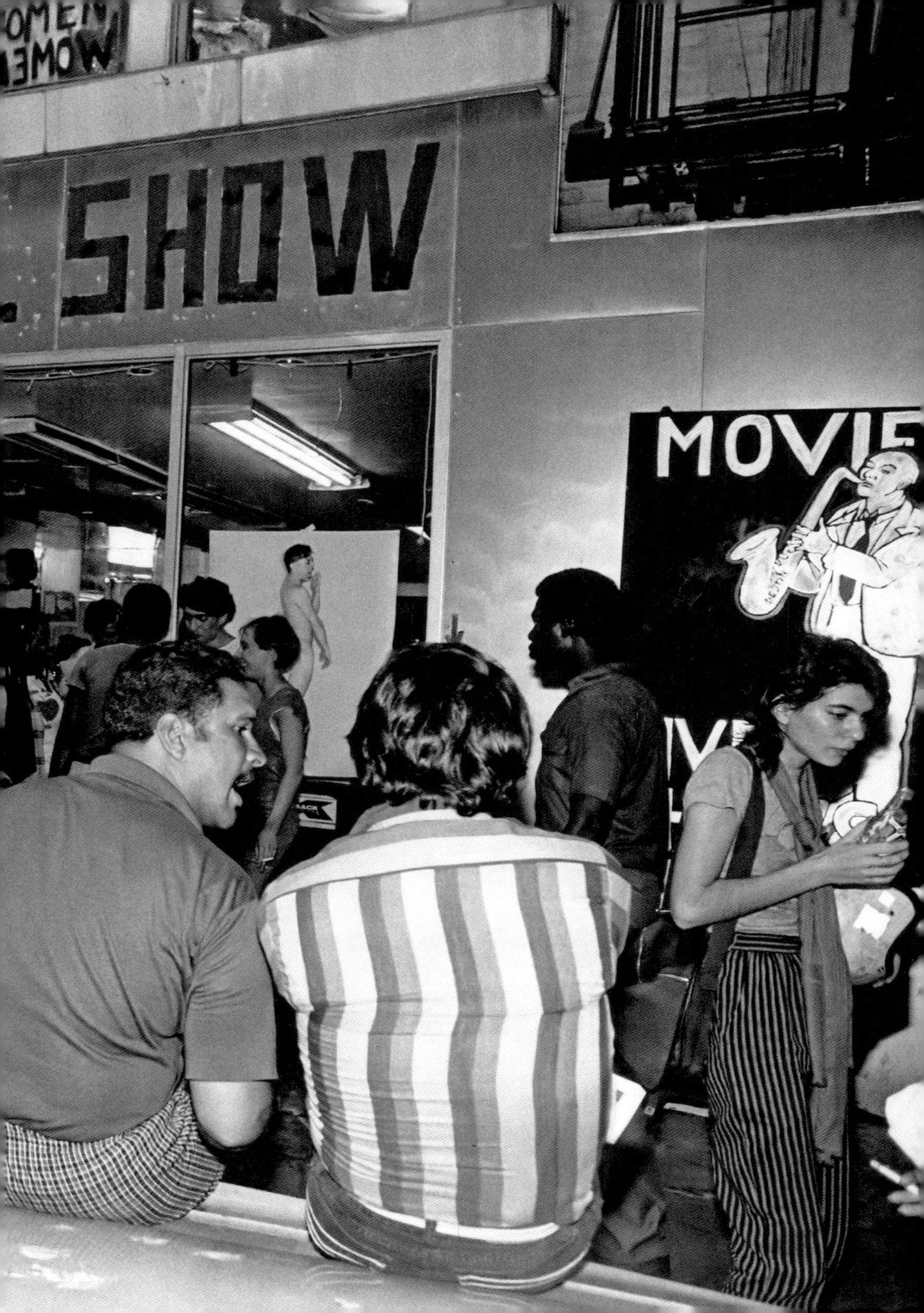

WOMEN
WOMEN
SHOW
MOVIE

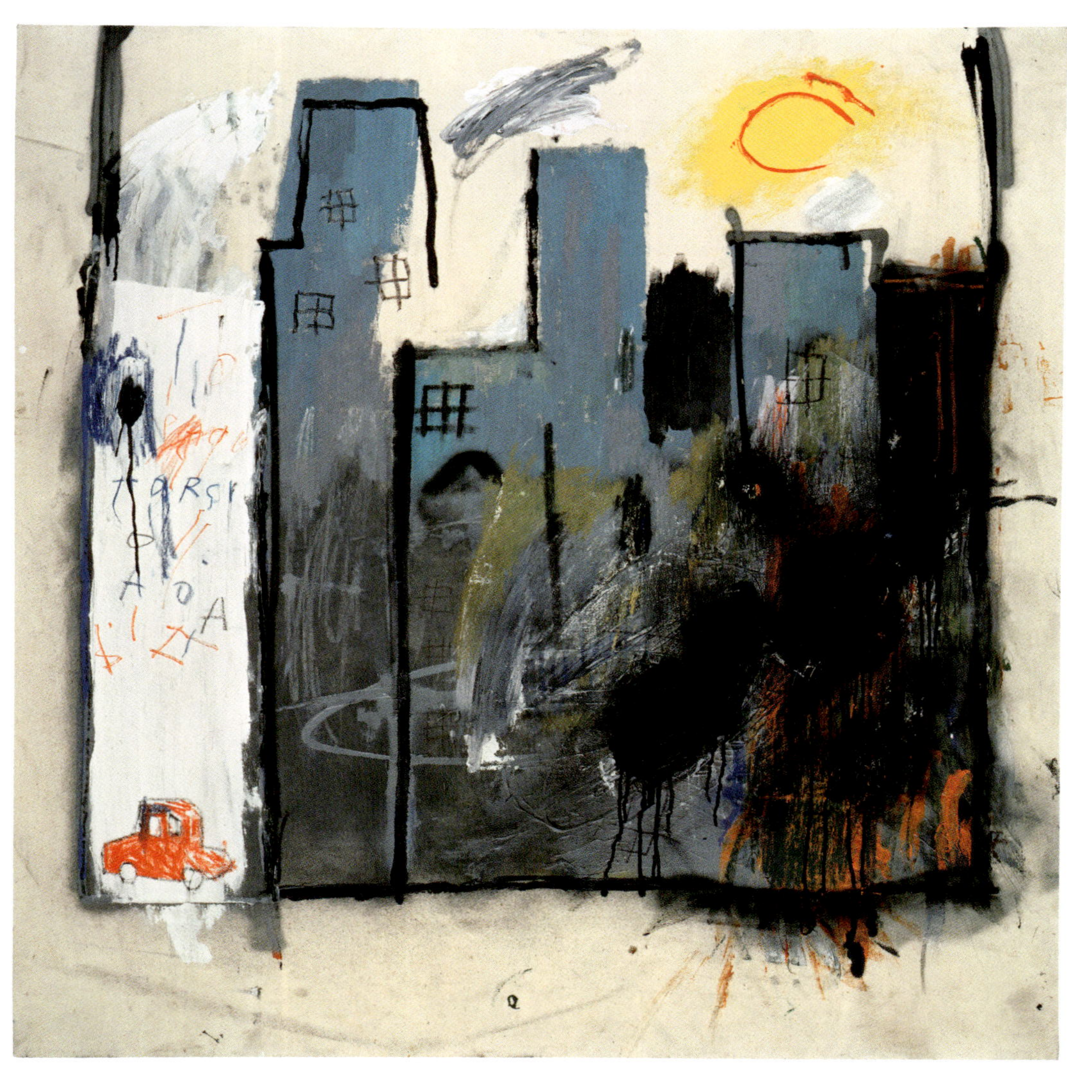

Untitled, 1980–1981
Acrylic, spray paint,
and oilstick on canvas,
122 x 122 cm / 48 x 48 inches

The Box, 1980–1981
Acrylic, oilstick, spray paint, paper collage,
and plaster on wood box, 82 x 46 x 5.5 cm /
32 ¹/₄ x 18 x 2 ¹/₄ inches

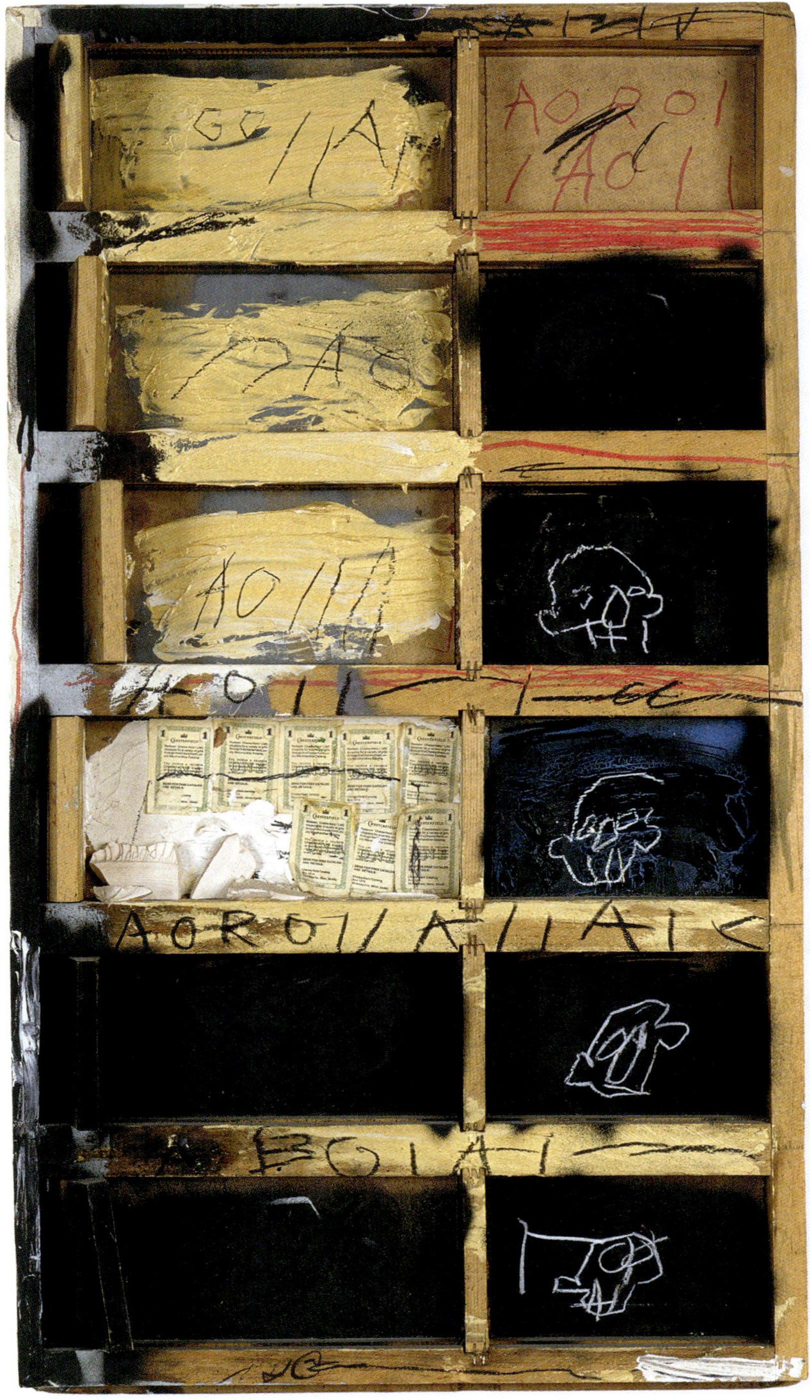

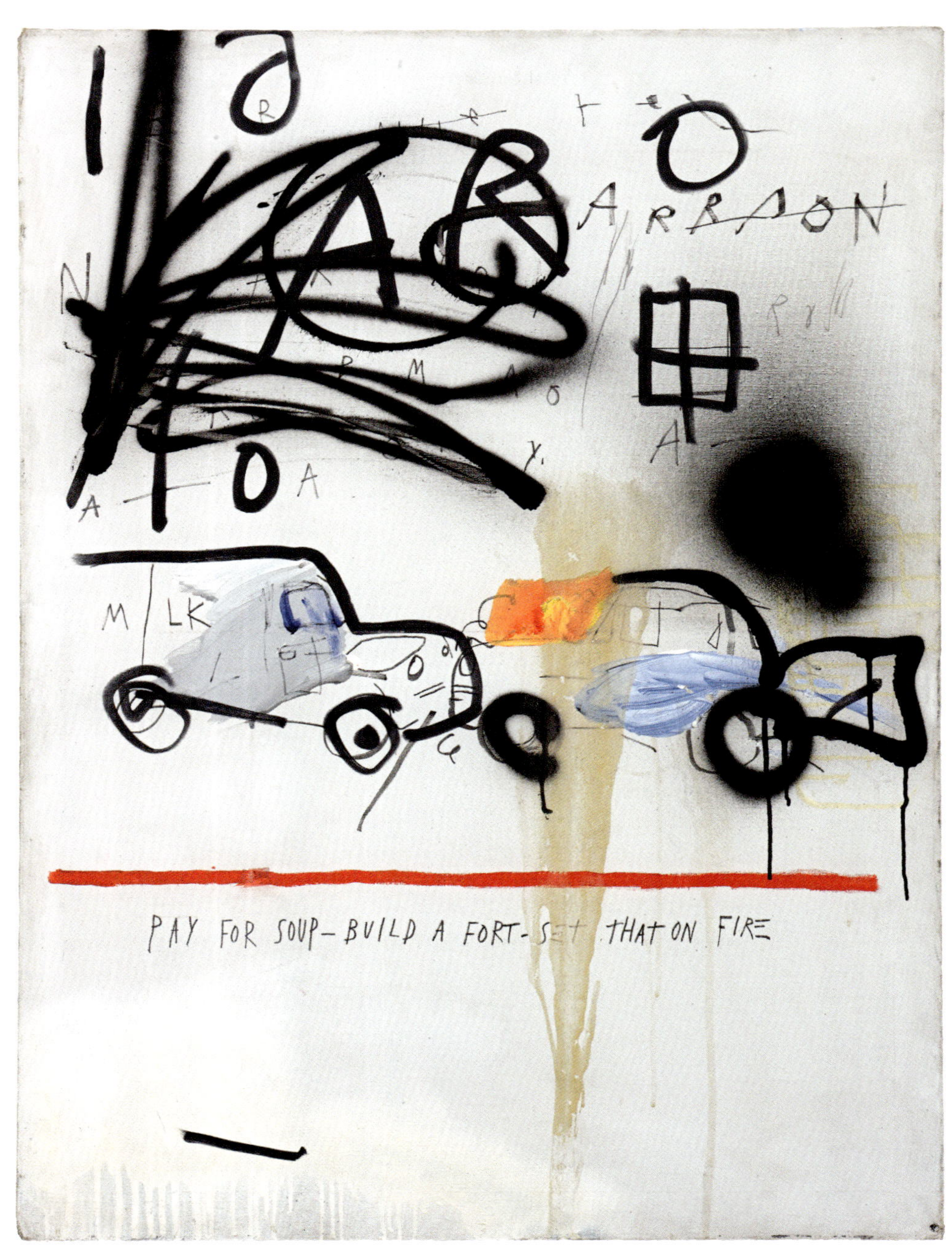

Untitled, 1980
Acrylic, spray paint, marker, and varnish
on canvas, 101.5 x 75.5 cm / 40 x 29 ³/₄ inches

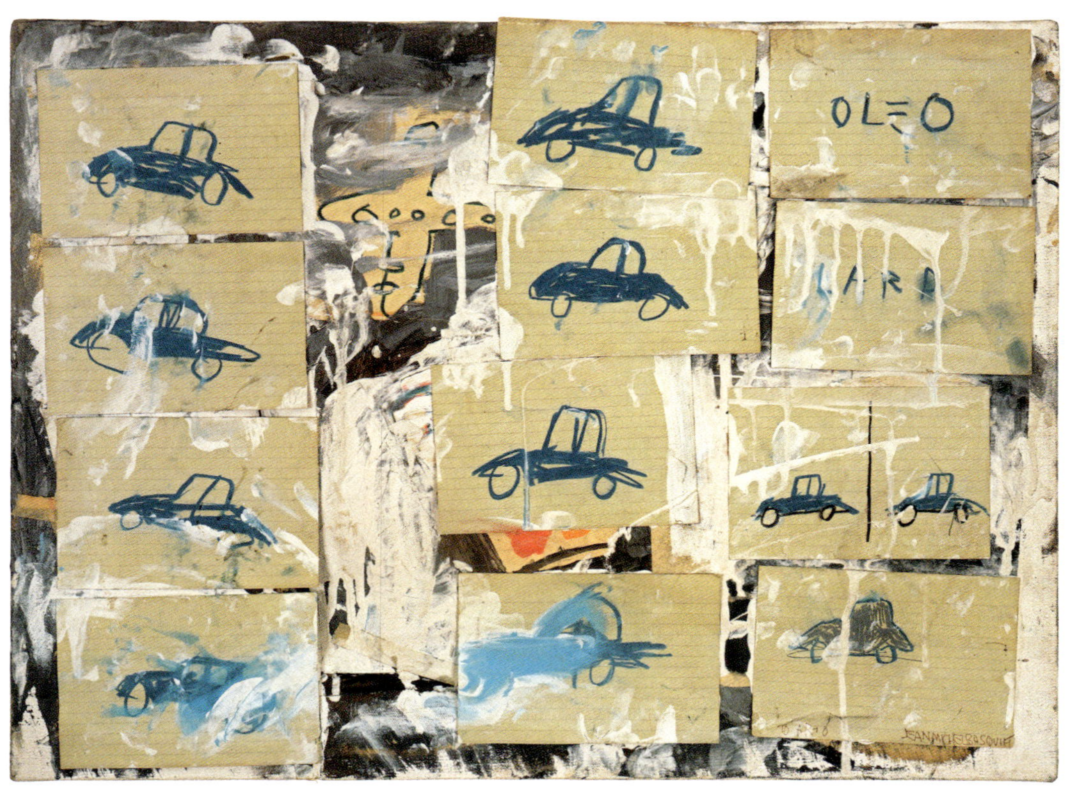

Untitled, 1980
Acrylic, oilstick, paper collage, and masking tape
on canvas, 47 x 62 cm / 18 ¹/₂ x 24 ¹/₂ inches

Pages 94/95: **Untitled**, 1980
Acrylic and oilstick on canvas mounted on
wooden supports, 109 x 180.5 cm / 43 x 71 inches

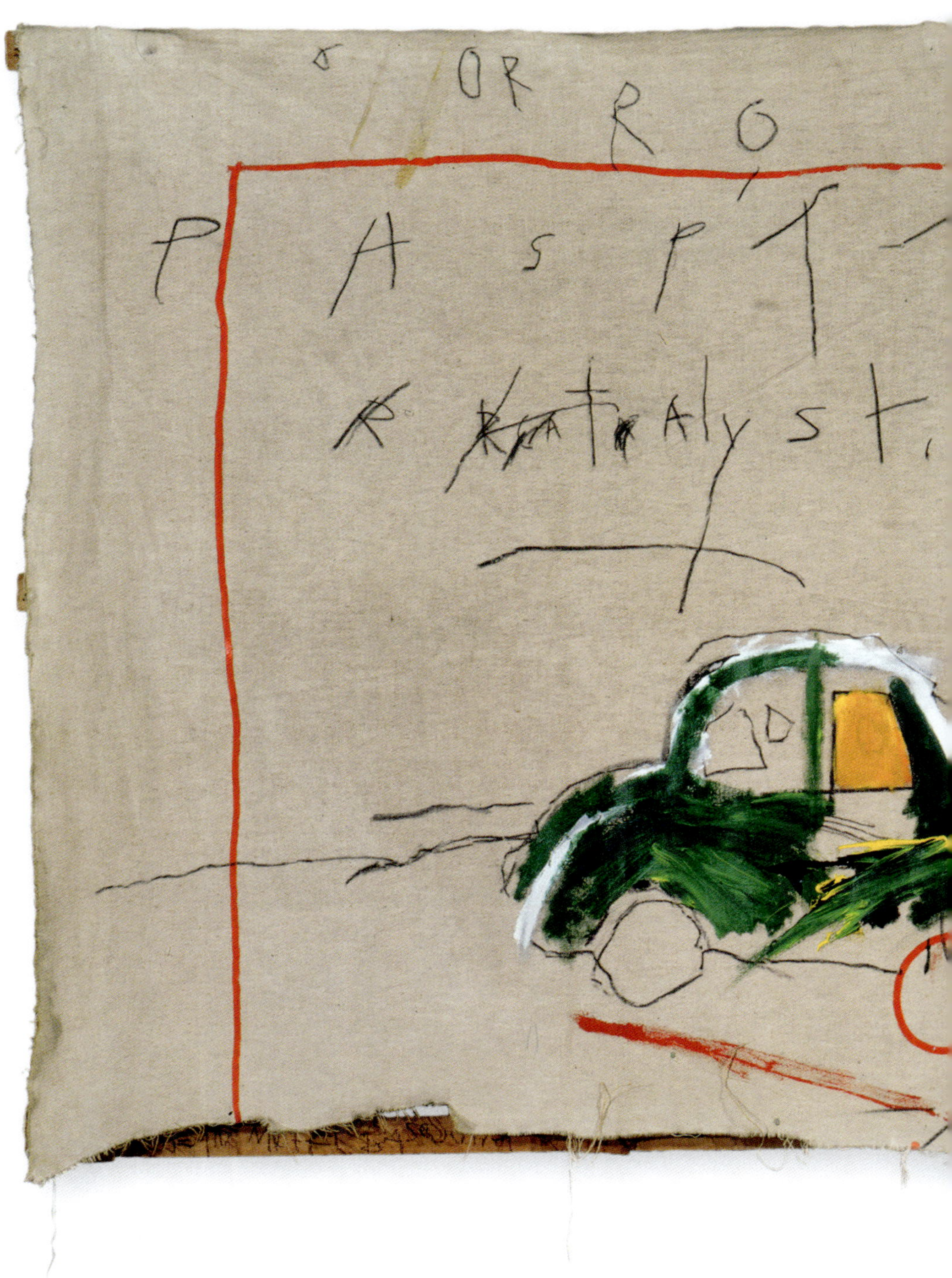
OR
R O
PASPT
KATALYST

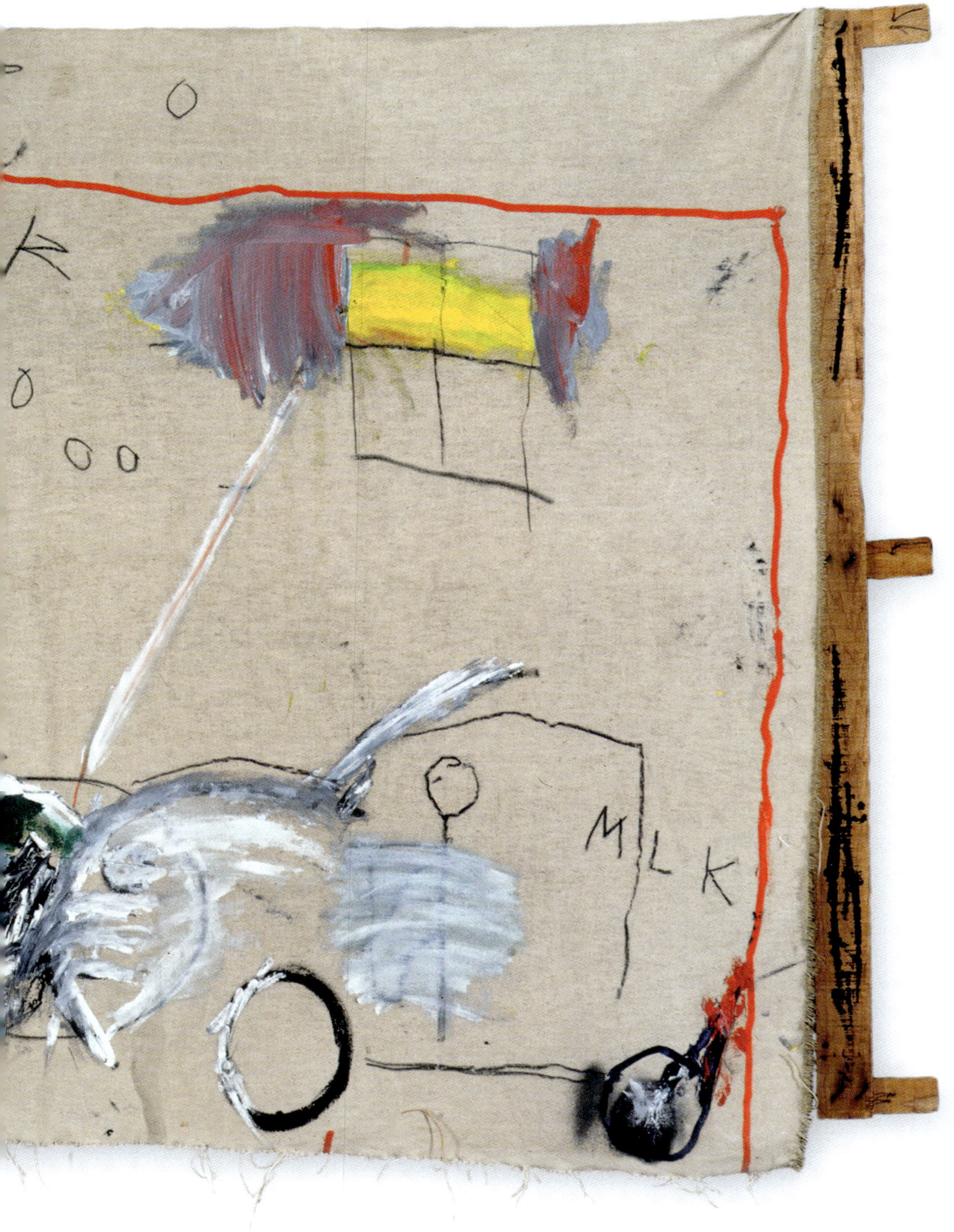
MLK

II.

1981
New York New Wave

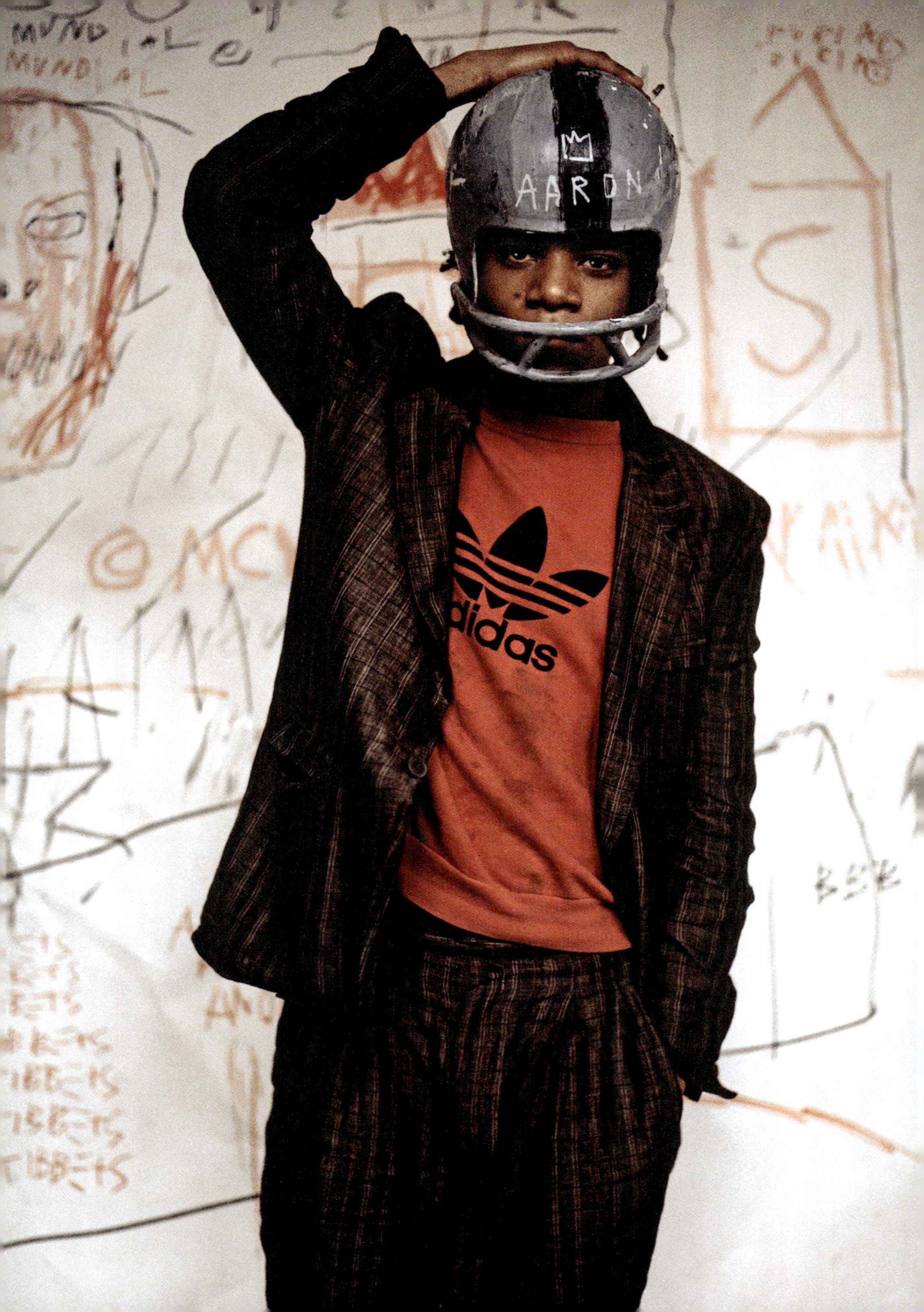

In February, the exhibition *New York/New Wave* opens at P.S.1 in Long Island City, organized by Diego Cortez. It is a huge, sprawling show aiming to introduce the full range of the current artistic counterculture, with over a hundred artists including Fab 5 Freddy, Nan Goldin, Keith Haring, Robert Mapplethorpe, and Kenny Scharf, but also kindred spirits of earlier generations such as William Burroughs and Andy Warhol. Beside other works throughout the display, Basquiat receives a complete wall to hang his paintings and tags the other artists' names on the walls. Peter Schjeldahl, who covers the exhibition for the *Village Voice*, is immediately won over by the new work: "The most impressive individual in the show after Mapplethorpe is Jean-Michel Basquiat, a 20-year-old Haitian-Puerto-Rican New Yorker and formerly the aphoristic graffitist known as 'Samo.' I would not have suspected from Samo's generally grotty defacements of my neighborhood the graphic and painterly talents revealed here, in dashing works on surfaces including canvas, scrap lumber, sheet metal, and foam rubber."[2]

The artist's friend Glenn O'Brien is convinced that Basquiat has now fully arrived. In his review of the exhibition for *Interview* he writes: "As it turns out, a graffiti artist also happens to be the greatest painter in the show. Look out world, Jean-Michel Basquiat is known to some as Samo, but that's inaccurate. He and Al Diaz were Samo. Now Jean is just Jean. He doesn't paint on trains. Maybe a wall now and then. But also on canvas, primed and unprimed, wood, paper, steel, whatever. He uses paint, crayon, xerox, Chesterfield coupons, whatever. He's not afraid of any color, even gold. He is, obviously, an agent of color, sent from where color comes from to make things more colorful, beautiful, amazing, and funny. Some of it looks like child's play, and it is like child's play, but more advanced. I can't think of much better advanced child's play. Jean-Michel Basquiat's wild perfect paintings and drawings are all over the show, charging the atmosphere with art ions."[3] And indeed, with this exhibition the work is immediately gaining the attention of top-flight gallerists such as Bruno Bischofberger, Emilio Mazzoli, and Annina Nosei, and Basquiat's career is truly underway.

Meanwhile, the artist has moved into 68 East 1st Street with his new girlfriend Suzanne Malouk, he exhibits in group shows organized by Haring and later by Fab 5 Freddy and Futura in the Mudd Club, and appears in a cameo role as a DJ in Blondie's video for their song "Rapture." In May, he has his first solo exhibition in the gallery of Emilio Mazzoli in Modena, Italy, still under the name Samo. Back in New York, gallerist Annina Nosei shows a pronounced interest in Basquiat's work, and since he has no studio to produce new paintings, she offers him spaces in the basement of her SoHo venue (pp. 6/7). Then, in October, he takes part in the group show *Public Address* at Nosei's gallery, which comprises politically charged work by Keith Haring, Jenny Holzer, Barbara Kruger, and others, reserving a separate room for several large paintings by Basquiat. His work sells immediately, and after the exhibition Nosei becomes his main gallerist. Working in the basement studio, he produces large numbers of canvases, which often sell even before they are finished. Artistically also,

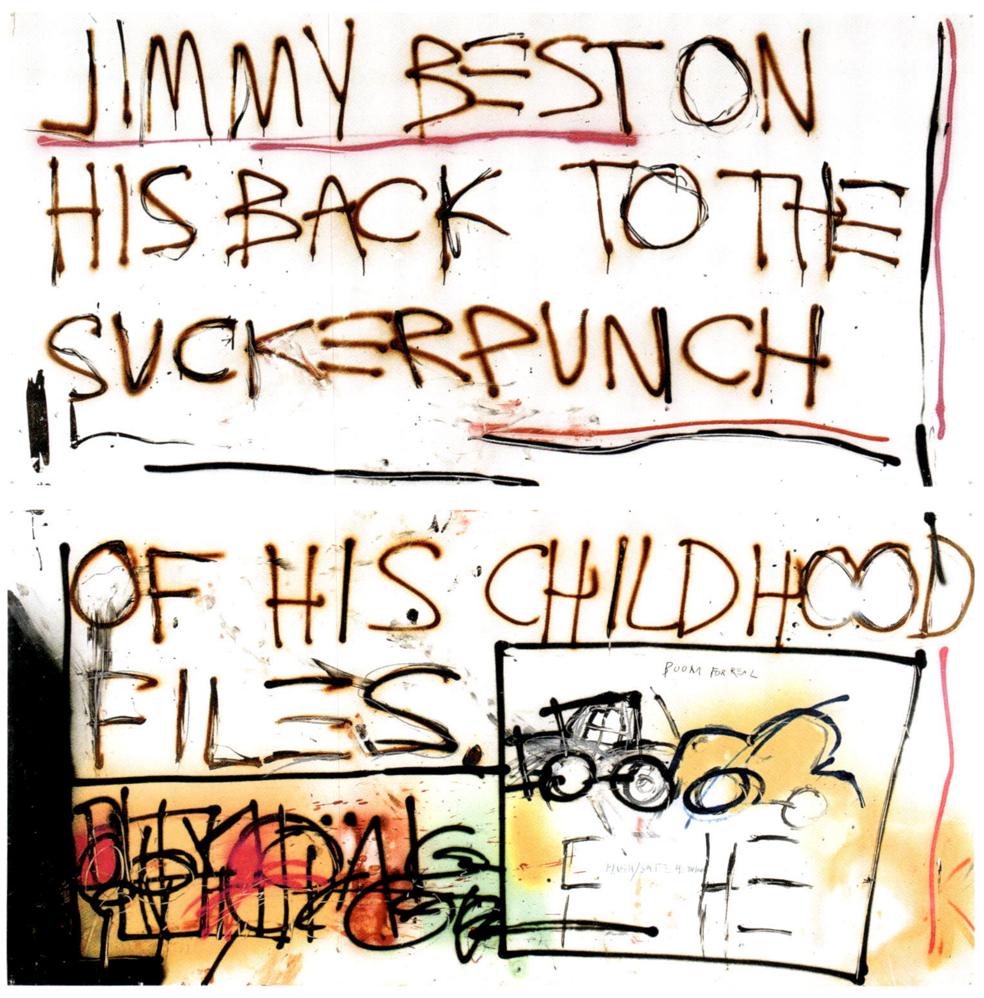

he develops quickly, and while at the beginning of the year his canvases had a simple, still somewhat graffiti-like quality to them, now the compositions become more complex and his use of color is bold and expressive. Still, working in the gallery's basement will prove growingly inconvenient, both because the dealer brings unannounced buyers who disturb the work process, and because of the politically awkward arrangement of a black artist being kept below a gallery to churn out new work.

Jimmy Best, 1981
Spray paint and oilstick on metal panel,
diptych: 244 x 244 cm / 96 x 96 inches

Page 97: Jean-Michel Basquiat,
New York 1981. Photo Edo Bertoglio

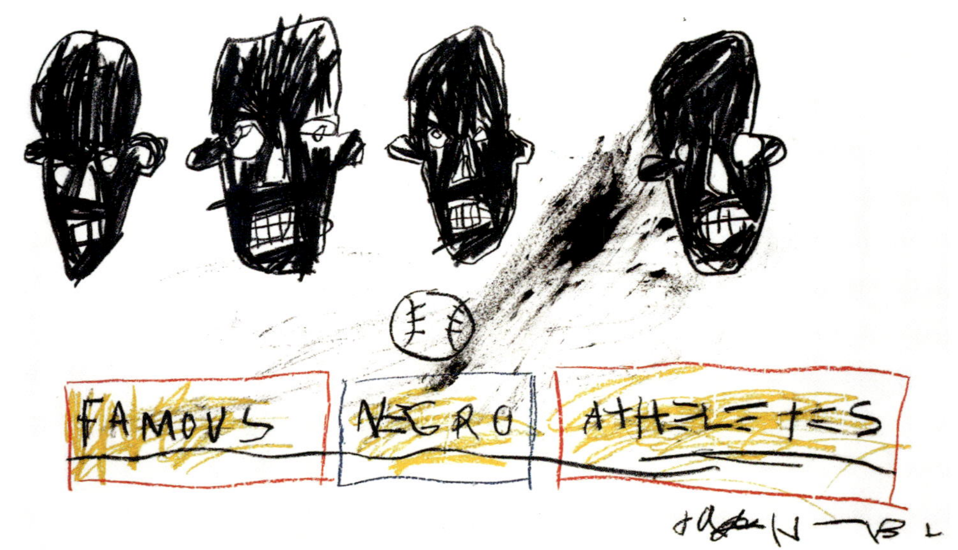

Famous Negro Athletes, 1981
Oilstick on paper,
71 x 89 cm / 28 x 35 inches

Untitled (Refrigerator), 1981
Acrylic, marker, and collage on refrigerator,
140 x 63.5 x 57 cm / 55 x 25 x 22 ¹/₂ inches

With Basquiat on the cusp of the big time, poet and art critic René Ricard publishes "The Radiant Child," an article in the December *Artforum* that focuses its stocktaking of a new street-born aesthetic on Basquiat: "I'm always amazed by how people come up with things. Like Jean-Michel. How did he come up with those words he puts all over everything? Their aggressively handmade look fits his peculiarly political sensibility. He seems to have become the gutter and his world view very much that of the downtrodden and dispossessed … His is also the elegance of the clochard who lights up a megot with his pinkie raised. If Cy Twombly and Jean Dubuffet had a baby and gave it up for adoption, it would be Jean-Michel. The elegance of Twombly is there but from the same source (graffiti) and so is the brut of the young Dubuffet. Except the politics of Dubuffet needed a lecture to show, needed a separate text, whereas in Jean-Michel they are integrated by the picture's necessity. I'd rather have a Jean-Michel than a Cy Twombly. I do not live in the classical city. My neighborhood is unsafe. Also, I want my home to look like a pile of junk to burglars."[4]

[1–4] *See Endnotes on page 508.*

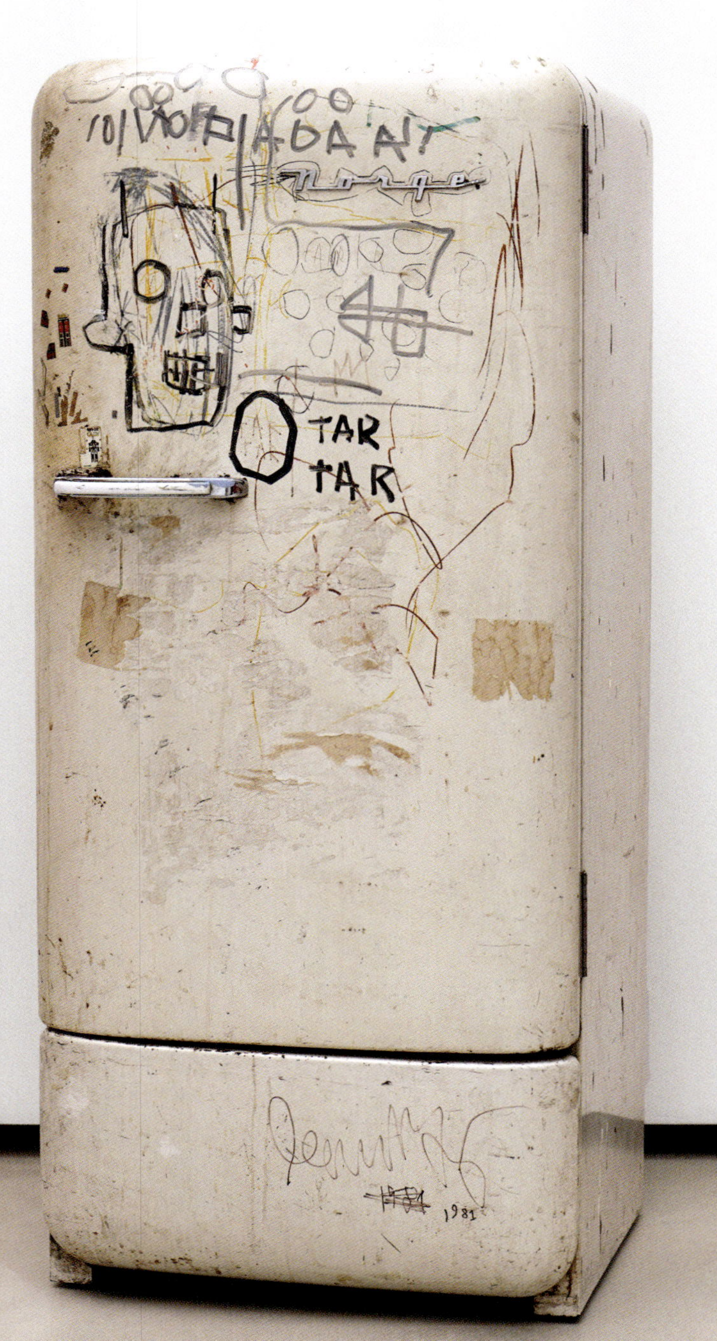

Asbestos, 1981–1982
Acrylic on paper mounted on canvas,
282 x 272 cm / 111 x 107 inches

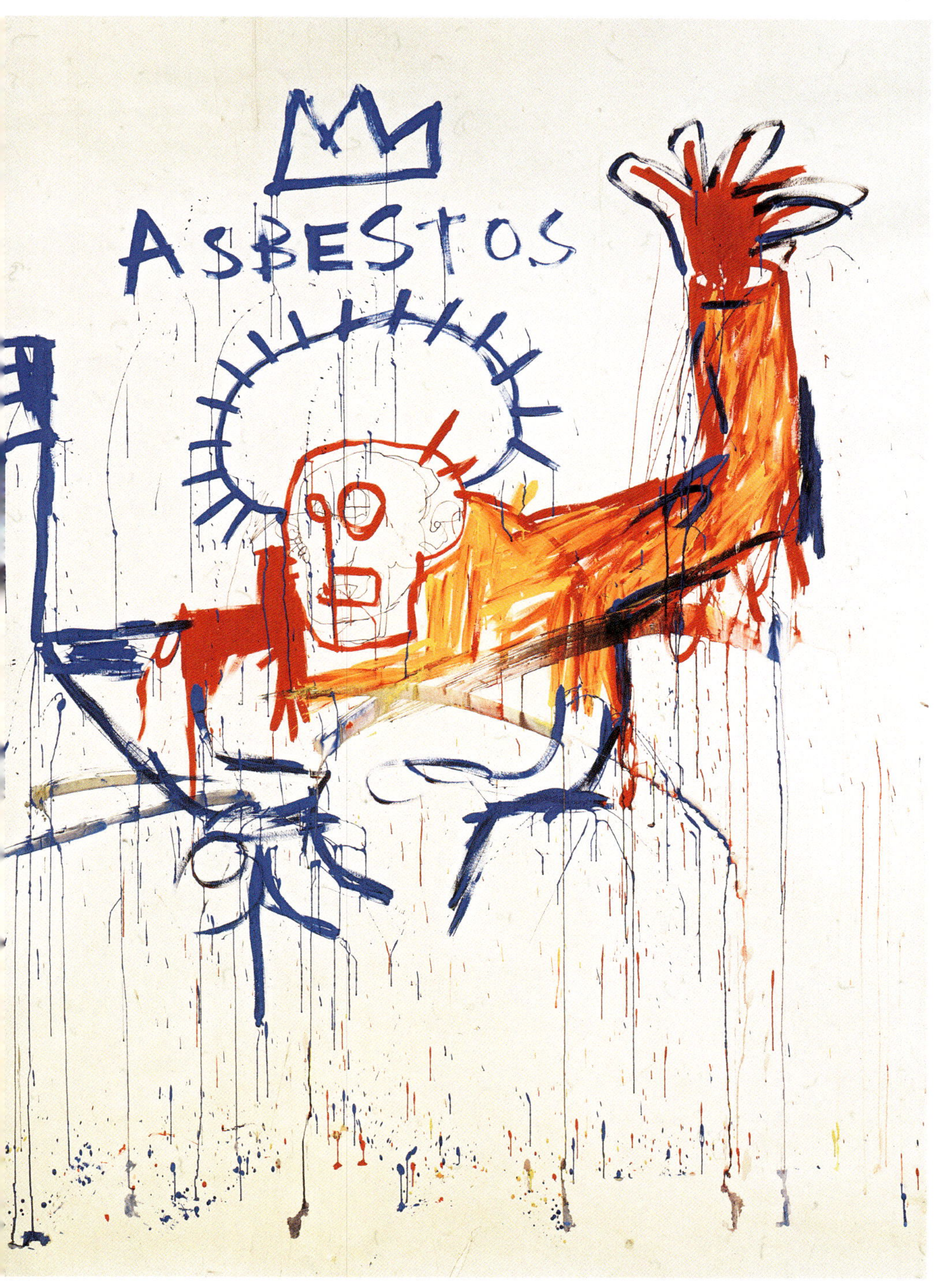

ASBESTOS

Untitled, 1981
Acrylic, oilstick, and pencil on canvas,
183 x 152.5 cm / 72 x 60 inches

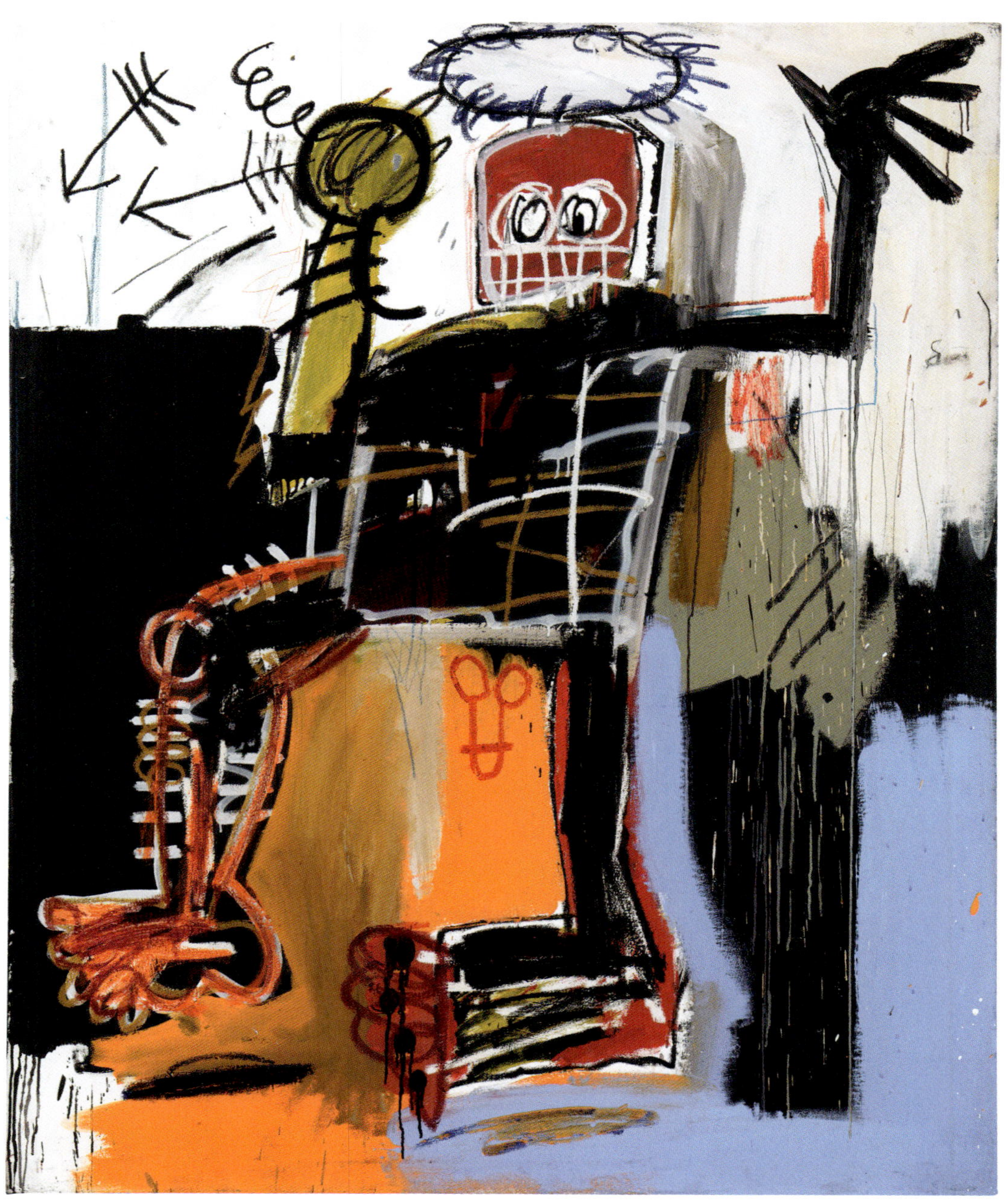

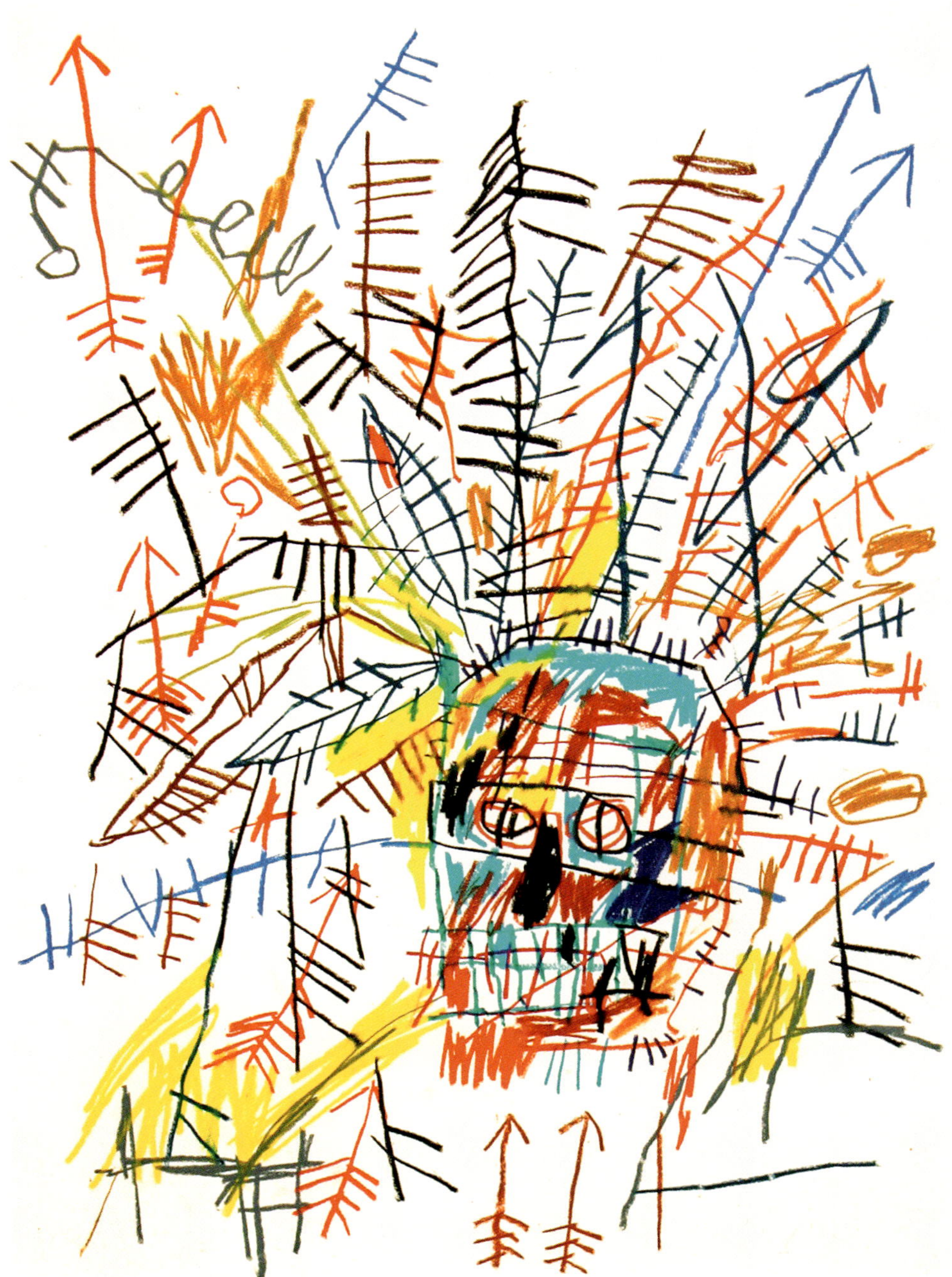

Untitled (Indian Head), 1981
Oilstick on paper, 61 x 45.5 cm /
24 x 18 inches

Untitled, 1981
Acrylic, oilstick, and marker on paper,
76 x 56 cm / 30 x 22 inches

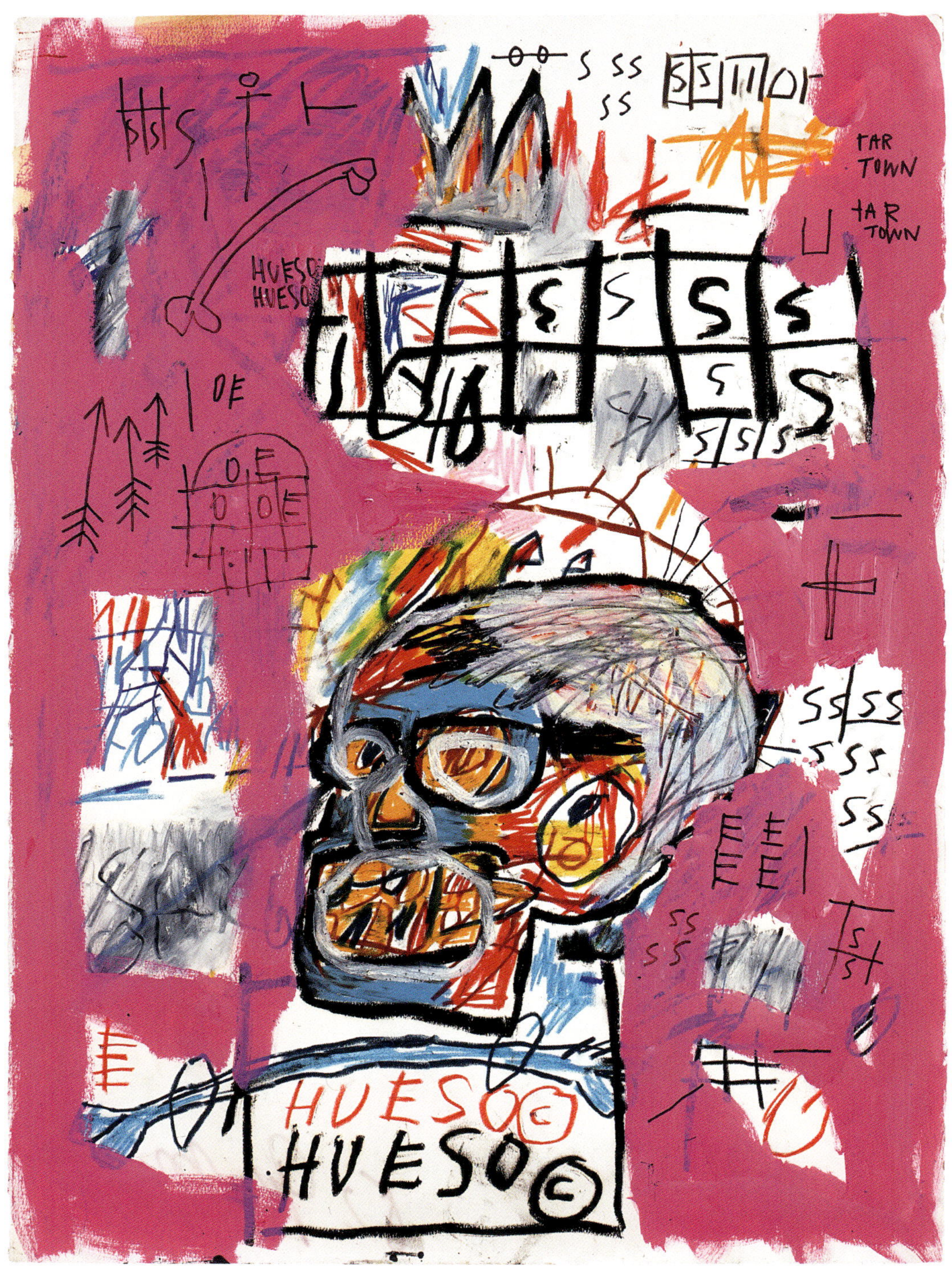
TAR TOWN
TAR TOWN
HUESO
HUESO
OE
OE
O OE
HUESO
HUESO

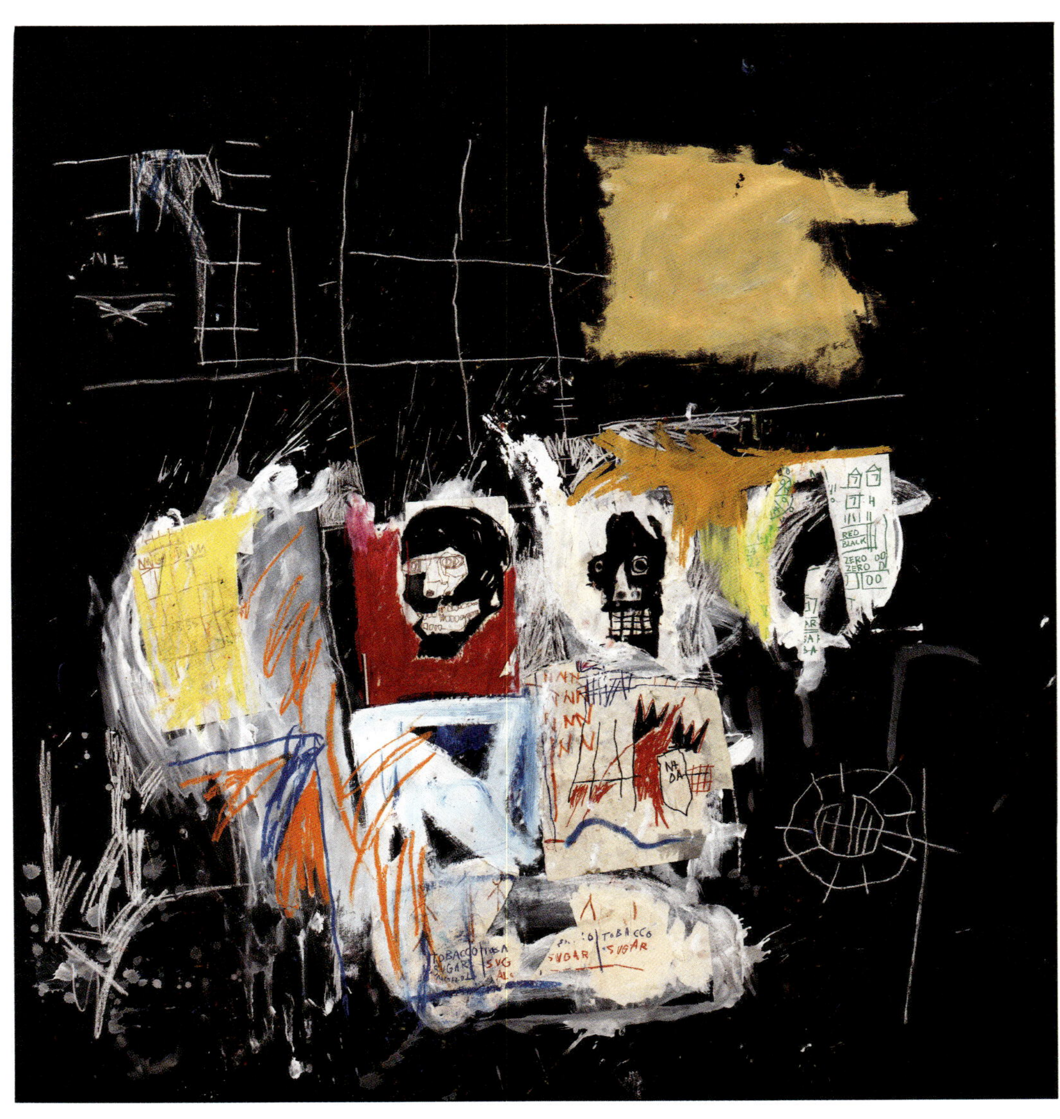

Untitled, 1981
Acrylic, oilstick, chalk, and paper collage on
black paper, 150 x 141 cm / 59 x 55 ¹/₂ inches

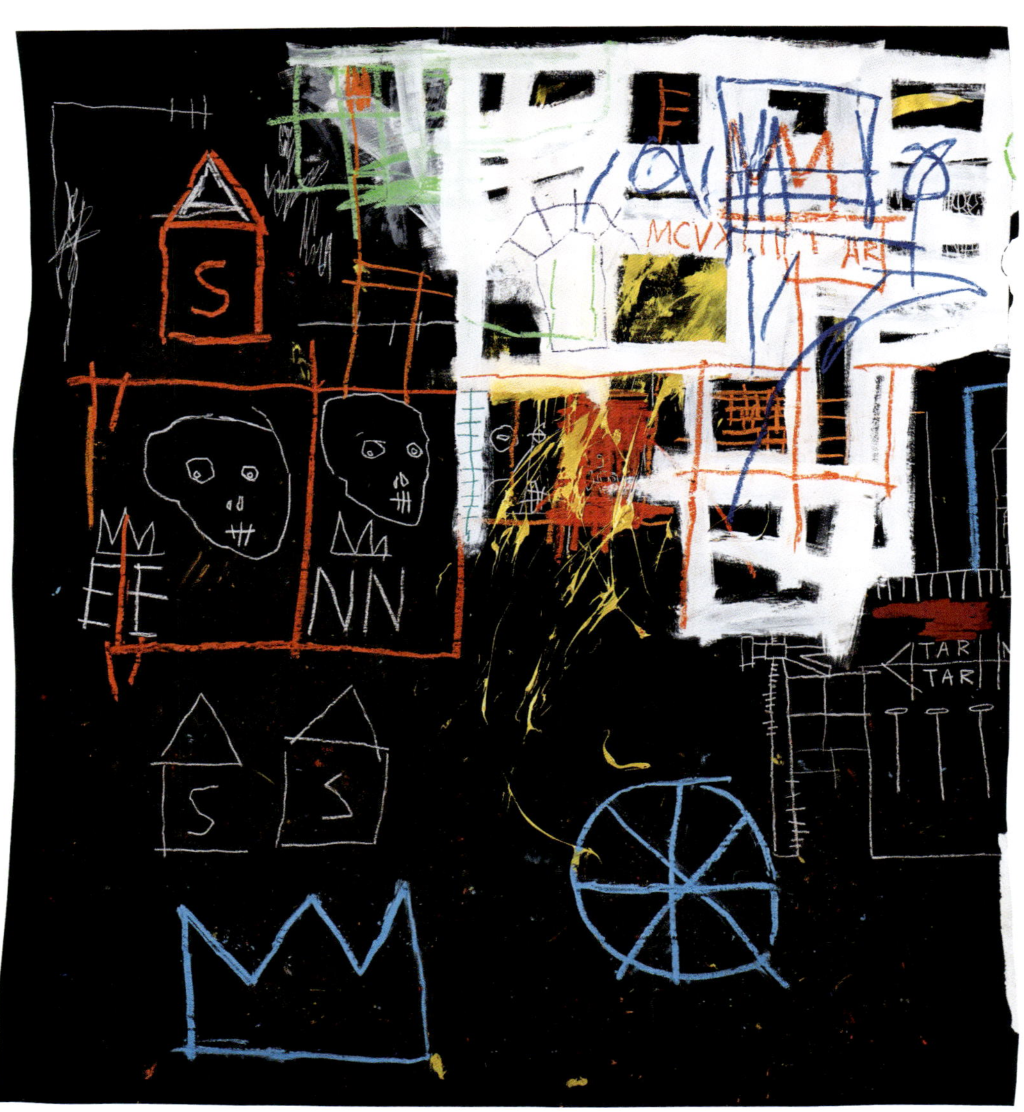

Untitled, 1981
Acrylic, oilstick, and chalk on black paper,
150 x 137 cm / 59 x 54 inches

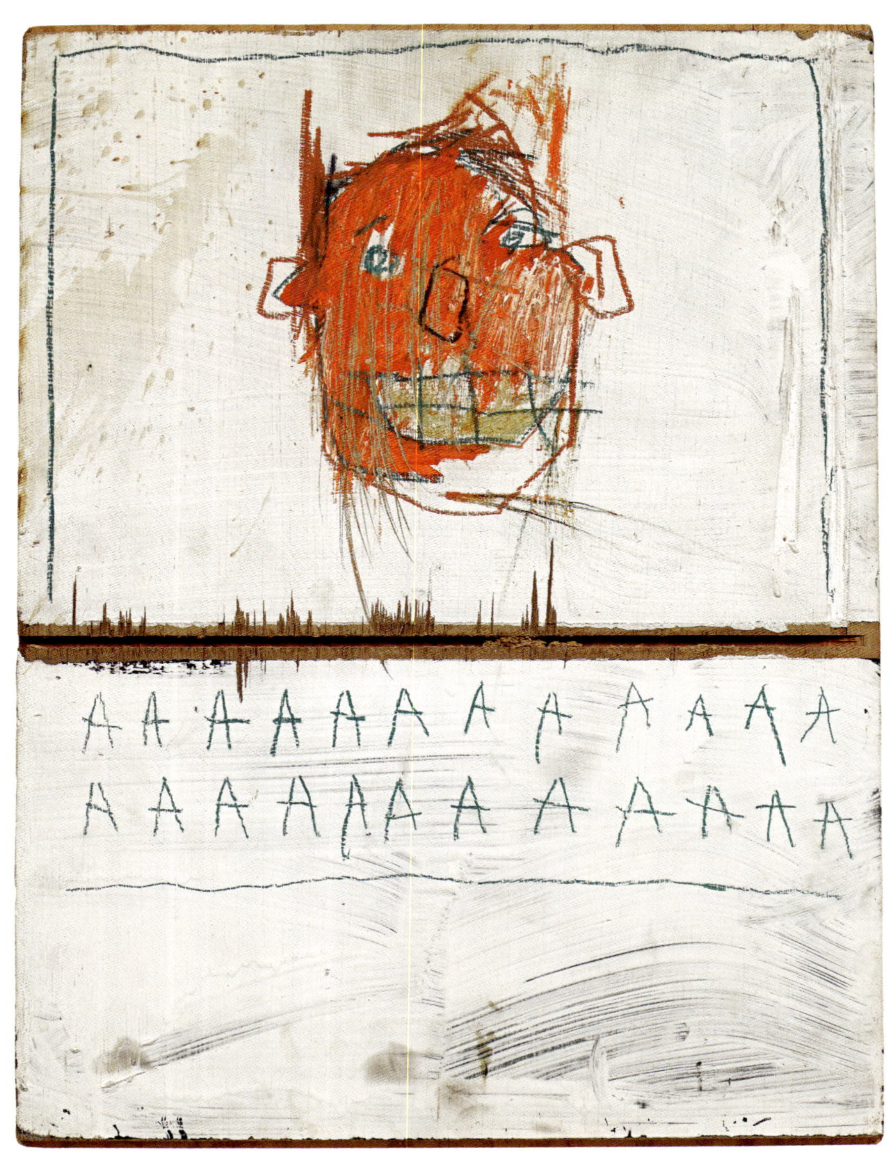

Untitled, 1981
Acrylic, oil, and oilstick on wood,
61 x 45.5 cm / 24 x 18 inches

Untitled, 1981
Acrylic, oil, and oilstick on wood panel,
82.5 x 47 cm / 32 $^1/_2$ x 18 $^1/_2$ inches

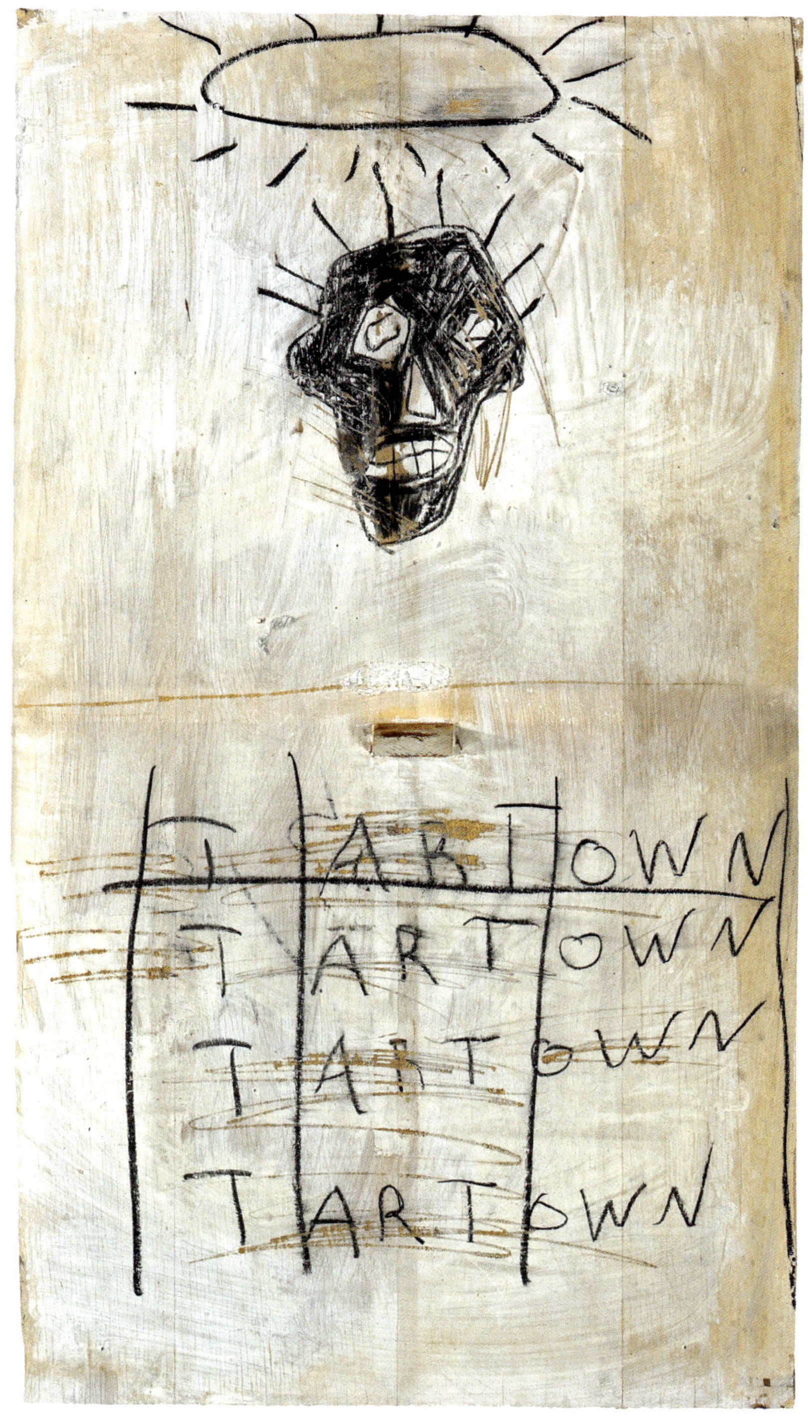

TARTOWN
TARTOWN
TARTOWN
TARTOWN

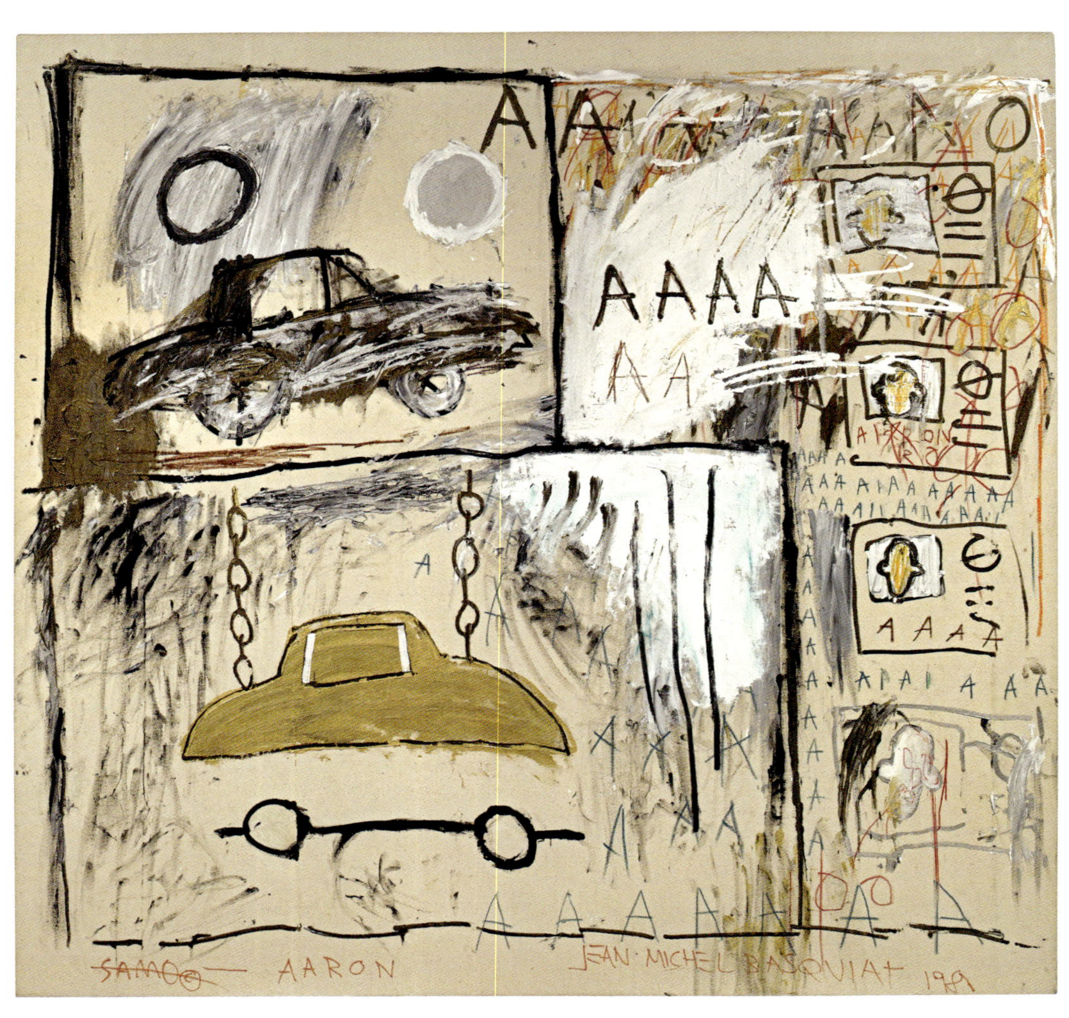

Cadillac Moon, 1981
Acrylic and oilstick on canvas,
162 x 172 cm / 63 ³/₄ x 67 ³/₄ inches

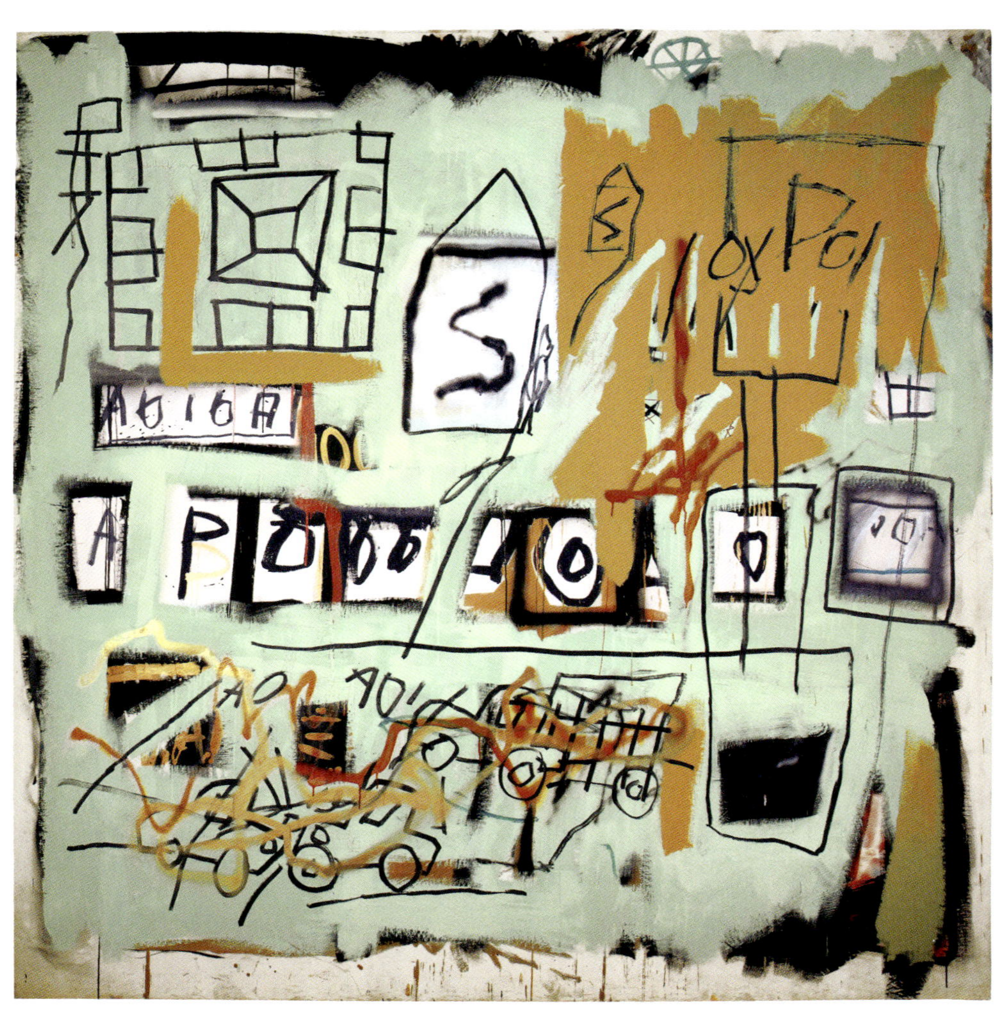

Untitled, 1981
Acrylic and spray paint on canvas,
203 x 203 cm / 80 x 80 inches

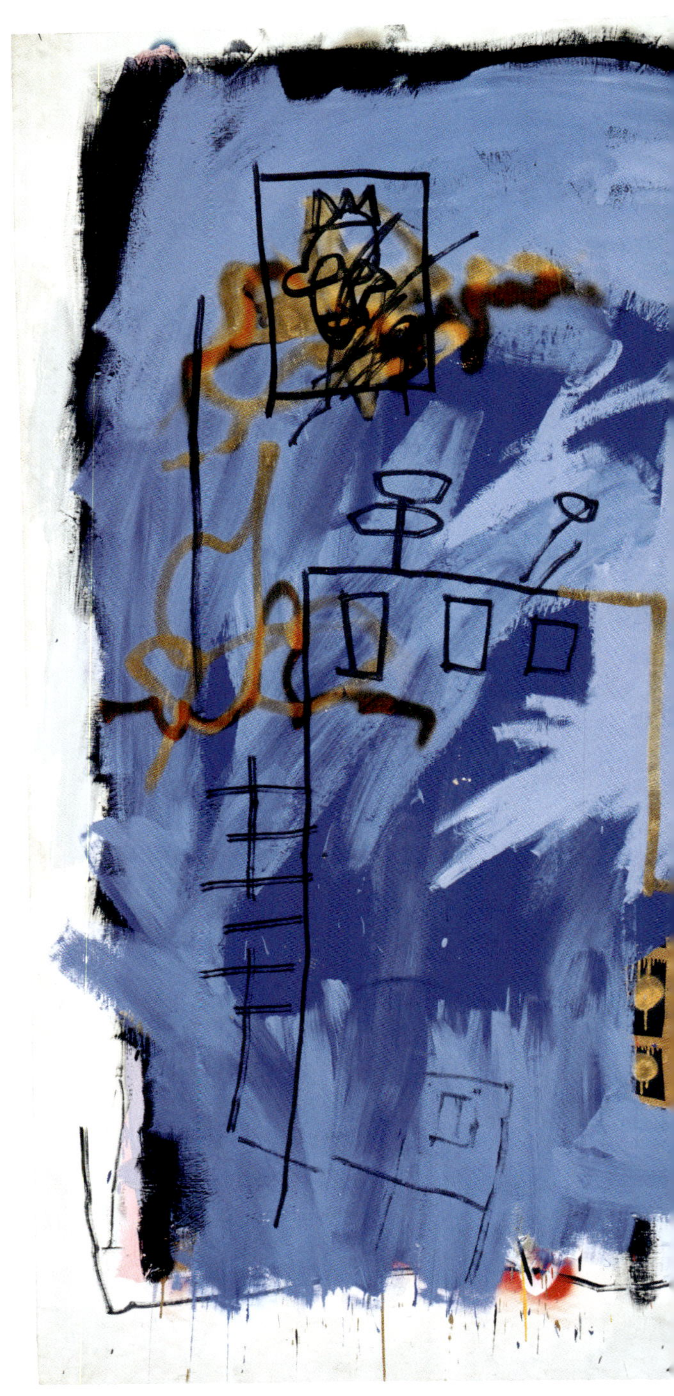

Untitled (Blue Airplane), 1981
Acrylic, oilstick, and spray paint
on canvas, 218.5 x 264 cm /
86 x 104 inches

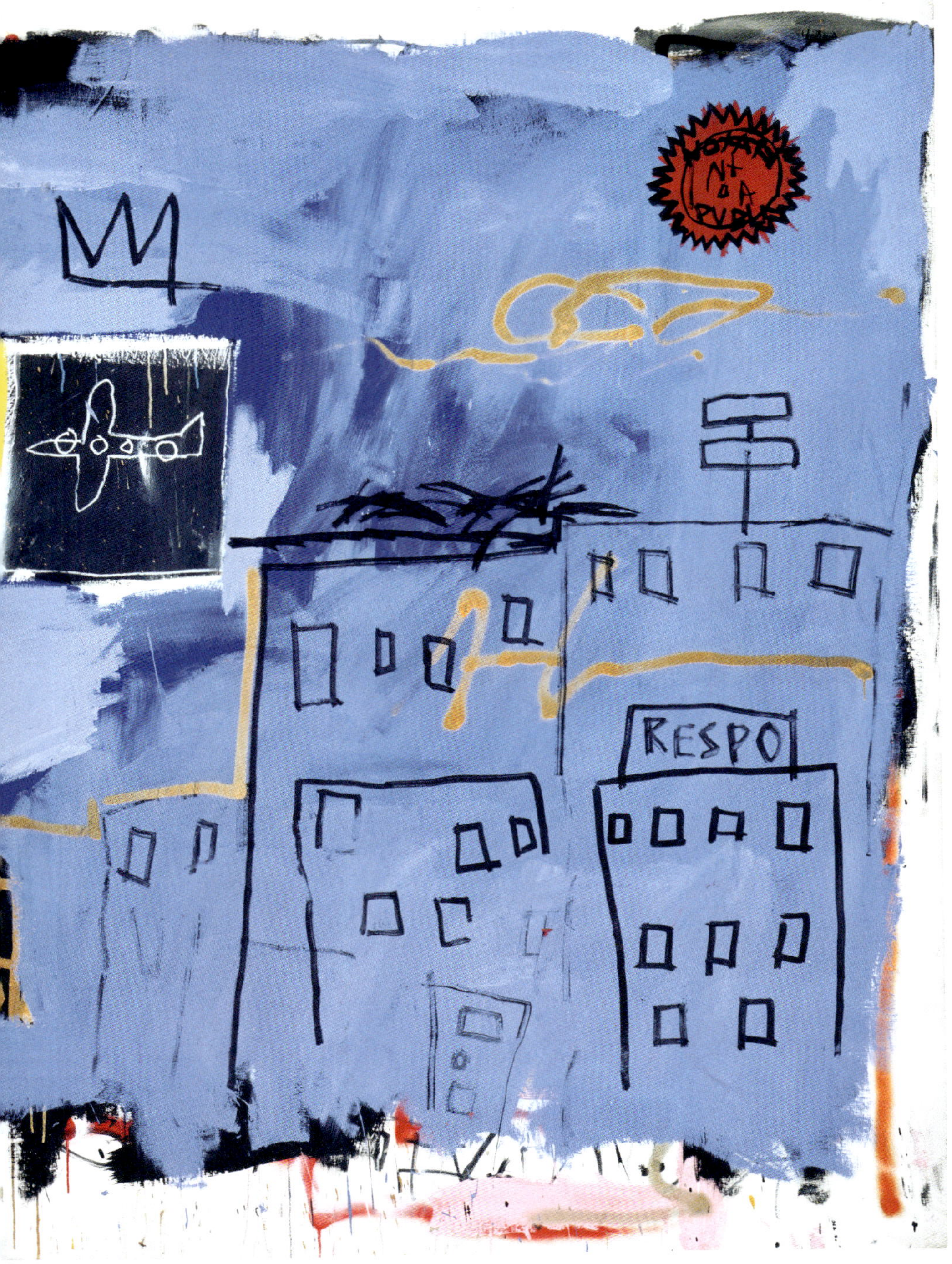
WORTH
N¹
0 A
PUDDLE
RESPO

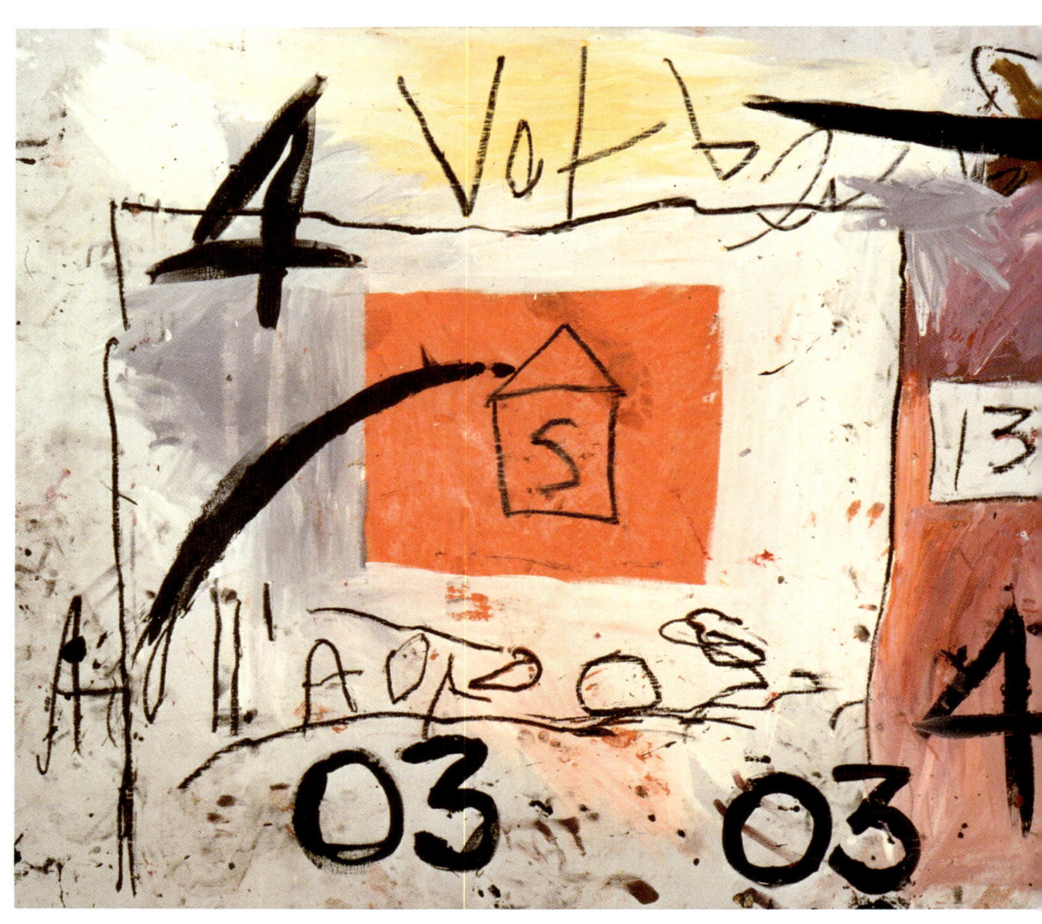

Untitled, 1981
Acrylic and oilstick on canvas,
127 x 302 cm / 50 x 119 inches

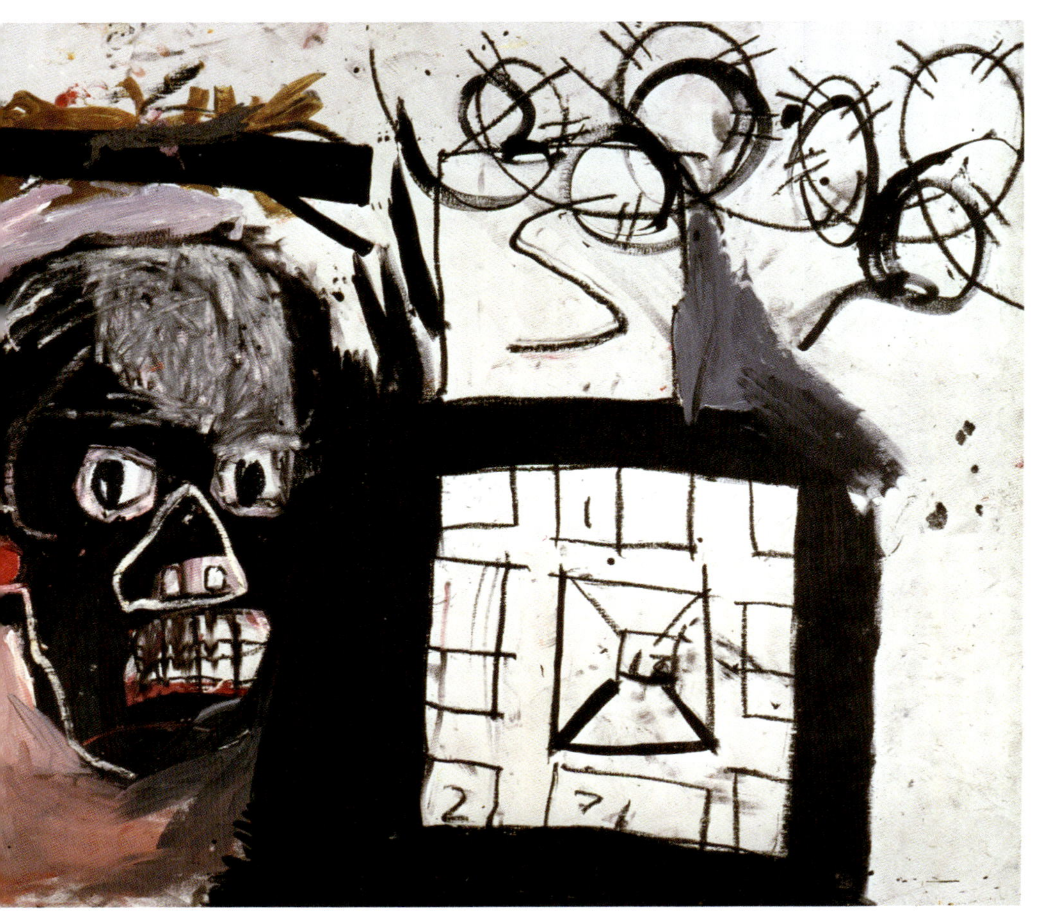

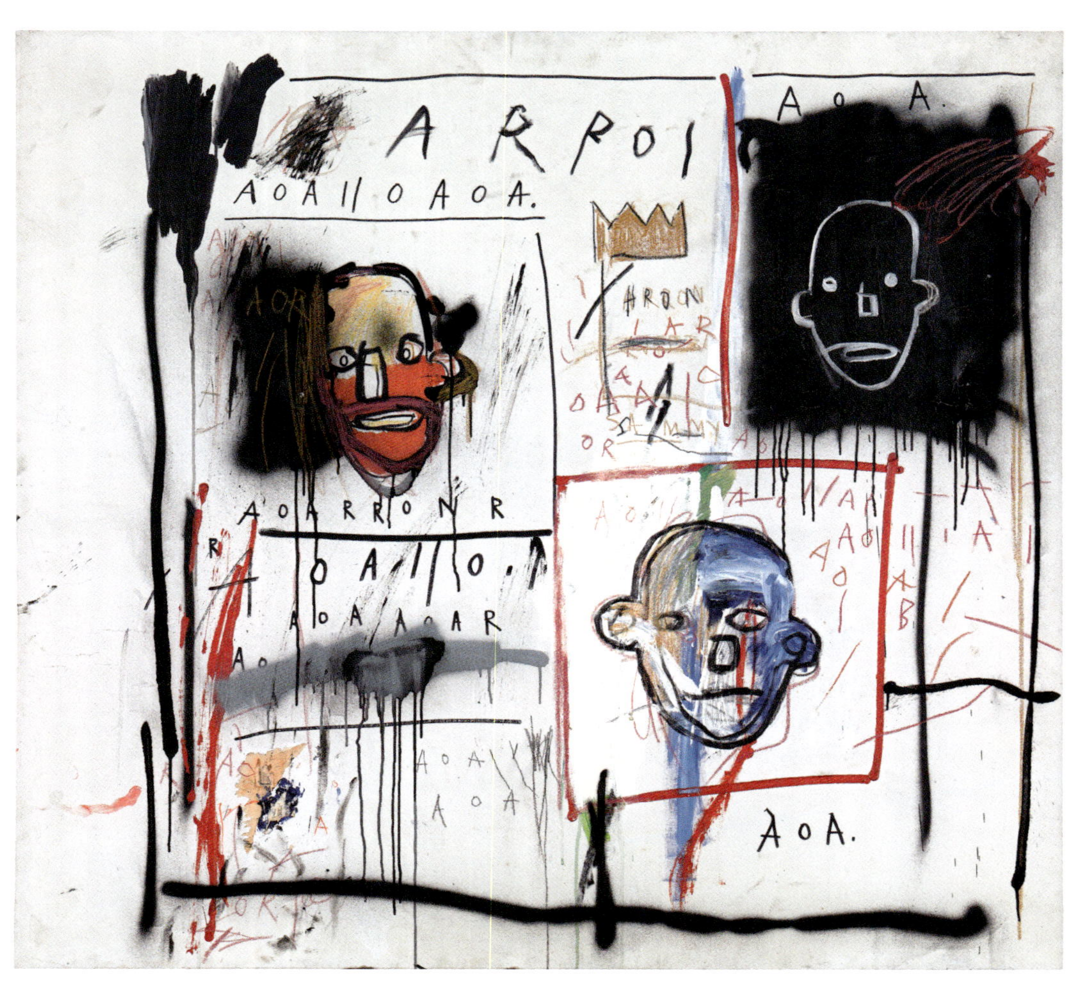

Untitled, 1981
Acrylic, oilstick, and spray paint on canvas,
130 x 143 cm / 51 $^1/_4$ x 56 $^1/_4$ inches

Untitled, 1981
Acrylic on window shade,
130 x 93 cm / 51 $^1/_4$ x 36 $^1/_2$ inches

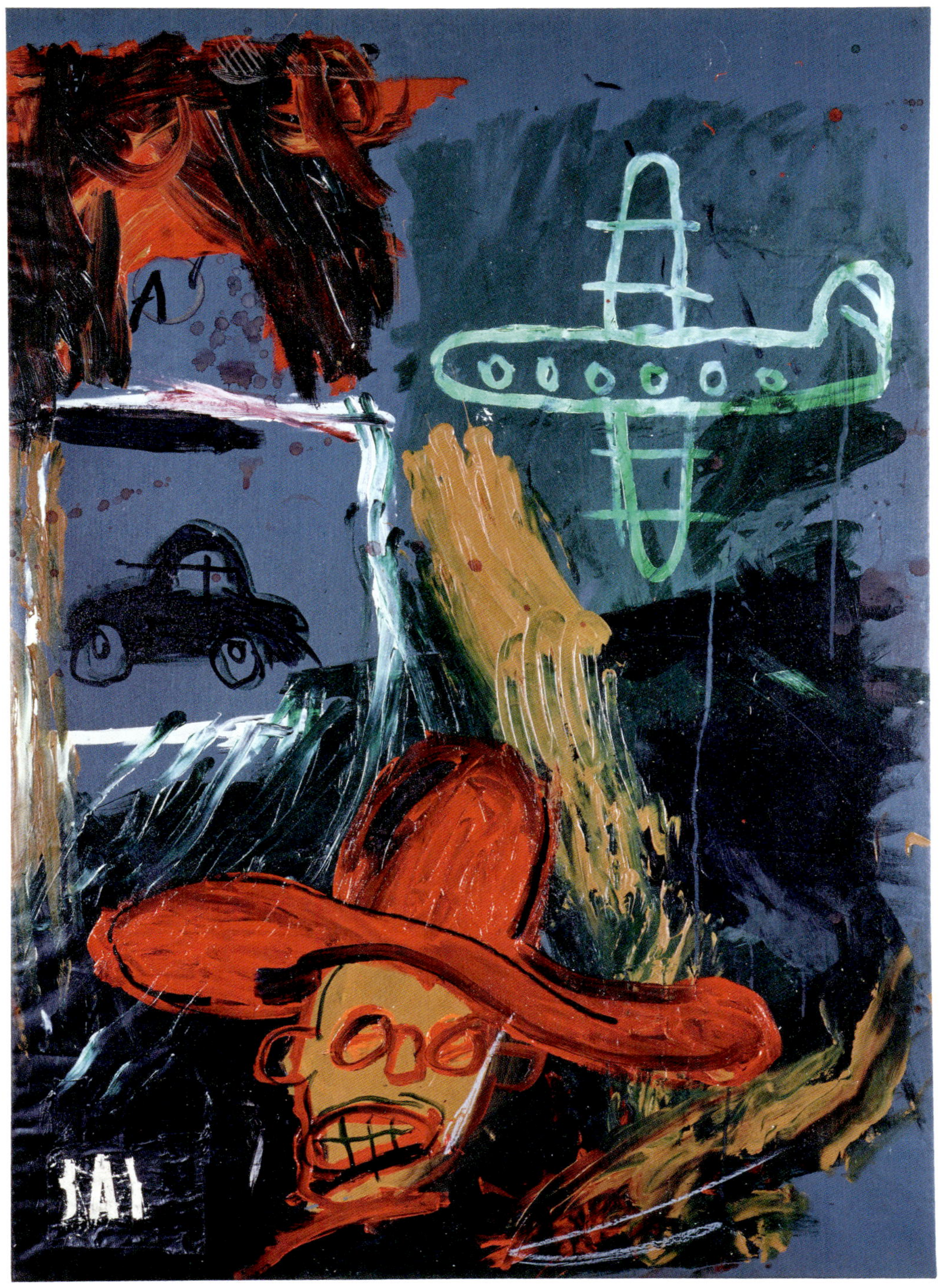

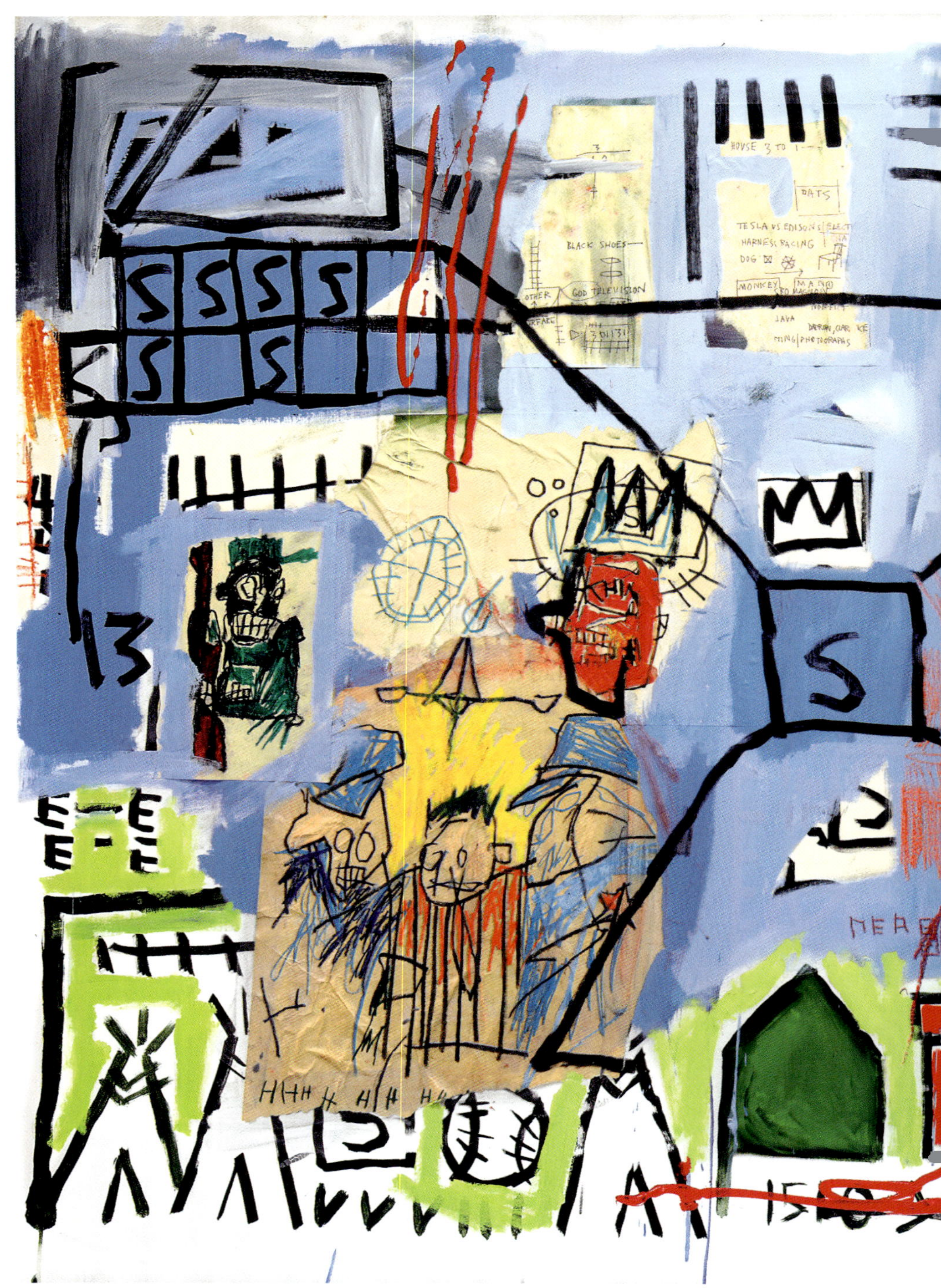
HOVSE 3 TO 1
OATS
TESLA VS EDISON'S ELECT
HARNESS RACING
DOG
BLACK SHOES
OTHER
GOD TELEVISION
MONKEY
MANO
JAVA
MING PHOTOGRAPHS
13
S S S S S
S S
HHH H HH HA

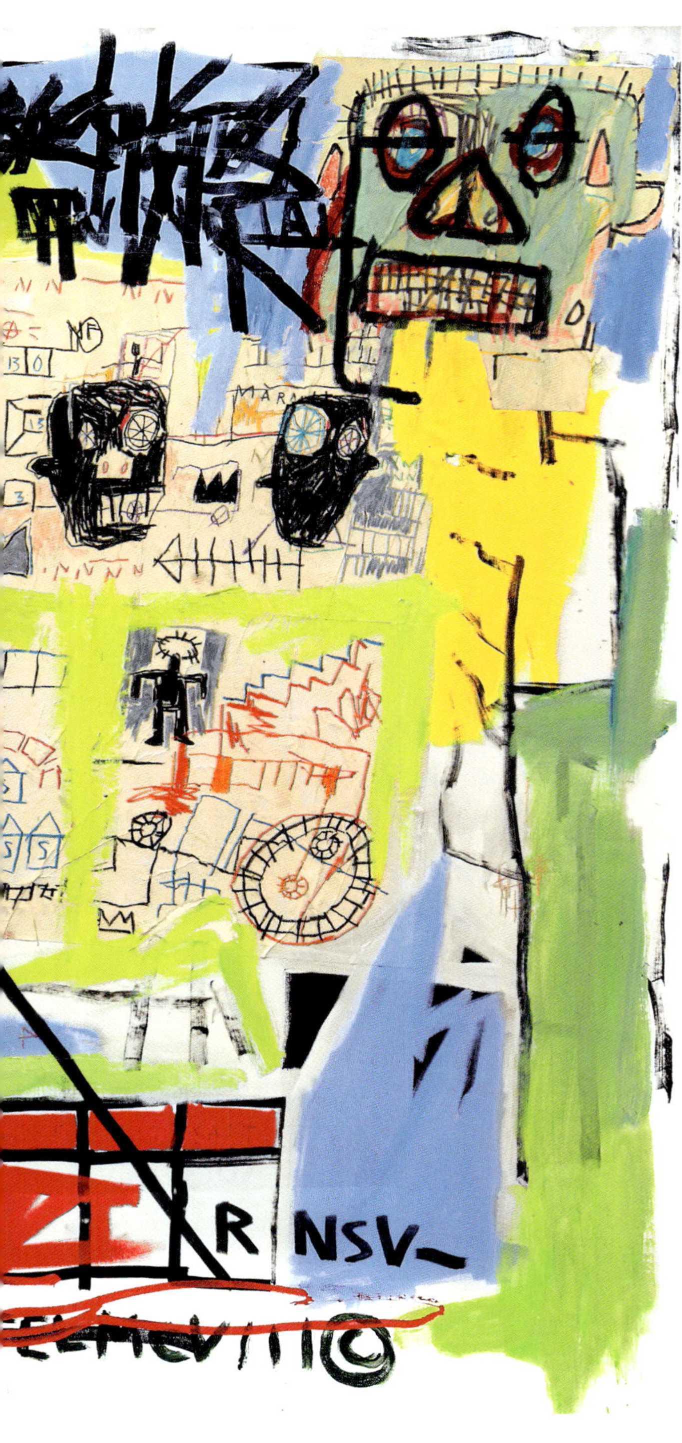

Untitled, 1981
Acrylic, marker, paper collage,
oilstick, and crayon on canvas,
123 x 157.5 cm / 48 ¹/₂ x 62 inches

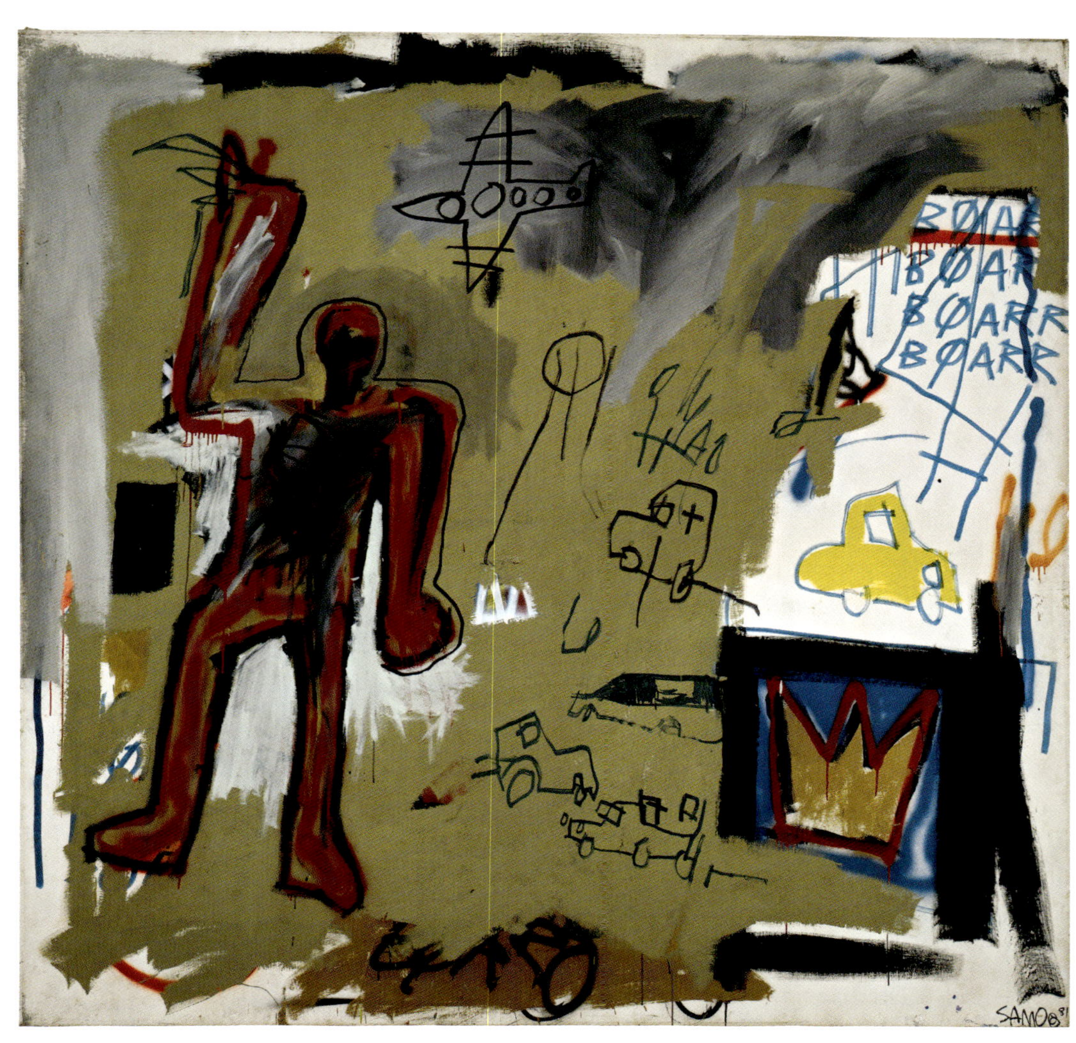

Untitled (Red Man), 1981
Acrylic, oilstick, and spray paint
on canvas, 204.5 x 211 cm / 80 $^1/_2$ x 83 inches

Untitled (Self-Portrait – The King), 1981
Acrylic, oil, oilstick, and paper collage on wood
and mirror, 118.5 x 87.5 cm / 46 $^3/_4$ x 34 $^1/_2$ inches

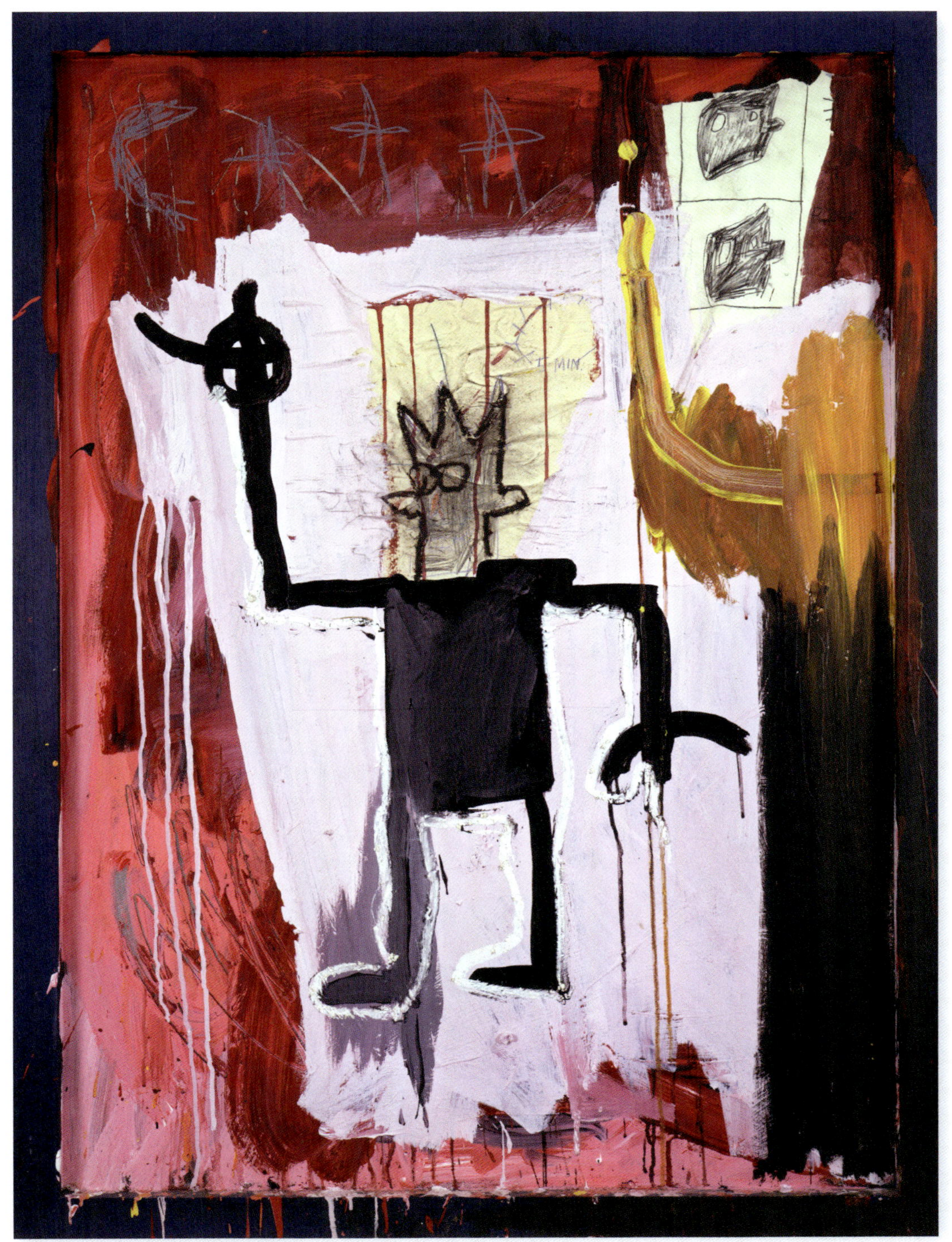

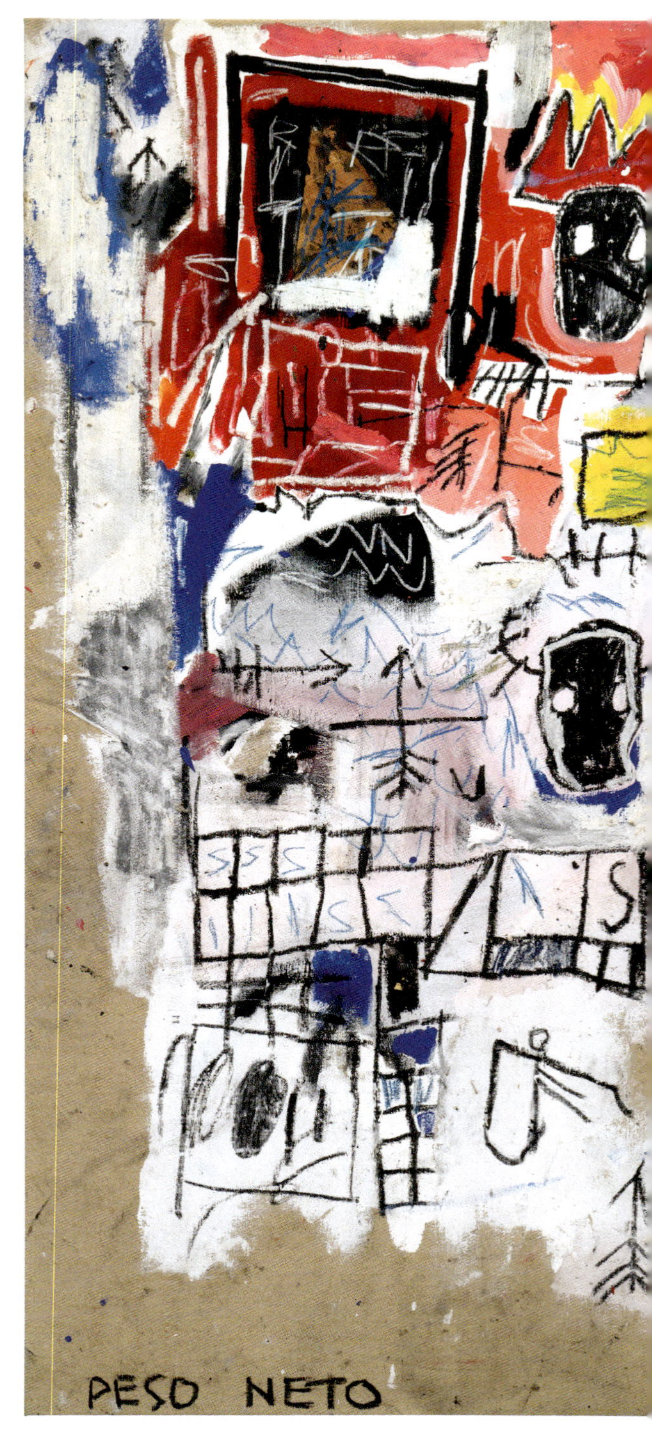

Crowns (Peso Neto), 1981
Acrylic, oilstick, and paper collage
on canvas, 183 x 239 cm /
72 x 94 inches

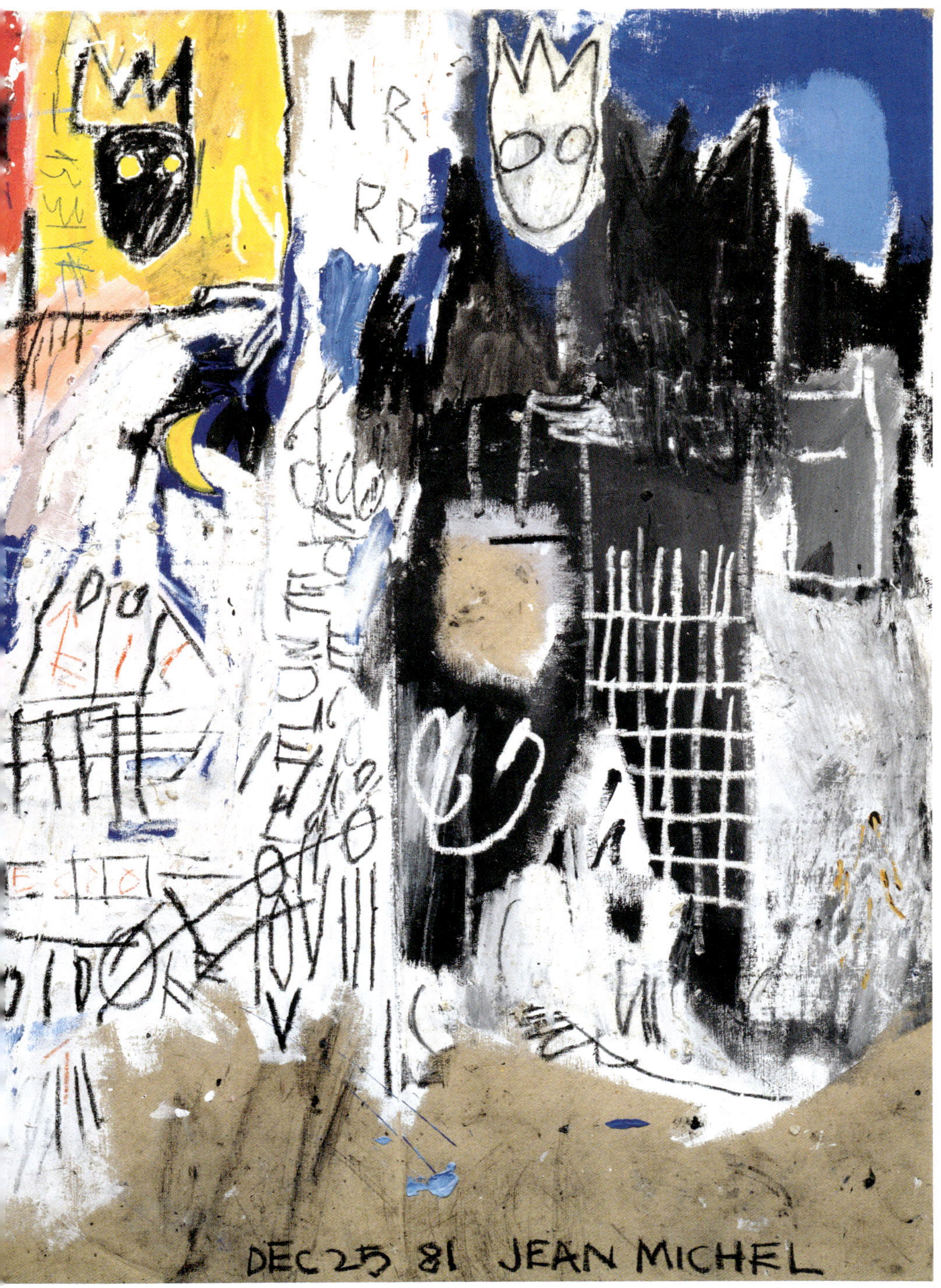
N R
R R
DEC 25 81 JEAN MICHEL

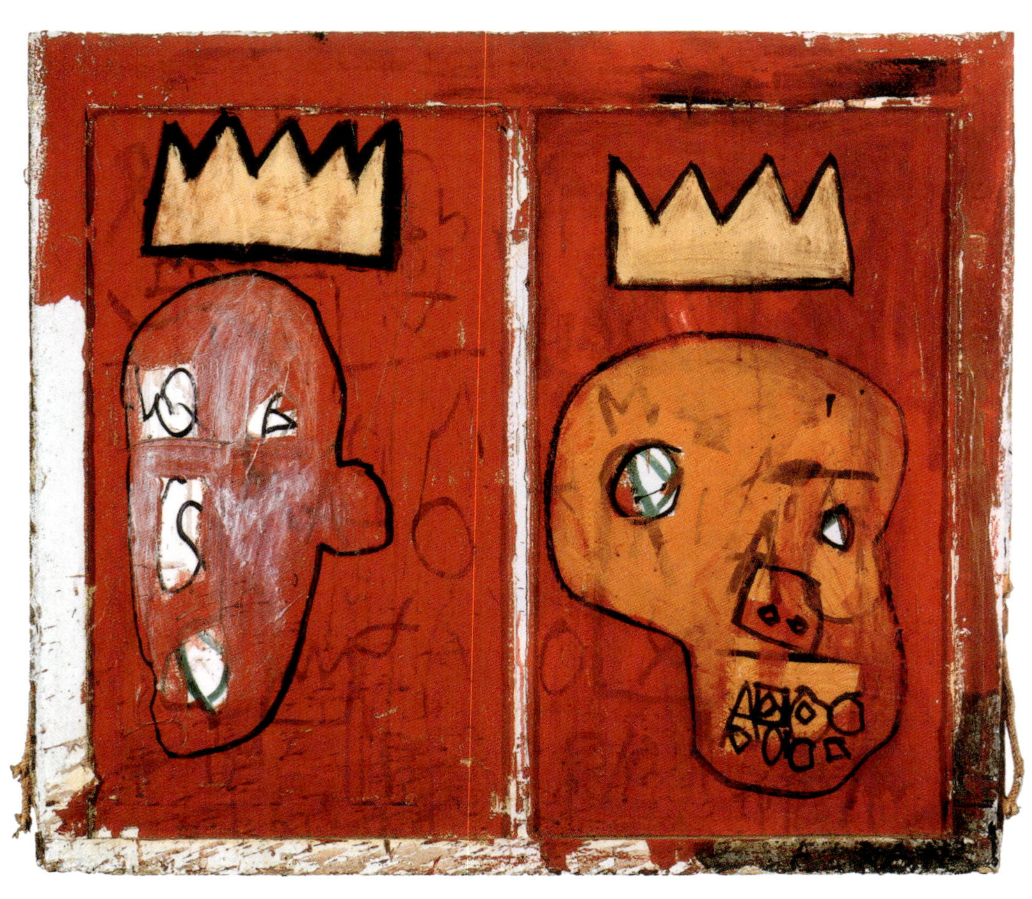

Red Kings, 1981
Acrylic on glass and wood,
81 x 93.5 cm / 32 x 36 ³/₄ inches

Pork, 1981
Acrylic, oil, and oilstick on glass and wood,
211 x 85.5 cm / 83 x 33 ²/₃ inches

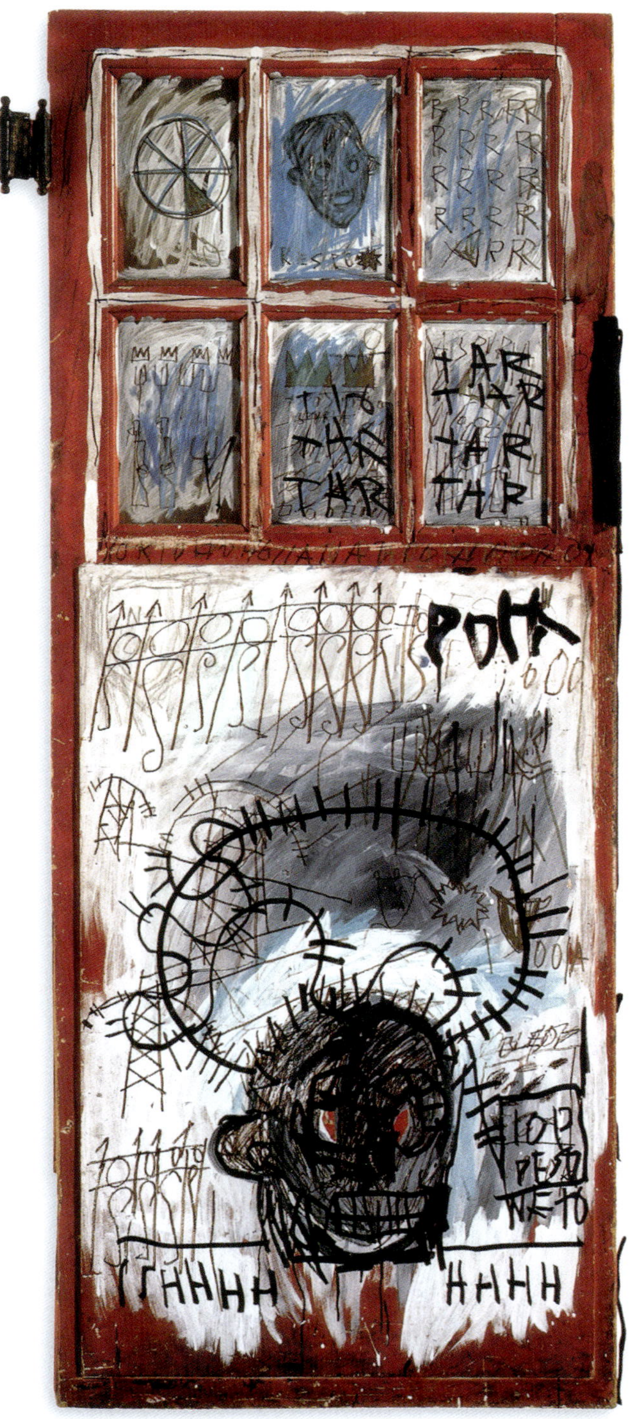

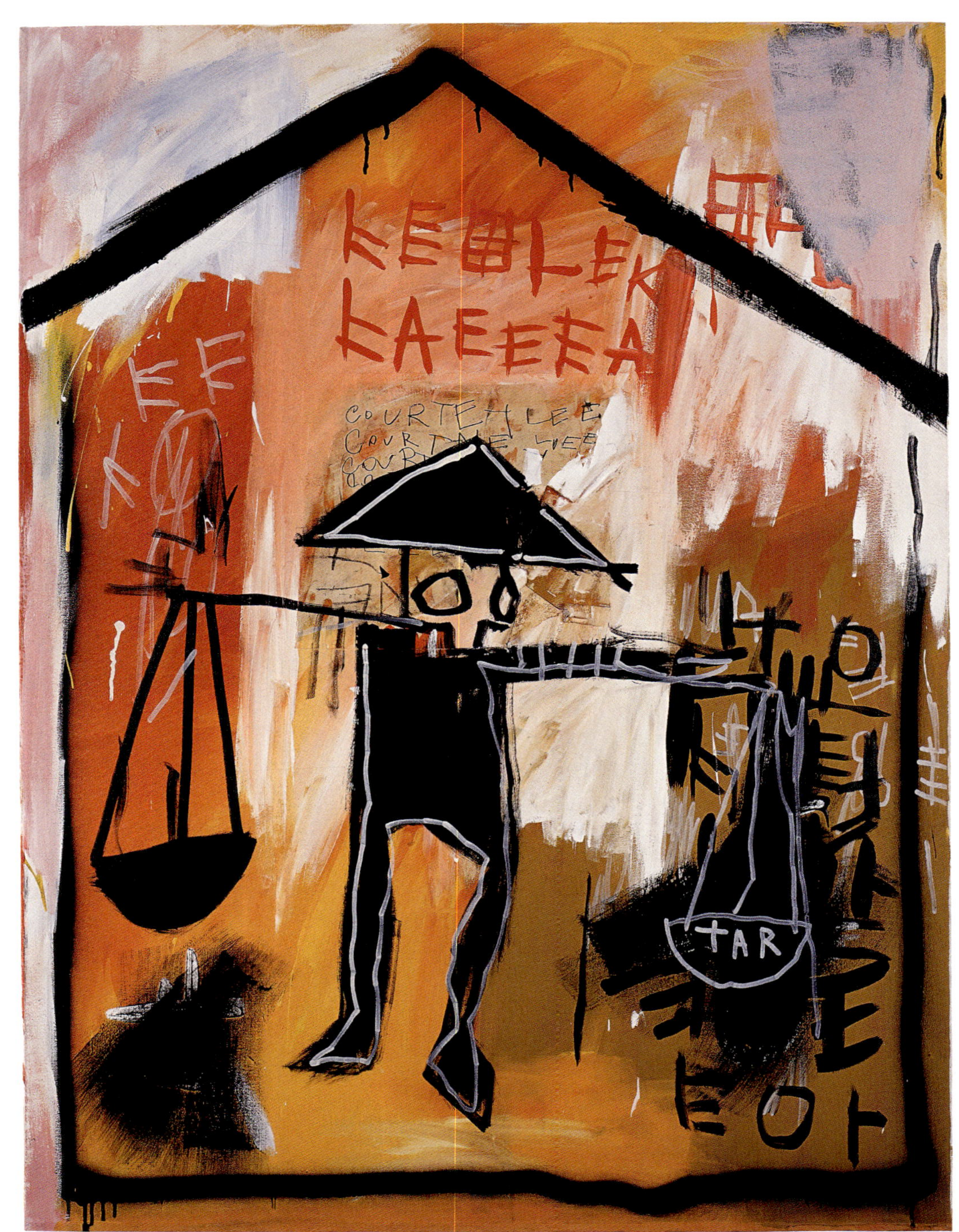
KEOLEK
KAEEEA
COURTEH LEE
COURTNE LEE
COURTNE LEE
TAR

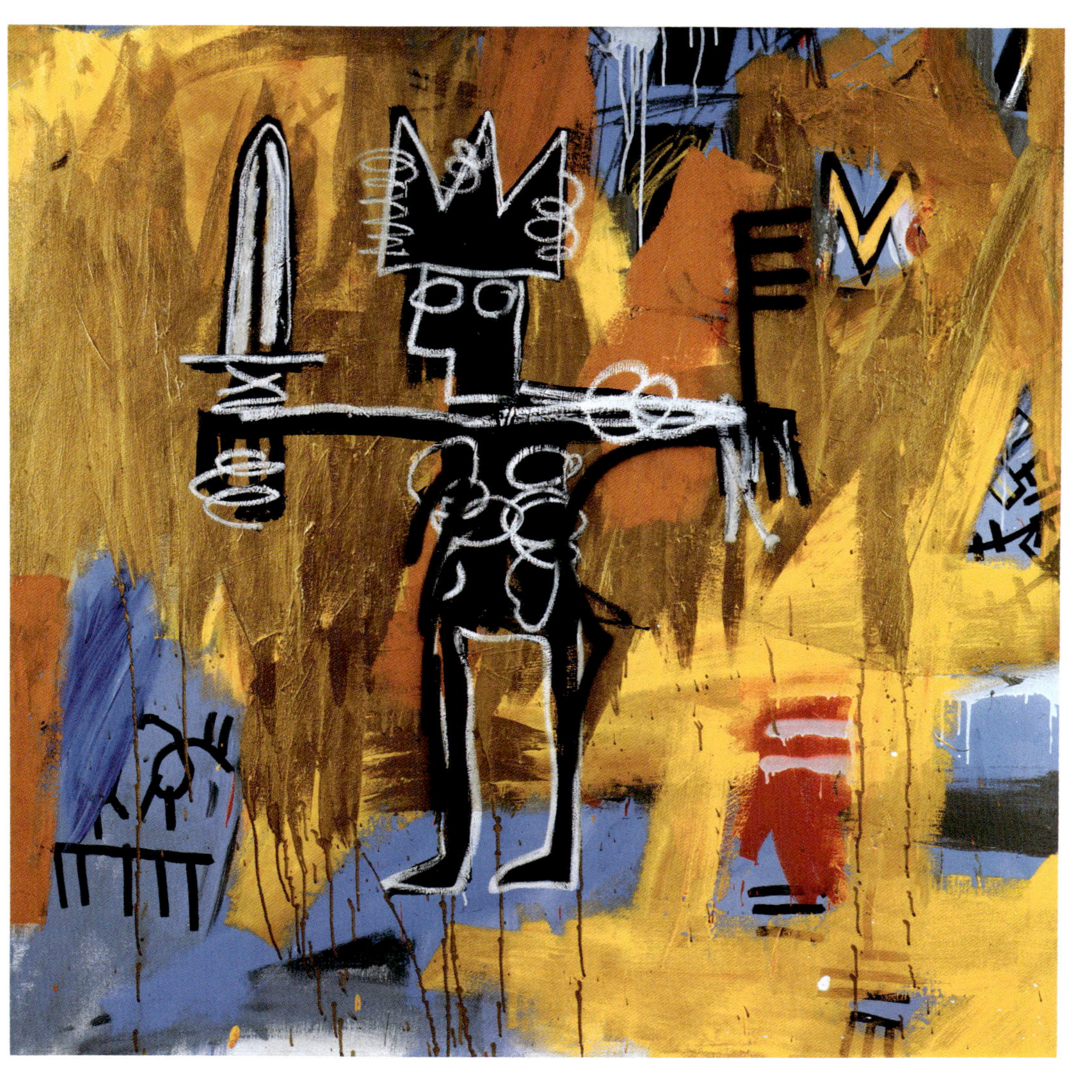

Untitled (Chinese Man Orange), 1981
Acrylic, ink, paper collage, and spray enamel
on canvas, 122 x 91.5 cm / 48 x 36 inches

Untitled (Julius Caesar on Gold), 1981
Acrylic and oilstick on canvas,
127 x 127 cm / 50 x 50 inches

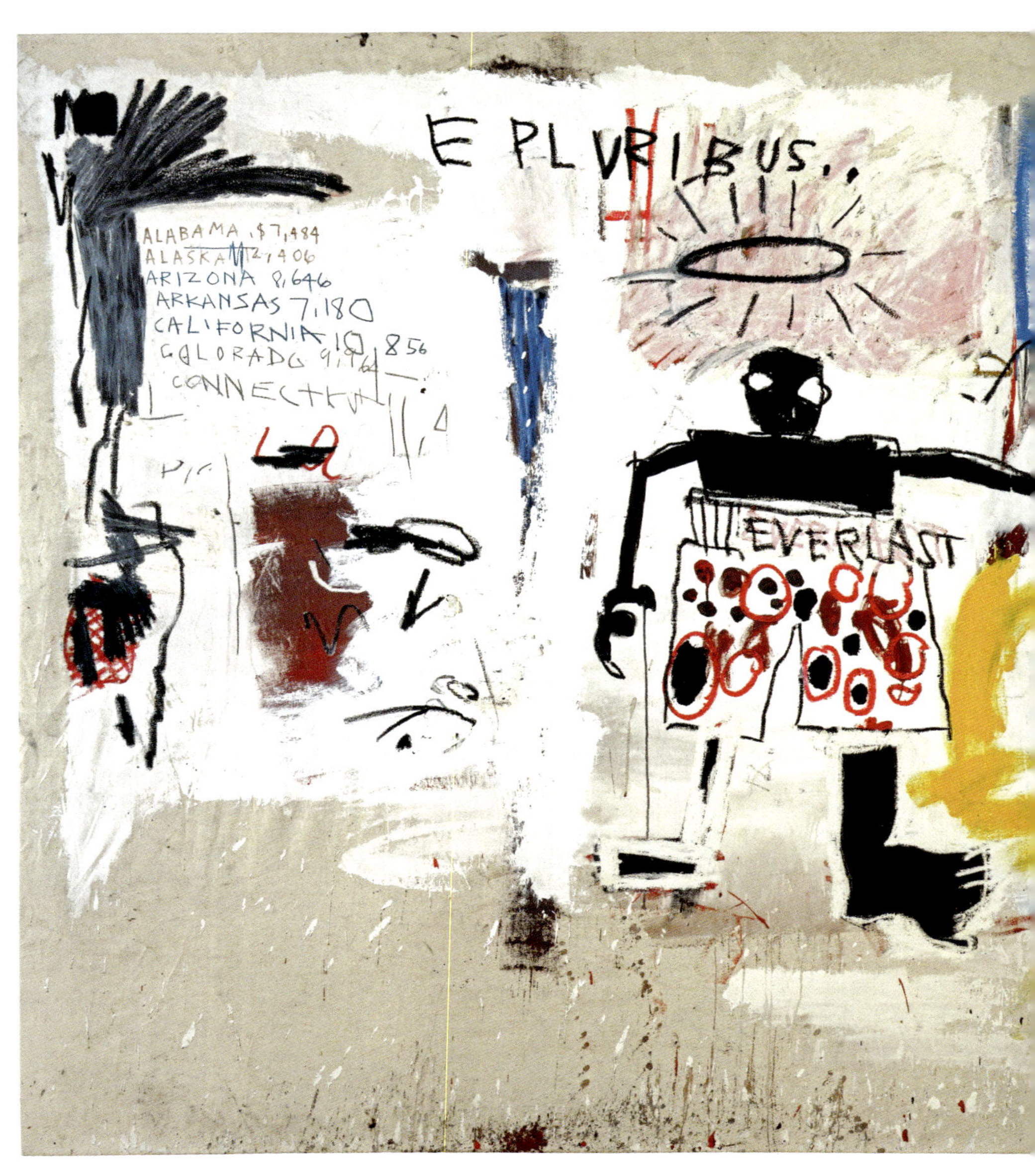

Per Capita, 1981
Acrylic and oilstick on canvas,
203 x 381 cm / 80 x 150 inches

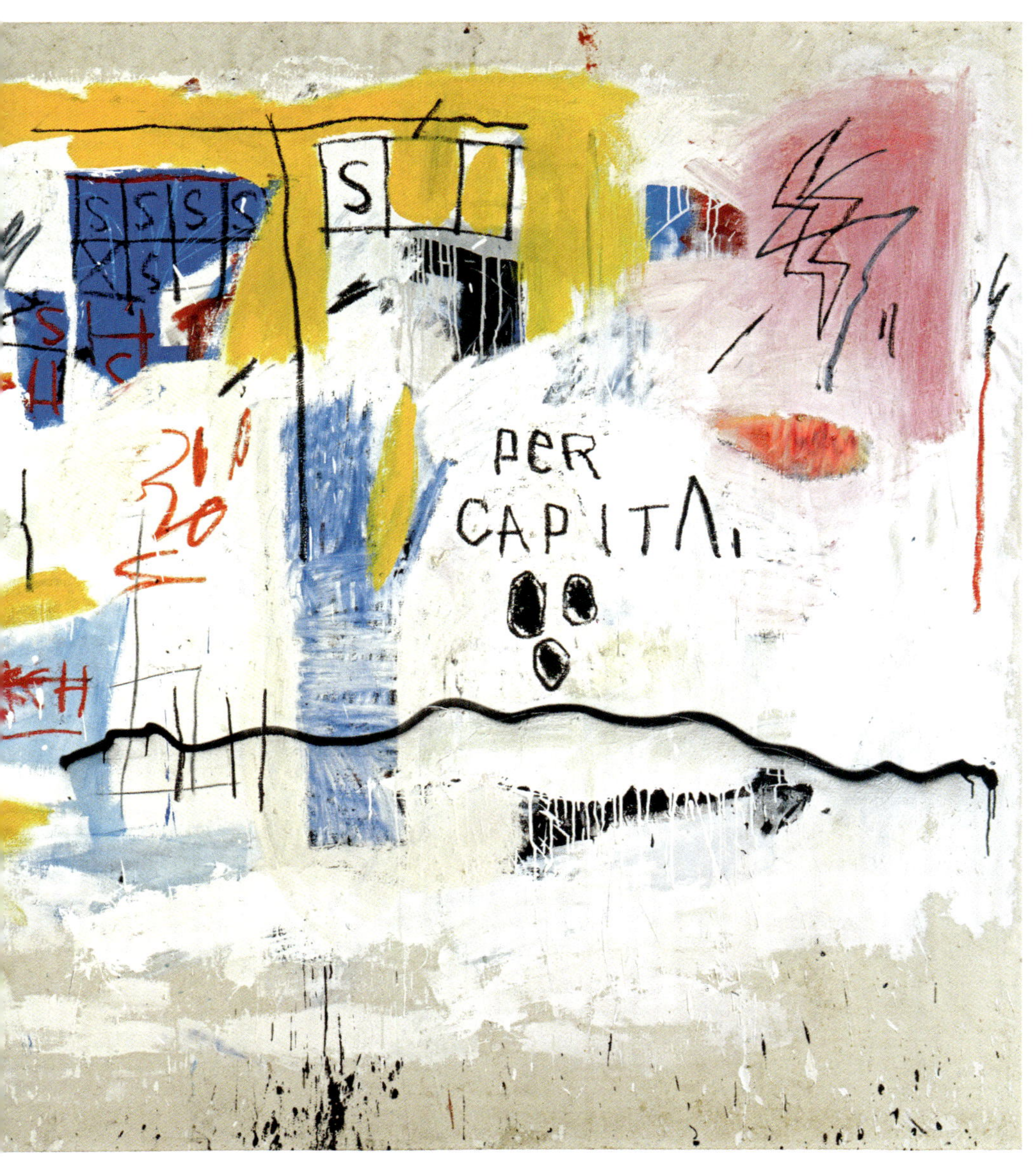

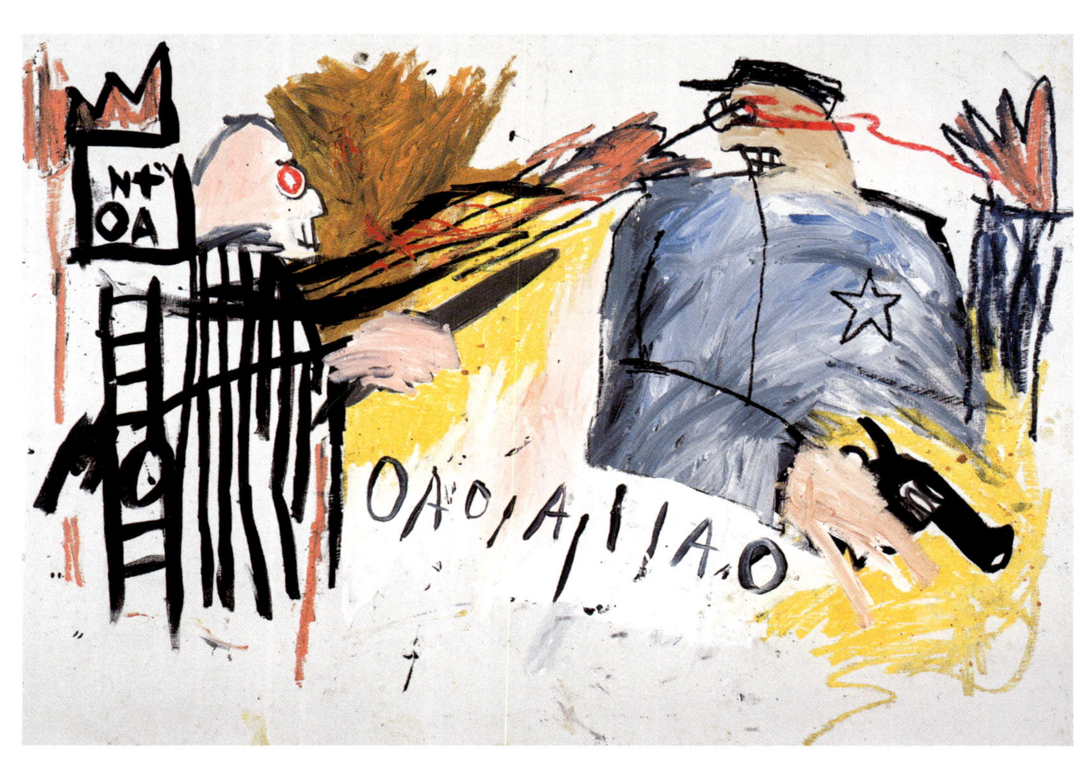

Untitled (Sheriff), 1981
Acrylic and oilstick on canvas,
131 x 188 cm / 51 ¹/₂ x 74 inches

Untitled, 1981
Acrylic and photocopy collage on wood,
122 x 76 cm / 48 x 30 inches

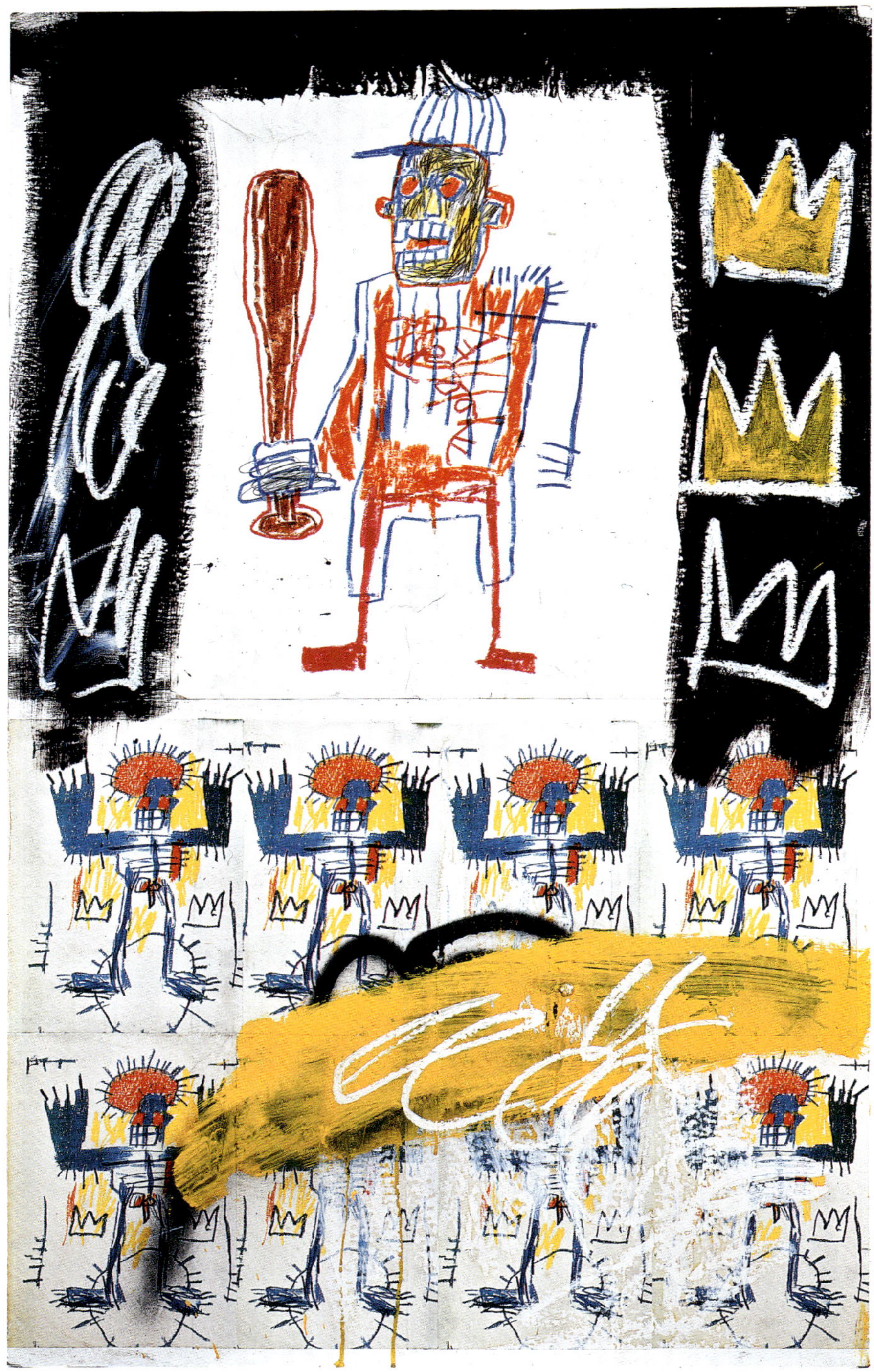

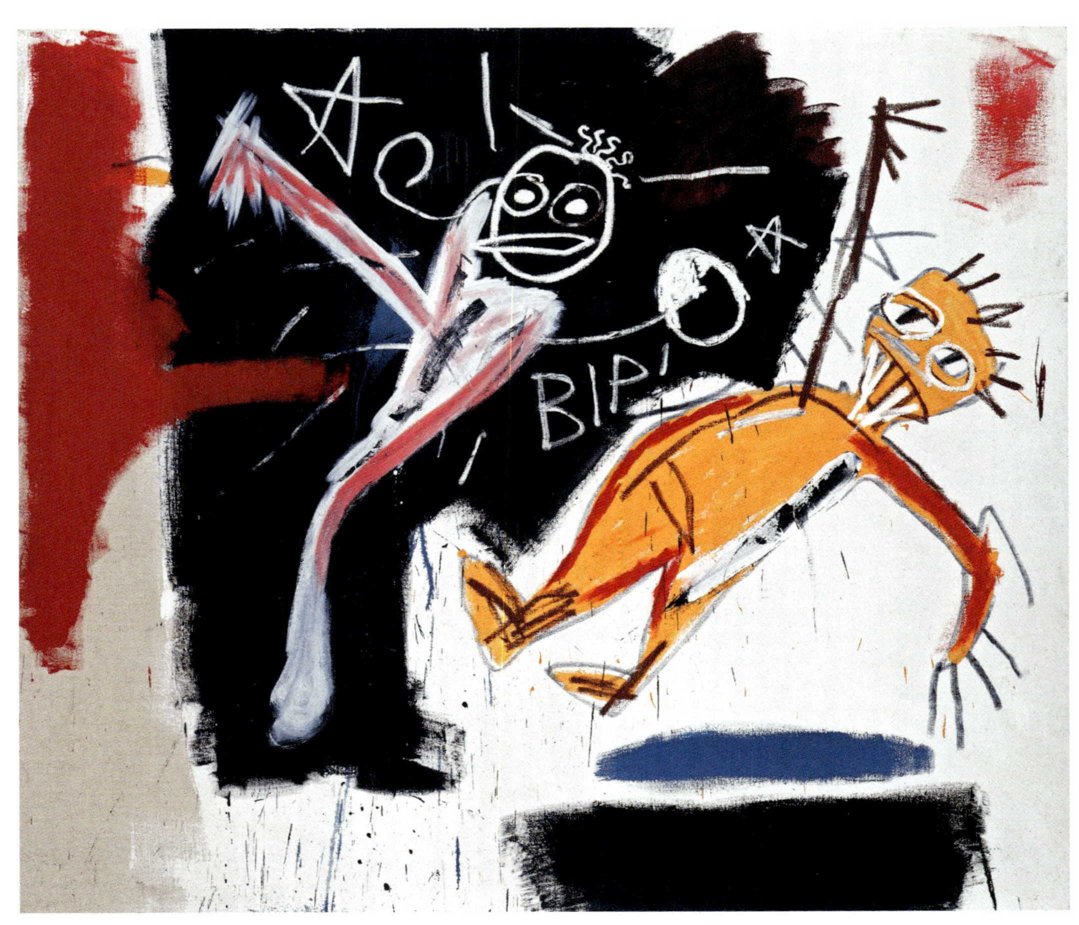

Untitled (Bip), 1981
Acrylic and oilstick on canvas,
183 x 213.5 cm / 72 x 84 inches

Number 1, 1981
Acrylic, enamel, spray paint, oilstick, felt pen, and
paper collage on canvas, 142 x 86.5 cm / 56 x 34 inches

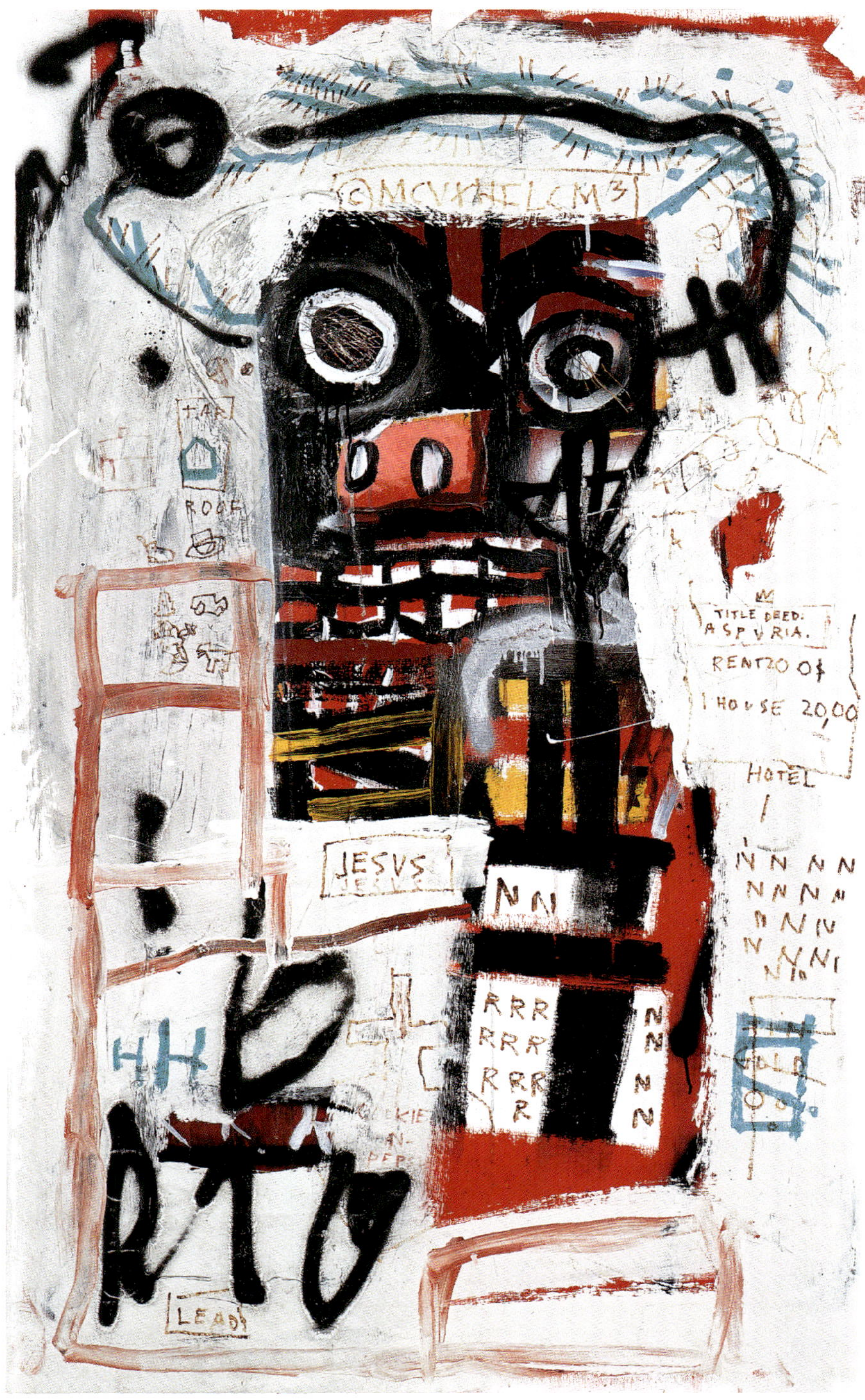

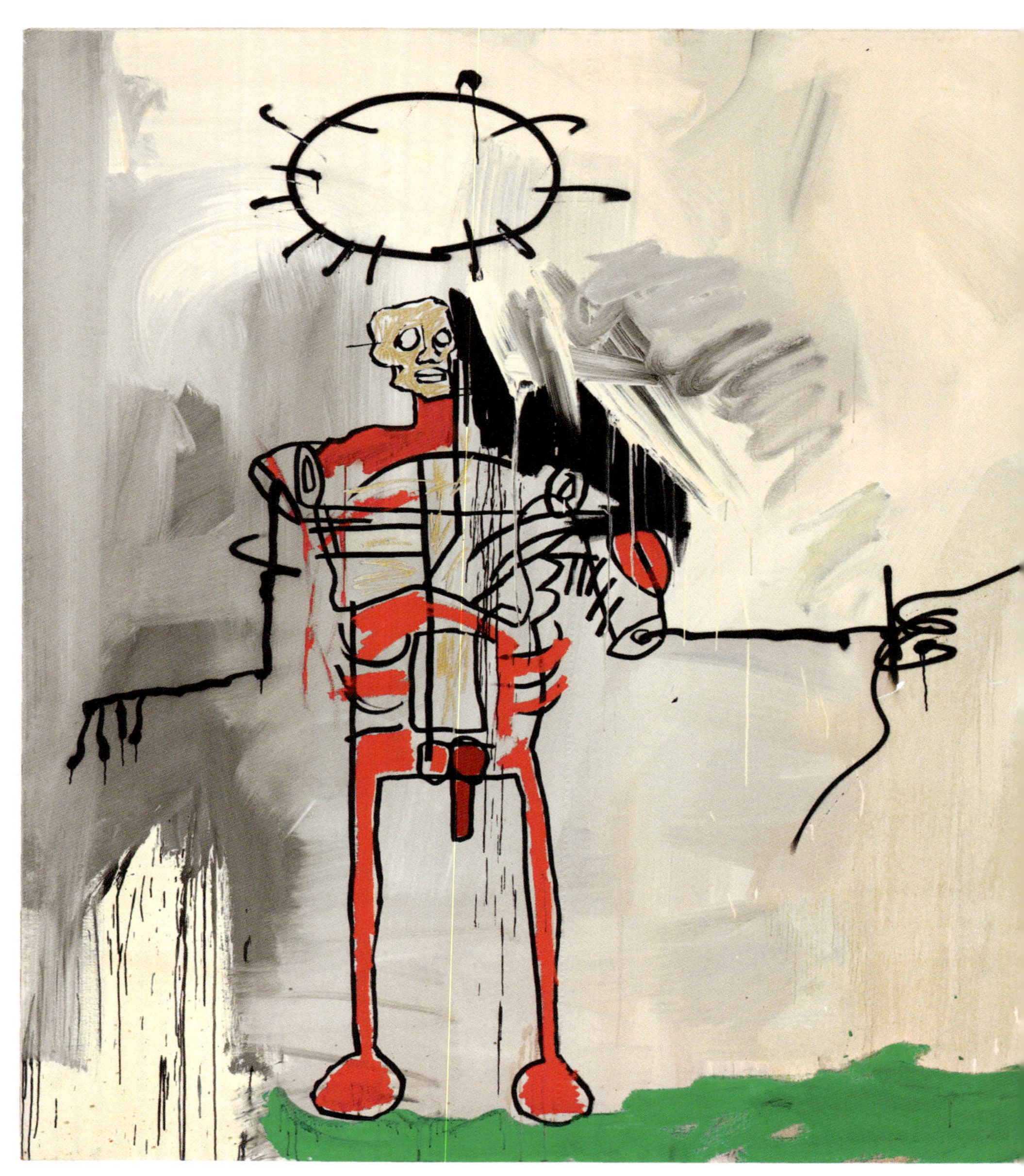

The Field next to the Other Road, 1981
Acrylic, enamel, spray paint, oilstick, and ink
on canvas, 221 x 401.5 cm / 87 x 158 inches

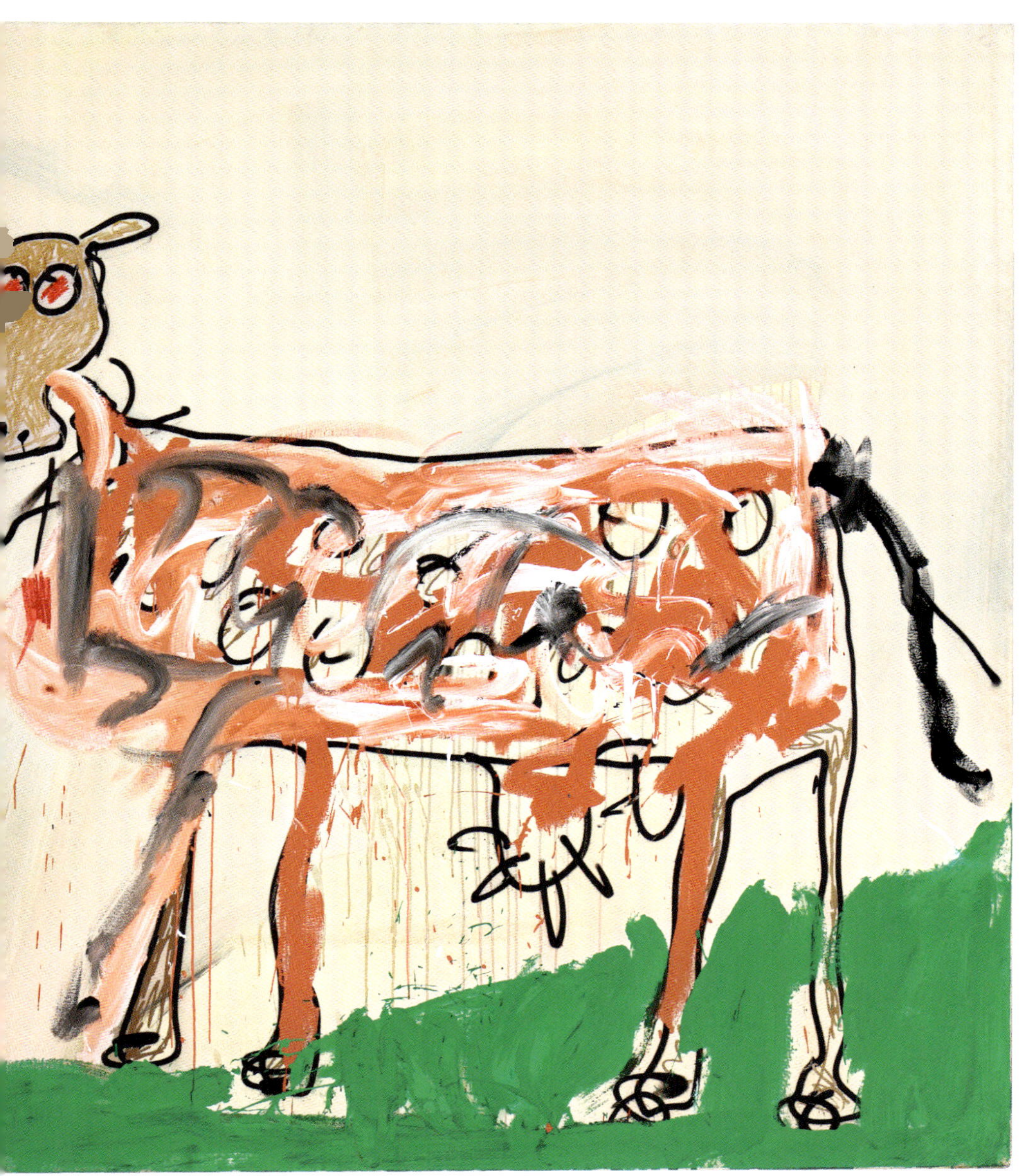

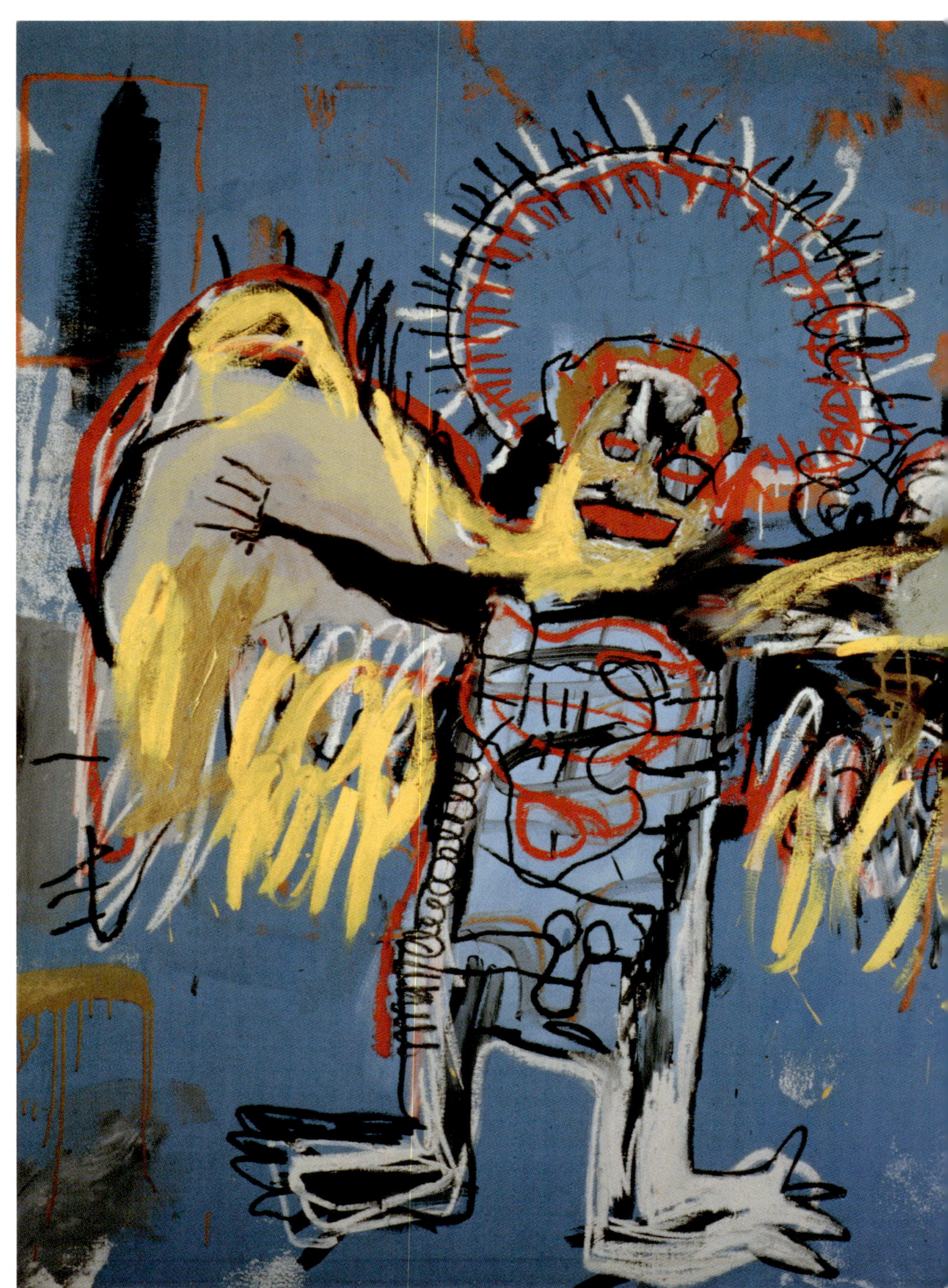

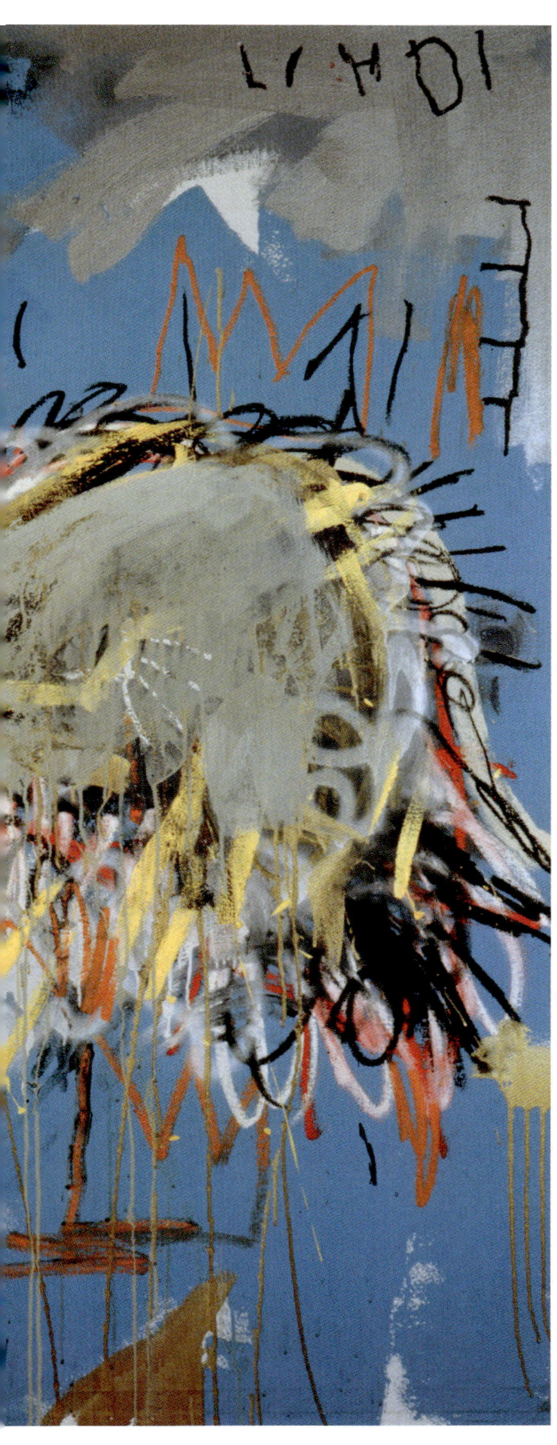

Untitled (Fallen Angel), 1981
Acrylic and oilstick on canvas,
168 x 197.5 cm / 66 ¹/₄ x 77 ³/₄ inches

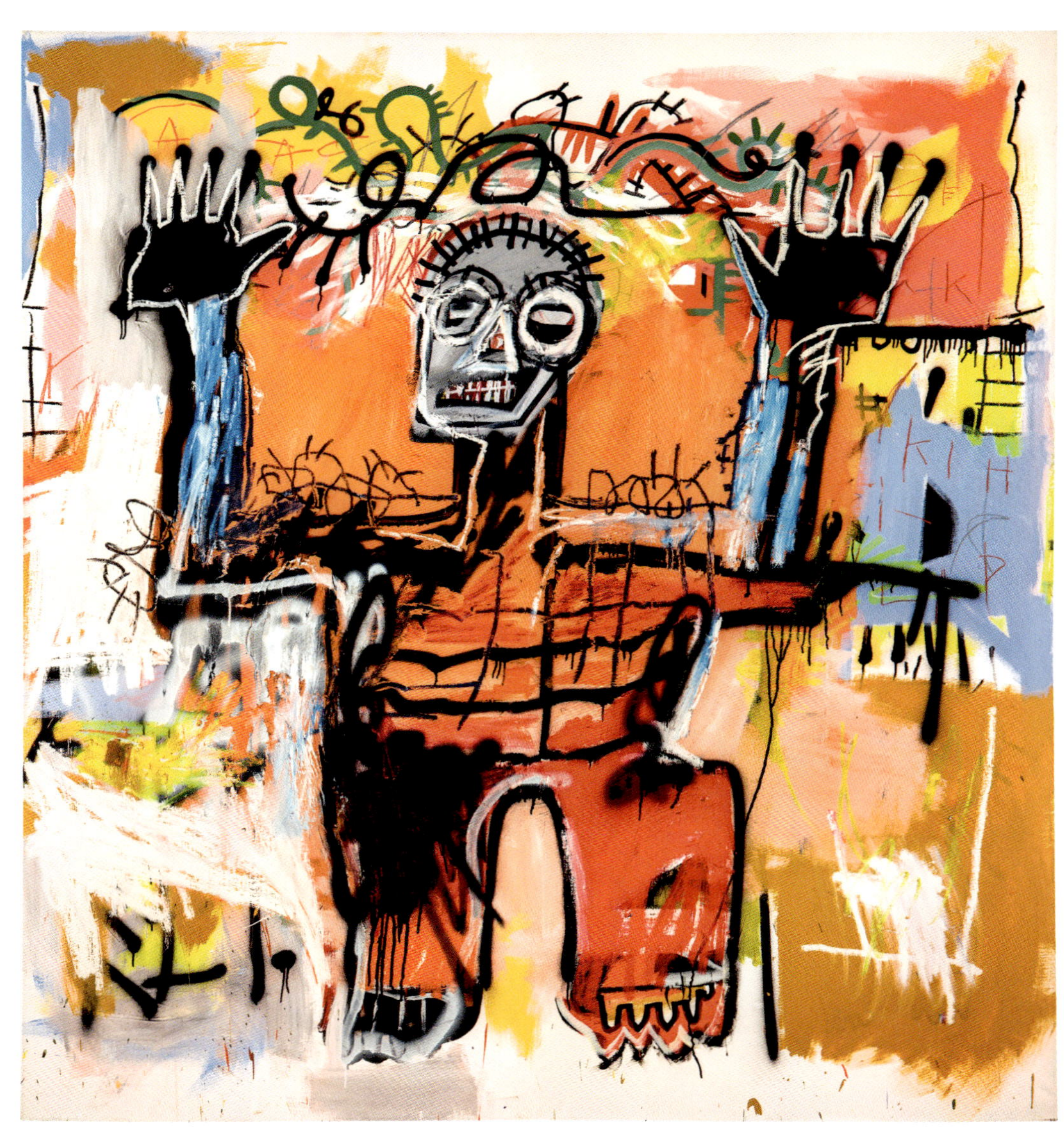

Untitled, 1981
Acrylic, oilstick, and spray paint on canvas,
199.5 x 183 cm / 78 ¹/₂ x 72 inches

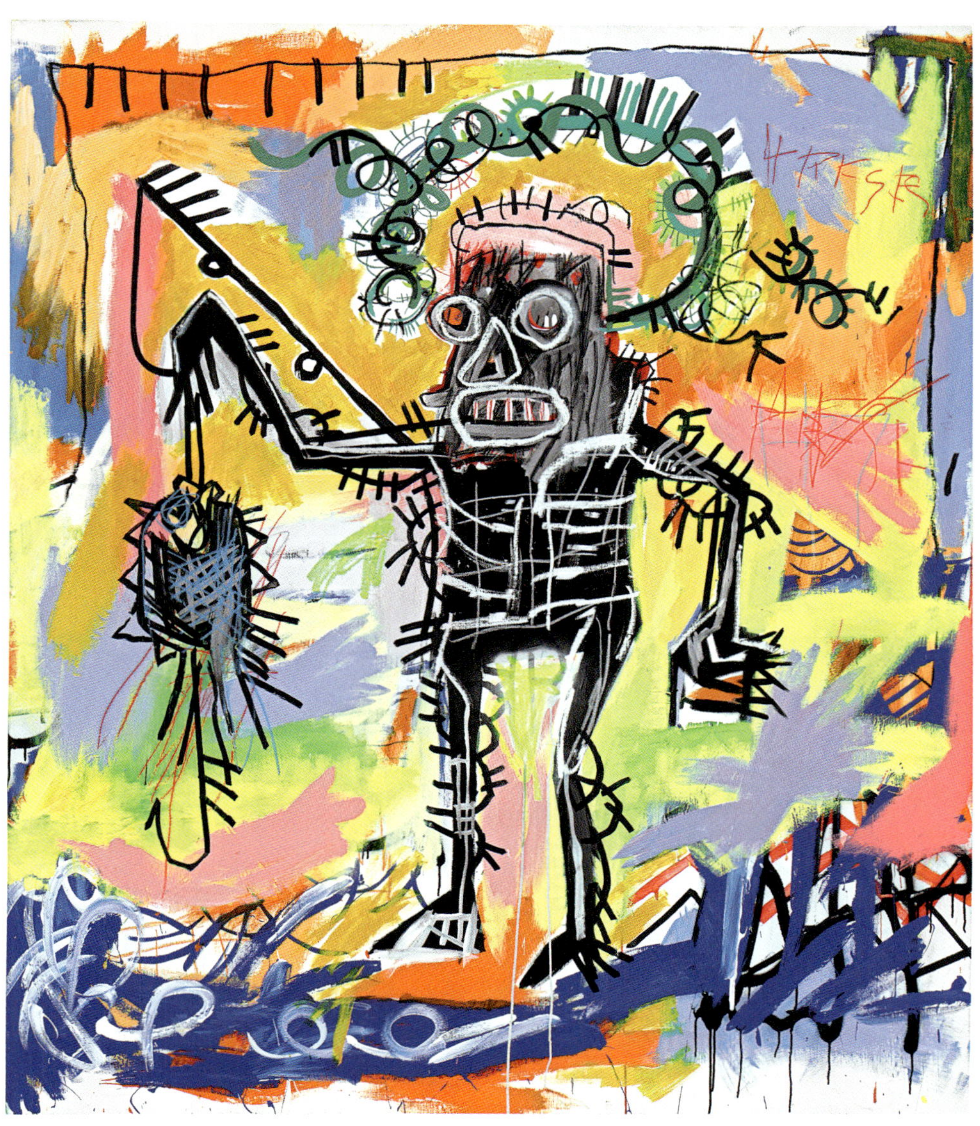

Untitled, 1981
Acrylic and oilstick on canvas,
198 x 173 cm / 78 x 68 inches

Pages 142/143: **Untitled**, 1981
Acrylic, oilstick, and metallic spray enamel
on canvas, 172.5 x 261.5 cm / 68 x 103 inches

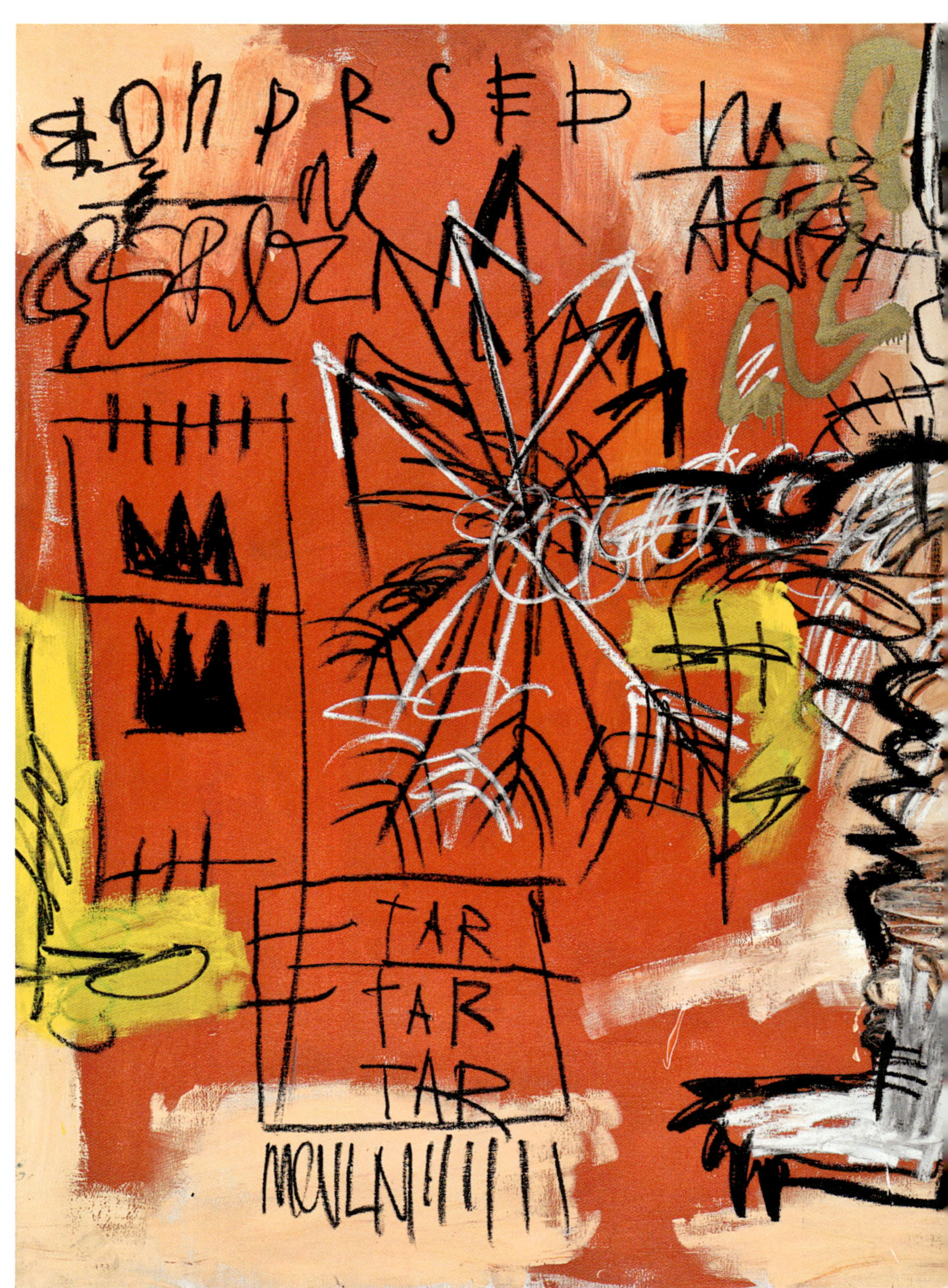

ON PRSED
BROZ
TAR
TAR
TAR
MOULN

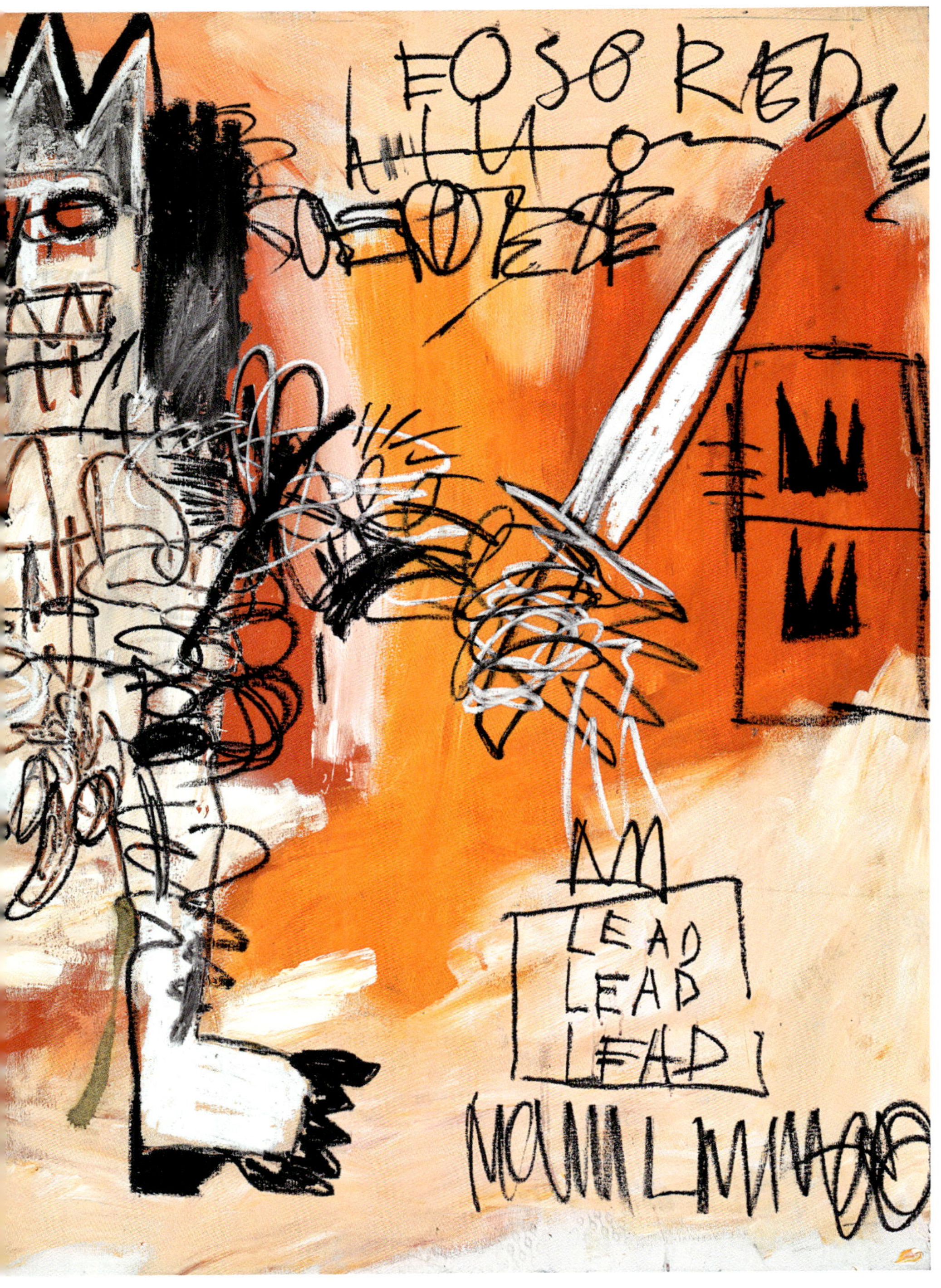
EOSO RED
LEAD
LEAD
LEAD

La Hara, 1981
Acrylic and oilstick on wood,
183 x 121.5 cm / 72 x 47 ³/₄ inches

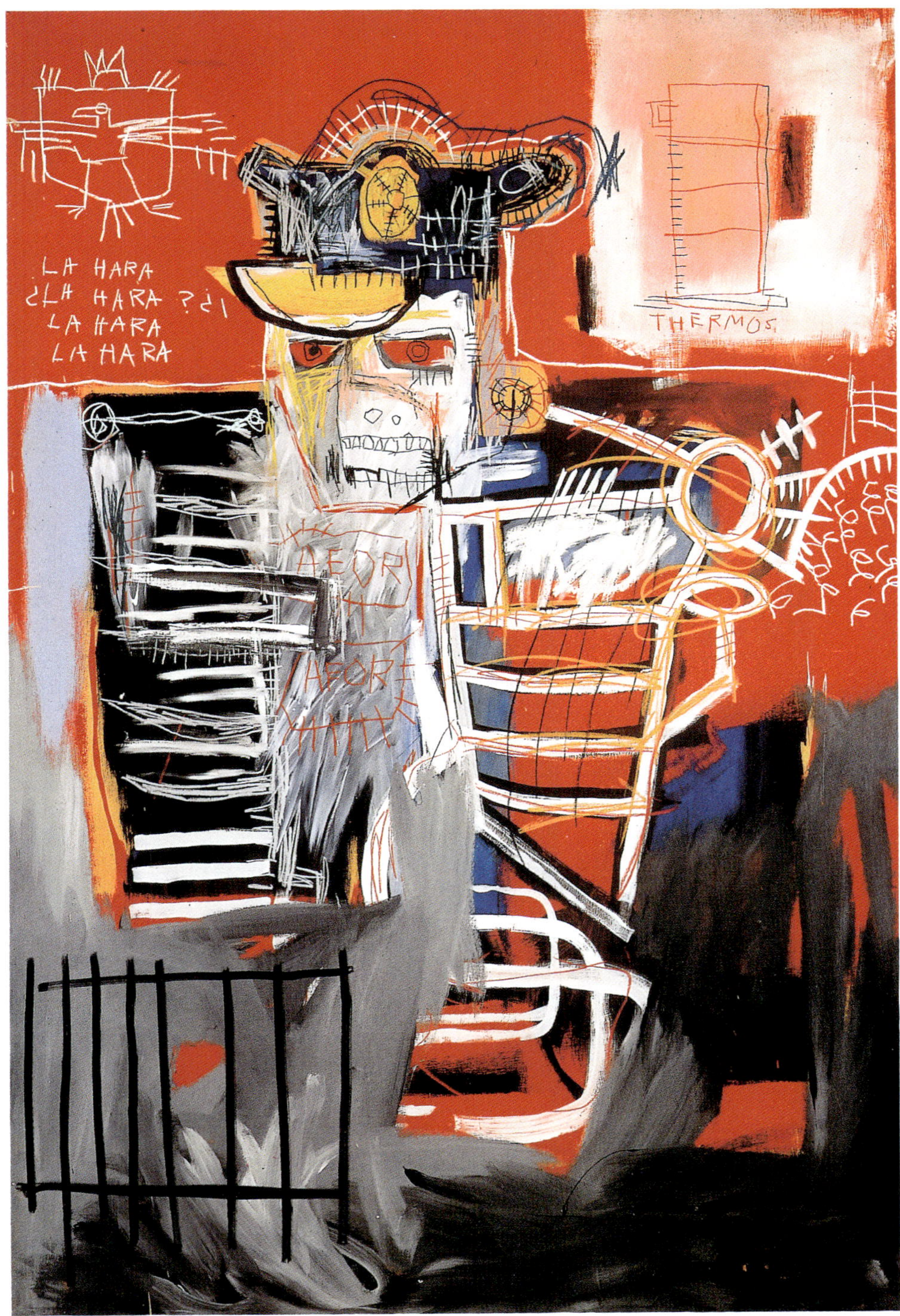
LA HARA
¿LA HARA?¿!
LA HARA
LA HARA
THERMOS

Untitled (Skull), 1981
Acrylic and oilstick on canvas,
207 x 175.5 cm / 81 ¹/₄ x 69 inches

Pages 148/149: **Bird on Money**, 1981
Acrylic and oilstick on canvas,
167.5 x 228.5 cm / 66 x 90 inches

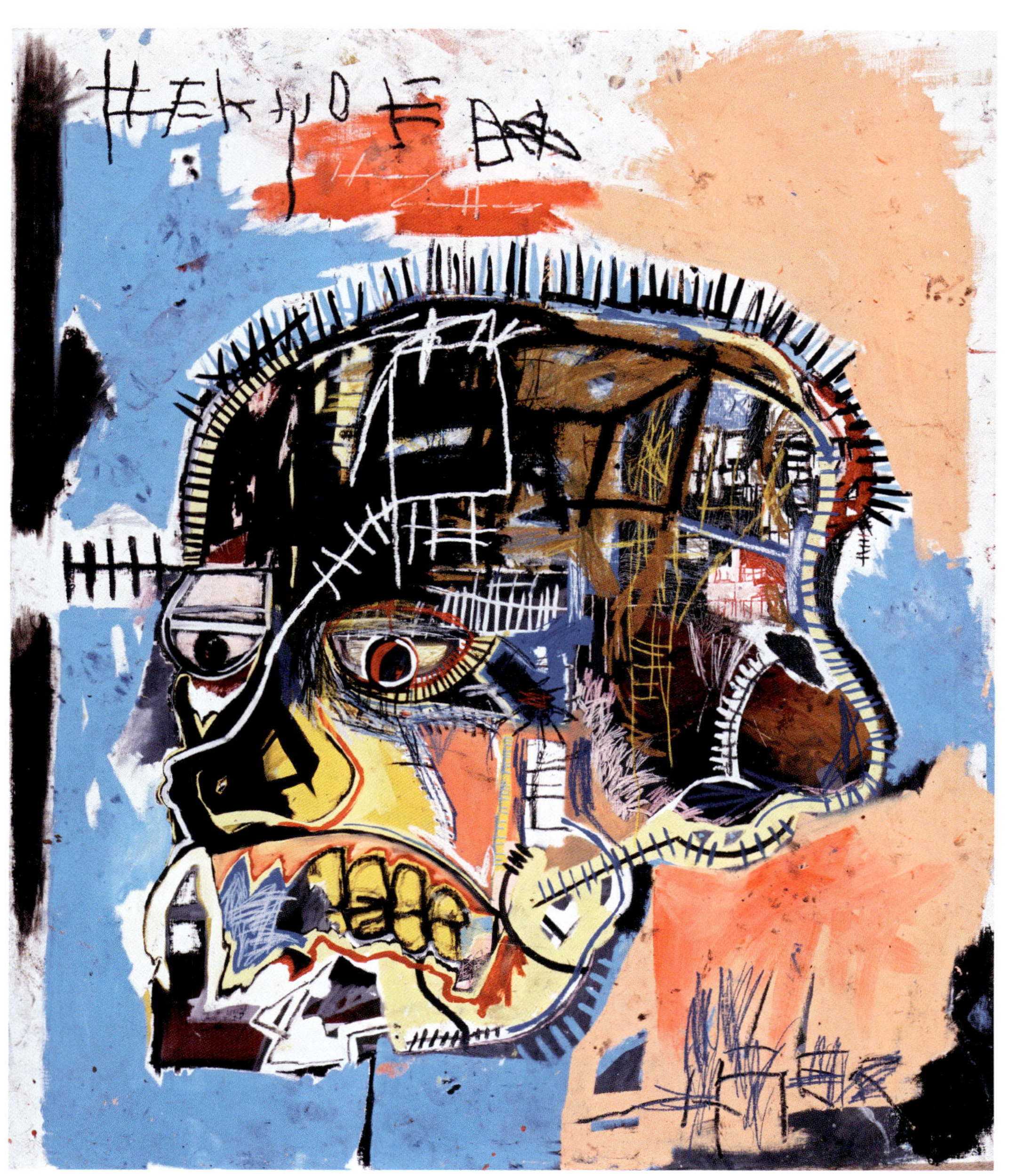

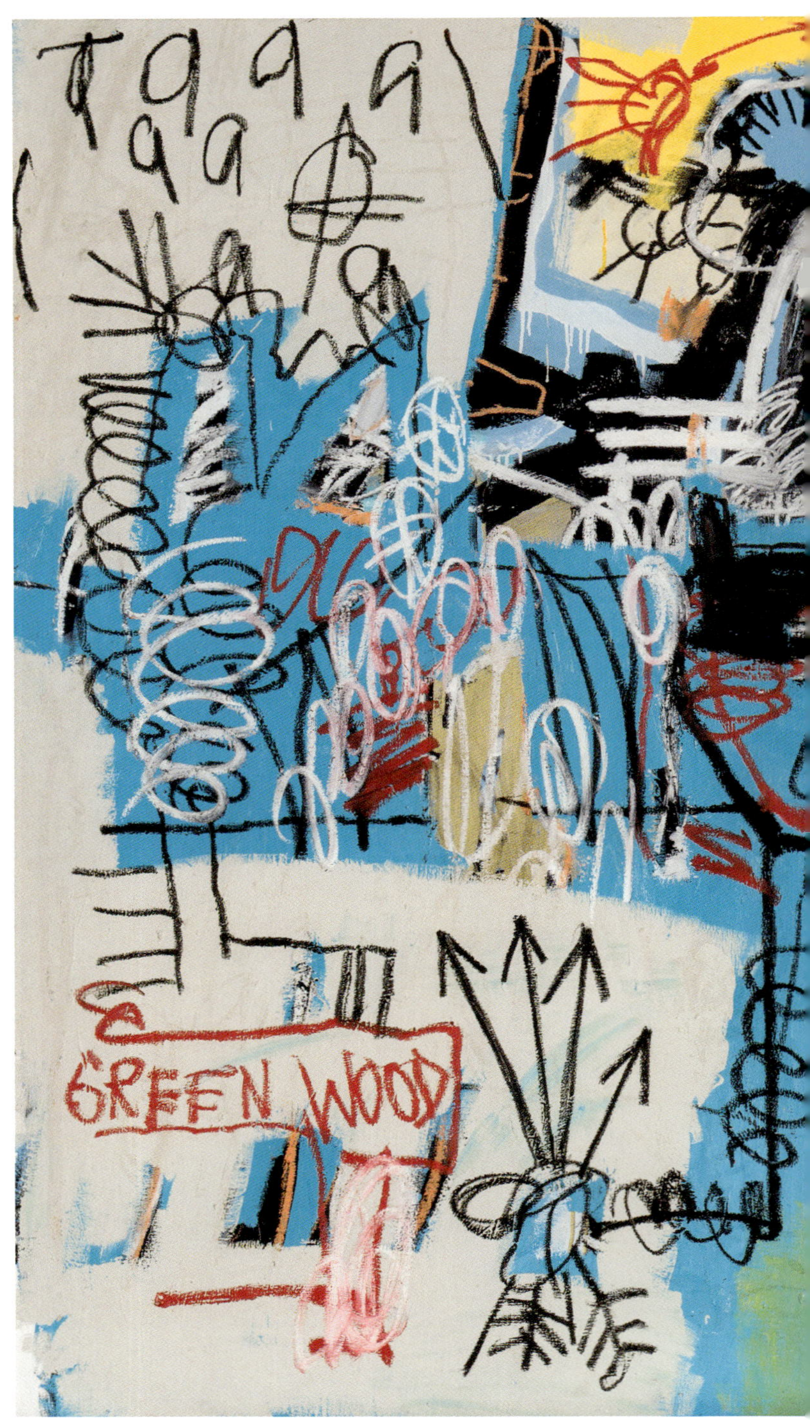

GREEN WOOD

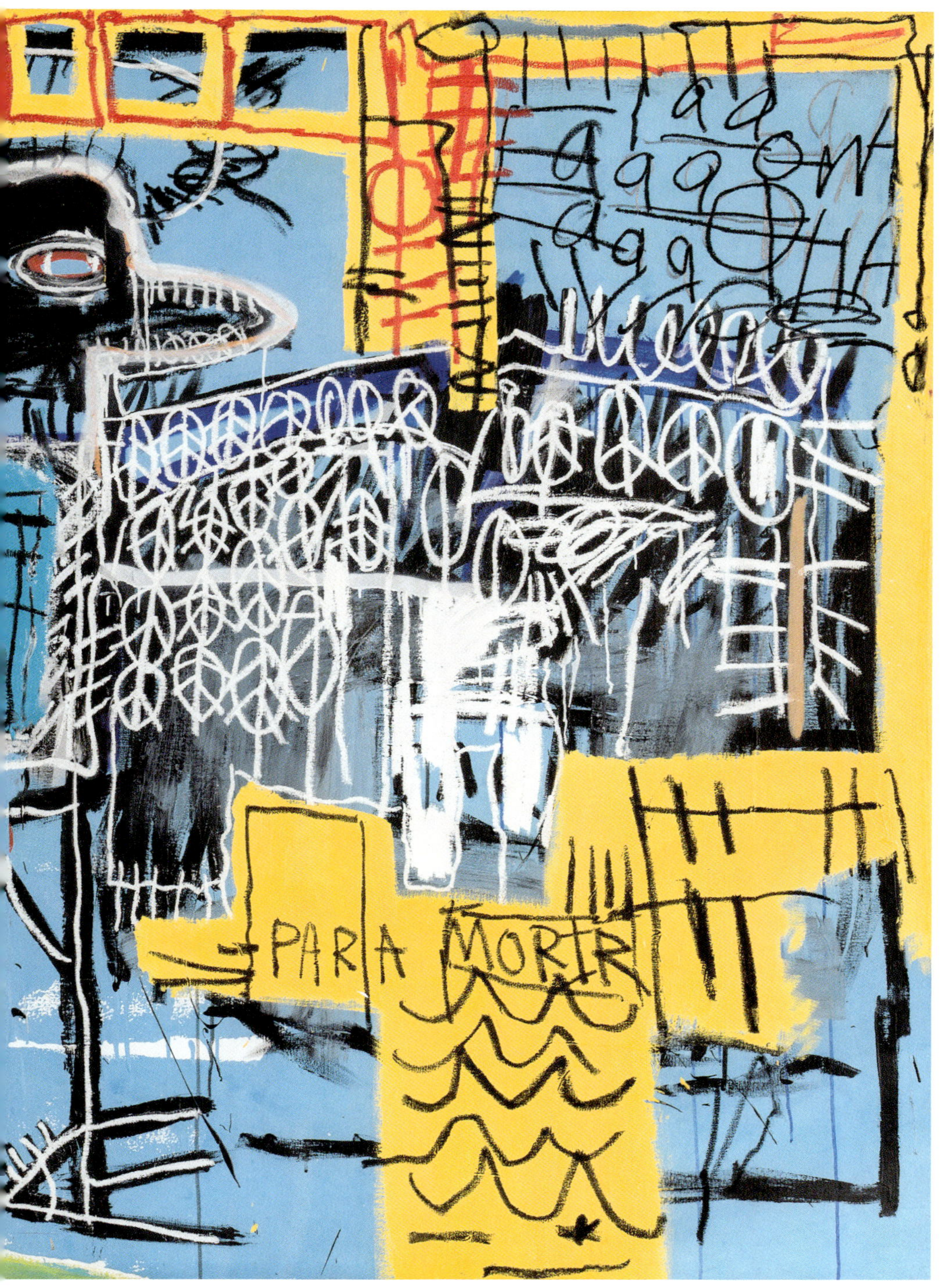
PARA MORIR

III

1982
A Hollywood Scenario

"What has propelled him so quickly is the unmistakable eloquence of his touch. The linear quality of his phrases and notations, whether 'graffiti' or 'art,' shows innate subtlety—he gives us not gestural indulgence, but an intimately calibrated relationship to surface instead … These paintings are tentative rather than stiff, ambitious rather than cynical, giddy maybe—but not complacent."

—LISA LIEBMANN, *ART IN AMERICA*, 1982[1]

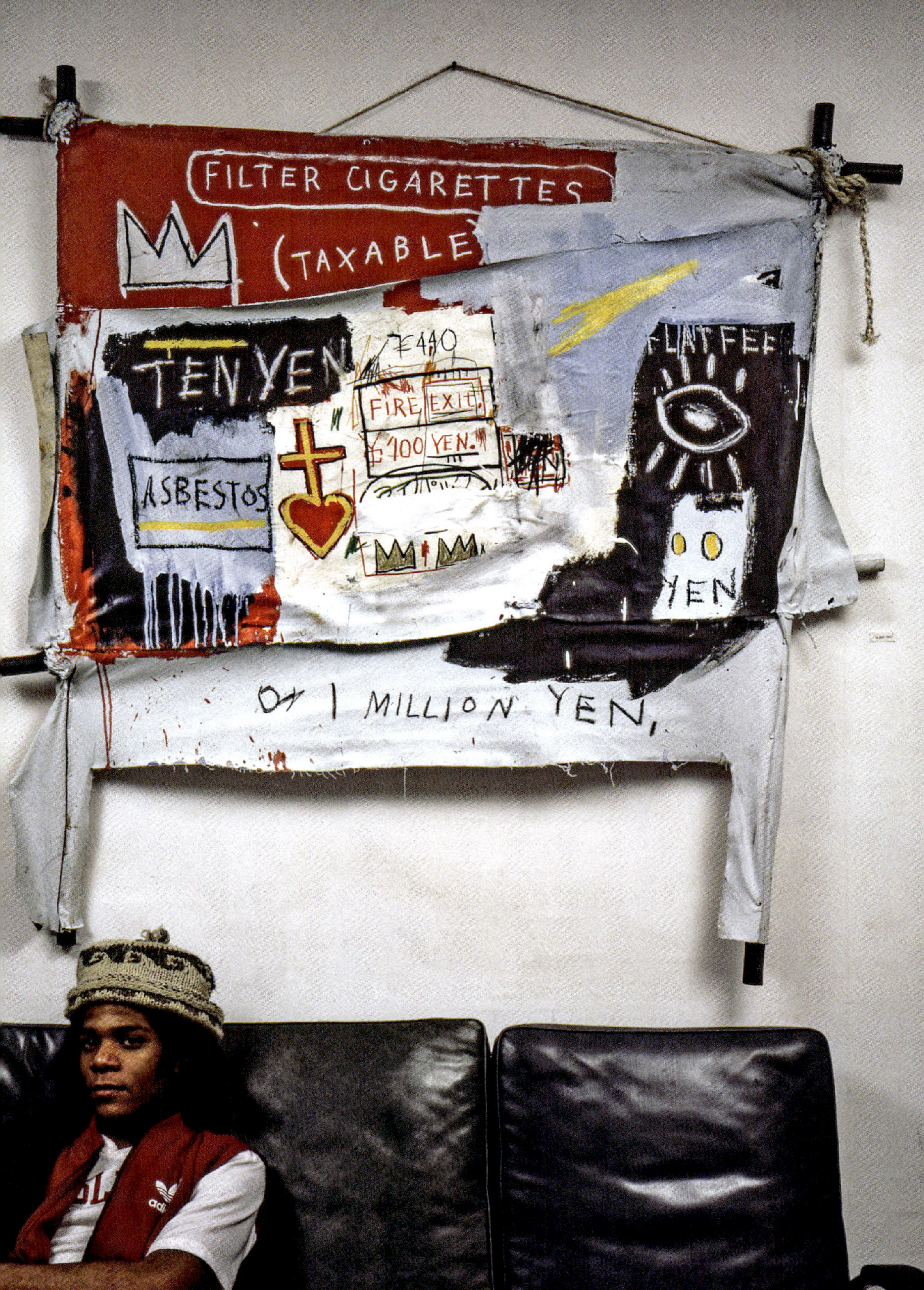

FILTER CIGARETTES
(TAXABLE
¥440
TEN YEN
FIRE EXIT
¥100 YEN.
ASBESTOS
FLINT FEE
YEN
OR 1 MILLION YEN,

Basquiat's first solo exhibition in the U.S. opens in March at Annina Nosei's gallery. It is a huge success, selling out immediately and receiving very favorable reviews. Basquiat is now "entirely capable of fulfilling his considerable promise," Lisa Liebmann closes her article.[2] There is a new thematic drift to his work, as Jeanne Silverthorne discerns in *Artforum*: "Painting after painting features boxers, winners and/or losers. The repeated gesture of the dazed champion raising his arm above his head in victory is uncomfortably close to that of the Statue of Liberty bearing her torch aloft … While only one of the contenders wears the crown (literally), the loser is often saintly, boasting a halo—as, frequently, do skulls. To lose is to be holy is to be dead? Yet this is shadow boxing; that is, one's competition in Basquiat's ring of social Darwinism is oneself, and the desire to win ends in the destruction of that possibly nobler *doppelgänger*. Every victory is a betrayal."[3]

Basquiat has moved to a new flat in 151 Crosby Street with Suzanne Mallouk. He meets Shenge Ka Pharaoh, an artist from Barbados, a friend with whom to discuss a growing interest in African topics, and later his studio assistant. In March, he takes part in a group exhibition in Modena, organized by curator Achille Bonito Oliva, featuring the Transavanguardia movement of Italian and American artists who find new approaches to figurative painting. His next big solo show is at Gagosian in Los Angeles in April. William Wilson breathlessly reviews it for the *L.A. Times*: "Imagine a Hollywood scenario where a New York kid-gang subway graffiti painter turns out to be an artistic prodigy. It doesn't sound like a very promising movie but it's an intriguing aesthetic idea, and Jean-Michel Basquiat is the man for the part. This 22-year- old kid from Brooklyn makes his L.A. debut with a dozen of the most vigorous Neo-Expressionist paintings I have seen to date. They are, in fact, so lacking in the wan sense of futility and jejune intellectual pretension often associated with the movement one could attend closely to an argument that they are not New Wave pictures at all."[4]

Basquiat remains in Los Angeles after the show. Aiming for an even rawer, almost makeshift look, he develops a new kind of stretcher with the canvas leaving the corners of the crossbars exposed; these are built for him by Shenge. In June he visits Germany, where he is youngest of all artists ever invited to *documenta*, the conceptually minded exhibition organized every five years in Kassel. "His strength comes not so much from the social-commentary aspect of his work," a review in *Arts Magazine* reads, "but from his Twombly-esque lyrical qualities."[5] In September, Basquiat shows at Bruno Bischofberger's gallery in Zürich. Following that, Bischofberger becomes his exclusive dealer for Europe.

Basquiat crosses paths with Andy Warhol again, who notes in an October entry of his diary: "Down to meet Bruno Bischofberger (cab $7.50). He brought Jean-Michel Basquiat with him. He's the kid who used the name 'Samo' when he used to sit on the sidewalk in

Untitled (Black Skull), 1982
Acrylic, oilstick, and spray paint on canvas,
183 x 152.5 cm / 72 x 60 inches

Page 151: Jean-Michel Basquiat
with *One Million Yen,* New York 1982.
Photo Tseng Kwong Chi

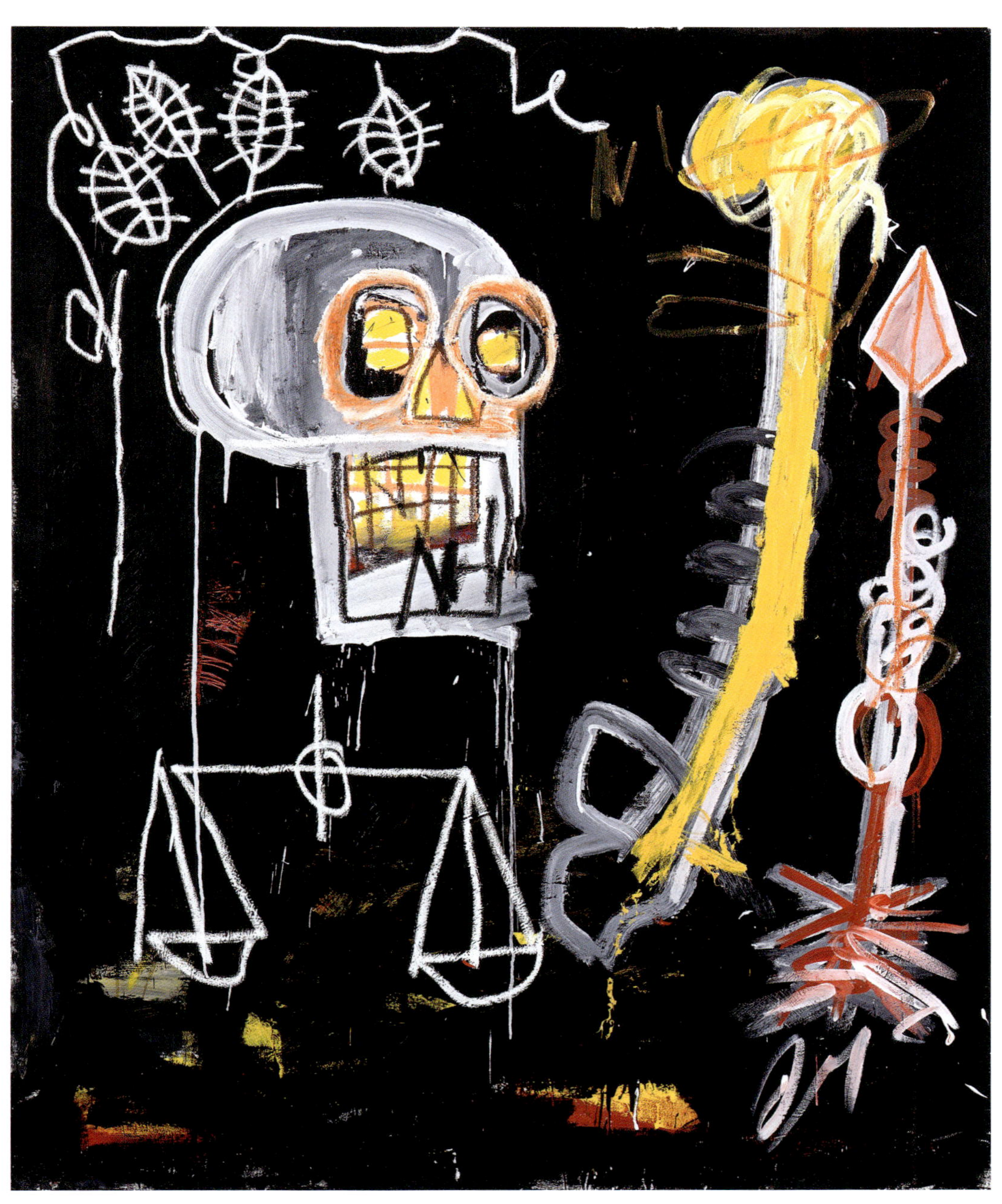

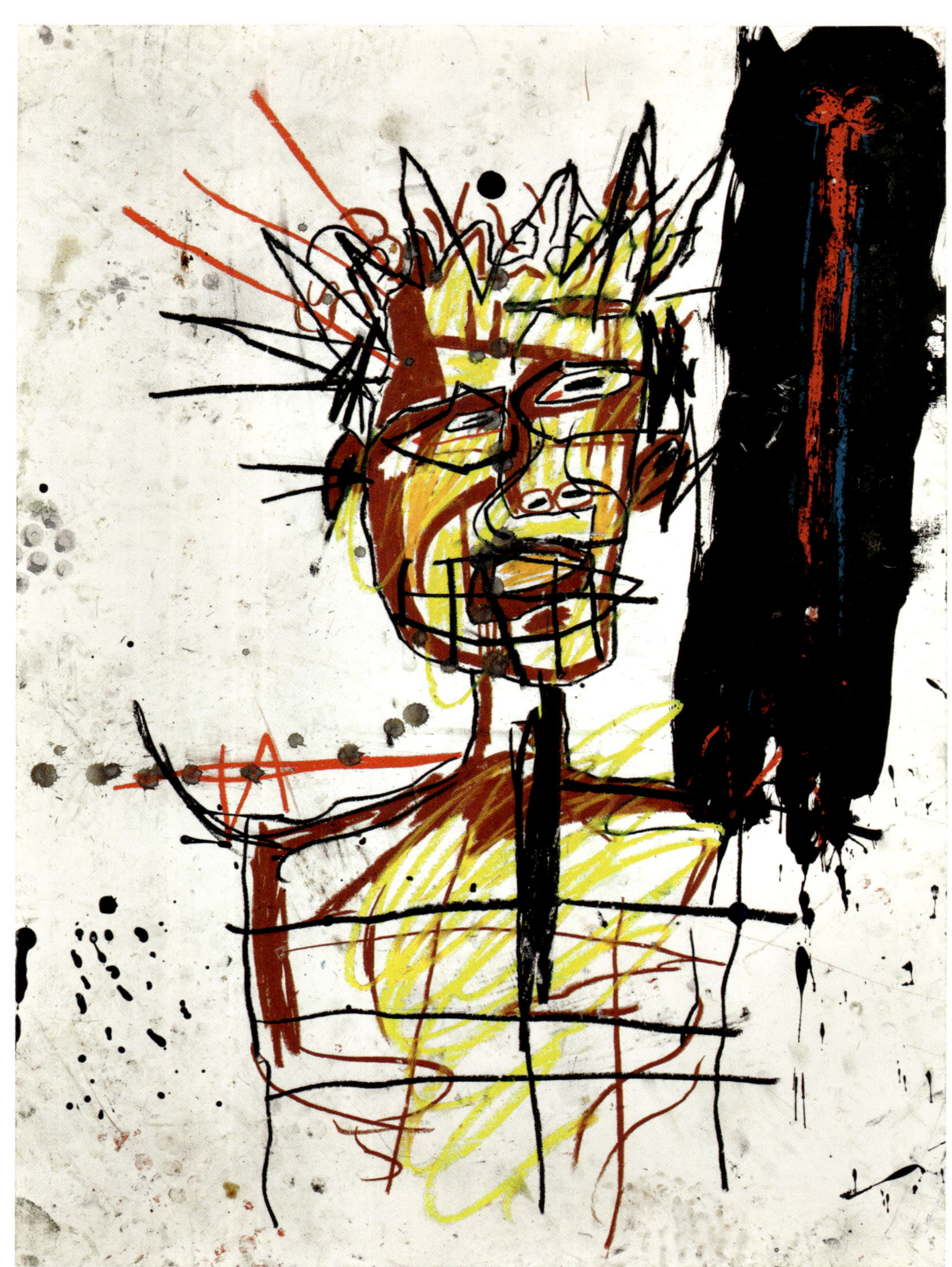

Greenwich Village and paint T-shirts, and I'd give him $10 here and there … And so had lunch for them and then I took a Polaroid and he went home and within two hours a painting was back, still wet, of him and me together. And I mean, just getting to Christie Street must have taken an hour."[6] This is their first real meeting and Warhol is impressed both with the bravura painting (*Dos Cabezas,* p. 199) and the young artist's boldness.

In November, Basquiat exhibits at the Fun Gallery, a newly opened East-Village off-space, against the wishes of his gallerist Annina Nosei. The show is an artistic triumph, with Basquiat's paintings carefully staged, as Nicolas A. Moufarrege describes: "He was at home; the hanging was perfect, the paintings more authentic than ever. Basquiat wrote on the windows of the gallery, waxed for the purpose, and like the ones in his paintings, his lists read like alchemical and historical texts."[7] Susan Hapgood in her review for *Flash Art* is equally impressed with the work's viscerality: "Basquiat is cynical about society's values, yet hasn't given up heroes altogether— *St. Joe Louis Surrounded by Snakes* greets the viewer in Fun Gallery's vitrine (pp. 156/157). In *Jawbone of an Ass,* the list of Greeks and Romans, and the three-foot-long date (Roman numerals, of course), ridicule the concept of educational credentials. He must be mulling all of this over after having entered the Paris-Zürich-New York star circuit … Gut emotions lie behind the phrases and images, not the desire to make neo-expressionist commodities."[8]

[1–8] *See Endnotes on page 508.*

Untitled, 1982
Acrylic and oilstick on paper,
76 x 56 cm / 30 x 22 inches

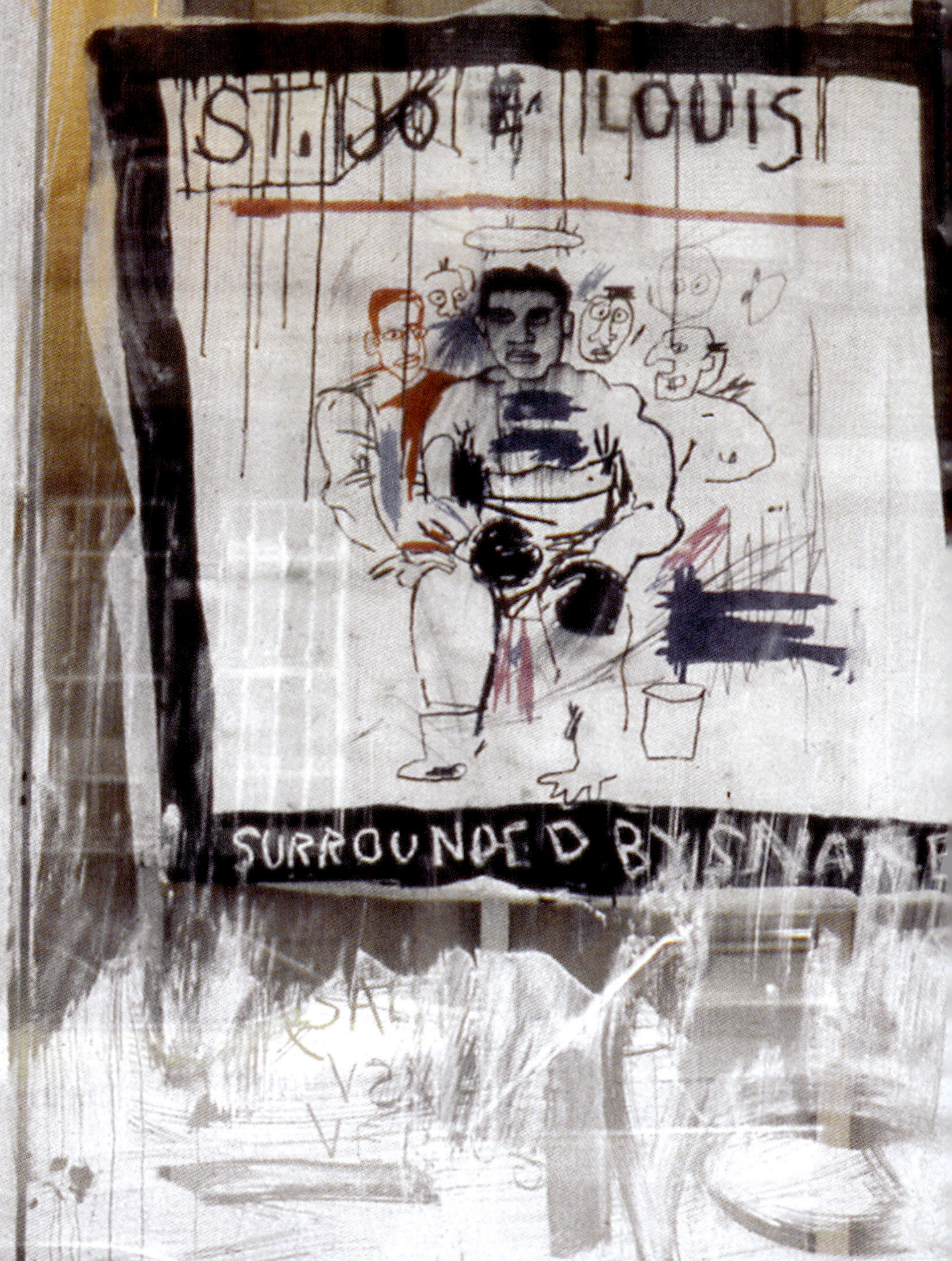
ST. JO LOUIS
SURROUNDED BY SNAKE

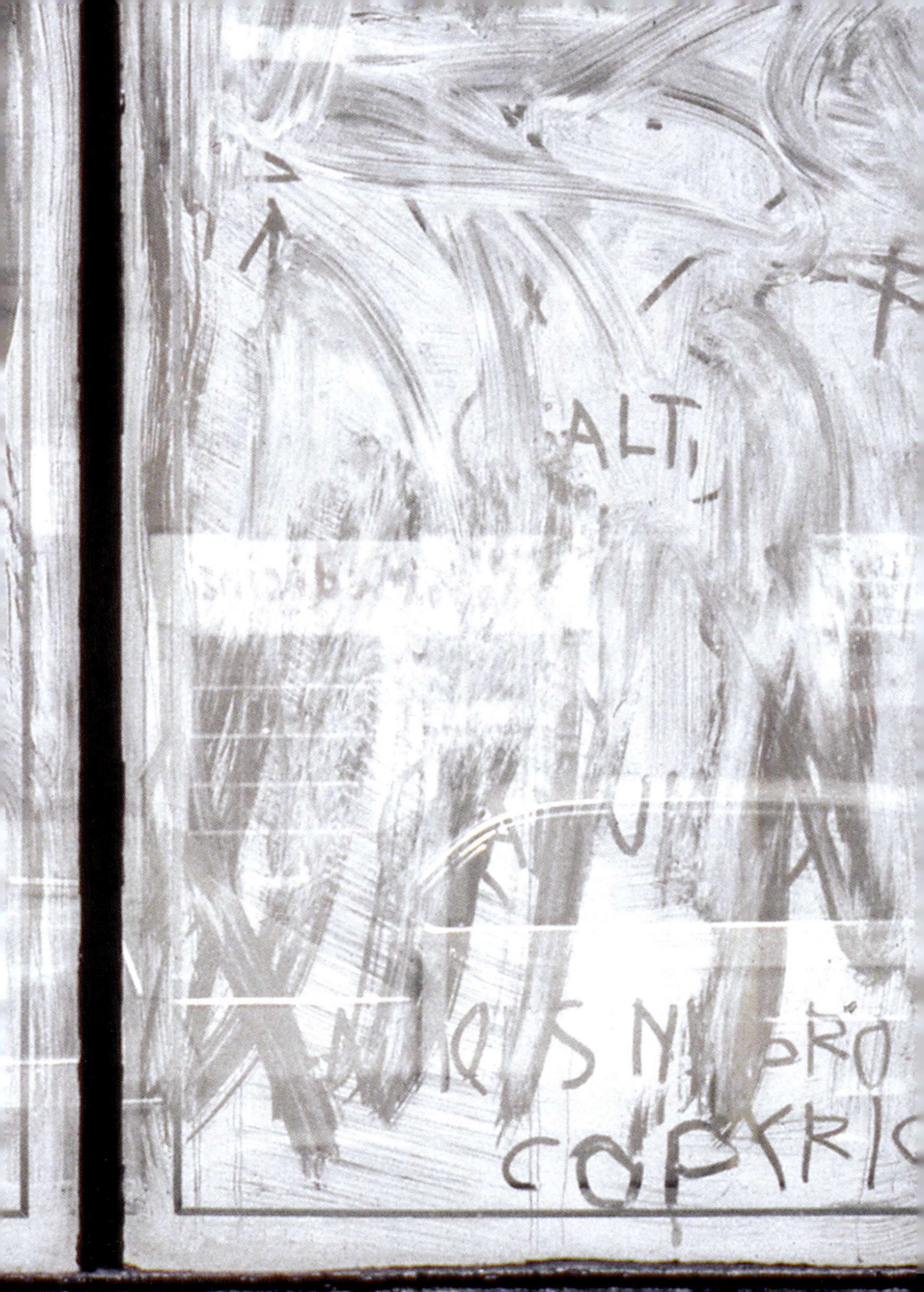
ALT
S N RO
COPERIC

Untitled, 1982
Acrylic on canvas,
183.5 x 172.5 cm / 72 $^{1}/_{4}$ x 68 inches

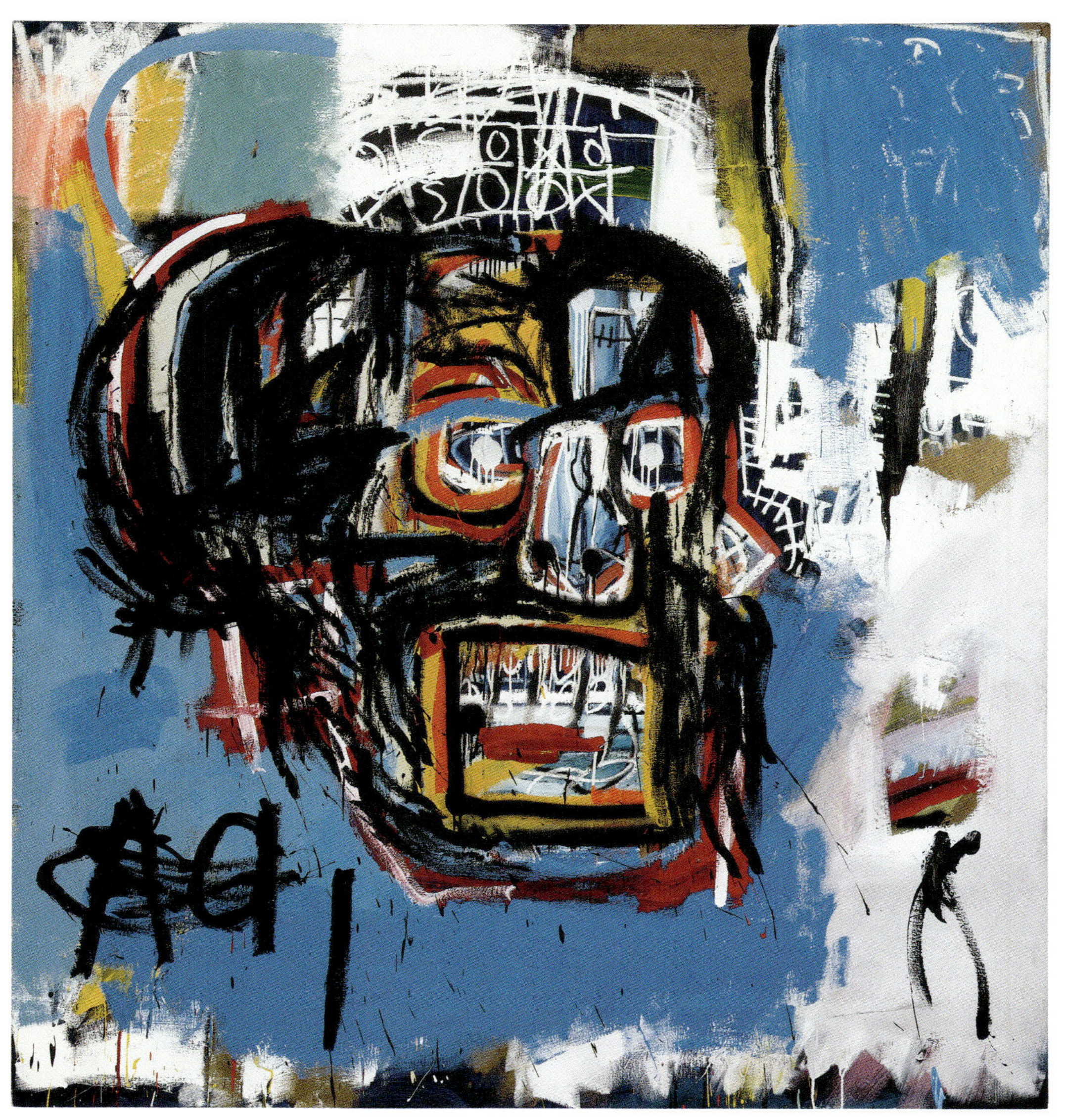

Dustheads, 1982
Acrylic and oilstick on canvas,
183 x 211 cm / 72 x 83 inches

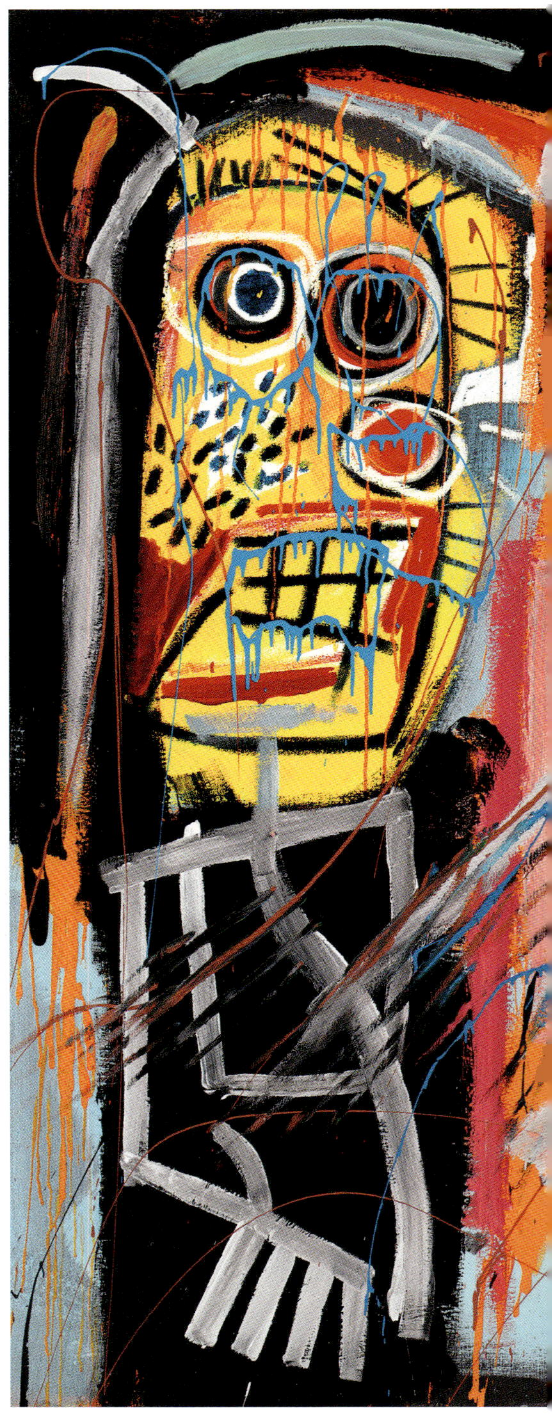

Page 162: **Untitled**, 1982
Oilstick on paper,
152.5 x 101.5 cm / 60 x 40 inches

Page 163: **Untitled**, 1982
Oilstick on paper,
152.5 x 101.5 cm / 60 x 40 inches

Page 164: **Untitled**, 1982
Oilstick and ballpoint pen on paper,
152.5 x 101.5 cm / 60 x 40 inches

Page 165: **Self-Portrait with Suzanne**, 1982
Oilstick on paper, 152.5 x 101.5 cm /
60 x 40 inches

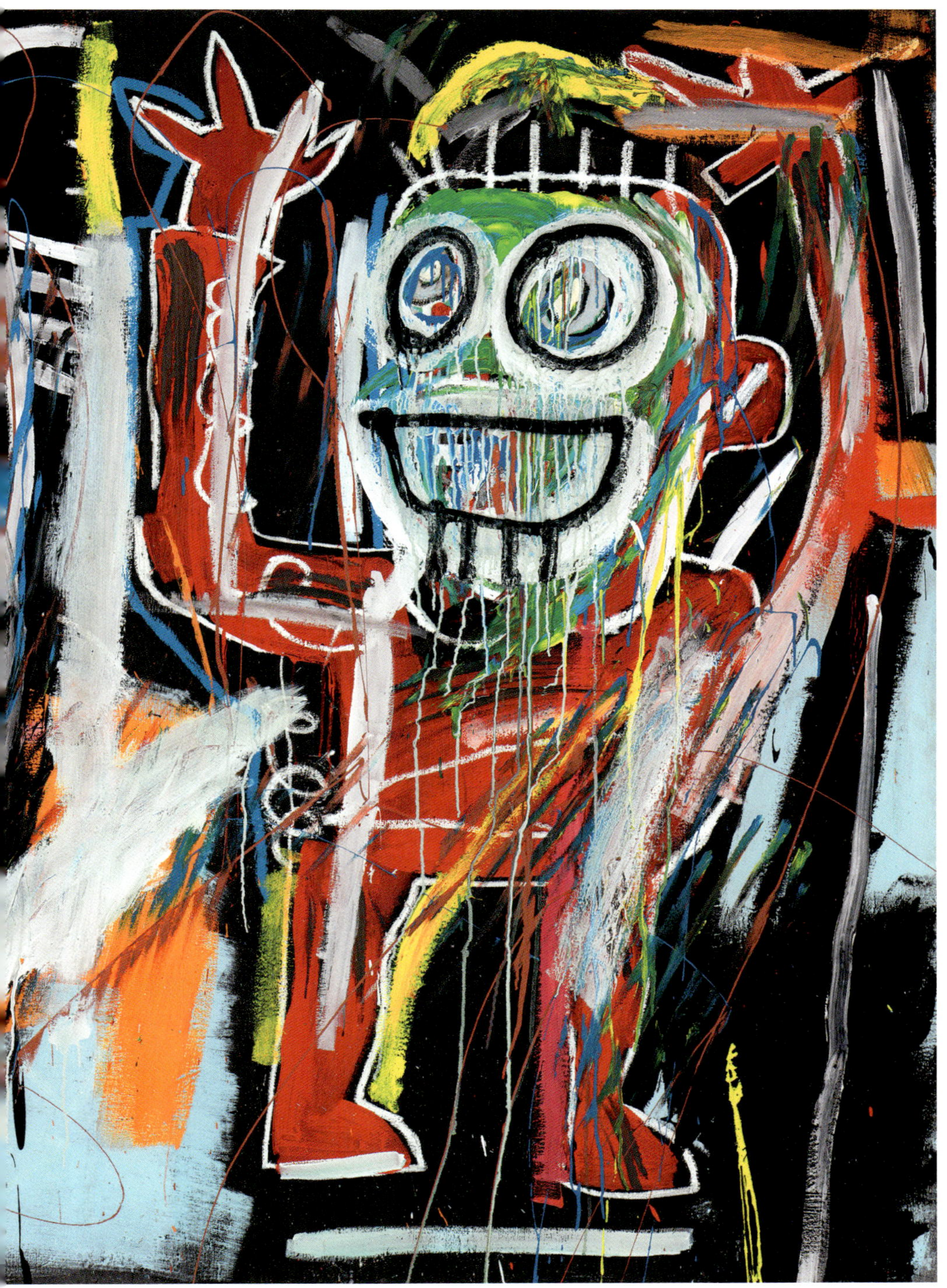

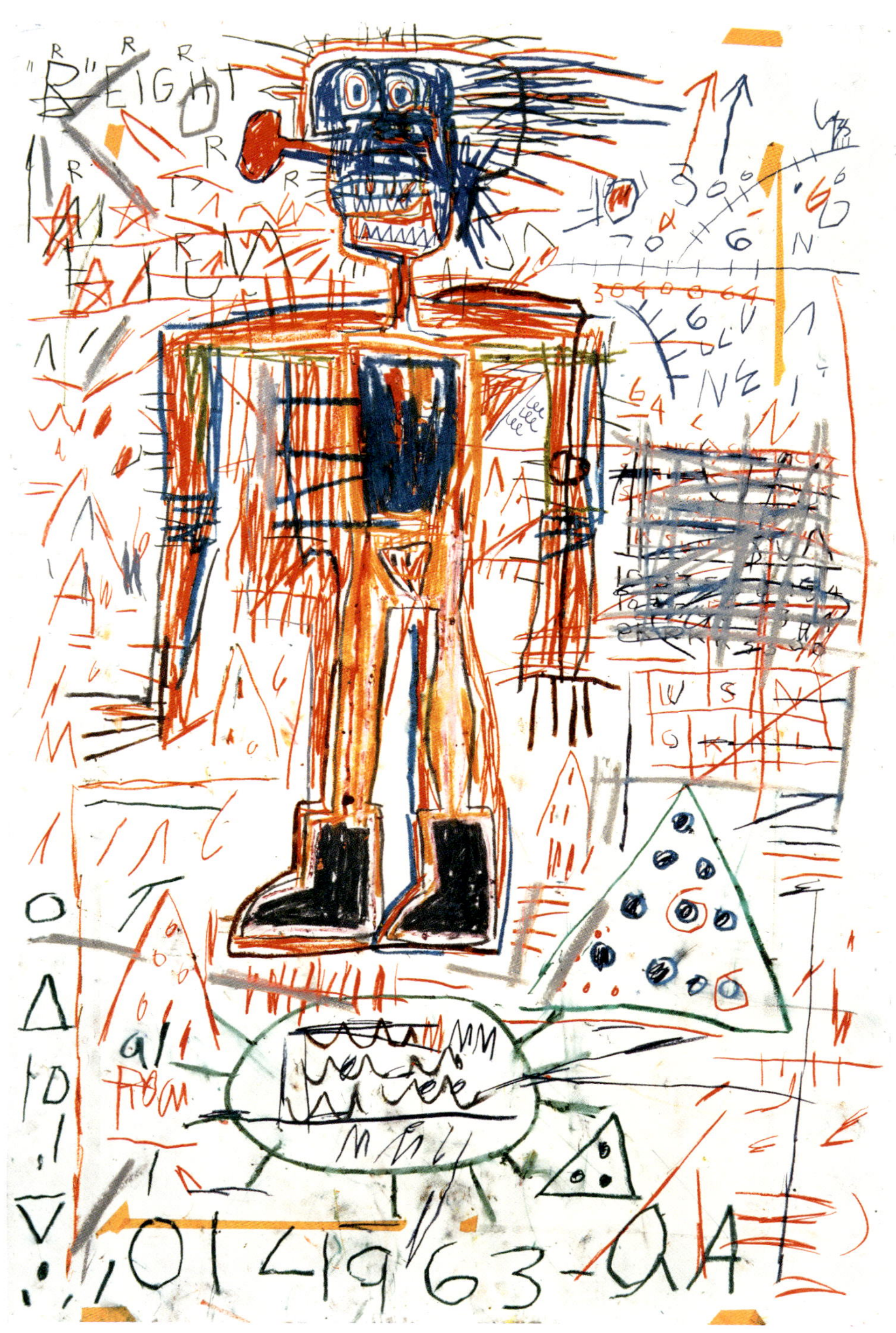
"R" EIGHT
1963
162

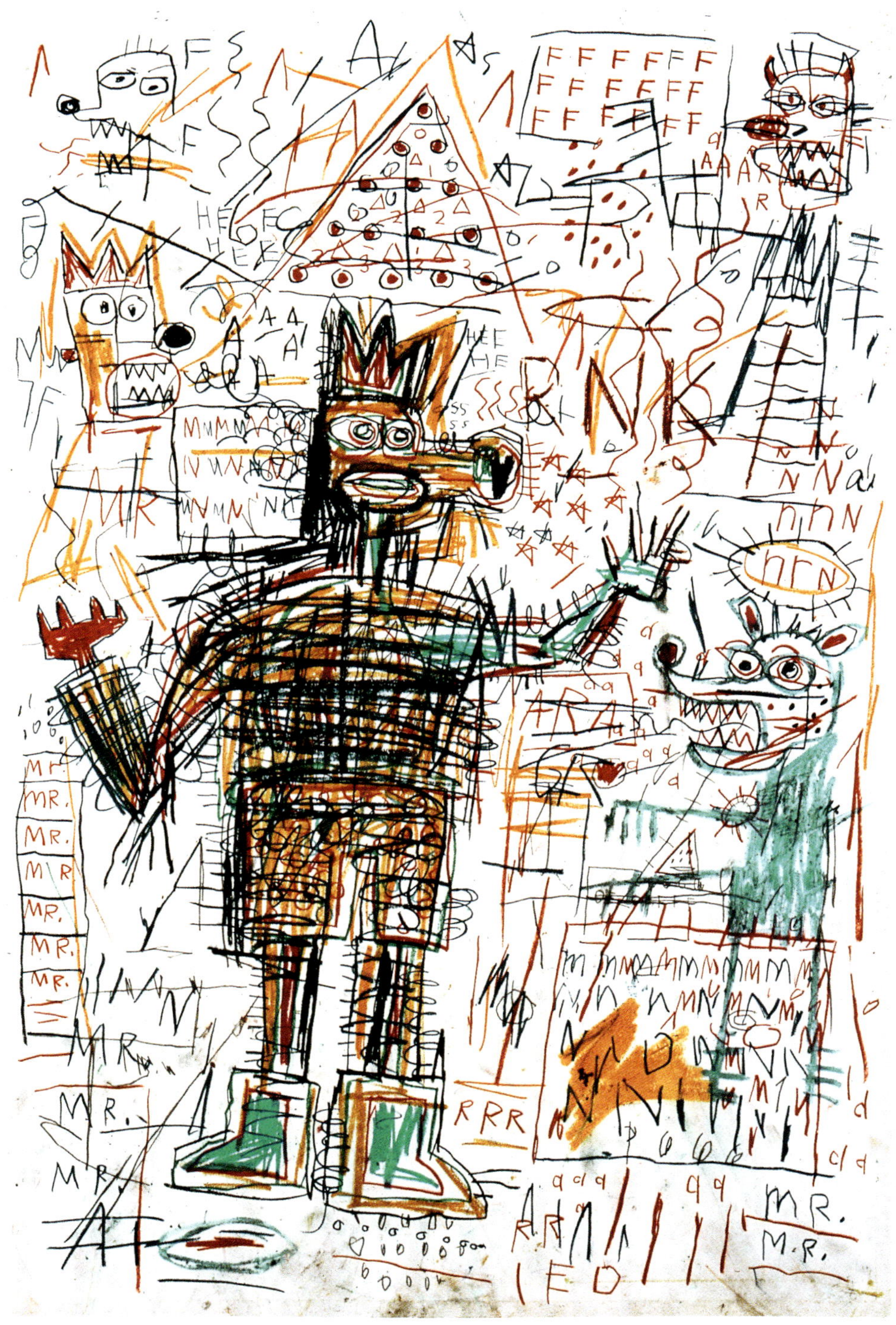

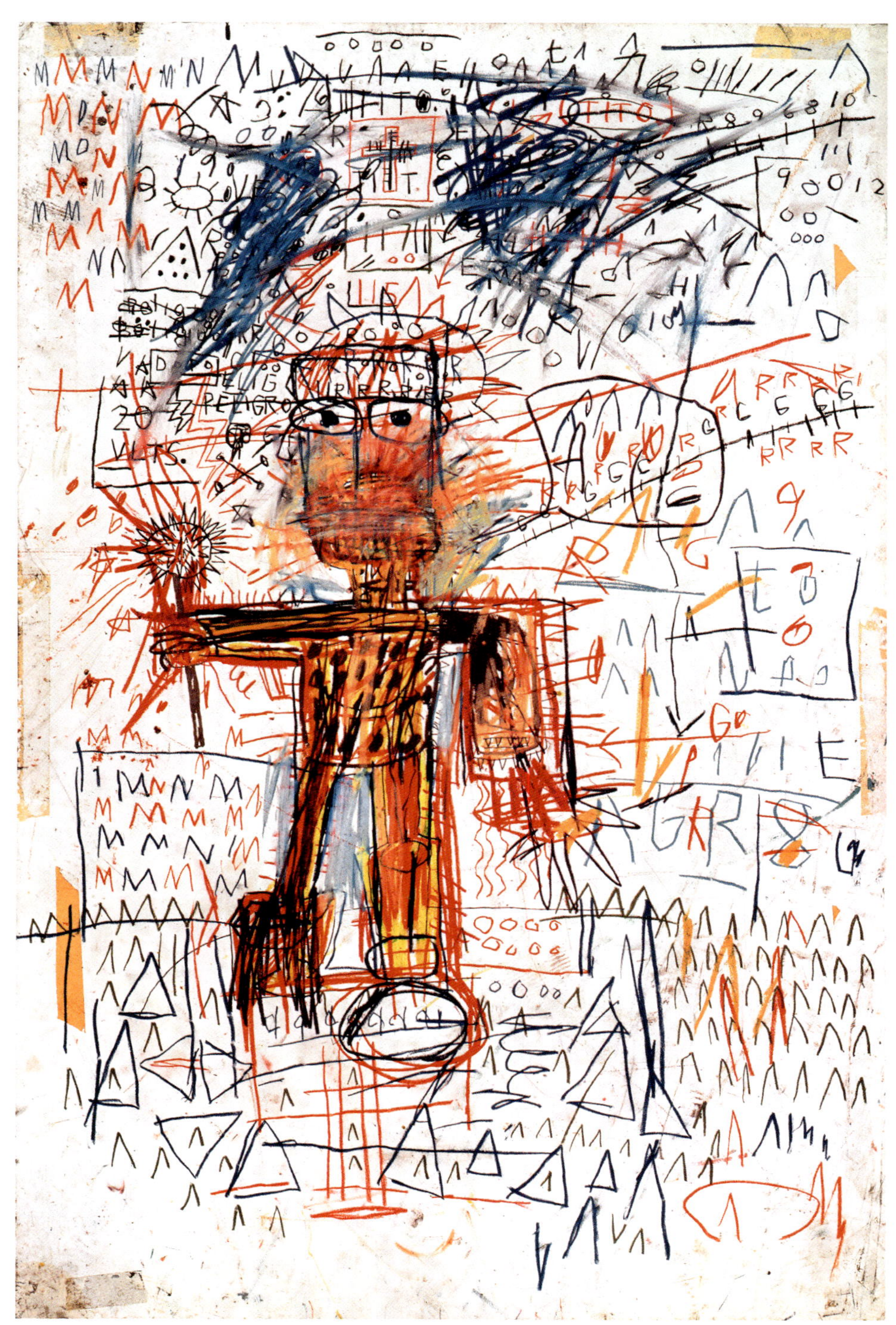

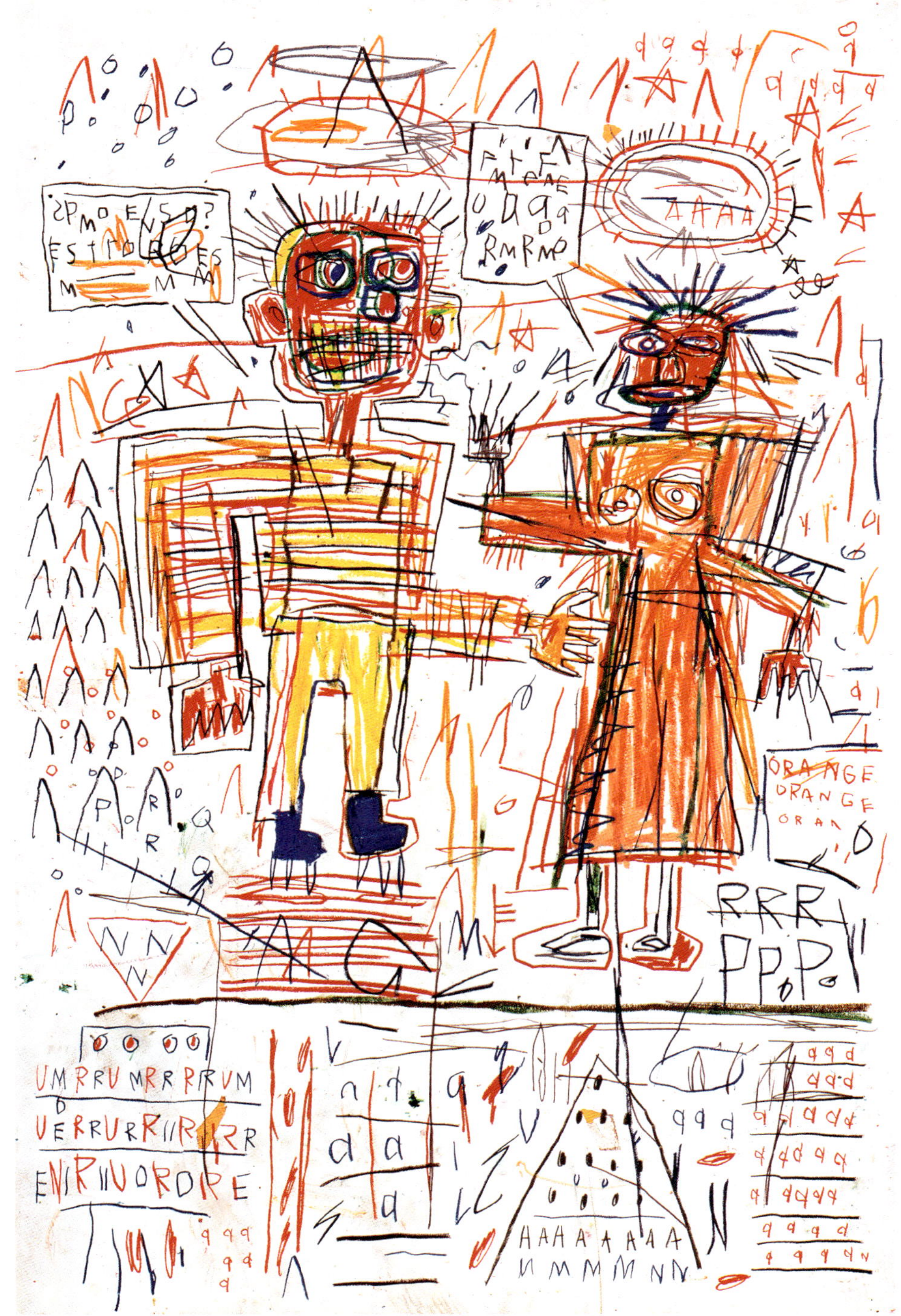

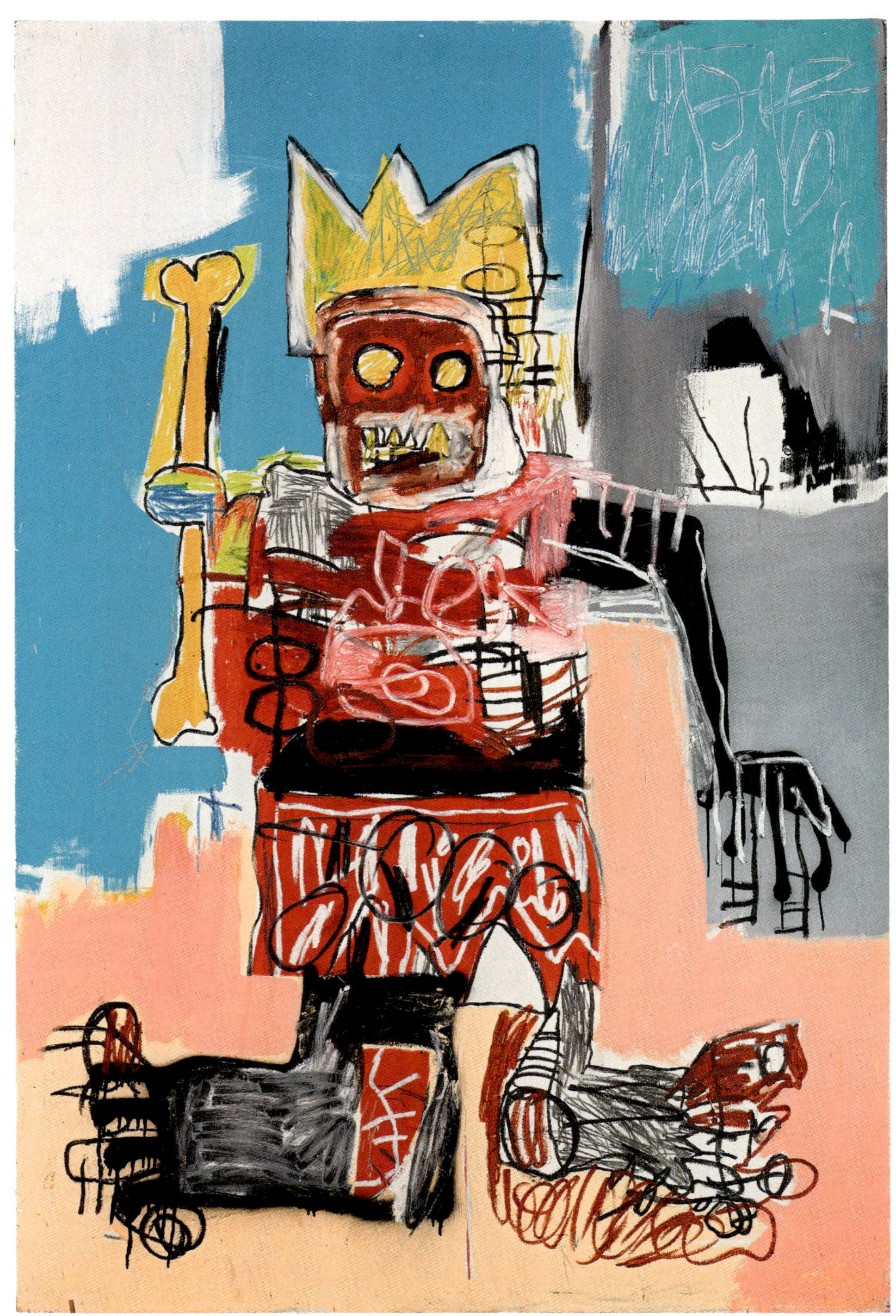

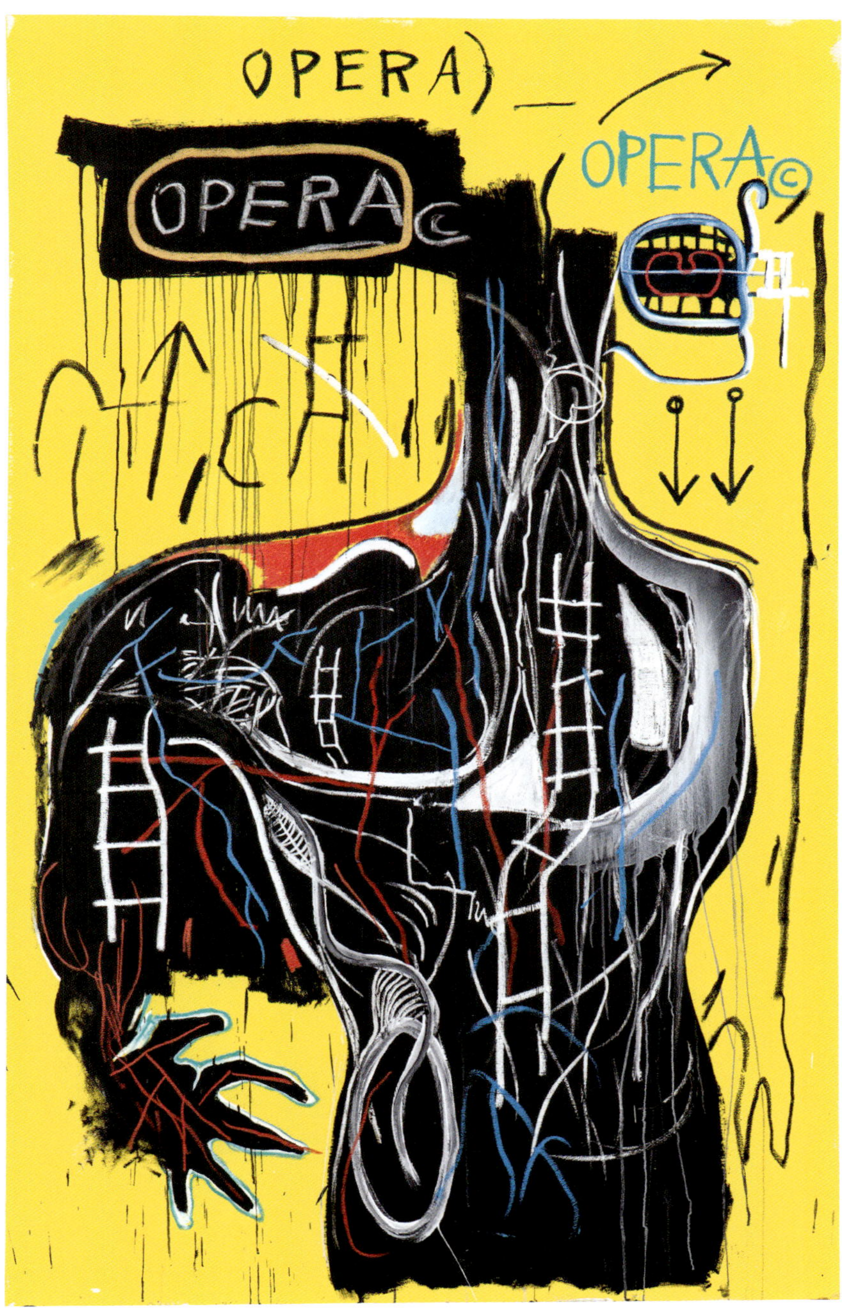

Untitled, 1982
Acrylic and oilstick on wood,
183 x 122 cm / 72 x 48 inches

Anybody Speaking Words, 1982
Acrylic and oilstick on canvas,
244 x 156 cm / 96 x 61 ¹/₂ inches

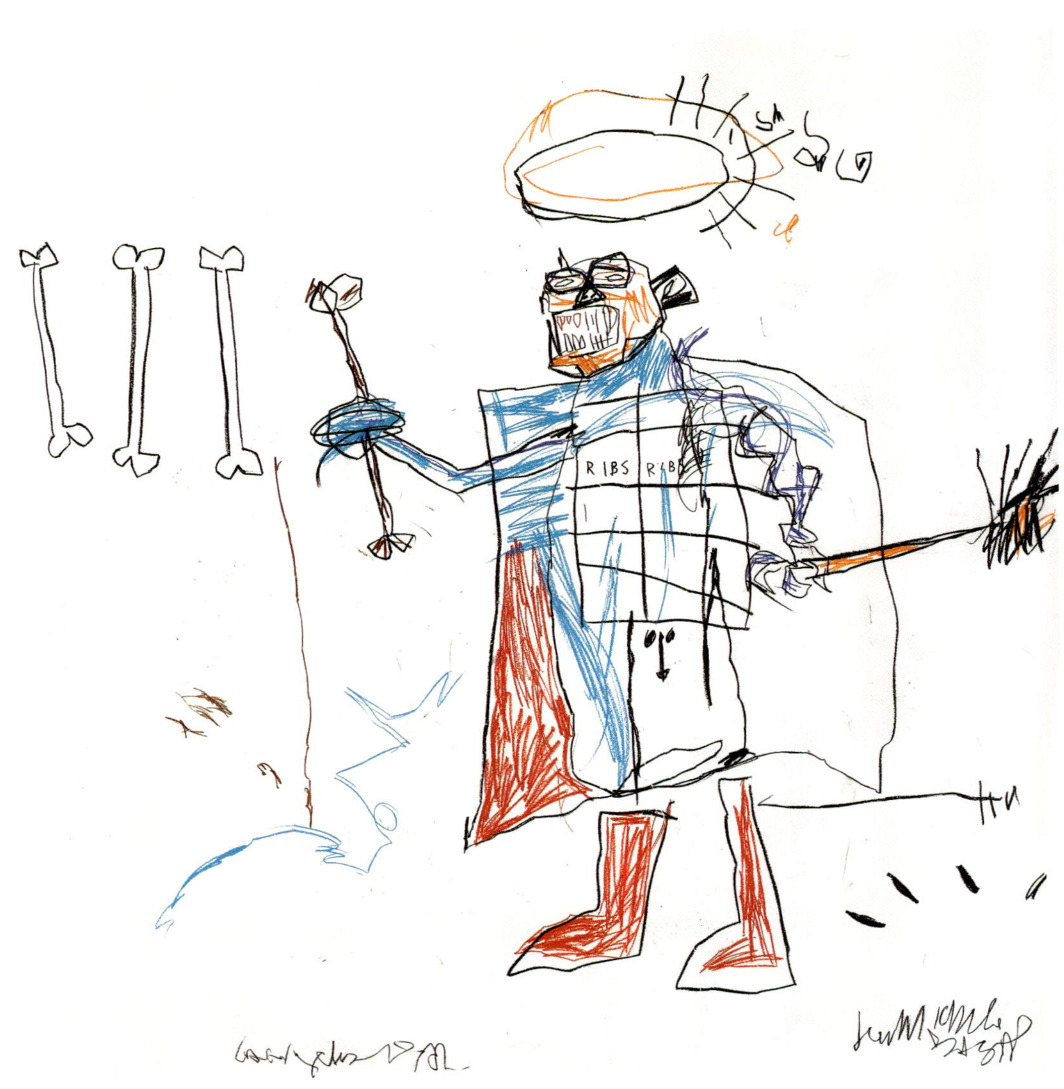

Ribs Ribs, 1982
Oilstick on paper,
246.5 x 243 cm / 97 x 95 ³/₄ inches

Loin, 1982
Acrylic, oilstick, and pastel on canvas,
183 x 122 cm / 72 x 48 inches

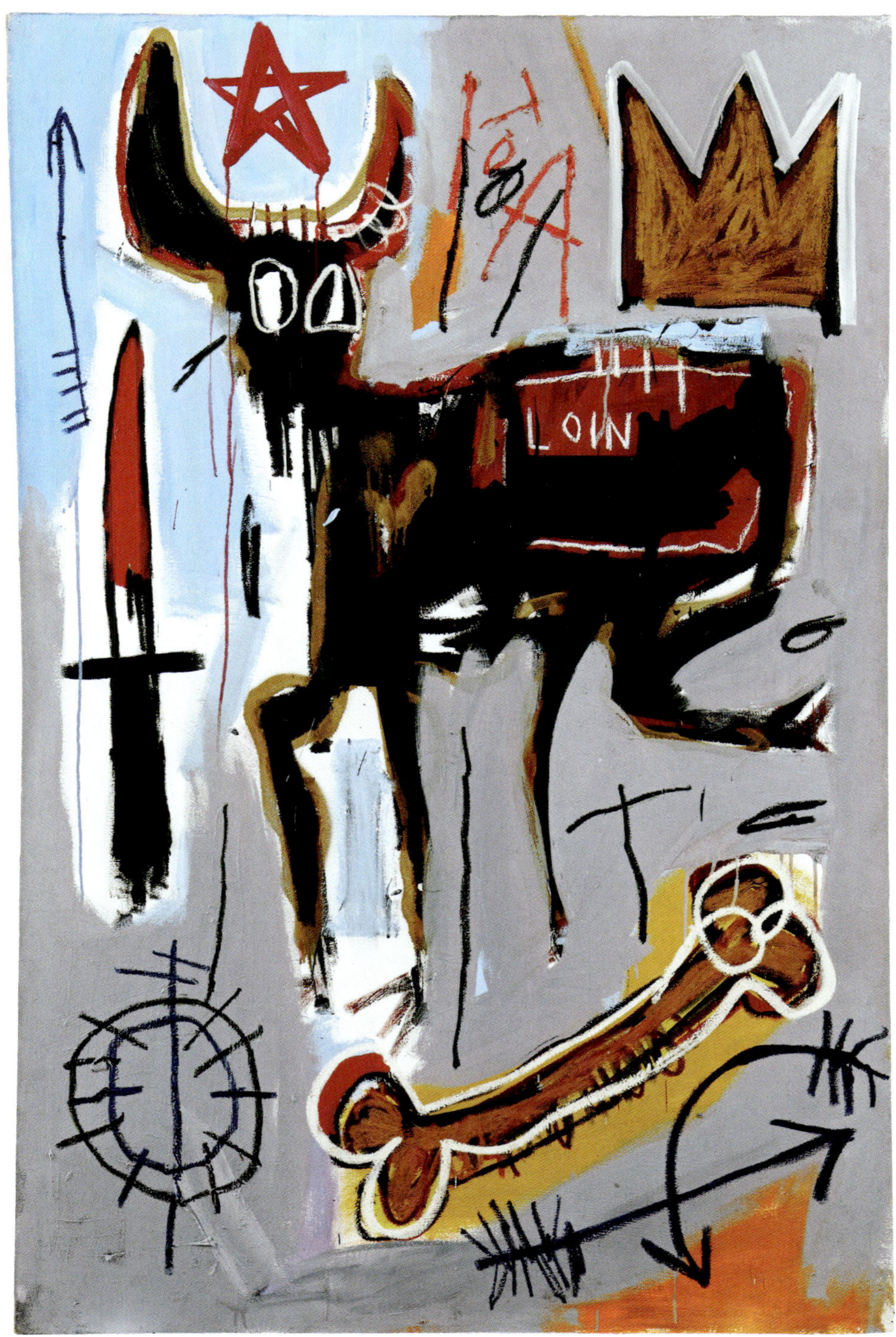

LOIN

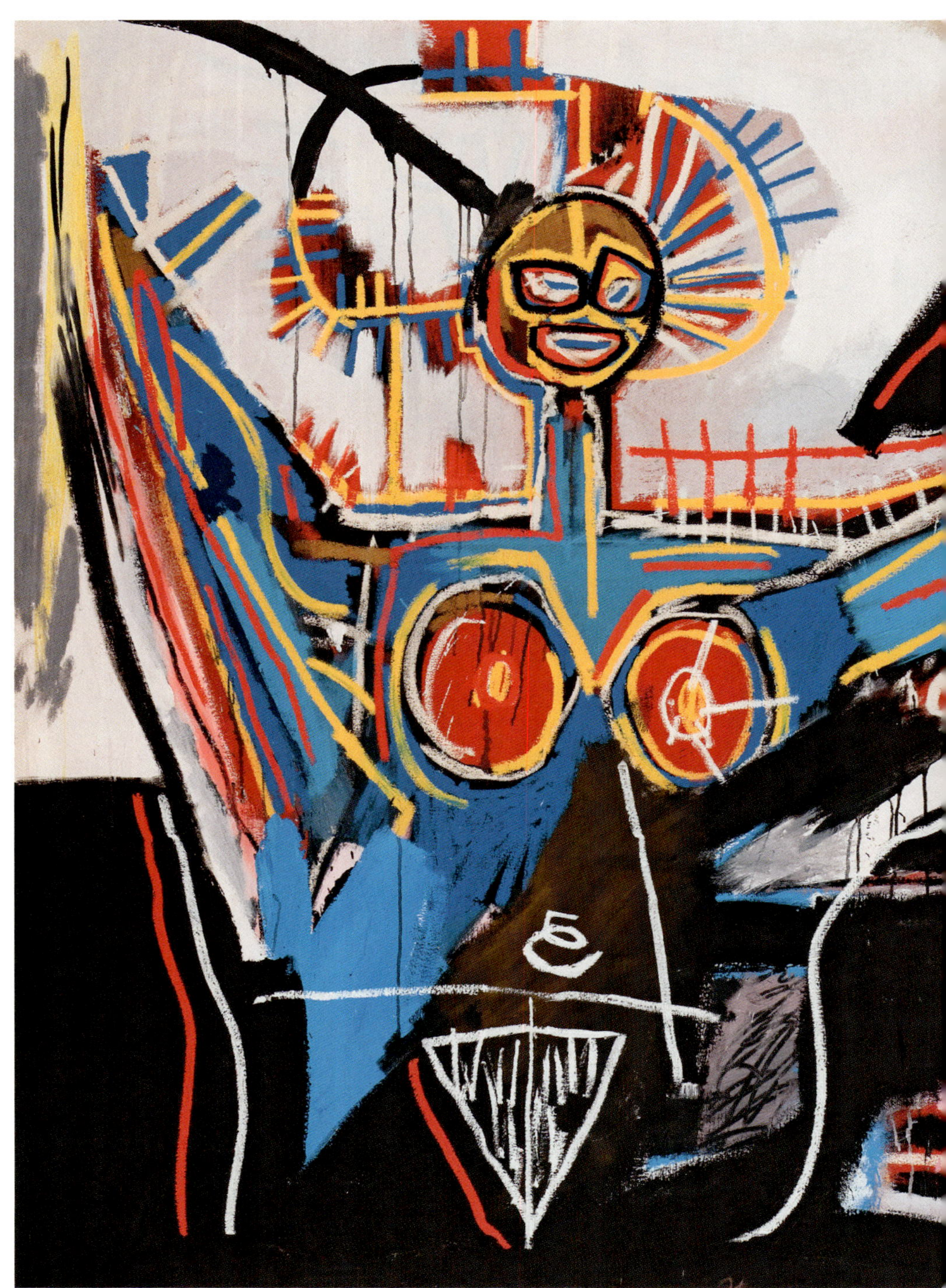

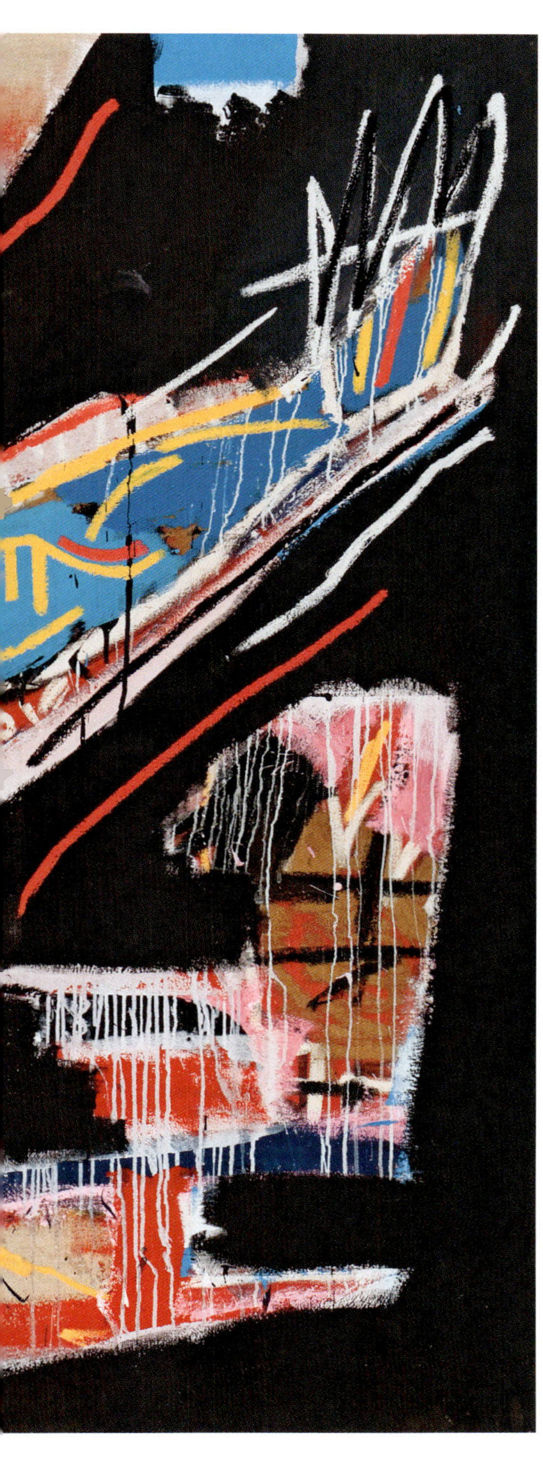

Mater, 1982
Acrylic and oilstick on canvas,
183 x 213.5 cm / 72 x 84 inches

Pages 172/173: **Untitled**, 1982
Acrylic, oilstick, spray paint, and
photocopy collage on canvas,
172.5 x 236 cm / 68 x 93 inches

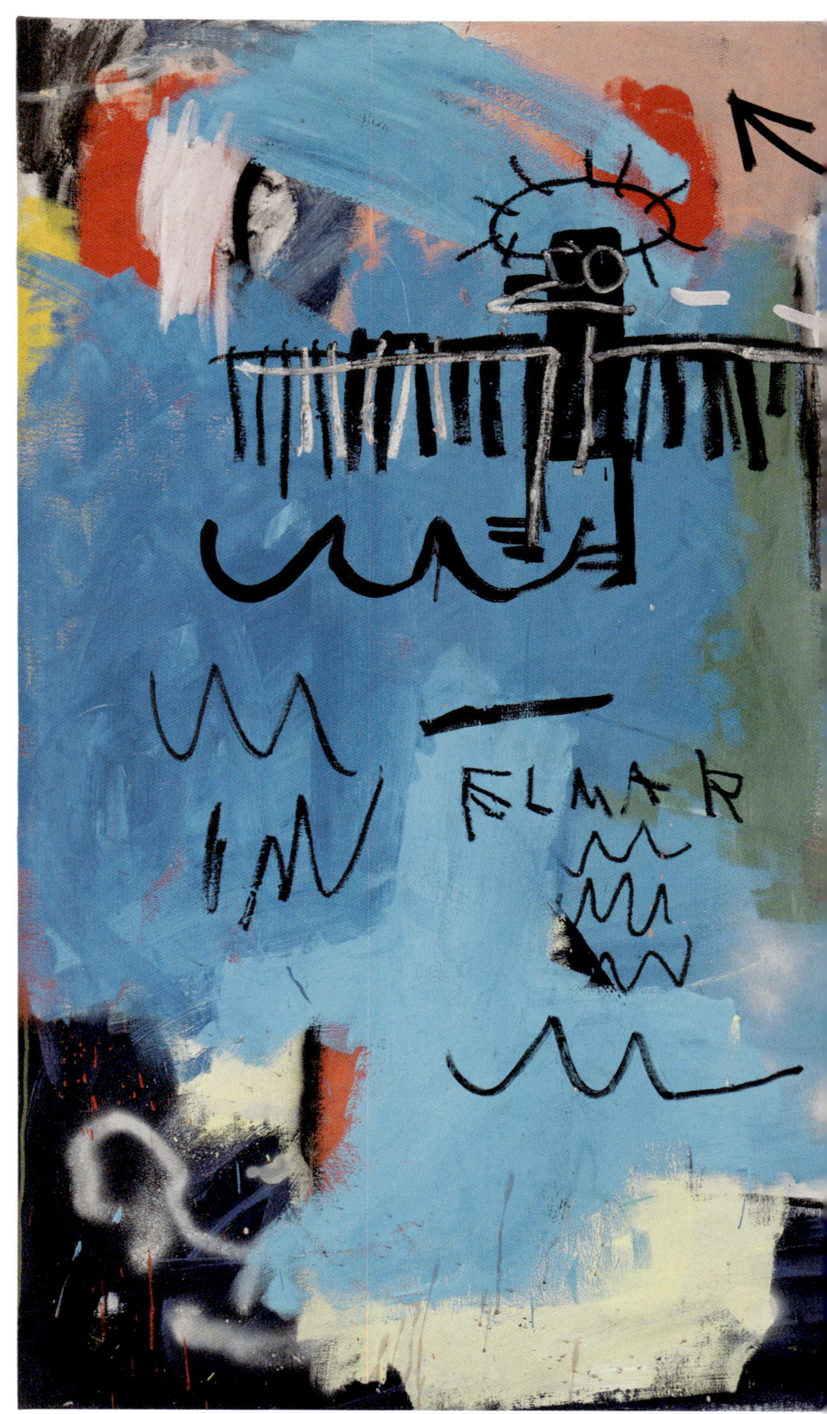

ELMAR

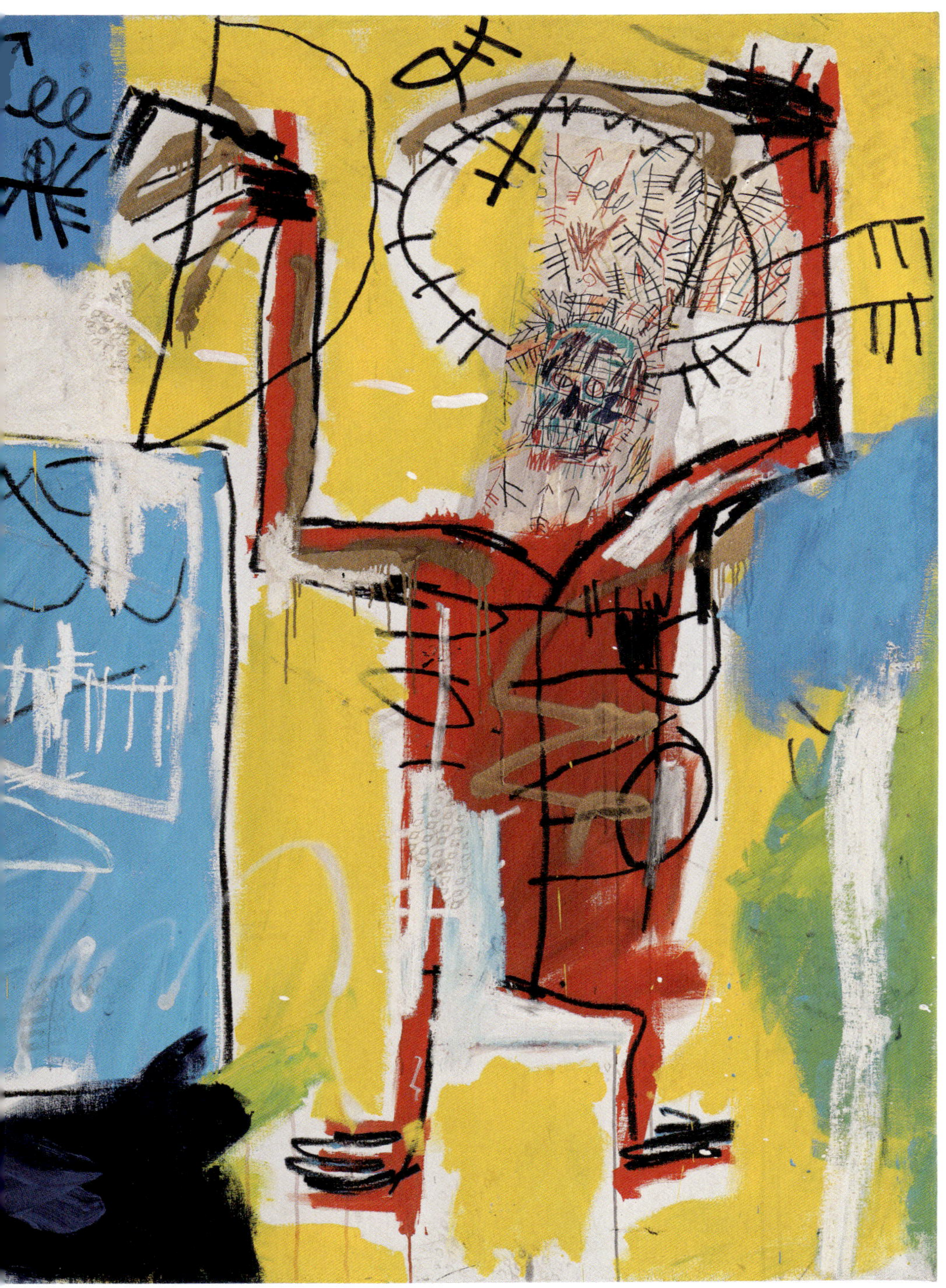

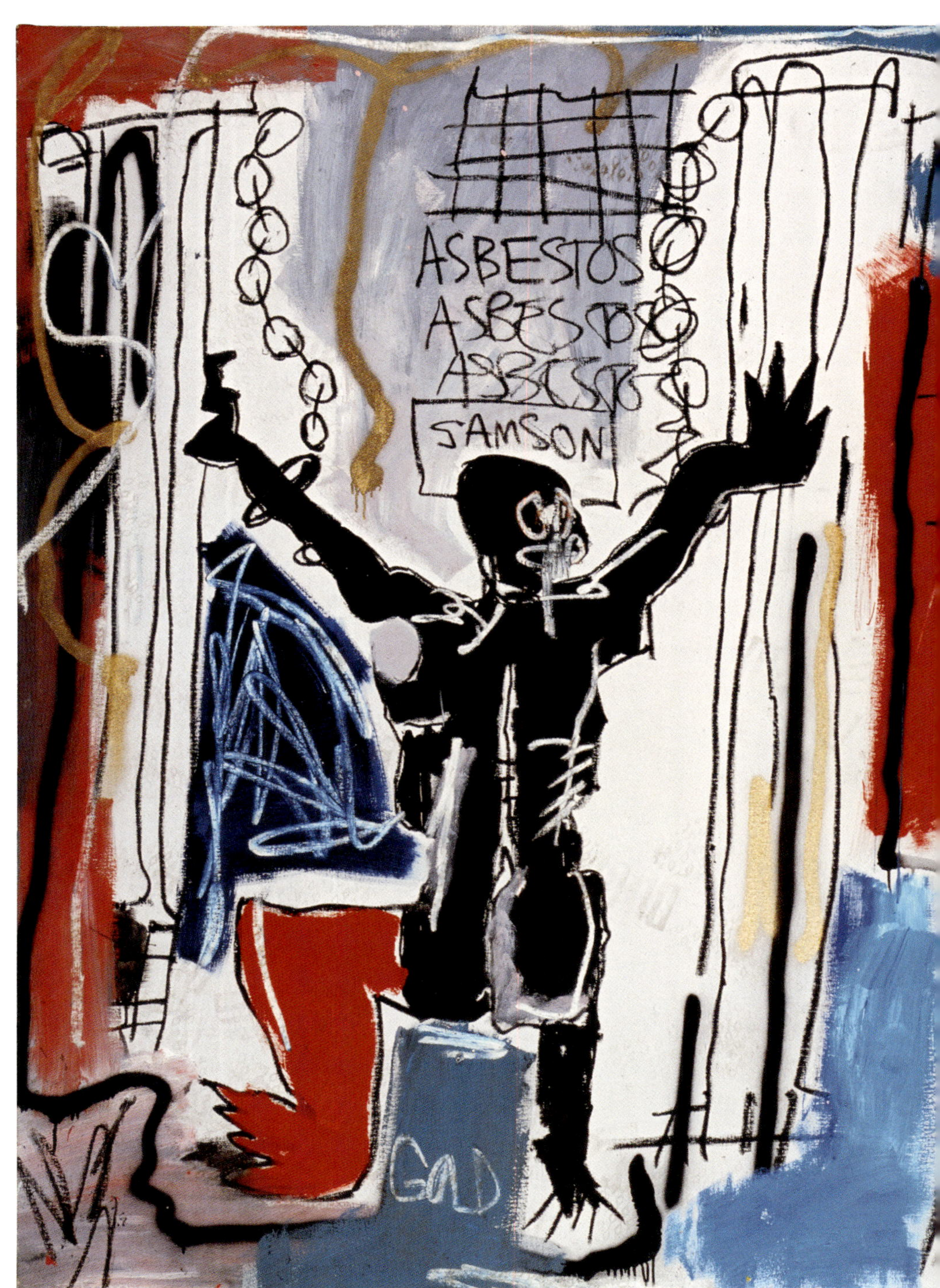

ASBESTOS
ASBESTOS
ASBESTOS
SAMSON
GOD

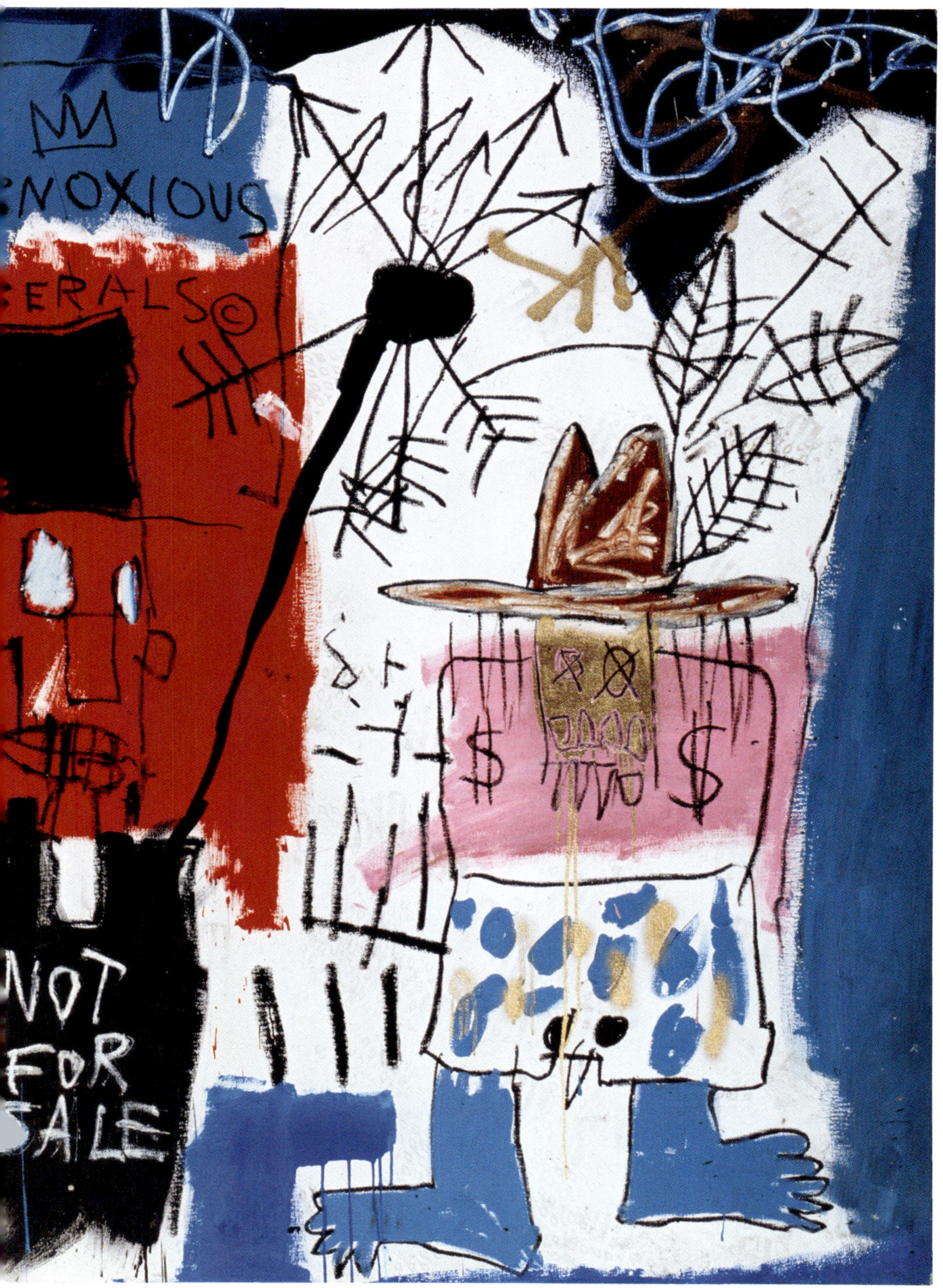
NOXIOUS
BERALS©
$
$
NOT
FOR
SALE

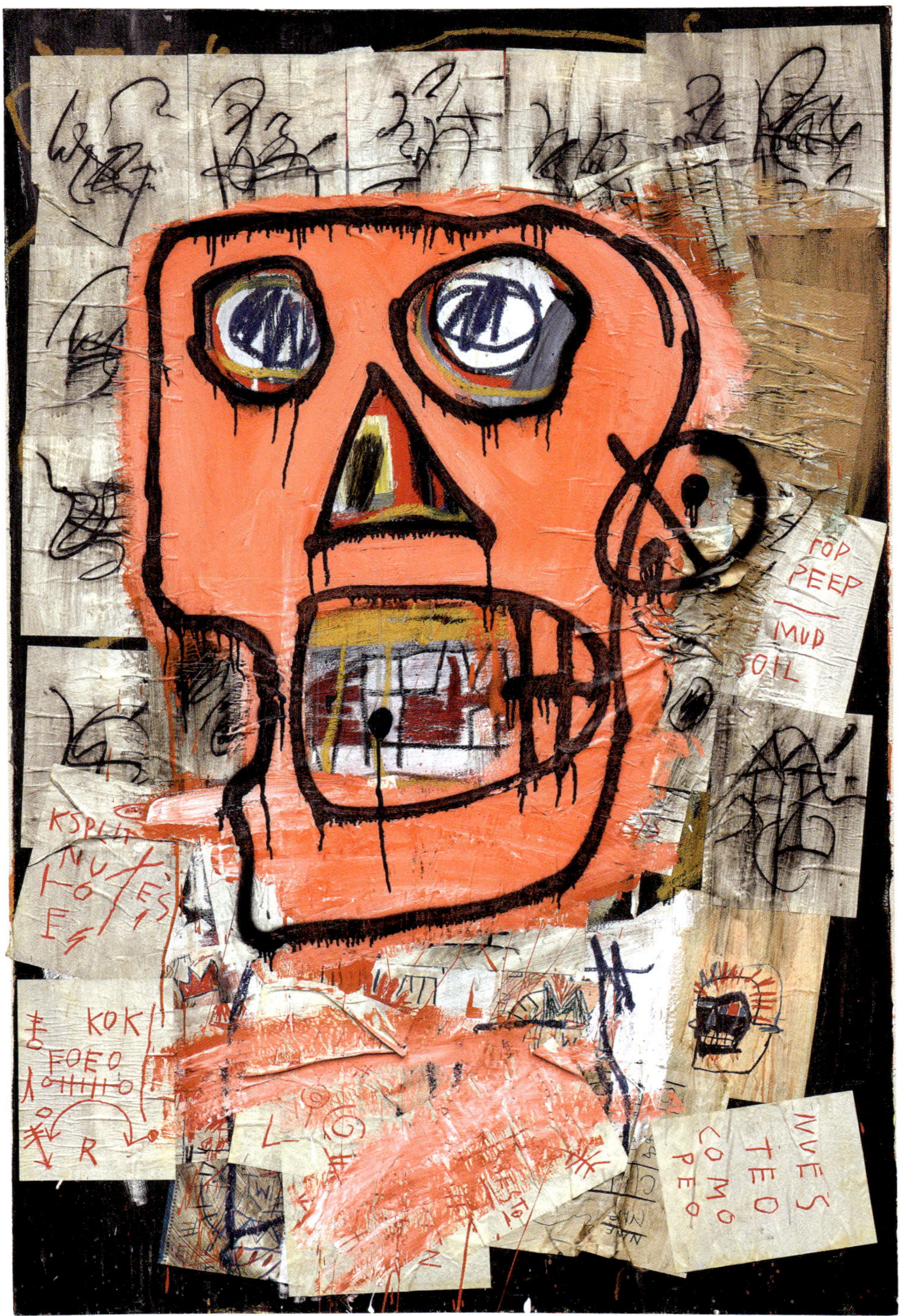
FOP
PEEP
MUD
SOIL
KSPLIT
NU/ES
TO
E
KOK
FOEO
O
R
NUES
TEO
COMO
PEO

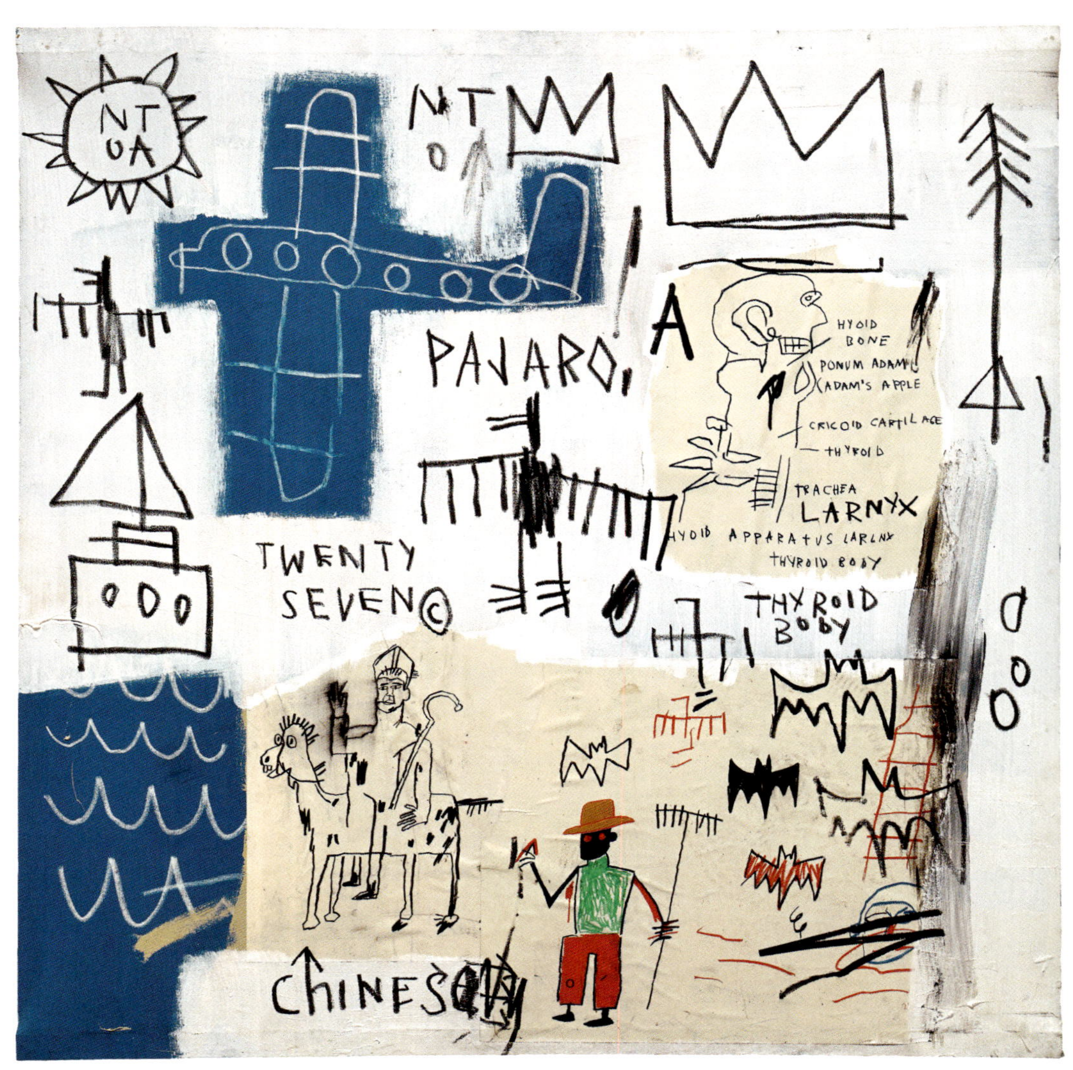

The Pilgrimage, 1982
Acrylic, marker, and oilstick on paper mounted
on canvas, 152.5 x 152.5 cm / 60 x 60 inches

The Ruffians, 1982
Acrylic, oilstick, and photocopy collage on canvas,
174 x 148.5 cm / 68 ½ x 58 ½ inches

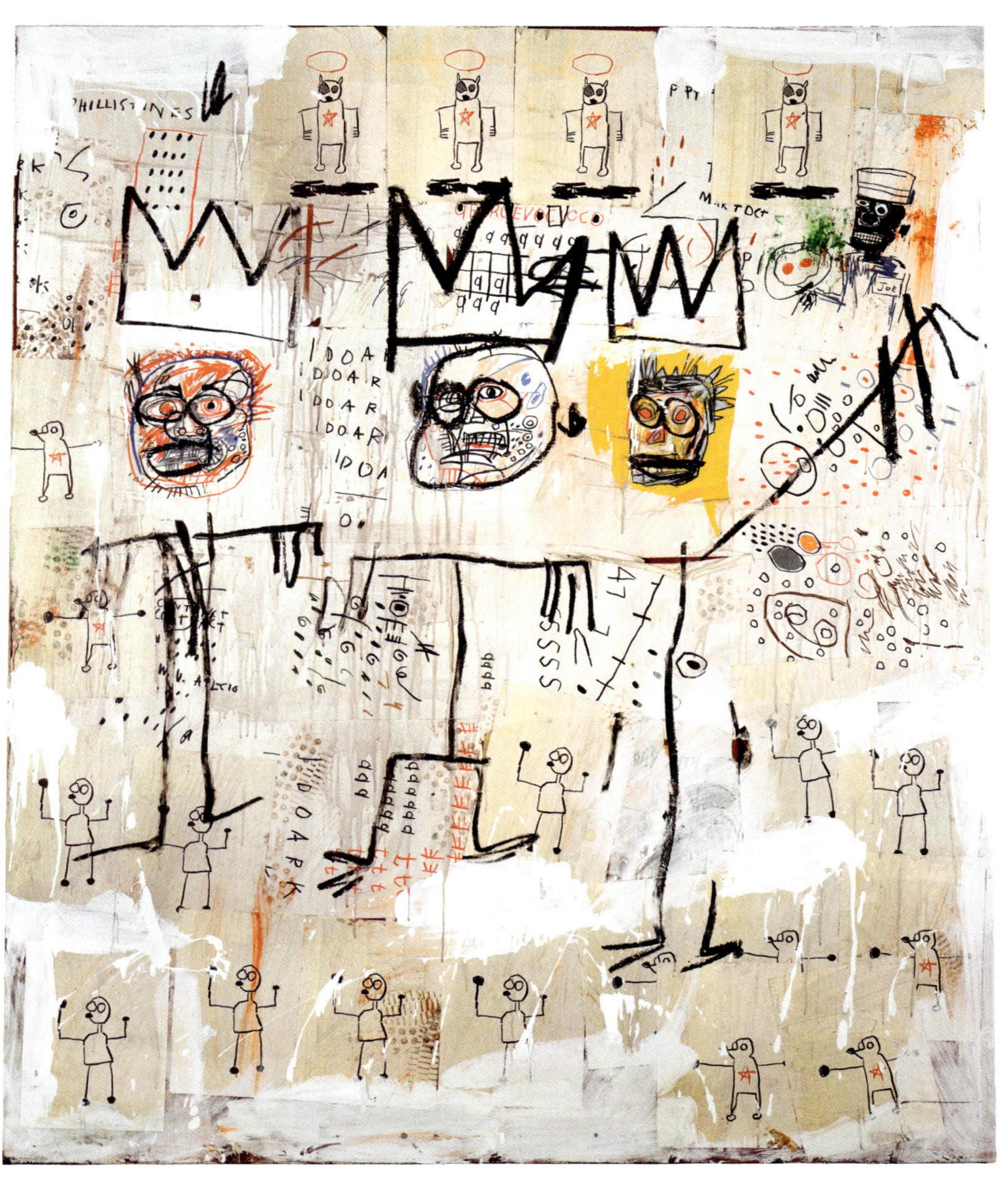

Leonardo da Vinci's Greatest Hits, 1982
Acrylic, oilstick, and paper collage on canvas,
polyptych: 213.5 x 198 cm / 84 x 78 inches

Pages 182/183: **Do Not Revenge**, 1982
Acrylic and oilstick on canvas,
132 x 213.5 cm / 52 x 84 inches

Page 184: **Charles the First**, 1982
Acrylic and oilstick on canvas, triptych:
198 x 158 cm / 78 x 62 inches

Page 185: **Four Big**, 1982
Acrylic, oilstick, and paper collage on
canvas, 200.5 x 155 cm / 79 x 61 inches

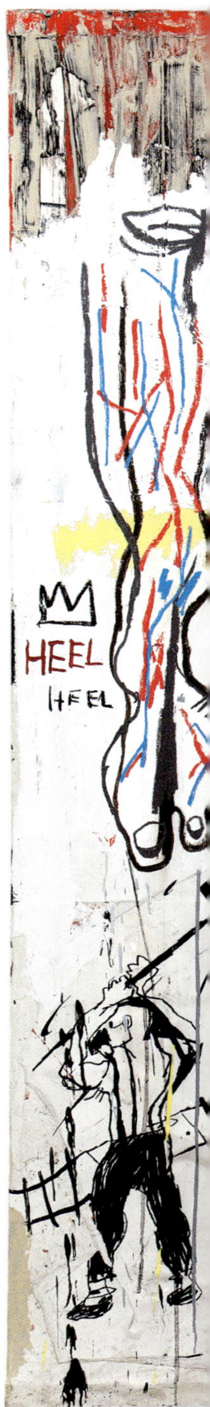

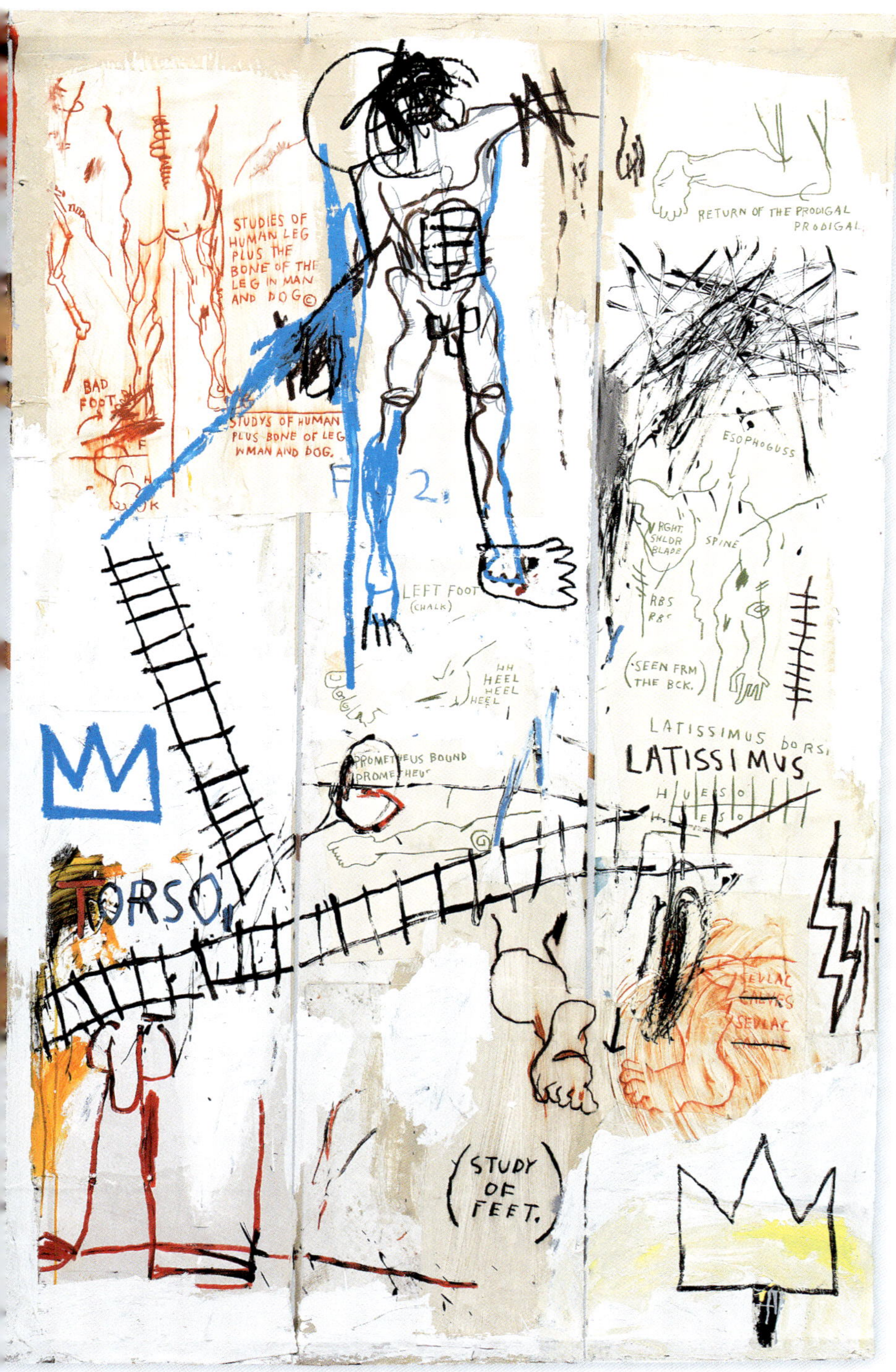
STUDIES OF
HUMAN LEG
PLUS THE
BONE OF THE
LEG IN MAN
AND DOG©
BAD FOOT
STUDYS OF HUMAN
PLUS BONE OF LEG
W MAN AND DOG.
LEFT FOOT
(CHALK)
HH
HEEL
HEEL
HEEL
PROMETHEUS BOUND
PROMETHEUS
TORSO.
RETURN OF THE PRODIGAL
PRODIGAL.
ESOPHOGUSS
RGHT.
SHLDR
BLADE
SPINE
RBS
RBS
(SEEN FRM
THE BCK.)
LATISSIMUS DORSI
LATISSIMUS
HUESO
HUESO
SEVLAC
CALVES
SEVLAC
STUDY
OF
FEET.

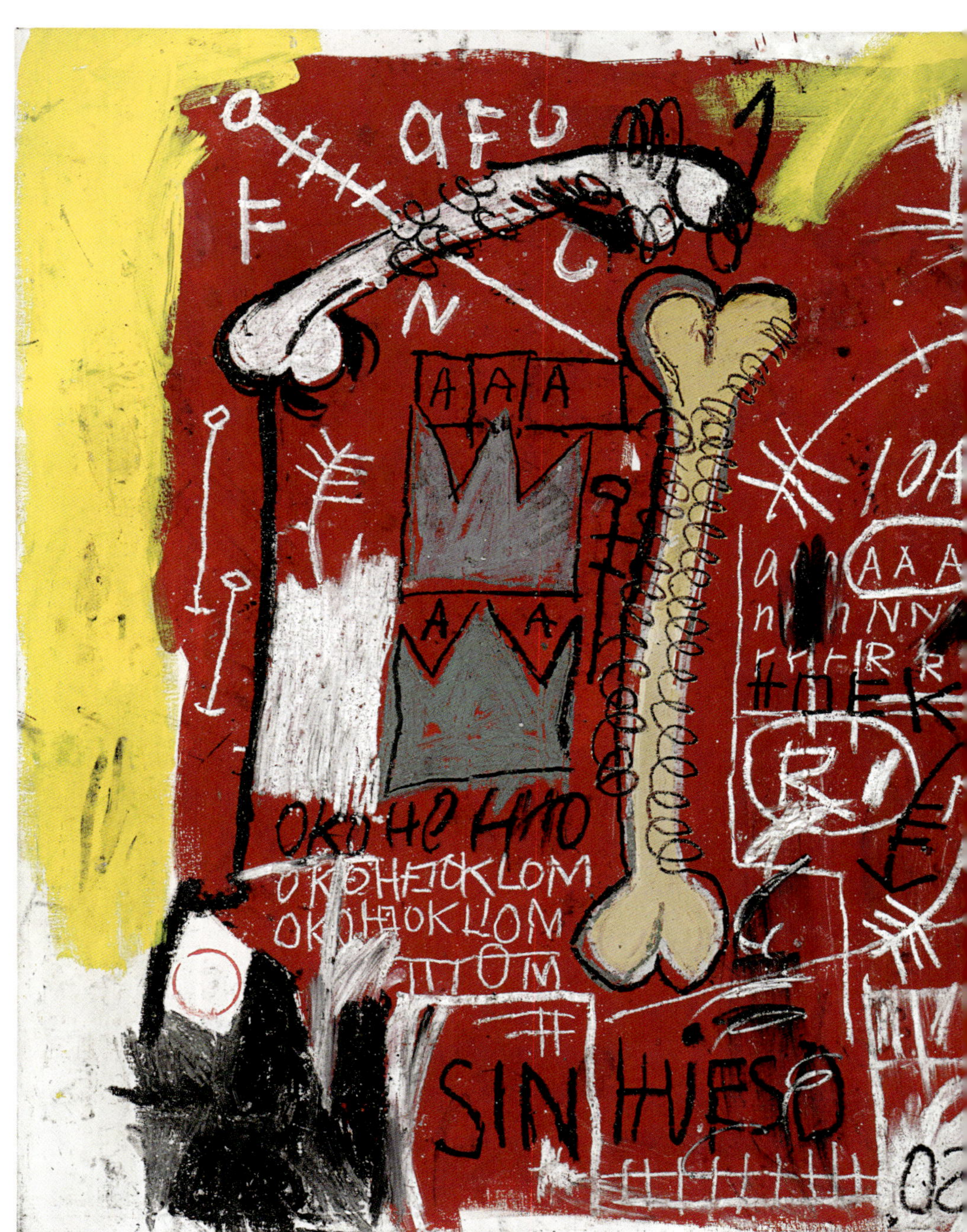

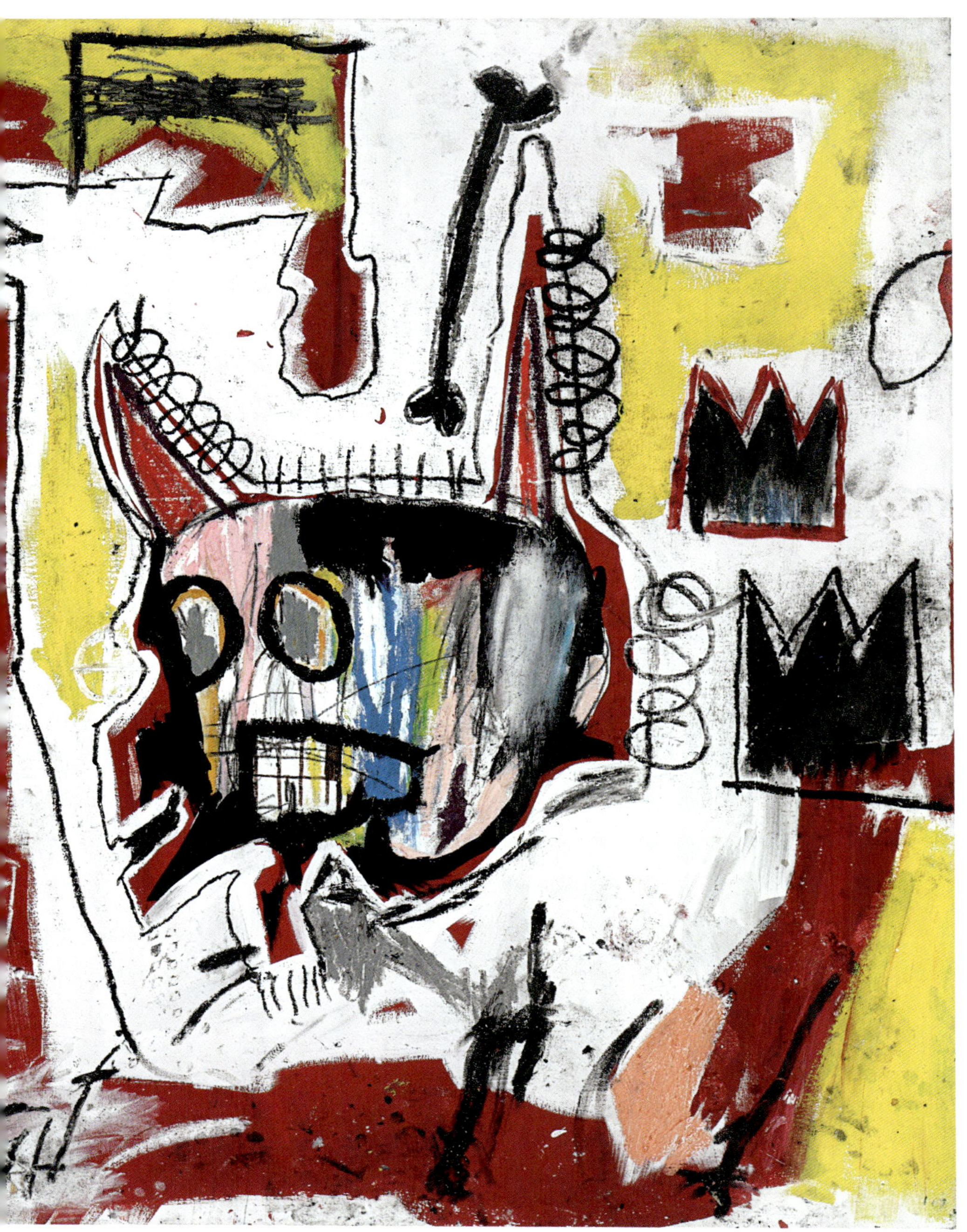

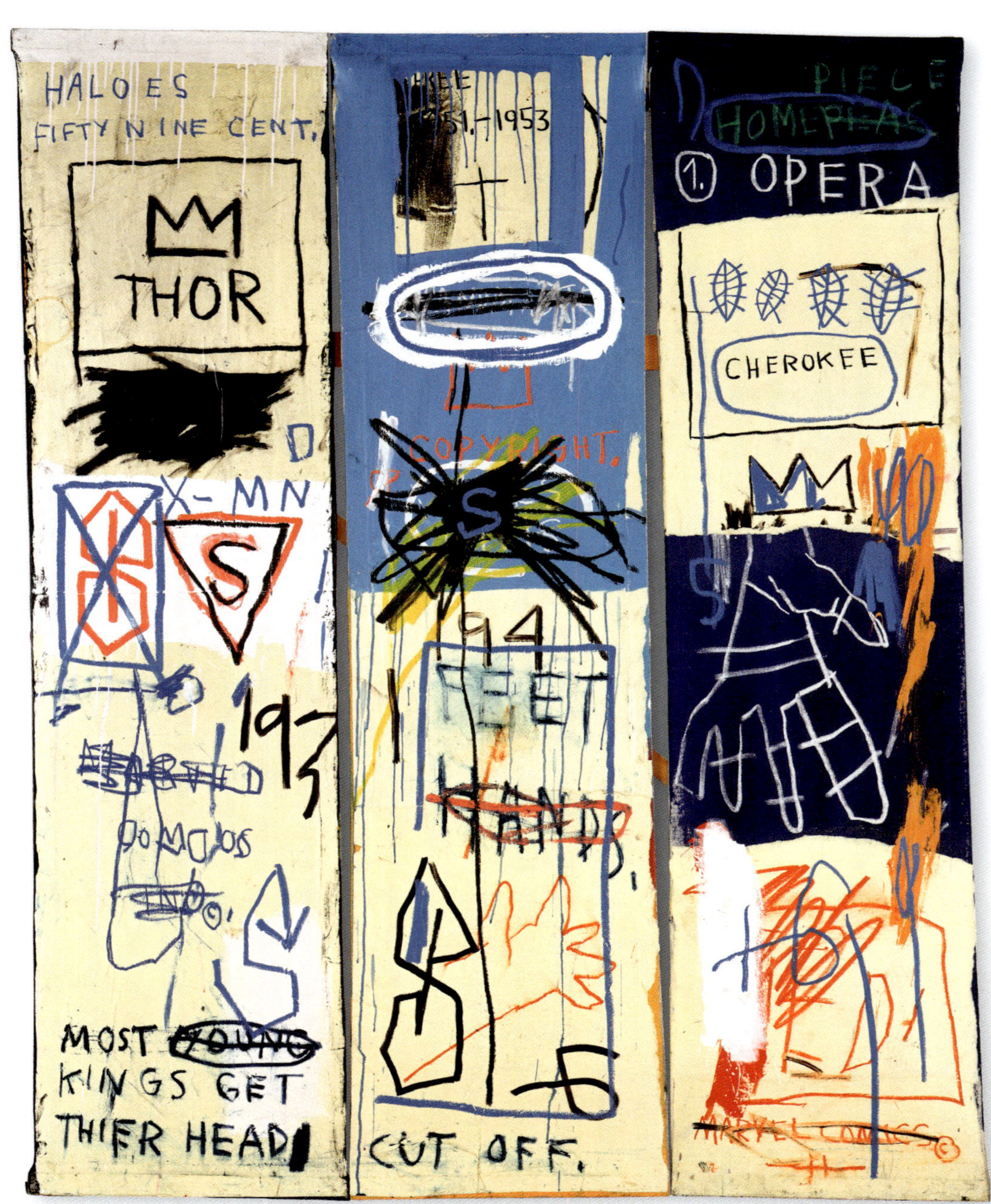

HALOES
FIFTY NINE CENT,
THOR
X-MN
S
193
MOST YOUNG
KINGS GET
THIER HEAD
1951.-1953
COPYRIGHT.
S
94
FEET
HANDS
CUT OFF.
PIECE
HOMEPHAG
1. OPERA
CHEROKEE
MARVEL COMICS

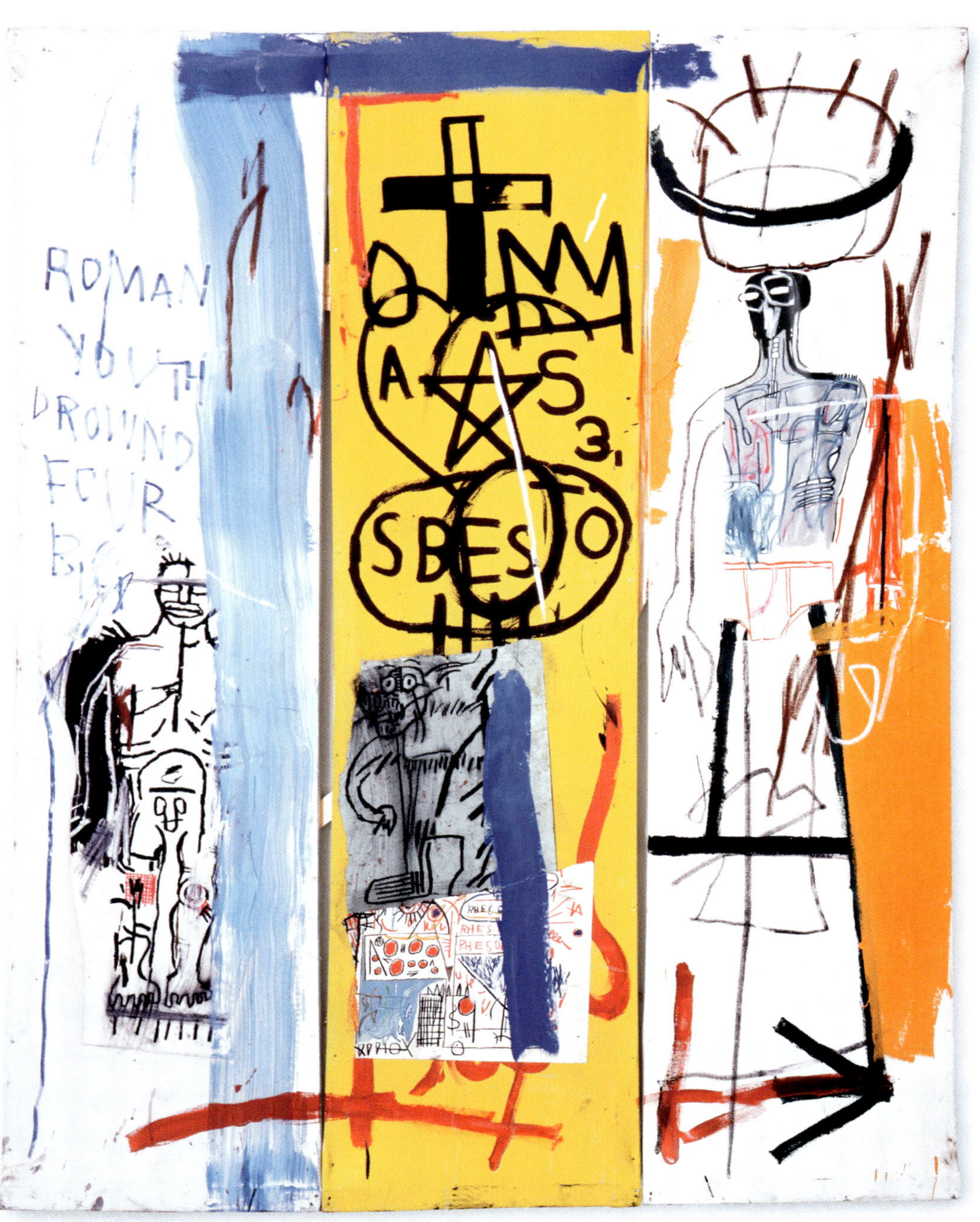

ROMAN
YOUTH
DROWND
FOUR
A S
3,
S BES O

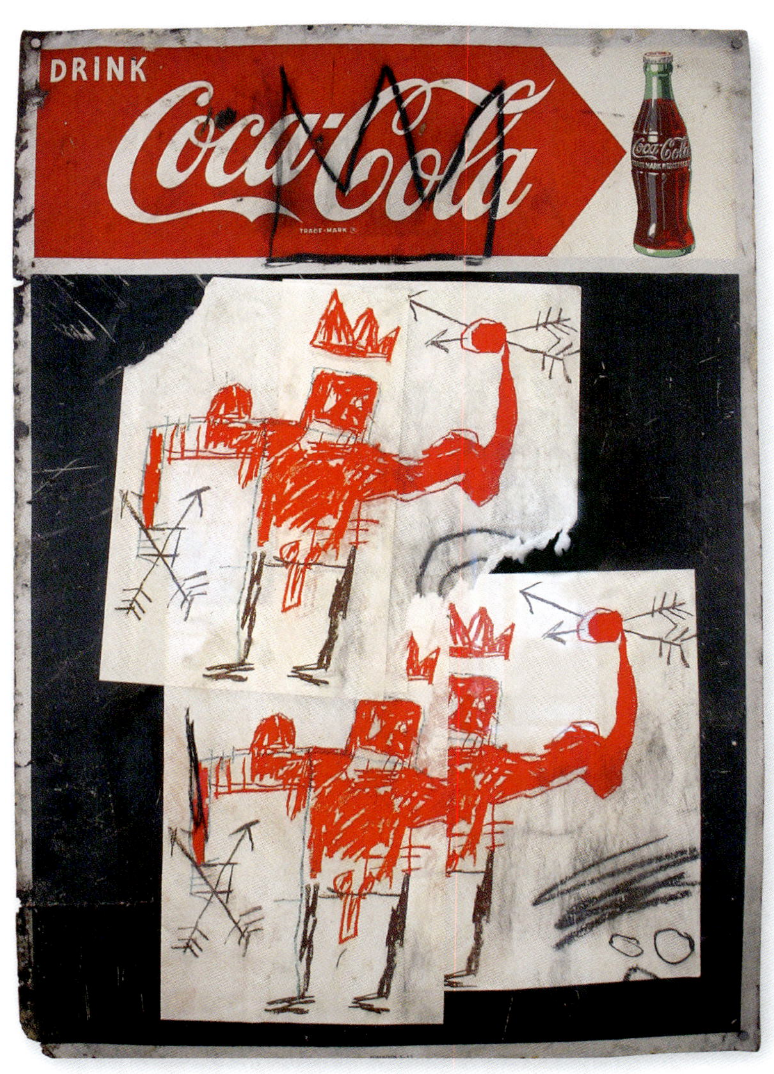

Untitled (Coca Cola), 1982
Oilstick and photocopy collage on metal,
71 x 51 cm / 28 x 20 inches

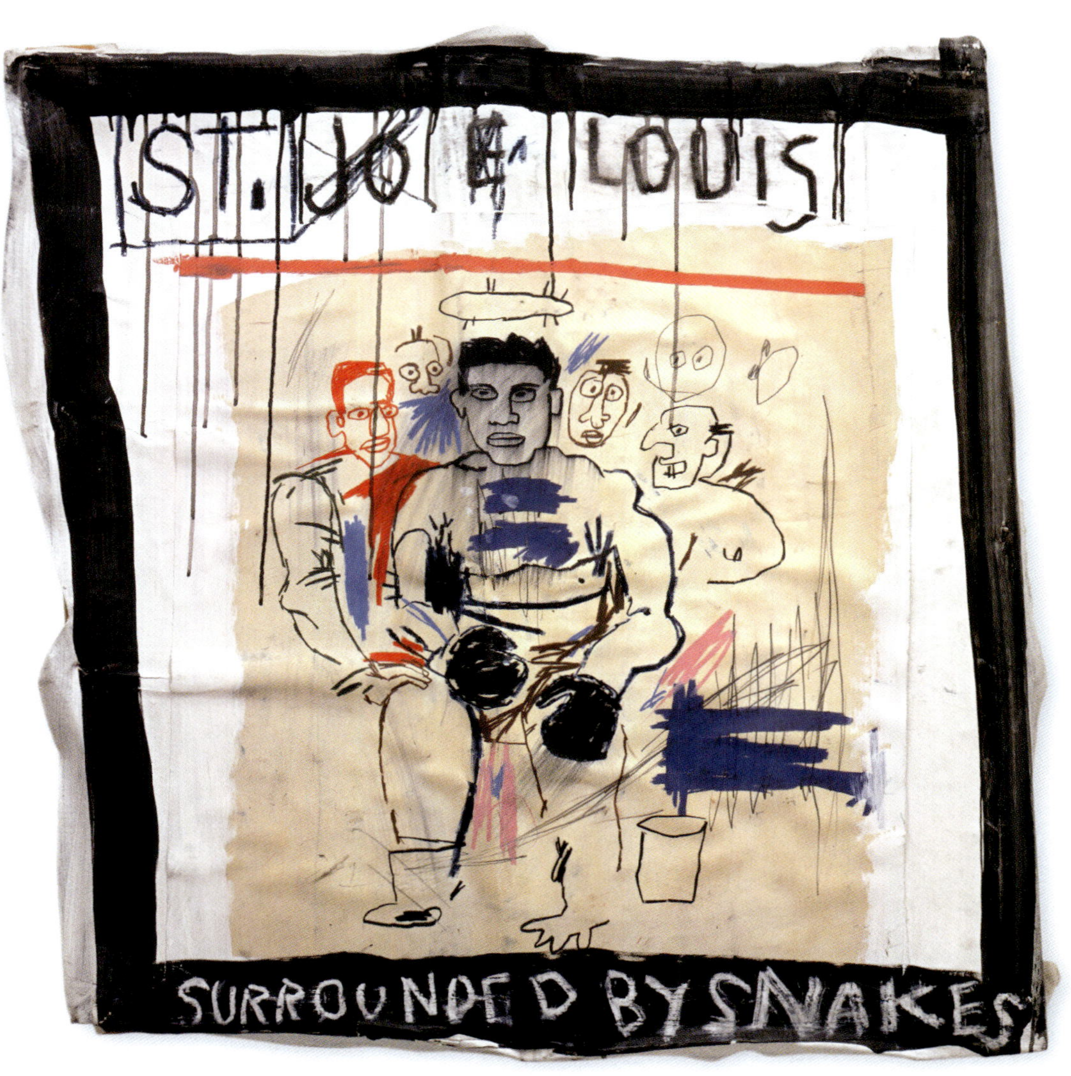

St. Joe Louis Surrounded by Snakes, 1982
Acrylic, oilstick, and paper collage on
canvas, 101.5 x 101.5 cm / 40 x 40 inches

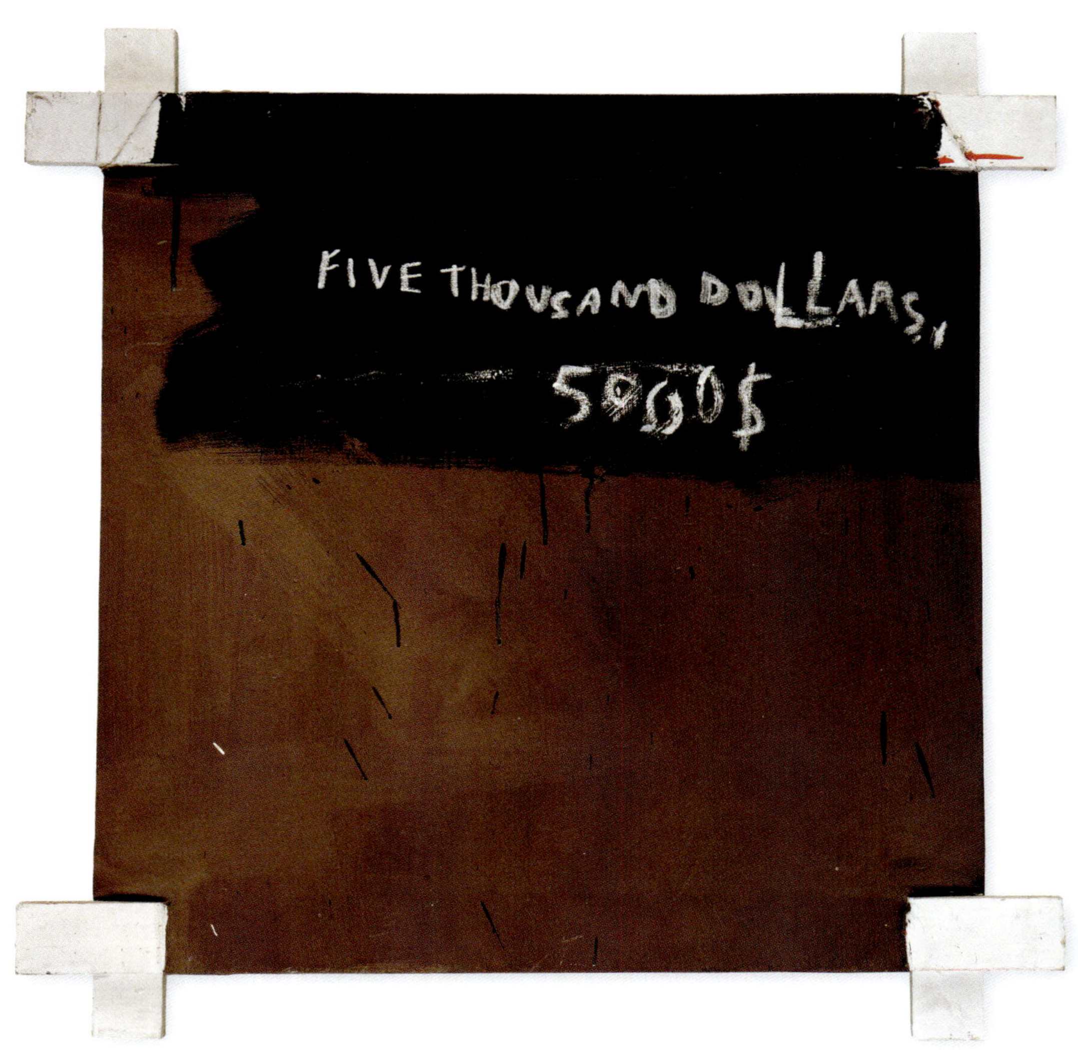

Untitled (Five Thousand Dollars), 1982
Acrylic and oilstick on canvas mounted on wooden
supports, 93.5 x 92.5 cm / 36 3/4 x 36 1/2 inches

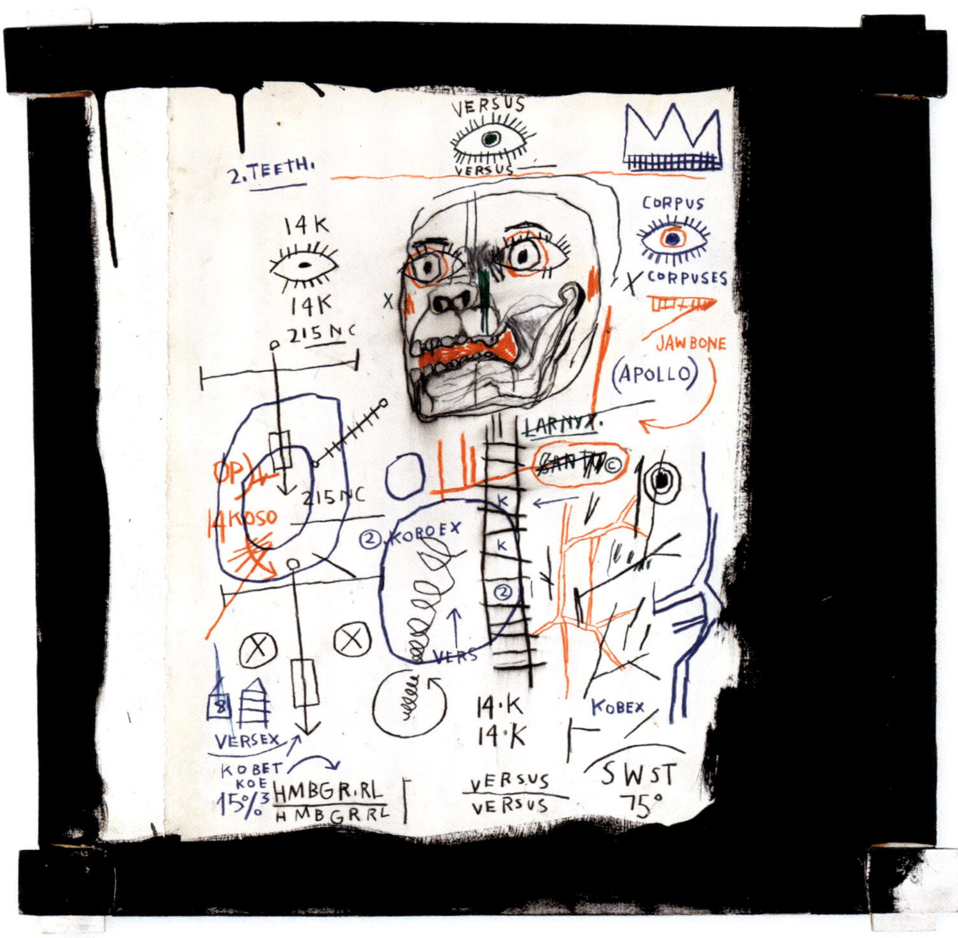

Santo 2, 1982
Acrylic, oilstick, and paper collage on canvas mounted
on wooden supports, 91.5 x 91.5 cm / 36 x 36 inches

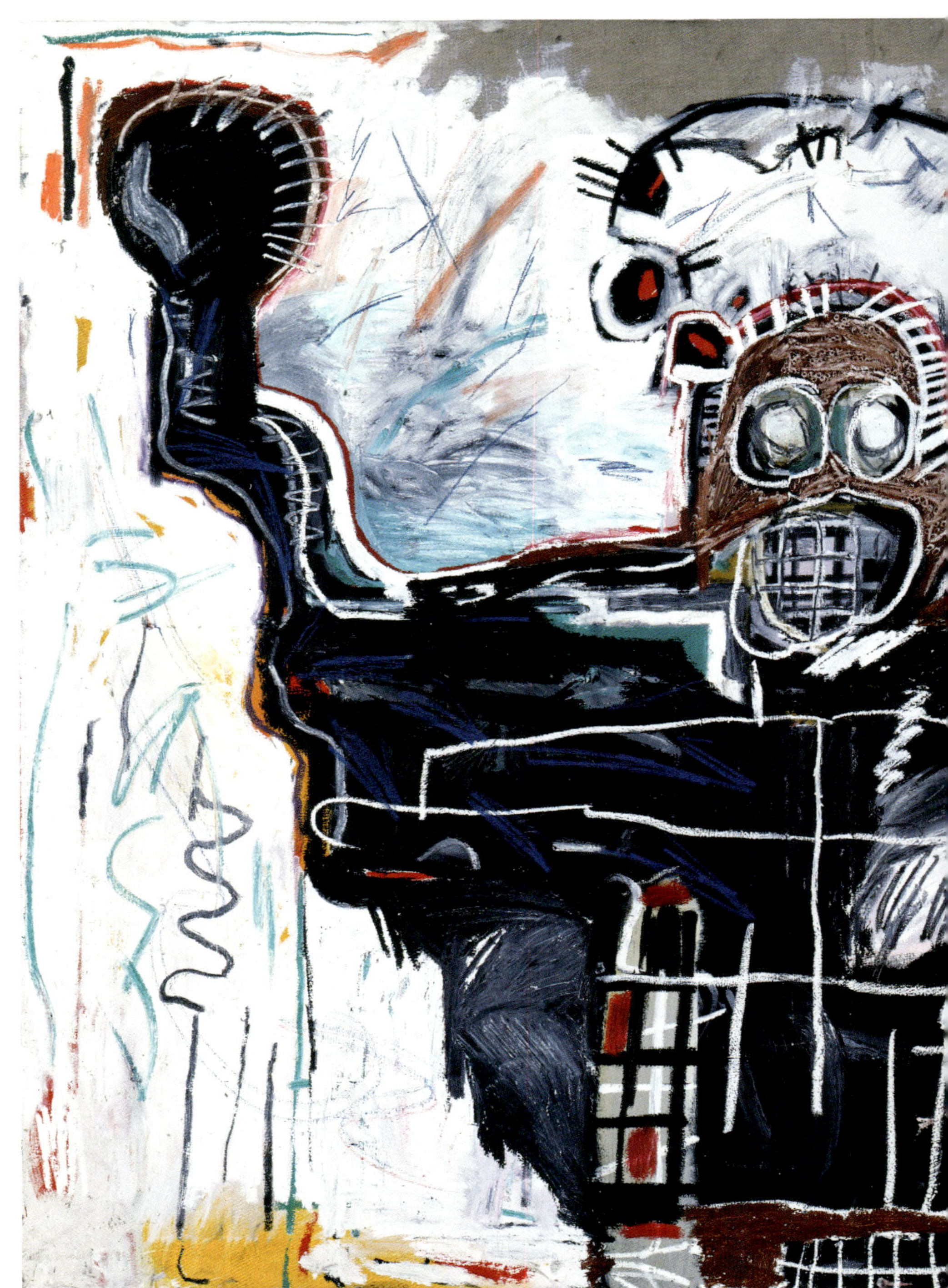

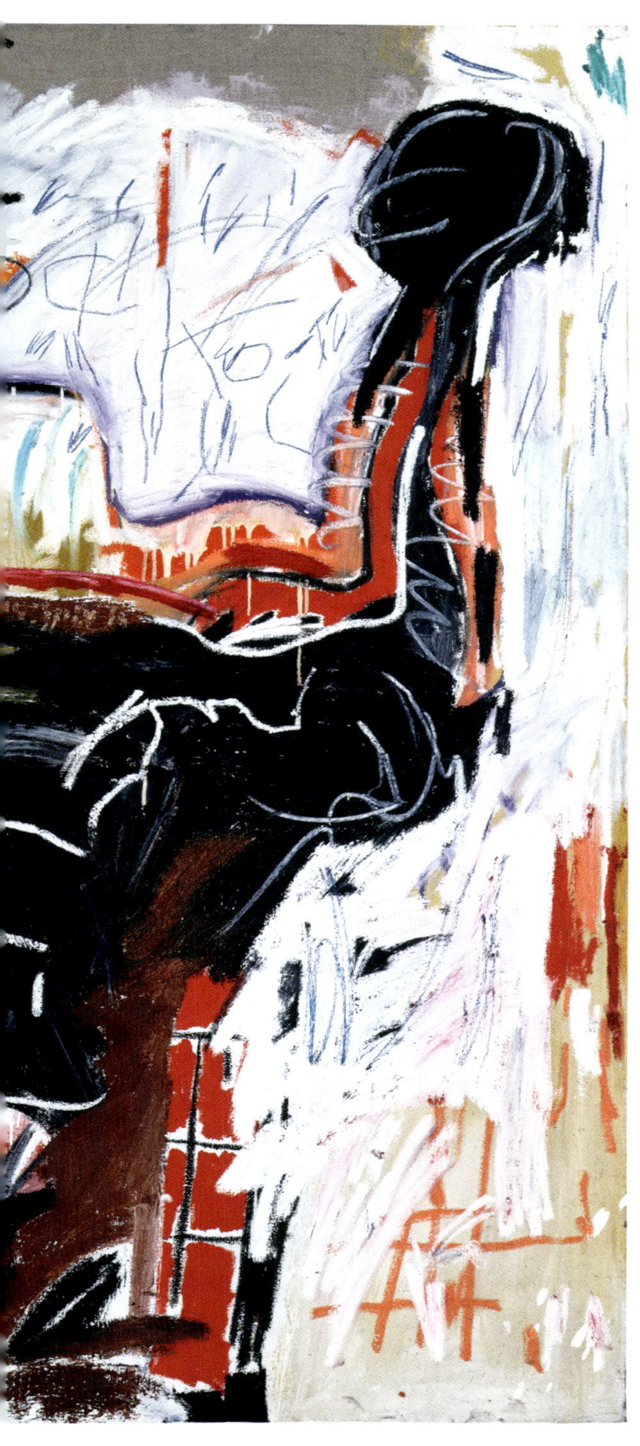

Untitled, 1982
Acrylic and oilstick on linen,
193 x 239 cm / 76 x 94 inches

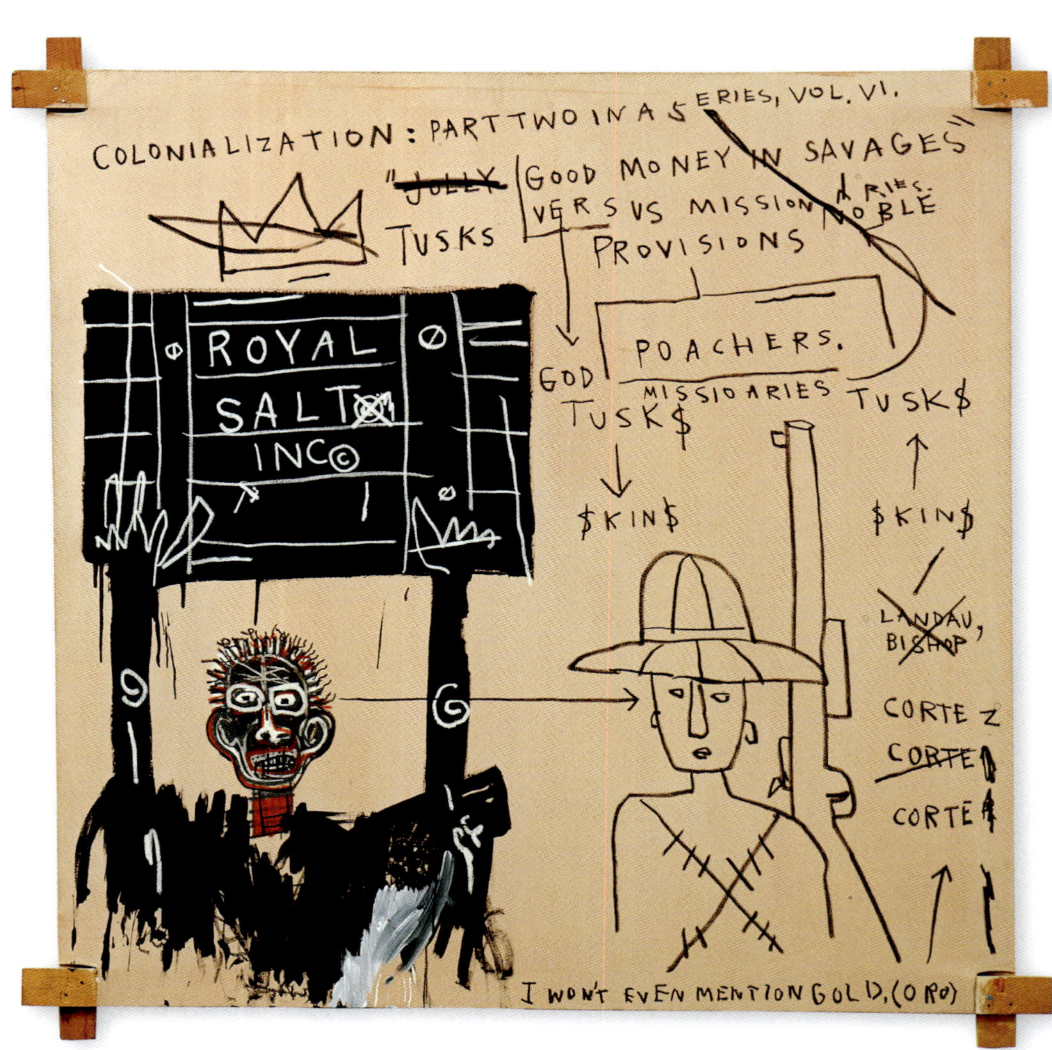

Native Carrying Some Guns,
Bibles, Amorites on Safari, 1982
Acrylic and oilstick on canvas mounted on
wooden supports, 183 x 183 cm / 72 x 72 inches

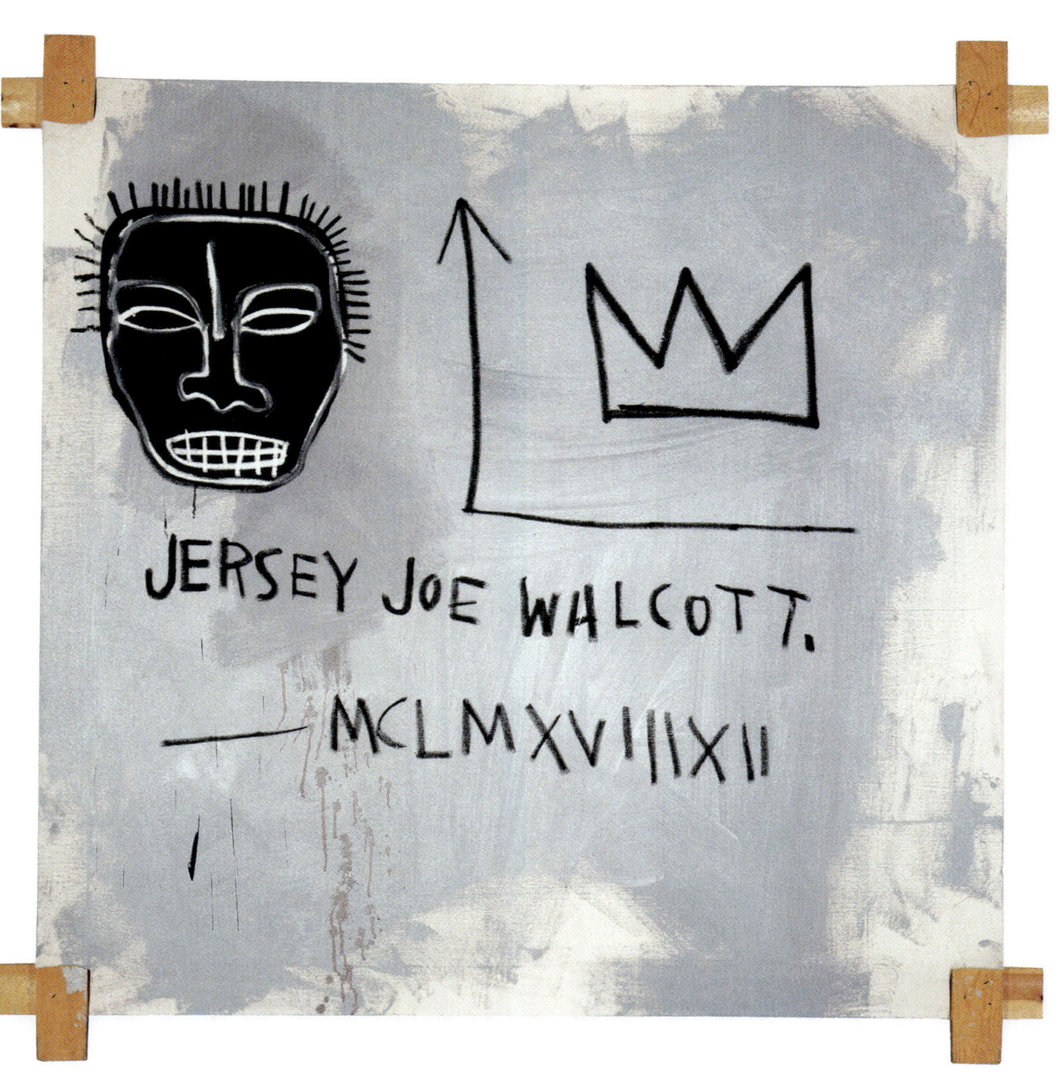

Jersey Joe Walcott, 1982
Acrylic and oilstick on canvas mounted on
wooden supports, 183 x 183 cm / 72 x 72 inches

Cassius Clay, 1982
Acrylic and oilstick on canvas,
122 x 101.5 cm / 48 x 40 inches

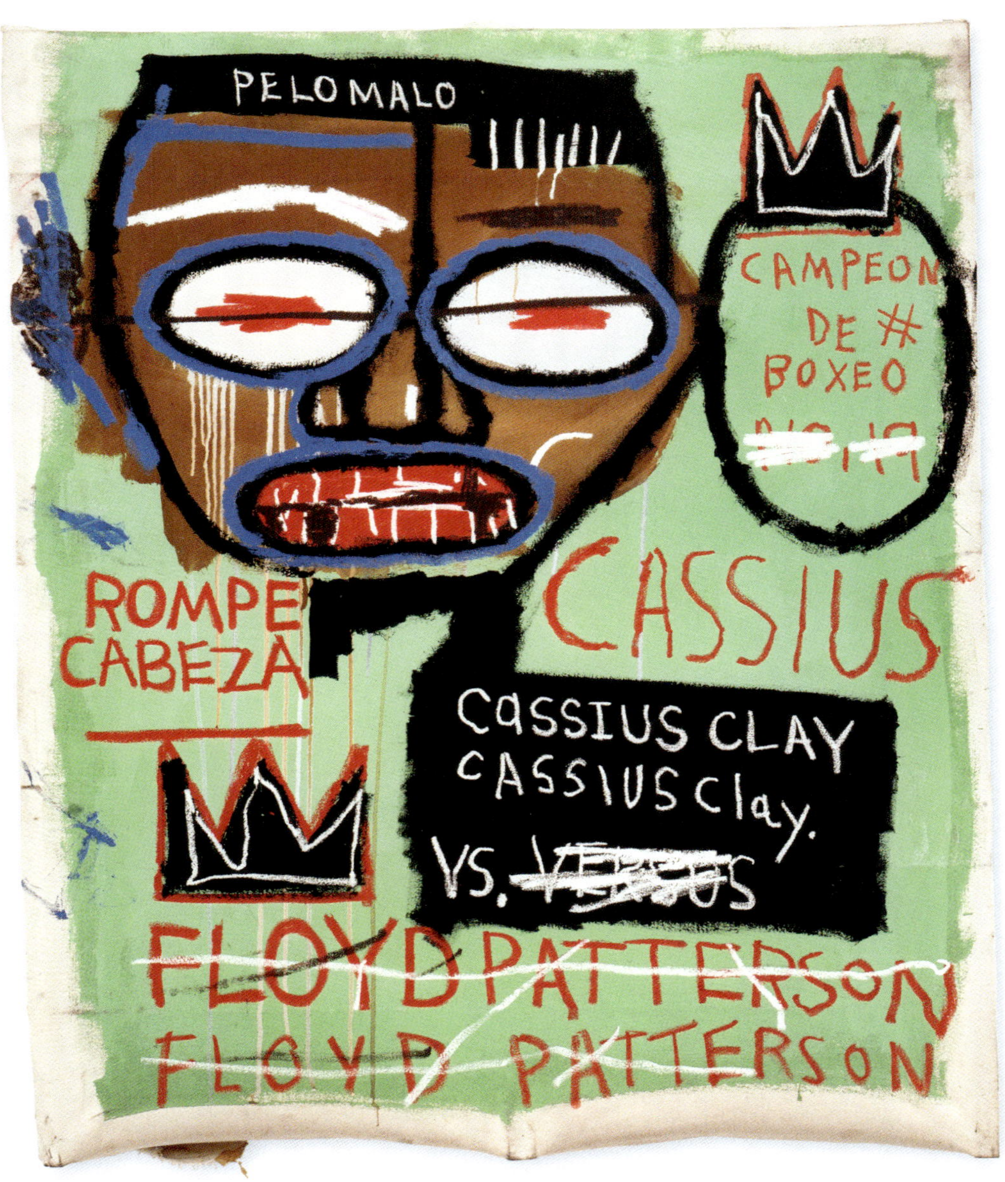

PELO MALO
CAMPEON DE # BOXEO
ROMPE CABEZA
CASSIUS
CASSIUS CLAY
CASSIUS clay.
VS. VERSUS
FLOYD PATTERSON
FLOYD PATTERSON

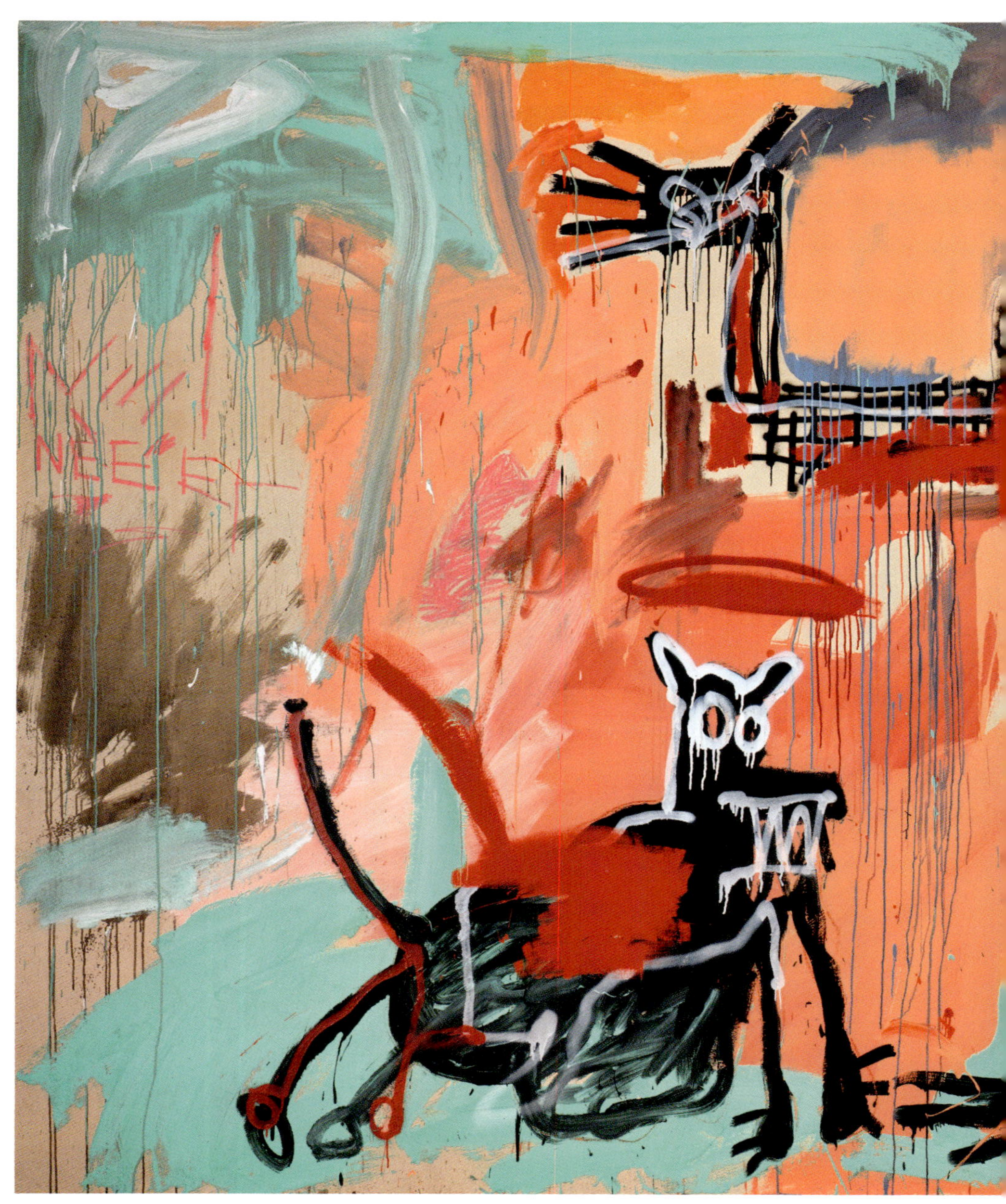

Boy and Dog in a Johnnypump, 1982
Acrylic, oilstick, and spray paint on canvas,
240 x 420.5 cm / 94 ¹/₂ x 165 ¹/₂ inches

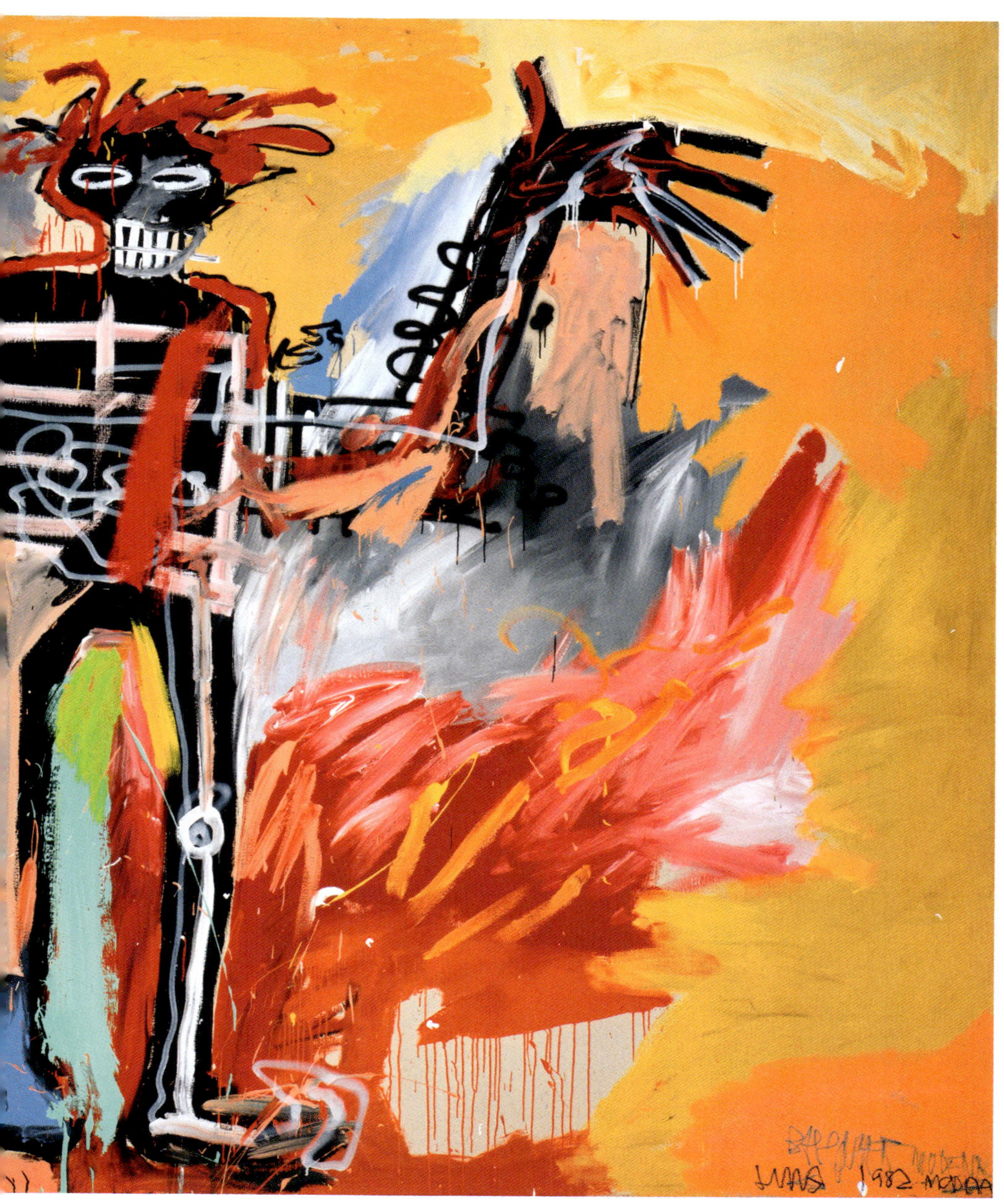

Dos Cabezas, 1982
Acrylic and oilstick on canvas mounted on wooden
supports, 152.5 x 152.5 cm / 60 x 60 inches

Pages 200/201: **Untitled (Two on Gold)**, 1982
Acrylic and oilstick on canvas,
203 x 317.5 cm / 80 x 125 inches

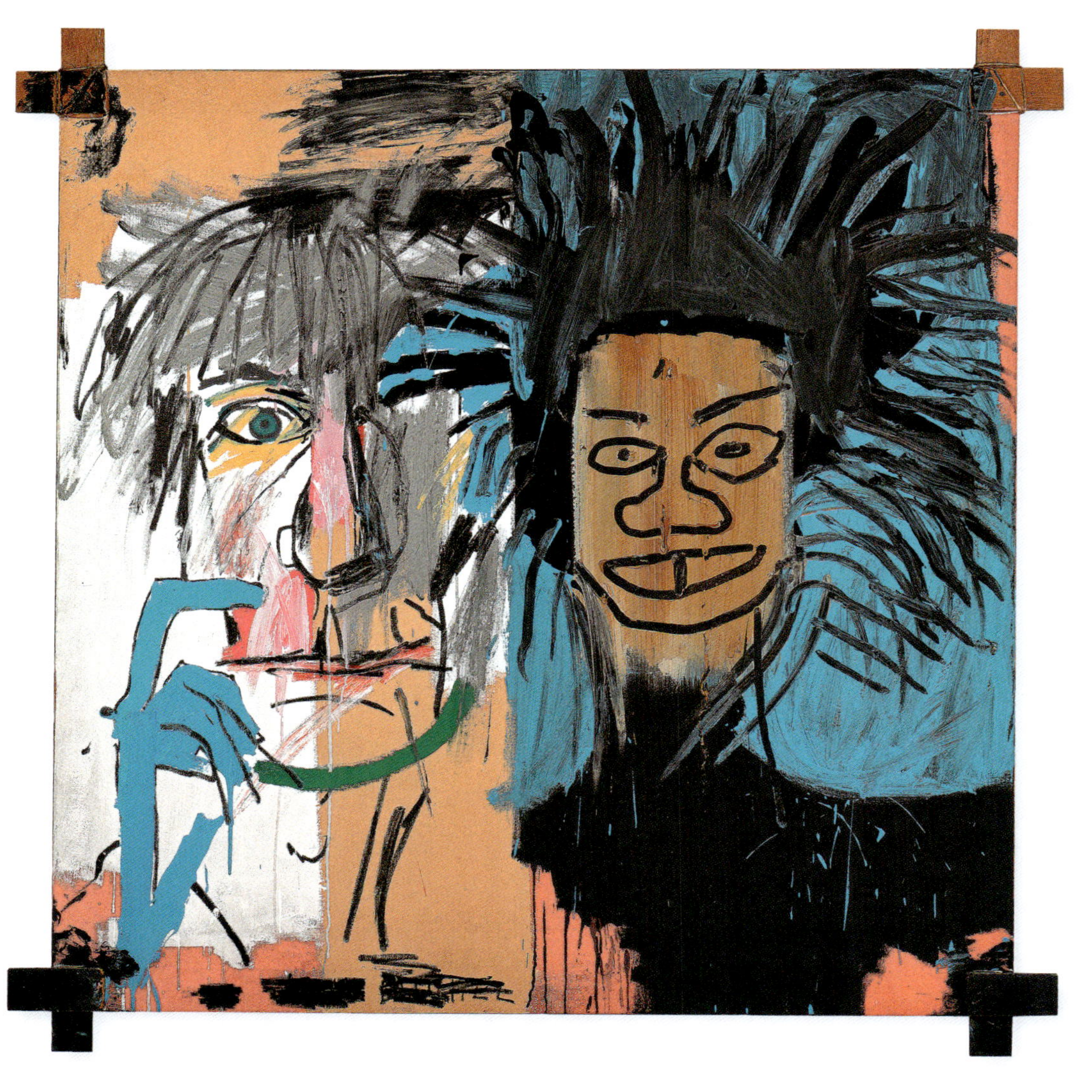

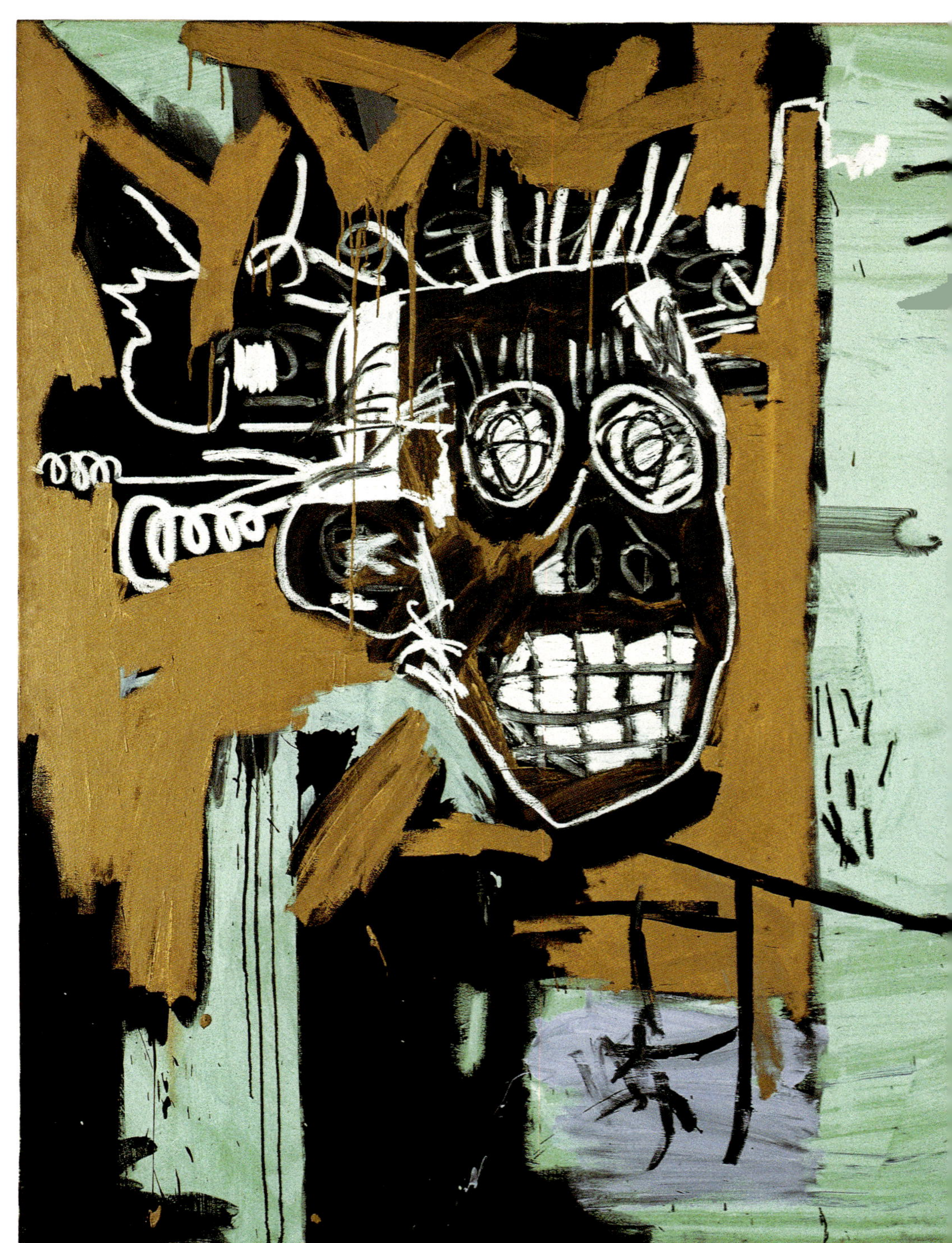

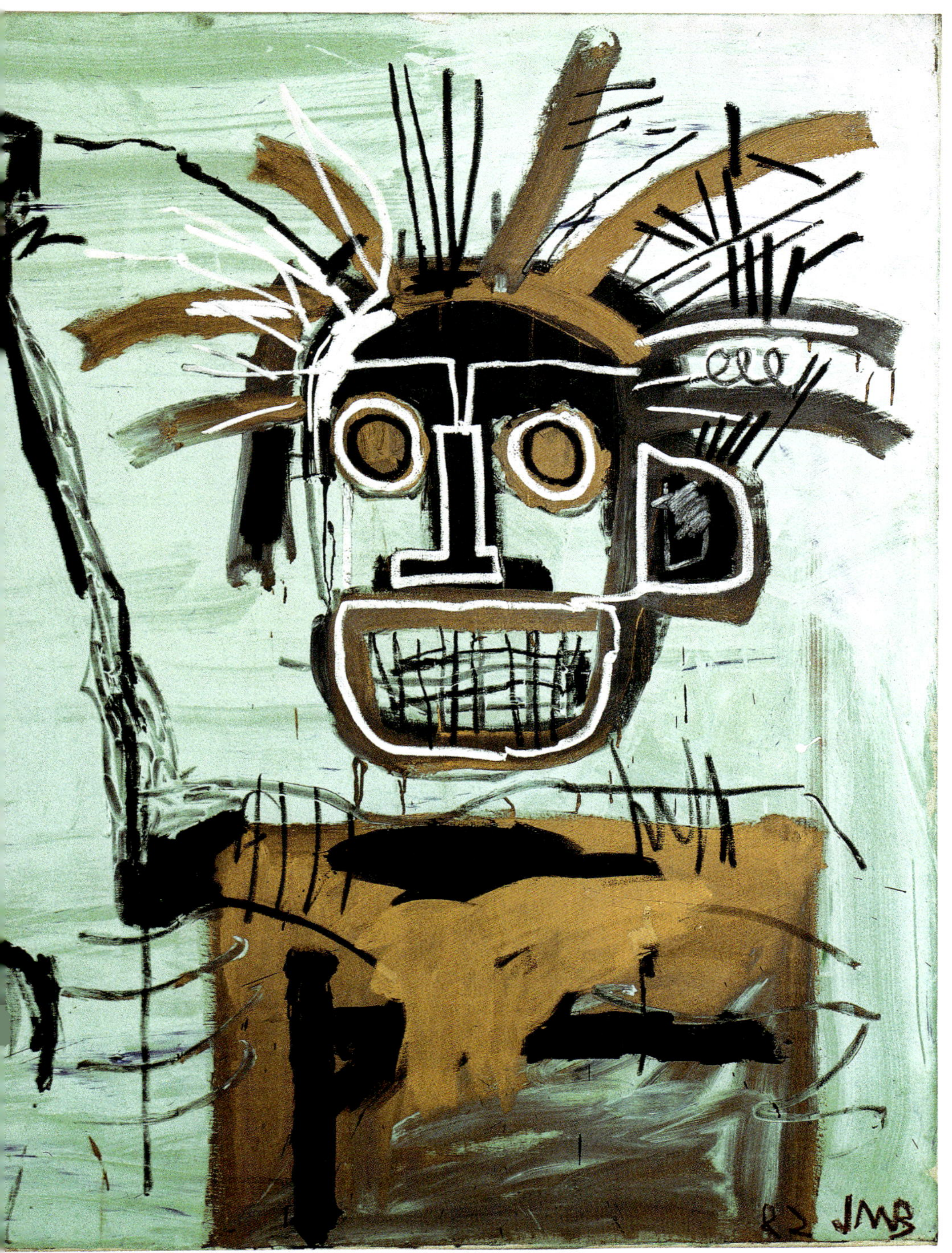

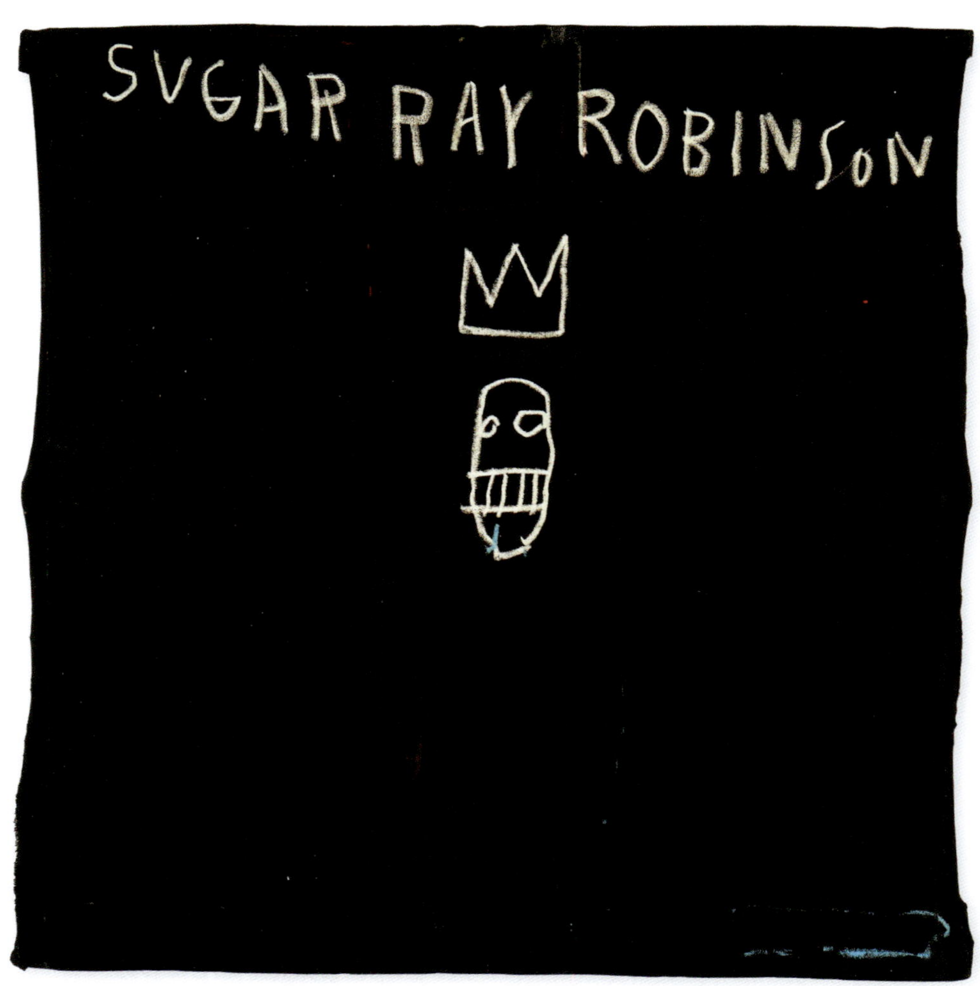

Untitled (Sugar Ray Robinson), 1982
Acrylic and oilstick on canvas,
106.5 x 106.5 cm / 42 x 42 inches

Tuxedo, 1982–1983
Silkscreen on canvas,
259 x 152.5 cm / 102 x 60 inches

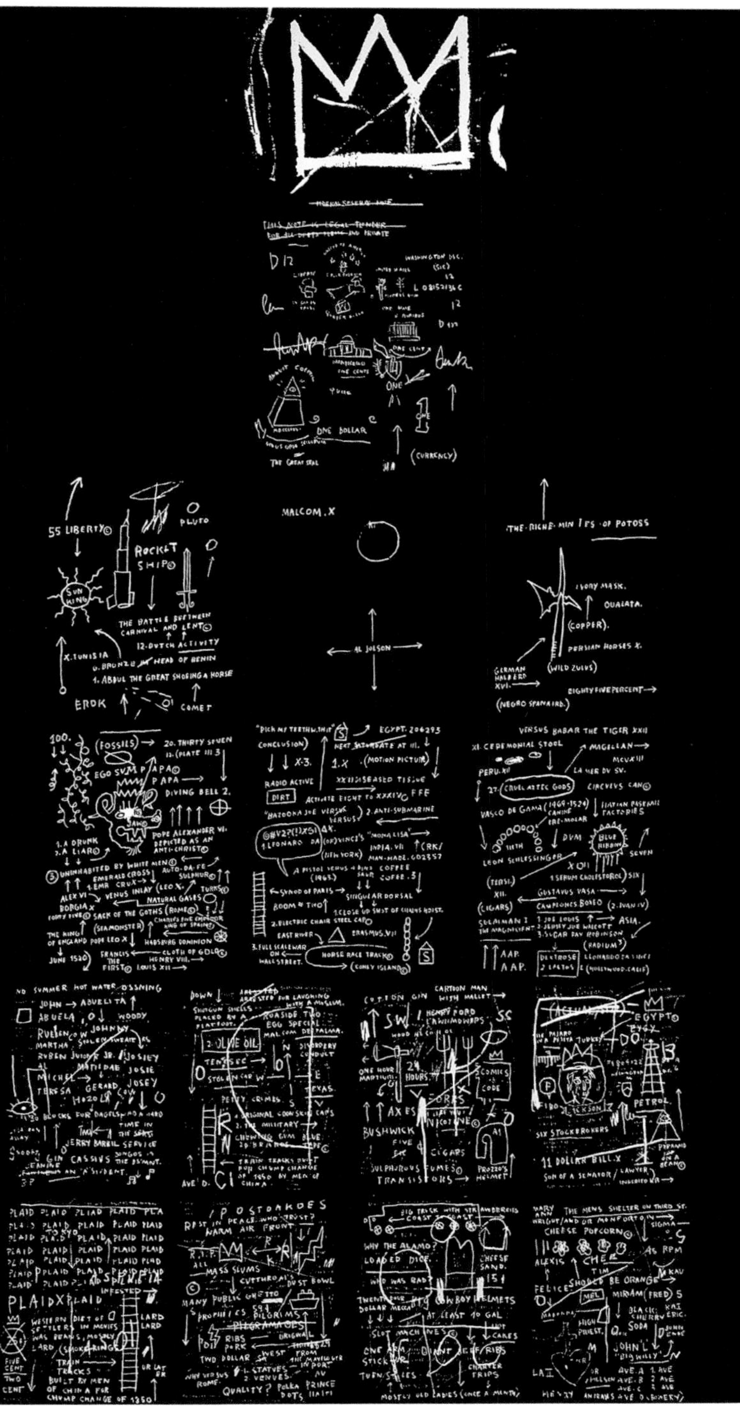

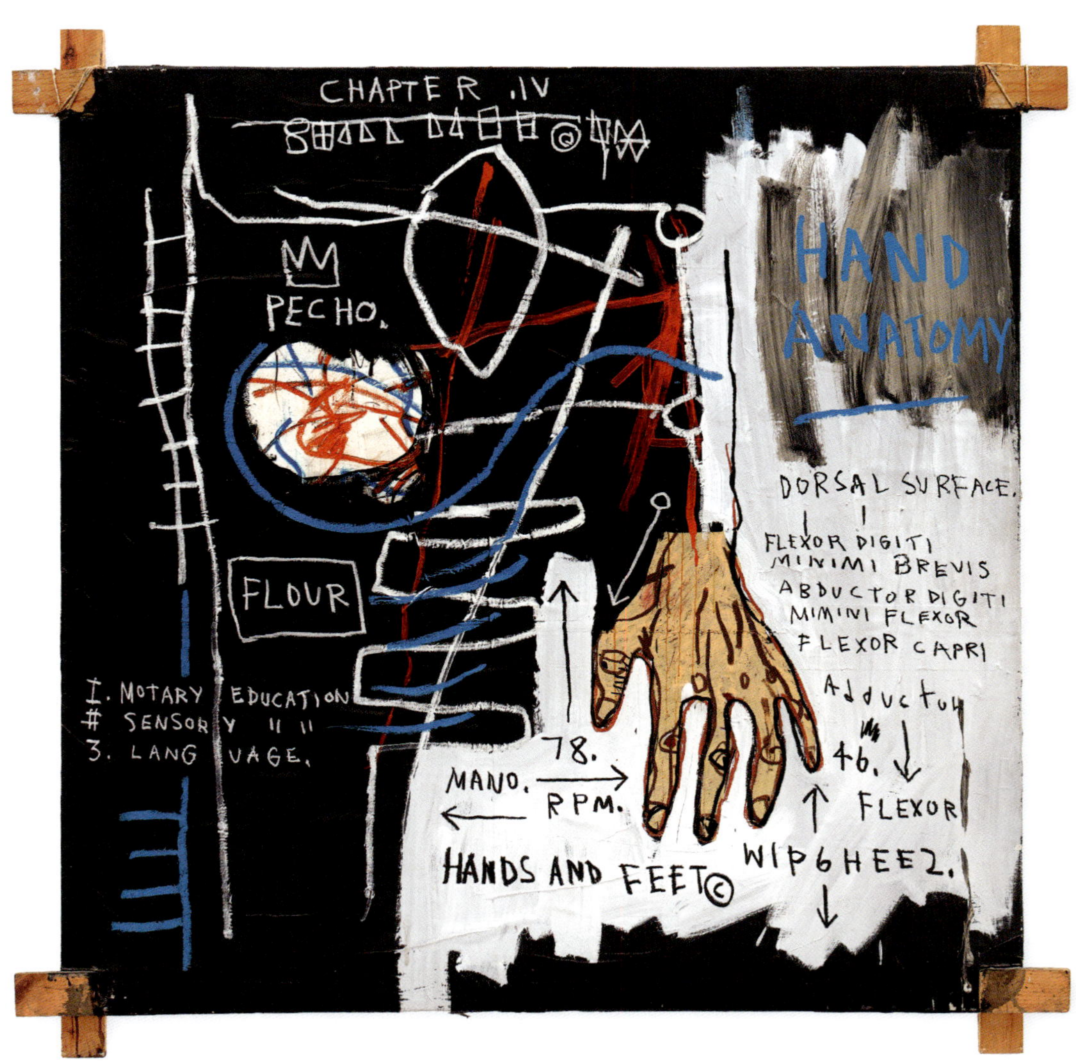

Untitled (Hand Anatomy), 1982
Acrylic, oilstick, and paper collage on canvas mounted
on wooden supports, 152.5 x 152.5 cm / 60 x 60 inches

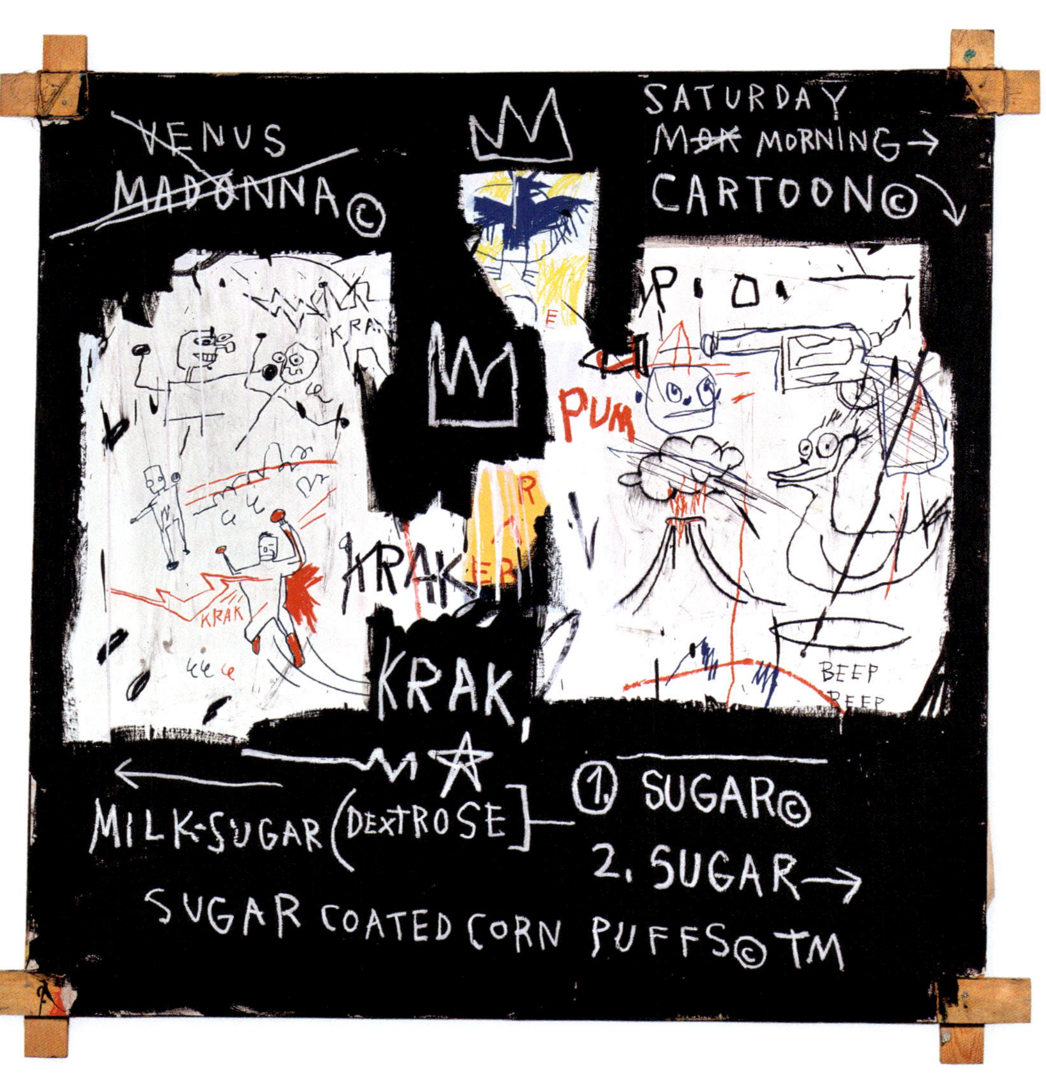

A Panel of Experts, 1982
Acrylic, oilstick, and paper collage on canvas mounted
on wooden supports, 152.5 x 152.5 cm / 60 x 60 inches

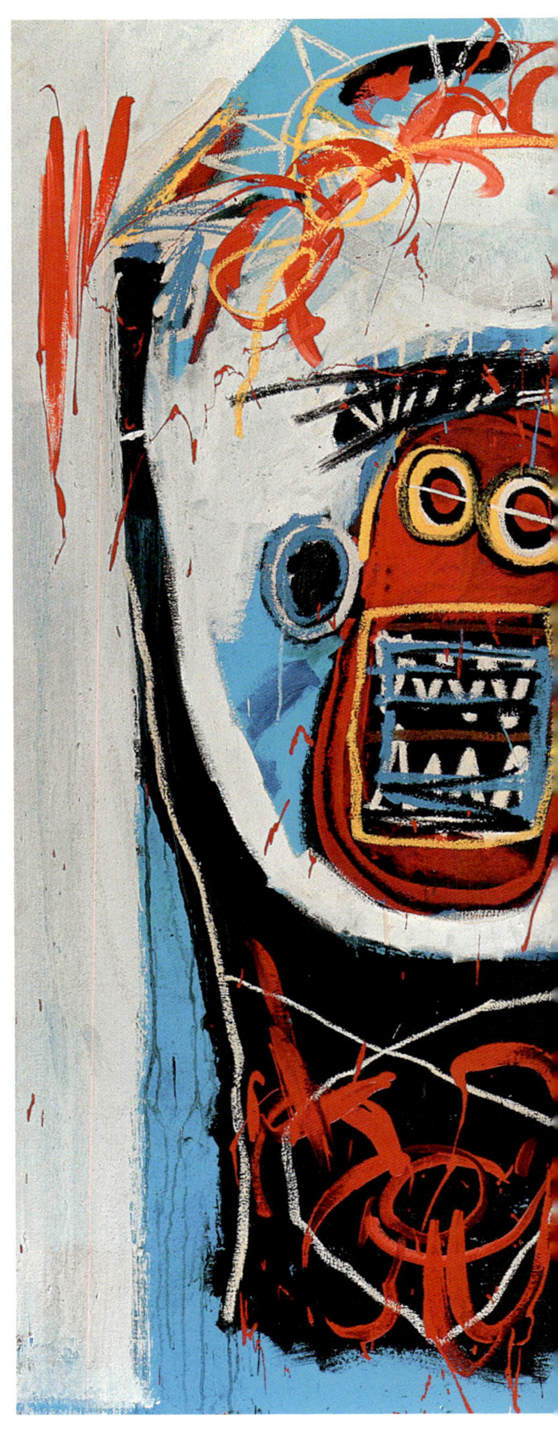

Palm Spring Jump, 1982
Acrylic and oilstick on canvas,
183 x 213.5 cm / 72 x 84 inches

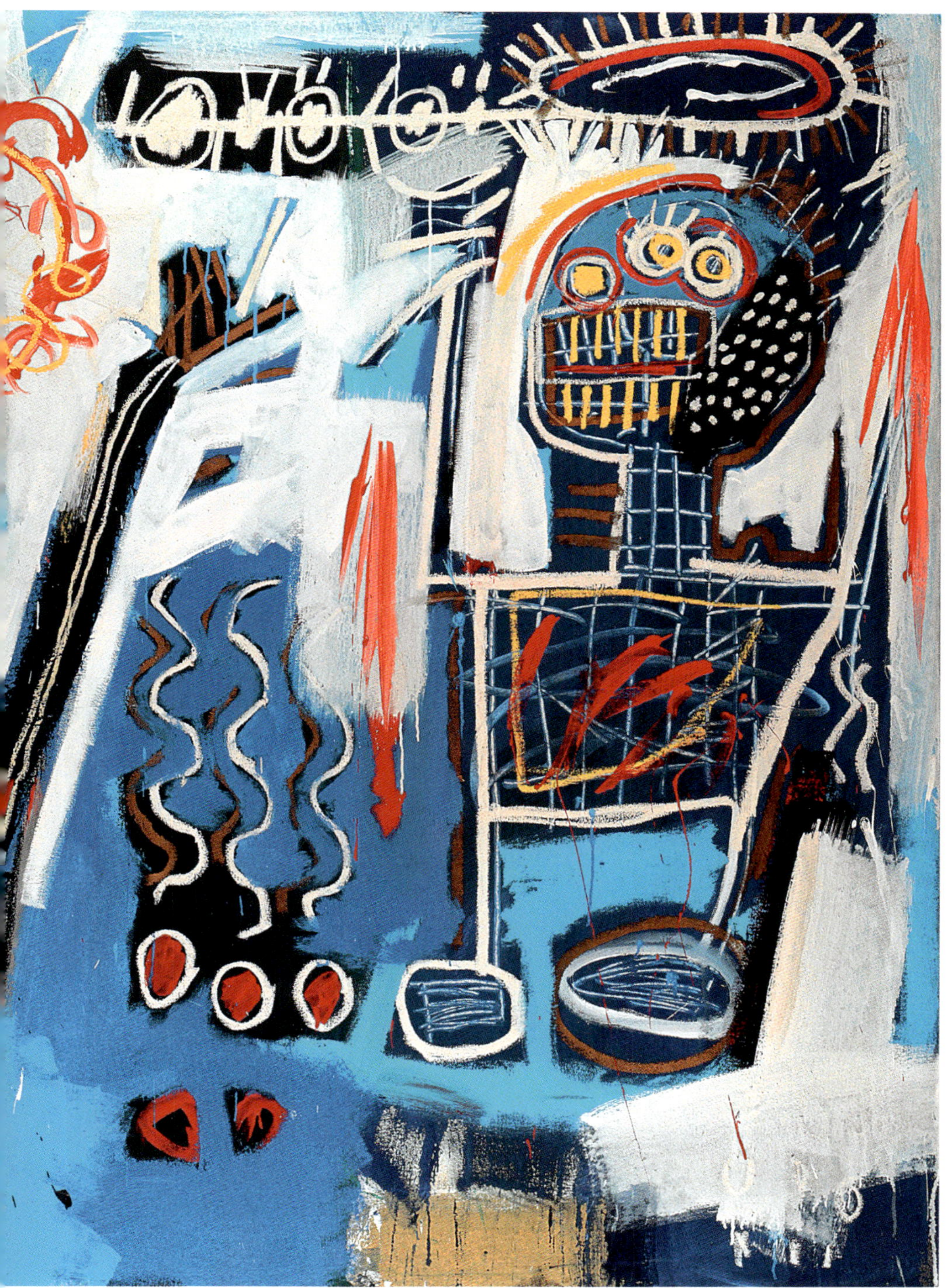

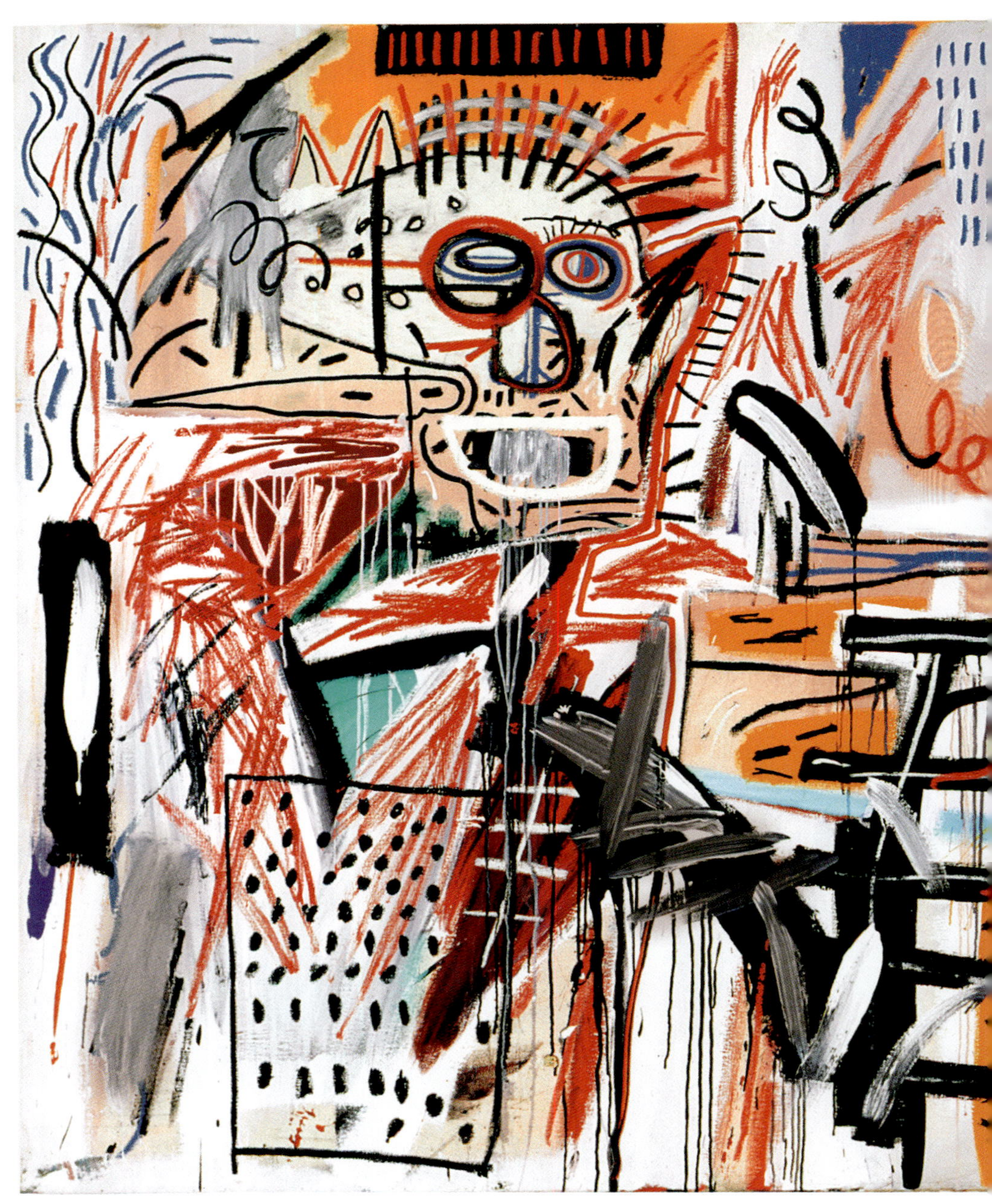

Philistines, 1982
Acrylic and oilstick on canvas,
183 x 312.5 cm / 72 x 123 inches

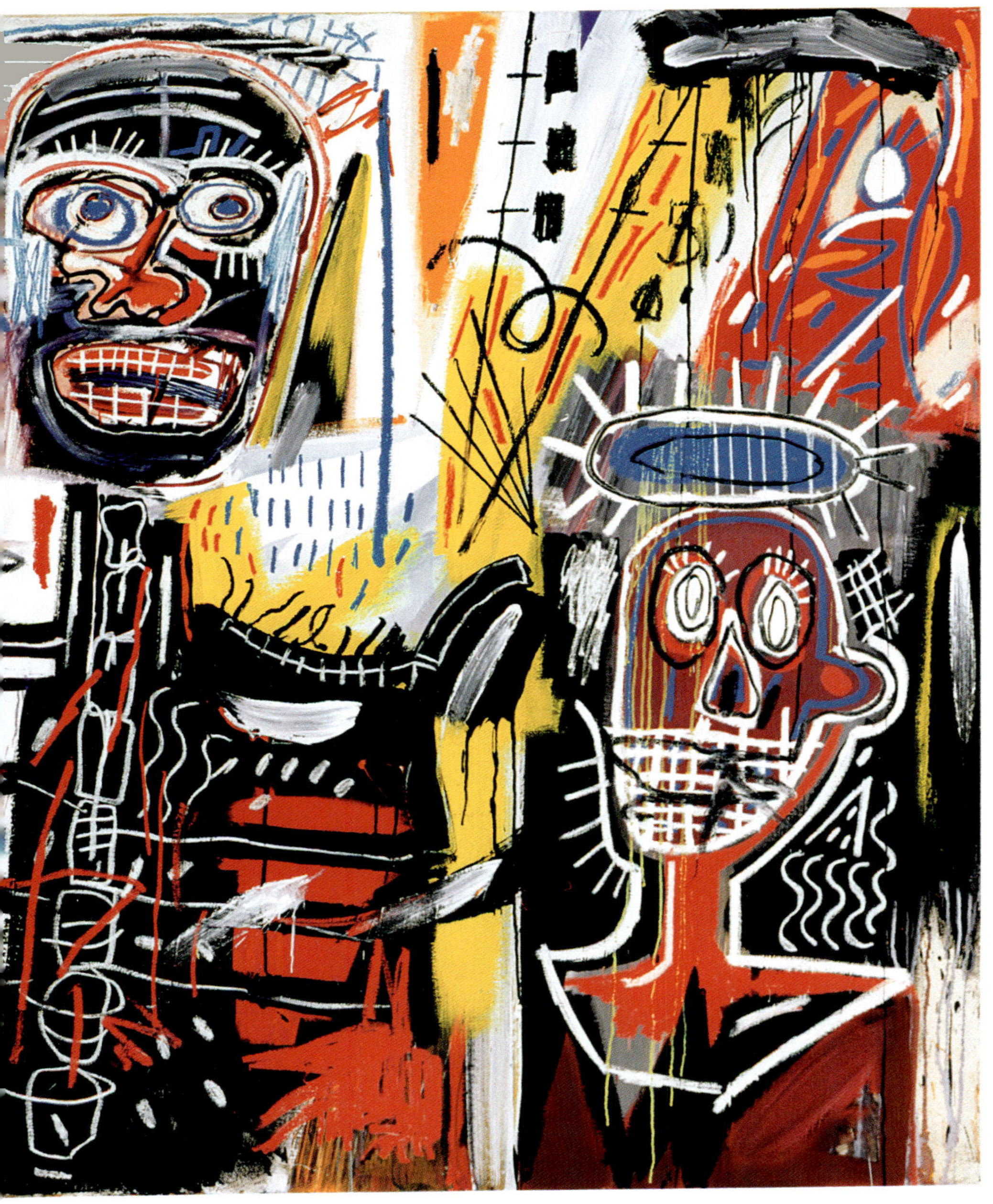

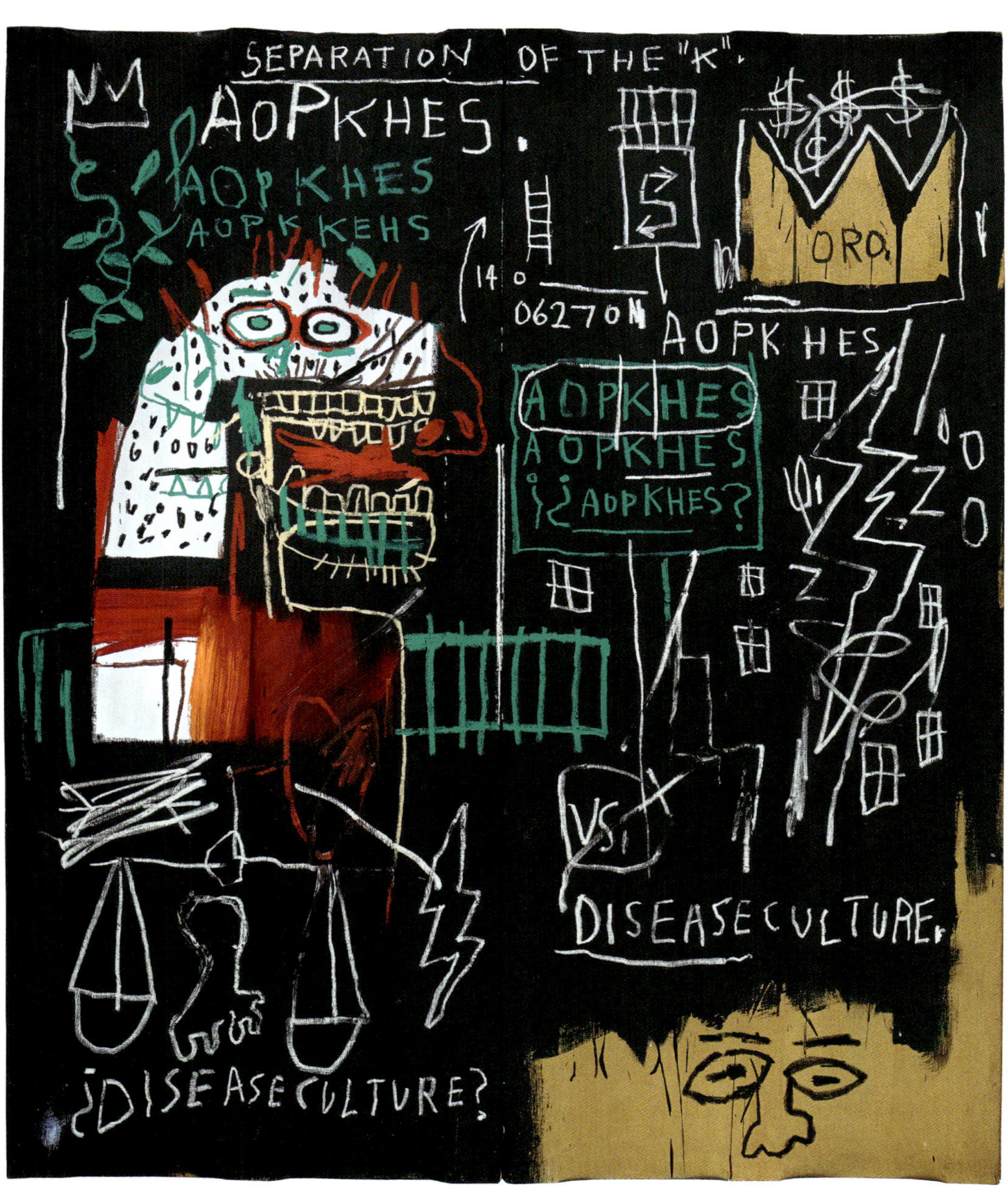

K, 1982
Acrylic and oilstick on canvas, diptych:
183 x 155 cm / 72 x 61 inches

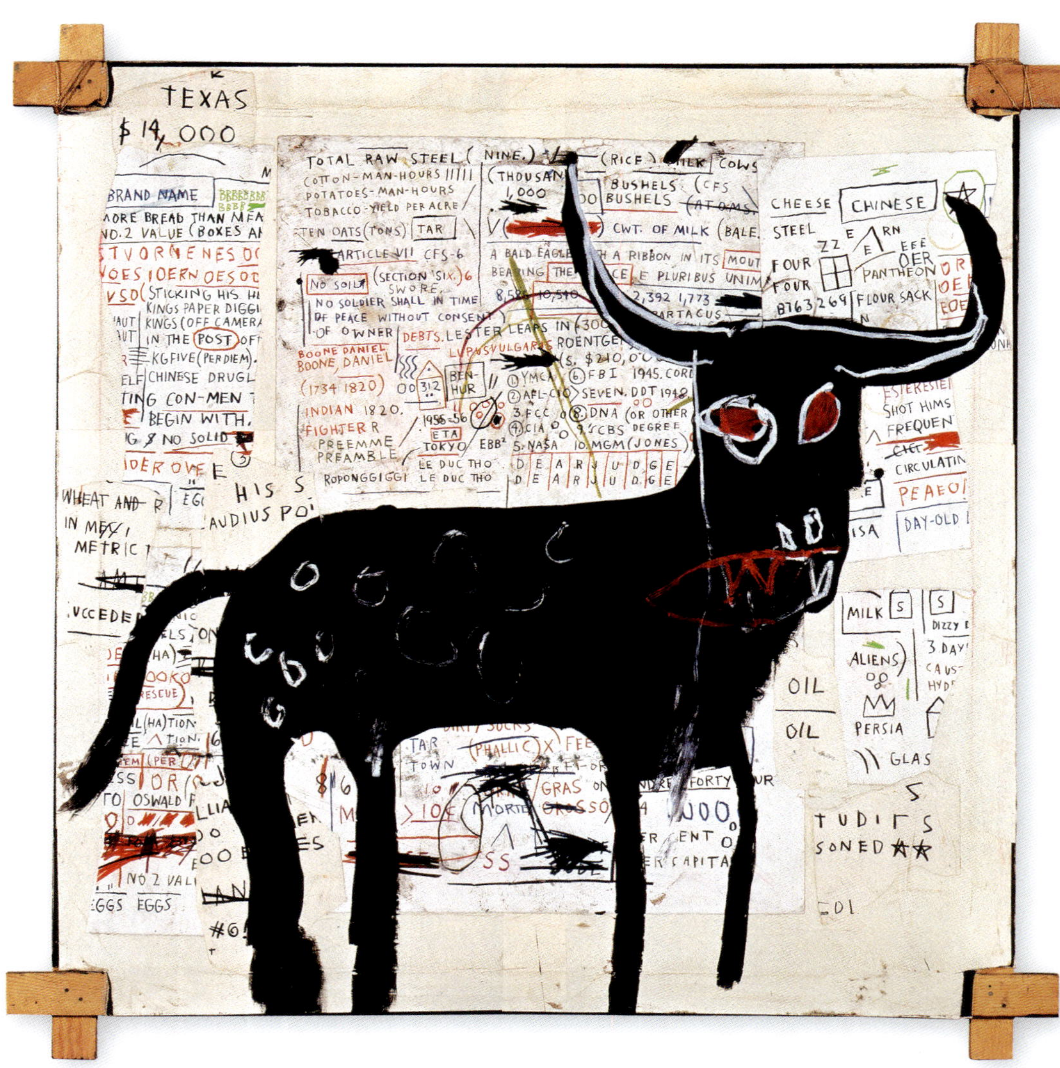

Beef Ribs Longhorn, 1982
Acrylic, oilstick, and paper collage on
canvas mounted on wooden supports,
152.5 x 152.5 cm / 60 x 60 inches

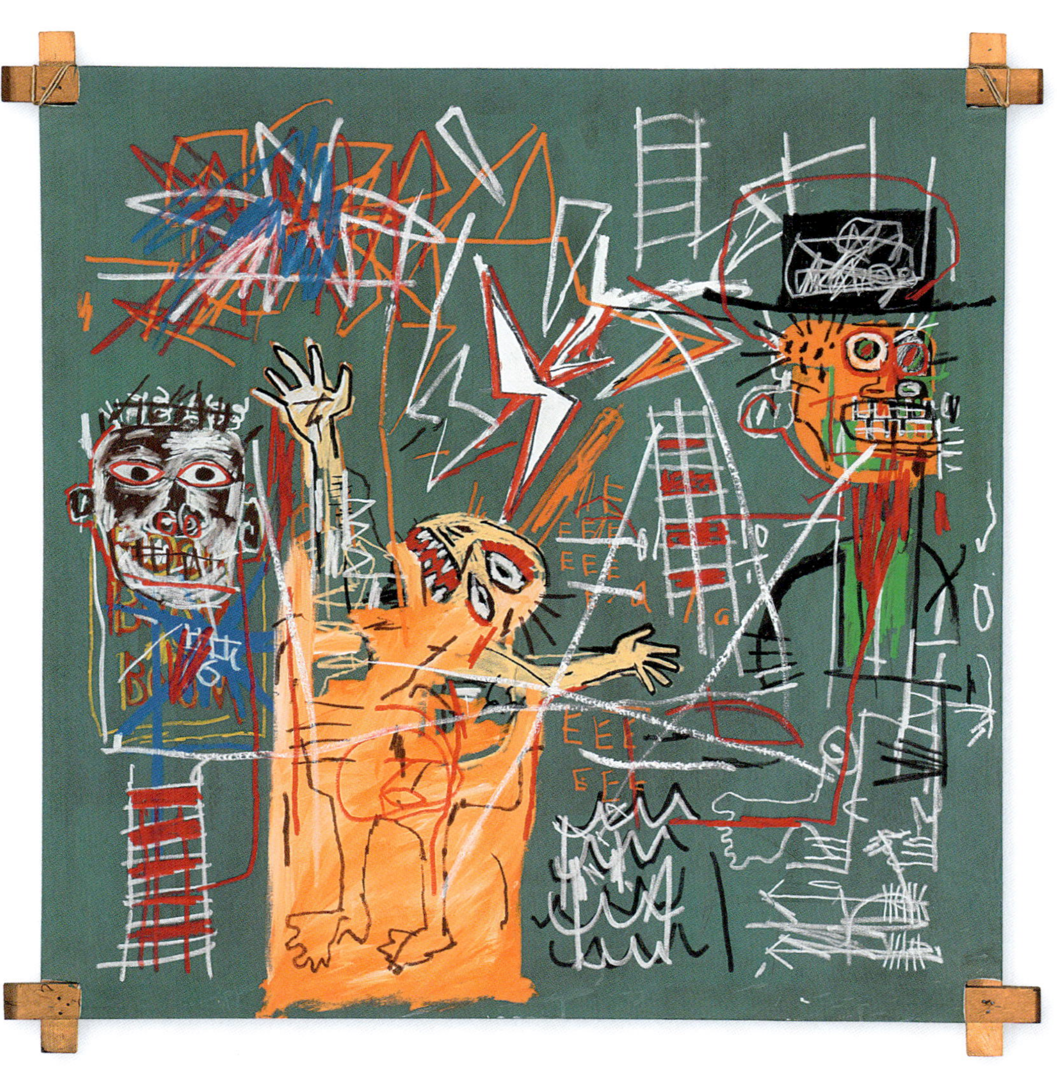

Man Struck by Lightning. Two Witnesses, 1982
Acrylic and oilstick on canvas mounted on wooden
supports, 182 x 182 cm / 71 $^3/_4$ x 71 $^3/_4$ inches

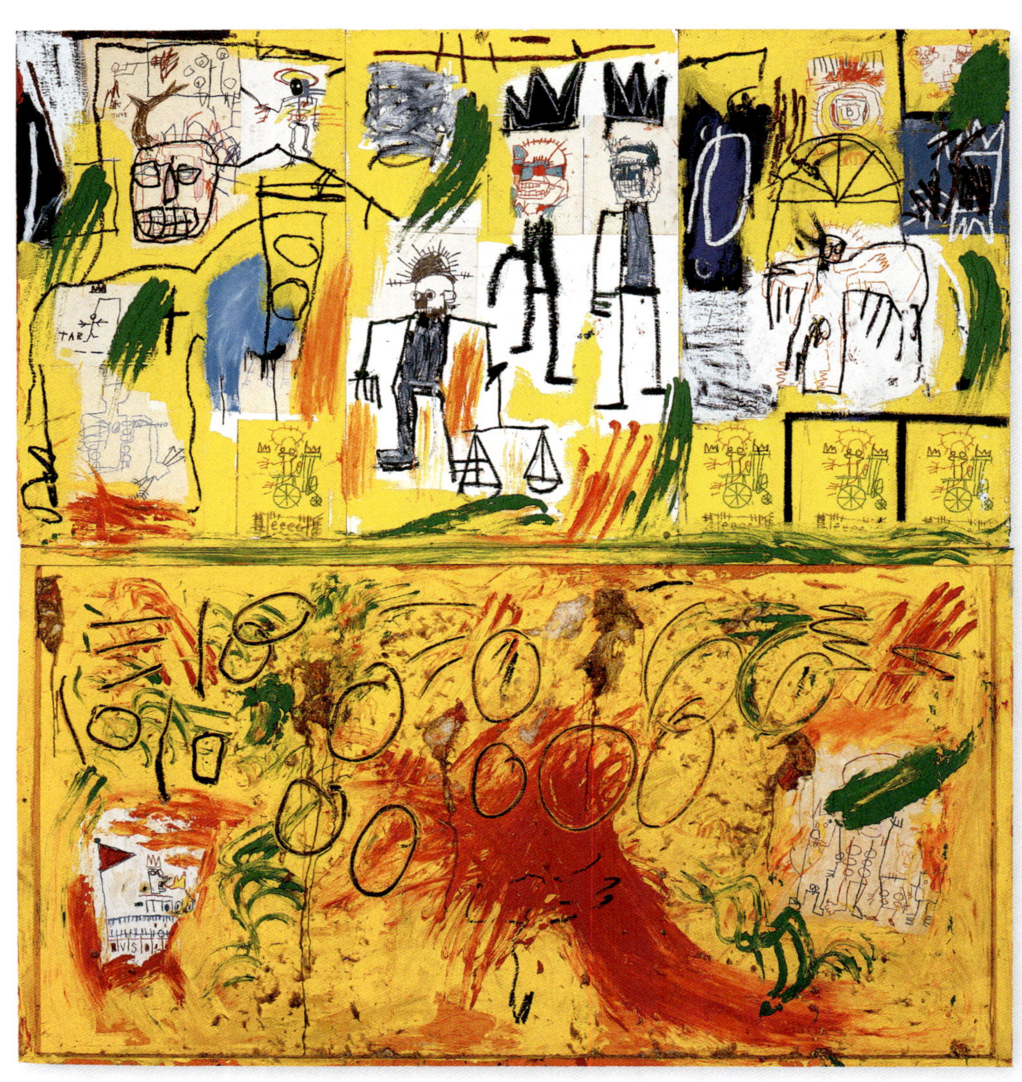

Untitled (Yellow Tar and Feathers), 1982
Acrylic, oilstick, paper collage, tar, and feather on
masonite, polyptych: 244 x 228.5 cm / 96 x 90 inches

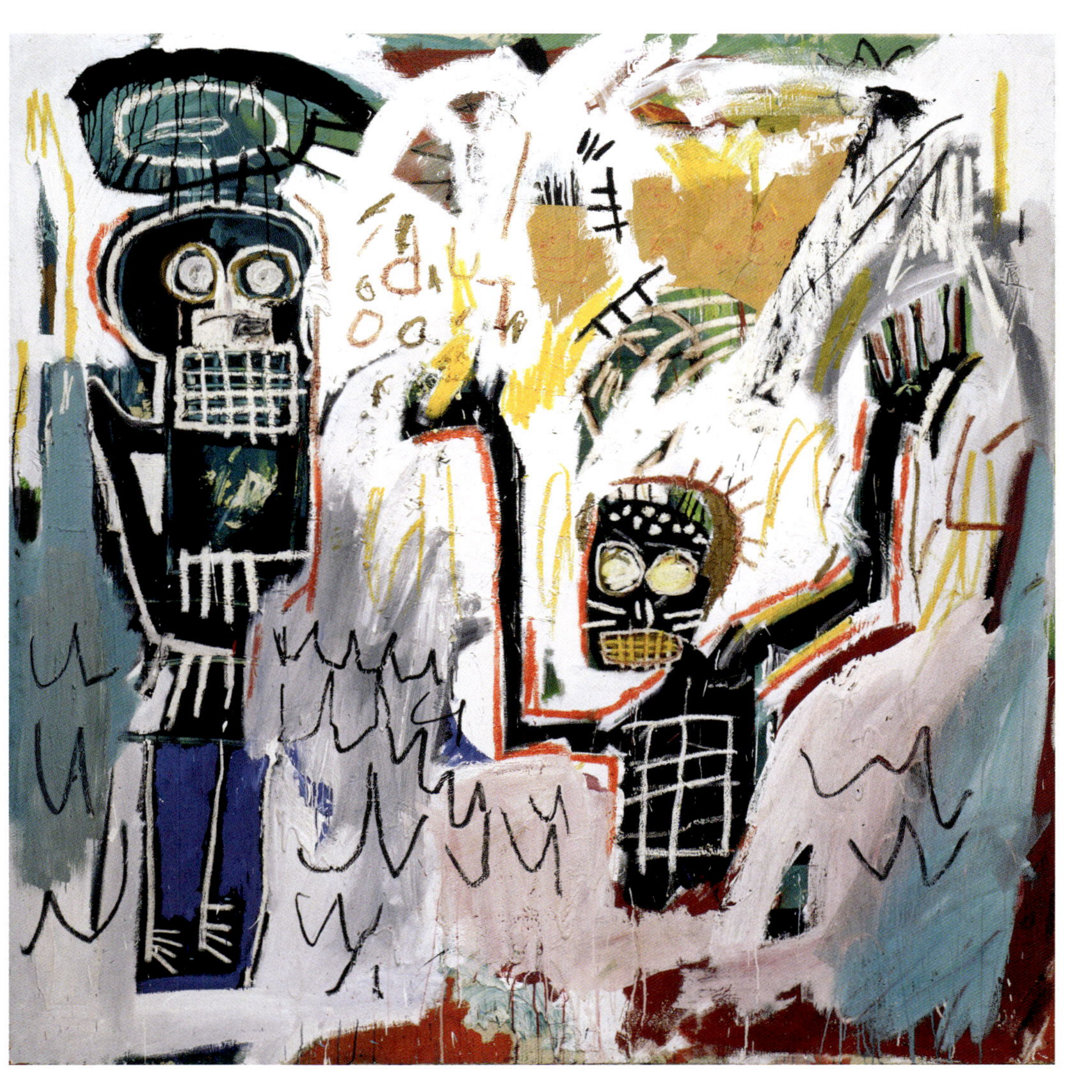

Untitled (Baptism), 1982
Acrylic, oilstick, and paper collage on
canvas, 233.5 x 233.5 cm / 92 x 92 inches

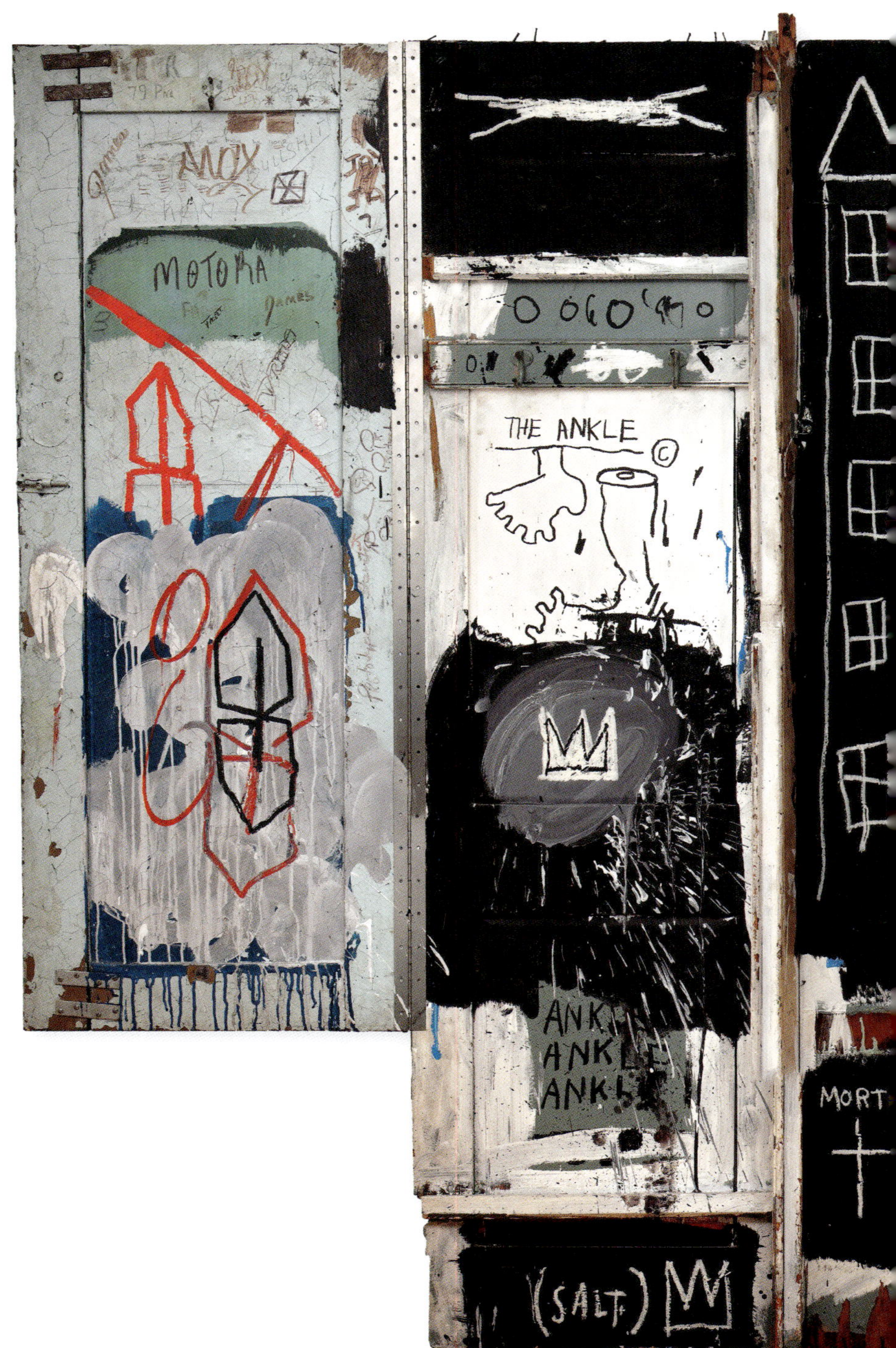
79 Pne
MOX
MOTORA
James
THE ANKLE
O O6O
ANKL
ANKLE
ANKL
MORT
(SALT)

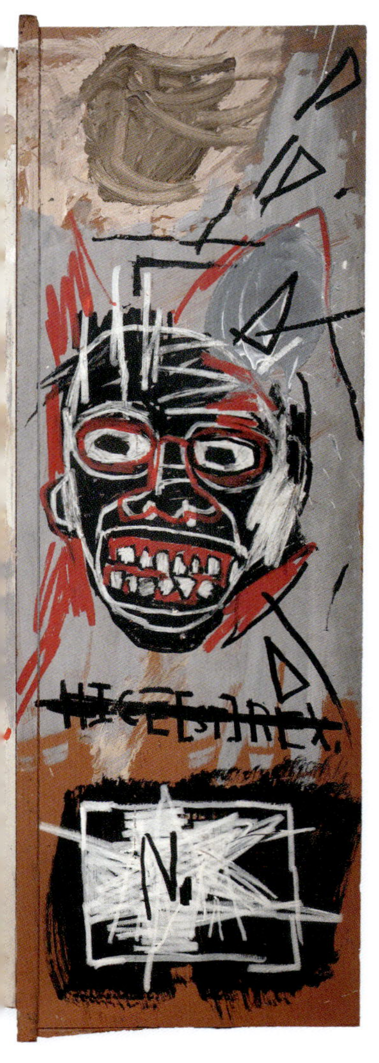

Portrait of the Artist as a Young Derelict, 1982
Acrylic, oil, ink, and oilstick on wood,
triptych: 204 x 208.5 cm / 80 x 82 inches

Pages 218/219: **Famous** (recto and verso), 1982
Acrylic and photocopy collage on wood,
182 x 90 x 53 cm / 71 ³/₄ x 35 ¹/₂ x 20 ³/₄ inches

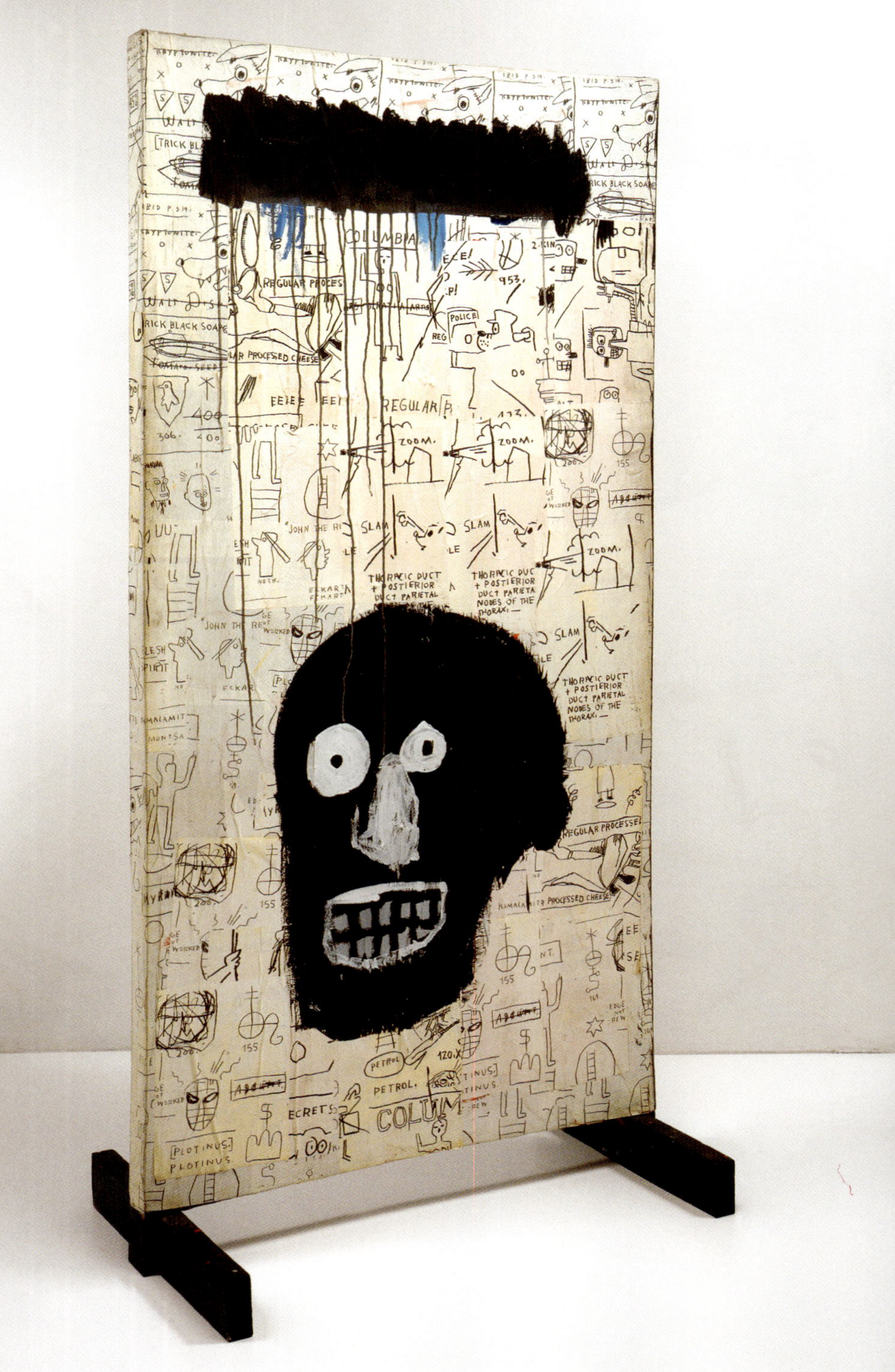

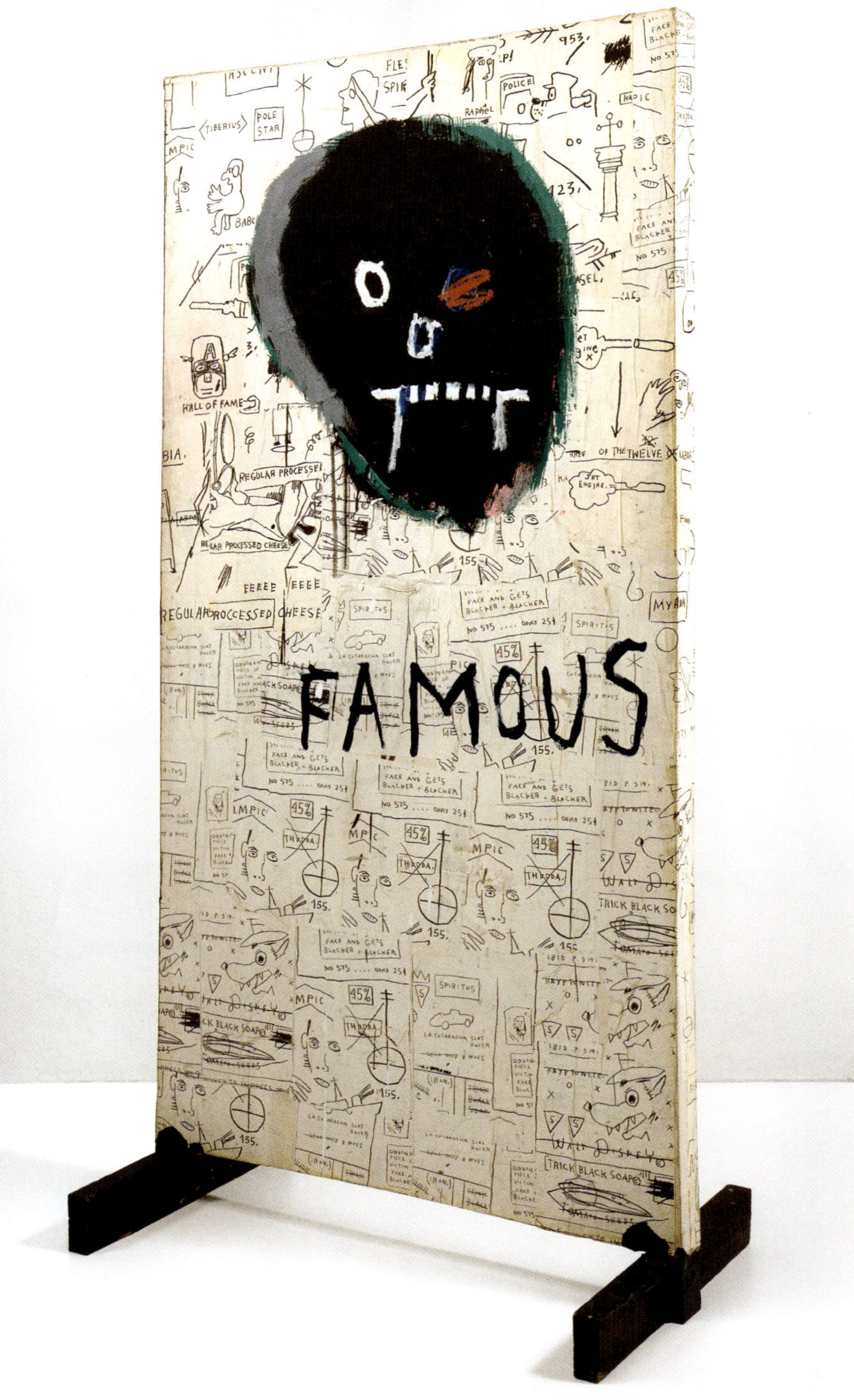

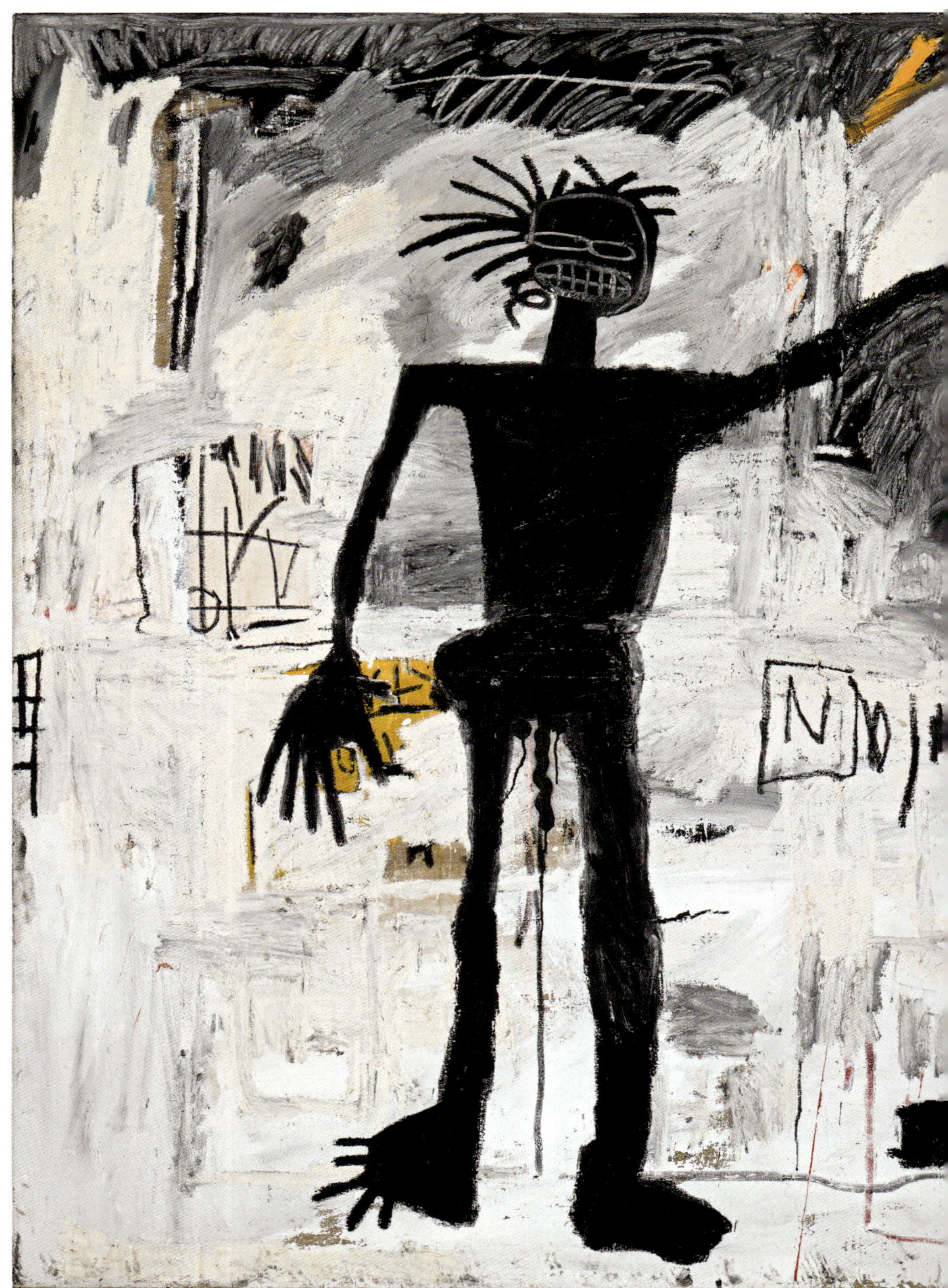

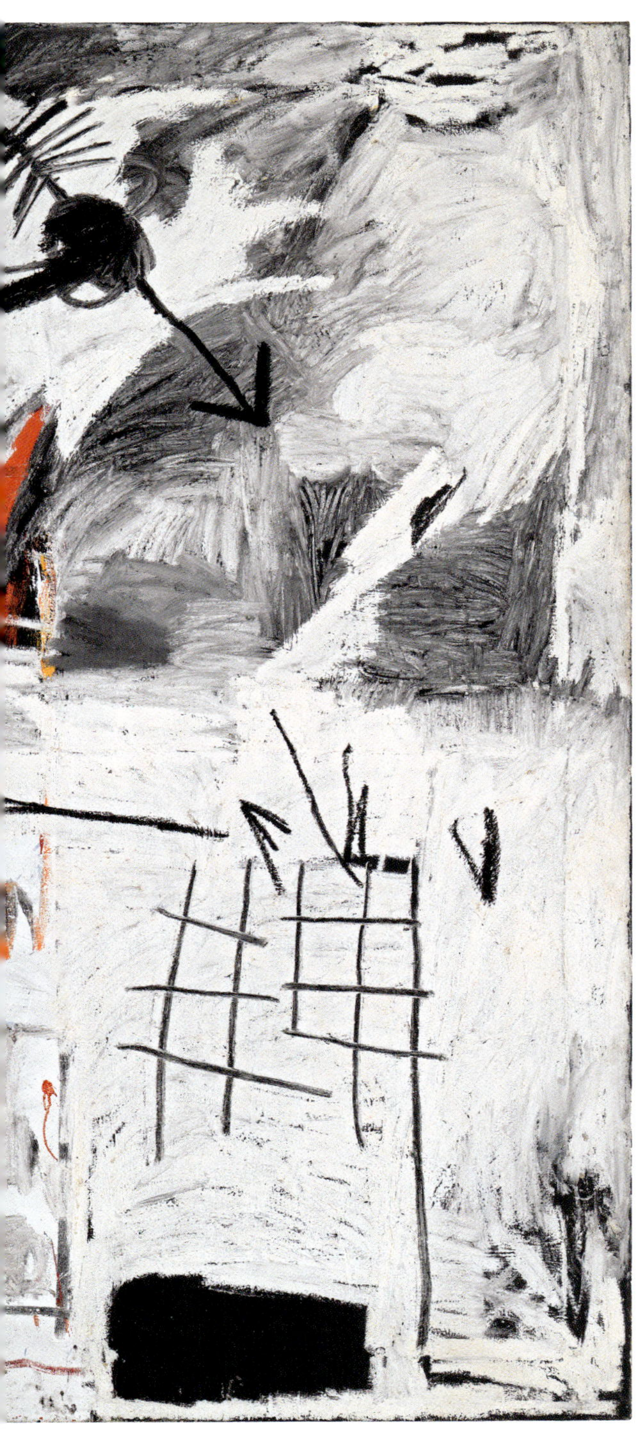

Self-Portrait, 1982
Acrylic and oilstick on linen,
193 x 239 cm / 76 x 94 inches

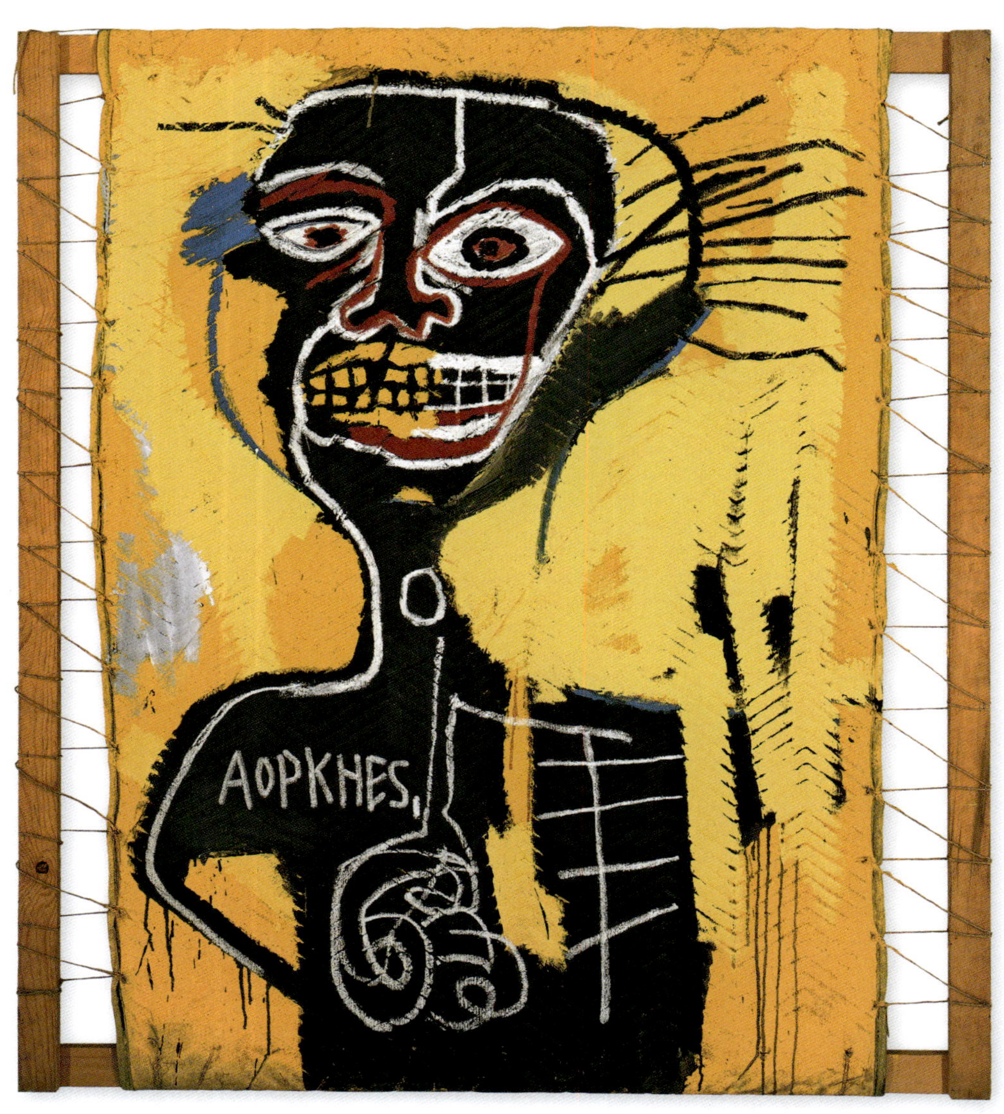

Cabeza, 1982
Acrylic and oilstick on blanket
mounted on wooden supports,
169.5 x 152.5 cm / 66 ³/₄ x 60 inches

Santo versus Second Avenue, 1982
Acrylic, oilstick, and paper collage on
canvas mounted on wooden supports,
137 x 106.5 cm / 54 x 42 inches

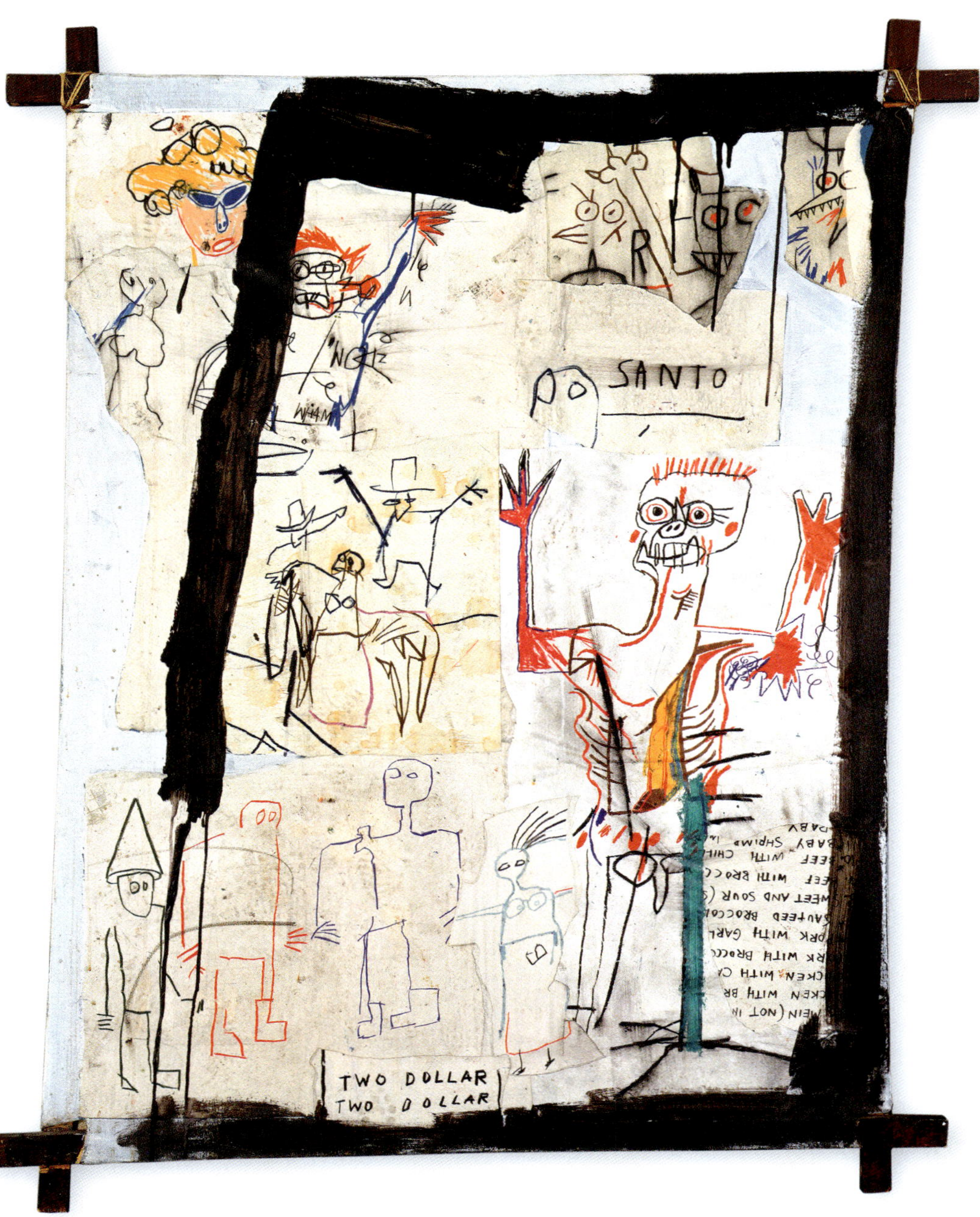

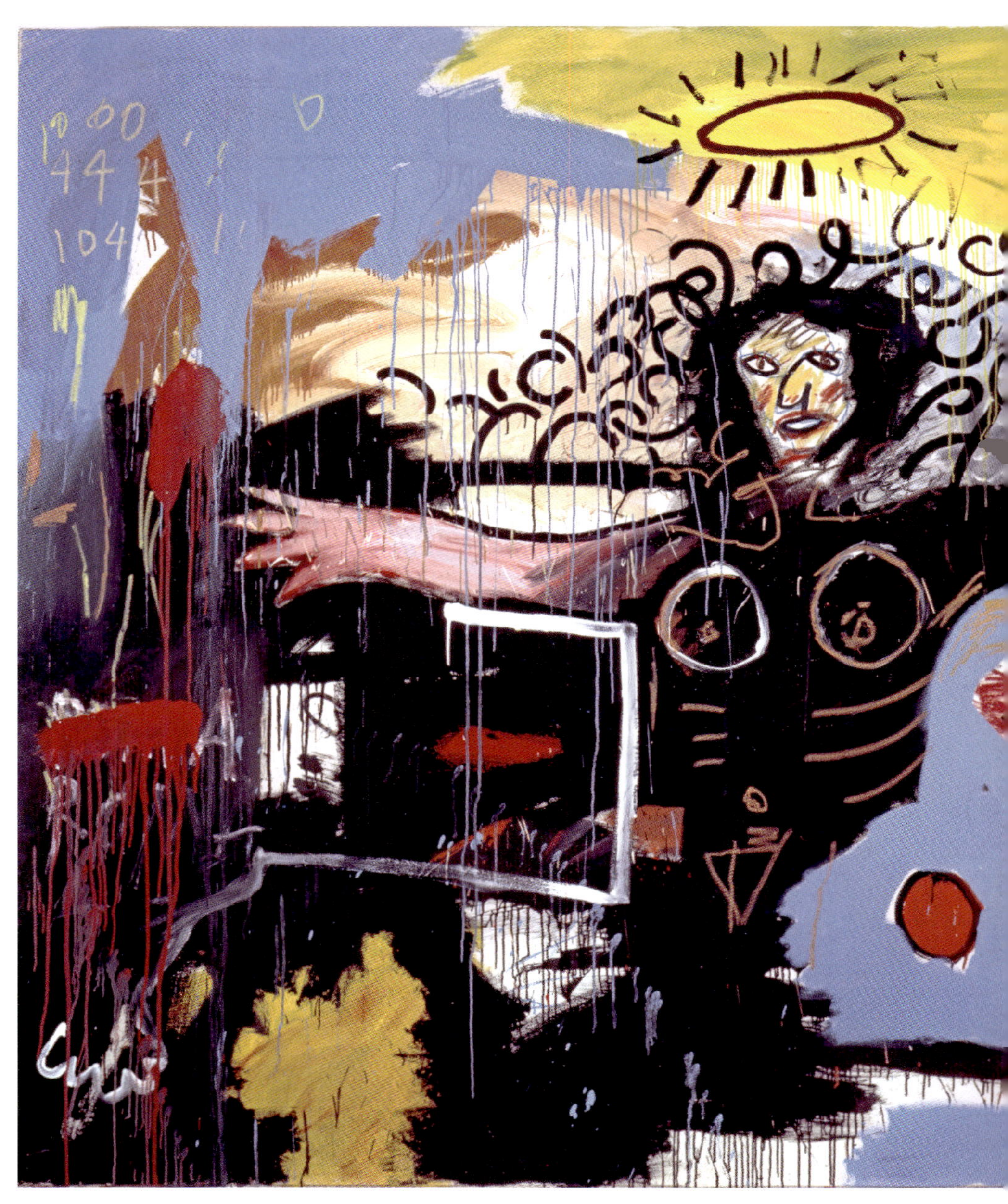

Untitled, 1982
Acrylic on canvas,
241 x 420 cm / 95 x 165 1/4 inches

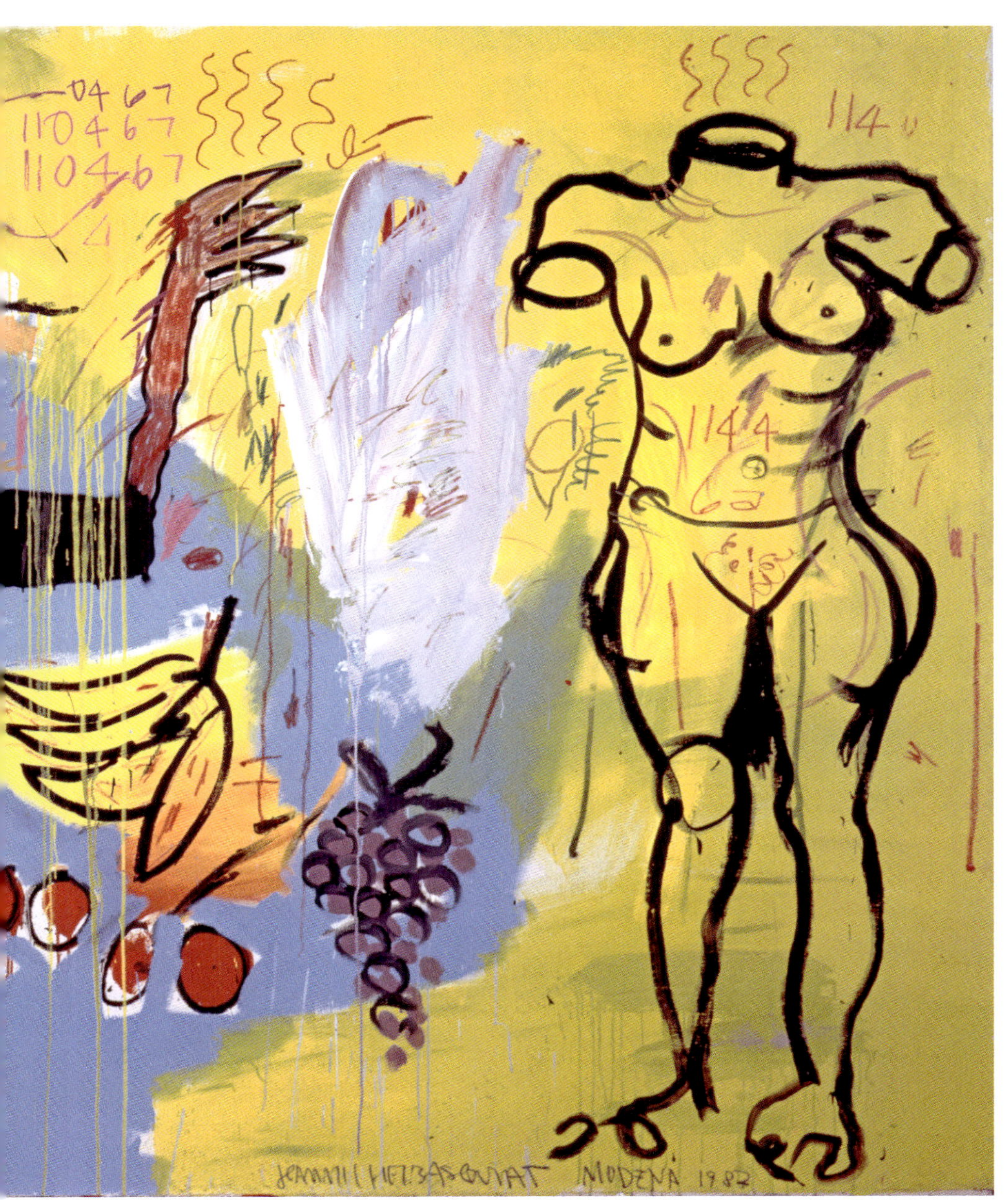
Jean Michel Basquiat MODENA 1982

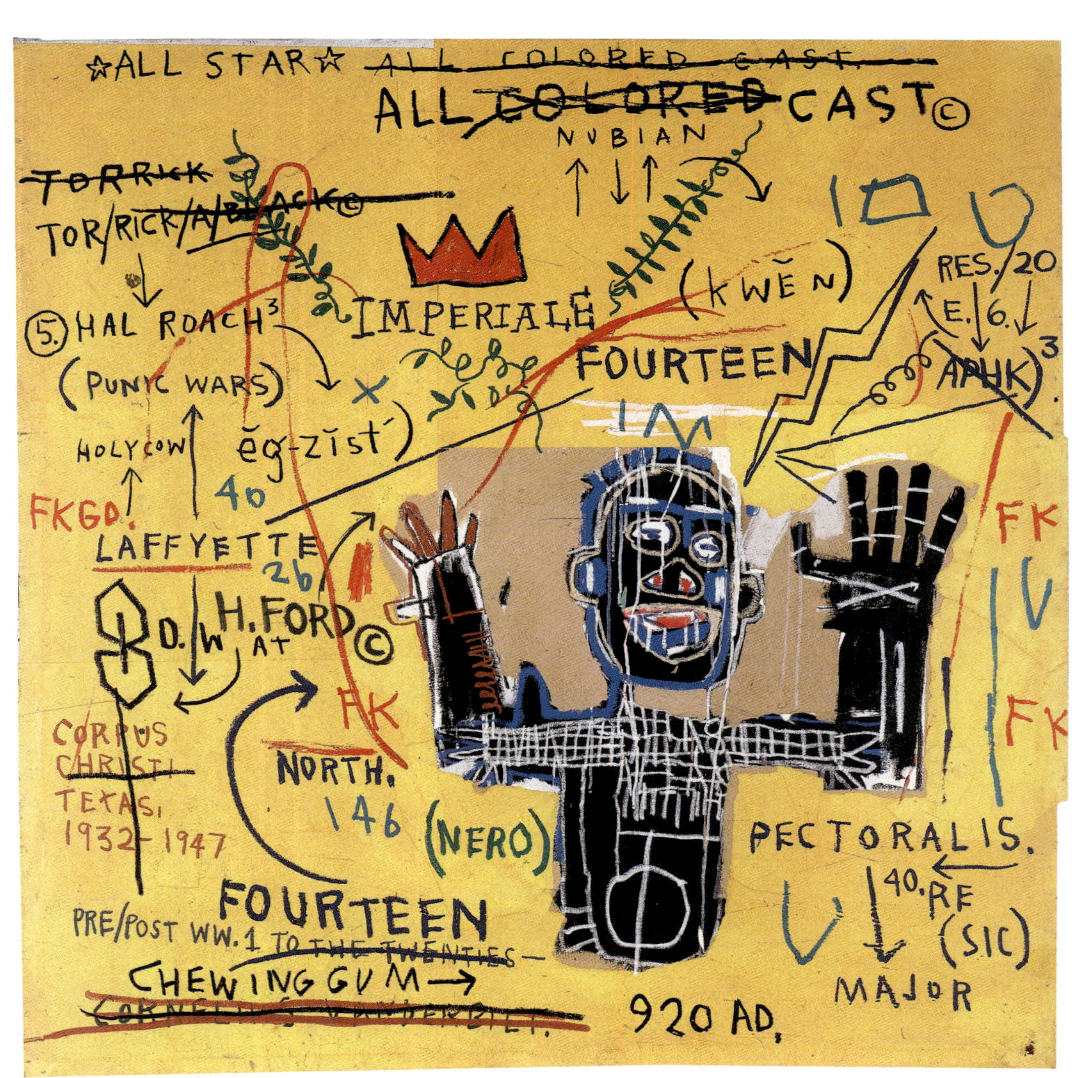

All Colored Cast (Part I), 1982
Acrylic and oilstick on canvas,
152.5 x 152.5 cm / 60 x 60 inches

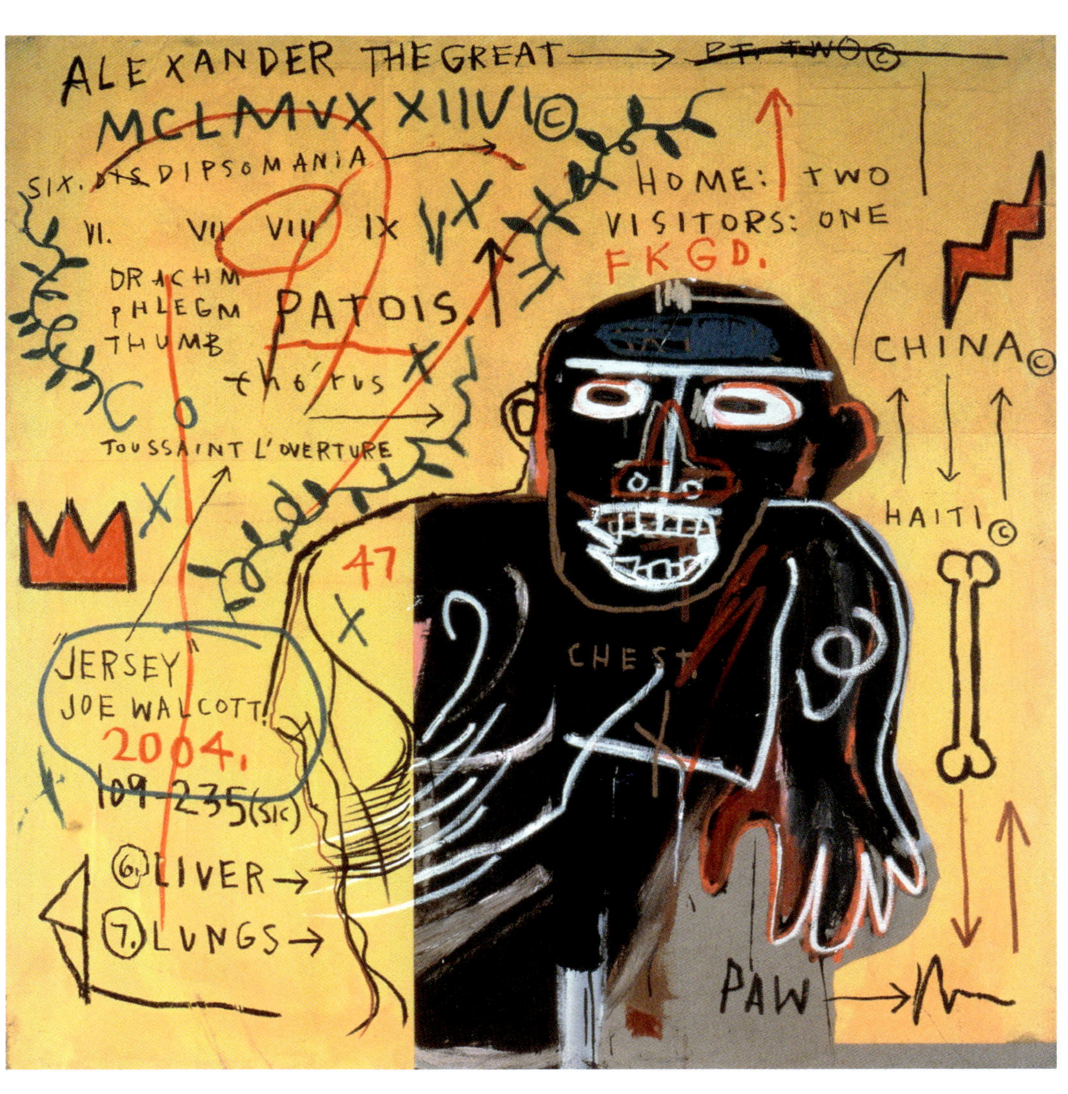

All Colored Cast (Part II), 1982
Acrylic and oilstick on canvas,
152.5 x 152.5 cm / 60 x 60 inches

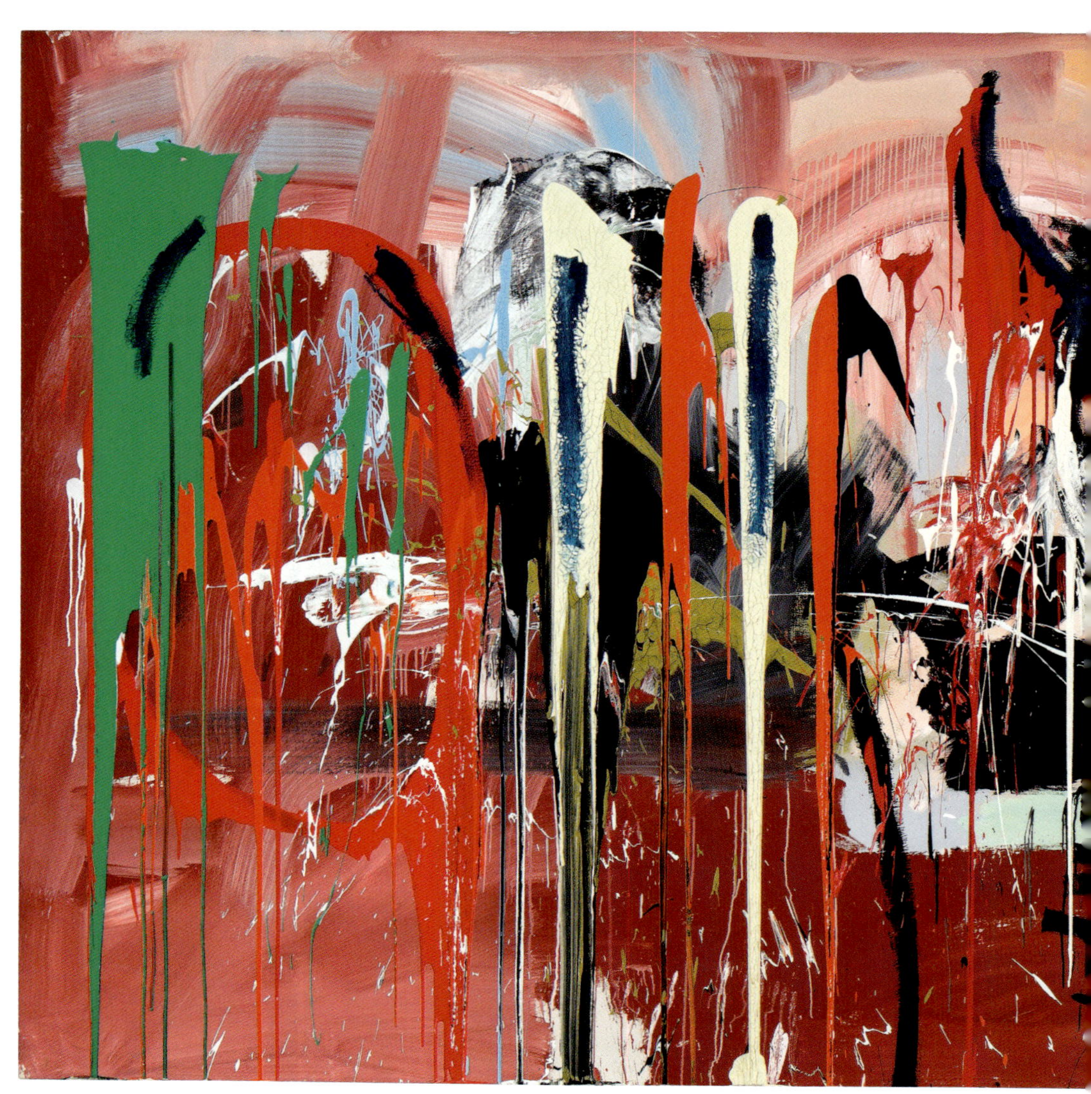

Untitled (Devil), 1982
Acrylic on canvas,
239 x 500 cm / 94 x 197 inches

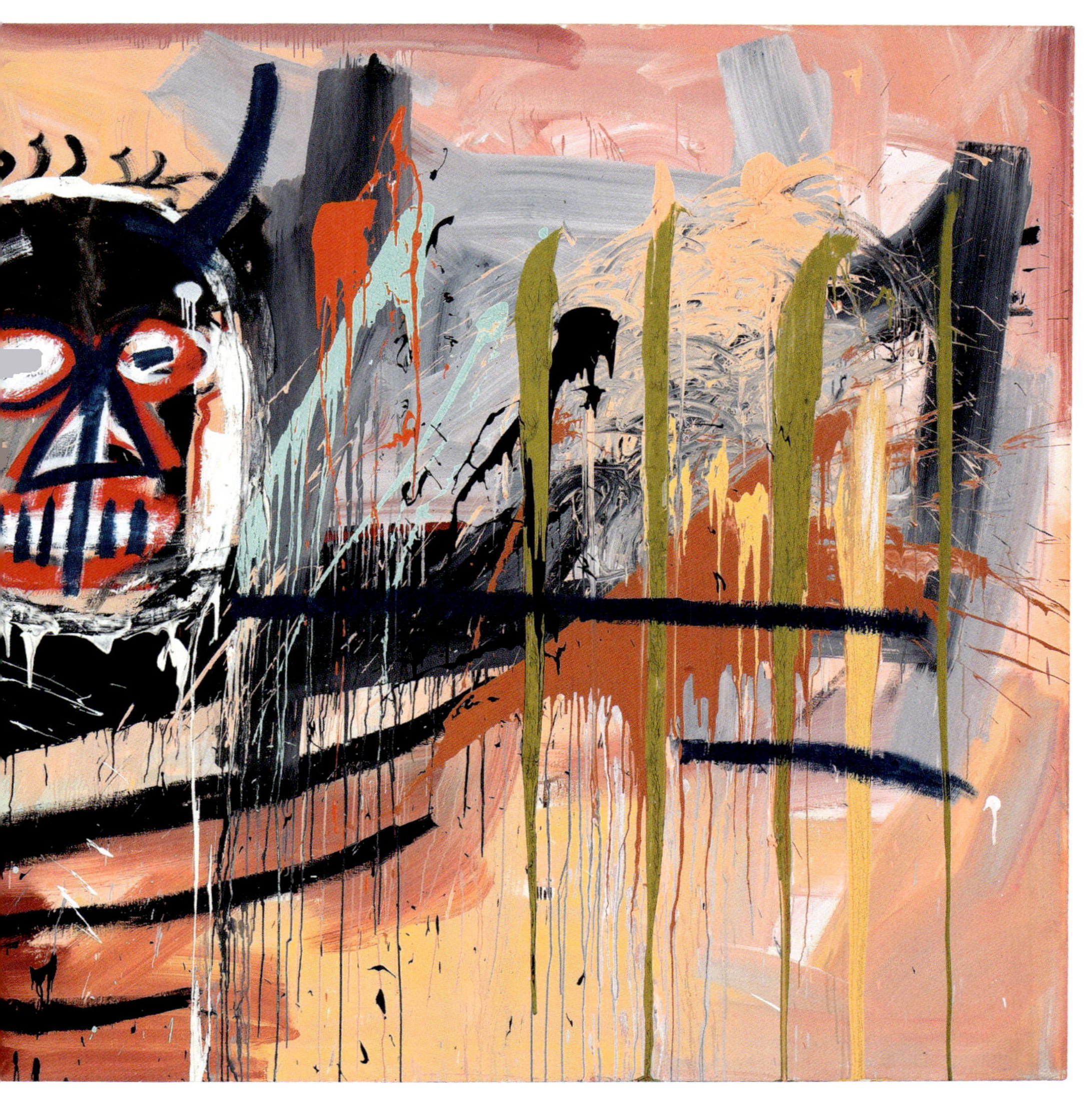

Self-Portrait as a Heel (Part Two), 1982
Acrylic and oilstick on canvas,
244 x 156 cm / 96 x 61 ¹/₂ inches

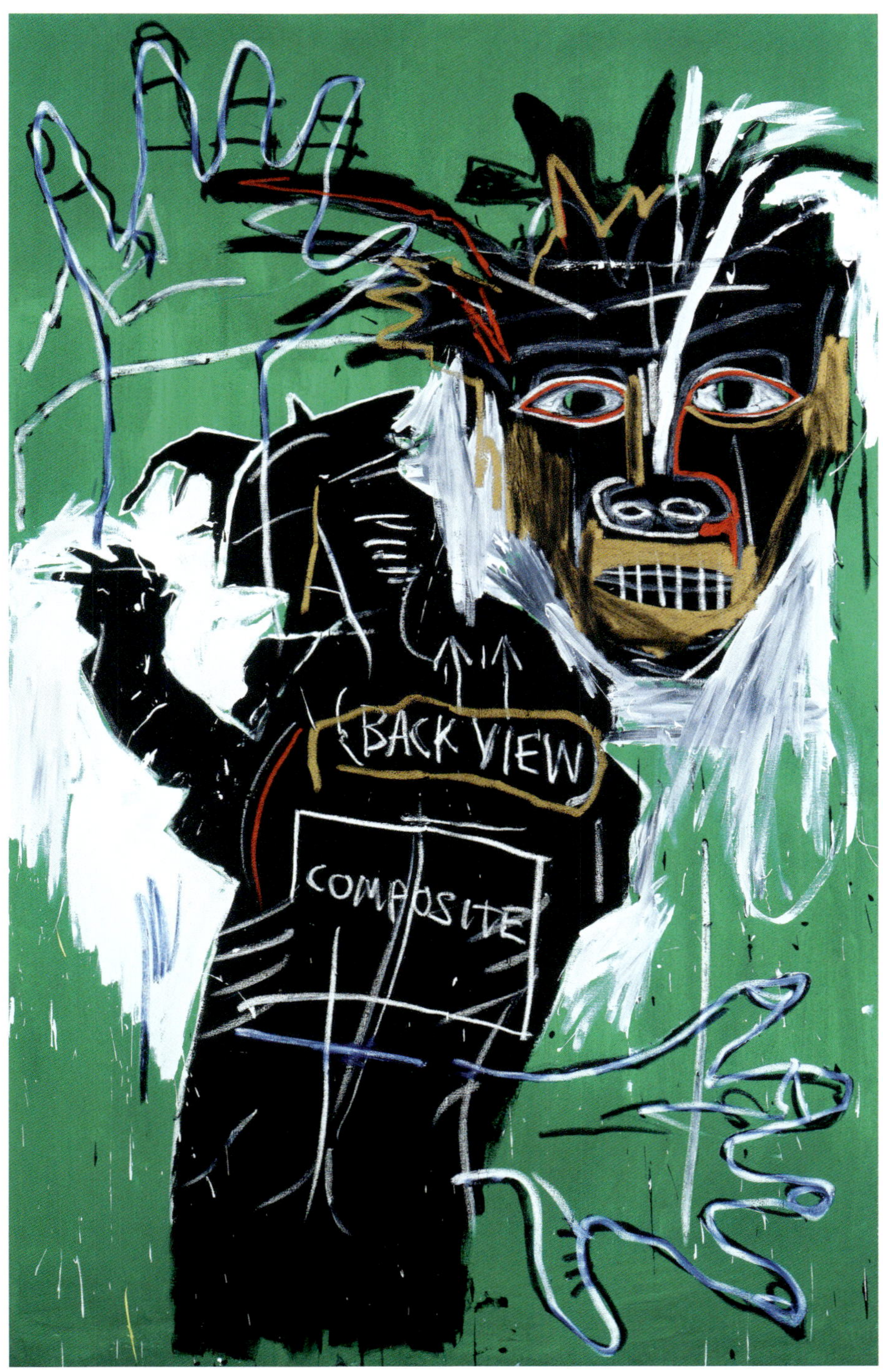

BACK VIEW
COMPOSITE

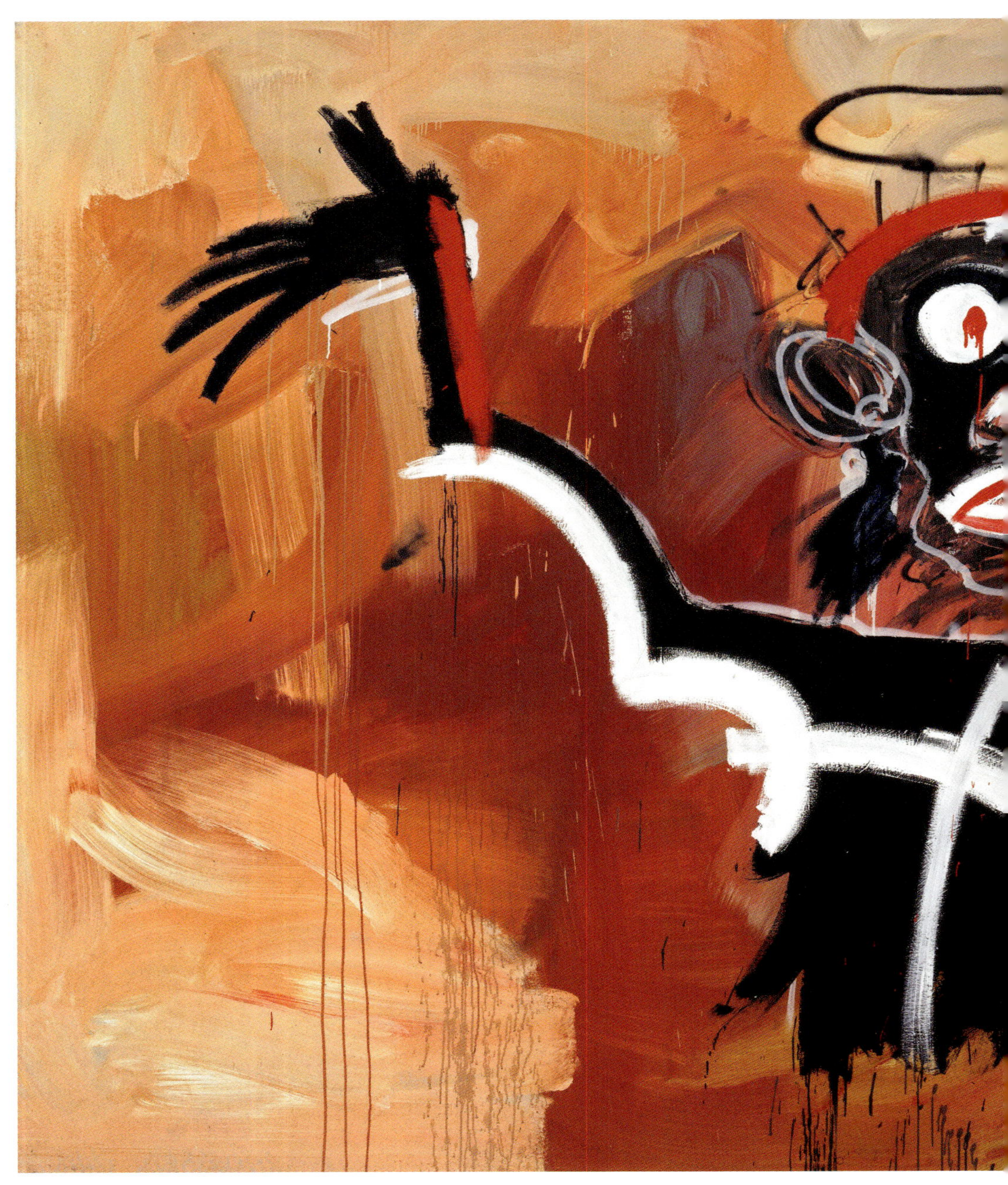

Untitled (Angel), 1982
Acrylic on canvas,
244 x 429 cm / 96 x 169 inches

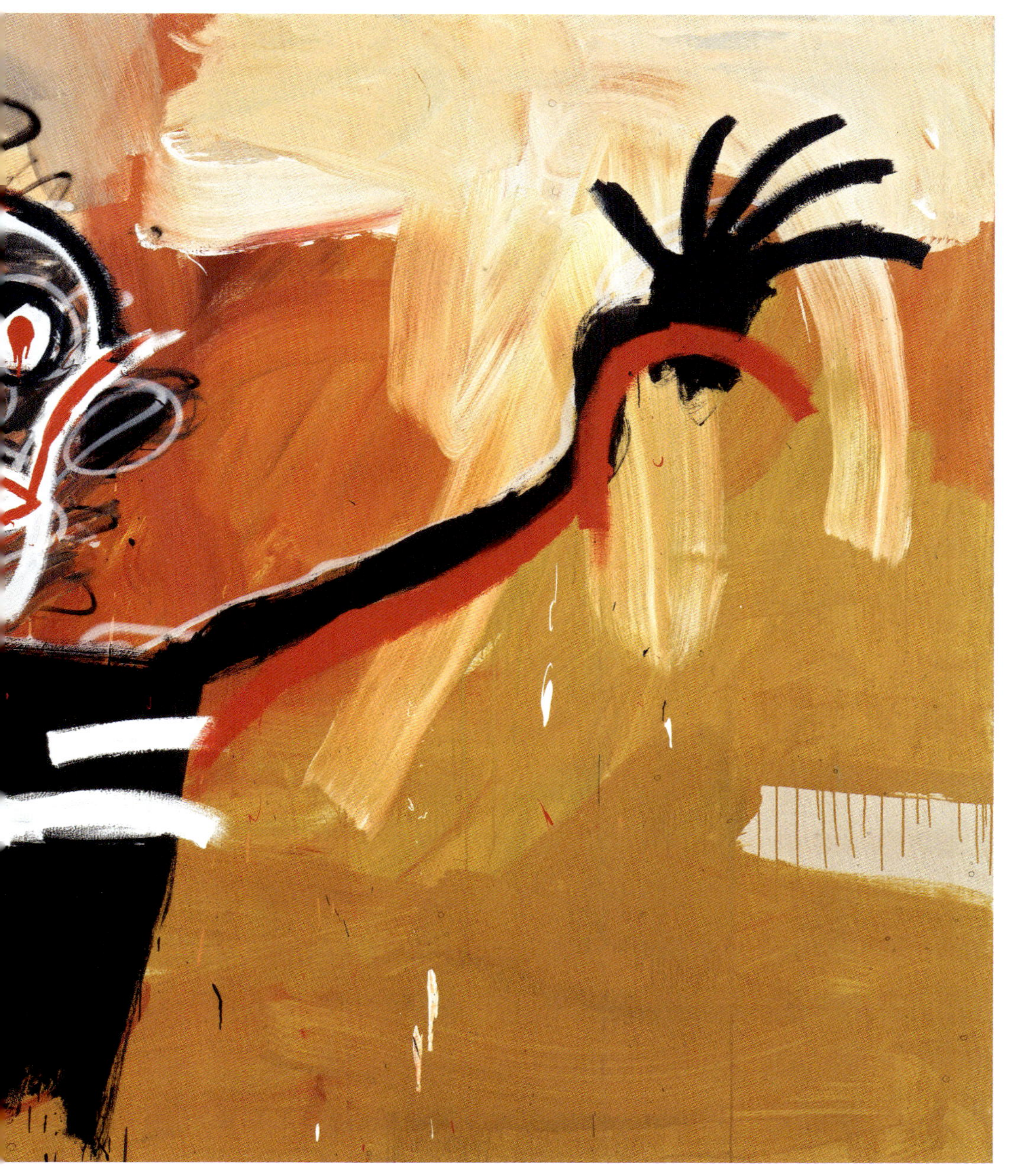

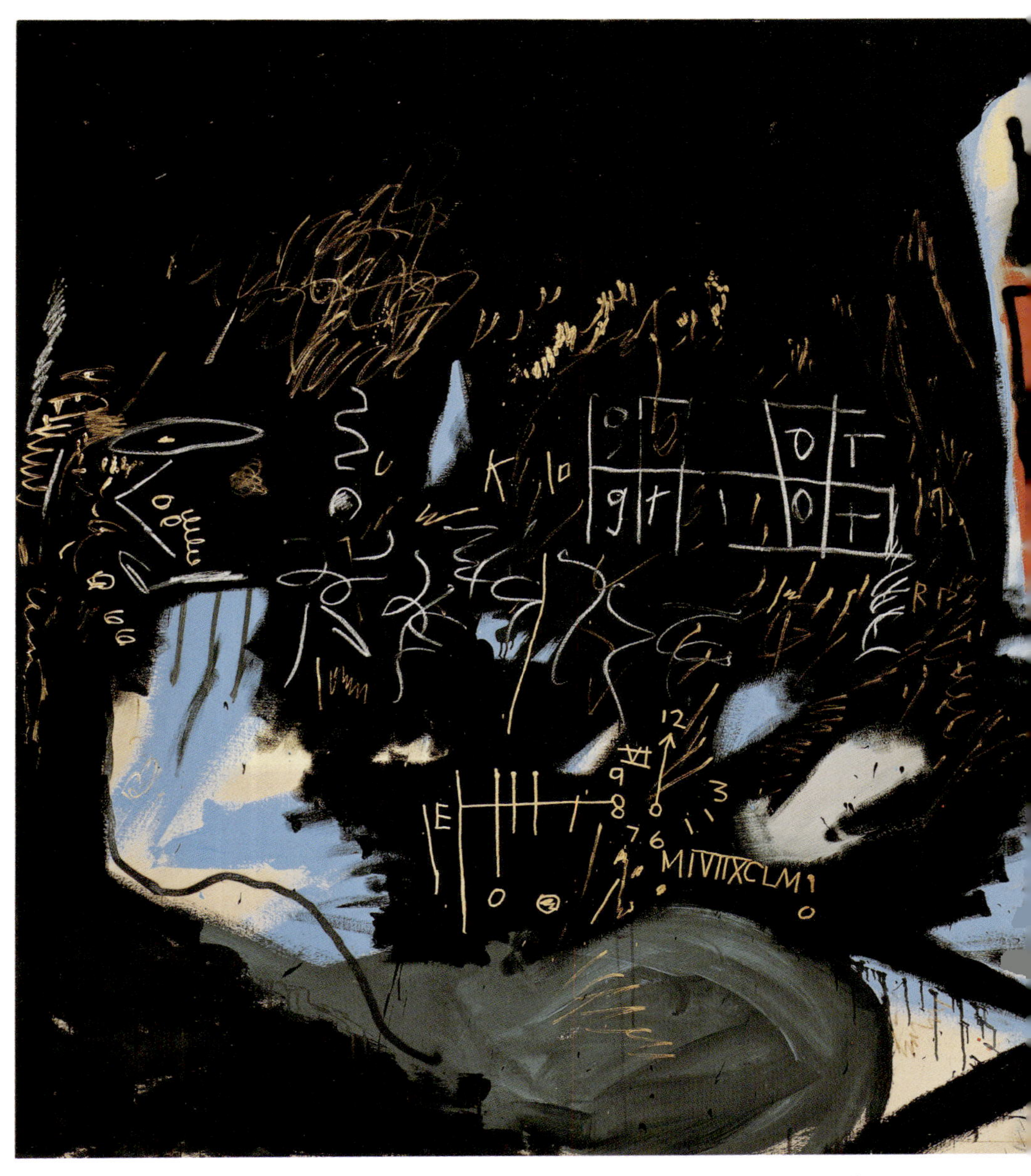

Profit I, 1982
Acrylic and spray paint on canvas,
220 x 400 cm / 86 ¹/₂ x 157 ¹/₂ inches

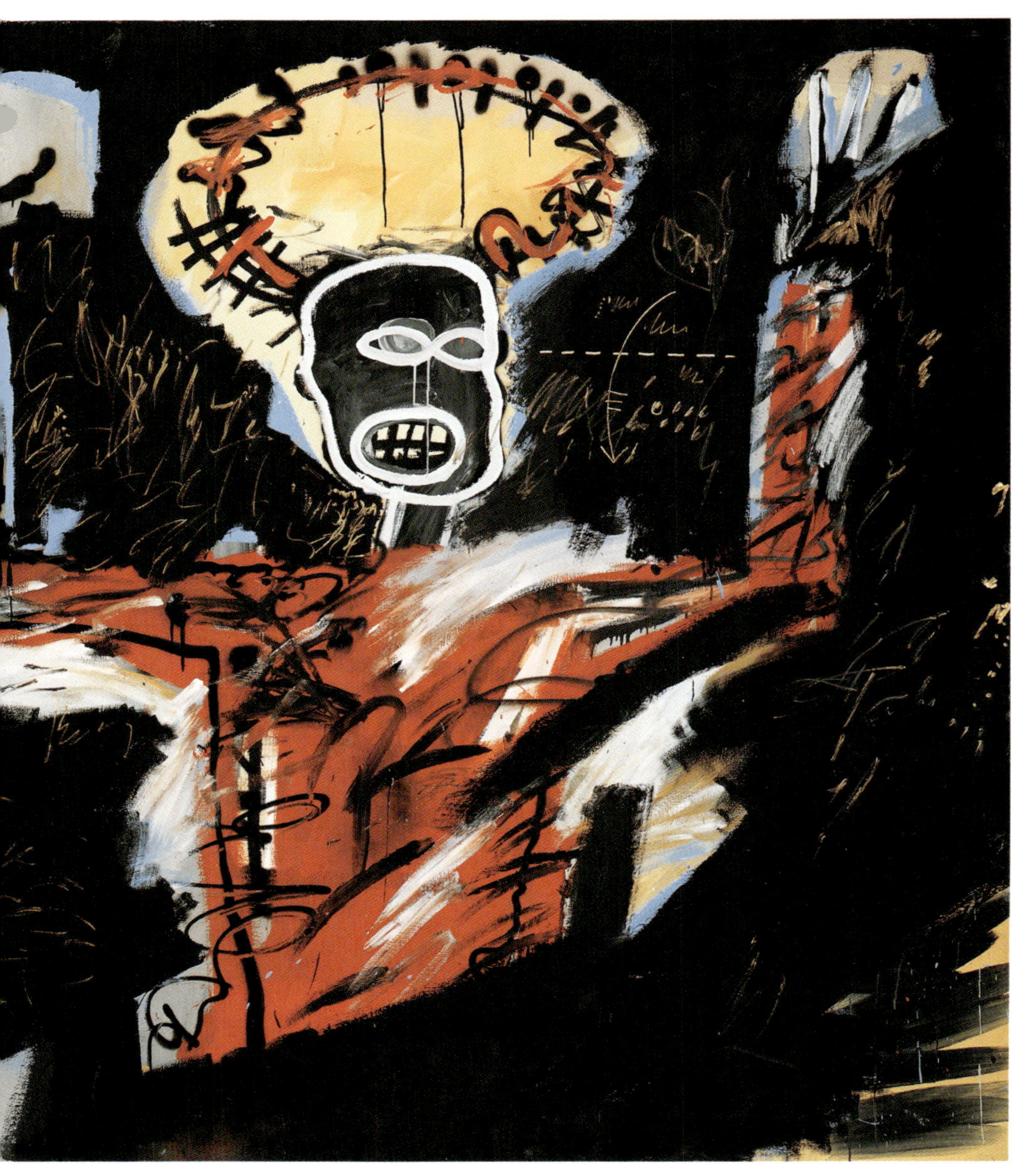

IV.

1983
A Graphic Punch

*Henry Geldzahler: "Is that something you've done from
your childhood, lists of things?" Jean-Michel Basquiat:
"That was from going to Italy, and copying names
out of tour books, and condensed histories."
HG: "Is the impulse to know a lot, or is the impulse
to copy things that strike you?" JMB: "Well, originally
I wanted to copy the whole history down, but it was too
tedious so I just stuck to the cast of characters."
HG: "So they're kinds of indexes to encyclopedias that
don't exist." JMB: "I just like the names."[1]*

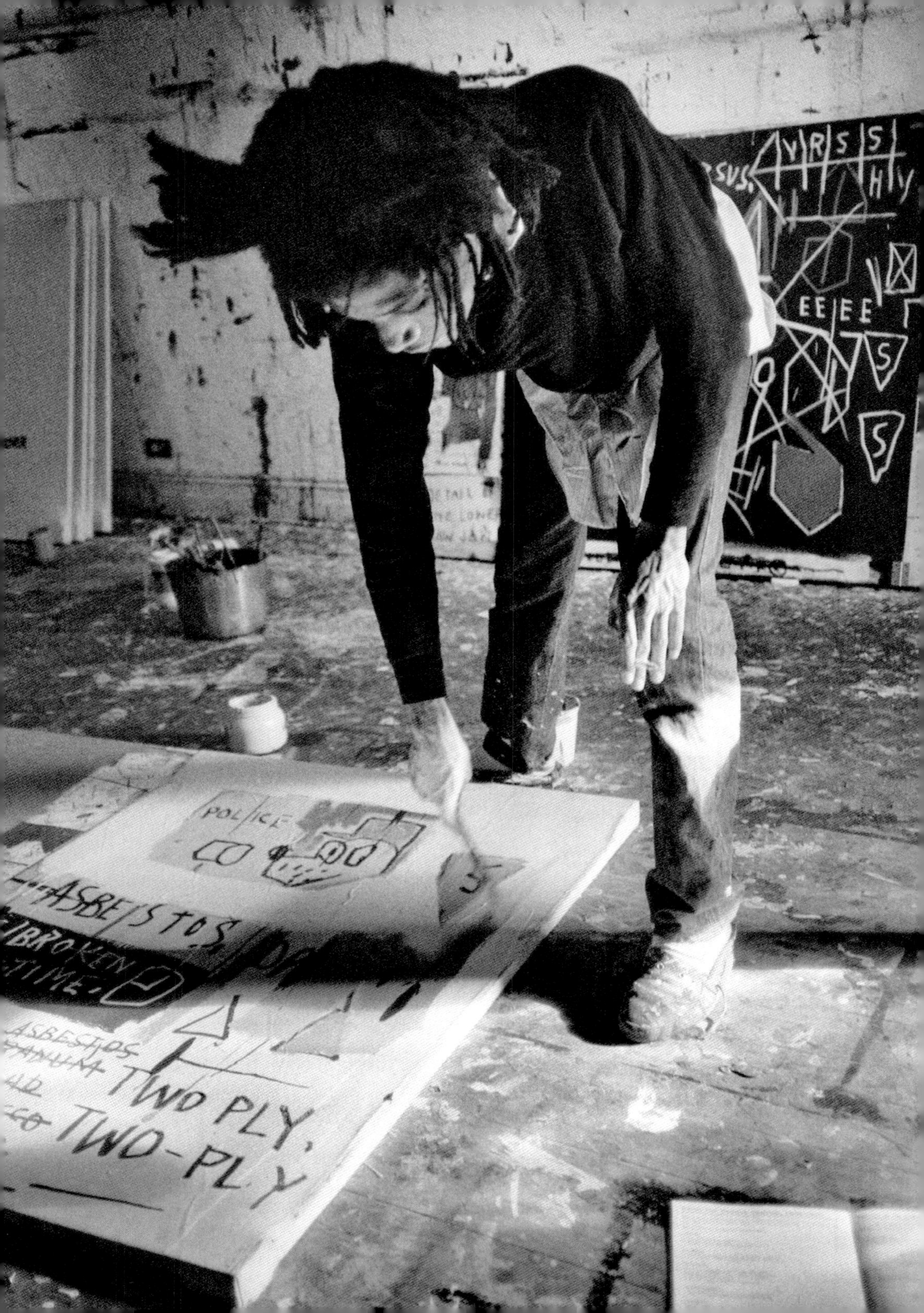
POLICE
ASBESTOS
BROKEN
TIME
ASBESTOS
TWO PLY.
TWO-PLY

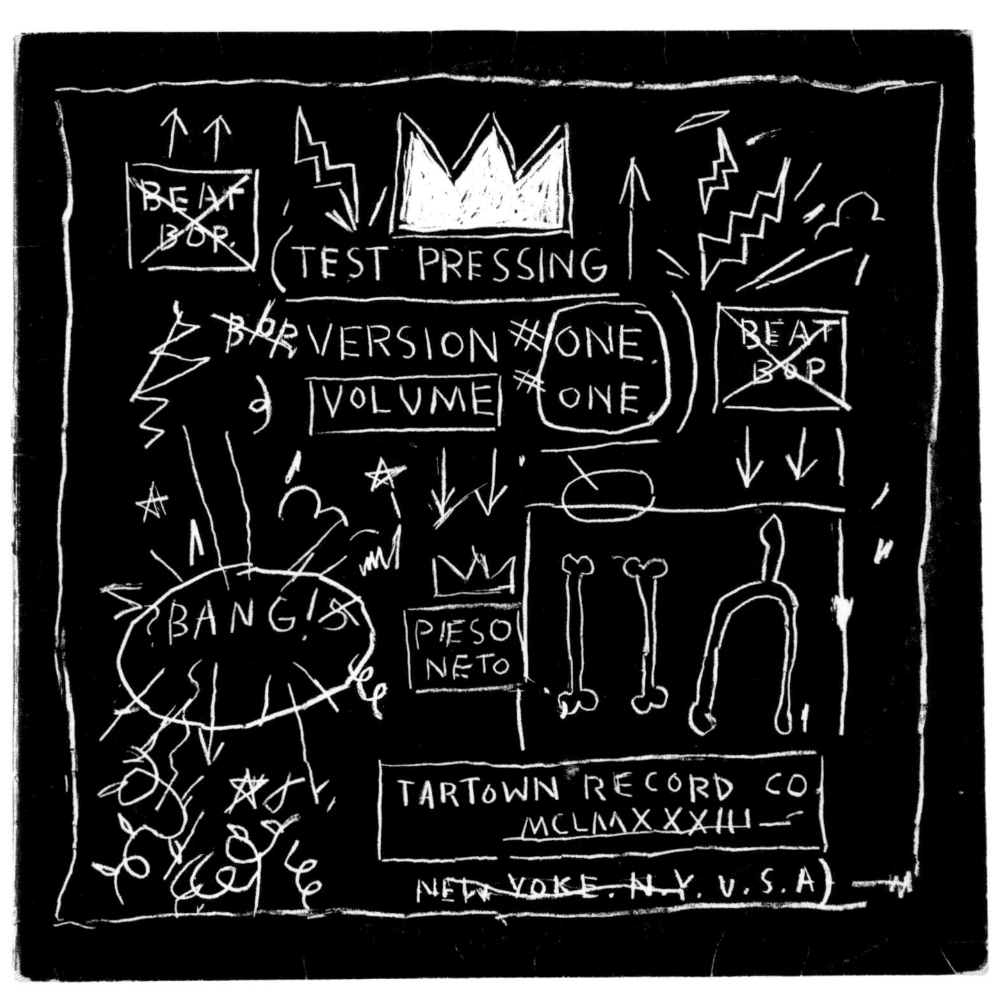

Rammellzee vs. K-Rob, "Beat Bop," 1983, 12-inch single released on Tartown, produced and cover designed by Jean-Michel Basquiat

Page 237: Jean-Michel Basquiat in his Crosby Street studio, New York 1983. Photo Roland Hagenberg

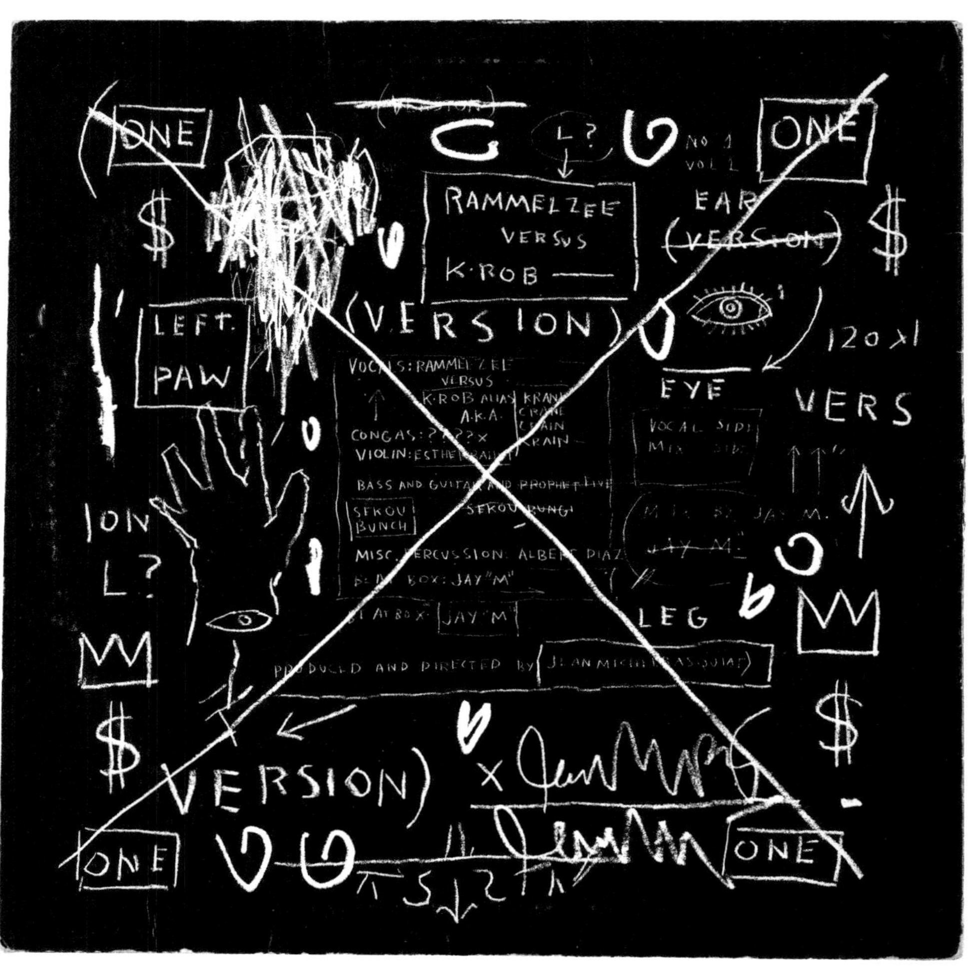

The January issue of Warhol's *Interview* magazine runs a conversation between Basquiat and Henry Geldzahler, accompanied with a portrait of the artist by James van der Zee (p. 497), a legendary photographer who was already central to the Harlem Renaissance of the 1920s. With characteristic hesitancy, Basquiat discusses his current life and work: HG: "Do you feel a hectic need to get a lot of work done?" JMB: "No. I just don't know what else to do with myself." HG: "Painting is your activity, and that's what you do …" JMB: "Pretty much. A little socializing." HG: "I've noticed in the recent work you've gone back to the idea of not caring how well stretched it is; part of the work seems to be casual." JMB: "Everything is well stretched even though it looks like it may not be."[2]

The artist also mentions a preference for very immediate images: "I like the ones where I don't paint as much as others, where it's just a direct idea." Some of these especially stark pictures of this year simply show sparse lettering in white on black blown up large, while his incredibly varied output also includes 20-feet-wide complex polyptychs with up to seven panels that can be folded together on hinges and carried out the studio door.

The 12-inch single "Beat Bop" by Rammellzee and K-Rob appears. This foundational hip hop track was originally planned as a battle rap between Basquiat and Rammellzee; in the end the artist funds and designs the release and receives a producer credit. In March, Basquiat participates in the Whitney Biennial; in May, he has another exhibition at Gagosian in Los Angeles, a city in which he now often stays. Suzanne Muchnic reviews the show for the *L.A. Times*: "In a show of recent paintings, many of them done in the last four months while he has been living in Los Angeles, we see art that delivers a graphic punch and conveys a convincing air of urban anxiety. It does so with the tools of Abstract Expressionism and language. Current works seem less painterly than the batch he showed here about a year ago, but what they lack in surface interest they make up in brutish stylishness."[3]

Basquiat starts dating Paige Powell, an editor for Warhol's *Interview* magazine. Since he now has no dealer in New York, he shows privately at her apartment. Through her, he also grows closer to Warhol, and in August he rents a new studio apartment at 57 Great Jones Street from the older artist, who a month later notes in his diary: "Jean-Michel called, he wanted some philosophy, he came over and we talked, and he's afraid he's just going to be a flash in the pan. And I told him not to worry, that he wouldn't be. But then I got scared because he's rented our building on Great Jones and what if he is a flash in the pan and doesn't have the money to pay his rent?"[4]

On September 15, graffiti artist Michael Stewart dies after a violent beating in New York City police custody. Basquiat is deeply shocked: he has known Stewart personally, and as a black man he feels as vulnerable to police brutality as the victim. In the aftermath, he

With Strings Two, 1983
Acrylic and oilstick on canvas,
244 x 152.5 cm / 96 x 60 inches

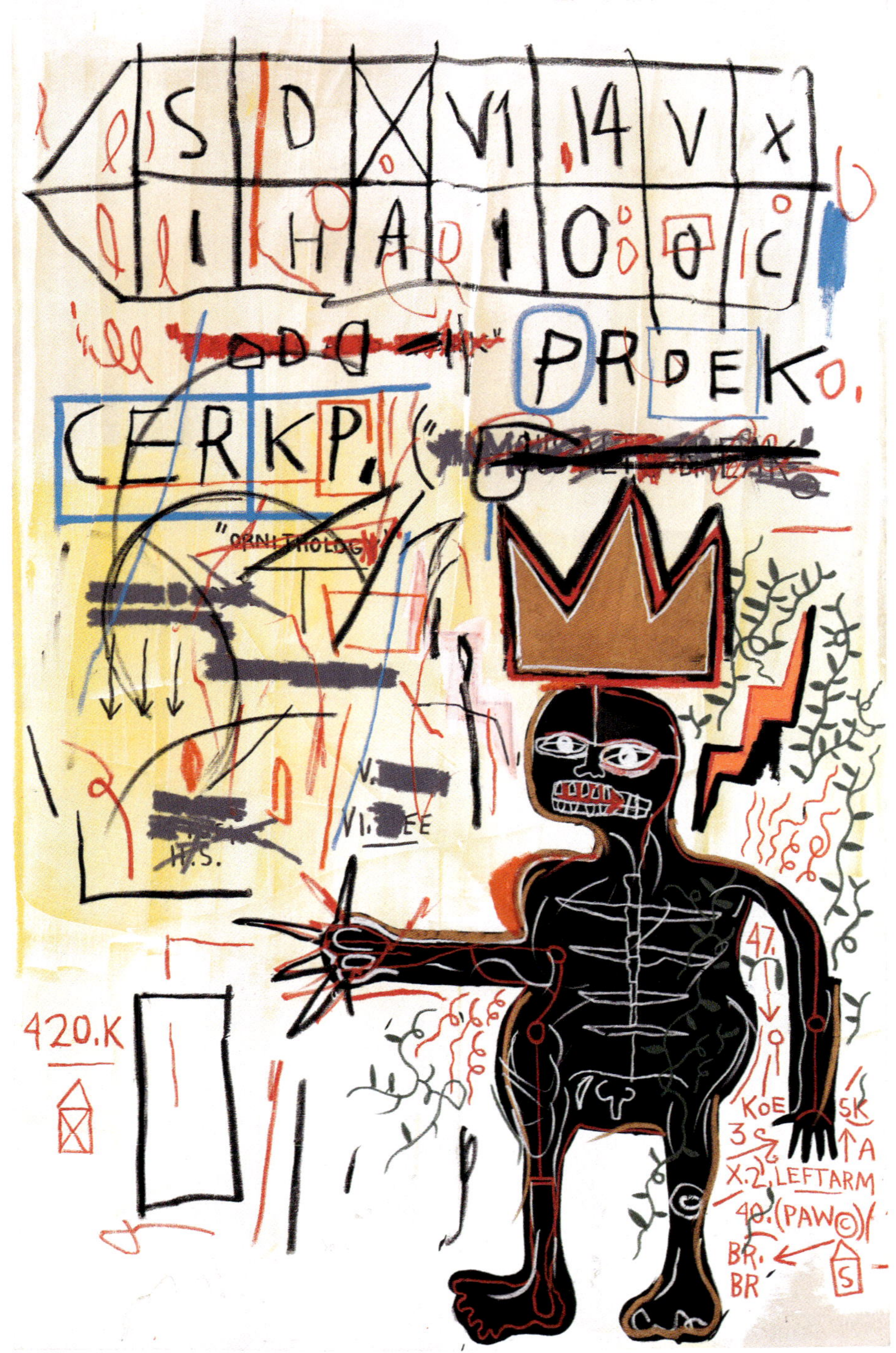
S D VI .14 V X
HA 1 O C
PR DE K,
CERKP.
"ORNITHOLOGY"
H.S.
VI. EE
420.K
47.
KoE 5K
3 A
X.2. LEFTARM
40.(PAW©)
BR.
BR

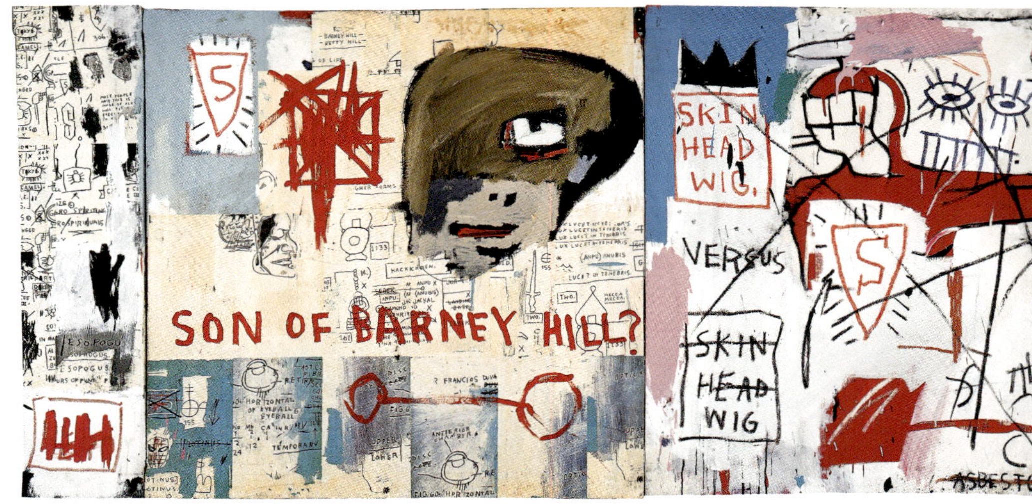

paints *Defacement (The Death of Michael Stewart)* (1983; pp. 74/75), originally on a wall in Keith Haring's studio, from which it is then transferred to canvas.

In October Basquiat travels with Warhol to Madrid, Zürich, and Milan, where he is interviewed for *Domus* magazine by Lisa Ponti: "You like this kind of nomadic life? two continents, different towns?" JMB: "Very much." LP: "You like to be called The Black Picasso?" JMB: "Not so much. It's flattering, but I think it is also demeaning." LP: "Do you think you are lucky?" JMB: "Talented, too." LP: "What do you think of the critics who say art is dead?" JMB: "When they were making Dada, when Picasso was around ... the same stuff about art being dead. Those guys are outside of art, you know, they aren't in it, you know what I mean? Too much free dinners for them, you know? They drink cheap wine at the openings, they get drunk, and they get nasty ..." LP: "Which are the people you like to discuss art with?" JMB: "I don't like to discuss art at all."[5]

Life Like Son of Barney Hill, 1983
Acrylic, oilstick, and photocopy collage on canvas, polyptych: 122 x 522 cm / 48 x 205 ¹/₂ inches

Pages 244/245: Jean-Michel Basquiat: New Paintings, exhibition view, Gagosian Gallery, Los Angeles 1983

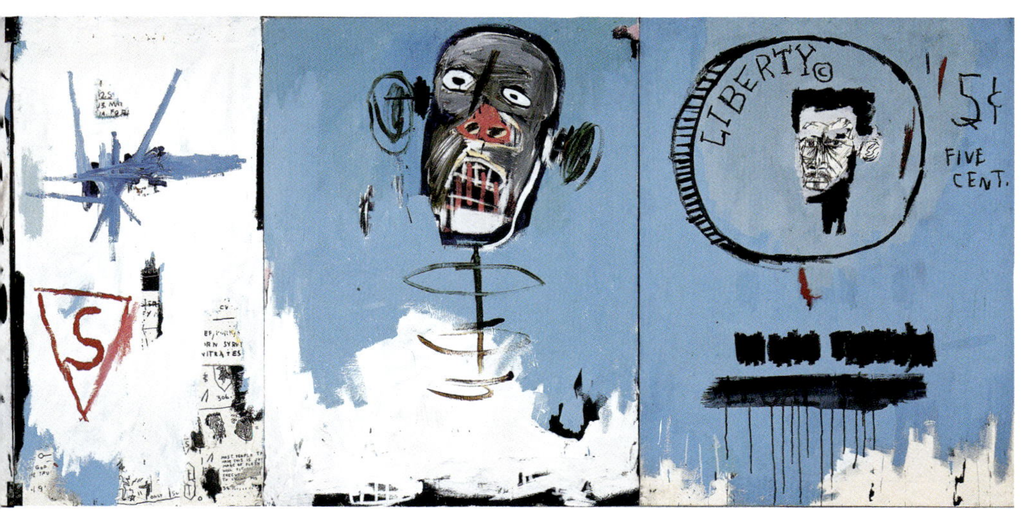

He travels to Tokyo with Bruno Bischofberger for an exhibition at Akira Ikeda Gallery. Initiated by Bischofberger, who is now his exclusive dealer worldwide, he begins collaborating on paintings together with Warhol and Francesco Clemente. Warhol's diary hints at the difficulties of the process involved, clearly worried that they will step on each other toes: "Jean-Michel came up to the office but he was out of it. Clemente brought up some of the paintings that the three of us are working on together, and Jean-Michel was so out of it he began painting away. Jean-Michel and Clemente paint each other out. There's about fifteen paintings that we're working on together."[6]

In December, Basquiat goes back to Los Angeles, then hires a studio in the district of Venice, where he spends the rest of the year with the singer Madonna, who has just released her first album.

[1–6] *See Endnotes on page 508.*

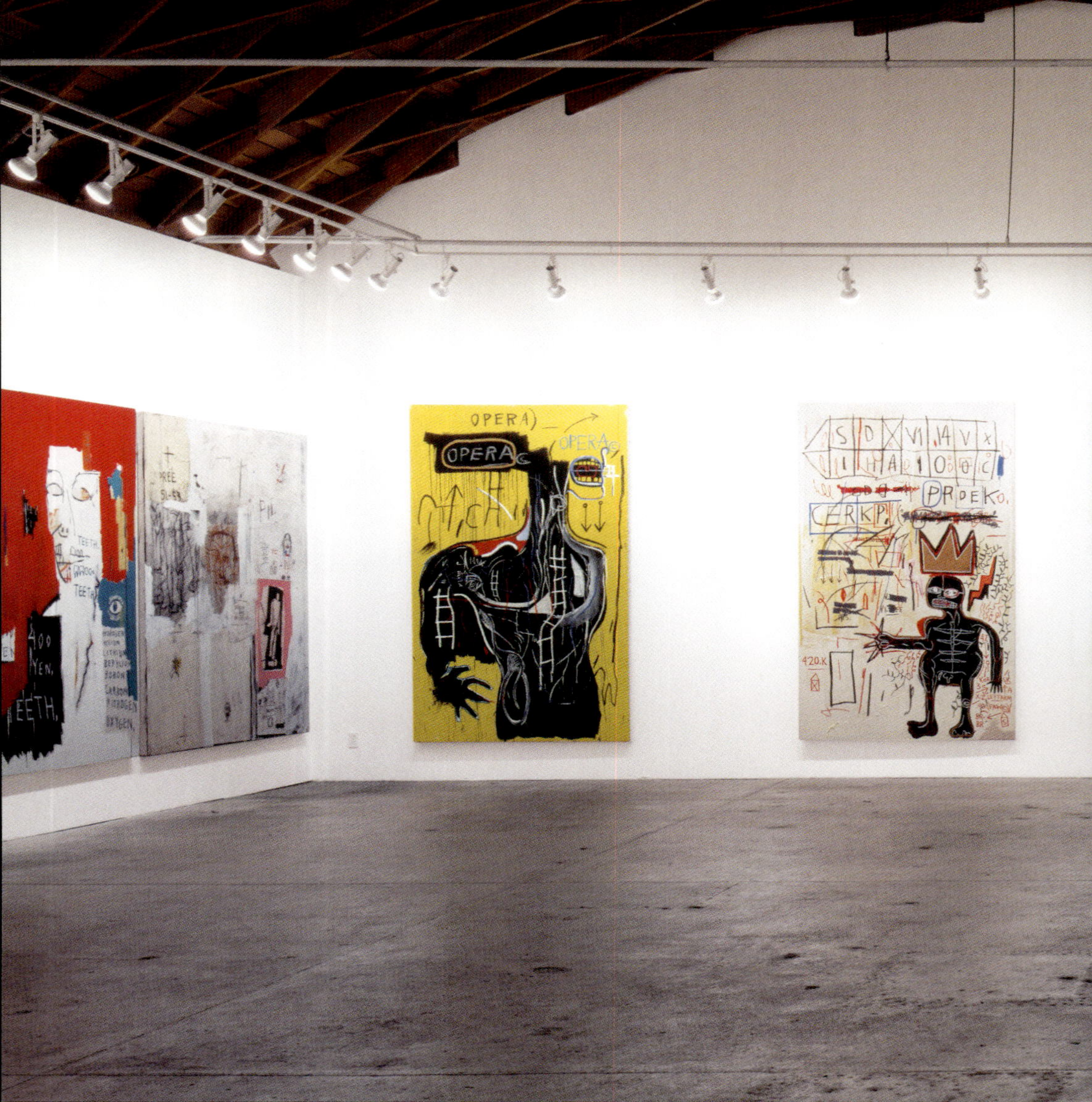

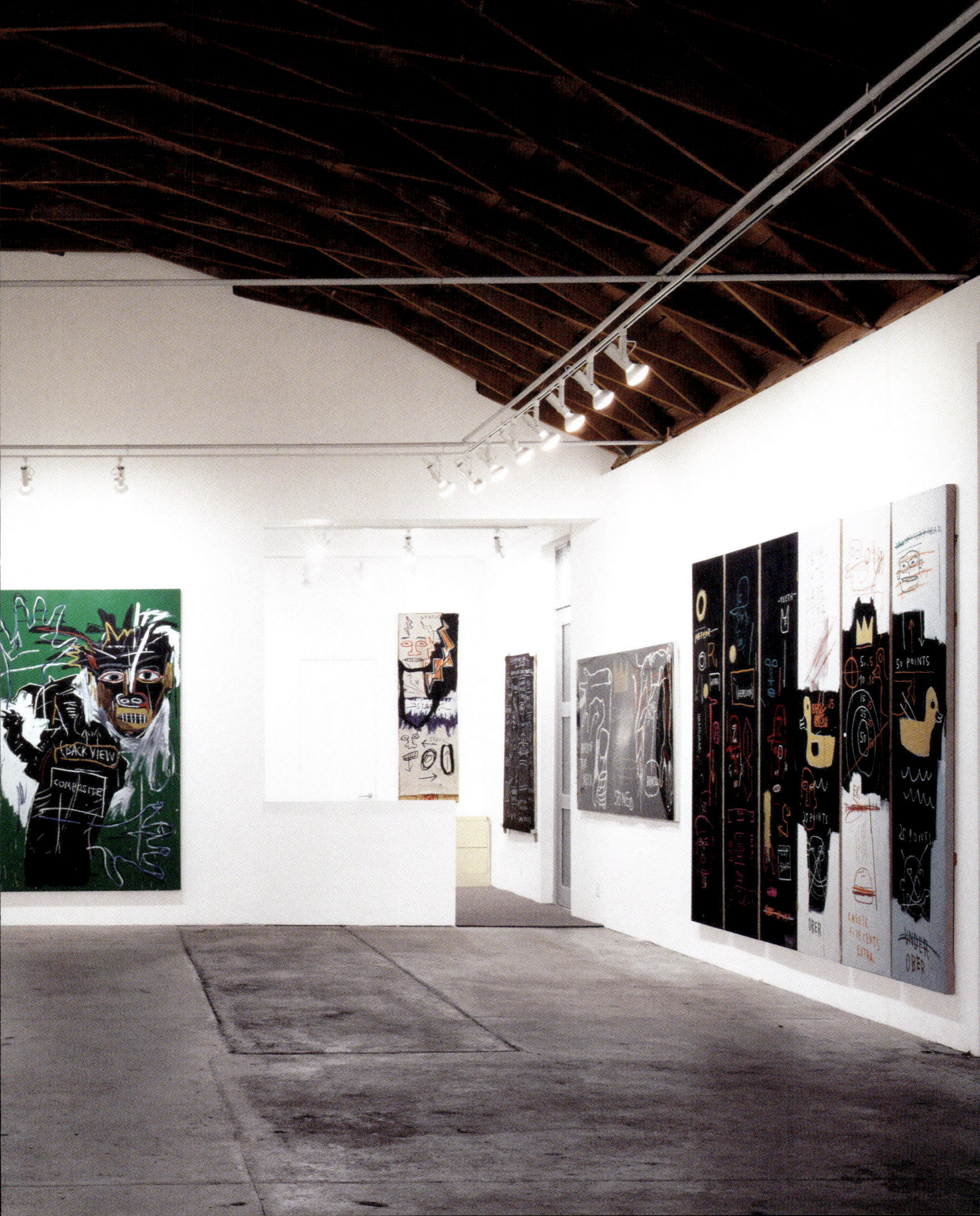

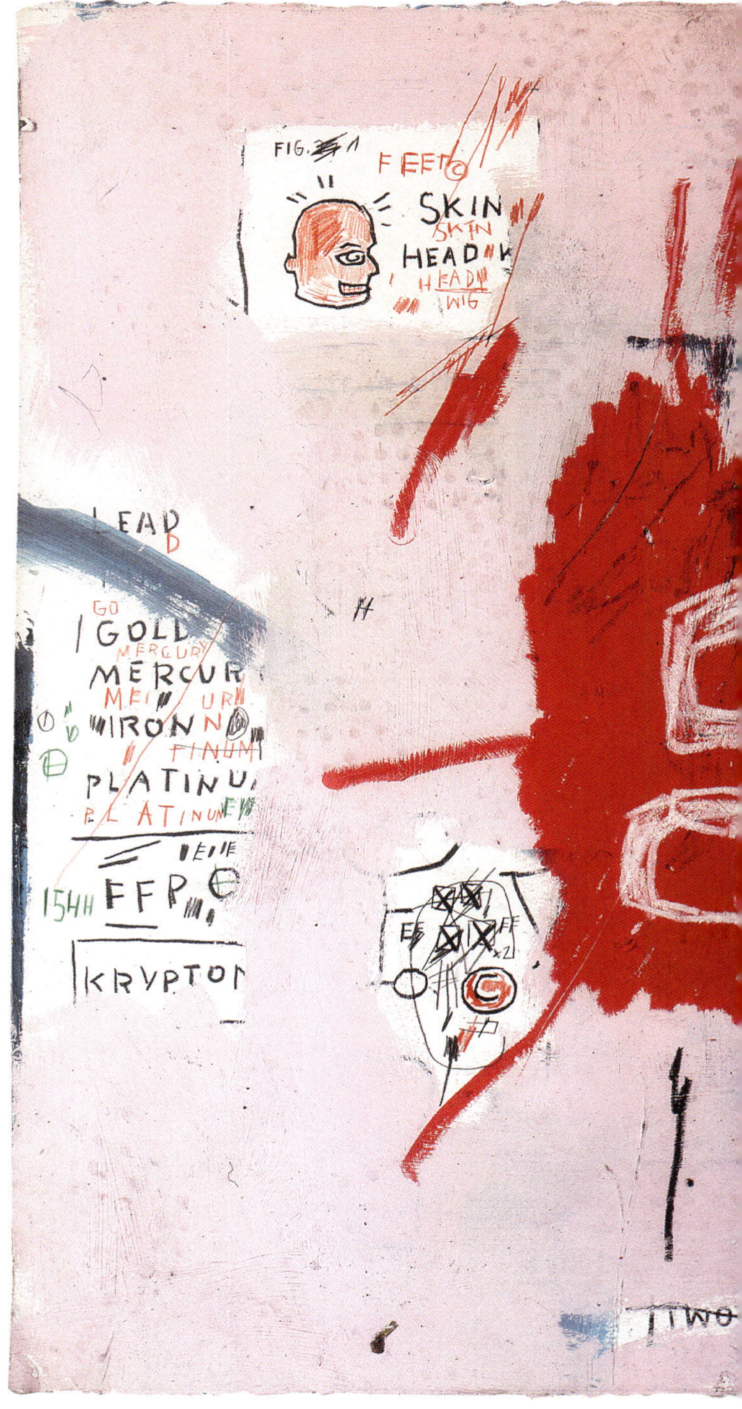

Pages 246–265: **From The Daros Suite**, 1982–1983
Acrylic, oilstick, pastel, crayon, charcoal, and pencil on paper, 32 sheets, each 57 x 76.5 cm / 22 $^1/_2$ x 30 inches

1. **Snakeman**
2. **Olympic**
3. **PPCD**
4. **Napoleon Stereotype as Portrayed**
5. **Ascent**
6. **Liberty**
7. **Leeches**
8. **Formless**
9. **King Alphonso**
10. **Large Body of Water**
11. **Dwellers in the Marshes**
12. **Boxer Rebellion**
13. **Undiscovered Genius**

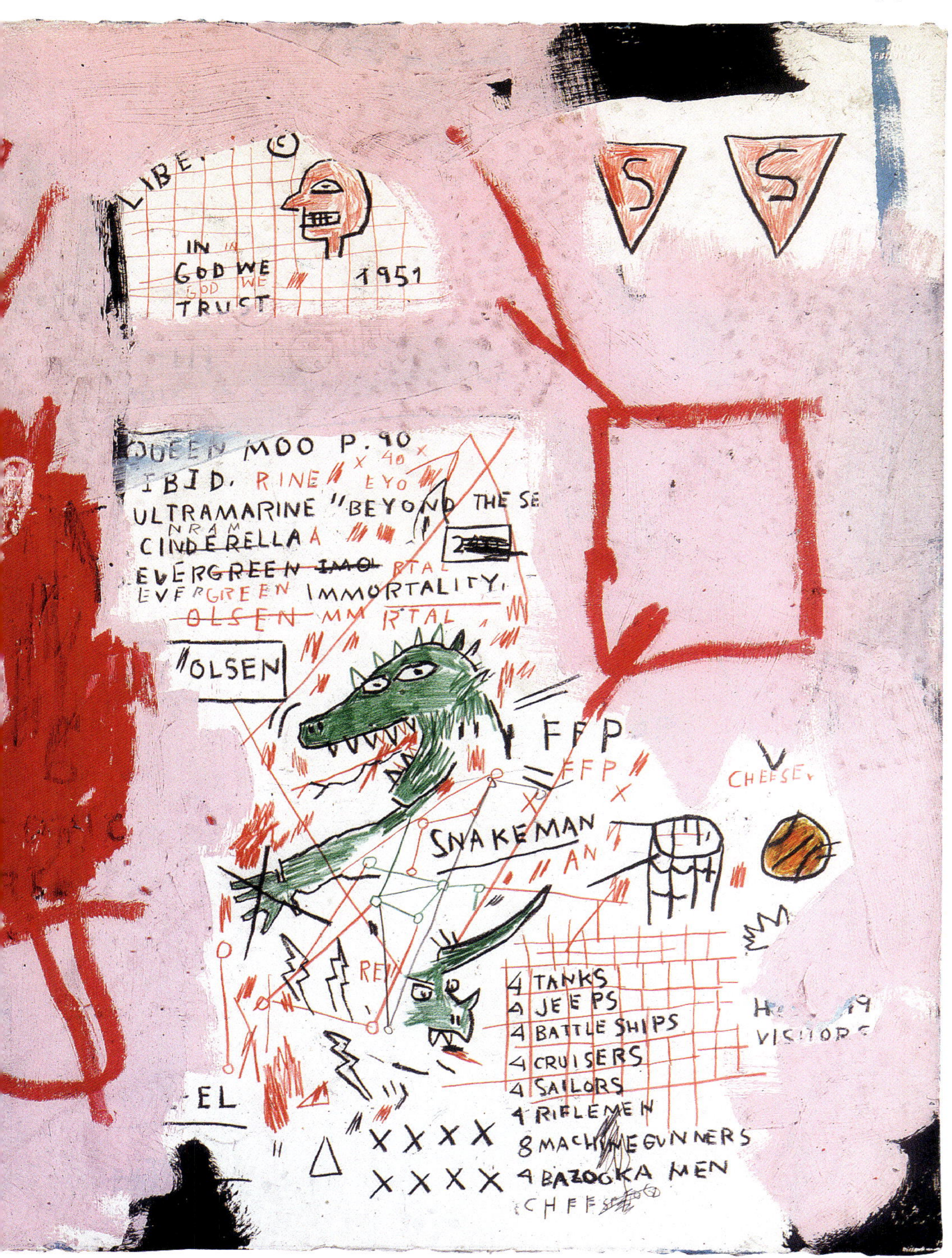

LIBE
IN GOD WE
GOD WE
TRUST
1951
S
S
QUEEN MOO P. 40
IBID. RINE EYO
ULTRAMARINE "BEYOND THE SE
NRAM
CINDERELLA A
EVERGREEN IMMORTAL
EVERGREEN IMMORTALITY,
OLSEN MM RTAL
OLSEN
FFP
FFP
CHEESE
SNAKEMAN
AN
4 TANKS
4 JEEPS
4 BATTLE SHIPS
4 CRUISERS
4 SAILORS
4 RIFLEMEN
8 MACHINE GUNNERS
4 BAZOOKA MEN
CHEESE
VISITORS
EL
XXXX
XXXX

SMITHS
N
N
LA CUCARACHA SLO
"SLOT RACER" TRAC
SELL ONLY EIGHT BOXES
SELL ONLY BOXES
79A,
(IRON)
MPIC
BLAC
SOAP
OLMPIC
SELL
GRIT.
2 FORTS
SPLIT
LUGPE
207,
SOAP
ONLY FIFTY
ONLY FIFTY

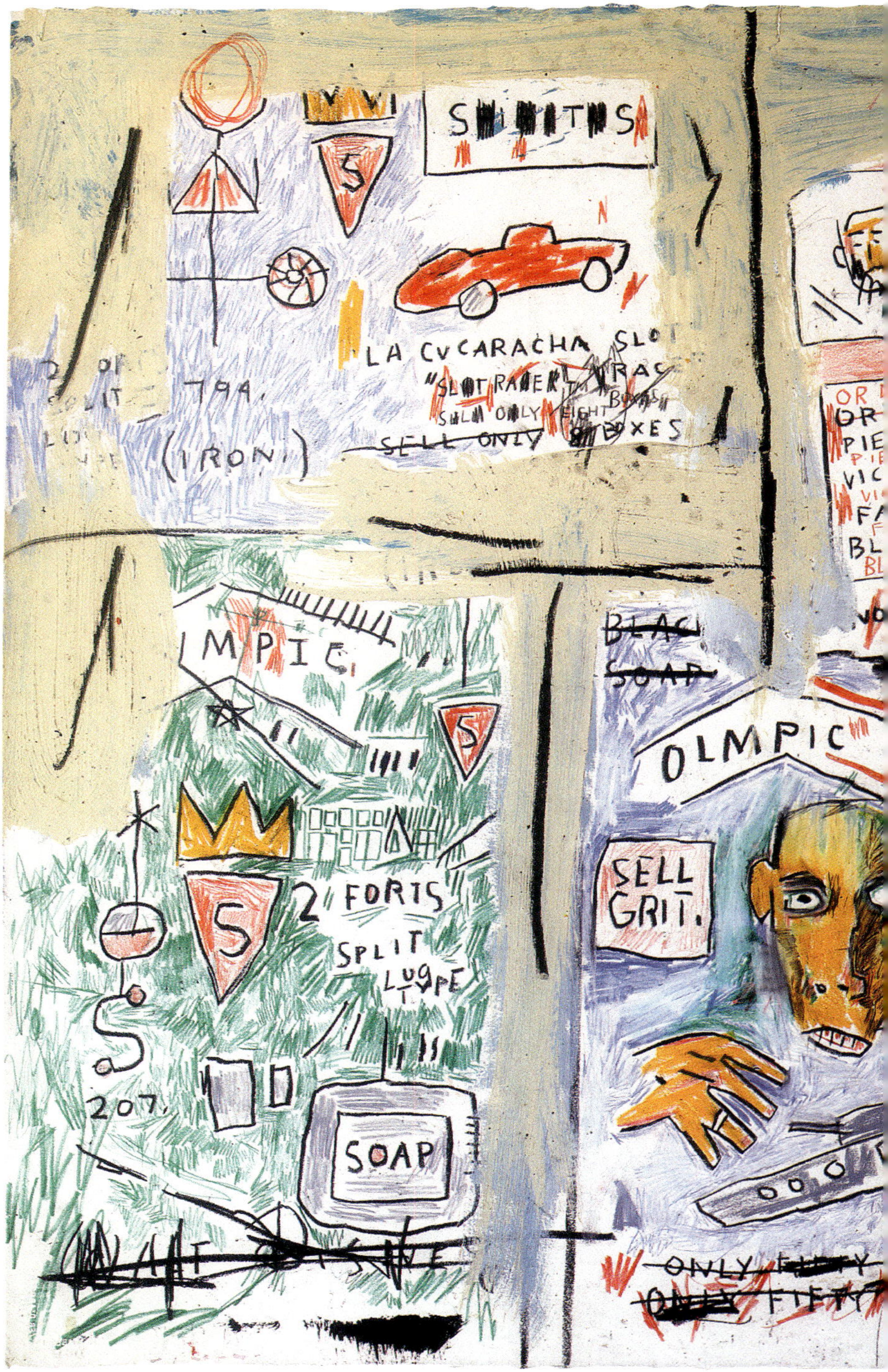

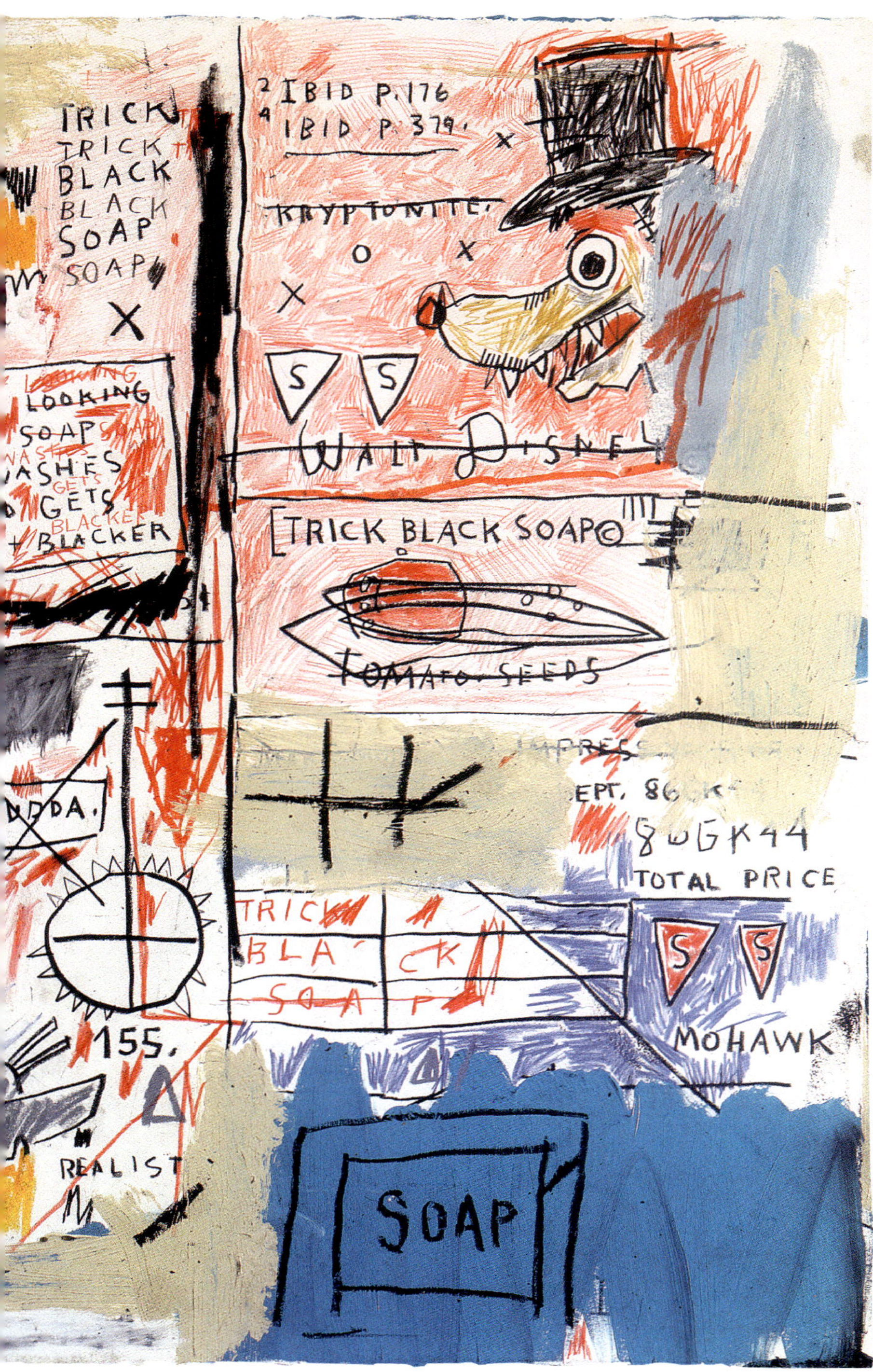
TRICK
TRICK
BLACK
BLACK
SOAP
SOAP
X
LOOKING
LOOKING
SOAP
WASHES
ASHES
GETS
GETS
BLACKER
BLACKER
2 IBID P. 176
4 IBID P. 379
KRYPTONITE
WALT DISNEY
TRICK BLACK SOAP©
TOMATO SEEDS
IMPRESS
EPT. 86
TOTAL PRICE
MOHAWK
DDA.
155.
REALIST
SOAP

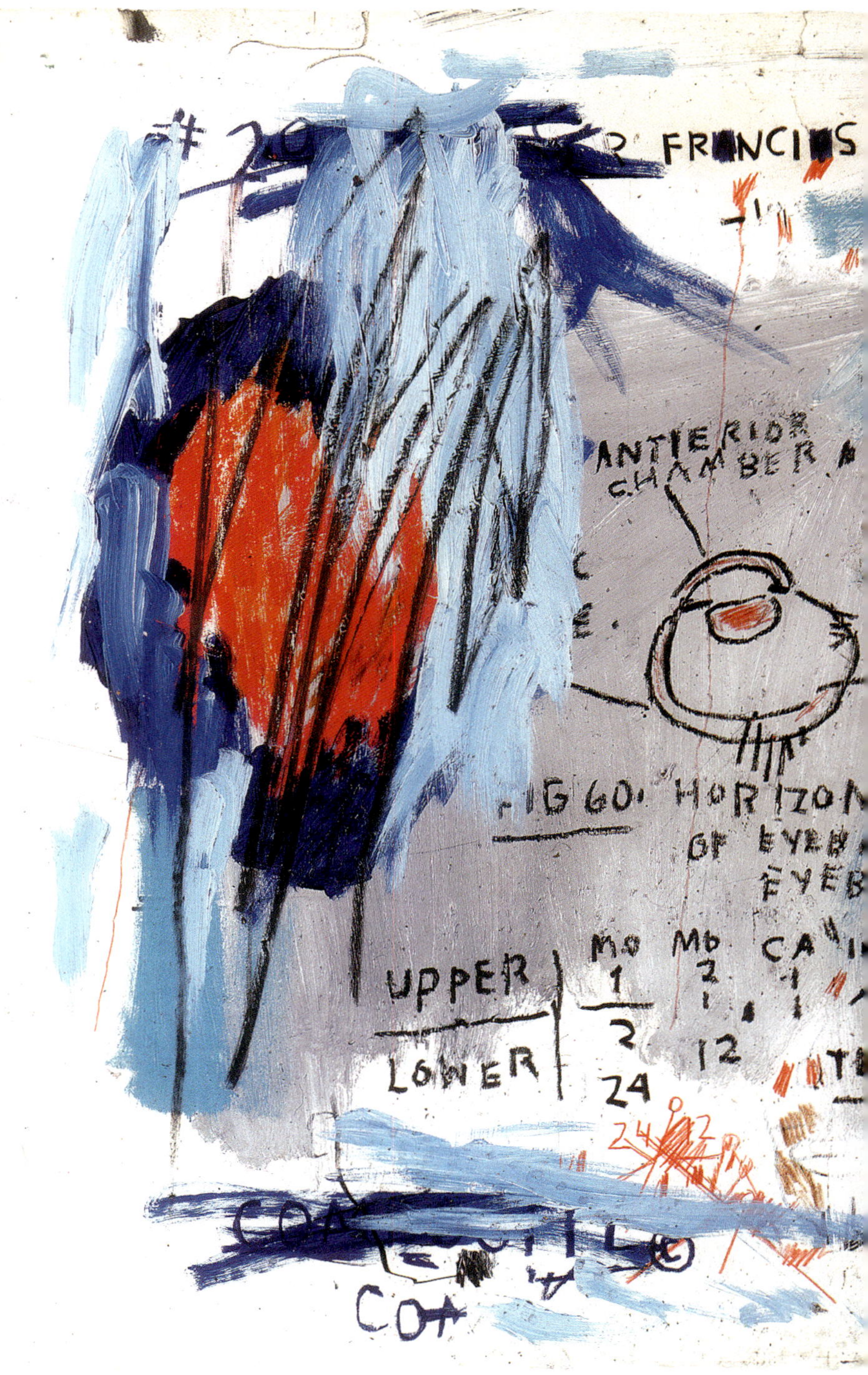
3
#2
FRANCIS
ANTIERIOR
CHAMBER
FIG 60. HORIZON
OF EYEB
EYEB
UPPER
LOWER
MO MO CA
1 2
2
24
24
CO
CO

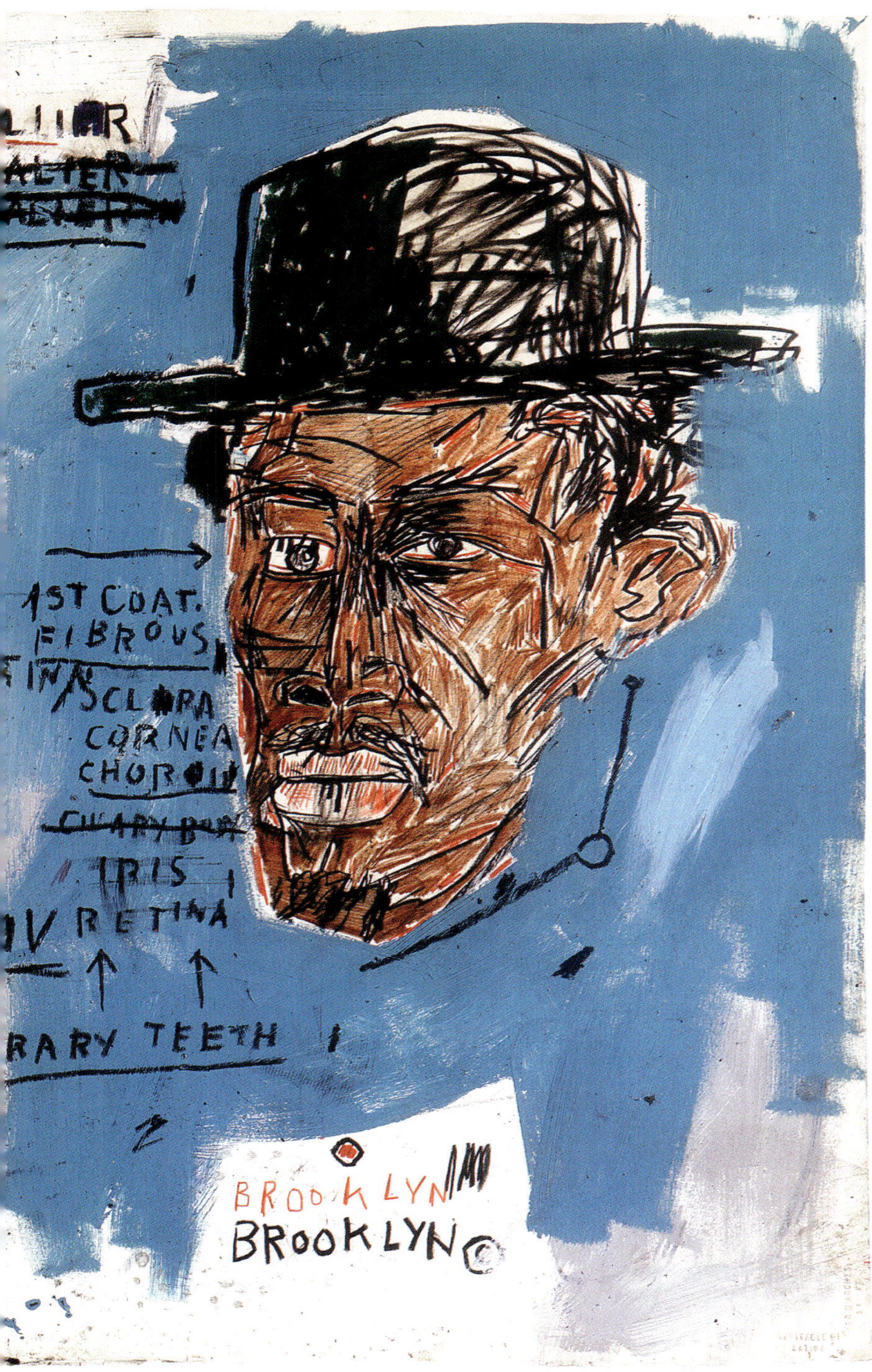
LIIAR
ALTER
1ST COAT.
FIBROUS
SCLERA
CORNEA
CHOR
CILIARY BODY
IRIS
IV RETINA
RARY TEETH
BROOKLYN
BROOKLYN©

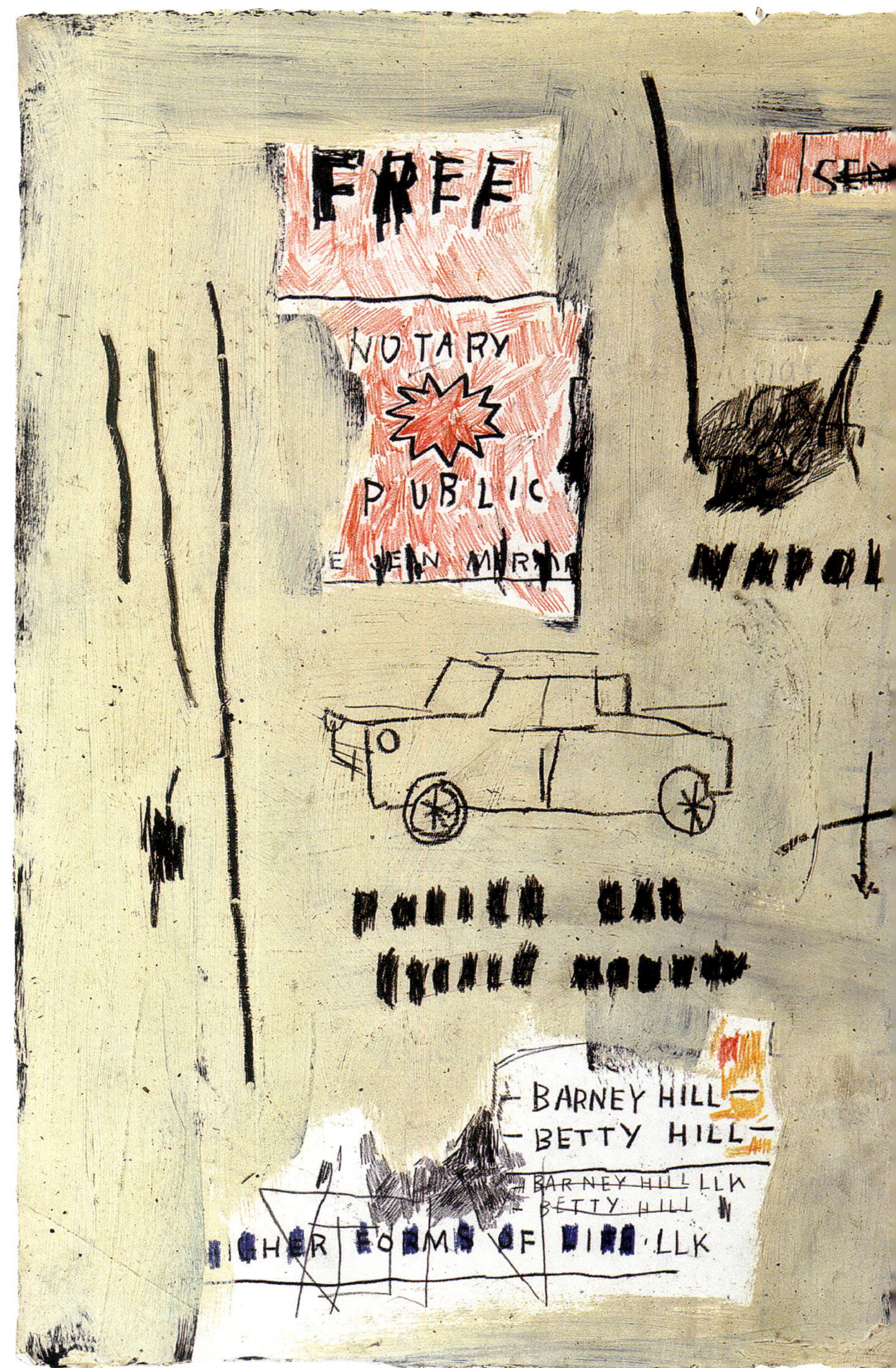
FREE
SE
NOTARY
PUBLIC
E JEAN MI
NAPOL
BARNEY HILL
BETTY HILL
BARNEY HILL LLK
BETTY HILL
HIGHER FORMS OF NIRA LLK

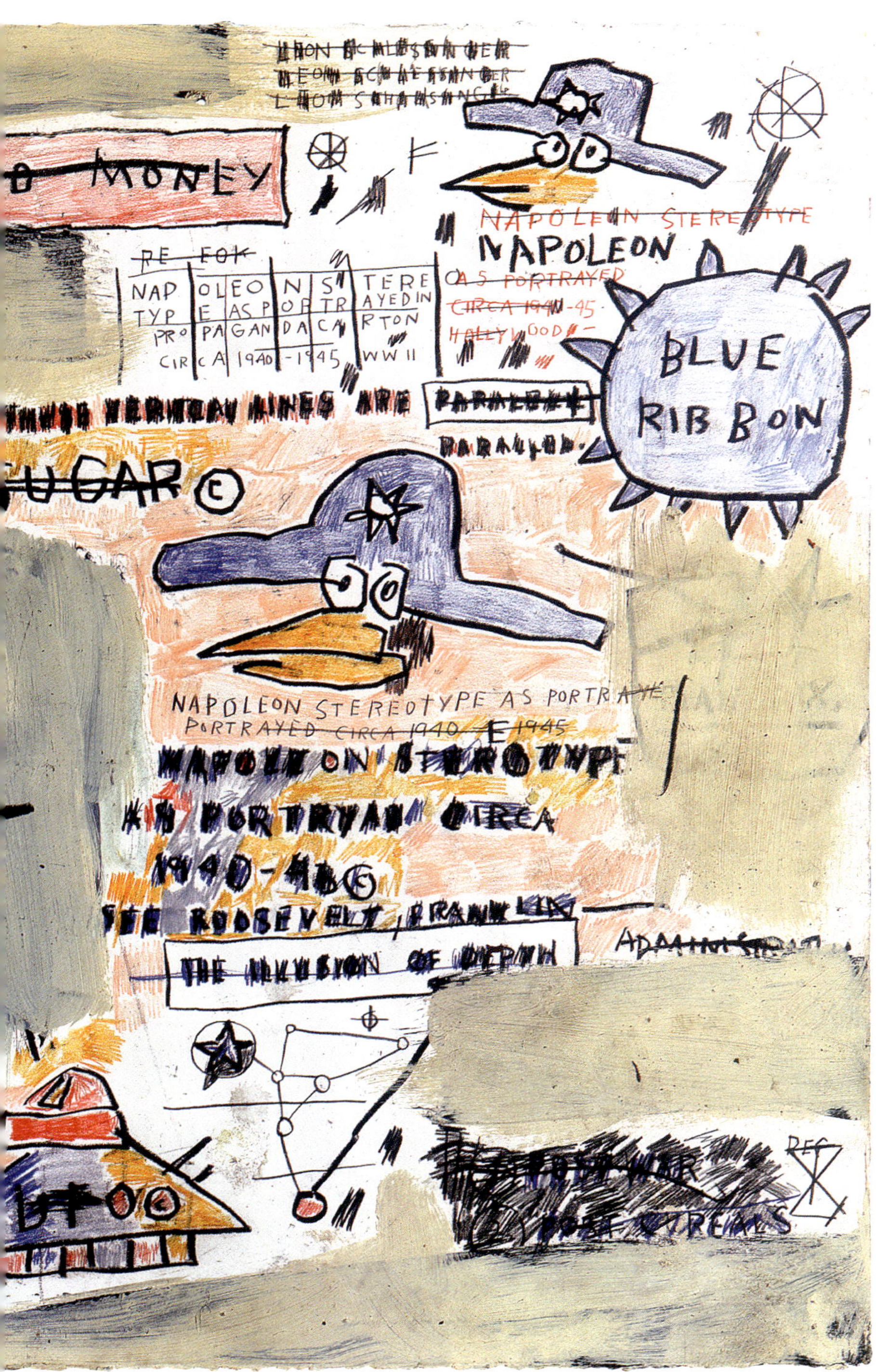
LEON SCHLESINGER
LEON SCHLESINGER
LEON SCHLESINGER
MONEY
NAPOLEON STEREOTYPE
NAPOLEON
AS PORTRAYED
CIRCA 1940-45
HOLLYWOOD
RE FOK
NAPOLEON STEREO
TYPE AS PORTRAYED IN
PROPAGANDA CARTON
CIRCA 1940-1945 WWII
ALL VERTICAL LINES ARE
PARALLEL
PARALLEL
BLUE
RIBBON
SUGAR ©
NAPOLEON STEREOTYPE AS PORTRAYE
PORTRAYED CIRCA 1940 1945
NAPOLEON STEREOTYPE
AS PORTRYAD CIRCA
1940-1946 ©
SEE ROOSEVELT, FRANKLIN
ADMINISTRAT
THE ILLUSION OF DEPTH
REG

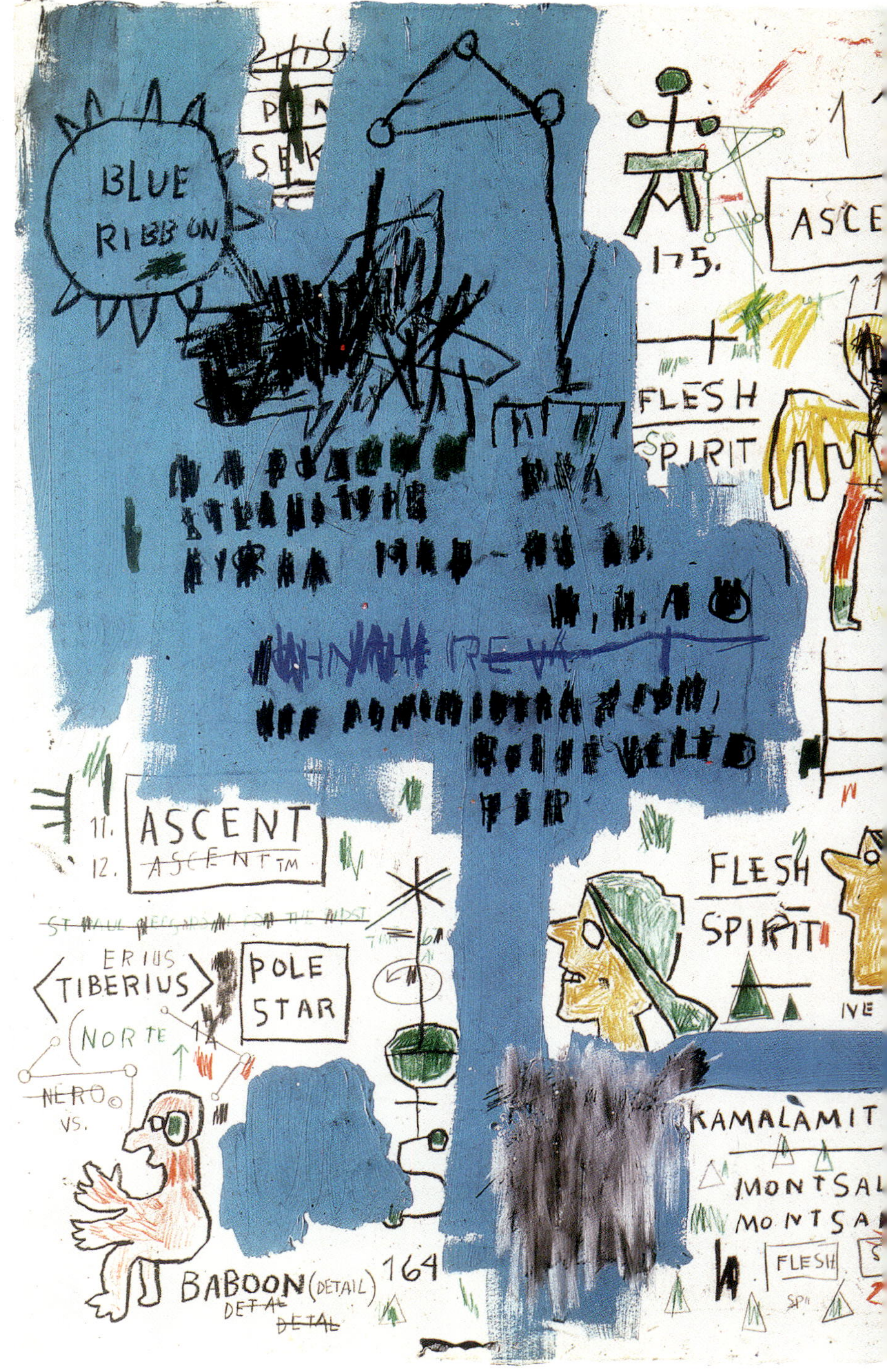
BLUE
RIBBON
P[N]
SE[K]
175.
FLESH
SPIRIT
ASCE[NT]
11. ASCENT
12. ASCENT TM
ST PAUL [RECKONS] [FOR] THE [MOST]
ERIUS
TIBERIUS
NORTE
NERO
VS.
POLE
STAR
FLESH
SPIRIT
IVE
KAMALAMIT
MONTSAL
MONTSA
FLESH
SPI
BABOON (DETAIL) 164
DETAIL
DETAIL

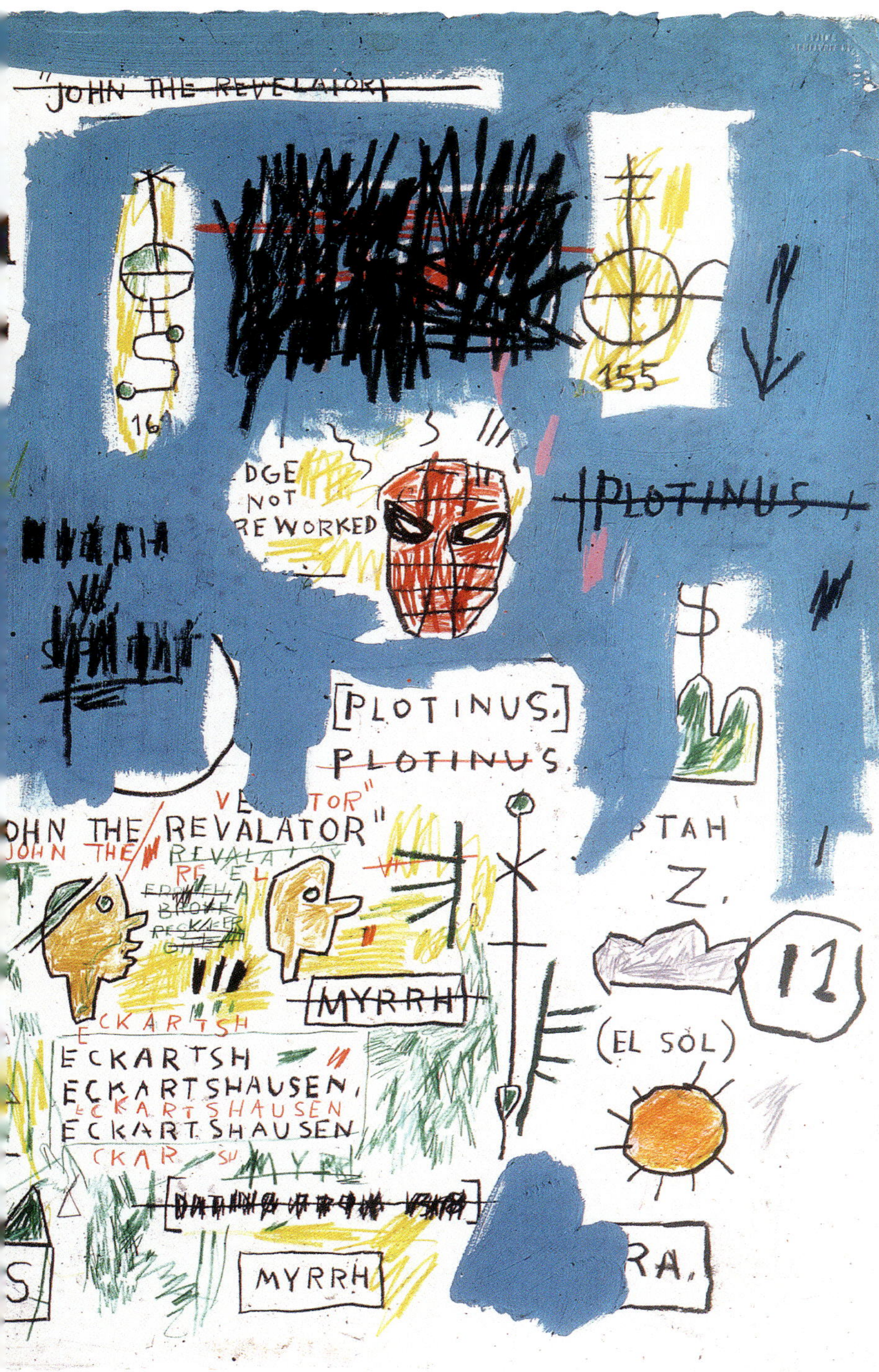
"JOHN THE REVELATOR"
155
16
DGE
NOT
REWORKED
PLOTINUS
PLOTINUS.
PLOTINUS.
"VECTOR"
JOHN THE / REVALATOR"
JOHN THE / REVALATOR
PTAH
Z.
12
(EL SOL)
MYRRH
ECKARTSH
ECKARTSH
ECKARTSHAUSEN,
ECKARTSHAUSEN
ECKART.SHAUSEN
CKAR SH
MYRRH
MYRRH
S
RA.

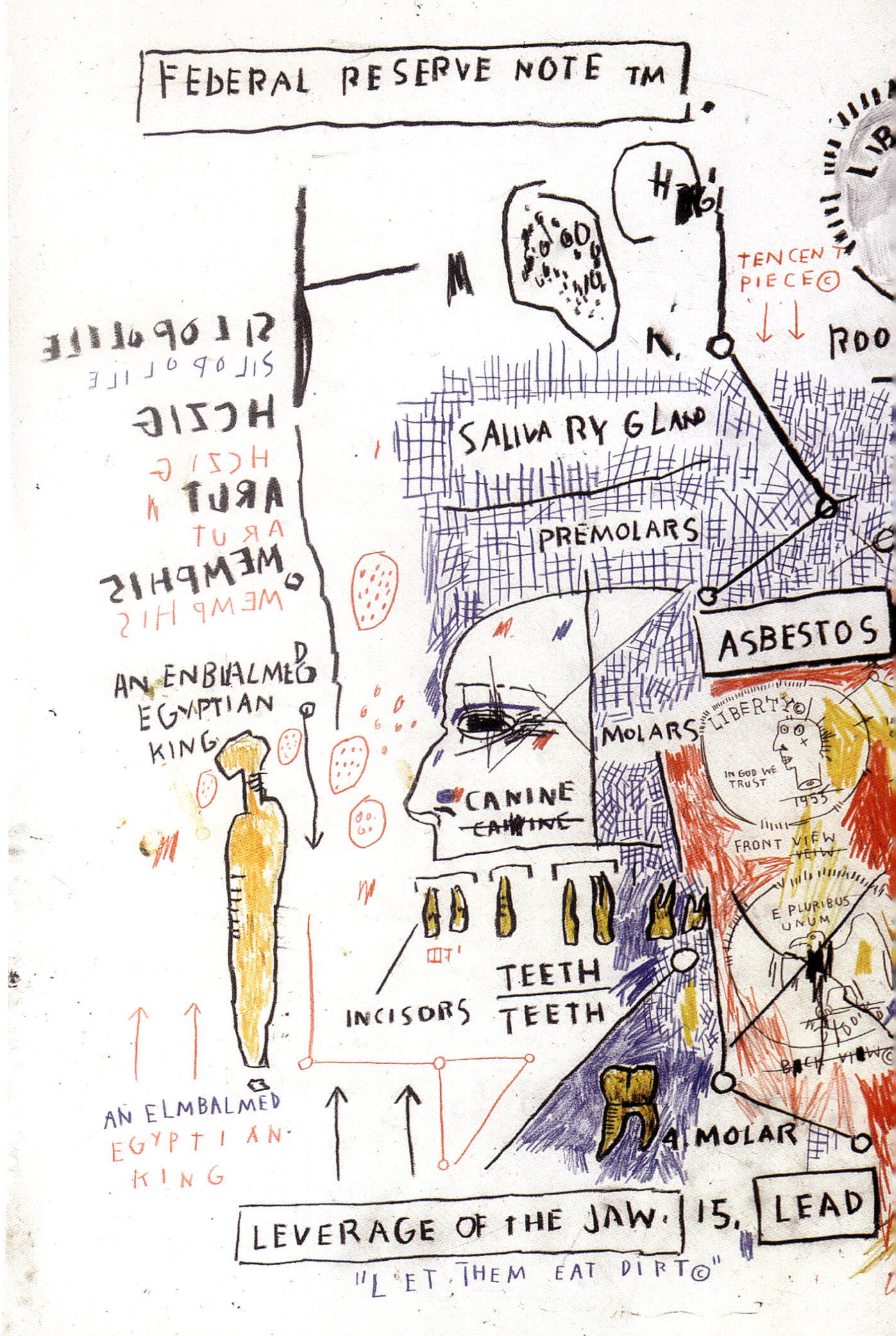
FEDERAL RESERVE NOTE TM
SILOPOLITE
SILOPOLITE
HCZIG
HCZIG
ARUT
ARUT
MEMPHIS
MEMPHIS
AN ENBIALMED
EGYPTIAN
KING
AN ELMBALMED
EGYPTIAN
KING
TEN CENT
PIECE©
ROO
SALIVARY GLAND
PREMOLARS
ASBESTOS
MOLARS
LIBERTY©
IN GOD WE
TRUST
1955
FRONT VIEW
E PLURIBUS
UNUM
BACK VIEW©
CANINE
CANINE
INCISORS
TEETH
TEETH
A. MOLAR
LEVERAGE OF THE JAW. 15. LEAD
"LET THEM EAT DIRT©"
LIB
LIB

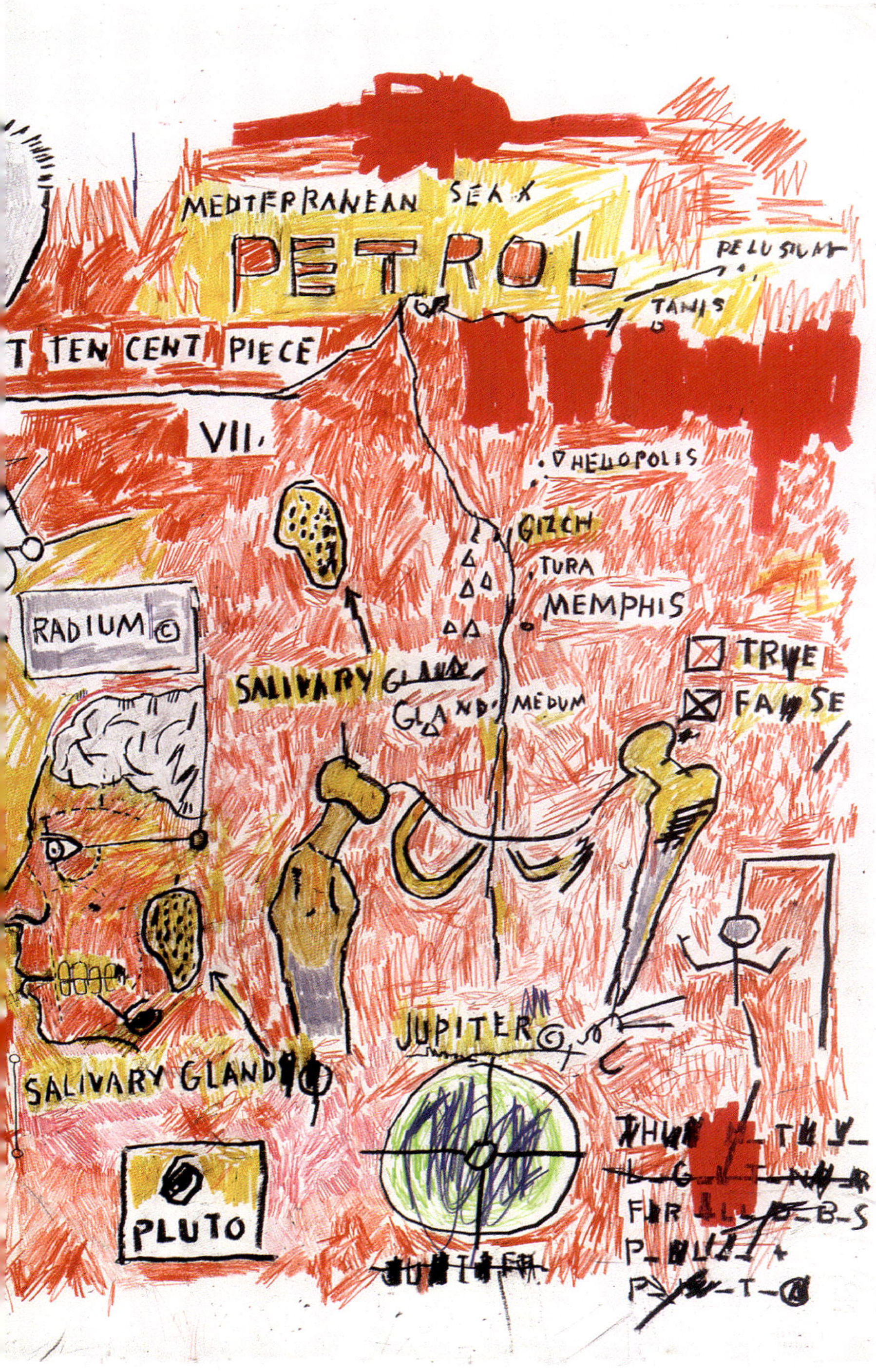
MEDITERRANEAN SEA
PETROL
PELUSIUM
TANIS
T TEN CENT PIECE
VII.
HELIOPOLIS
GIZEH
TURA
MEMPHIS
RADIUM ©
SALIVARY GLAND
GLAND MEDUM
TRUE
FALSE
JUPITER
SALIVARY GLAND
PLUTO

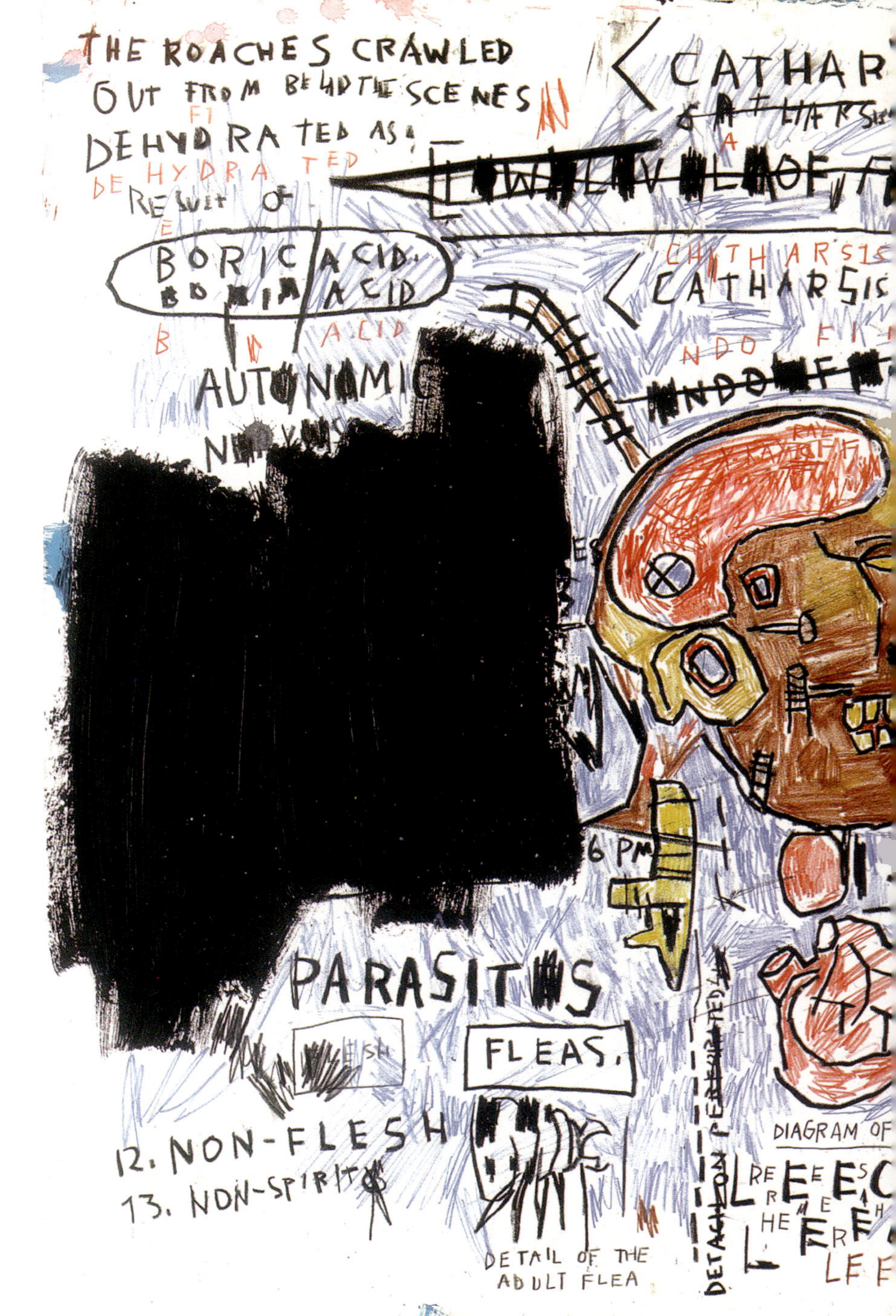

THE ROACHES CRAWLED
OUT FROM BEHIND THE SCENES
DEHYDRATED AS A
DEHYDRATED
RESULT OF
BORIC ACID
BORIC ACID
B ACID
AUTONAMIC
NERVOUS
CATHAR
CATHARSIS
OF
CATHARSIS
NDO F
6 PM
PARASITS
FLEAS
12. NON-FLESH
13. NON-SPIRITS
DETAIL OF THE
ADULT FLEA
DIAGRAM OF
DETACHON PEDICULOIDES
LEE
LEE

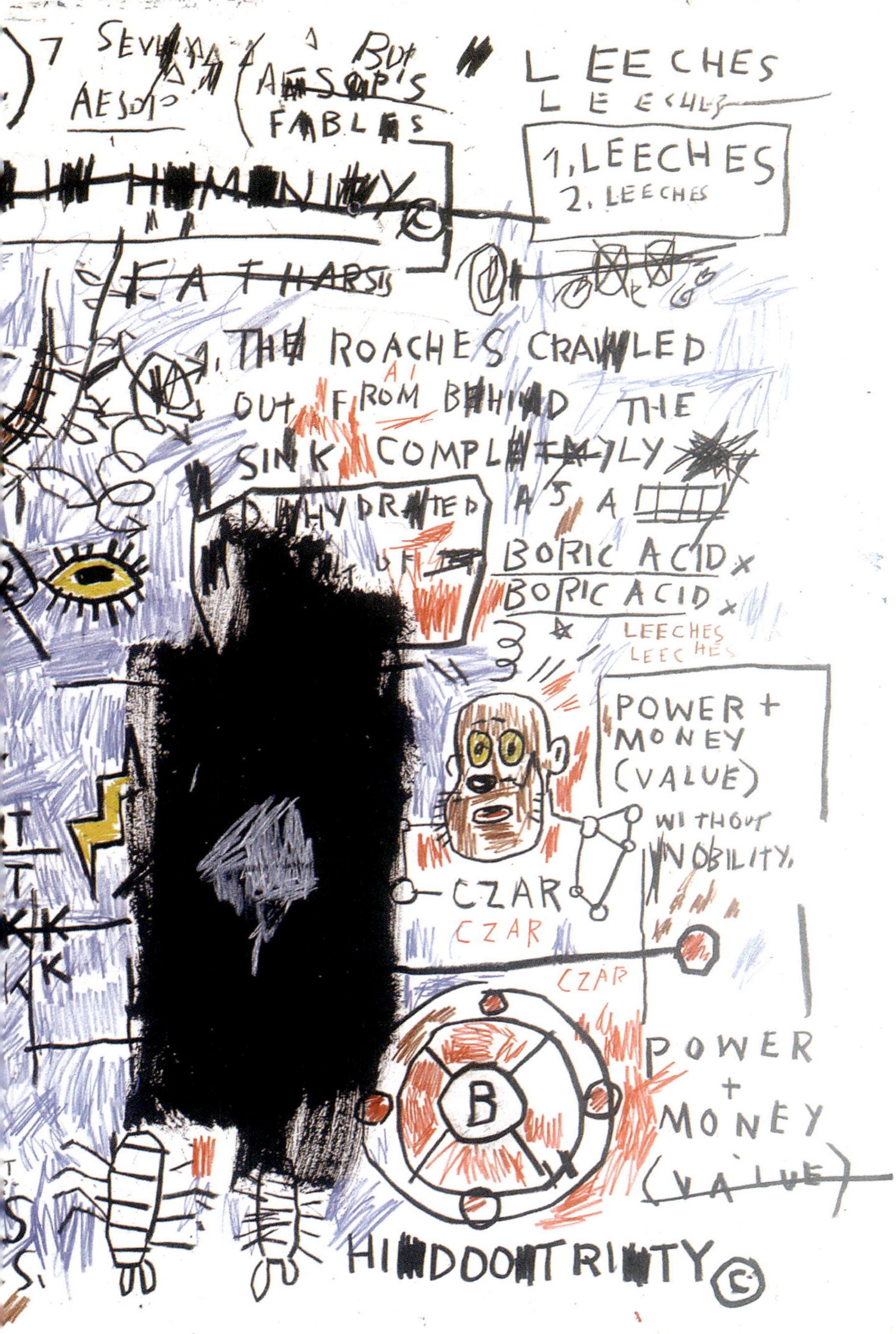
7 SEVEN A BUT AESOP'S
AESOP (AESOP'S FABLES
HUMANITY
LEECHES
LEECHES
1. LEECHES
2. LEECHES
CATHARSIS
1. THE ROACHES CRAWLED
OUT FROM BEHIND THE
SINK COMPLETELY
HYDRATED AS A
BORIC ACID
BORIC ACID
LEECHES
LEECHES
POWER +
MONEY
(VALUE)
WITHOUT
NOBILITY.
CZAR
CZAR
CZAR
B
POWER
+
MONEY
(VALUE)
HINDOO TRINITY

BIRTH OF EARTH ©

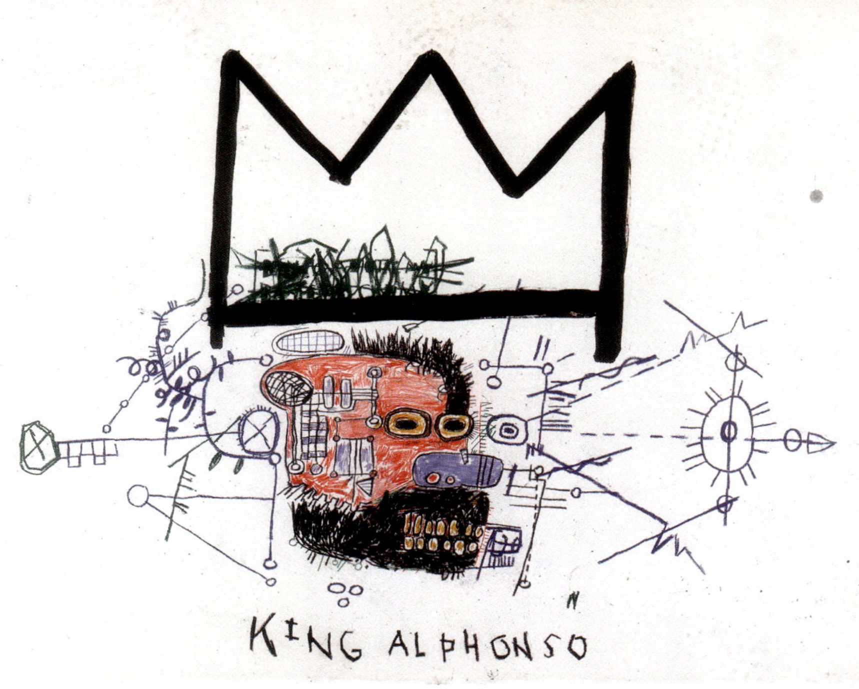
KING ALPHONSO

10

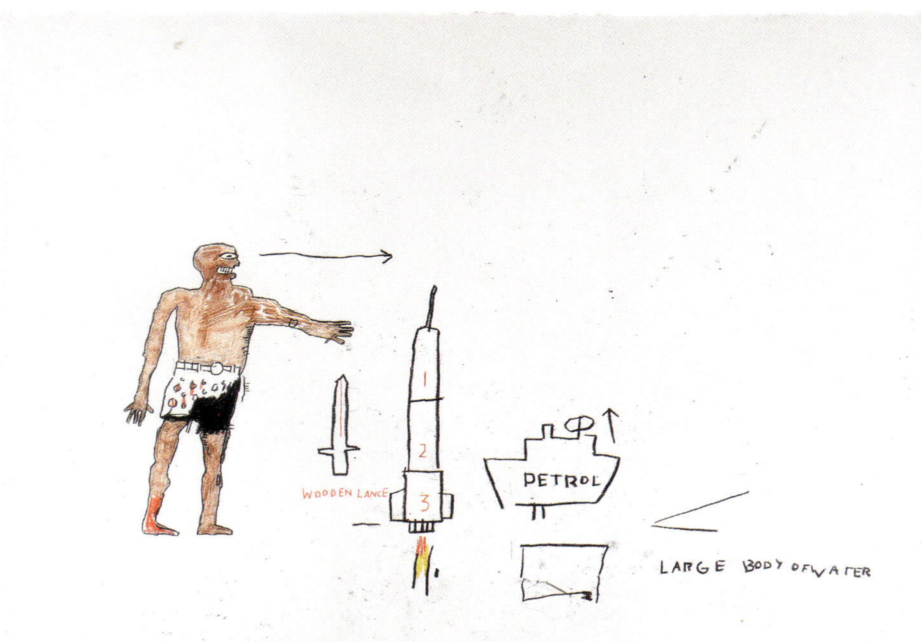

11

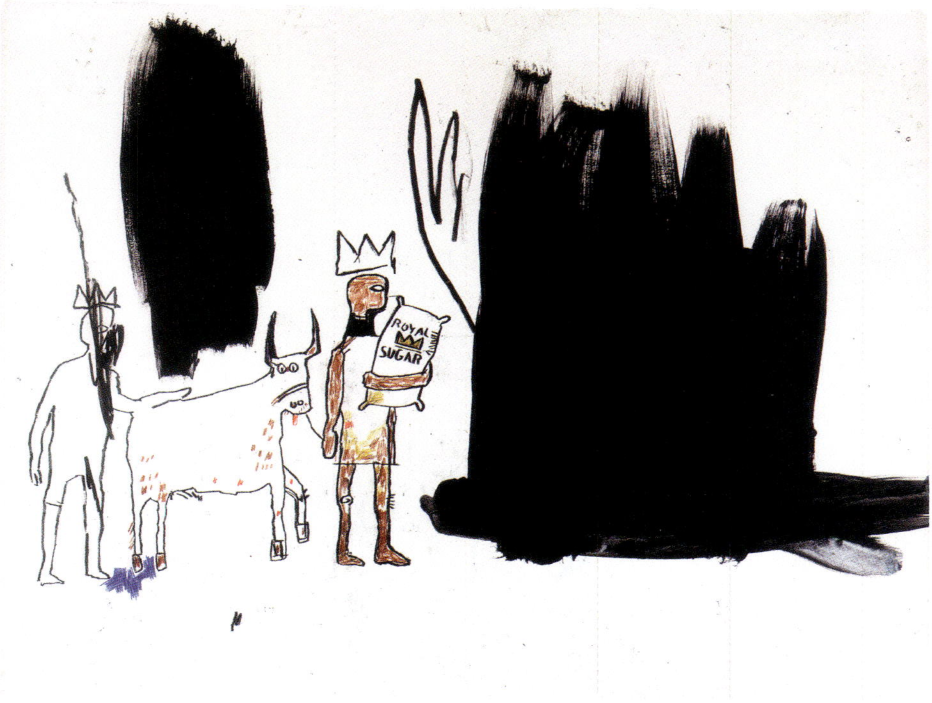

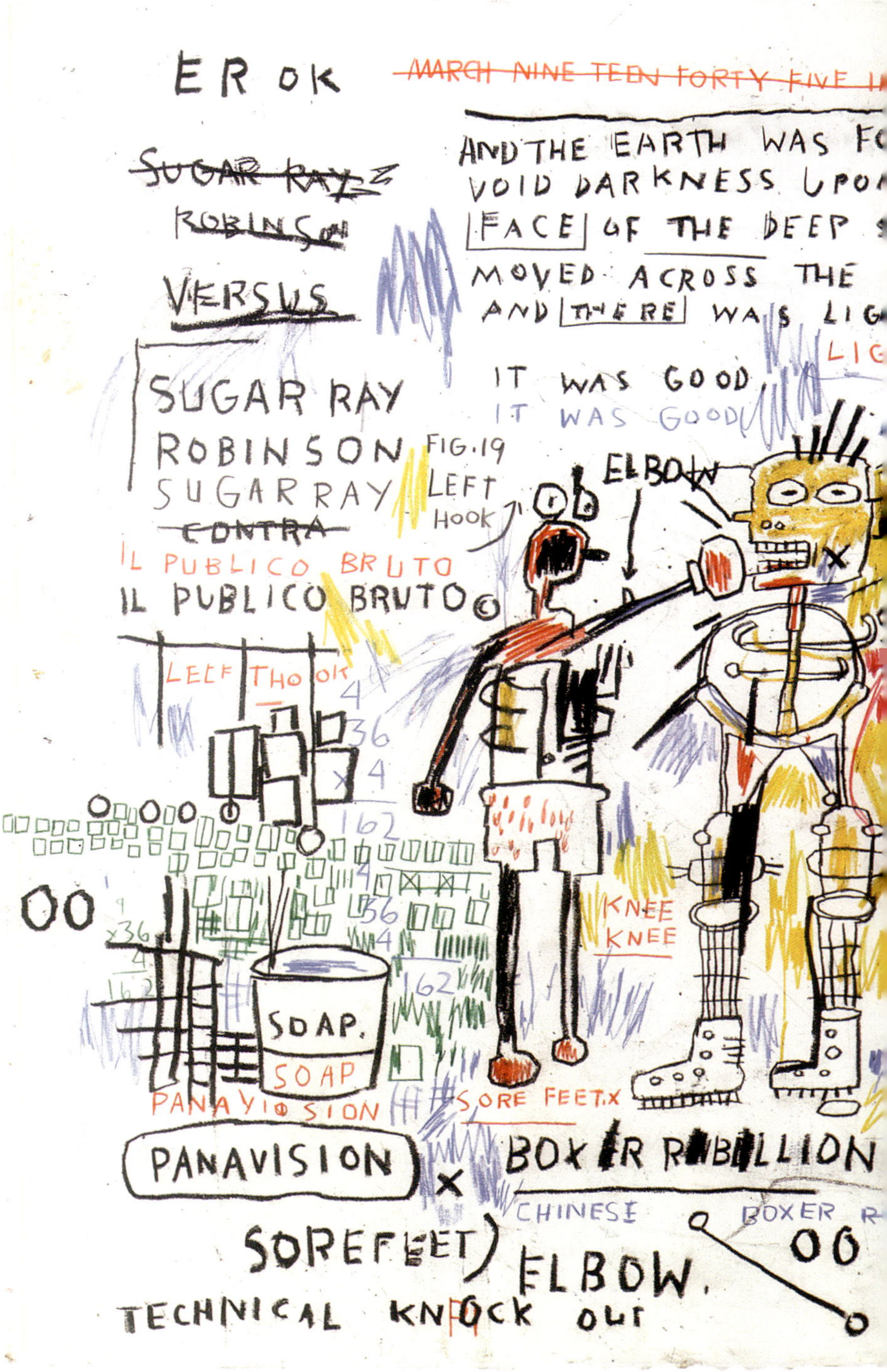

ER OK ~~MARCH NINE TEEN FORTY FIVE~~

~~SUGAR RAY~~
~~ROBINSON~~

VERSUS

SUGAR RAY
ROBINSON
SUGAR RAY
~~CONTRA~~
IL PUBLICO BRUTO
IL PUBLICO BRUTO ©

AND THE EARTH WAS FO
VOID DARKNESS UPON
FACE OF THE DEEP
MOVED ACROSS THE
AND THERE WAS LIG

IT WAS GOOD
IT WAS GOOD
LIG

FIG. 19
LEFT
HOOK

ELBOW

LEFT THOOK

4
36
4
162

00

4
×36
4
162

SOAP.
SOAP

PANAVISION

PANAVISION ×

SORE FEET. X

KNEE
KNEE

BOXER REBELLION

CHINESE   BOXER R

00

SOREFEET)
ELBOW.

TECHNICAL KNOCK OUT

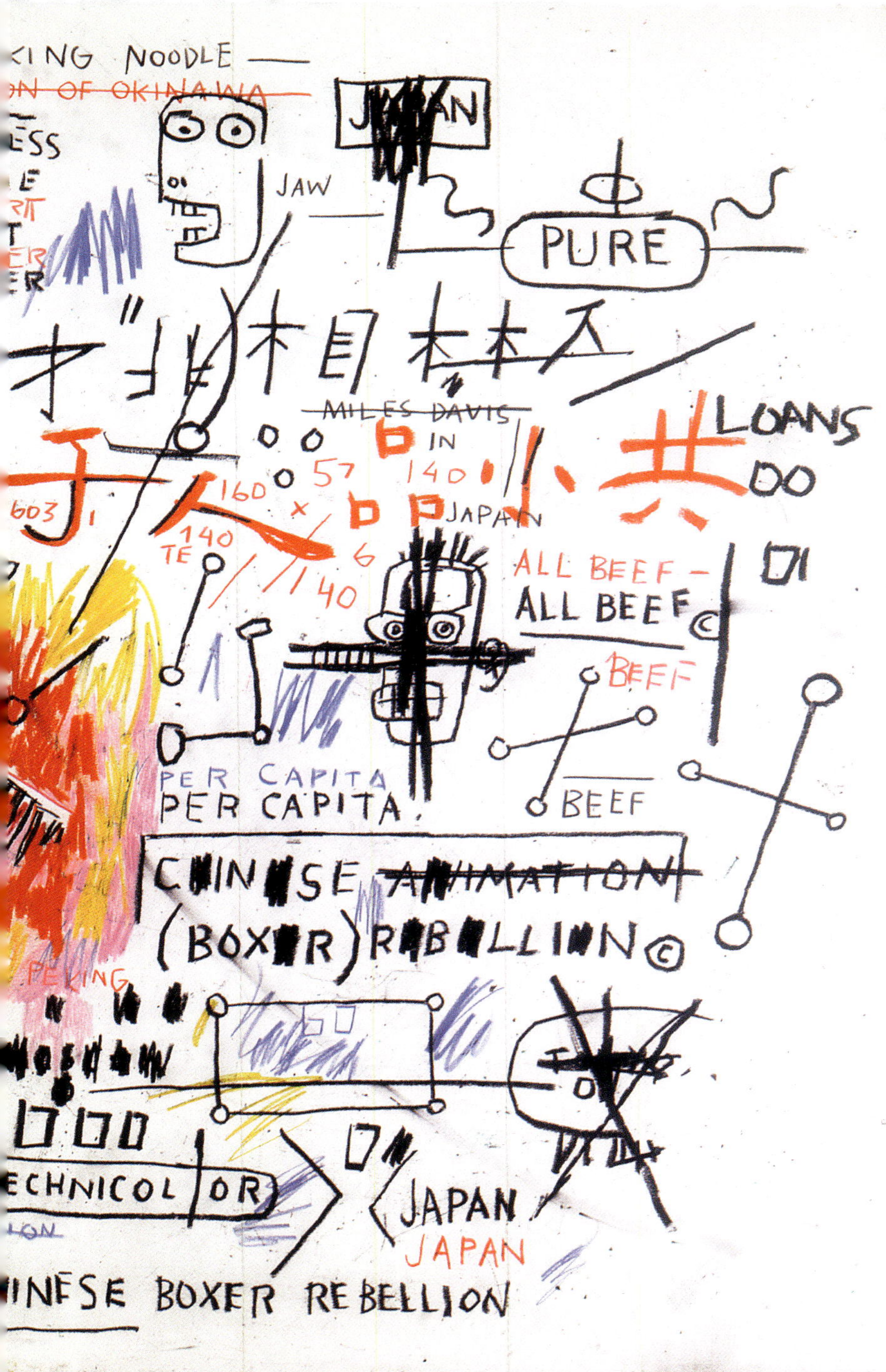
KING NOODLE
ON OF OKINAWA
ESS
E
R
R
JAPAN
JAW
PURE
MILES DAVIS
IN
57 140
160 JAPAN
603
140
TE
LOANS
OO
OI
ALL BEEF —
ALL BEEF ©
BEEF
BEEF
PER CAPITA
PER CAPITA.
CHINESE ANIMATION
(BOXER) REBELLION ©
PEKING
TECHNICOLOR
ON
JAPAN
JAPAN
INESE BOXER REBELLION

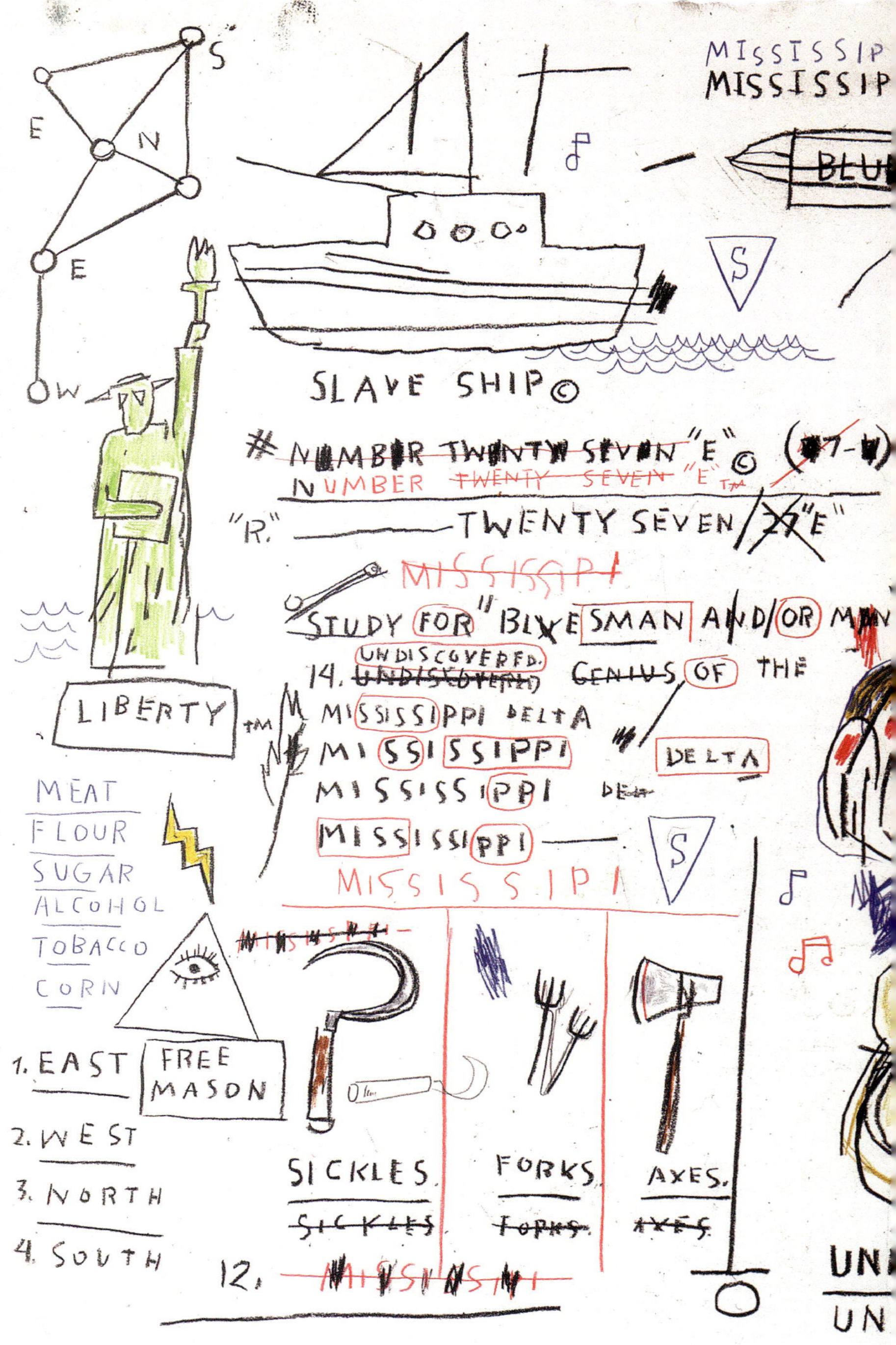
S
E
N
E
W
MISSISSIP
MISSISSIP
BLU
S
SLAVE SHIP ©
NUMBER TWENTY SEVEN "E" © (#7-
NUMBER TWENTY SEVEN "E" ™
"R." TWENTY SEVEN "27"E"
MISSISSIP
STUDY FOR "BLUESMAN AND/OR M
14. UNDISCOVERED. GENIUS OF THE
MISSISSIPPI DELTA
MISSISSIPPI DELTA
MISSISSIPPI DEL
MISSISSIPPI
MISSISSIPI
MISSISSIP
LIBERTY ™
MEAT
FLOUR
SUGAR
ALCOHOL
TOBACCO
CORN
FREE
MASON
1. EAST
2. WEST
3. NORTH
4. SOUTH
12.
SICKLES
SICKLES
FORKS
FORKS
AXES.
AXES
S
UN
UN

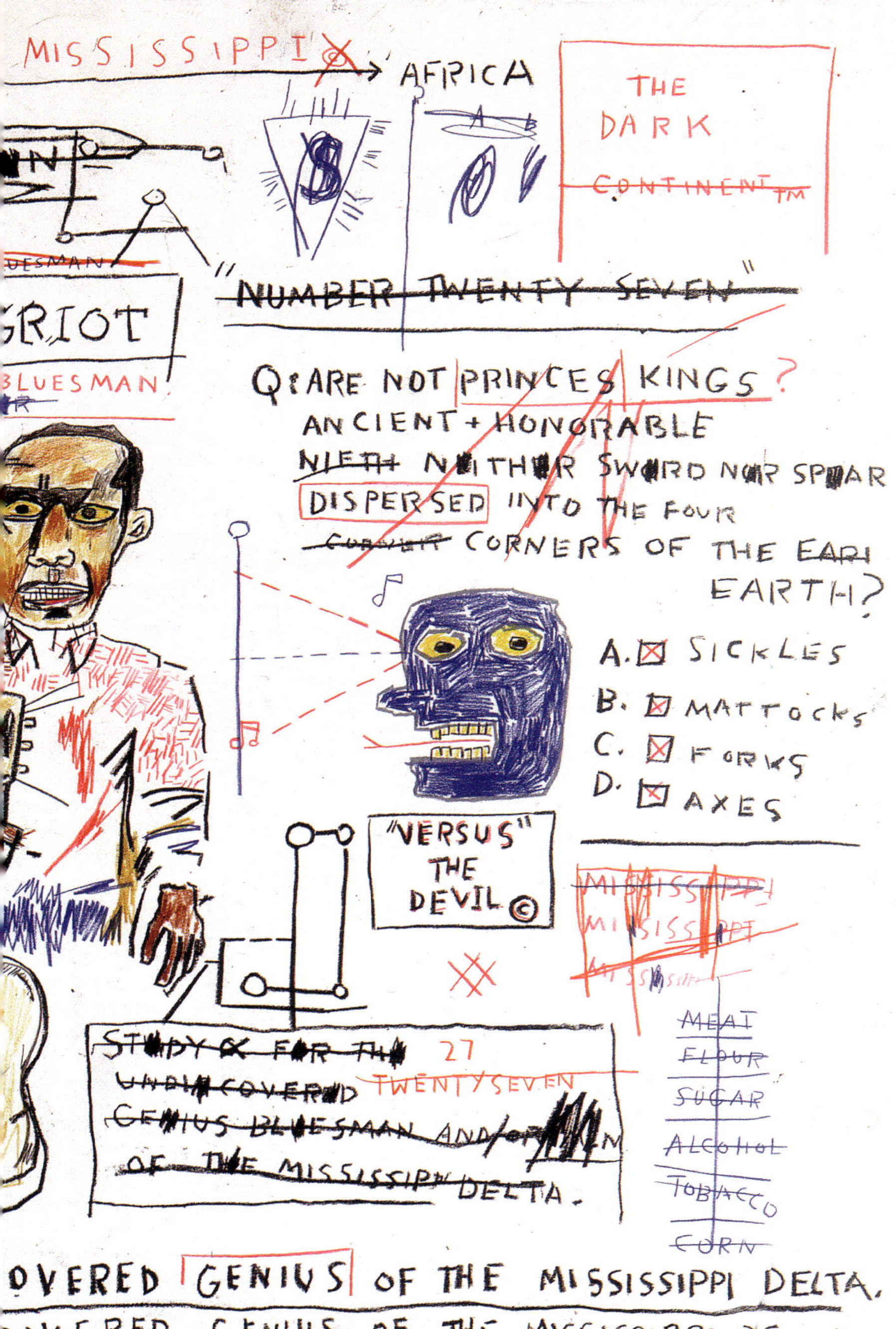
MISSISSIPPI → AFRICA
THE DARK CONTINENT TM
"NUMBER TWENTY SEVEN"
Q: ARE NOT PRINCES KINGS?
ANCIENT + HONORABLE
NIETH NEITHER SWORD NOR SPEAR
DISPERSED INTO THE FOUR
CORNERS OF THE EARI EARTH?
A. ☒ SICKLES
B. ☒ MATTOCKS
C. ☒ FORKS
D. ☒ AXES
"VERSUS" THE DEVIL ©
GRIOT
BLUESMAN
DESMAN
MISSISSIPPI
MISSISSIPPI
MISSISSIPPI
MEAT
FLOUR
SUGAR
ALCOHOL
TOBACCO
CORN
STUDY FOR THE 27
UNDISCOVERED TWENTY/SEVEN
GENIUS BLUESMAN AND/OR M
OF THE MISSISSIPPI DELTA.
OVERED GENIUS OF THE MISSISSIPPI DELTA.
OVERED GENIUS OF THE MISSISSIPPI DELTA.

Untitled (1960), 1983
Acrylic and oilstick on paper mounted
on wood, 91.5 x 61 cm / 36 x 24 inches

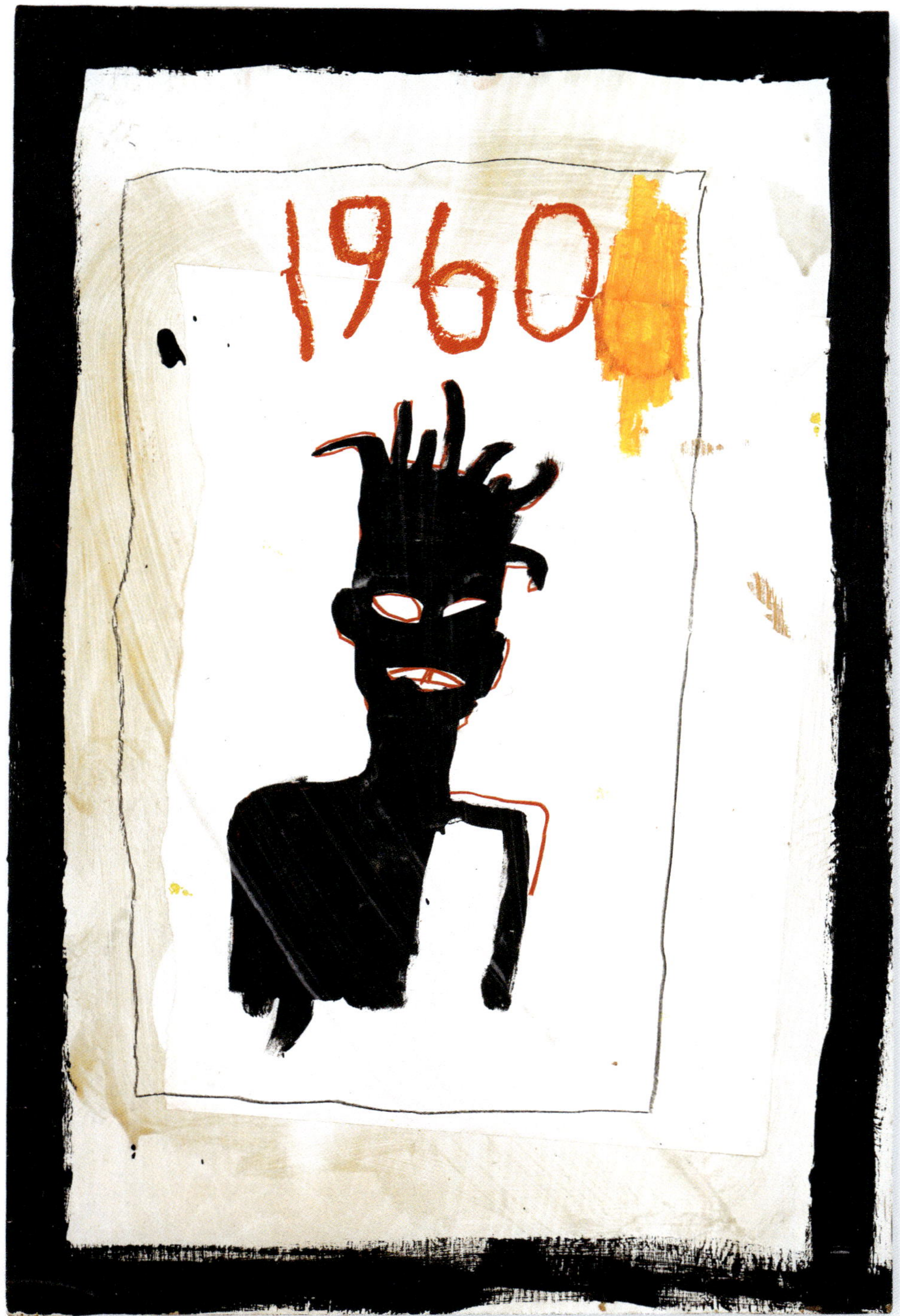
1960

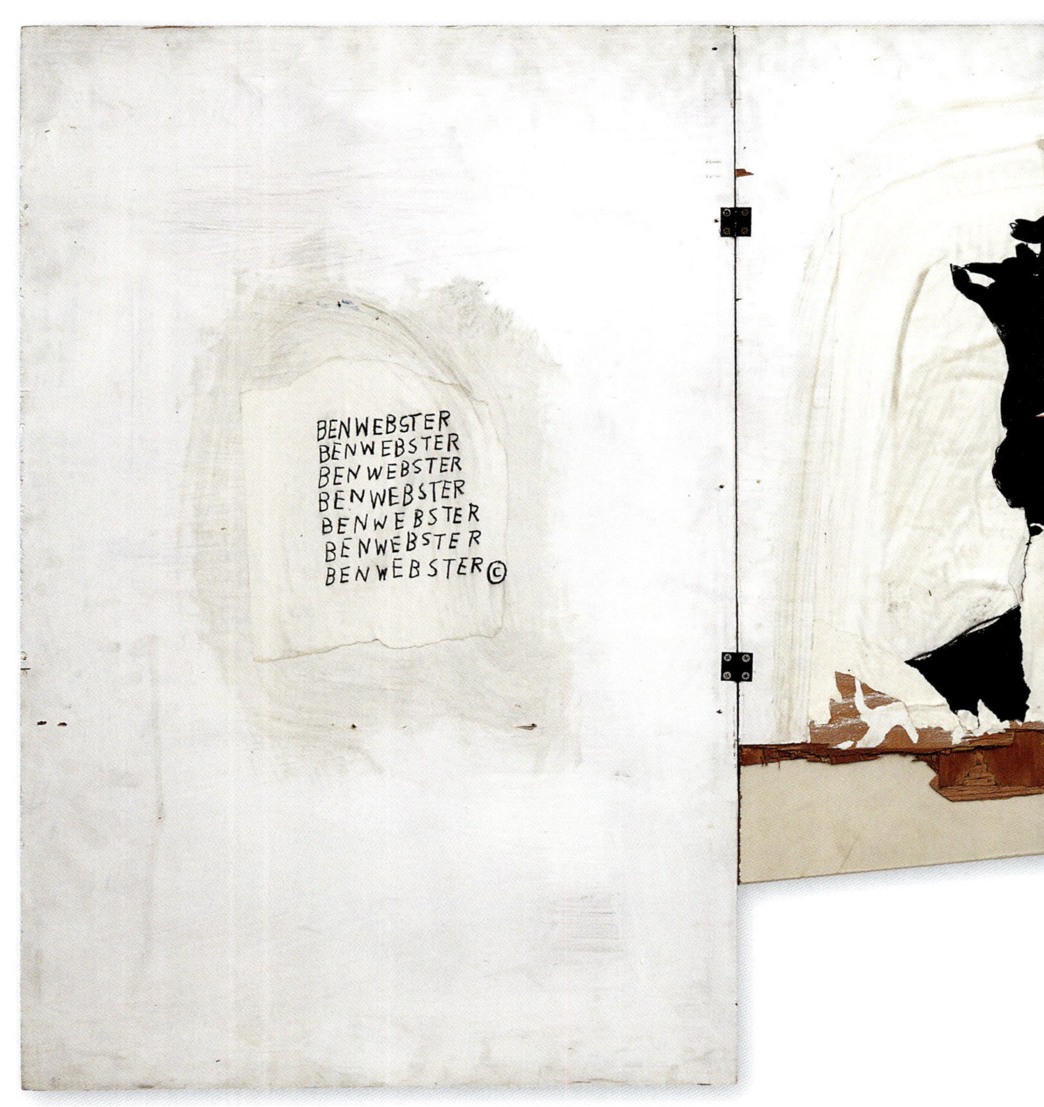

Self-Portrait, 1983
Acrylic, oil, oilstick, and paper collage on wood,
triptych: 101.5 x 178 cm / 40 x 70 inches

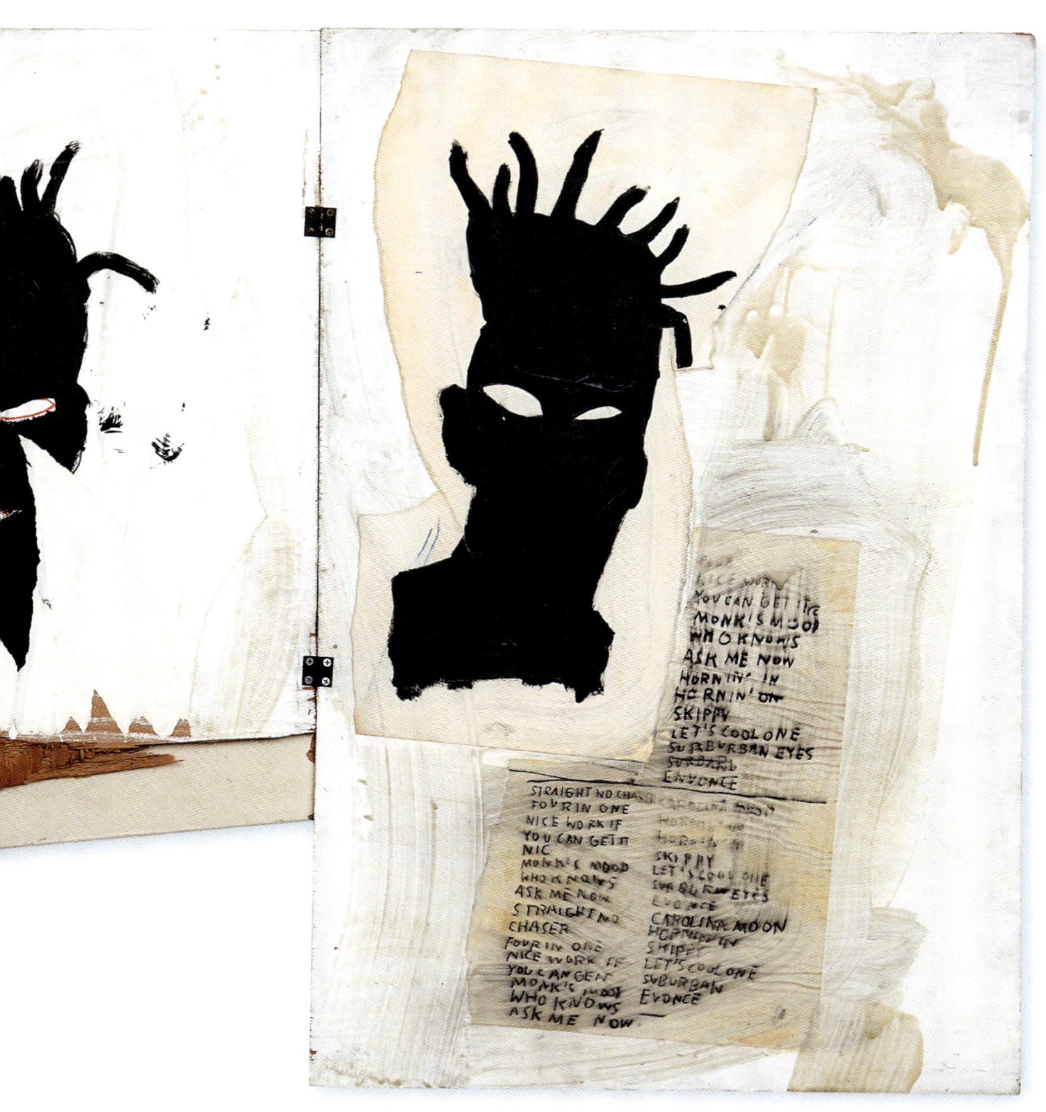

Discography I, 1983
Acrylic and oilstick on canvas,
167.5 x 152.5 cm / 66 x 60 inches

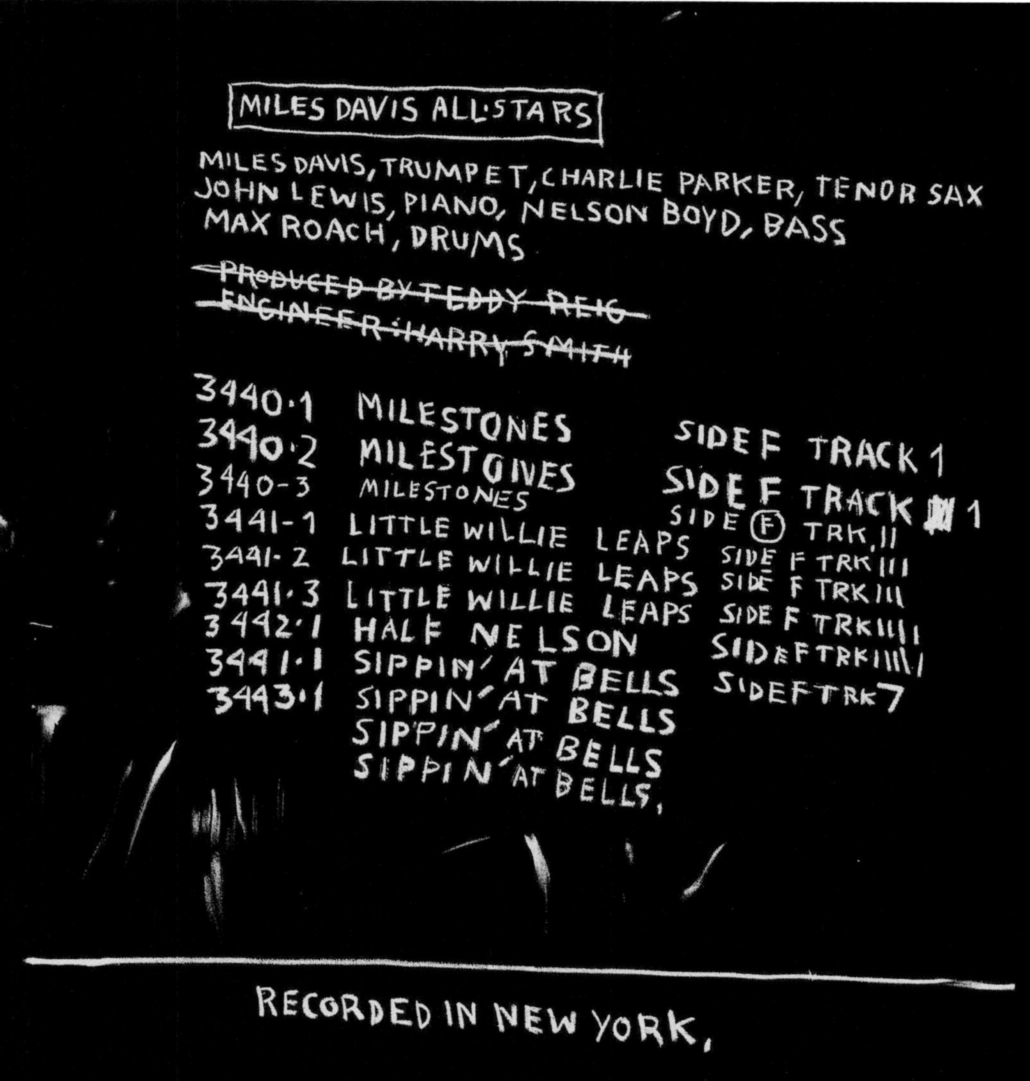

Discography II, 1983
Acrylic and oilstick on canvas,
167.5 x 152.5 cm / 66 x 60 inches

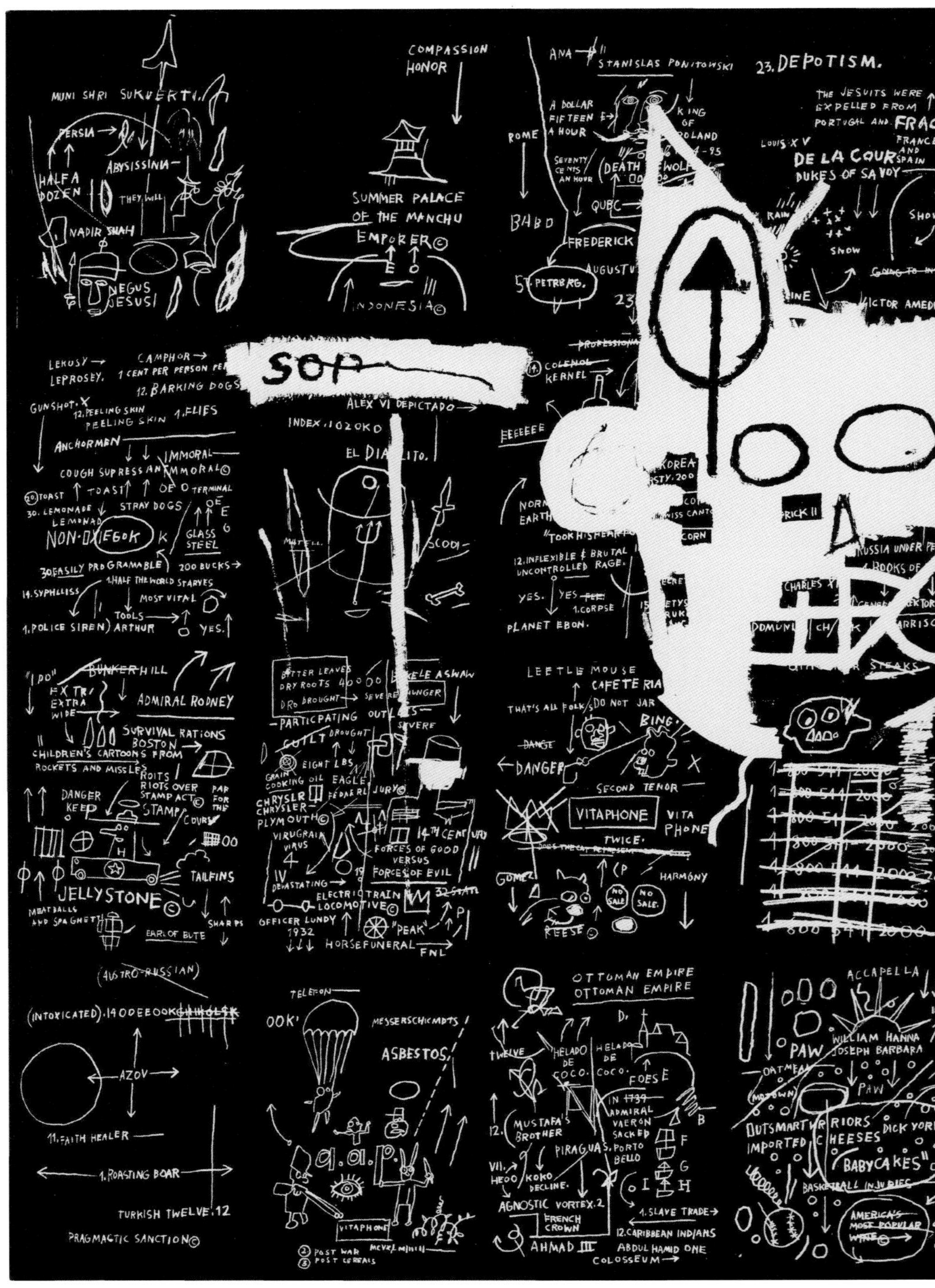

COMPASSION
HONOR
ANA
STANISLAS PONITOWSKI
23. DEPOTISM.
MUNI SHRI SUKVERTI.
A DOLLAR
FIFTEEN
A HOUR
KING
OF
POLAND
THE JESUITS WERE
EXPELLED FROM
PORTUGAL AND
FRAC
FRANCE
AND
SPAIN
PERSIA
ABYSISSINIA
ROME
SEVENTY
CENTS
AN HOUR
DEATH WOLF
LOUIS XV
DE LA COUR
DUKES OF SAVOY
HALF A
DOZEN
THEY WILL
SUMMER PALACE
OF THE MANCHU
EMPORER
BABD
QUBC
FREDERICK
RAIN
SNOW
NADIR SHAH
AUGUSTU
ST. PETRBRG.
SNOW
GOING TO INT
NEGUS
JESUSI
INDONESIA
23
VICTOR AMEDU
LEKOSY
LEPROSEY.
CAMPHOR
1 CENT PER PERSON PE
12. BARKING DOGS
SOP
COLENOL
KERNEL
PROFESSIONA
GUNSHOT. X
12. PEELING SKIN
PEELING SKIN 1. FLIES
ALEX VI DEPICTADO
EEEEEEE
ANCHORMEN
INDEX .1020KO
EL DIABLITO.
KOREA
STY. 200
COUGH SUPRESS AN IMMORAL
IMMORAL
OF O TERMINAL
NORM
EARTH
COT
SWISS CANTO
RICK II
TOAST TOAST
OE
30. LEMONADE STRAY DOGS
LEMONAD
OE
NON-OXIE GOK
GLASS
STEEL
MATELL.
TOOK HIS HEA
12. INFLEXIBLE & BRUTAL
UNCONTROLLED RAGE.
CORN
EASILY PROGRAMABLE
200 BUCKS
RUSSIA UNDER PET
BOOKS OF
14. SYPHLLISS
1. HALF THE WORLD STARVES
MOST VITAL
SCODI
YES. YES
1. CORPSE
CHARLES X
ETYS
RUK
EKTORI
1. POLICE SIREN) ARTHUR
TOOLS
YES.
PLANET EBON.
DDMUN
CH
ARRISO
STEAKS
"I DO"
BUNKER HILL
BETTER LEAVES
DRY ROOTS 40000
DRo DROUGHT
KELE ASWAN
SEVERE HUNGER
LEETLE MOUSE
CAFETERIA
EX TR
EXTRA
WIDE
ADMIRAL RODNEY
PARTICPATING OUTLE S
SEVERE
THAT'S ALL FOLK/S DO NOT JAR
BING.
SURVIVAL RATIONS
BOSTON
CHILDREN'S CARTOONS FROM
ROCKETS AND MISSLES
GUILT
DROUGHT
DANGE
SECOND TENOR
DANGER
EIGHT LBS
GRAIN
COOKING OIL EAGLE
VITAPHONE
VITA
PHONE
ROITS
RIOTS OVER
STAMP ACT PAR
FOR THE
CHRYSLR
CHRYSLER
PLYMOUTH
FEDERL JURY
TWICE.
DANGER
KEEP
STAMP
COURS
VIRUGRAI
VIRUS
14TH CENT UR
FORCES OF GOOD
VERSUS
FORCES OF EVIL
GOMEZ
(P
HARMONY
H
TAILFINS
IV
DEVASTATING
ELECTRIC TRAIN
LOCOMOTIVE
32 STATI
NO
SALE
NO
SALE.
JELLYSTONE
OFFICER LUNDY
1932
"PEAK"
FNL
REESE
MEATBALLS
AND SPAGHETT
SHARPS
HORSEFUNERAL
EARL OF BUTE
(AUSTRO-RUSSIAN)
TELEFON
OTTOMAN EMPIRE
OTTOMAN EMPIRE
ACCAPELLA
(INTOXICATED). 14 ODEEOOK
OOK'
MESSERSCHICMDTS
PAW
WILLIAM HANNA
JOSEPH BARBARA
ASBESTOS.
TWELVE
HELADO
DE
COCO.
HELADO
DE
COCO.
FOESE
OATMEA
PAW
AZOV
IN 1739
ADMIRAL
VAERON
SACKED
OUTSMART RIORS
IMPORTED CHEESES
DICK YORK
11. FAITH HEALER
12.
MUSTAFA'S
BROTHER
PIRAGUAS, PORTO
BELLO
BABYCAKES
1. ROASTING BOAR
VII.
HEOO
KOKO
DECLINE.
I H
BASKETBALL INJURIES
TURKISH TWELVE. 12
AGNOSTIC VORTEX. 2
FRENCH
CROWN
1. SLAVE TRADE
AMERICA'S
MOST POPULAR
WINE
PRAGMACTIC SANCTION
VITAPHONE
POST WAR
POST CEREALS
AHMAD III
12. CARIBBEAN INDIANS
ABDUL HAMID ONE
COLOSSEUM

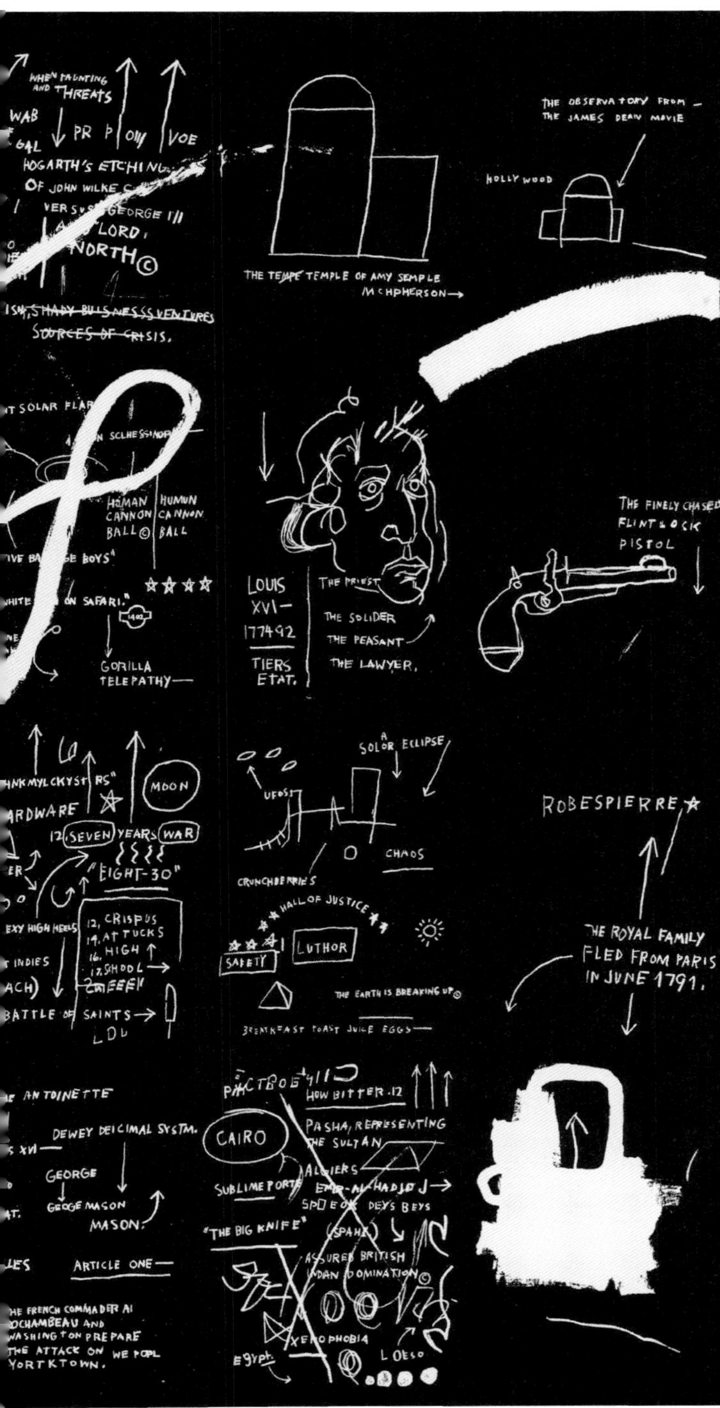

Untitled, 1983
Silkscreen on canvas,
146.5 x 192 cm /
57 3/4 x 75 1/2 inches

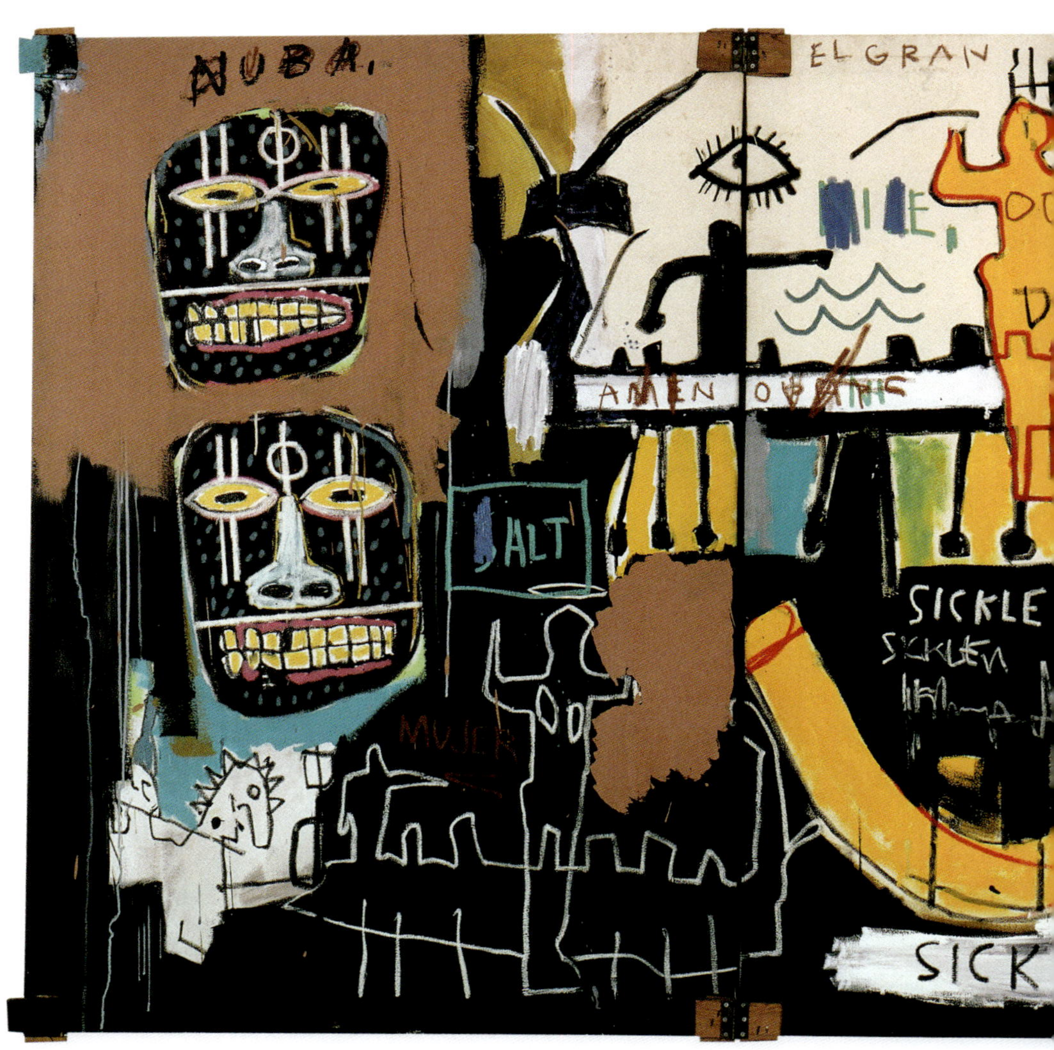

El Gran Espectaculo (History of Black People), 1983
Acrylic and oilstick on canvas mounted on wooden
supports, triptych: 172.5 x 358 cm / 68 x 141 inches

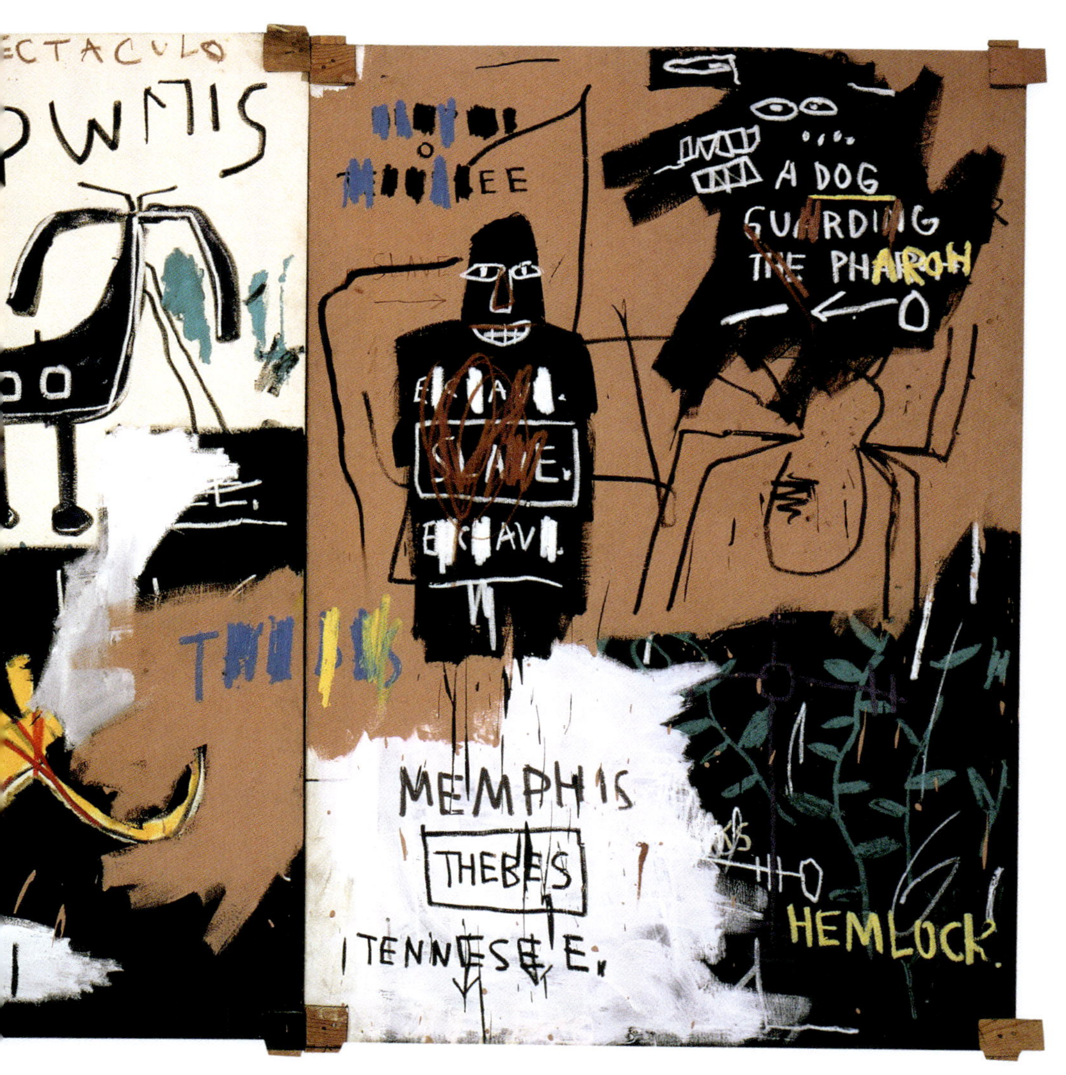
ECTACULO
PWMIS
EE
SLAVE
MEMPHIS
THEBES
TENNESEE.
A DOG
GUARDING
THE PHAROH
HEMLOCK.

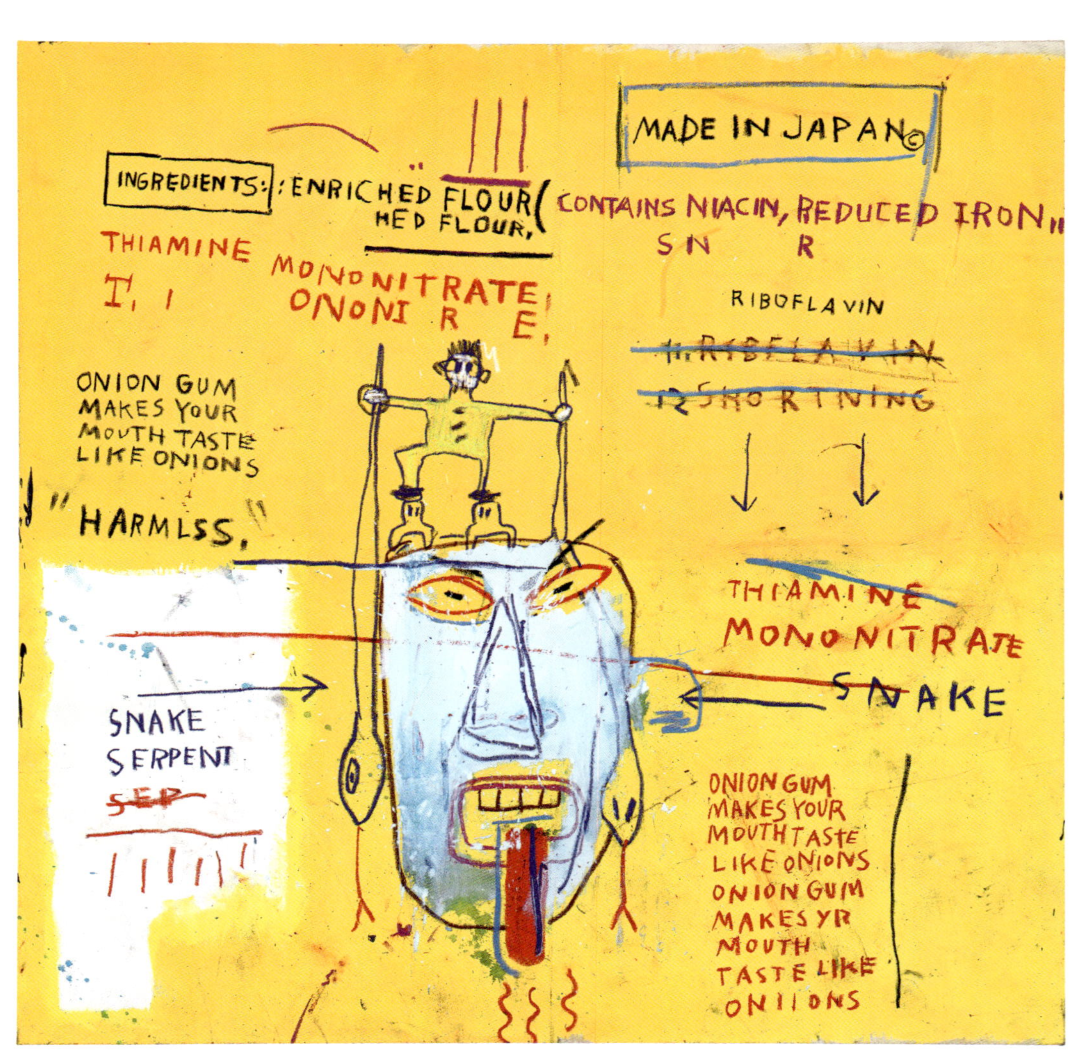

Onion Gum, 1983
Acrylic and oilstick on canvas,
197 x 203 cm / 77 ¹/₂ x 80 inches

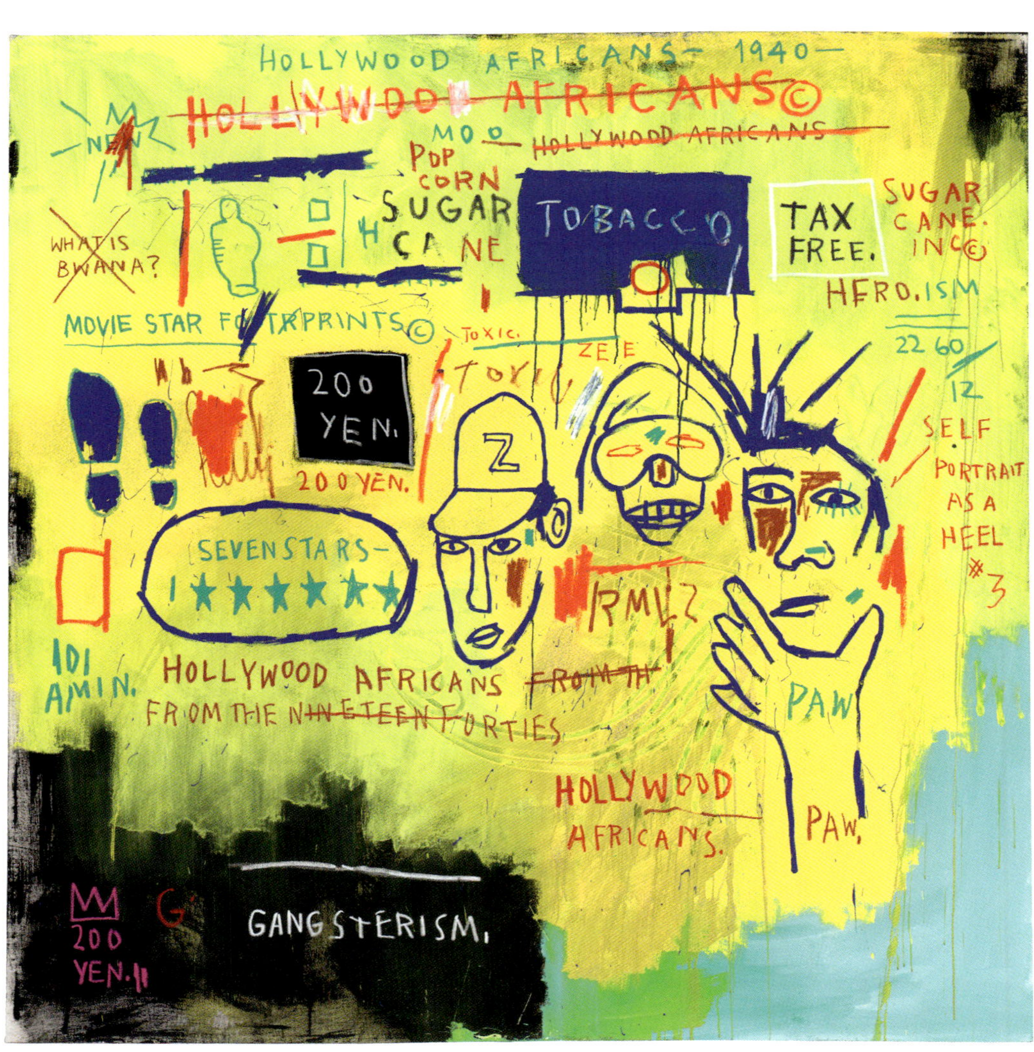

Hollywood Africans, 1983
Acrylic and oilstick on canvas,
213.5 x 213.5 cm / 84 x 84 inches

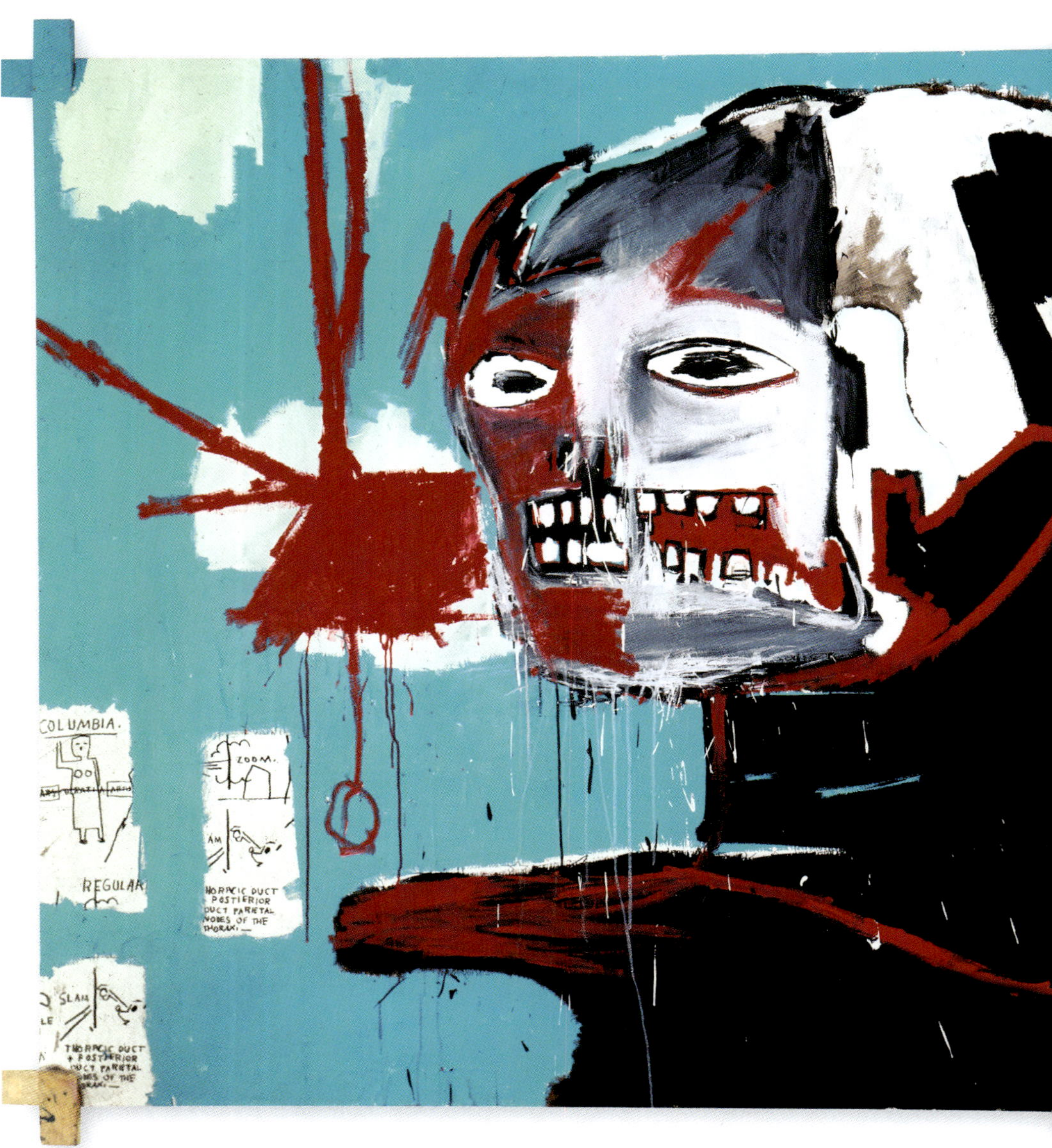

La Colomba, 1983
Acrylic, oilstick, and photocopy collage
on canvas mounted on wooden supports,
diptych: 183 x 365.5 cm / 72 x 144 inches

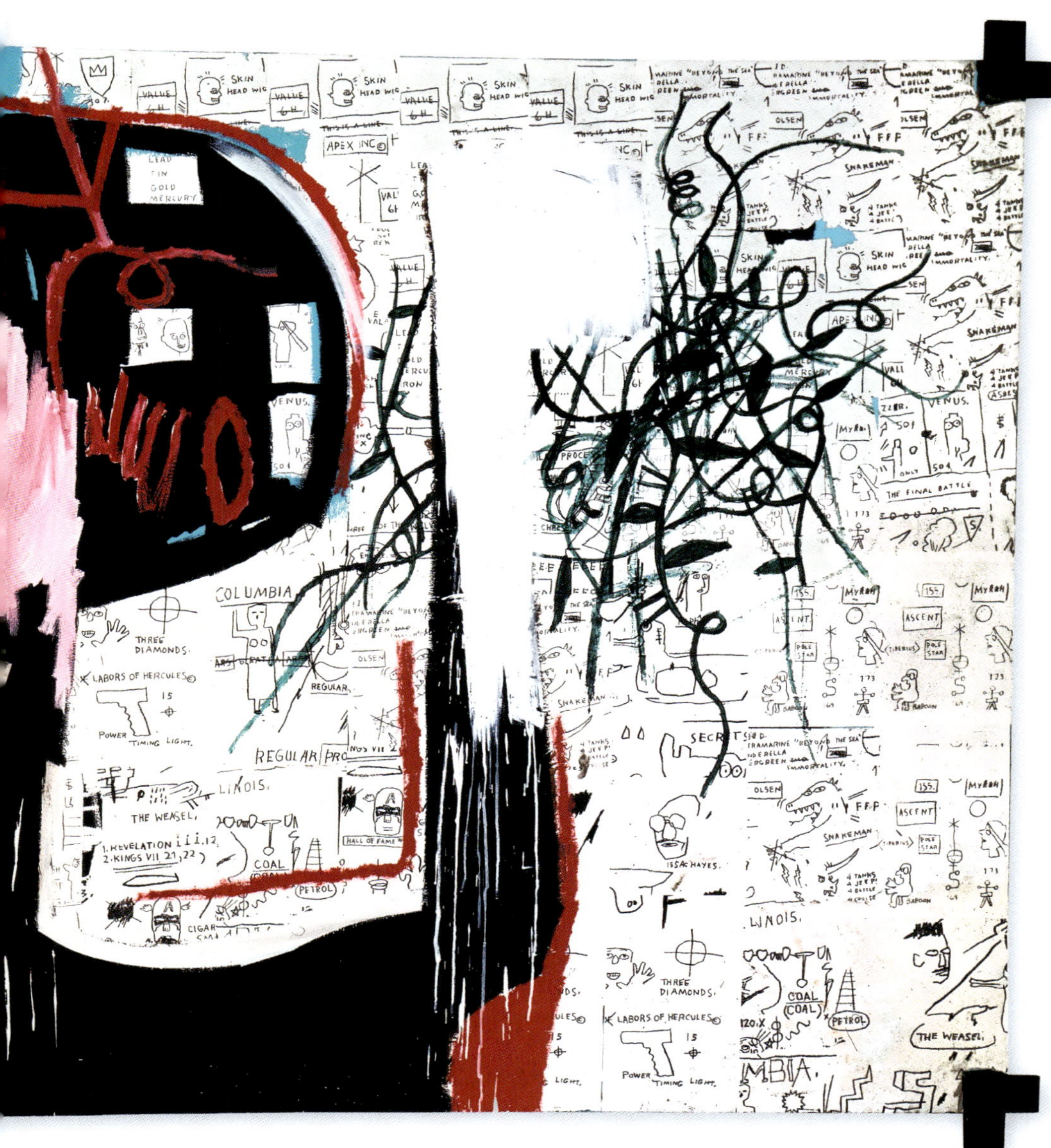

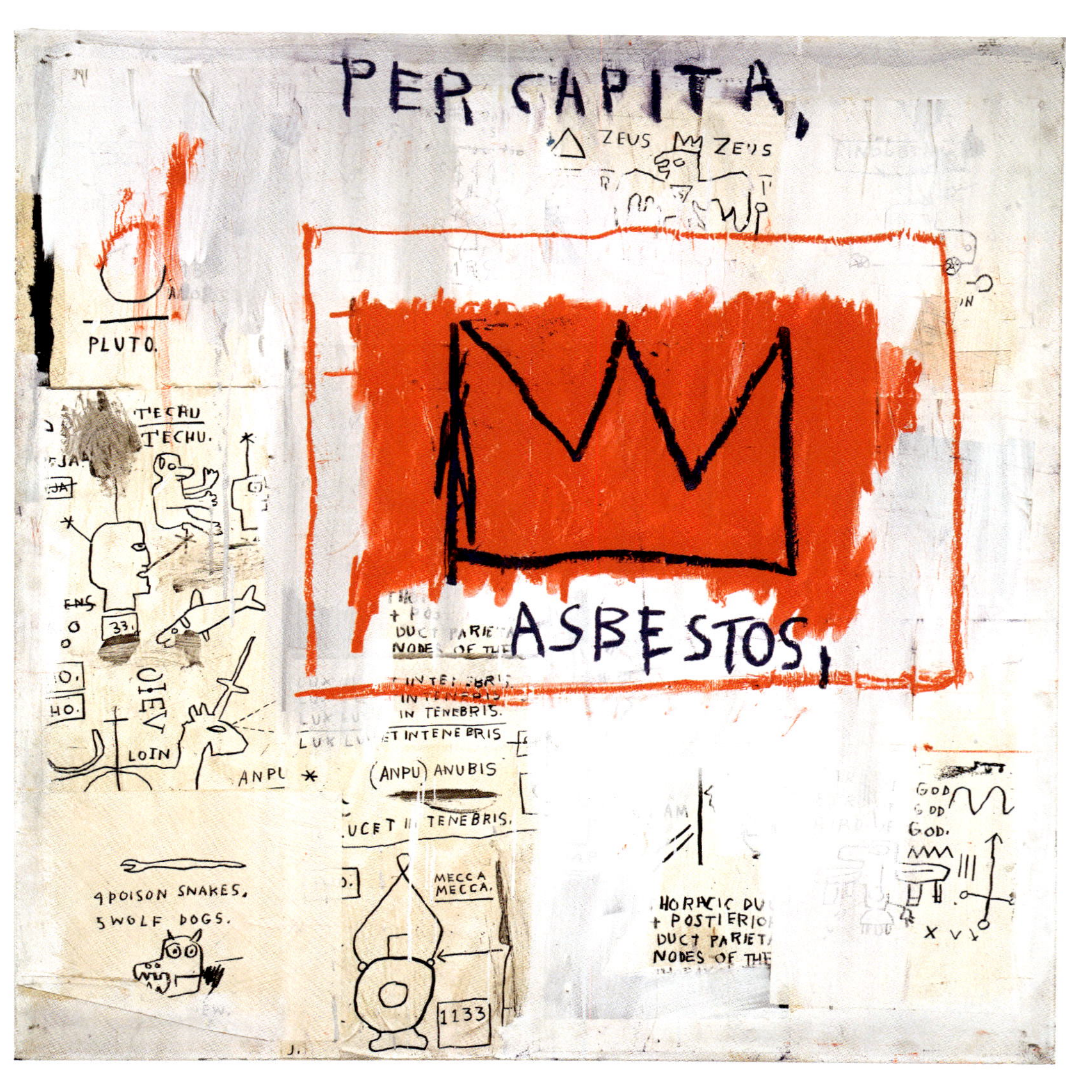

Untitled (Per Capita), 1983
Acrylic, oilstick, and photocopy
collage on aluminum,
89 x 89 cm / 35 x 35 inches

Danny Rosen, 1983
Acrylic, oilstick, and paper collage on
canvas mounted on wooden supports,
223.5 x 122 cm / 88 x 48 inches

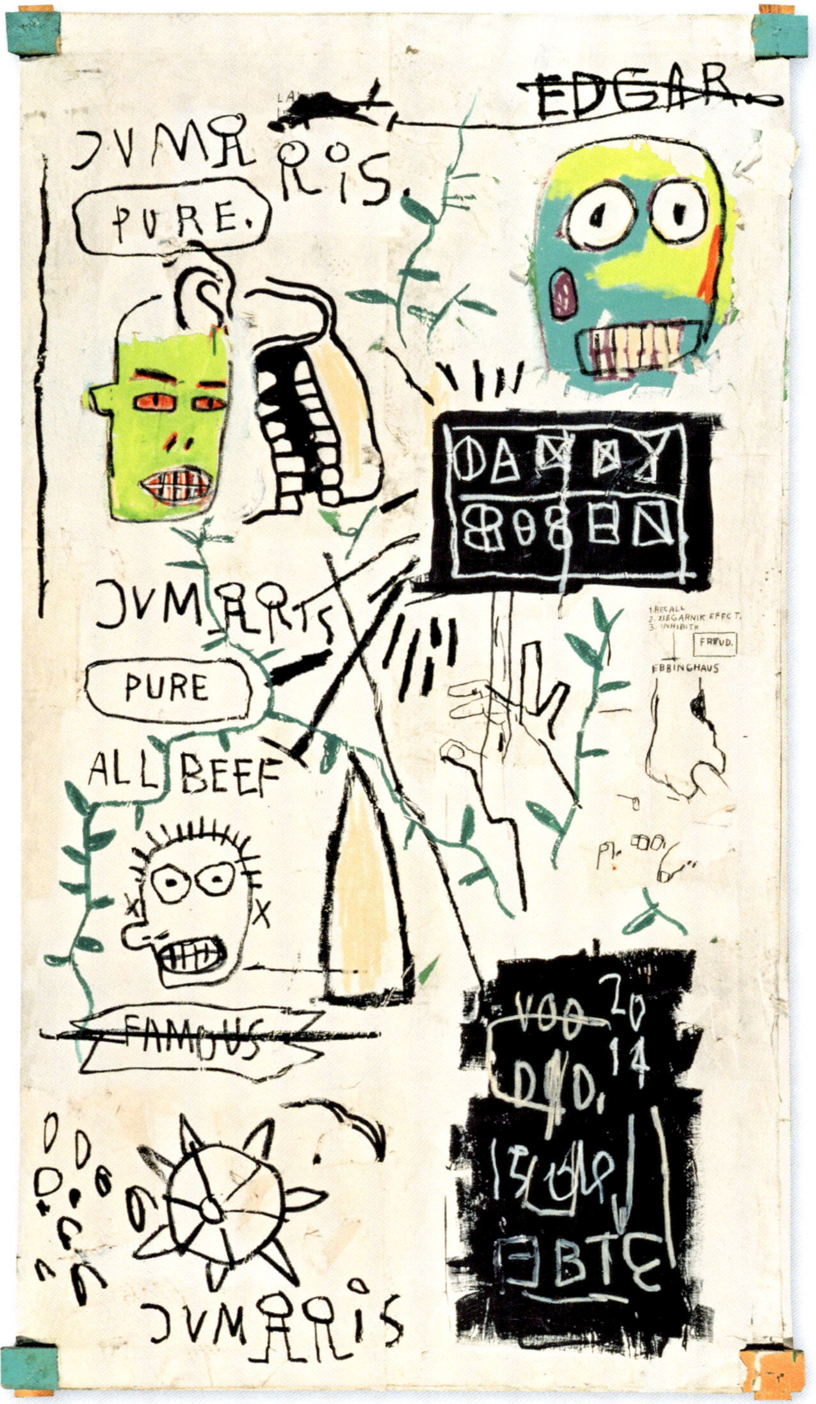
EDGAR
JVMA RIS.
PURE,
JVMARIS
PURE
ALL BEEF
FAMOUS
JVMARIS
1. RECALL
2. ZIEGARNIK EFFECT.
3. INHIBIT
FREUD.
EBBINGHAUS

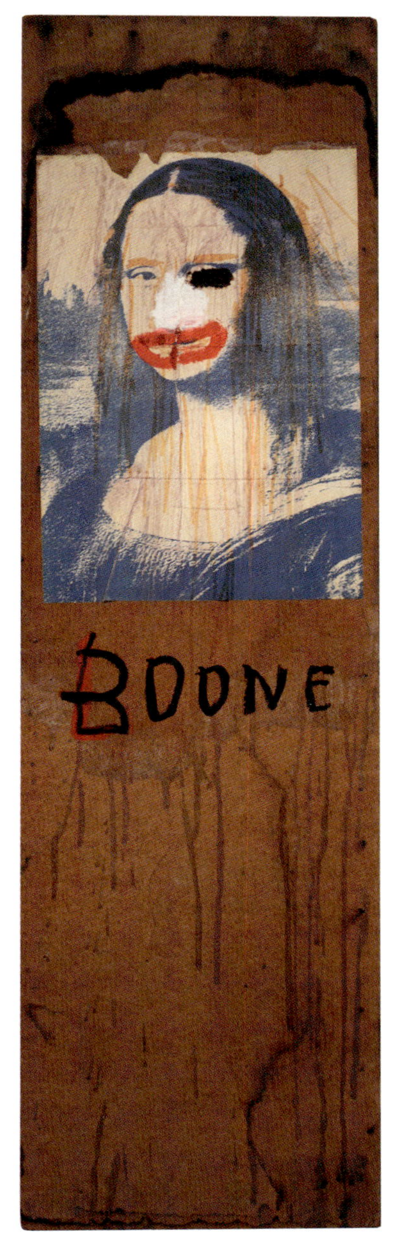

BOONE

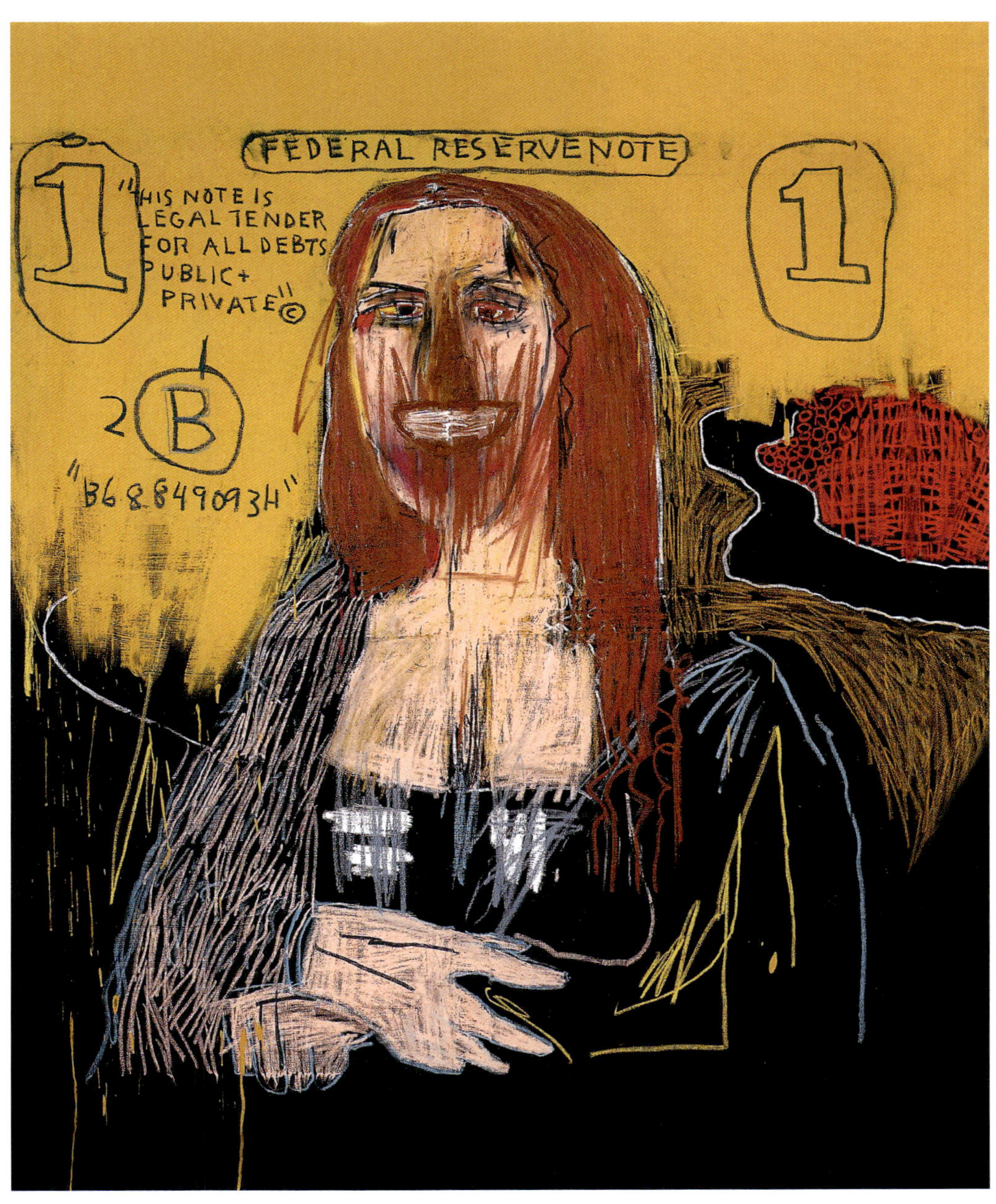

Boone, 1983
Paper collage, marker, and oilstick on masonite
mounted on panel, 104 x 30.5 cm / 41 x 12 inches

Mona Lisa, 1983
Acrylic and oilstick on canvas,
169.5 x 154.5 cm / 66 $^{3}/_{4}$ x 60 $^{3}/_{4}$ inches

Untitled, 1983
Acrylic and oilstick on canvas, triptych:
244 x 183 cm / 96 x 72 inches

Page 286: **Horn Players**, 1983
Acrylic and oilstick on canvas, triptych:
244 x 190.5 cm / 96 x 75 inches

Page 287: **Untitled**, 1983
Acrylic and oilstick on canvas, triptych:
246 x 191 cm / 97 x 75 $^1/_4$ inches

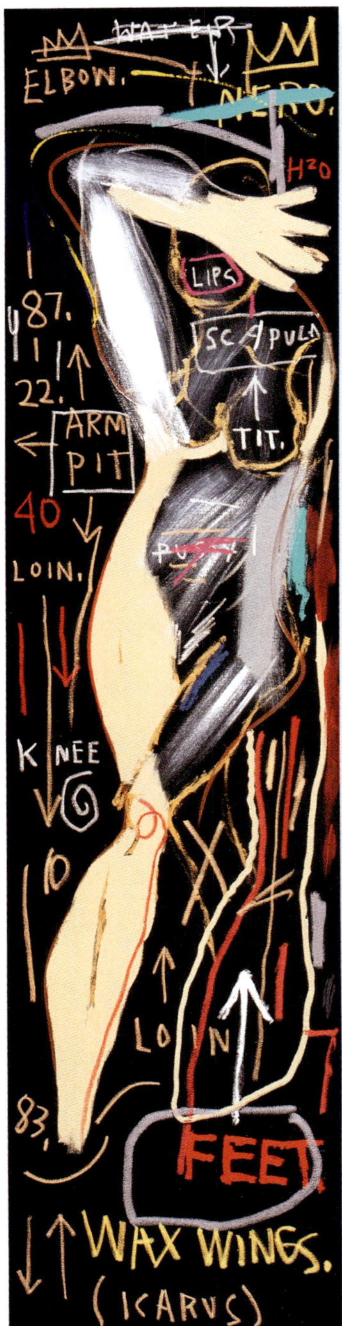

ELBOW.
NERO.
H2O
LIPS
SCAPULA
87.
22.
ARM PIT
40
LOIN.
TIT.
KNEE
LOIN
83.
FEET
WAX WINGS.
(ICARUS)

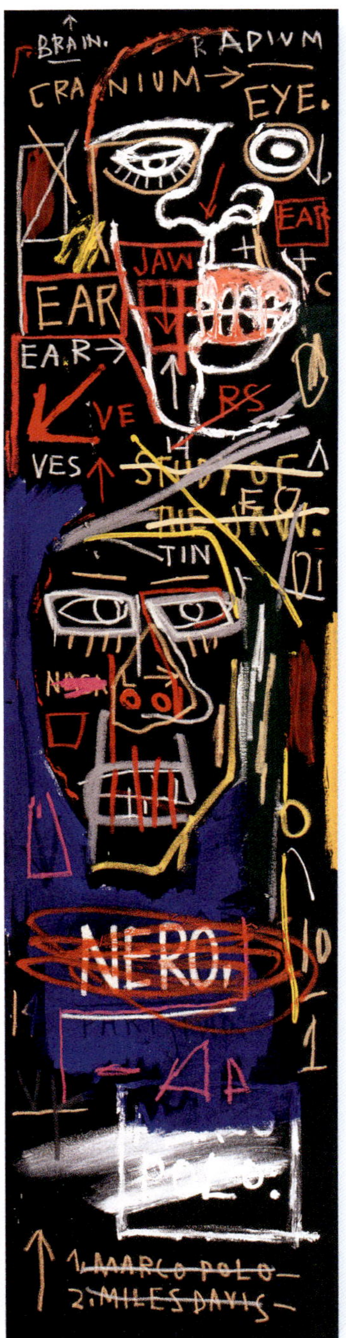

BRAIN.
RADIUM
CRANIUM
EYE.
EAR
JAW
EAR
EAR
VES
VES
STUDY OF
THE DRO.
TIN
NERO.
1. MARCO POLO
2. MILES DAVIS

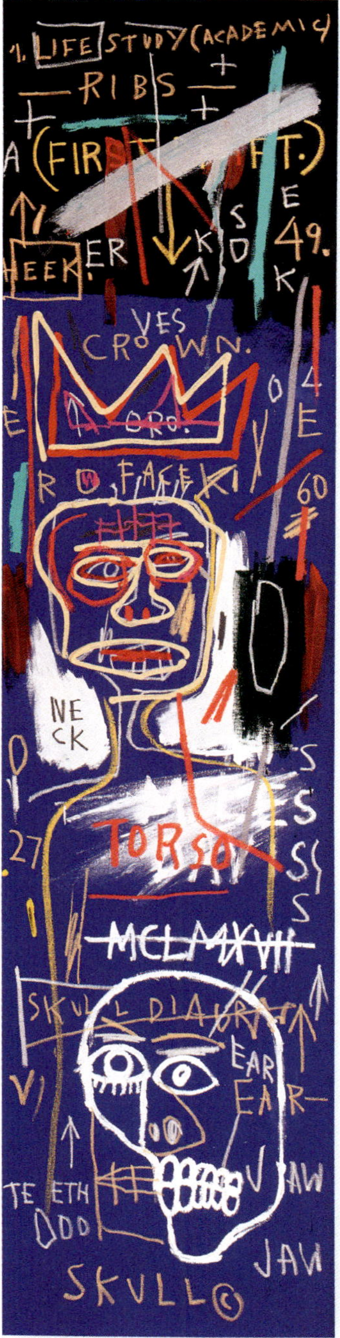

1. LIFE STUDY (ACADEMY)
RIBS
(FIRST
CHEEK.
ER
49.
VES
CROWN.
ORO.
FACE
60
NECK
TORSO
MCLMXVII
SKULL DIAGRAM
EAR
EAR
NECK
27
TEETH
JAW
SKULL
JAW

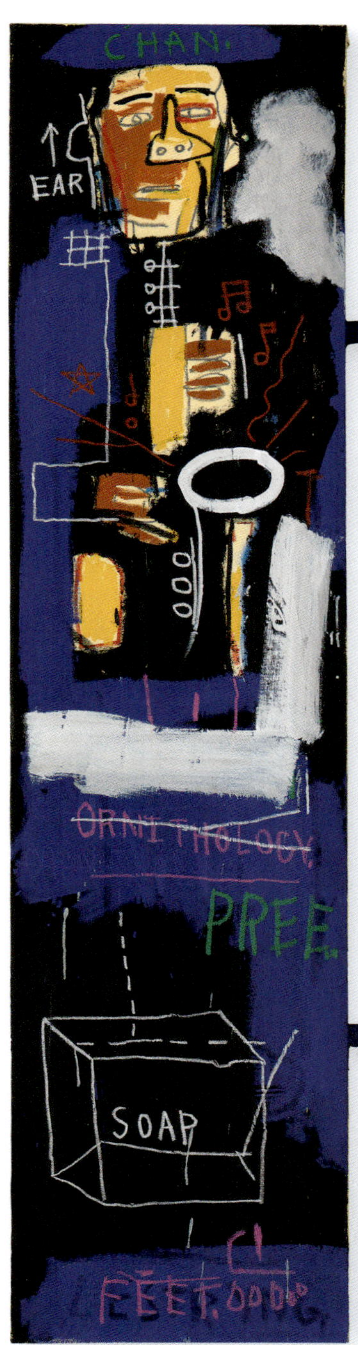

CHAN.
EAR
ORNITHOLOGY,
PREE.
SOAP
FEET.

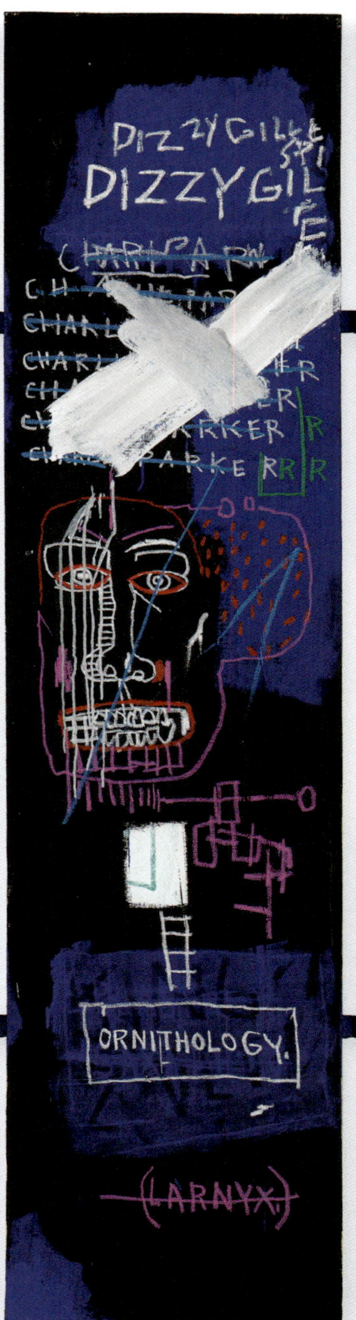

DIZZYGILLE
DIZZYGIL
CHARLPARK
CHARLIE PAR
CHARL
CHARL
CHARL PARKER
CHARL PARKER R R R
ORNITHOLOGY.
(LARNYX)

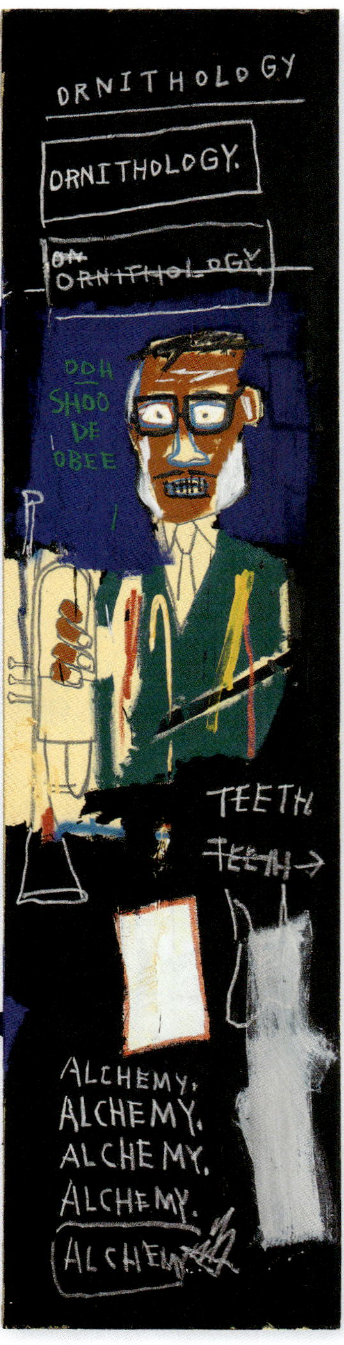

ORNITHOLOGY
ORNITHOLOGY.
ORNITHOLOGY
OOH
SHOO
DE
OBEE
TEETH
TEETH
ALCHEMY.
ALCHEMY.
ALCHEMY.
ALCHEMY.
ALCHEM

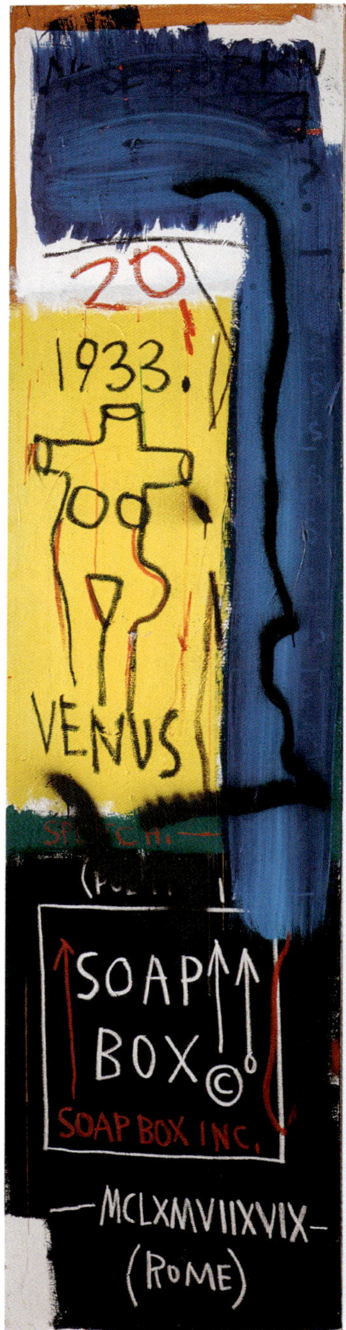
20
1933.
VENUS
SOAP
BOX ©
SOAP BOX INC.
MCLXMVIIXVIX
(ROME)

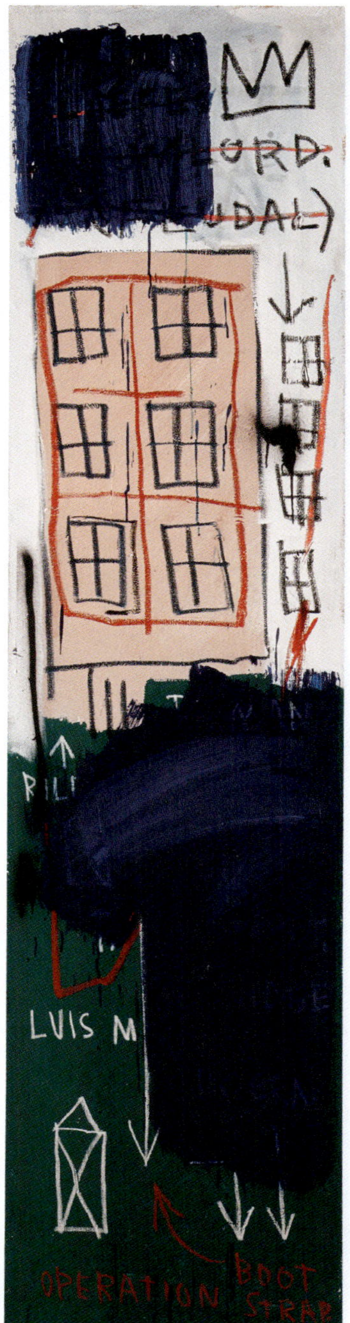
ORD.
(FEUDAL)
LUIS M
OPERATION
BOOT
STRAP

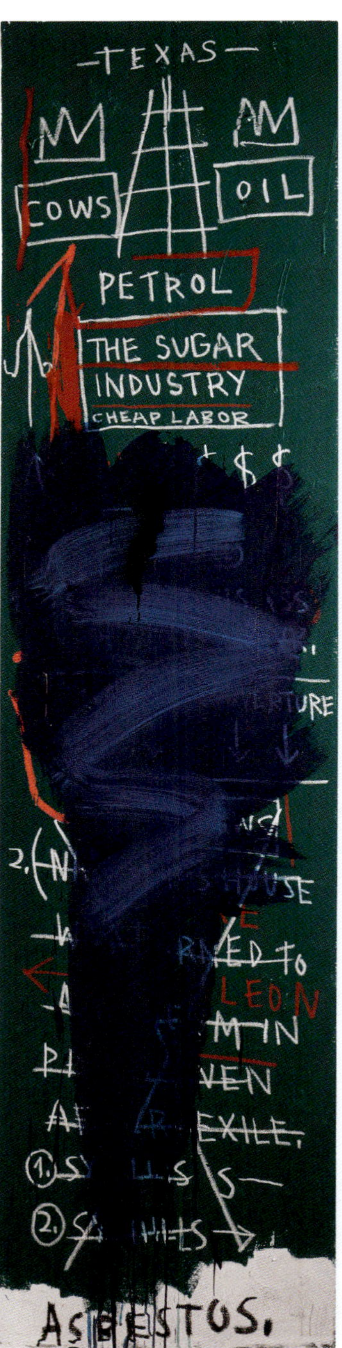
TEXAS
COWS
AM
OIL
PETROL
THE SUGAR
INDUSTRY
CHEAP LABOR
$$
LEON
EXILE
1.
2.
ASBESTOS.

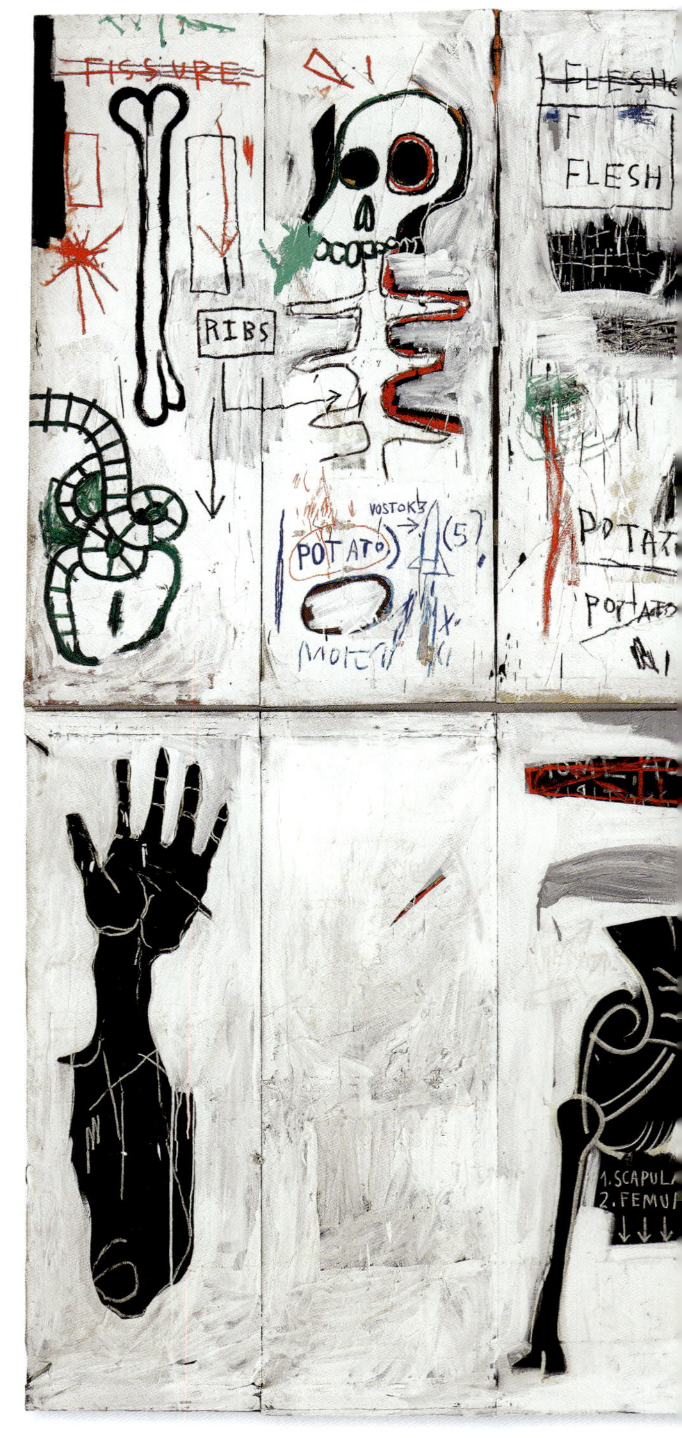

Flesh and Spirit, 1982–1983
Acrylic, oilstick, and gesso on
canvas, polyptych:
365.5 x 365.5 cm / 144 x 144 inches

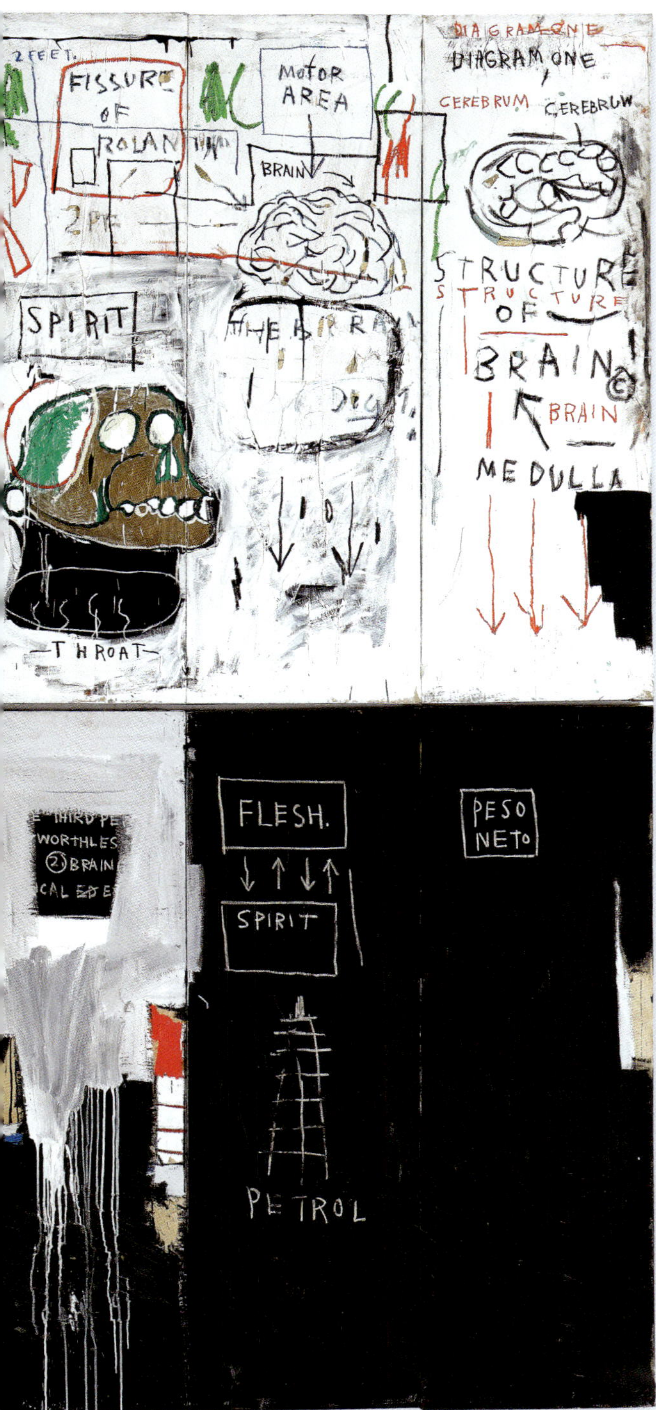
2 FEET.
FISSURE
OF
ROLAN
2 FE
MOTOR
AREA
BRAIN
DIAGRAM ONE
DIAGRAM ONE
CEREBRUM
CEREBRUW
STRUCTURE
STRUCTURE
OF
BRAIN
BRAIN
MEDULLA
SPIRIT
THROAT
THIRD PE
WORTHLES
2 BRAIN
CAL ED E
FLESH.
SPIRIT
PETROL
PESO
NETO

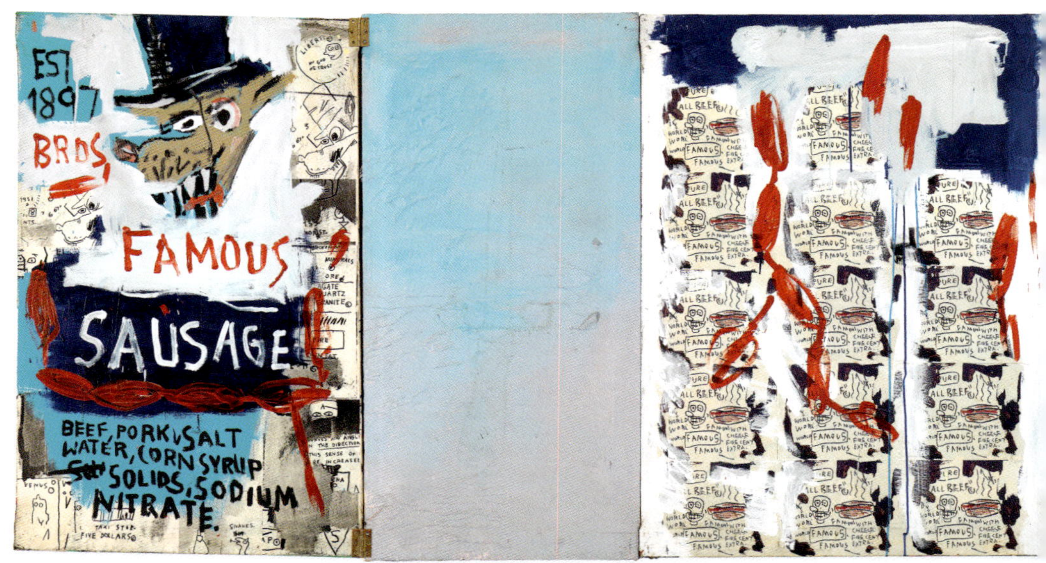

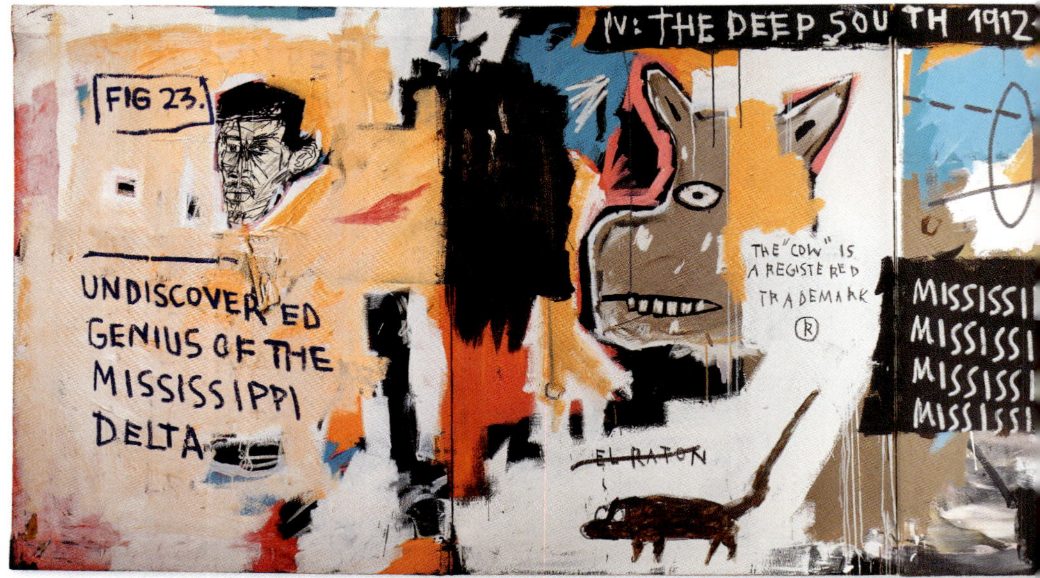

Brother's Sausage, 1983
Acrylic, oilstick, and photocopy collage on canvas,
polyptych: 122 x 476 cm / 48 x 187 ¹/₂ inches

Undiscovered Genius of the Mississippi Delta, 1983
Acrylic, oilstick, and paper collage on canvas,
polyptych: 122 x 467.5 cm / 48 x 184 inches

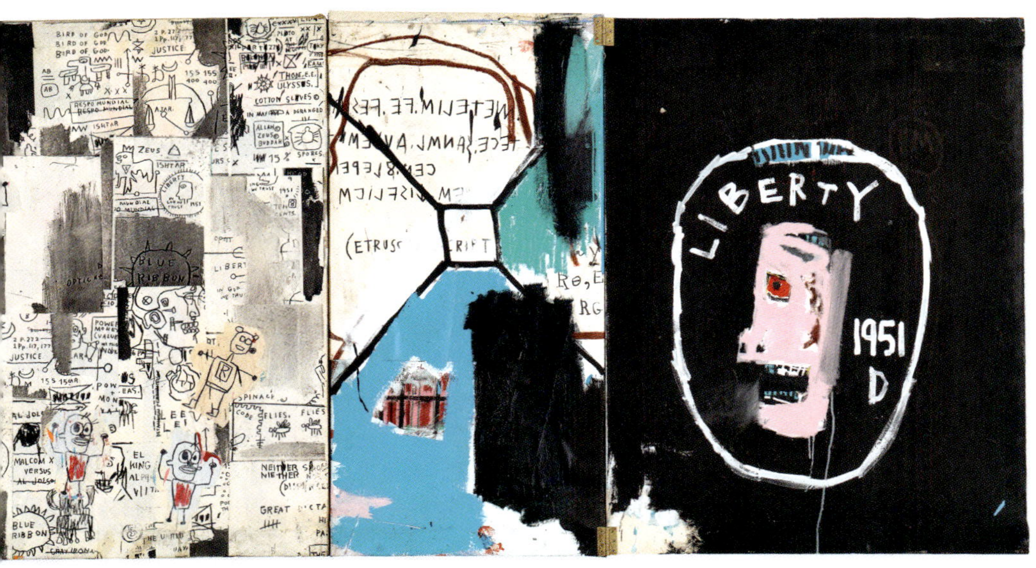

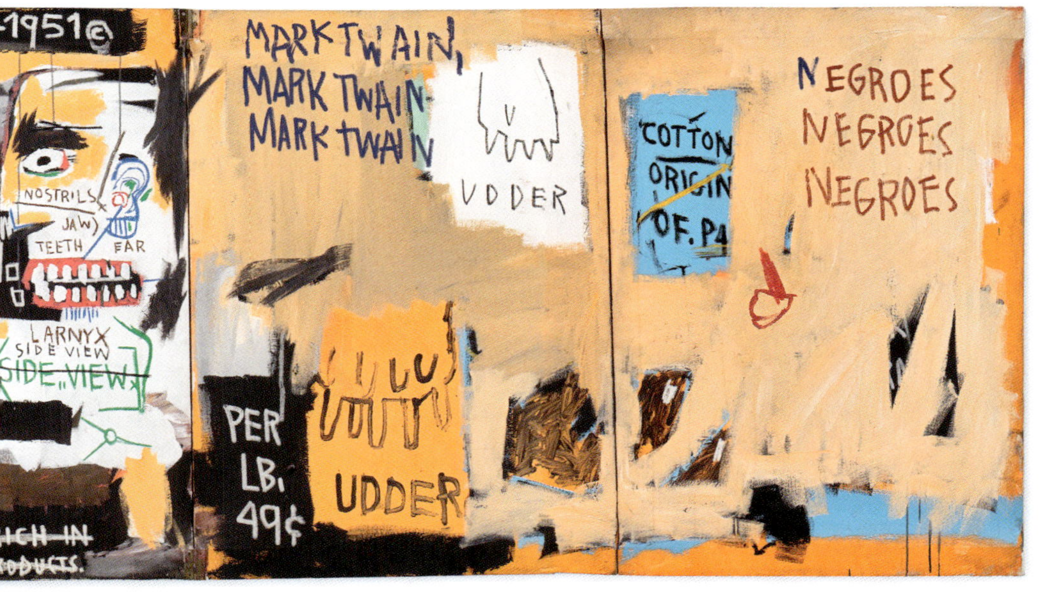

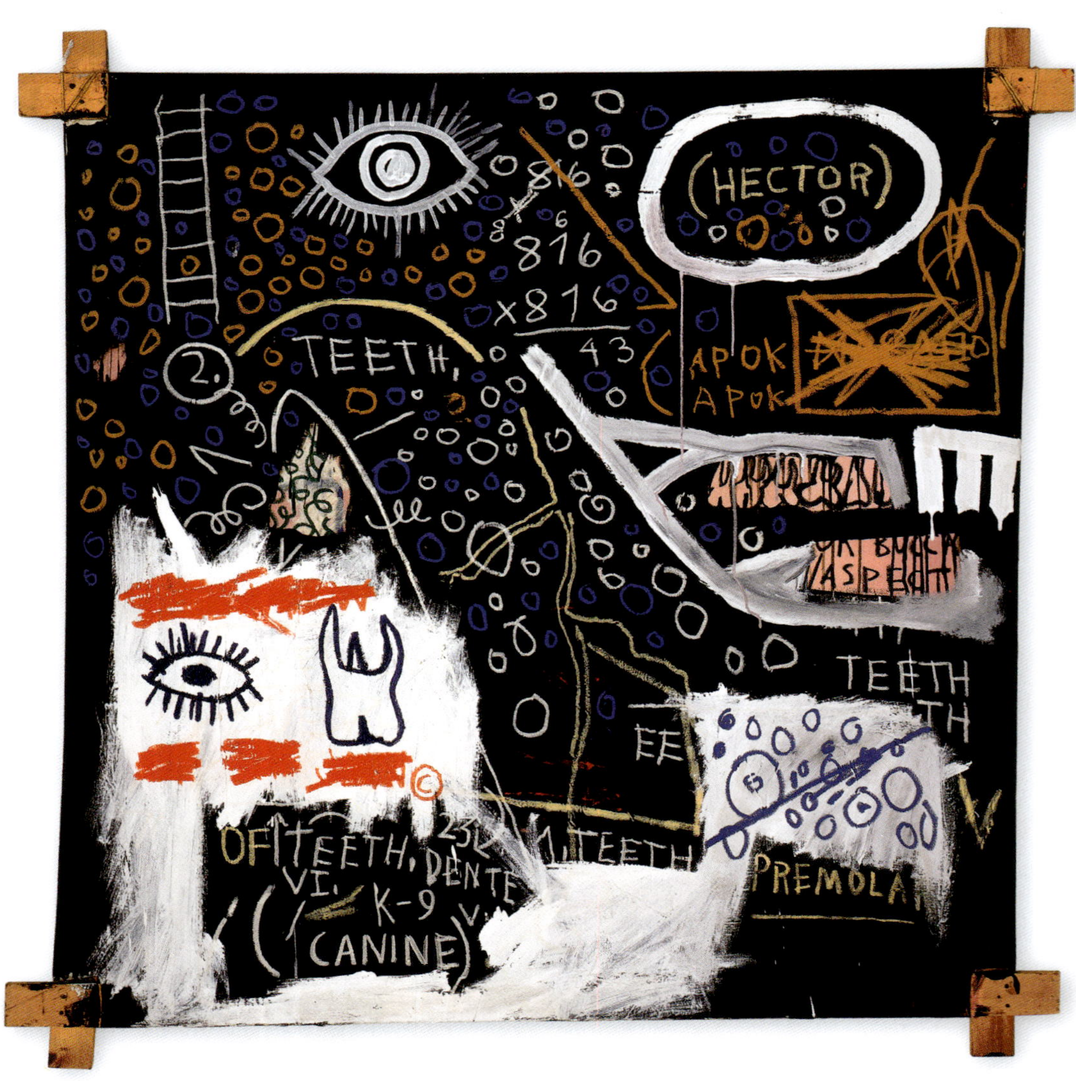

Hector, 1983
Acrylic and oilstick on canvas mounted on wooden
supports, 152.5 x 152.5 cm / 60 x 60 inches

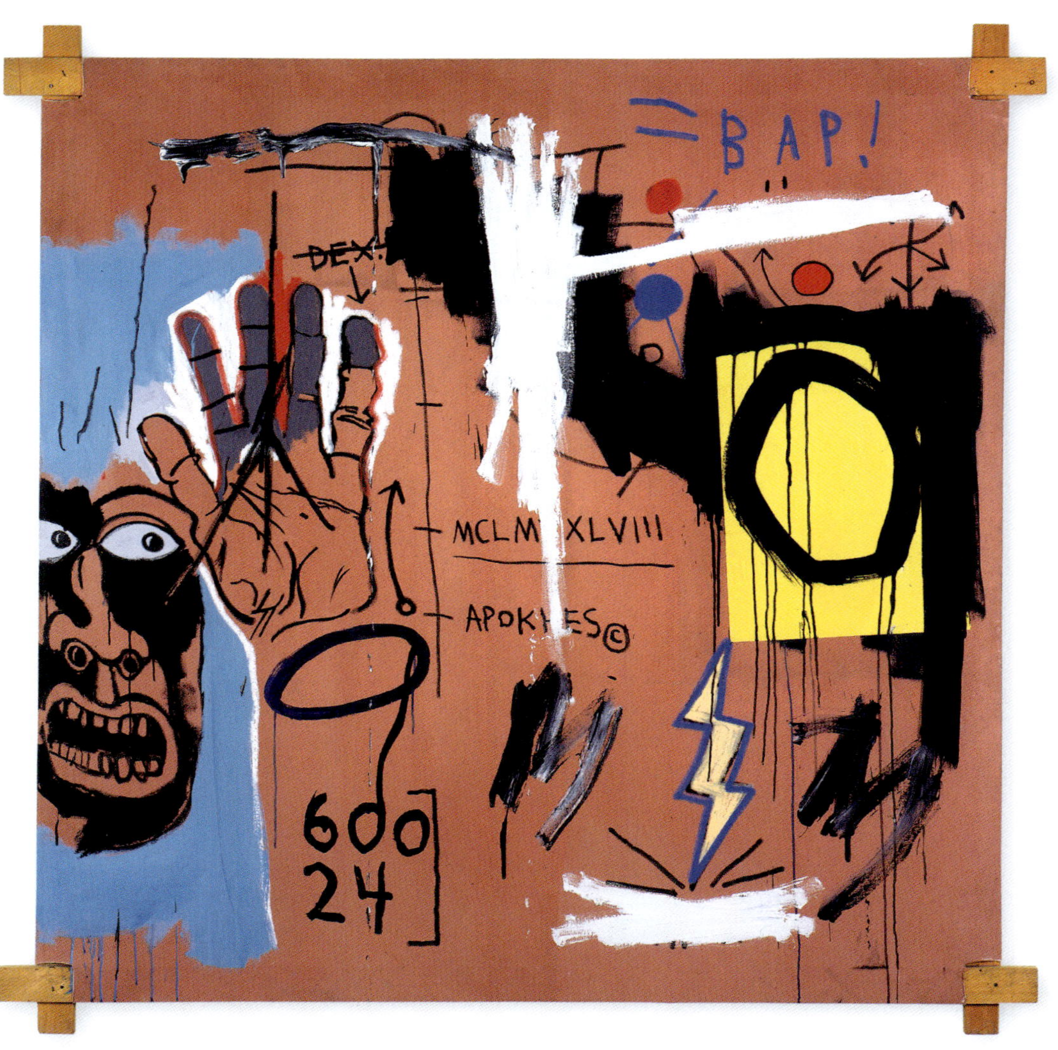

Bap, 1983
Acrylic, oilstick, and paper collage on canvas mounted
on wooden supports, 183 x 183 cm / 72 x 72 inches

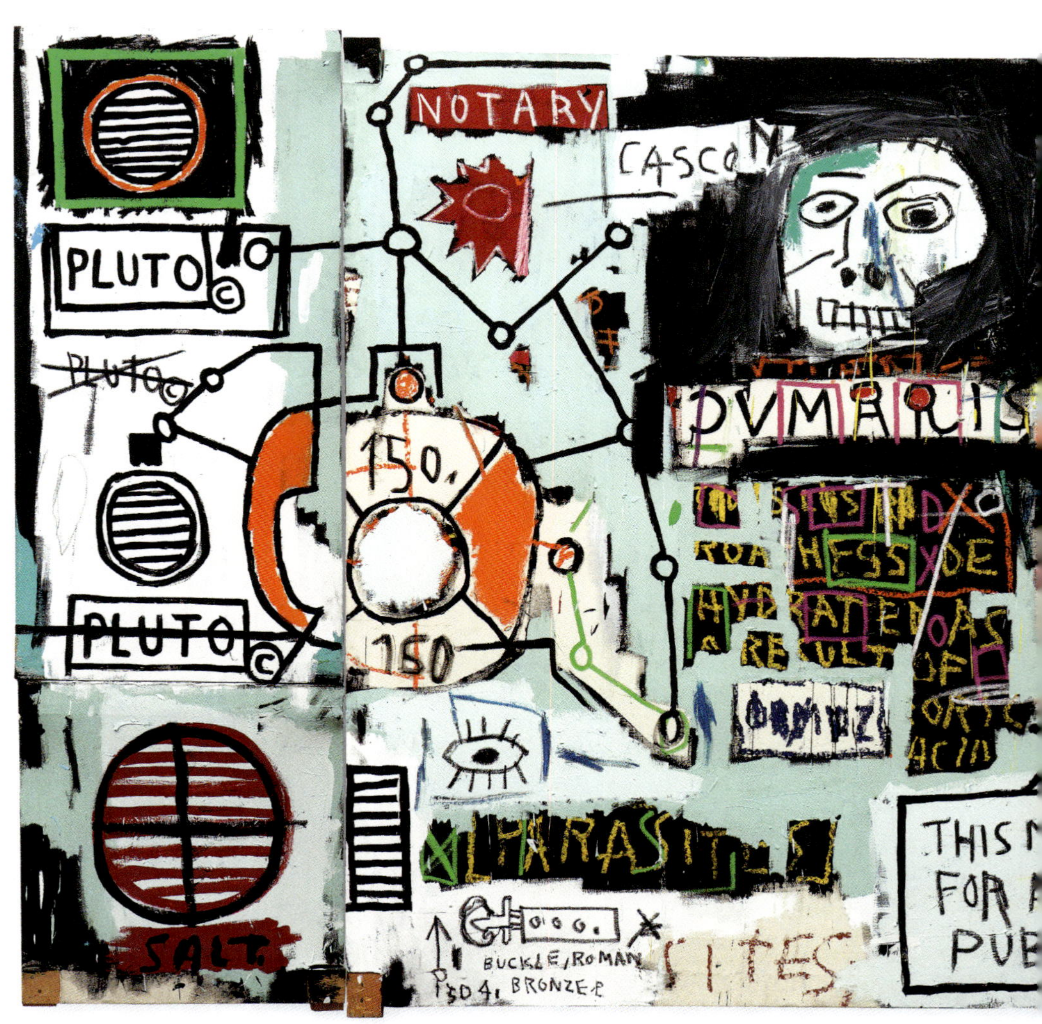

Notary, 1983
Acrylic, oilstick, and paper collage on
canvas mounted on wooden supports,
triptych: 180.5 x 401.5 cm / 71 x 158 inches

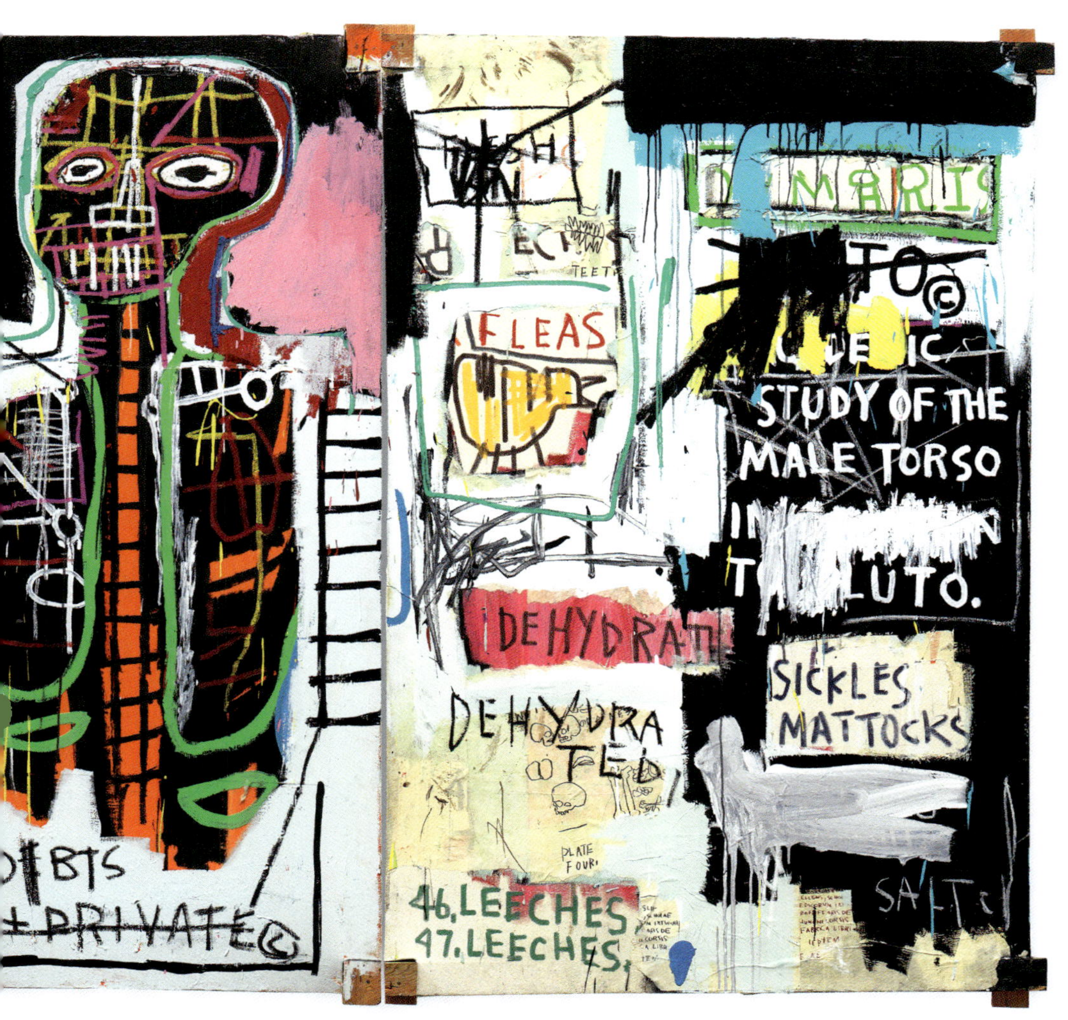
DEBTS
+ PRIVATE©
FRESH
ECTO
TEETH
FLEAS
DEHYDRAT
DEHYDRA TED
PLATE FOUR
46. LEECHES
47. LEECHES.
MARIS
TO©
STUDY OF THE
MALE TORSO
PLUTO.
SICKLES
MATTOCKS
SALT

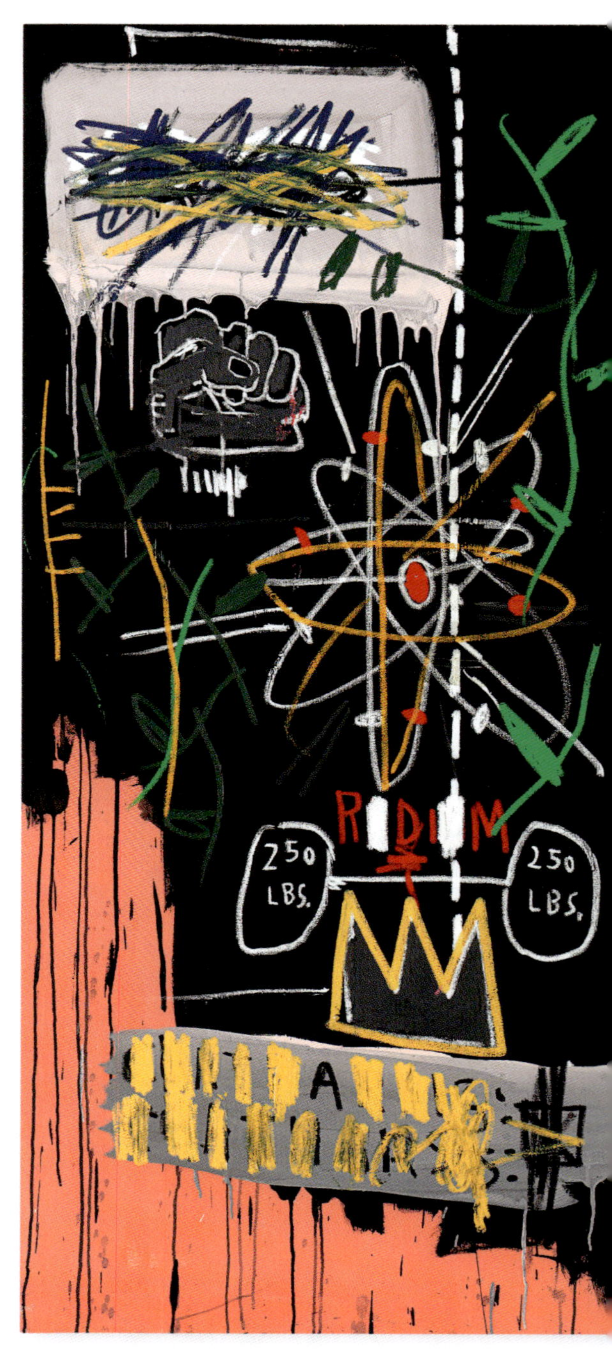

Catharsis, 1983
Acrylic and oilstick on
canvas, triptych:
183 x 233.5 cm / 72 x 92 inches

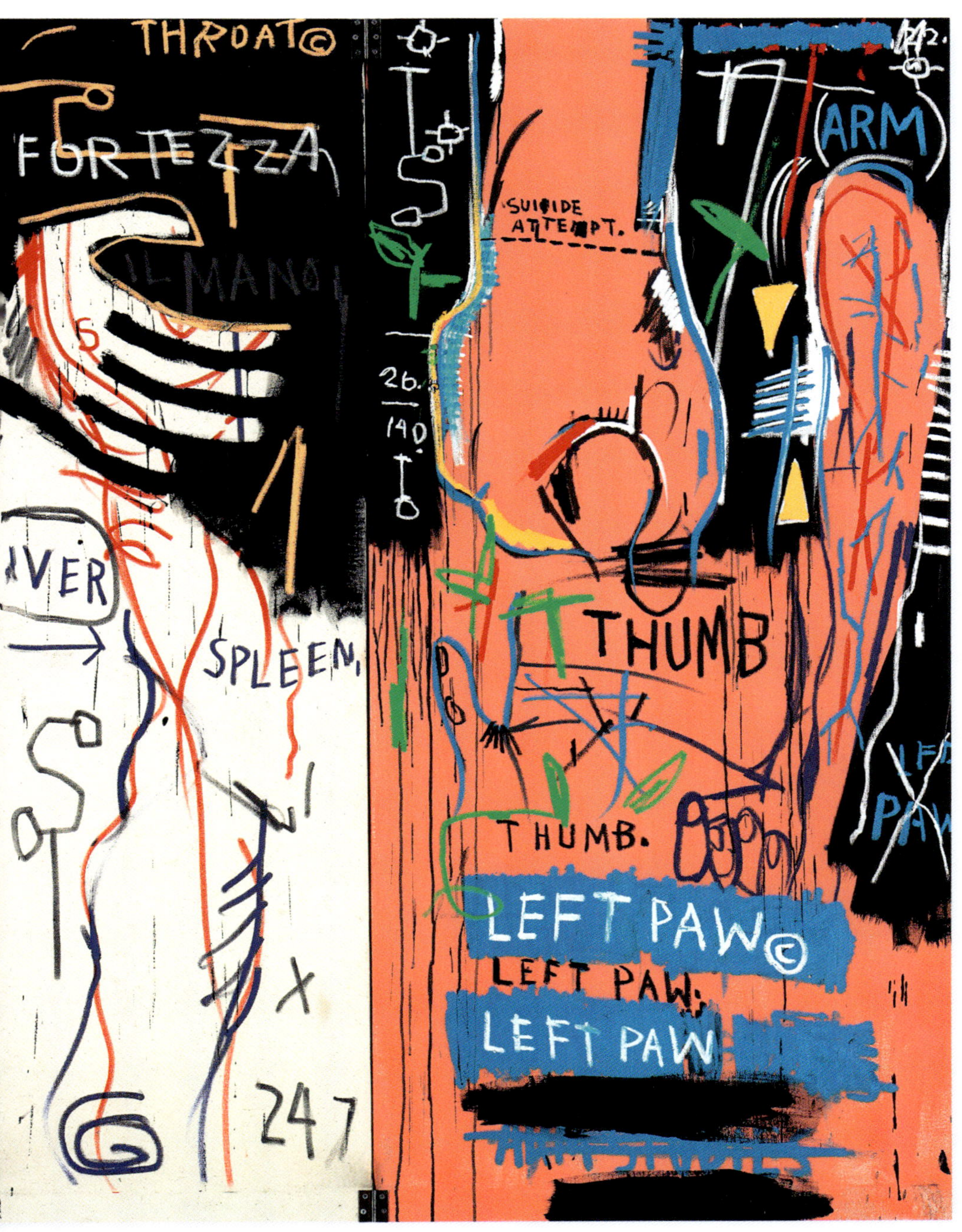

THROAT©
FORTEZZA
IL MANO
IVER
SPLEEN
247
SUICIDE ATTEMPT.
26.
140.
(ARM)
THUMB
THUMB.
LEFT PAW©
LEFT PAW;
LEFT PAW

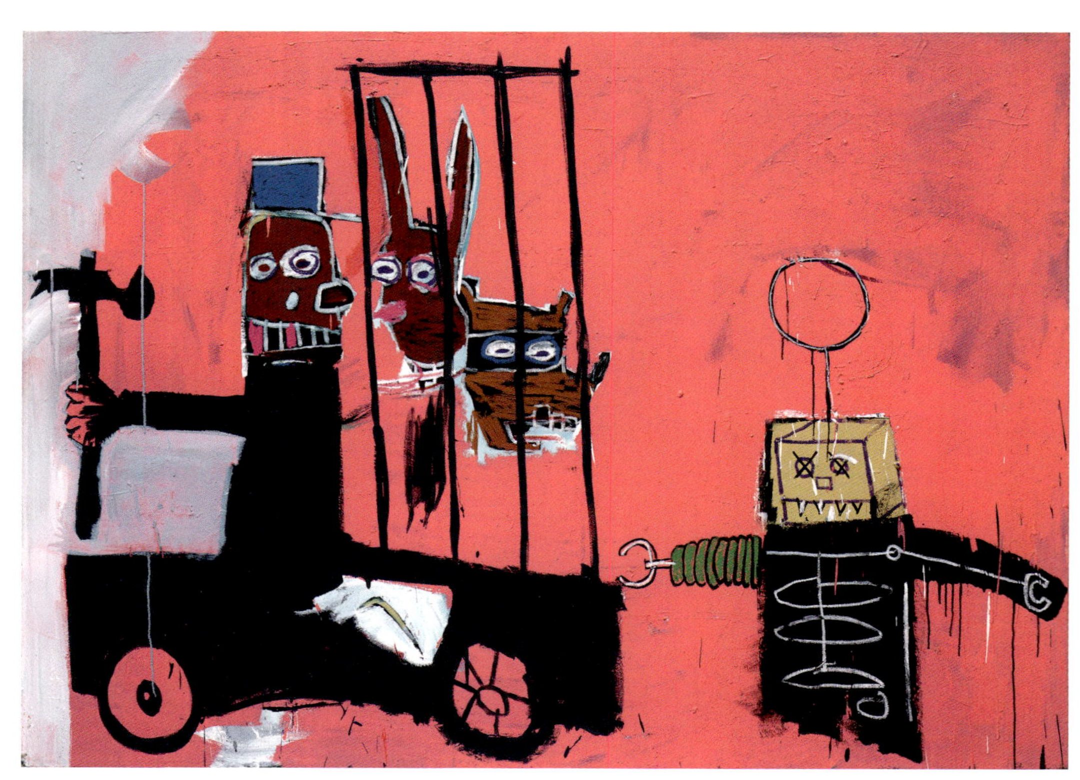

Molasses, 1983
Acrylic and oilstick on canvas,
152.5 x 213.5 cm / 60 x 84 inches

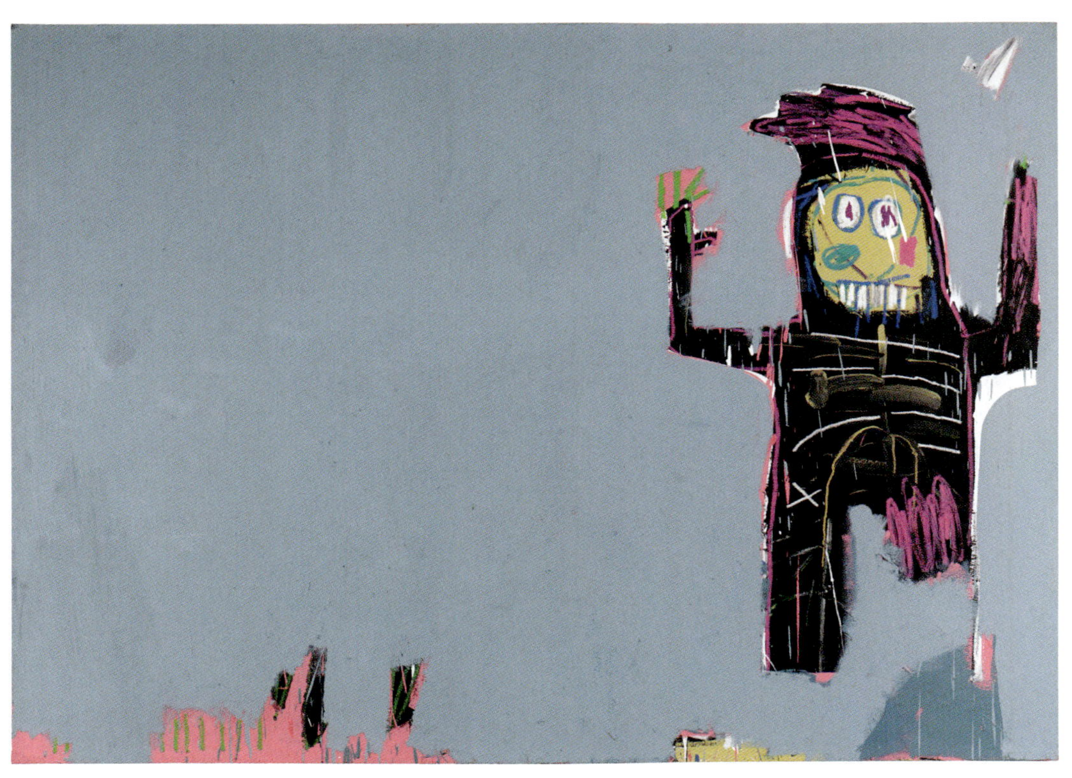

The Lake, 1983
Acrylic and oilstick on canvas,
153 x 213 cm / 60 ¹/₄ x 84 inches

Pages 300/301: **Hardware Store**, 1983
Acrylic, oilstick, and paper collage on canvas
mounted on wooden supports, diptych:
218 x 328 cm / 85 ³/₄ x 129 ¹/₈ inches

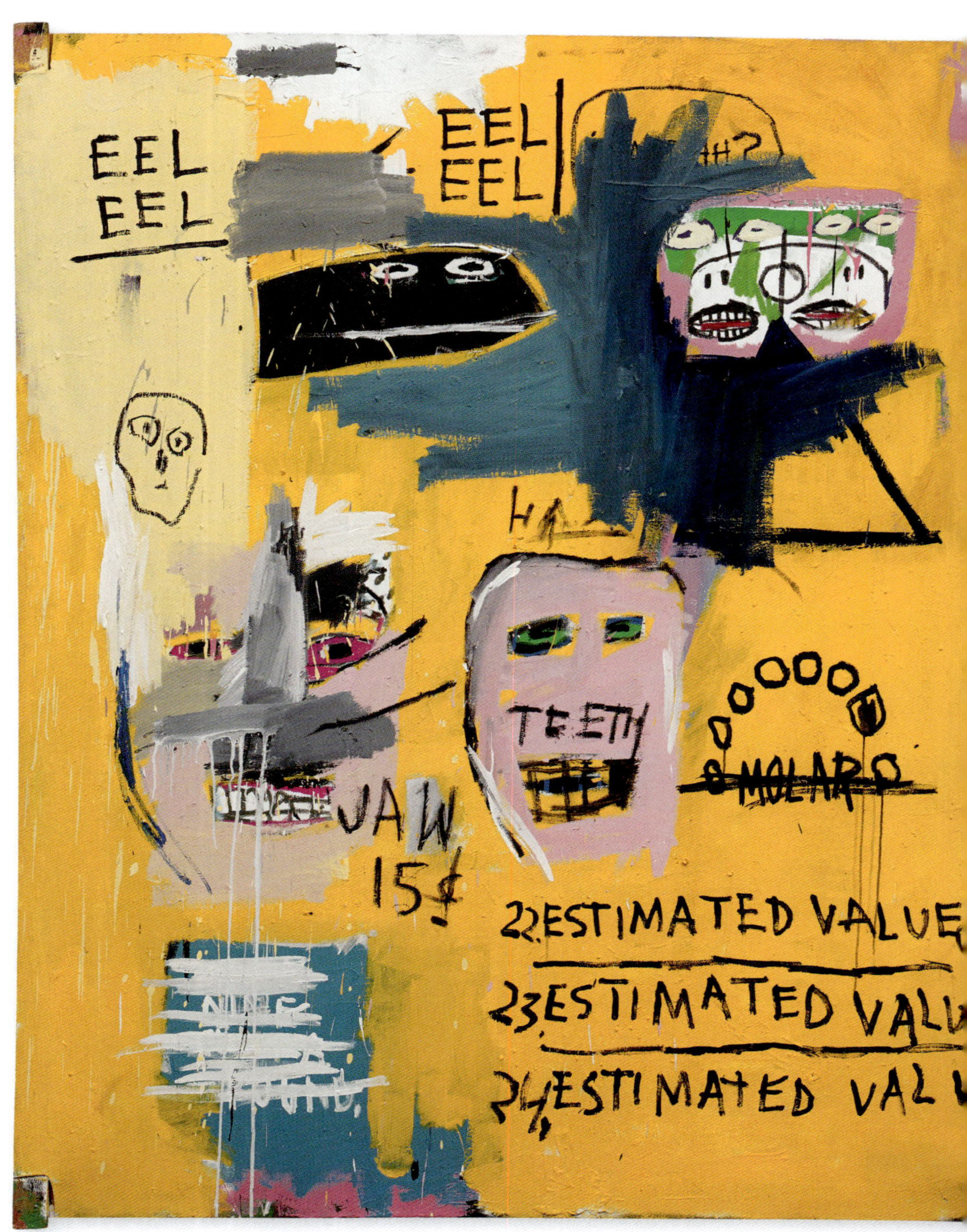

EEL
EEL
EEL
EEL
TEETH
JAW
15$
MOLARS
22ESTIMATED VALUE
23ESTIMATED VALU
24ESTIMATED VAL

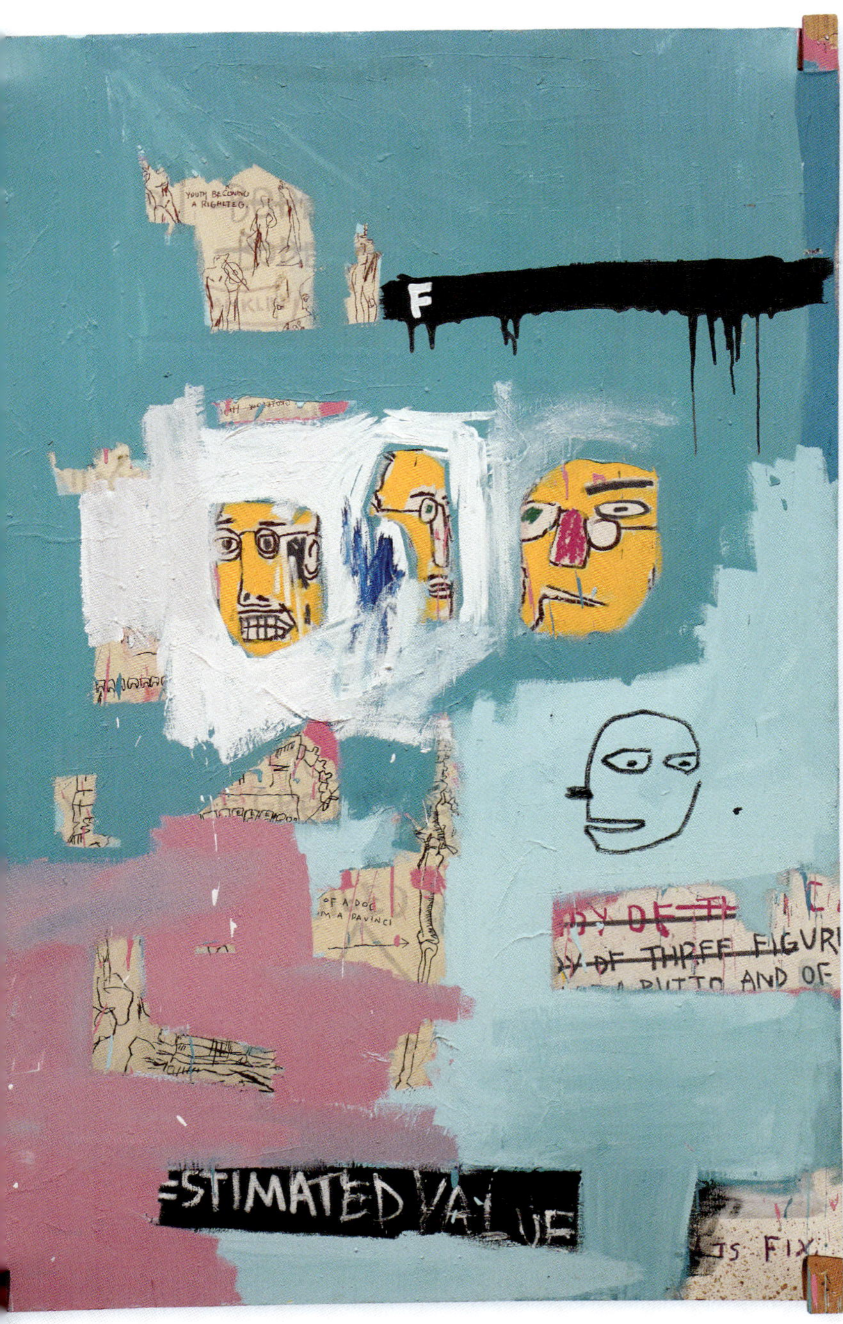

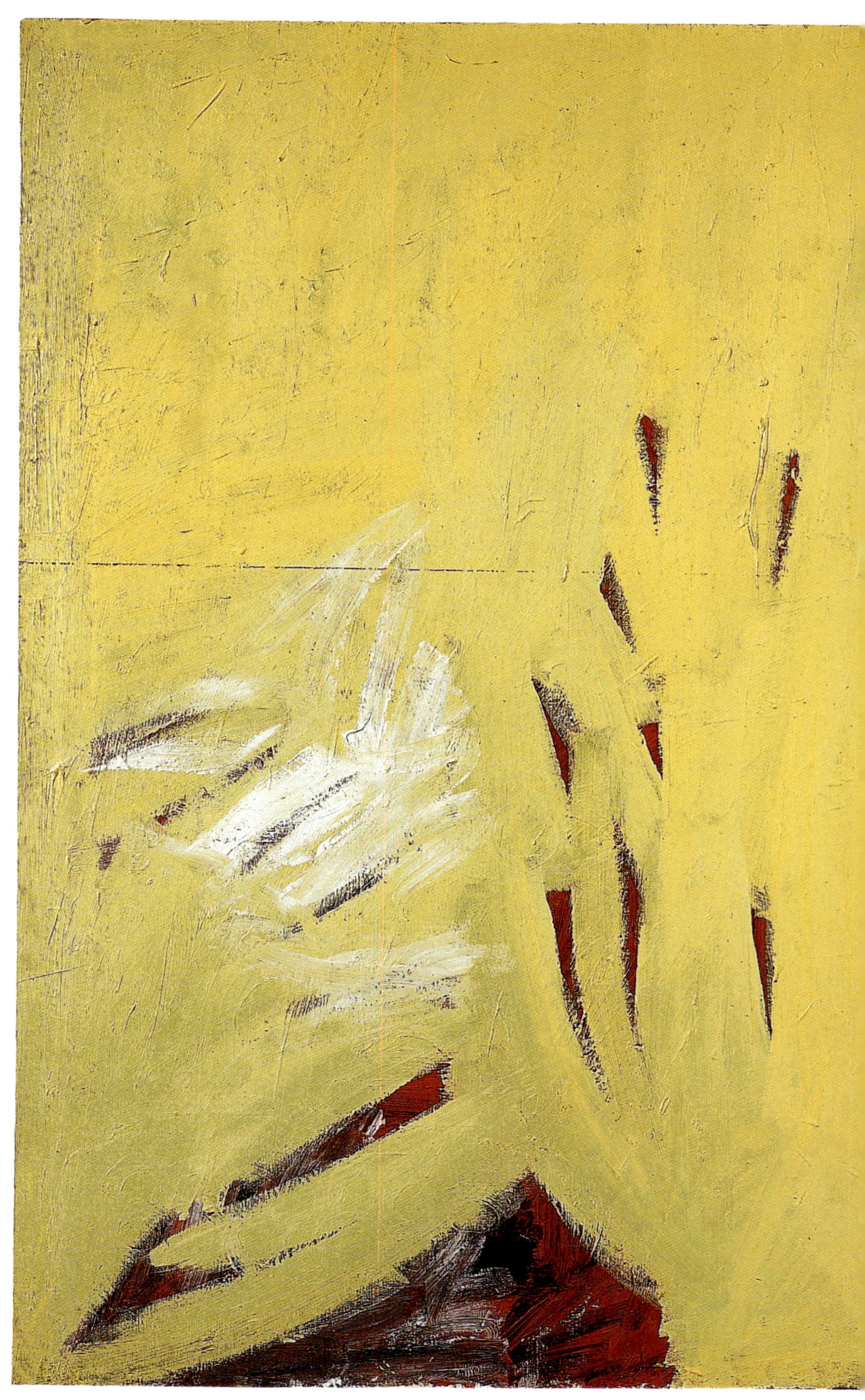

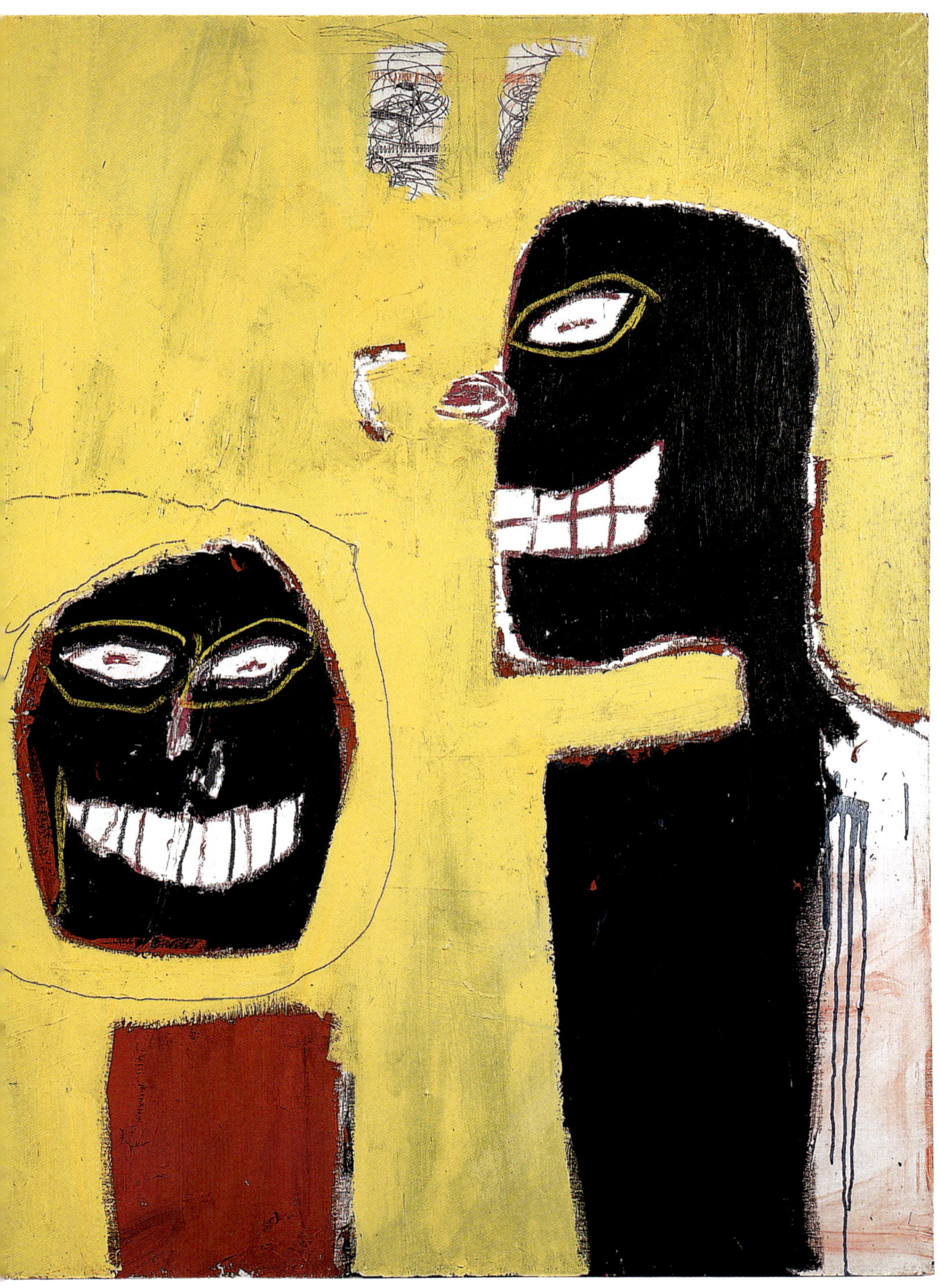

Pages 302/303: **Subjects**, 1983
Acrylic and oilstick on canvas,
165 x 230 cm / 65 x 90 $^1/_2$ inches

Jesse, 1983
Acrylic, oilstick, graphite, and paper collage
on canvas mounted on wooden supports,
216 x 180.5 cm / 85 x 71 inches

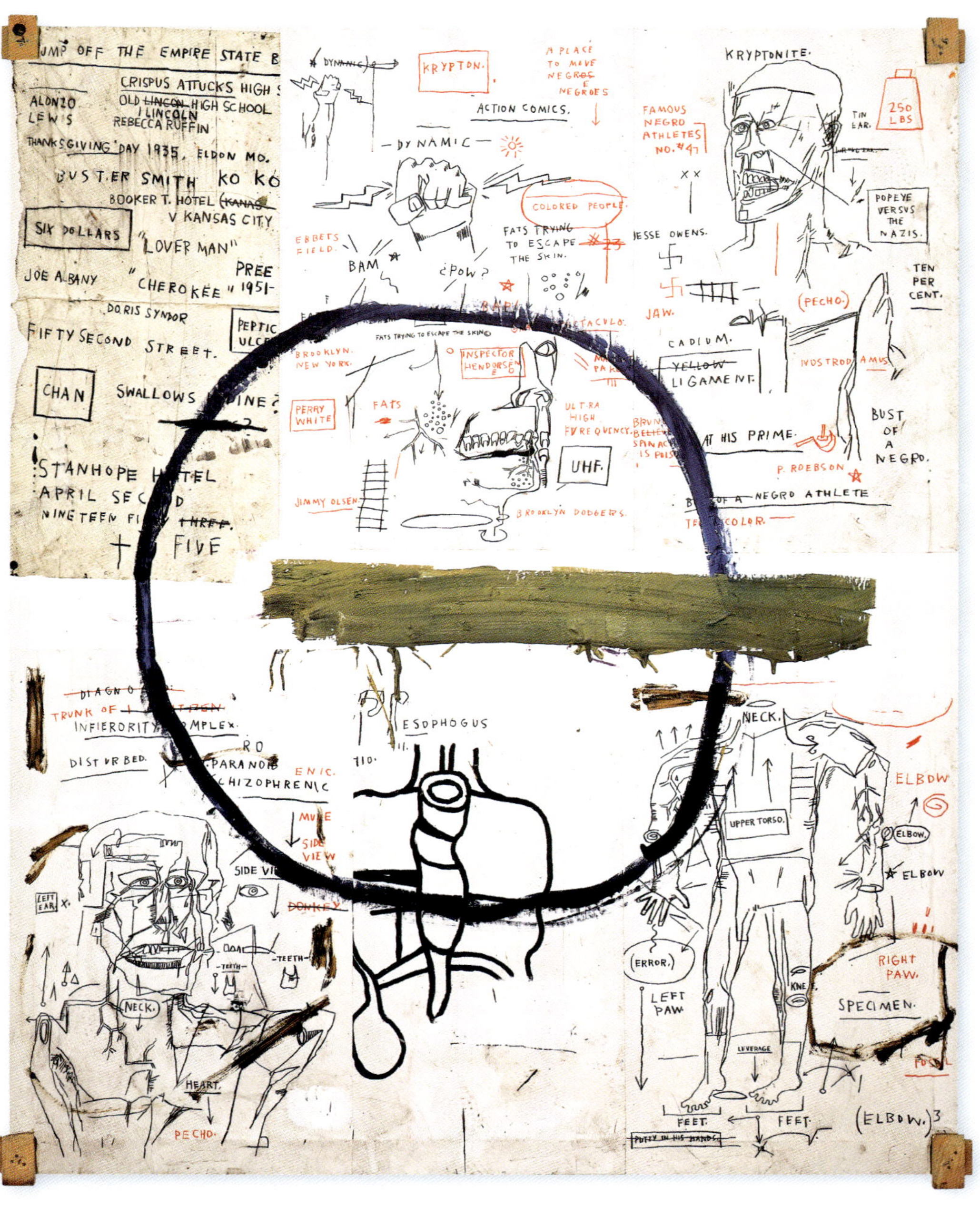
JUMP OFF THE EMPIRE STATE B
CRISPUS ATTUCKS HIGH S
ALONZO LEWIS
OLD LINCON HIGH SCHOOL
I LINCOLN
REBECCA RUFFIN
THANKSGIVING DAY 1935, ELDON MO.
BUSTER SMITH KO KO
BOOKER T. HOTEL (KANAS
V KANSAS CITY
SIX DOLLARS
"LOVER MAN"
PREE
JOE ALBANY "CHEROKEE" 1951-
DORIS SYNDOR
FIFTY SECOND STREET.
PEPTIC ULCE
CHAN SWALLOWS DINE?
STANHOPE HOTEL
APRIL SECOND
NINETEEN FI THREE
FIVE
DYNAMIC
KRYPTON.
A PLACE TO MOVE NEGROS E NEGROES
ACTION COMICS.
KRYPTONITE.
250 LBS
FAMOUS NEGRO ATHLETES NO. #47
TIN EAR.
POPEYE VERSUS THE NAZIS.
DYNAMIC
EBBETS FIELD
COLORED PEOPLE
FATS TRYING TO ESCAPE THE SKIN.
JESSE OWENS.
BAM
POW?
TEN PER CENT.
JAW.
(PECHO.)
FATS TRYING TO ESCAPE THE SKIN
CADIUM.
YELLOW LIGAMENT.
IVDSTRODAMUS
BROOKLYN, NEW YORK.
INSPECTOR HENDORSEN
PERRY WHITE
FATS
ULTRA HIGH FREQUENCY.
UHF.
AT HIS PRIME.
BUST OF A NEGRO.
JIMMY OLSEN
BROOKLYN DODGERS.
P. ROEBSON
BUST OF A NEGRO ATHLETE
TE COLOR.
DIAGNO
TRUNK OF
INFIERORITY OMPLEX.
NECK.
ESOPHOGUS
DISTURBED.
RO
PARANOID SCHIZOPHRENIC
ENIC
ELBOW
UPPER TORSO.
ELBOW.
MULE SIDE VIEW
SIDE VI
ELBOW
LEFT EAR
DONKEY
TEETH
TEETH
NECK.
ERROR.
RIGHT PAW.
LEFT PAW
KNEE.
SPECIMEN.
HEART.
LEVERAGE
PECHO.
FEET.
FEET.
(ELBOW.)3
PUTTY IN HIS HANDS.

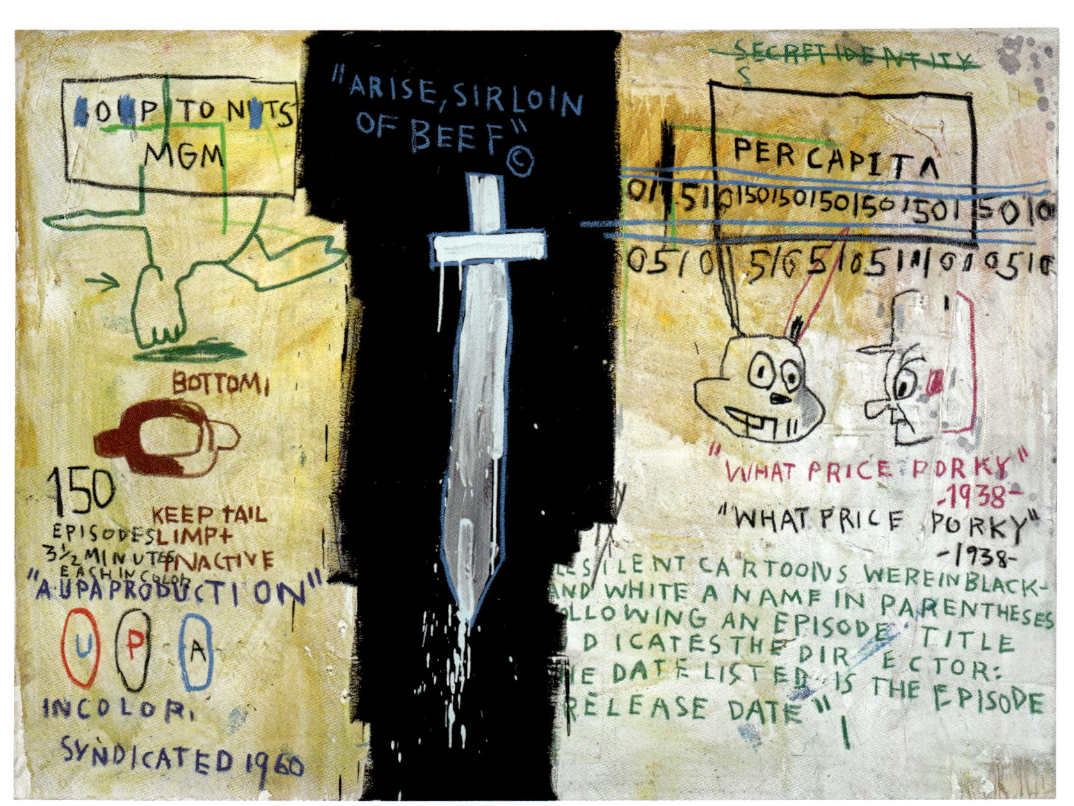

Job Analisis, 1983
Acrylic and oilstick on canvas,
141.5 x 187.5 cm / 55 ³/₄ x 74 inches

In Italian, 1983
Acrylic, oilstick, and marker on canvas
mounted on wooden supports, diptych:
225 x 203 cm / 88 ¹/₂ x 80 inches

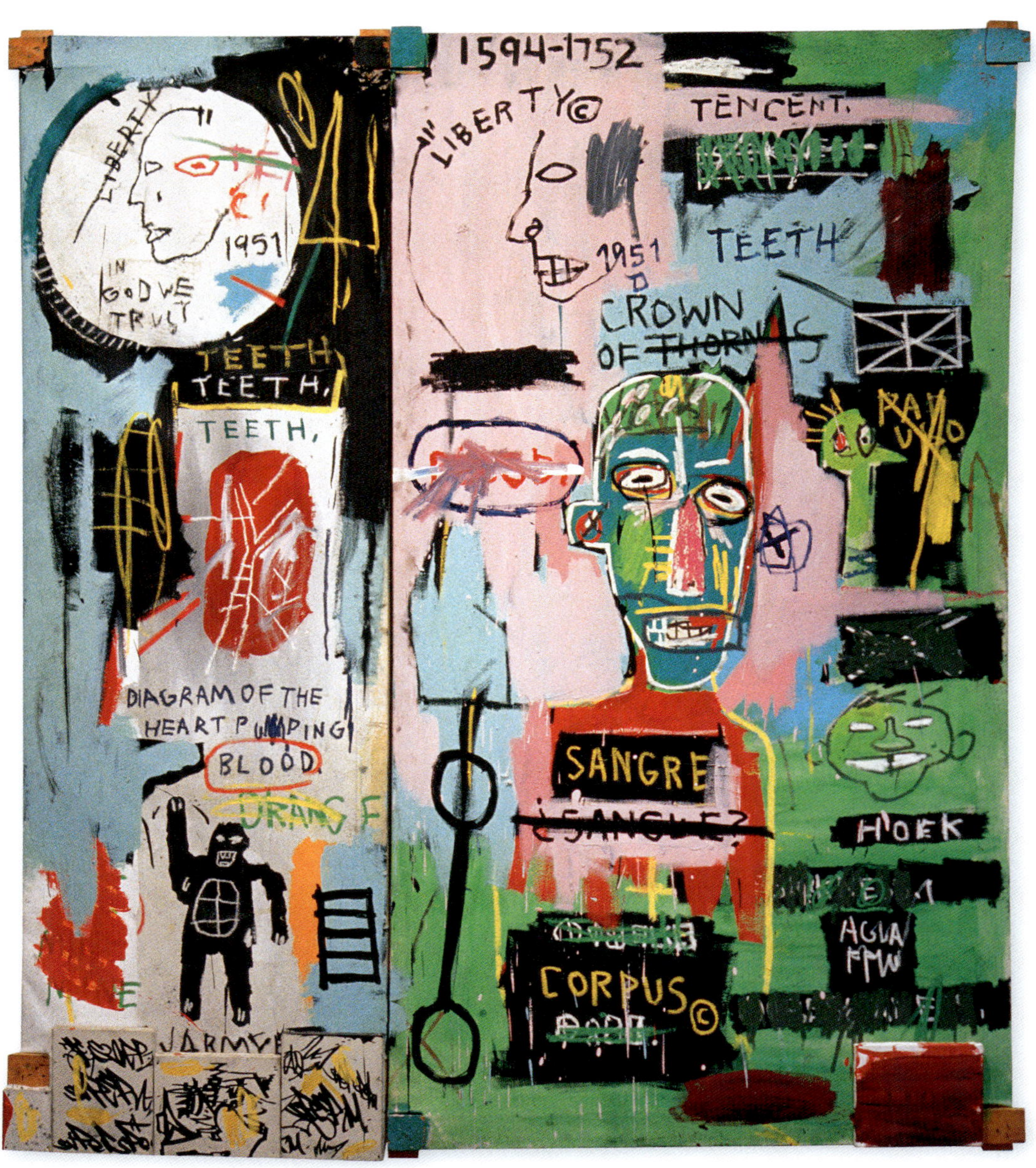
1594-1752
LIBERTY©
TENCENT.
LIBERTY©
1951
TEETH
D
CROWN
OF THORNS
LIBERTY
1951
IN GOD WE TRUST.
TEETH
TEETH,
TEETH,
RAYO
DIAGRAM OF THE
HEART PUMPING
BLOOD.
ORANGE
SANGRE
¿SANGRE?
HOEK
AGUA
FW
CORPUS©
JARME

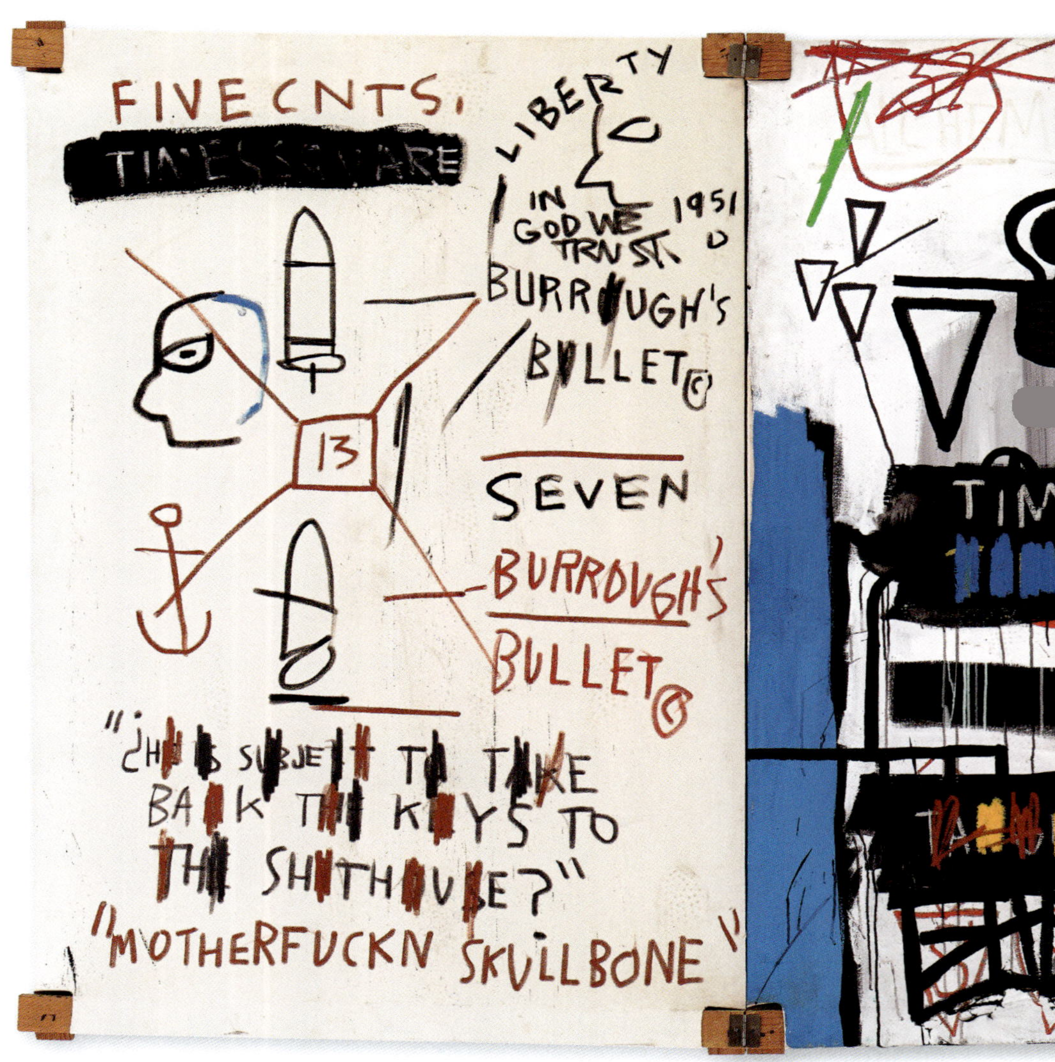

Five Fish Species, 1983
Acrylic and oilstick on canvas mounted
on wooden supports, triptych:
170 x 357 cm / 67 x 140 inches

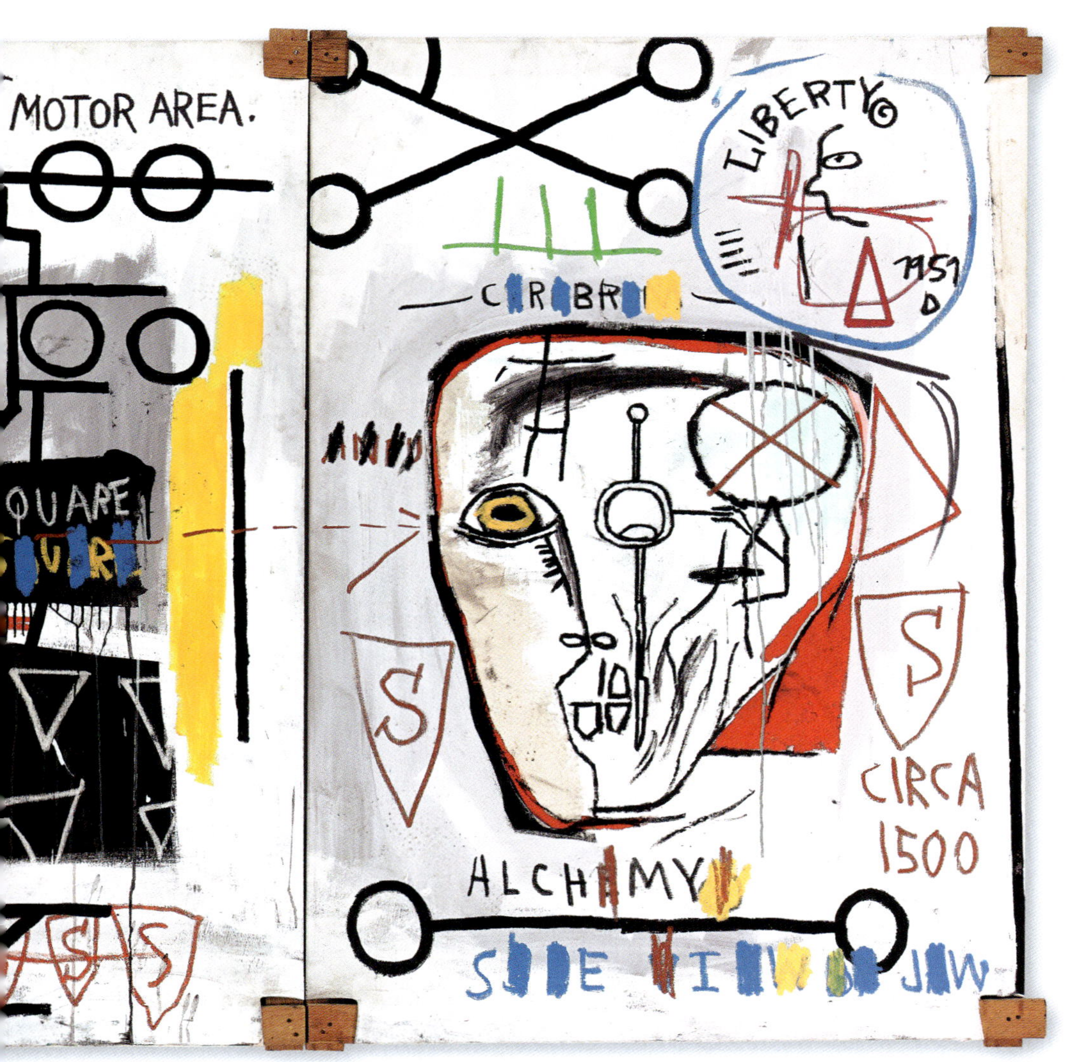

MOTOR AREA.
QUARE
LIBERTY
1951
CEREBRO
ALCHEMY
CIRCA 1500
S
S
S
S

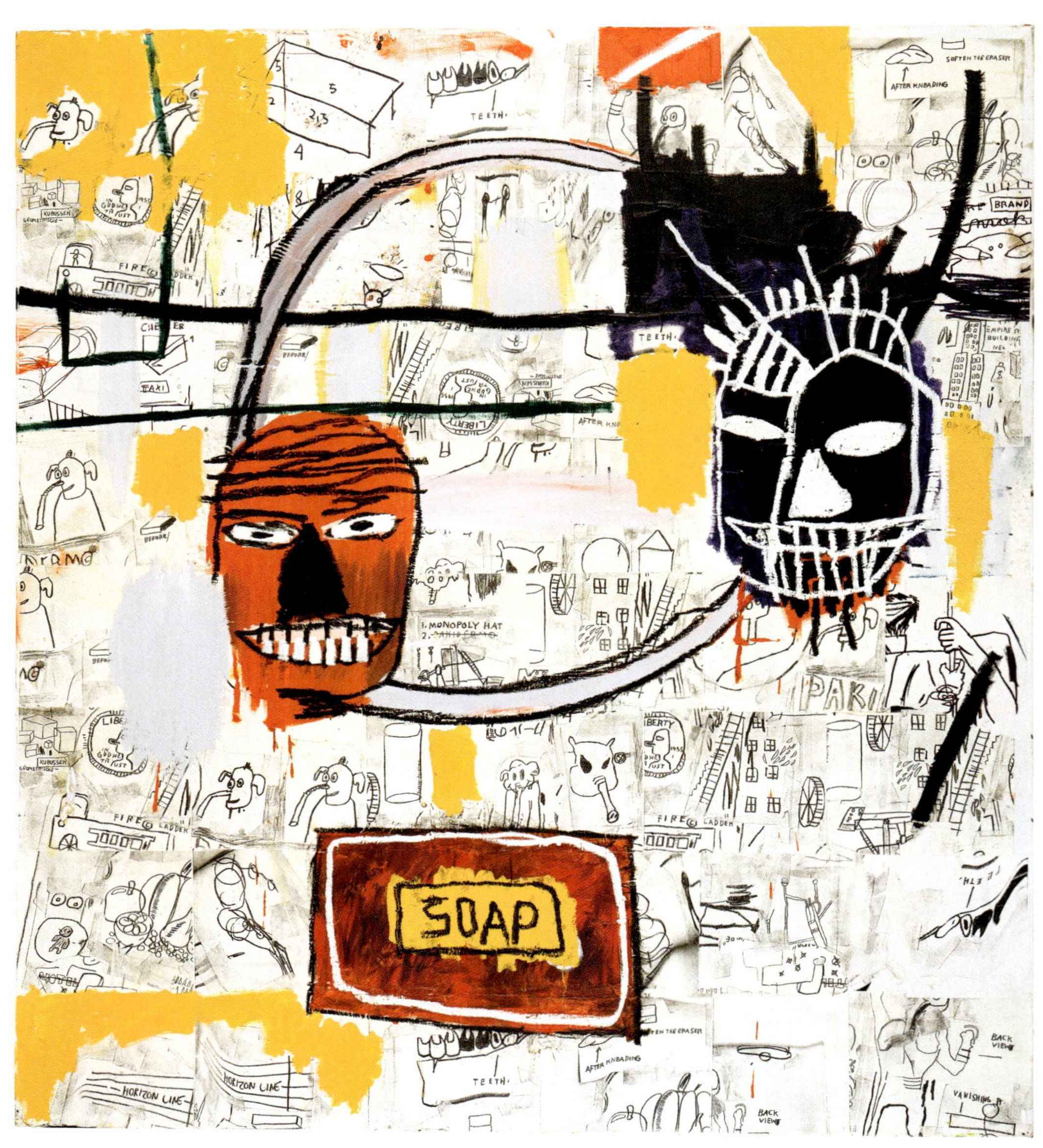

Untitled (Soap), 1983–1984
Acrylic, oilstick, and photocopy collage
on canvas, 167.5 x 152.5 cm / 66 x 60 inches

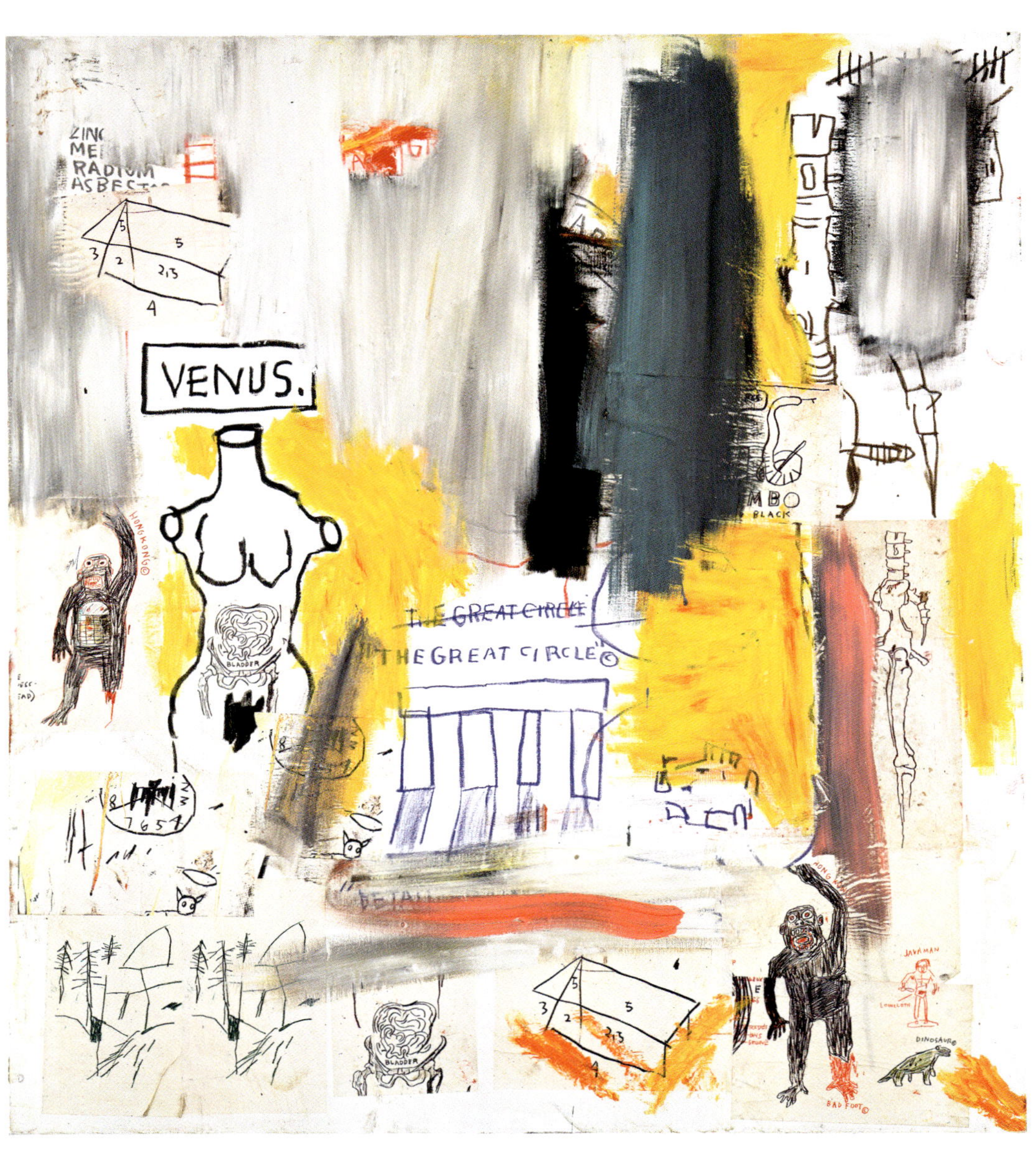

Untitled (Venus/The Great Circle), 1983
Acrylic, oilstick, and photocopy collage
on canvas, 167.5 x 152.5 cm / 66 x 60 inches

In This Case, 1983
Acrylic and oilstick on canvas,
196 x 188 cm / 77 ¹/₄ x 74 inches

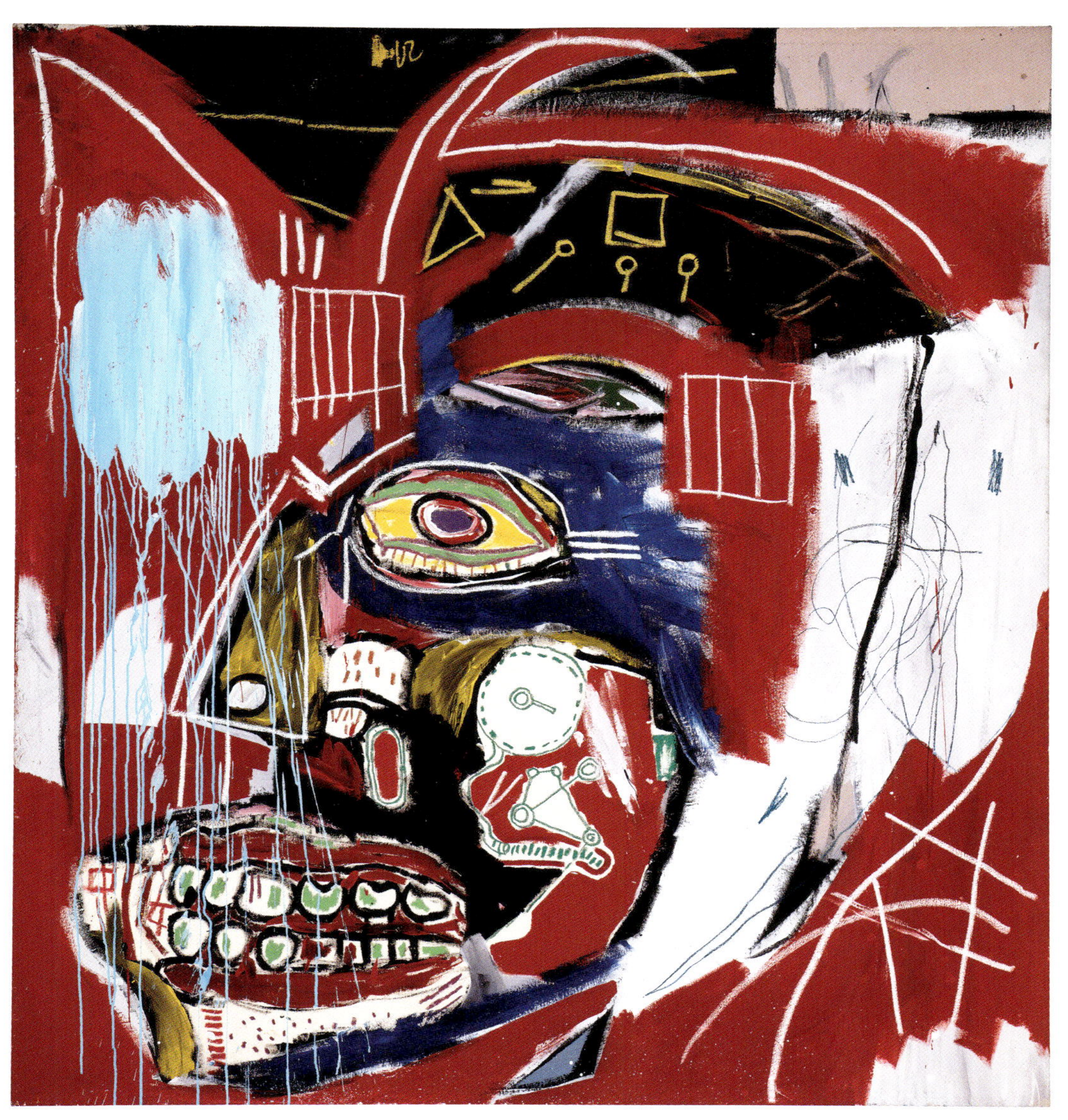

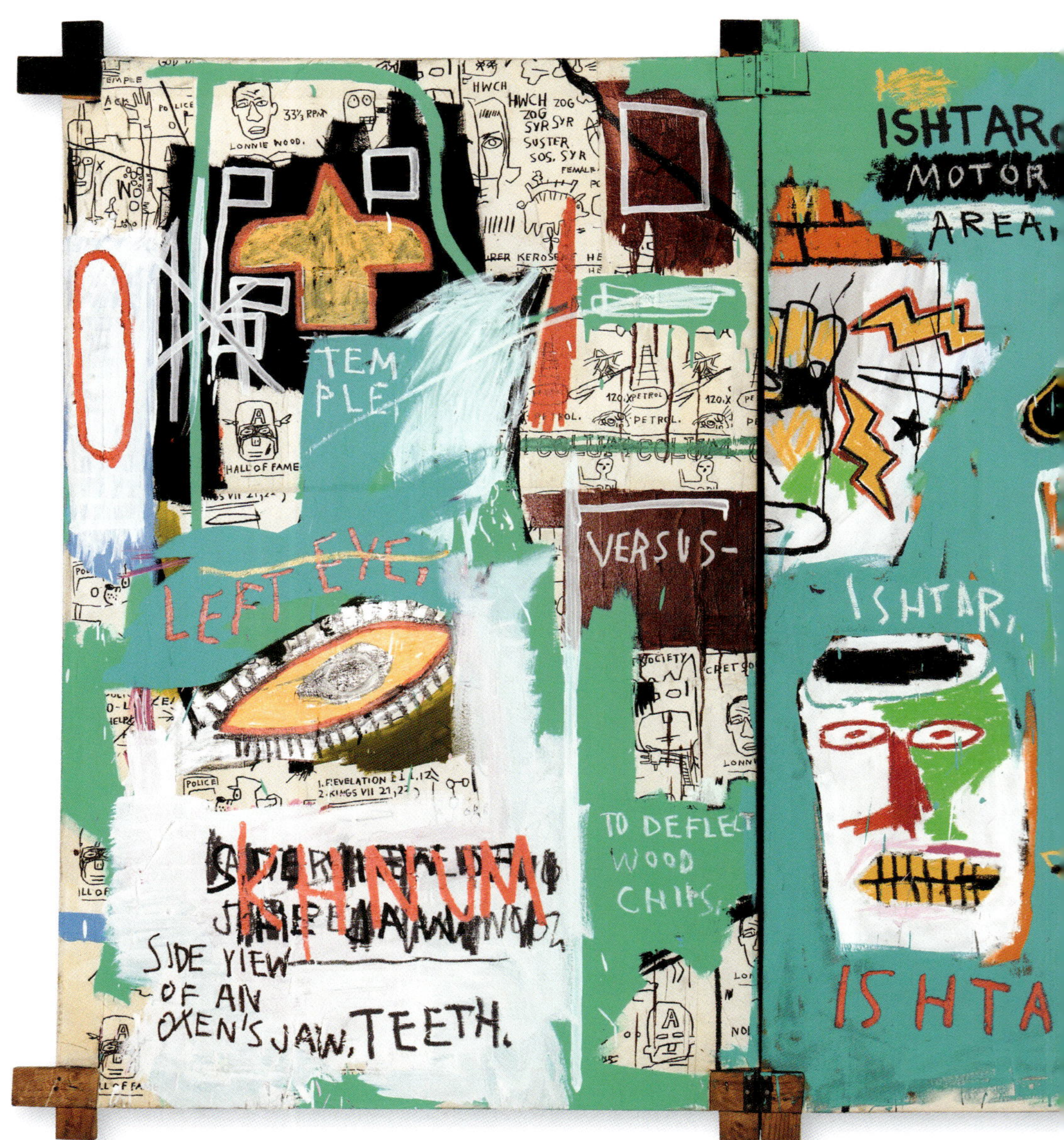

Ishtar, 1983
Acrylic, oilstick, and photocopy collage on
canvas mounted on wooden supports,
triptych: 183 x 352 cm / 72 x 138 ¹/₂ inches

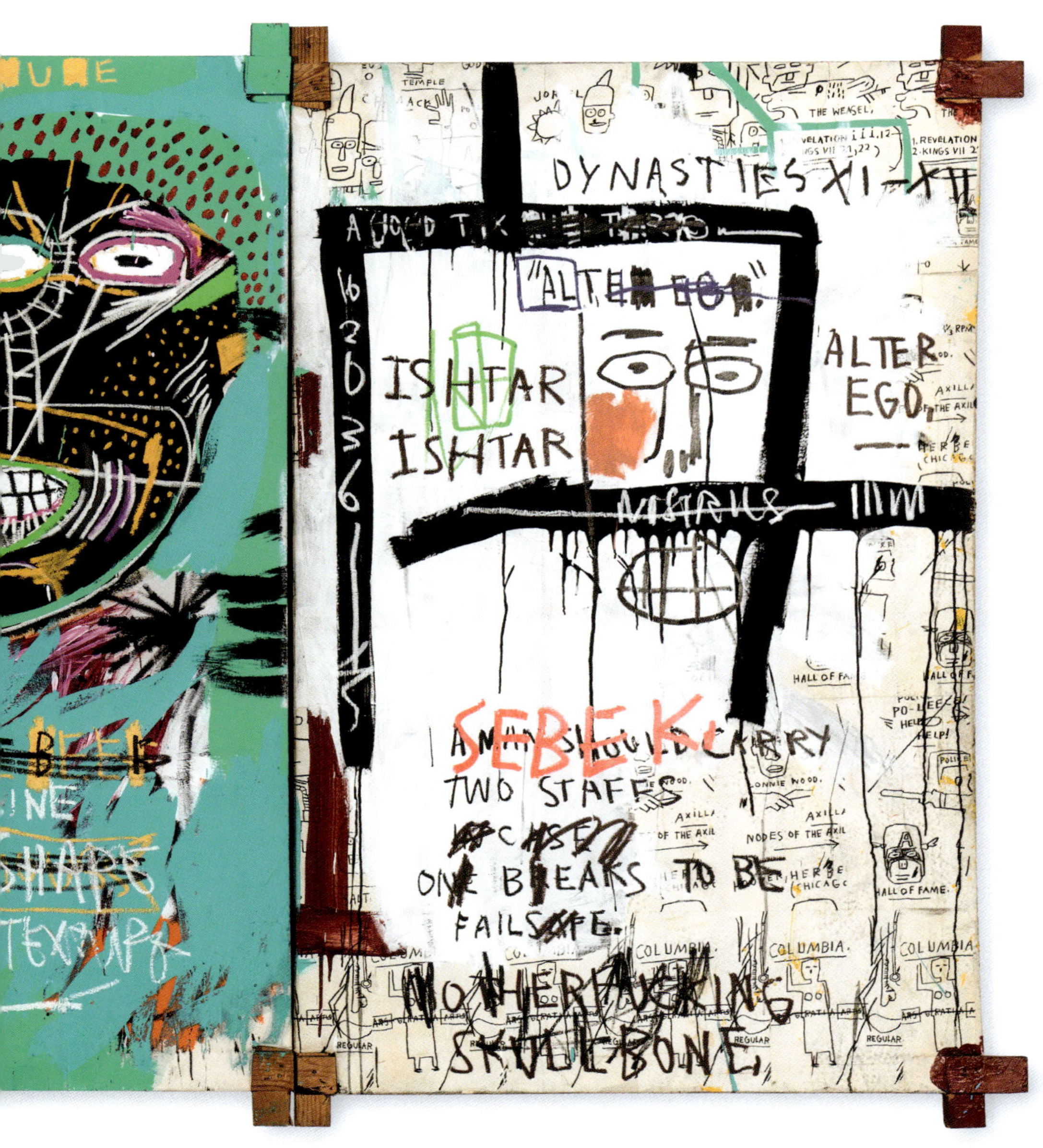
DYNASTIES XI
"ALTER EGO"
ISHTAR
ISHTAR
ALTER EGO
SEBEK
TWO STAFFS
ONE BREAKS
FAILSAFE.
MOTHERFUCKING
SKULLBONE.
THE WEASEL
TEMPLE
REVELATION
HALL OF FAME
COLUMBIA.
REGULAR
AXILLA
NODES OF THE AXIL

V.

1984
The Measure
of Success

"*There were wonderful works here—an Andy Warholish portrait, for example—and certain elements to my mind were new: a burning house, a fire truck, and a floral motif coexisted with the bones, machines, and so on. And throughout floated a disembodied eye, which seemed to allude both to the self—the 'I'—and to the witness or seer. But one sensed little of what Basquiat is witness to, or of why it bears accounting.*"

—KATE LINKER, *ARTFORUM*, 1984[1]

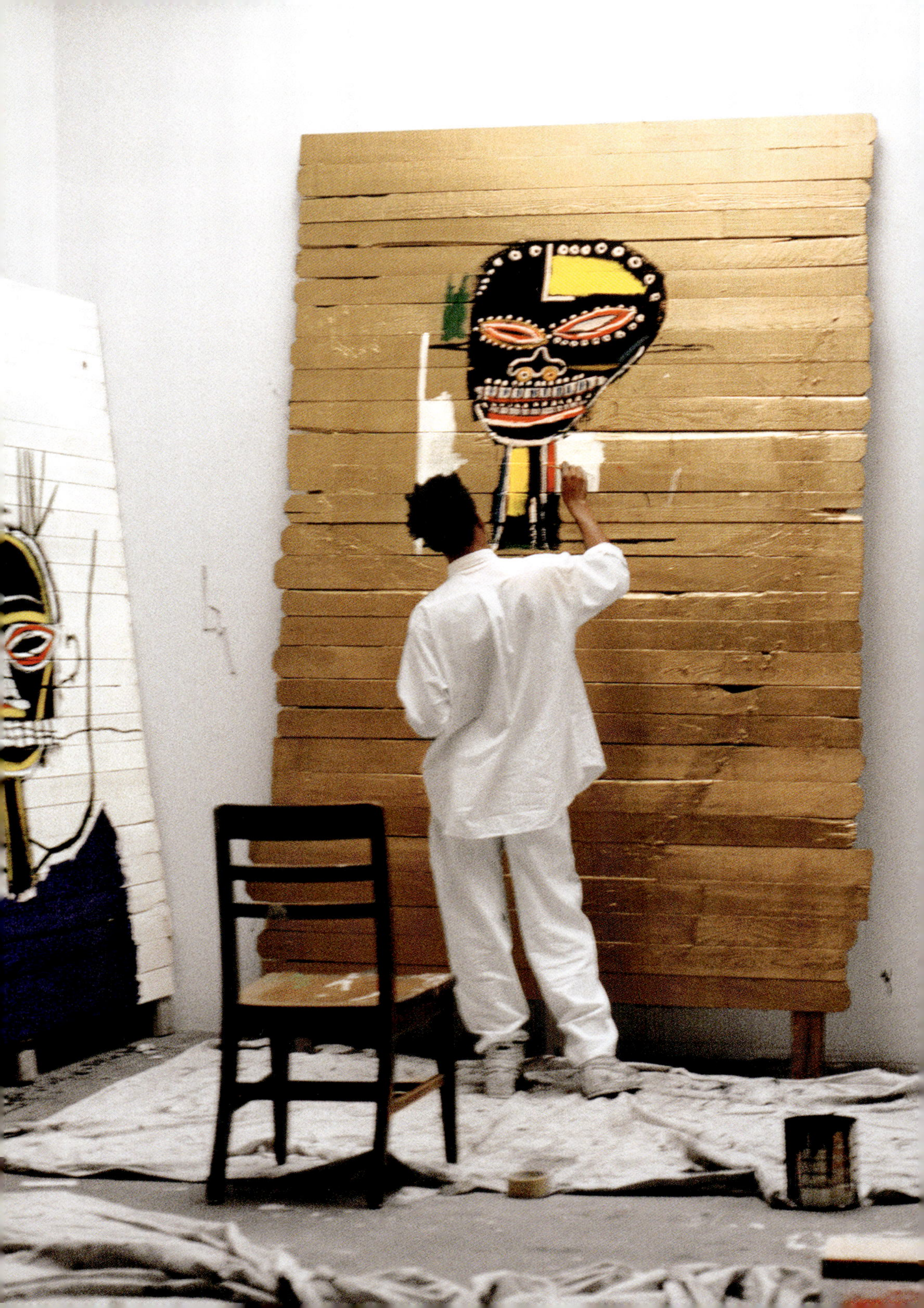

Basquiat spends the first two months of the year with family and friends in a remote part of Hawaii. While he does not work much, he feels he can recharge there, free of the hustle of the art world and his own extravagant lifestyle. Back in New York, he joins Mary Boone's gallery, and already in May she organizes a solo exhibition for him. Even if the show sells out immediately as always, for the first time reviews are mixed, possibly because Basquiat has decided to exhibit a large number of works in a crowded hang. Kate Linker in *Artforum*: "At his best the artist is quirky and whimsical, but how witty can you wax in some twenty-plus variations?"[2] In the *New York Times*, Vivien Raynor sees the young artist endangered by his quick rise to fame: "That Warhol has since done a likeness of Basquiat is a measure of the young contender's success. But it may also be a symptom of too much too soon, the more so since Basquiat has returned the compliment symbolically in the present show with a large painting of a partly peeled banana, titled *Brown Spots*. The young artist uses color well, applying it flatly … [or] more expressionistically in bright impastoed blocks. But more remarkable is the educated quality of his line and the stateliness of his compositions, both of which bespeak a formal training that, in fact, he never had … Right now, Basquiat is a very promising painter, who has a chance of becoming a very good one, as long as he can withstand the forces that would make of him an art-world mascot."[3] Donald Kuspit has similar misgivings: "The early work is of an original primitivism, with a graffiti heritage. The originality has quickly become stylized and somewhat self-conscious in this current show."[4]

That the young artist is taking these reviews to heart is suggested by an entry in Andy Warhol's diaries: "Jean-Michel came down to the office early. He was reading his big review in the *Voice*. They called him the most promising artist on the scene. And at least they didn't mention me and say he shouldn't be hanging around with me the way the *New York Times* thing did."[5] Despite of these dissenting critical voices, international recognition of Basquiat continues to grow. He is part of a group exhibition of recent art at the reopening of the newly renovated MoMA, and at the Fruitmarket Gallery in Edinburgh, he has his first museum solo exhibition, which afterwards travels to the ICA in London and the Museum Boymans-van Beuningen in Rotterdam.

His friendship with Warhol blossoms, they go to parties and work out together, and Warhol tries influencing the younger artist into a more responsible lifestyle: "Jean-Michel called at 8:00 in the morning and we philosophized. He got scared reading the Belushi book. I told him that if he wanted to become a legend, too, he should just keep going on like he was. But actually if he's even on the phone talking to me, he's okay."[6] In the studio, Basquiat is doing more than okay, and he develops several new directions in his work: some of the paintings have a freer use of color than ever, with drawings and words often

Page 317: Jean-Michel Basquiat in his
Market Street studio, Los Angeles 1984.
Photo Brian Williams

Gold Griot, 1984
Acrylic and oilstick on wood,
297 x 185.5 cm / 117 x 73 inches

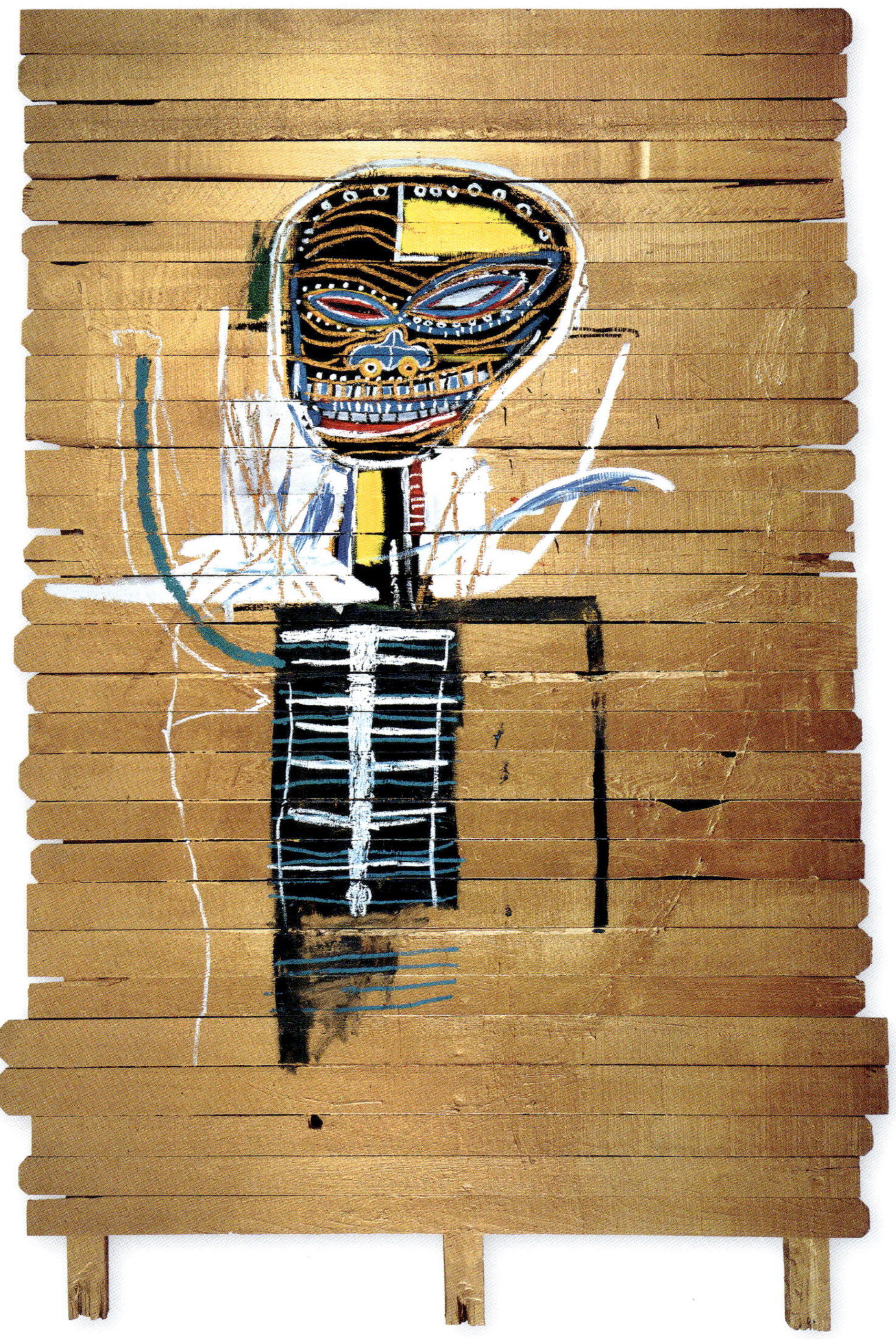

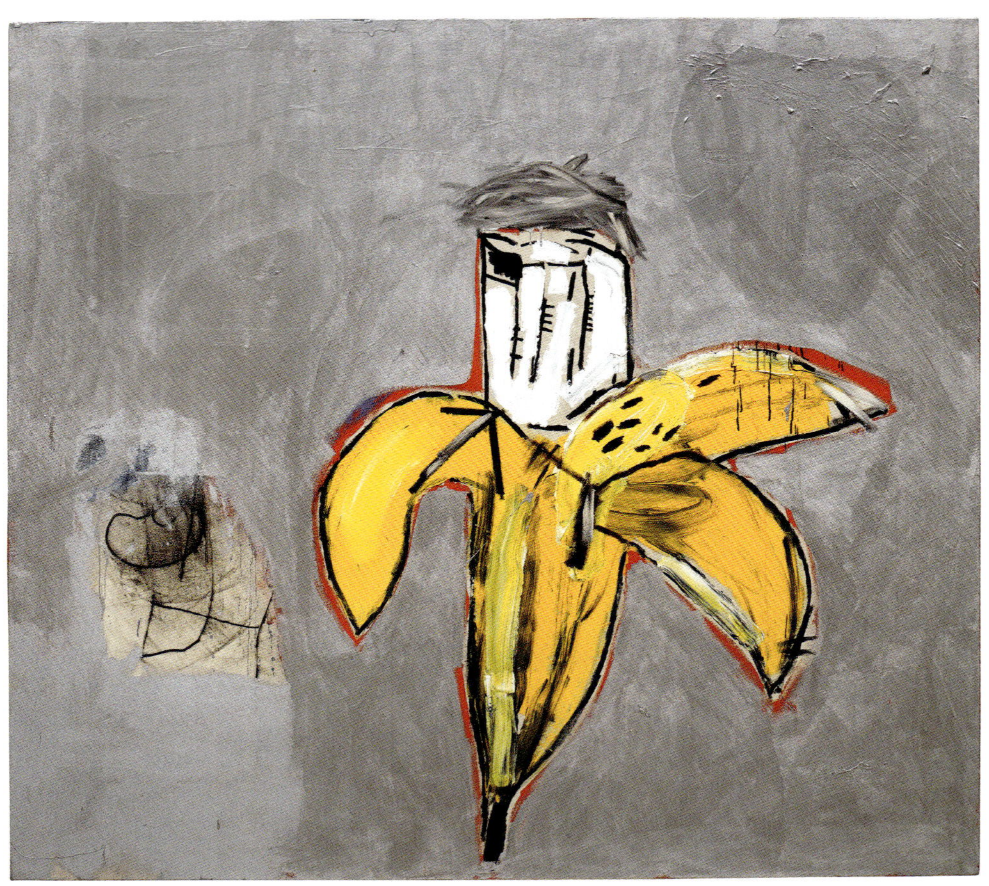

**Brown Spots (Portrait of
Andy Warhol as a Banana)**, 1984
Acrylic and oilstick on canvas,
193 x 213 cm / 76 x 83 ³/₄ inches

submerged in large areas of paint reminiscent of colorfield painting; other paintings are
executed on wooden slabs, sometimes as panels, sometimes knocked together as if they
were part of a hoarding.

In September, the collaborative paintings between Basquiat, Warhol, and Clemente
are shown at Bruno Bischofberger's gallery in Zürich. Max Wechsler reviews the exhibition for *Artforum*: "The respect each man has for the work of the others seems to have
been great enough that each essentially stuck to his own visual language and only rarely
and hesitantly intervened in the vision of his partners. Basquiat seems most to shake up
the works with his reactions and comments—which is fitting, considering the graffiti-like
scribbles that form his style."[7] In the following time, Basquiat and Warhol continue their

collaboration without their Italian colleague, and their relationship allows them to be less respectful of each other's art: "He would start most of the paintings," Basquiat later recalls, "he would put something very concrete or recognizable like a newspaper headline or a product logo and then I would sort of deface it and then I would try to get him to work some more on it and then I would do more work on it. I would try to get him to do at least two things. You know, he likes to do one hit and then have me do all the work after that … we used to paint over each other's stuff all the time."[8]

Late in the year, Basquiat meets Jennifer Goode at the nightclub Area, where he sometimes DJs. She is the sister of the owners and interior designer for its club nights. They start a relationship that will last for two years.

[1–8] *See Endnotes on page 508.*

Pages 322/323: Jean-Michel Basquiat, exhibition view, Mary Boone Gallery, New York 1984

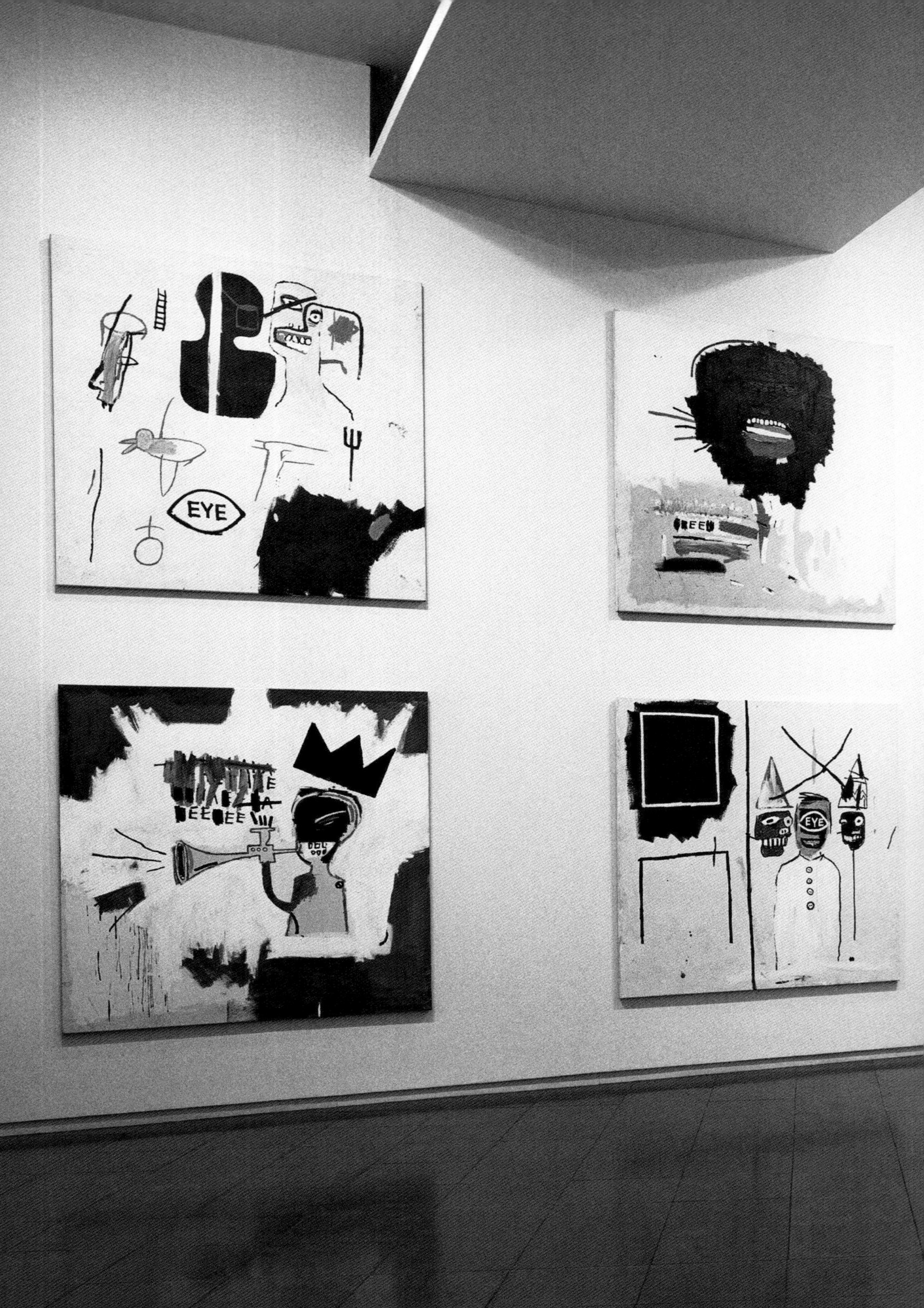

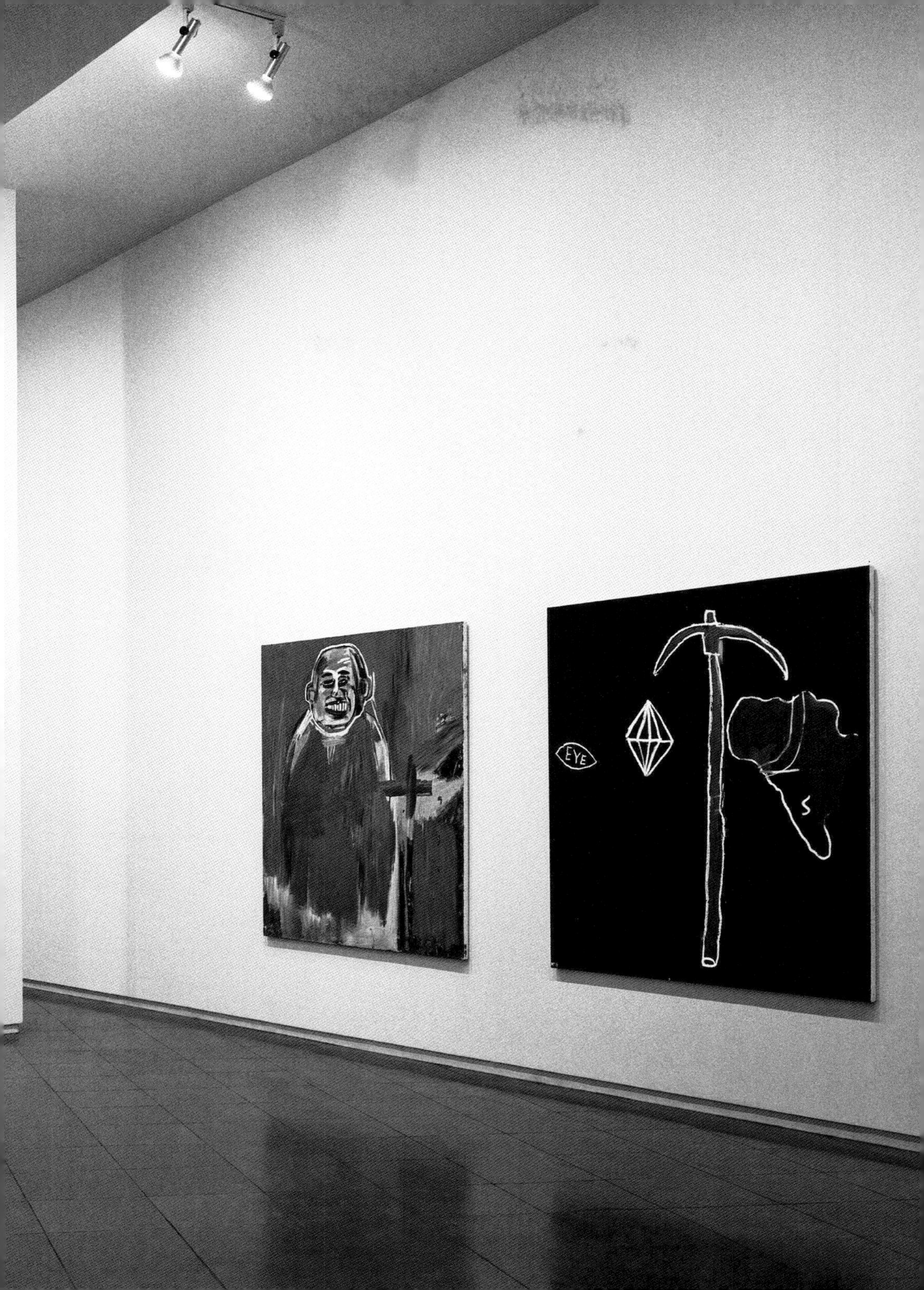

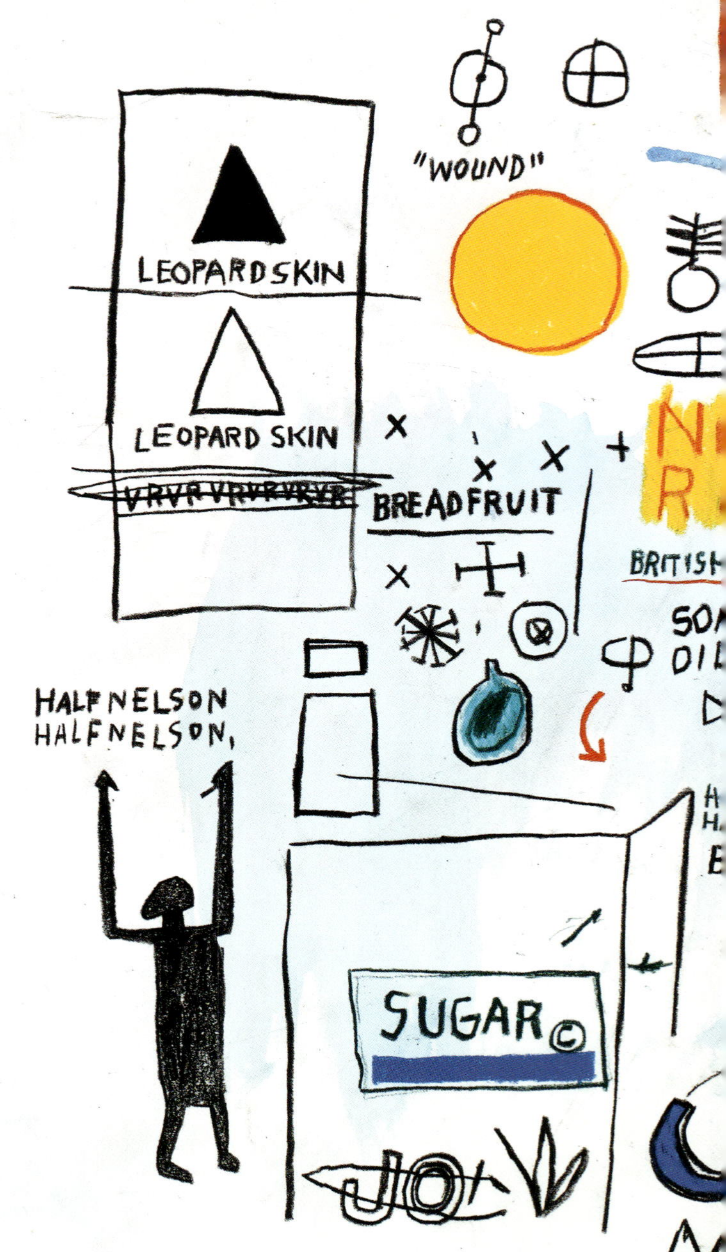

Untitled, 1984
Mixed media on paper, 56.5 x
76.5 cm / 22 ¹/₄ x 30 inches

Page 326: **Untitled,** 1984
Acrylic, graphite, oilstick,
paper collage, and masking
tape on paper, 76 x 56 cm /
30 x 22 inches

Page 327: **Untitled,** 1984
Acrylic, oilstick, and ink
on paper, 105.5 x 76 cm /
41 ¹/₂ x 30 inches

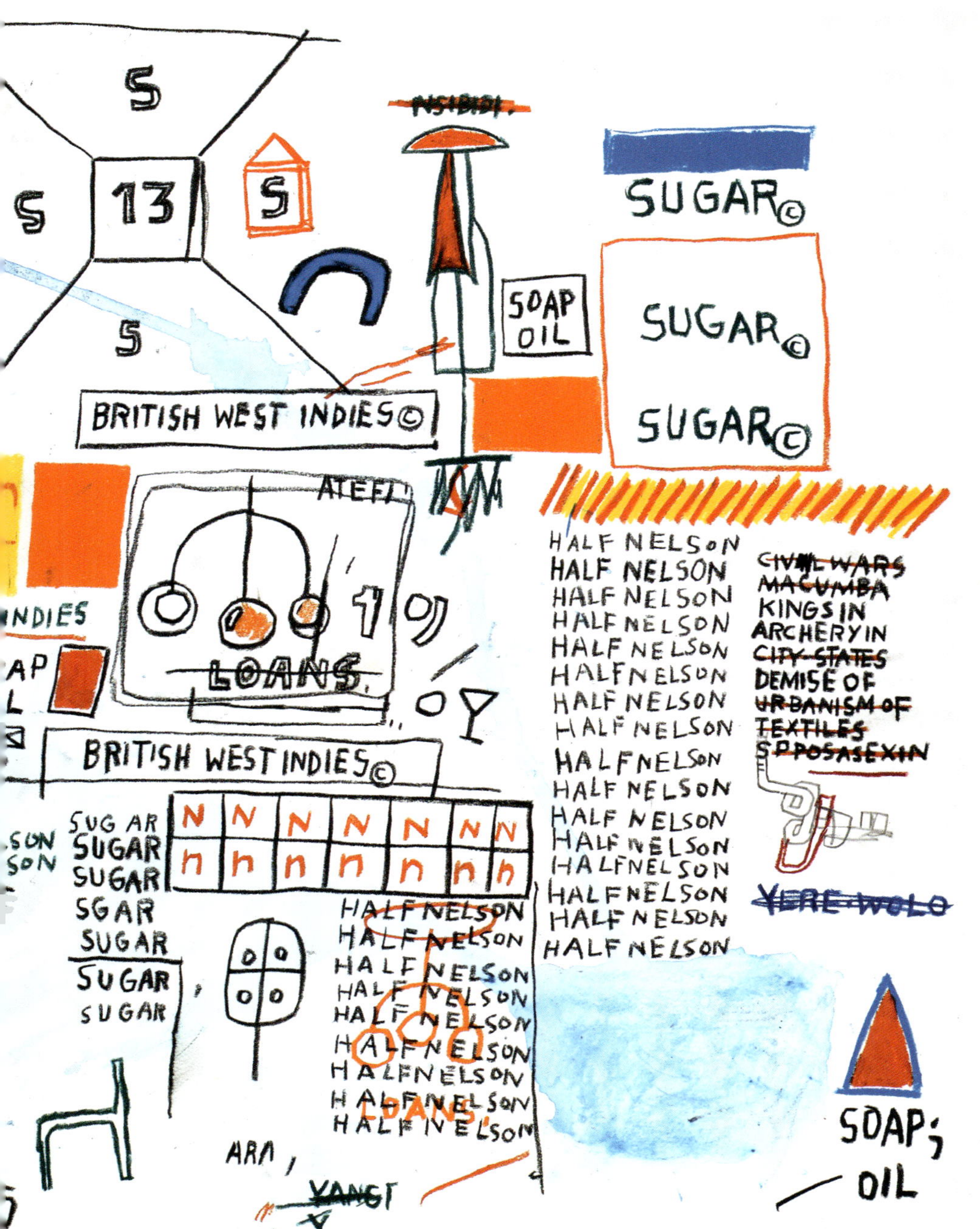
S
13
S
S
S
NSIBIDI
SOAP OIL
BRITISH WEST INDIES©
ATEFI
LOANS
SUGAR©
SUGAR©
SUGAR©
HALF NELSON
HALF NELSON
HALF NELSON
HALF NELSON
HALF NELSON
HALF NELSON
HALF NELSON
HALF NELSON
HALF NELSON
HALF NELSON
HALF NELSON
HALF NELSON
HALF NELSON
HALF NELSON
HALF NELSON
HALF NELSON
CIVIL WARS
MACUMBA
KINGS IN
ARCHERY IN
CITY-STATES
DEMISE OF
URBANISM OF
TEXTILES
SPPOSASEXIN
VERE WOLO
INDIES
AP
L
SON
SON
SUGAR
SUGAR
SUGAR
SGAR
SUGAR
SUGAR
SUGAR
N N N N N N
n n n n n n
HALF NELSON
HALF NELSON
HALF NELSON
HALF NELSON
HALF NELSON
HALF NELSON
HALF NELSON
HALF NELSON
HALF NELSON
LOANS
ARA
YANGT
Y
SOAP;
OIL

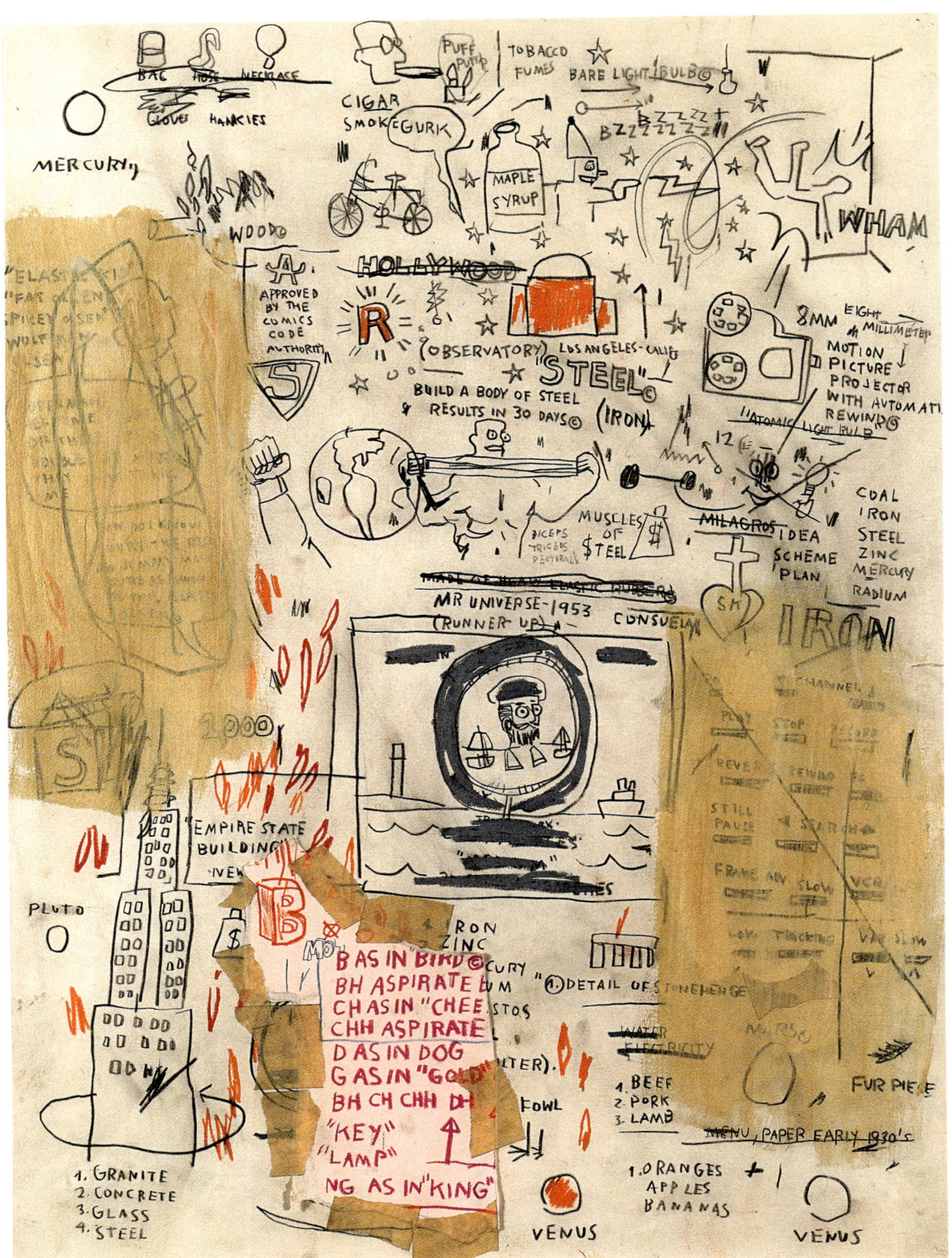
BAG NOSE NECKLACE
GLOVES HANKIES
MERCURY
CIGAR SMOKE GURK
PUFF PUFF
TOBACCO FUMES
BARE LIGHT BULB
WOOD
BZZZ ZZZ ZZ
MAPLE SYRUP
WHAM
HOLLYWOOD
APPROVED BY THE COMICS CODE AUTHORITY
R
S
(OBSERVATORY) LOS ANGELES - CALIF.
"STEEL"
BUILD A BODY OF STEEL
RESULTS IN 30 DAYS (IRON)
8MM EIGHT MILLIMETER
MOTION PICTURE PROJECTOR WITH AUTOMATIC REWIND
ATOMIC LIGHT BULB
12
MILAGROS
IDEA SCHEME PLAN
COAL IRON STEEL ZINC MERCURY RADIUM
"ELASTIC
FAT MEN
BICEPS TRICEPS PECTORALS
MUSCLES OF STEEL
SH
IRON
MADE OF HEAVY ELASTIC RUBBER
MR UNIVERSE - 1953 (RUNNER UP) CONSUELA
CHANNEL
PLAY STOP
REVERSE REWIND
STILL PAUSE SEARCH
FRAME ADV SLOW VCR
LOW TRACKING VAR SLOW
1000
EMPIRE STATE BUILDING
NEW
PLUTO
B
$
IRON ZINC MERCURY
B AS IN BIRD
BH ASPIRATE UM
CH AS IN "CHEESE" STOS
CHH ASPIRATE
D AS IN DOG
G AS IN "GOLD"
BH CH CHH DH
"KEY"
"LAMP"
NG AS IN "KING"
(1.) DETAIL OF STONEHENGE
WATER ELECTRICITY
MARS
FOWL
1. BEEF 2. PORK 3. LAMB
MENU, PAPER EARLY 1930's
FUR PIECE
1. GRANITE 2. CONCRETE 3. GLASS 4. STEEL
VENUS
1. ORANGES APPLES BANANAS
VENUS

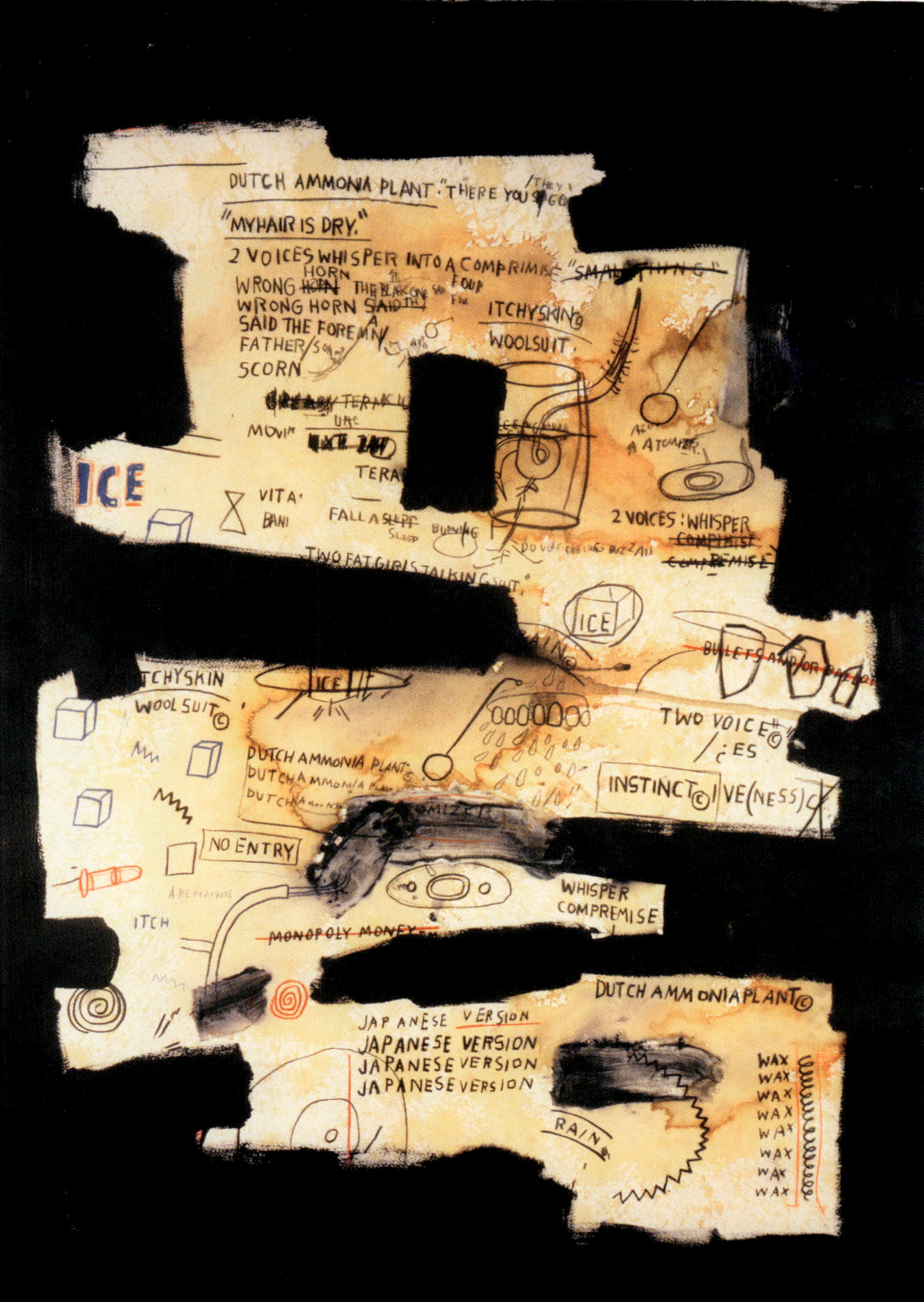
DUTCH AMMONIA PLANT. "THERE YOU GO
"MY HAIR IS DRY."
2 VOICES WHISPER INTO A COMPRIMISE "SMALL THING"
WRONG HORN THE BLACK ONE
WRONG HORN SAID
SAID THE FOREMAN
FATHER/SON
SCORN
ITCHYSKIN
WOOLSUIT
ICE
VITA-
BANI
MOVIN
TERA
FALL ASLEEP
A ATOMIZER
2 VOICES : WHISPER
COMPRIMIST
COMPREMISE
TWO FAT GIRLS TALKING SUIT
ICE
ITCHYSKIN
WOOLSUIT ©
BULLETS AND/OR
TWO VOICE ©
/ ¿ ES
DUTCH AMMONIA PLANT ©
DUTCH AMMONIA
DUTCH AMM
INSTINCT © IVE(NESS) ©
NO ENTRY
WHISPER
COMPREMISE
MONOPOLY MONEY
ITCH
DUTCH AMMONIA PLANT ©
JAPANESE VERSION
JAPANESE VERSION
JAPANESE VERSION
JAPANESE VERSION
RAIN
WAX
WAX
WAX
WAX
WAX
WAX
WAX
WAX

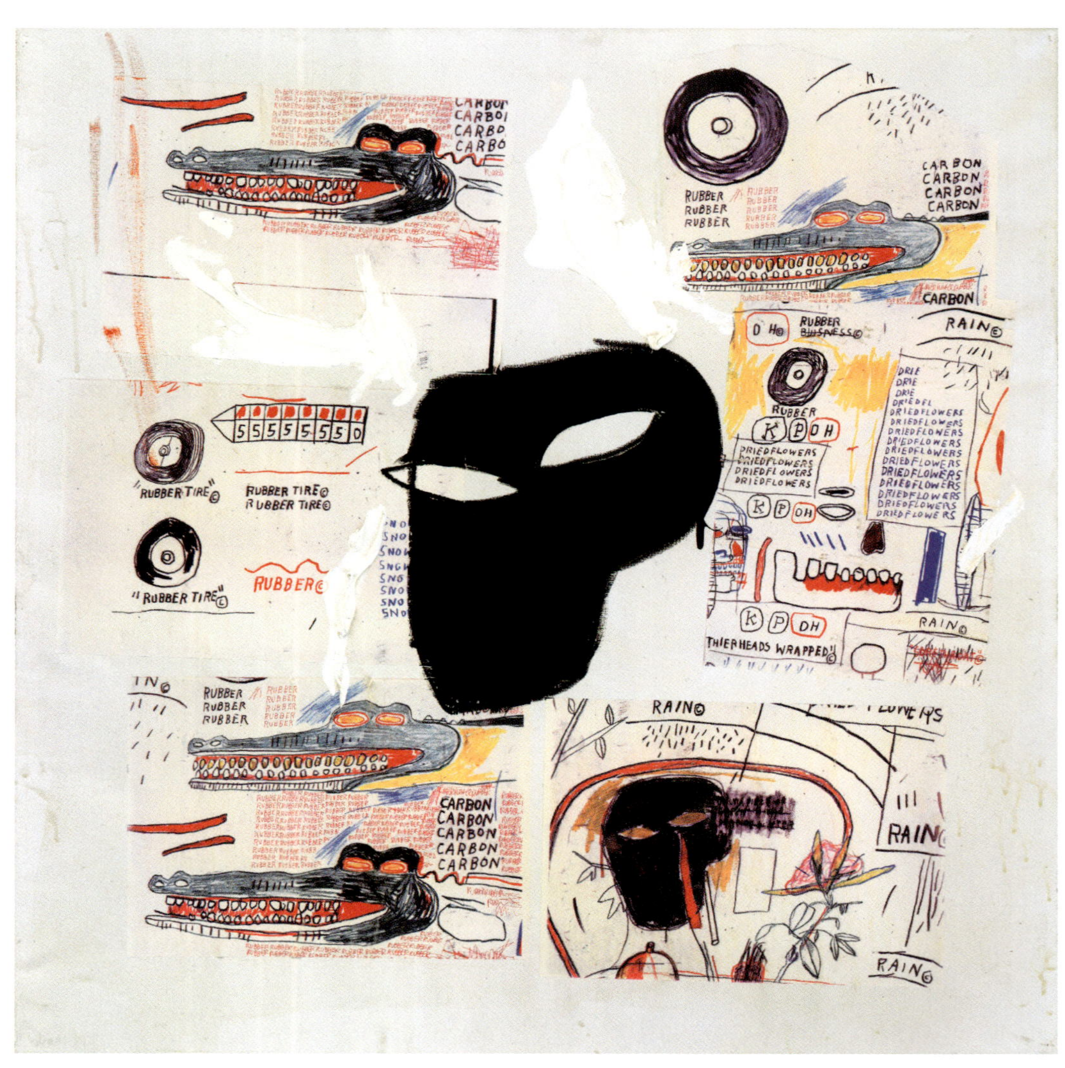

Dried Flowers, 1984
Mixed media and collage on canvas,
110 x 110 cm / 43 $^1/_3$ x 43 $^1/_3$ inches

M, 1984
Acrylic and oilstick on wood,
244 x 184.5 cm / 96 x 72 $^3/_4$ inches

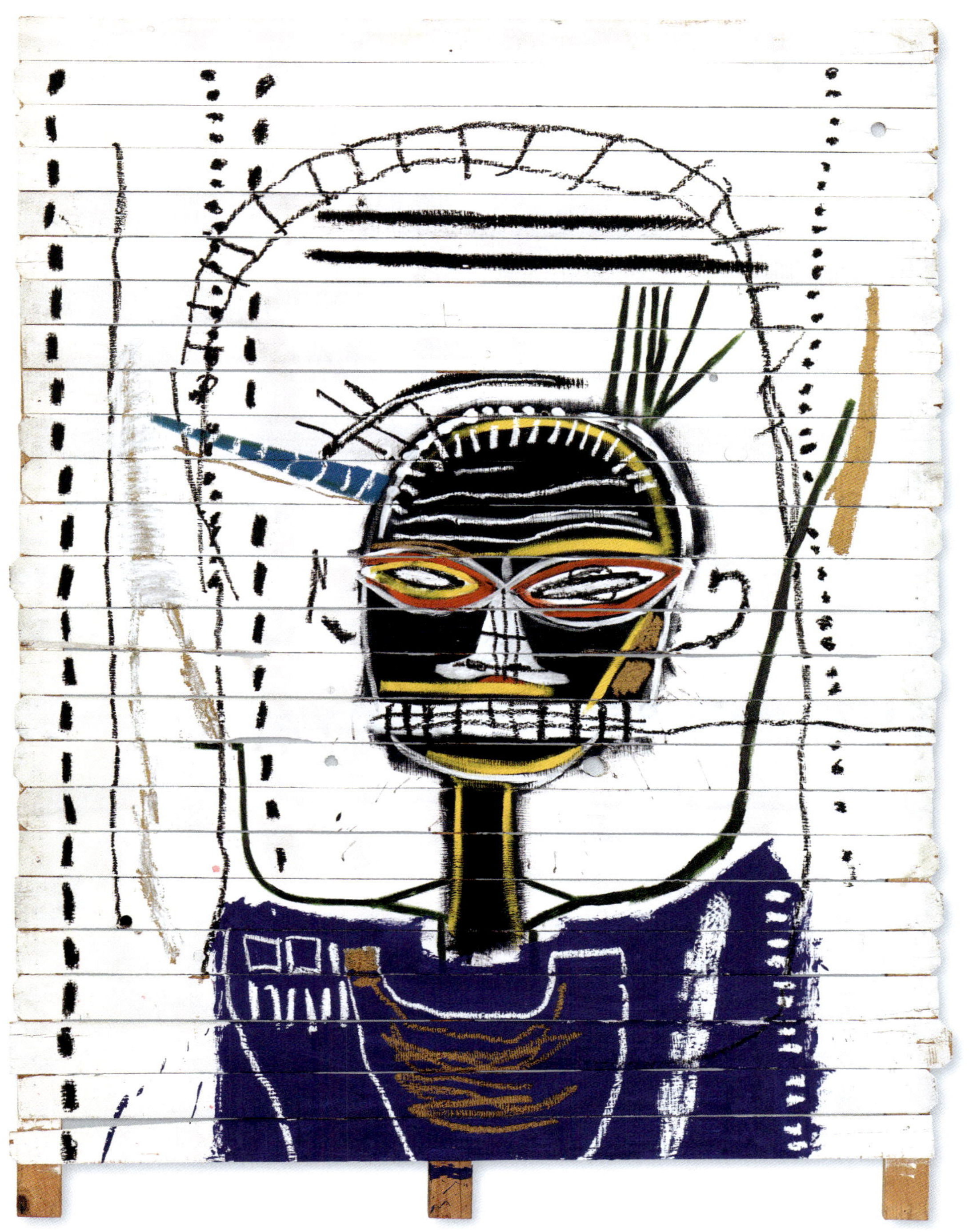

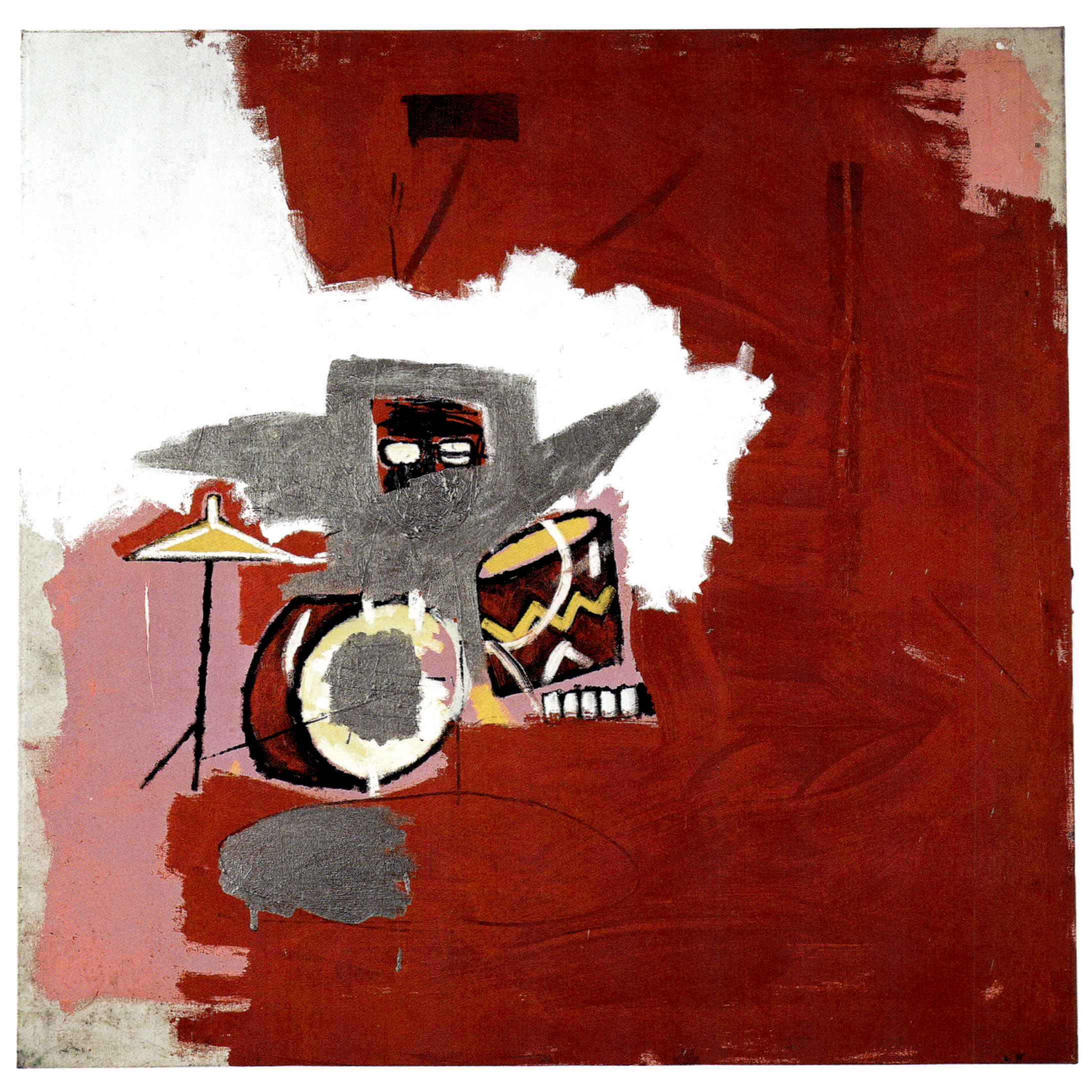

Max Roach, 1984
Acrylic and oilstick on canvas,
152.5 x 152.5 cm / 60 x 60 inches

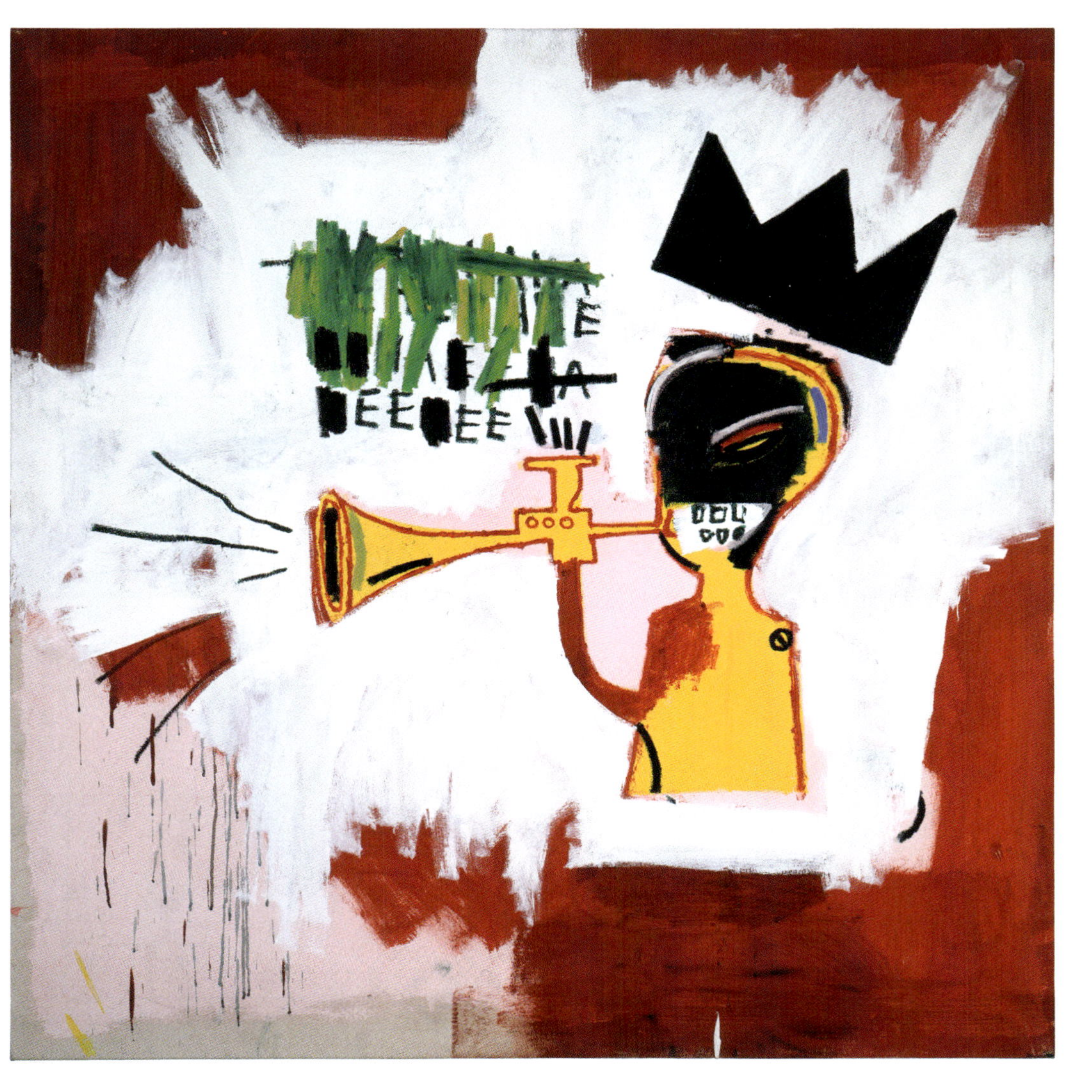

Trumpet, 1984
Acrylic and oilstick on canvas,
152.5 x 152.5 cm / 60 x 60 inches

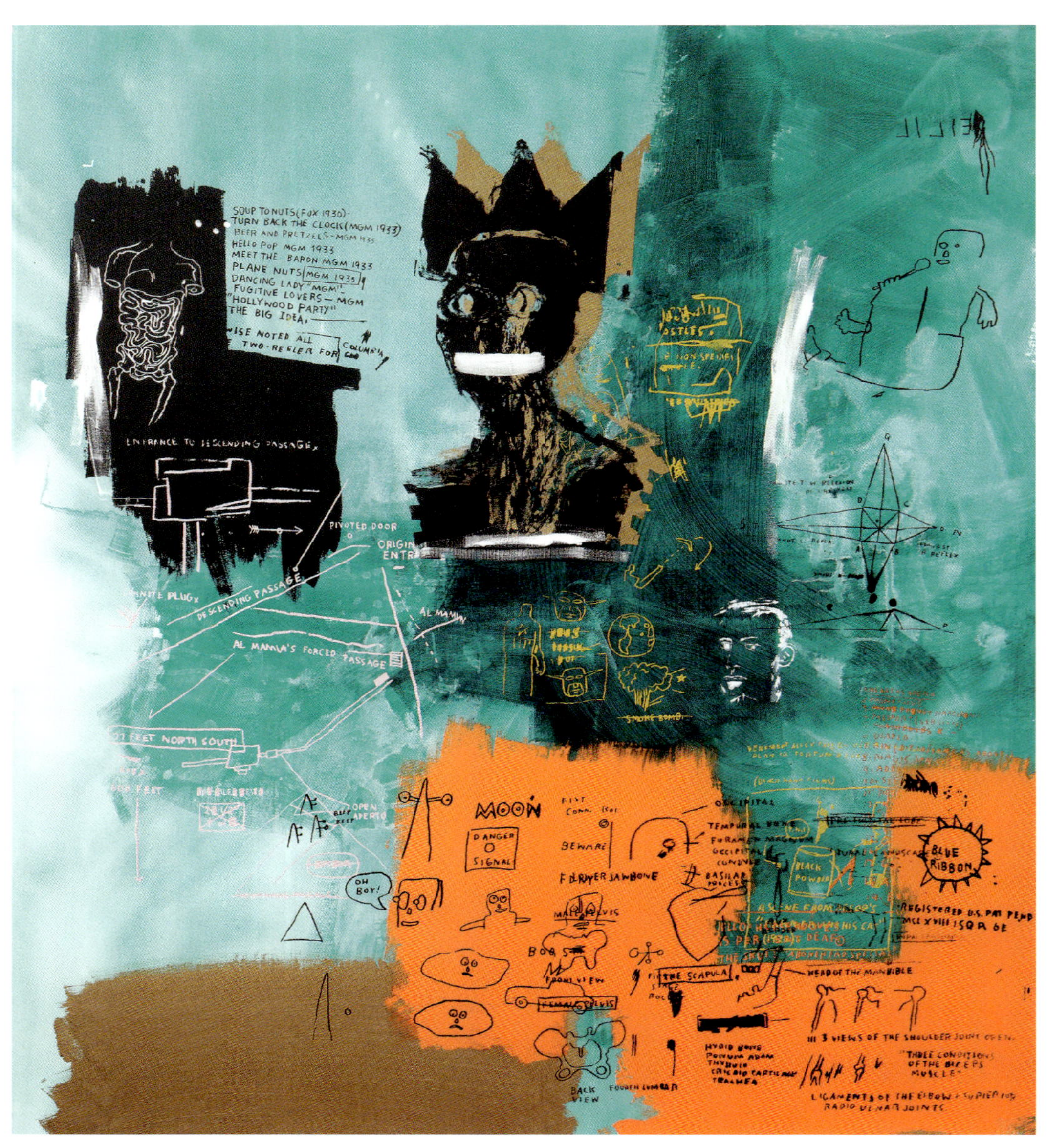

Untitled (from the series of
11 *Blue Ribbon Paintings*), 1984
Acrylic and silkscreen on canvas,
167.5 x 152.5 cm / 66 x 60 inches

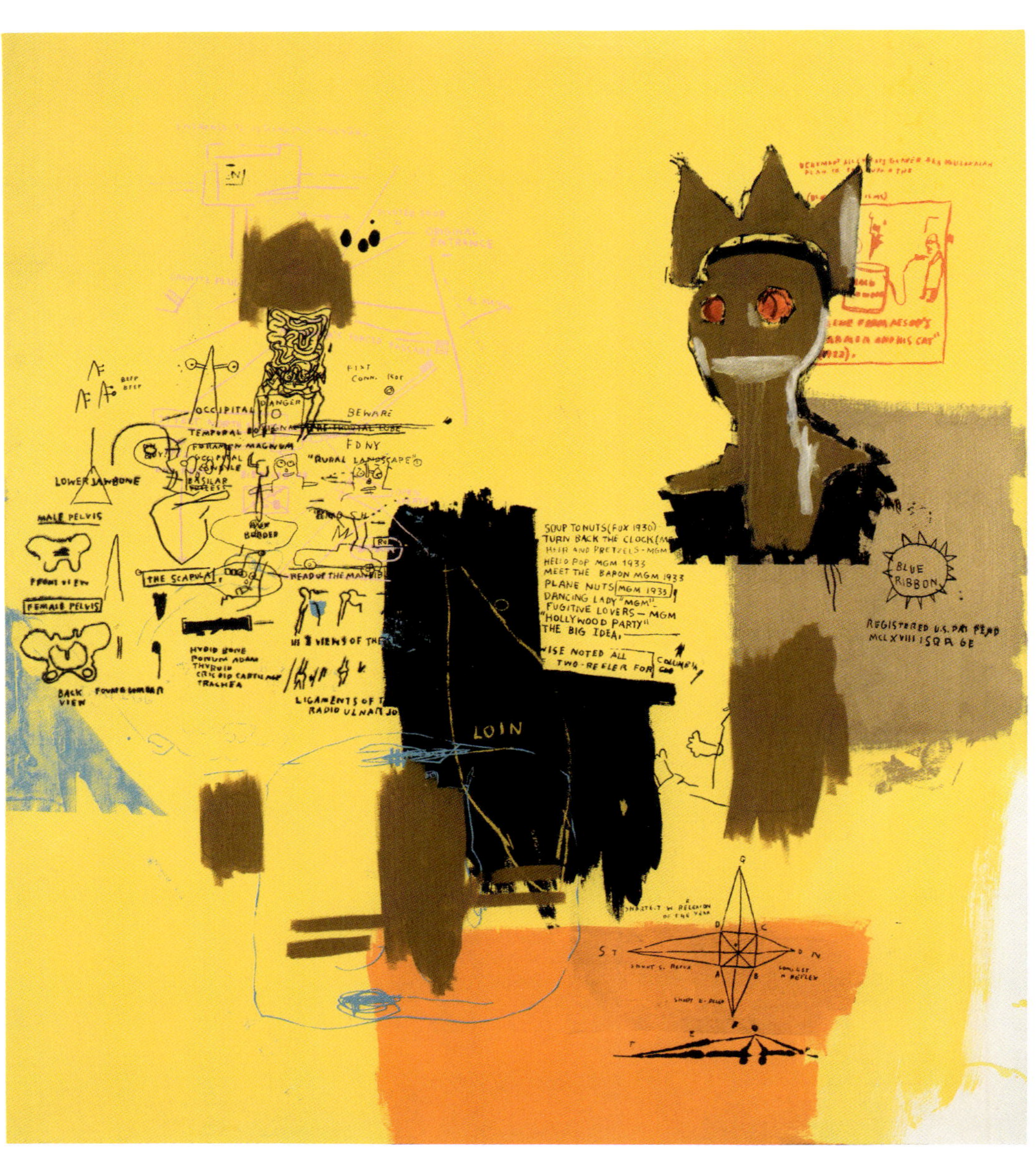

Untitled (from the series of
11 Blue Ribbon Paintings), 1984
Acrylic and silkscreen on canvas,
167.5 x 152.5 cm / 66 x 60 inches

Untitled (from the series of
11 Blue Ribbon Paintings), 1984
Acrylic and silkscreen on canvas,
167.5 x 152.5 cm / 66 x 60 inches

Page 336: **M.T.**, 1984
Acrylic and silkscreen on canvas,
218.5 x 172.5 cm / 86 x 68 inches

Page 337: **At Large**, 1984
Acrylic and oilstick on canvas,
218.5 x 172.5 cm / 86 x 68 inches

Page 338: **Pink Elephant with Fire Engine**, 1984
acrylic, oilstick, and silkscreen on canvas,
86 x 68 inches / 218.5 x 172.5 cm

Page 339: **Pyro**, 1984
acrylic and silkscreen on canvas,
86 ¹/₂ x 68 inches / 219.5 x 172.5 cm

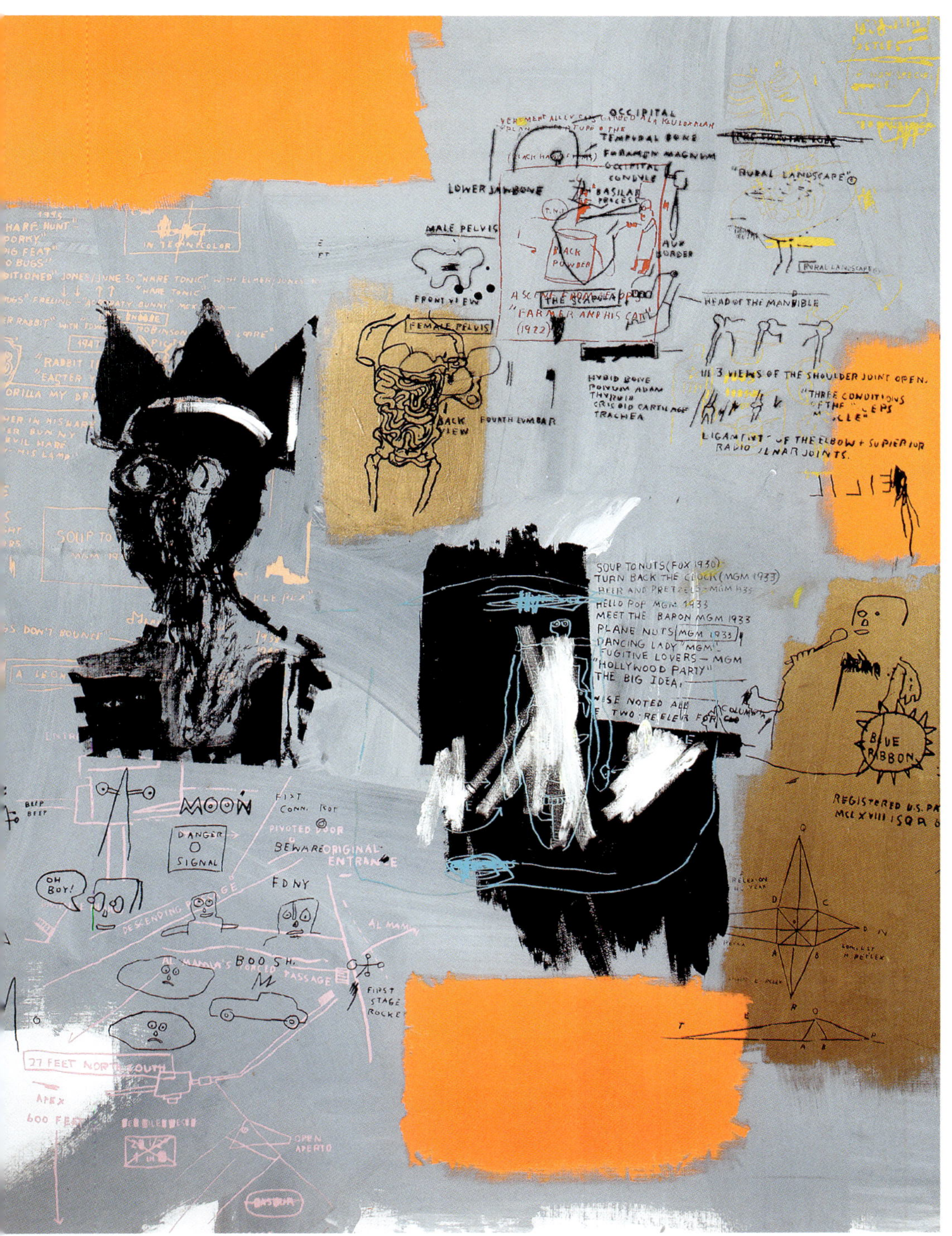

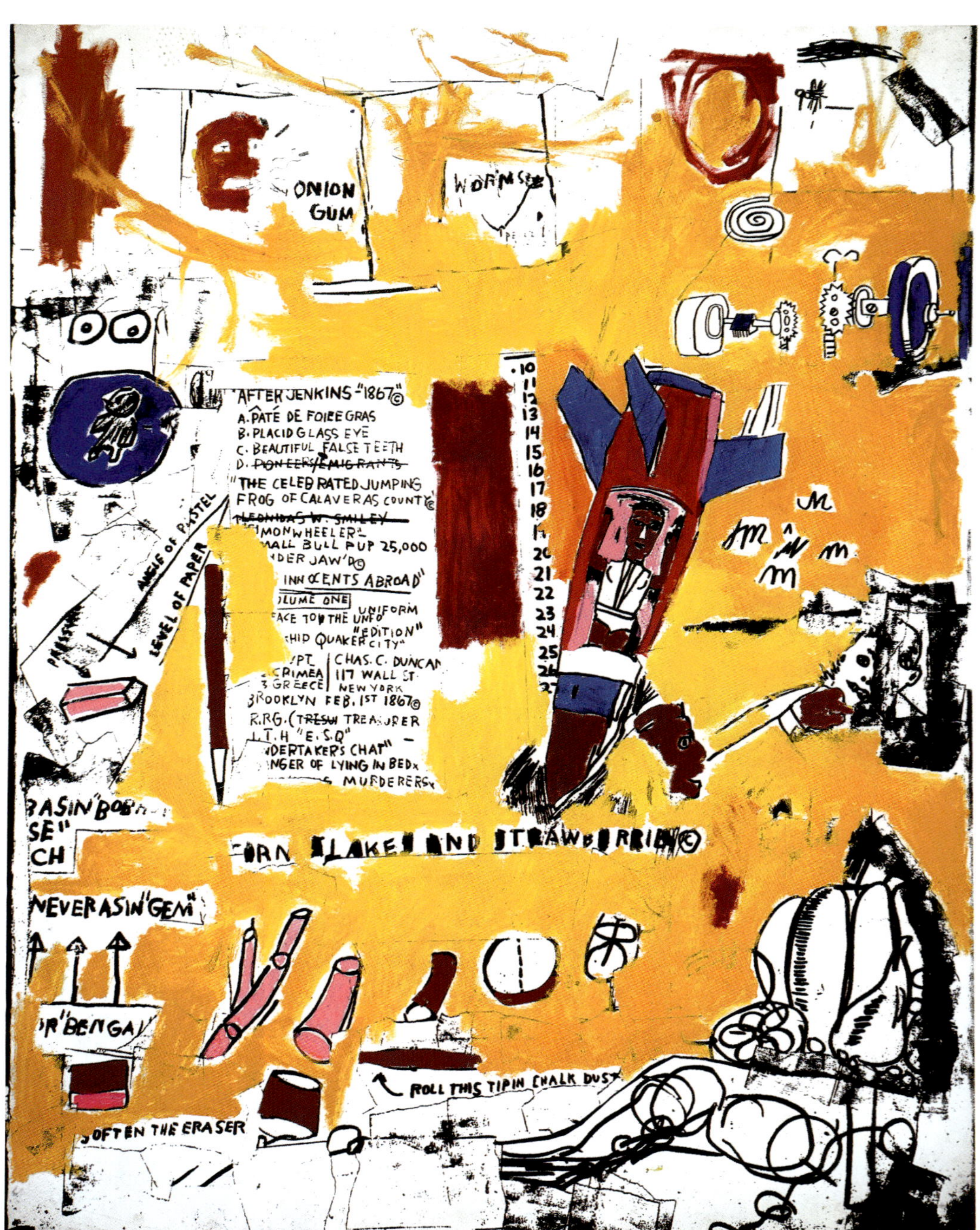
ONION GUM
WORMS
AFTER JENKINS "1867"©
A. PATÉ DE FOIE GRAS
B. PLACID GLASS EYE
C. BEAUTIFUL FALSE TEETH
D. PIONEERS/EMIGRANTS
"THE CELEBRATED JUMPING
FROG OF CALAVERAS COUNTY"©
LEONIDAS W. SMILEY
SIMON WHEELER
SMALL BULL PUP 25,000
UNDER JAW'D
INNOCENTS ABROAD"
VOLUME ONE
THE UNIFORM
"EDITION"
QUAKER CITY"
CHAS. C. DUNCAN
117 WALL ST.
NEW YORK
BROOKLYN FEB. 1ST 1867©
R.RG.(TRESH TREASURER
T.H "E.SQ"
UNDERTAKER'S CHAP"
DANGER OF LYING IN BED
MURDERERS
ANGLE OF PISTOL
LEVEL OF PAPER
BASIN BOB
SE"
CH
CORN FLAKES AND STRAWBERRIES©
NEVER A SIN "GEM"
OR "BENGAL"
ROLL THIS TIP IN CHALK DUST
SOFTEN THE ERASER

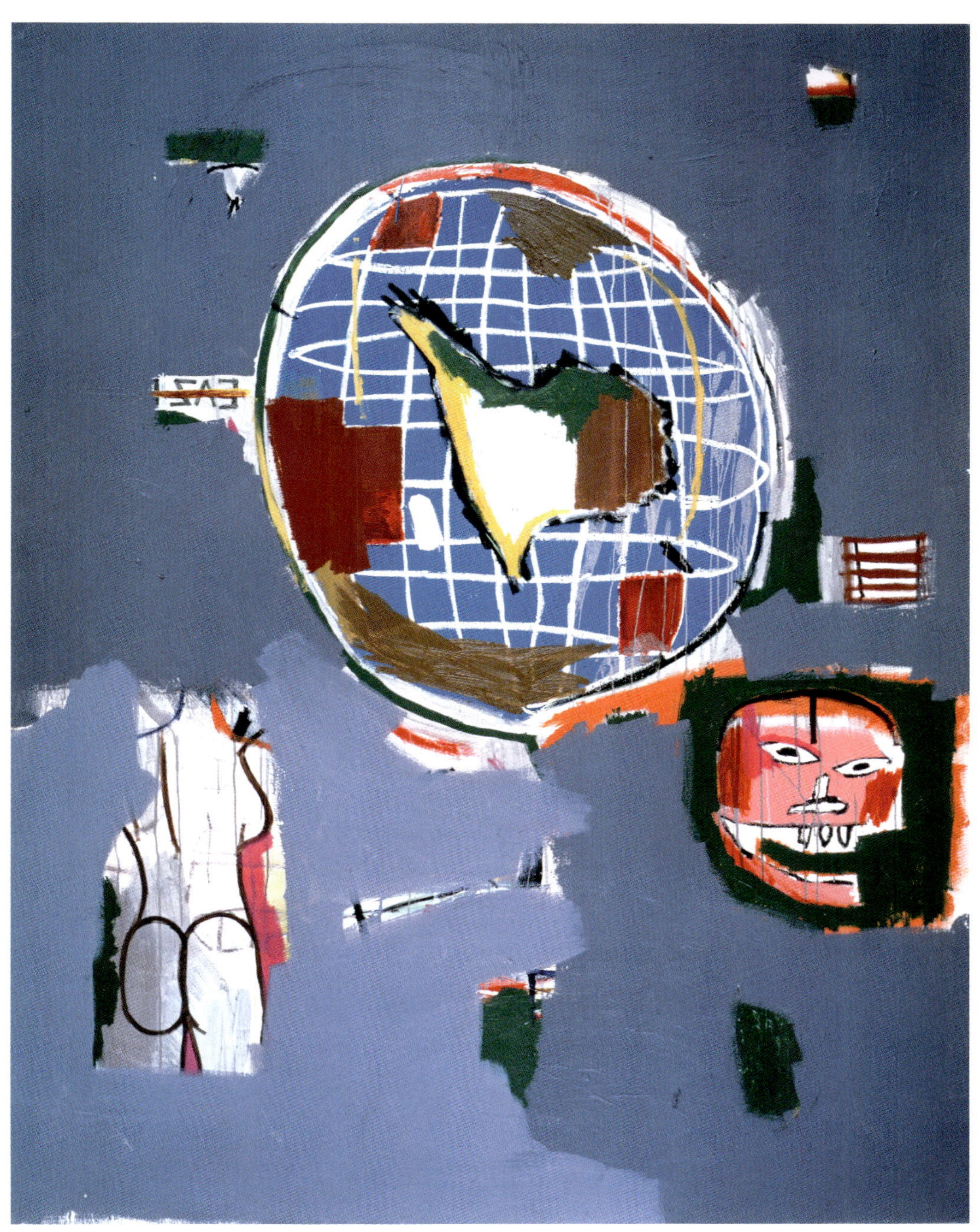

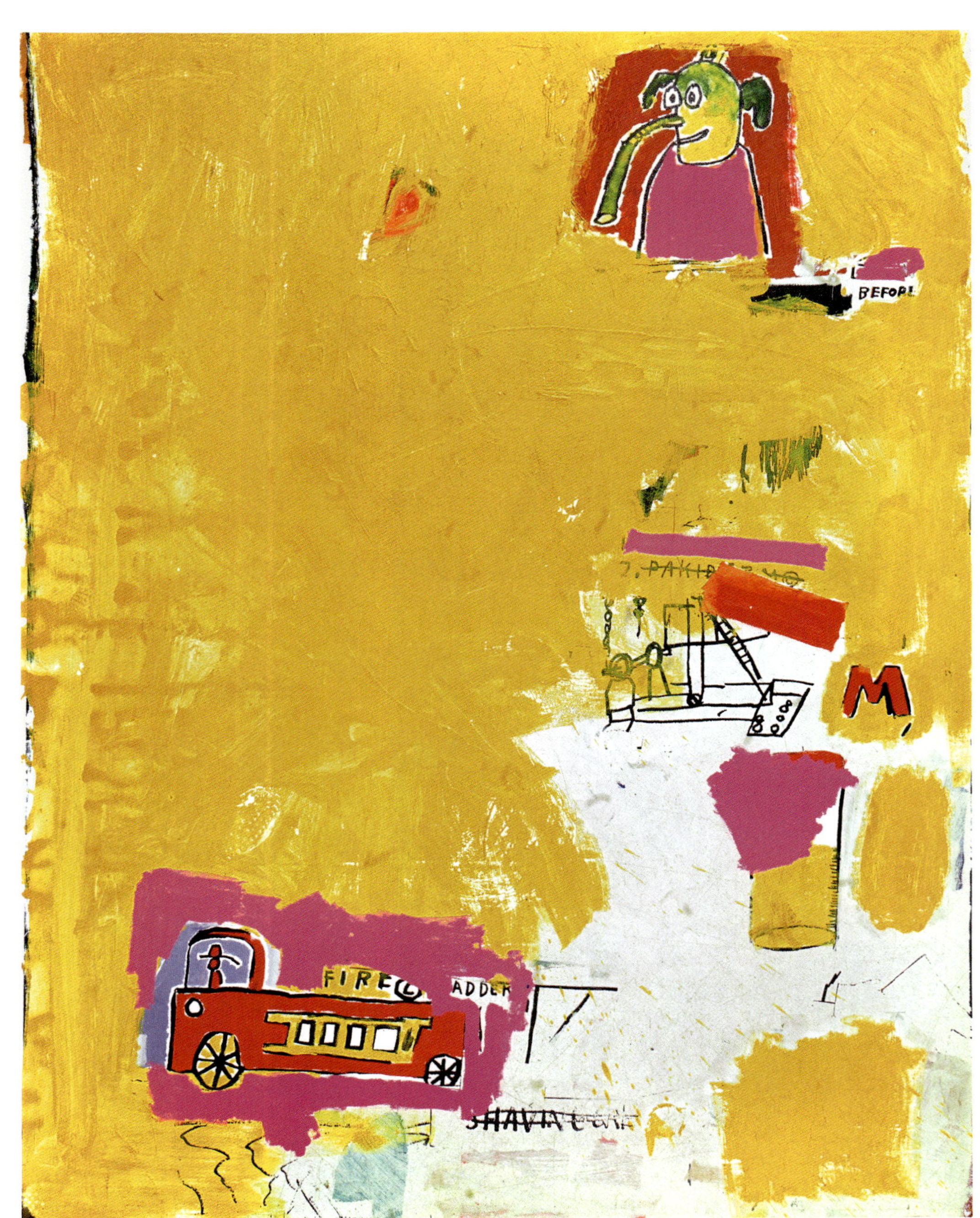
BEFORE
PAKISTANO
M
FIRE LADDER
SHAVING

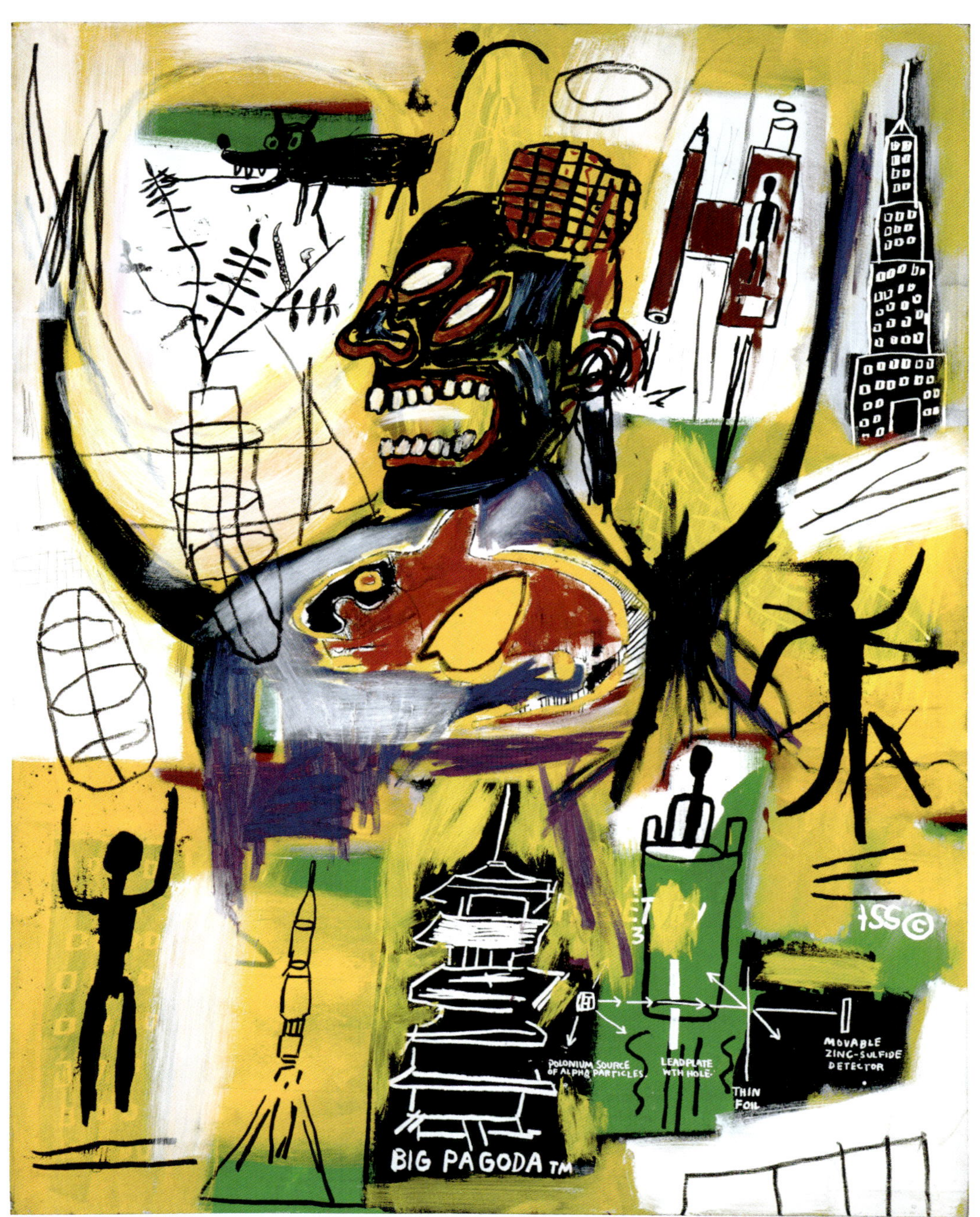
BIG PAGODA TM
POLONIUM SOURCE OF ALPHA PARTICLES
LEADPLATE WITH HOLE
THIN FOIL
MOVABLE ZINC-SULFIDE DETECTOR

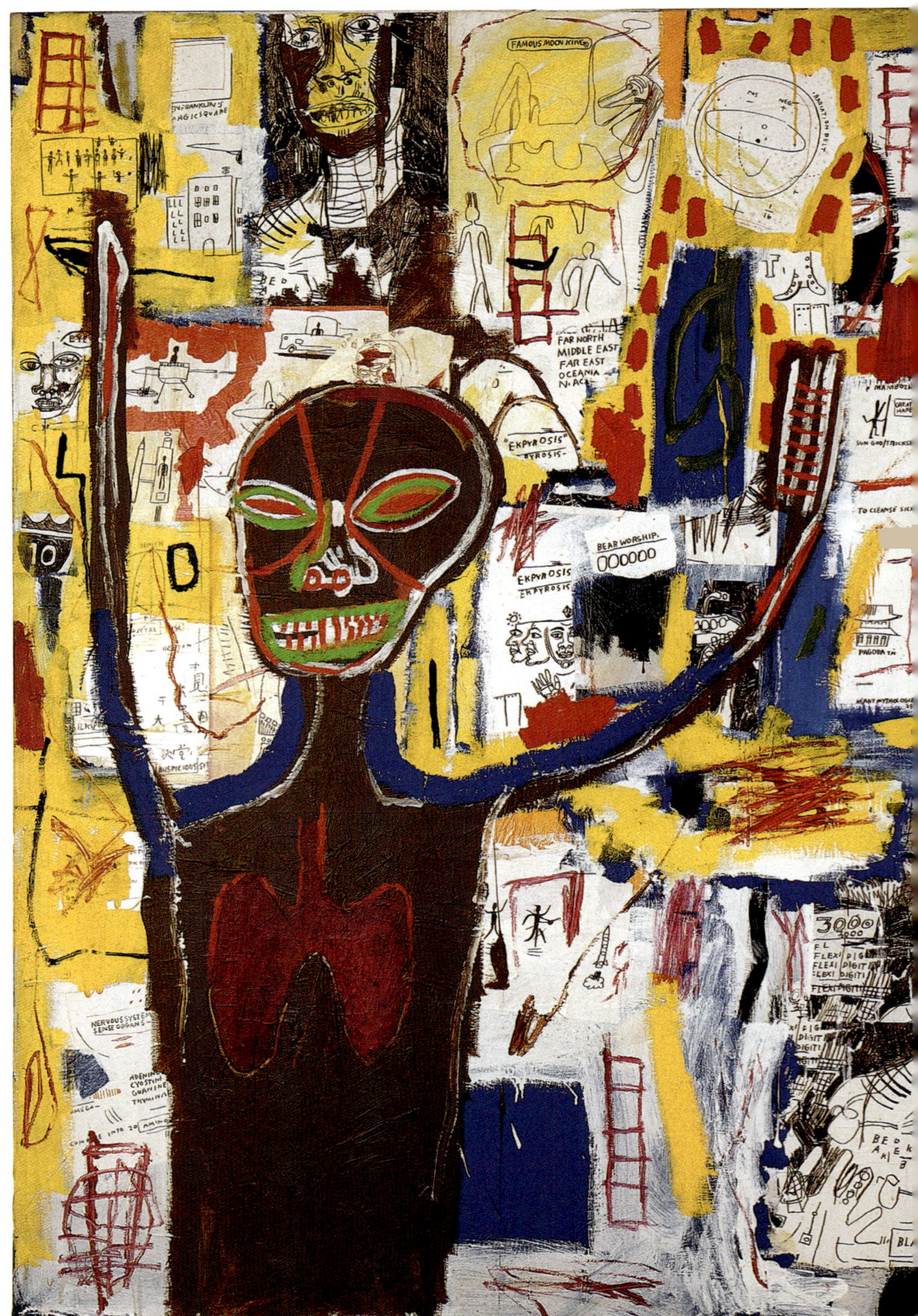

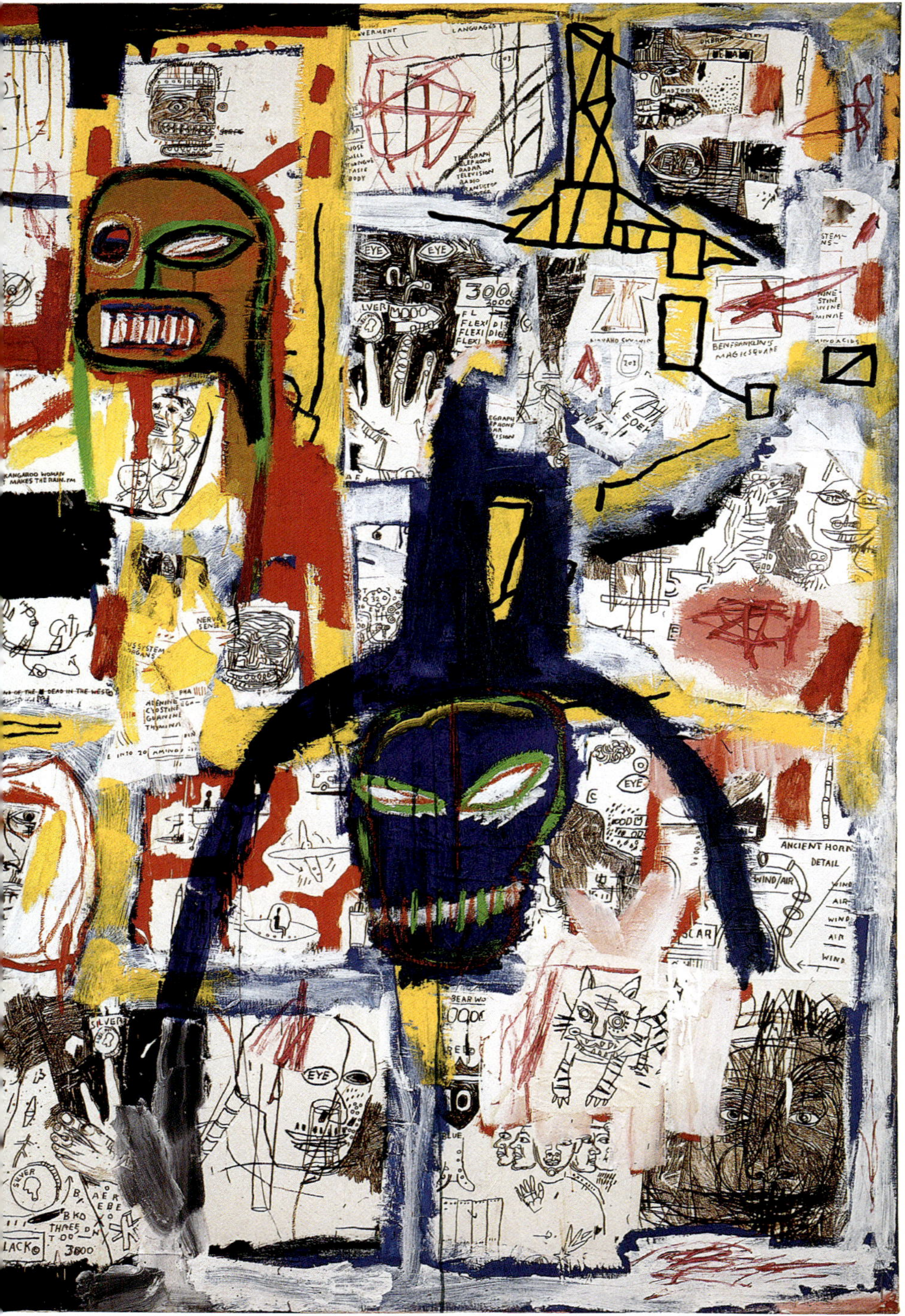

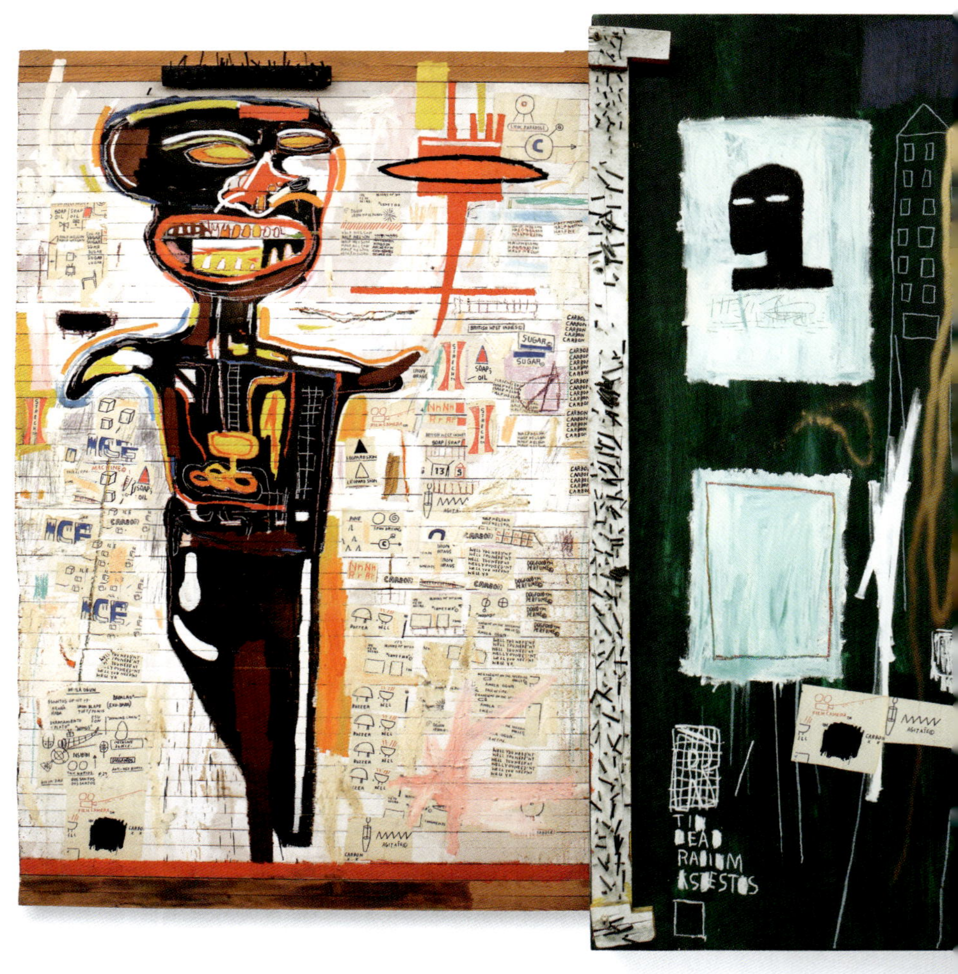

Pages 340/341: **Famous Moon King**, 1984
Acrylic, oilstick, and photocopy collage on
canvas, 180 x 261 cm / 70 ³/₄ x 102 ³/₄ inches

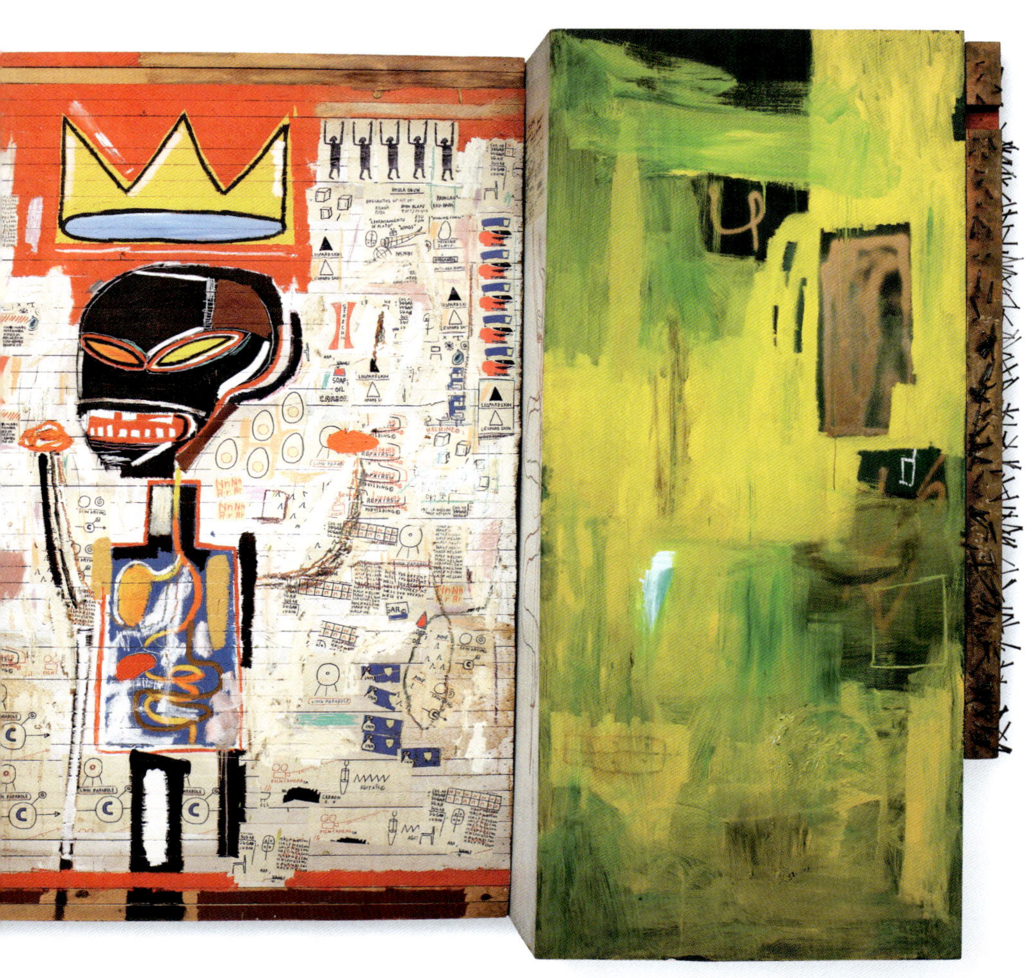

Grillo, 1984
Acrylic, oil, photocopy collage, oilstick,
and nails on wood, polyptych:
244 x 537 x 45.5 cm / 96 x 211 $^1/_2$ x 18 inches

Untitled, 1984
Acrylic and silkscreen on canvas,
218.5 x 172.5 cm / 86 x 68 inches

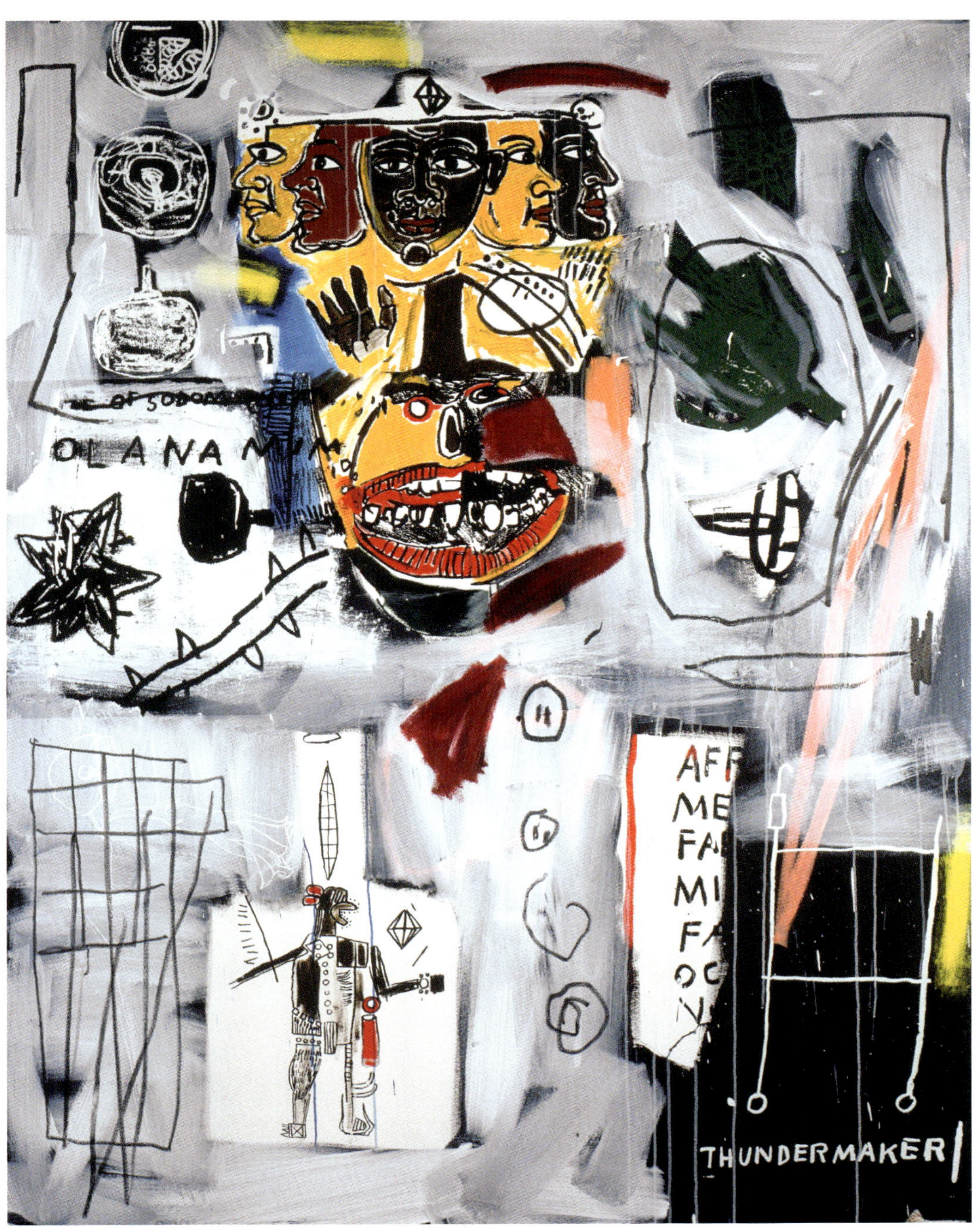
OLANAMI
AFR
ME
FA
MI
FA
O
THUNDERMAKER

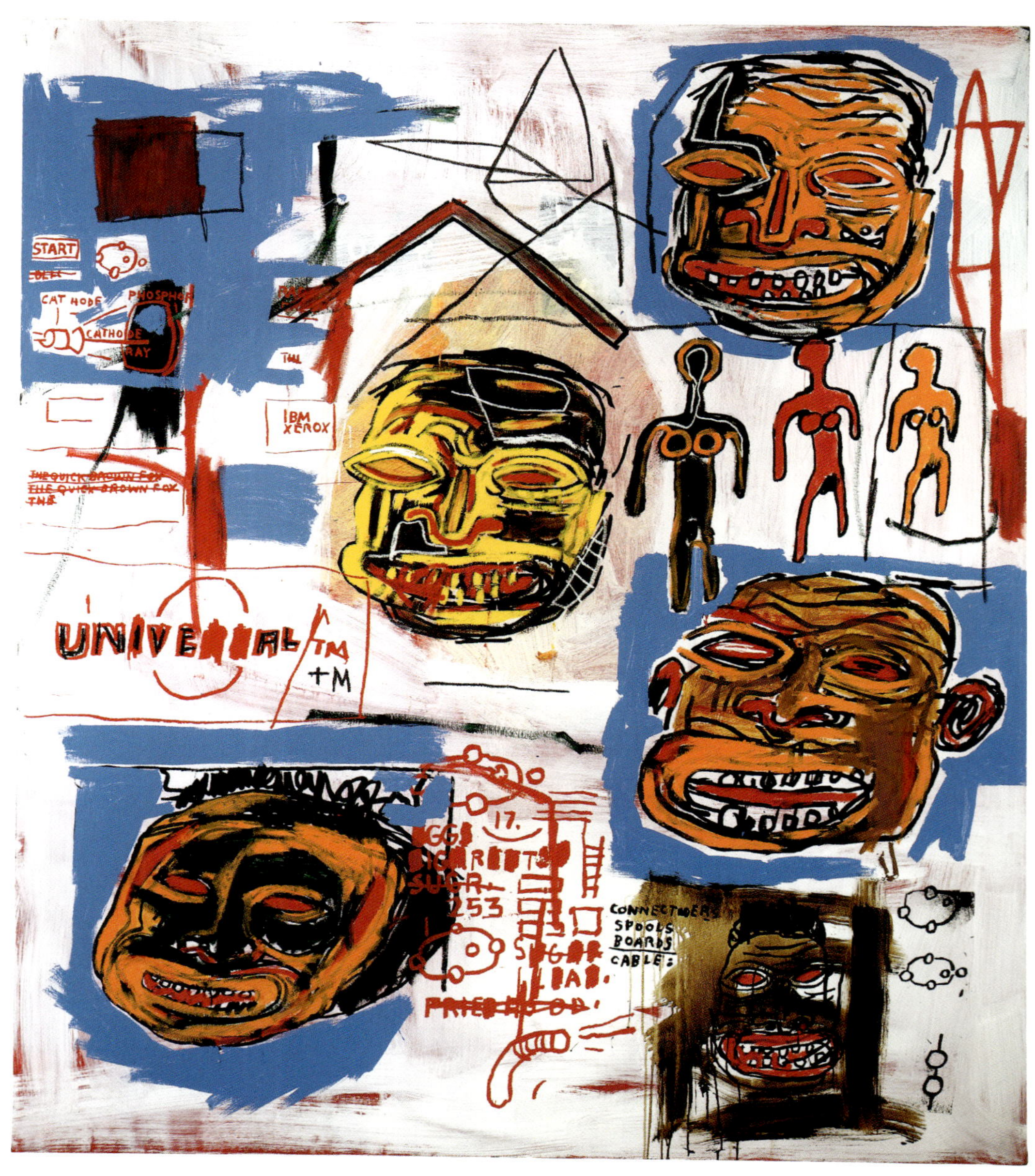

Cathode, 1984
Acrylic and silkscreen on canvas,
223.5 x 195.5 cm / 88 x 77 inches

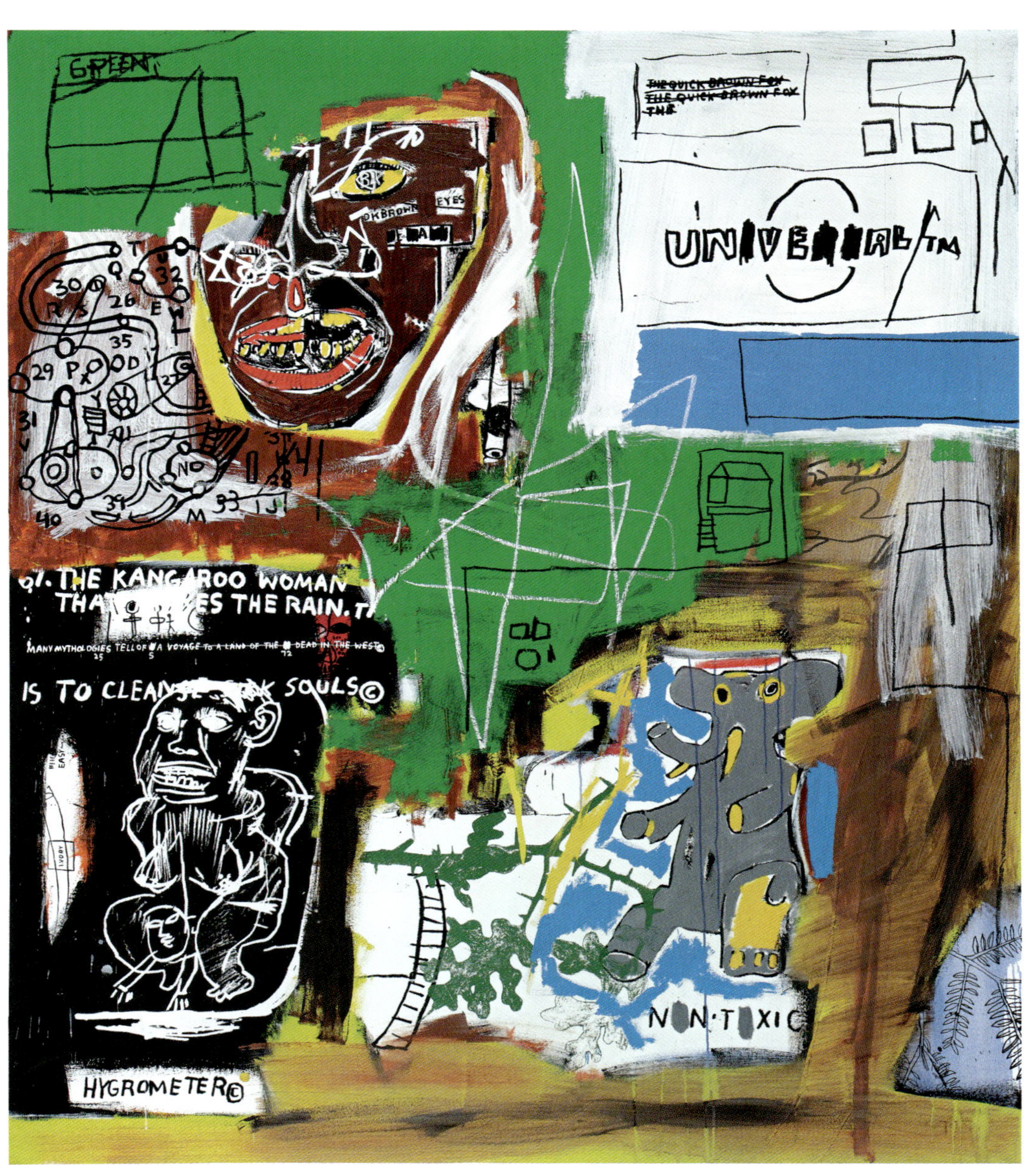

Sienna, 1984
Acrylic and silkscreen on canvas,
223.5 x 195.5 cm / 88 x 77 inches

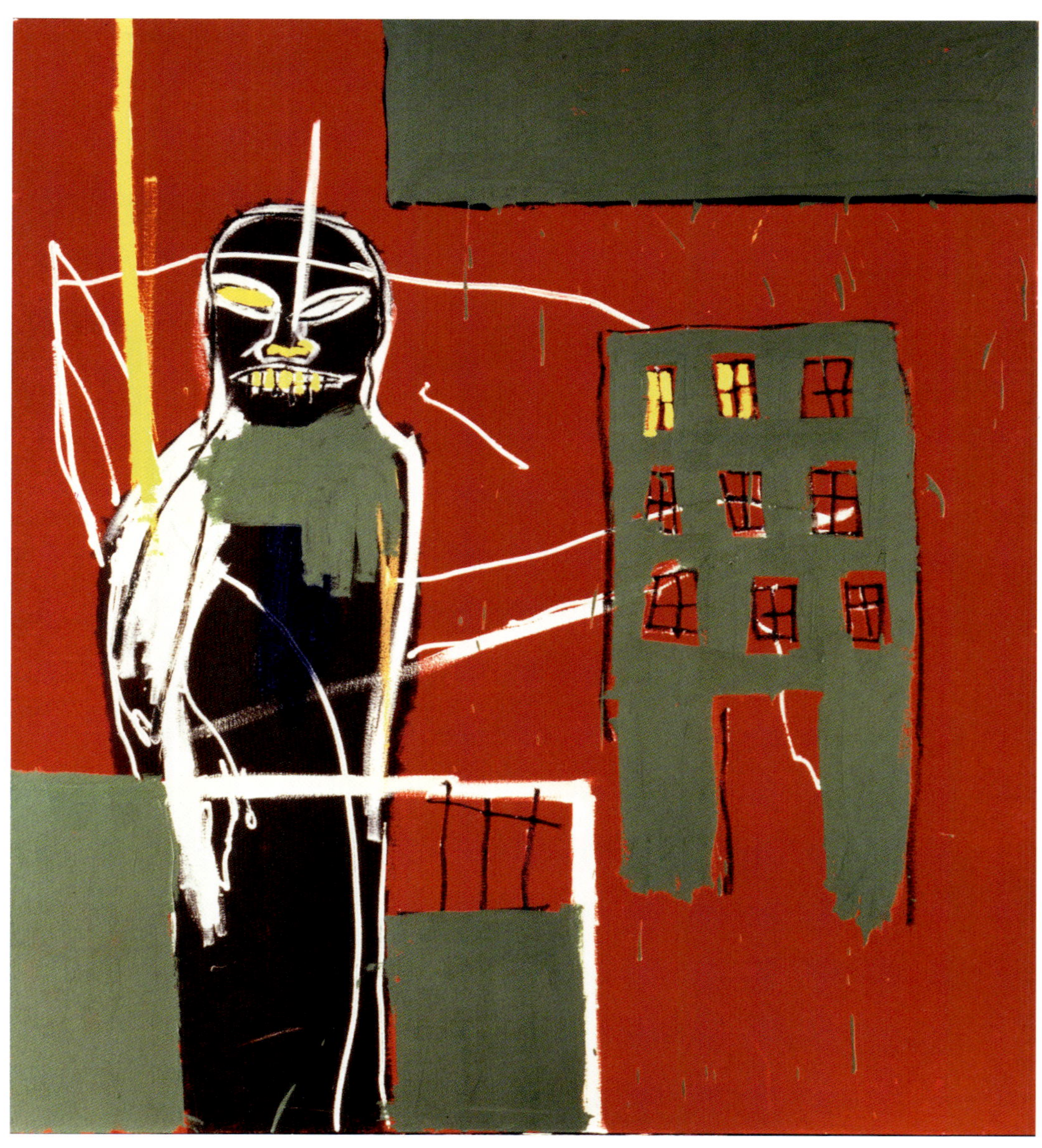

Pedestrian II, 1984
Acrylic and oilstick on canvas,
153 x 137 cm / 60 $^1/_4$ x 54 inches

Melting Point of Ice, 1984
Acrylic, oilstick, and silkscreen on canvas,
218.5 x 172.5 cm / 86 x 68 inches

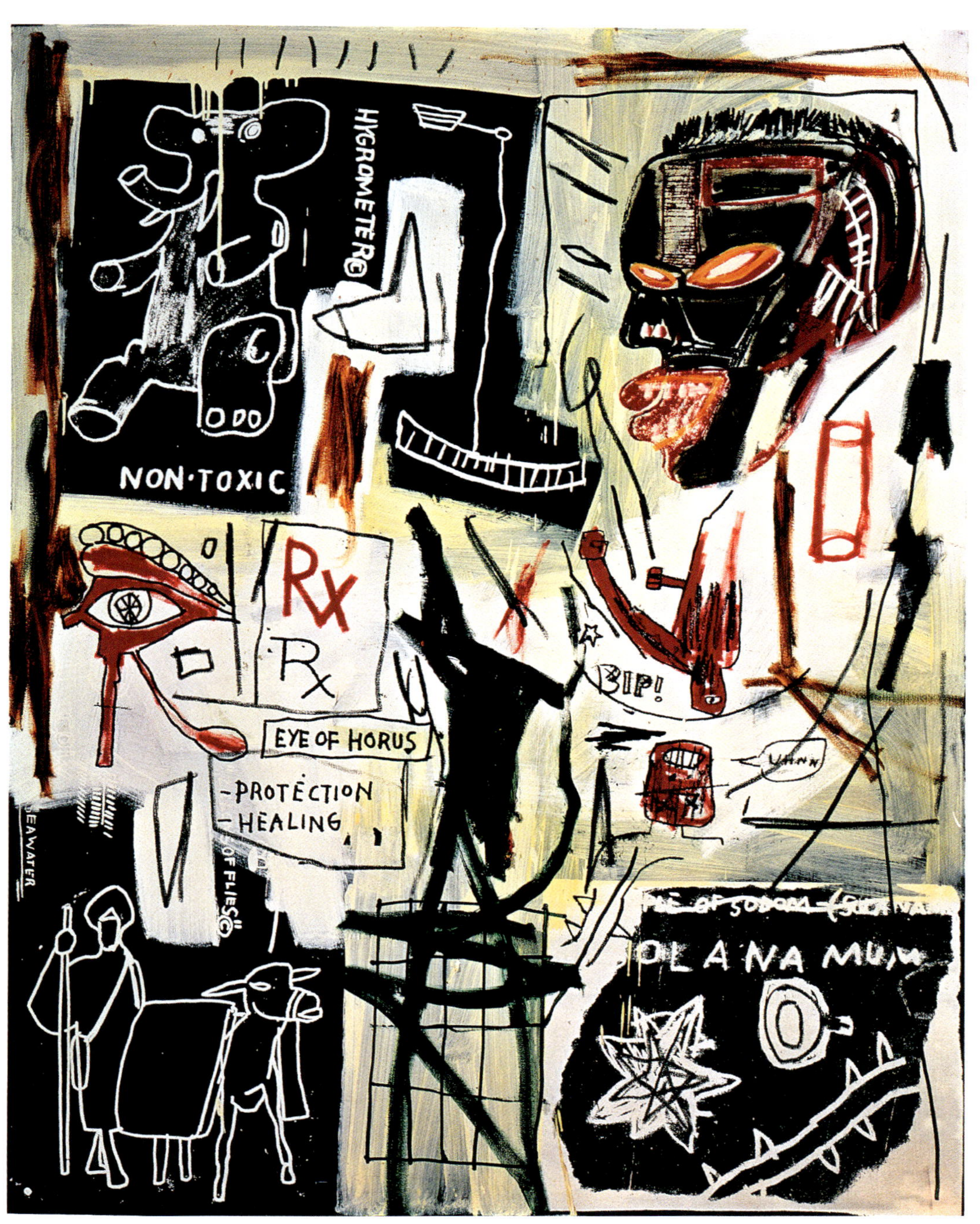
HYGROMETER©
NON·TOXIC
RX
RX
EYE OF HORUS
-PROTECTION
-HEALING
SEAWATER
OF FLIES"
BIP!
UHNN
ISLE OF SODOM
PLANA MUM

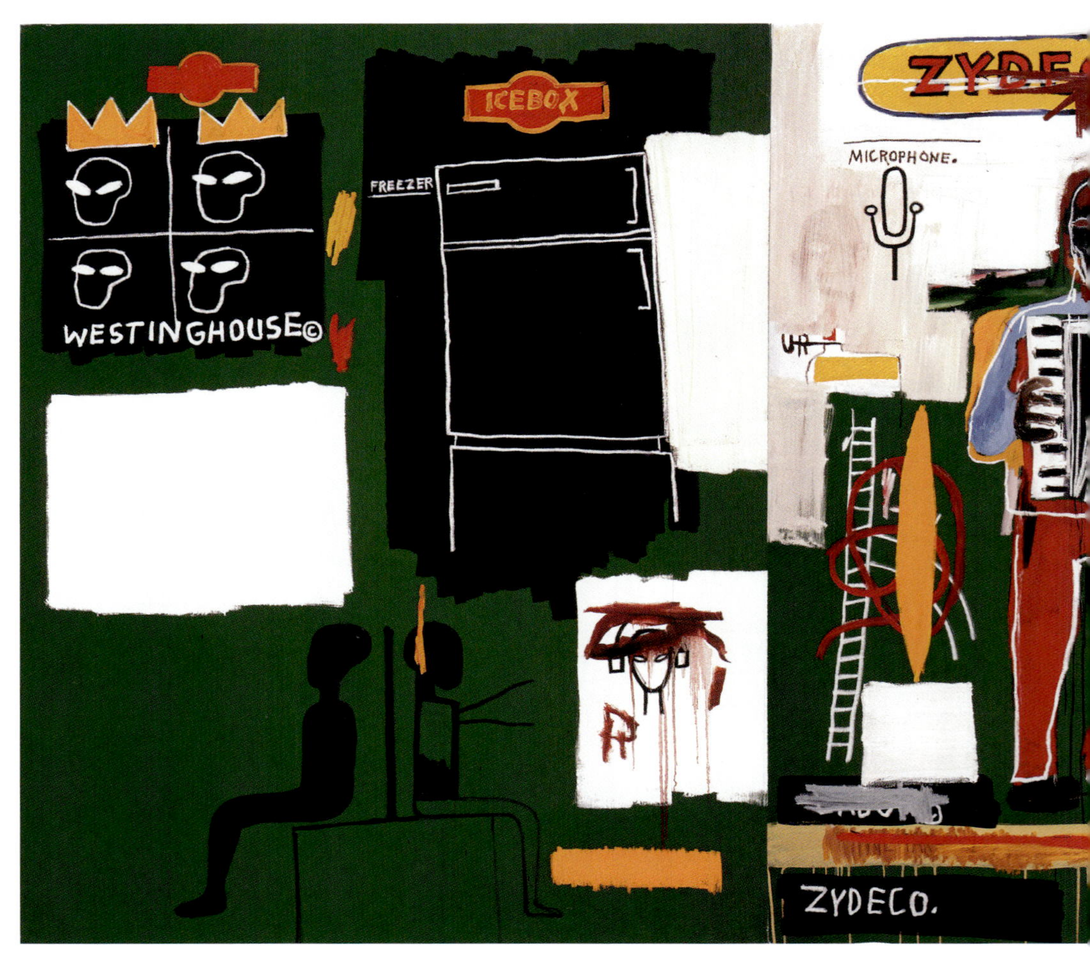

Zydeco, 1984
Acrylic and oilstick on canvas, triptych:
218.5 x 518 cm / 86 x 204 inches

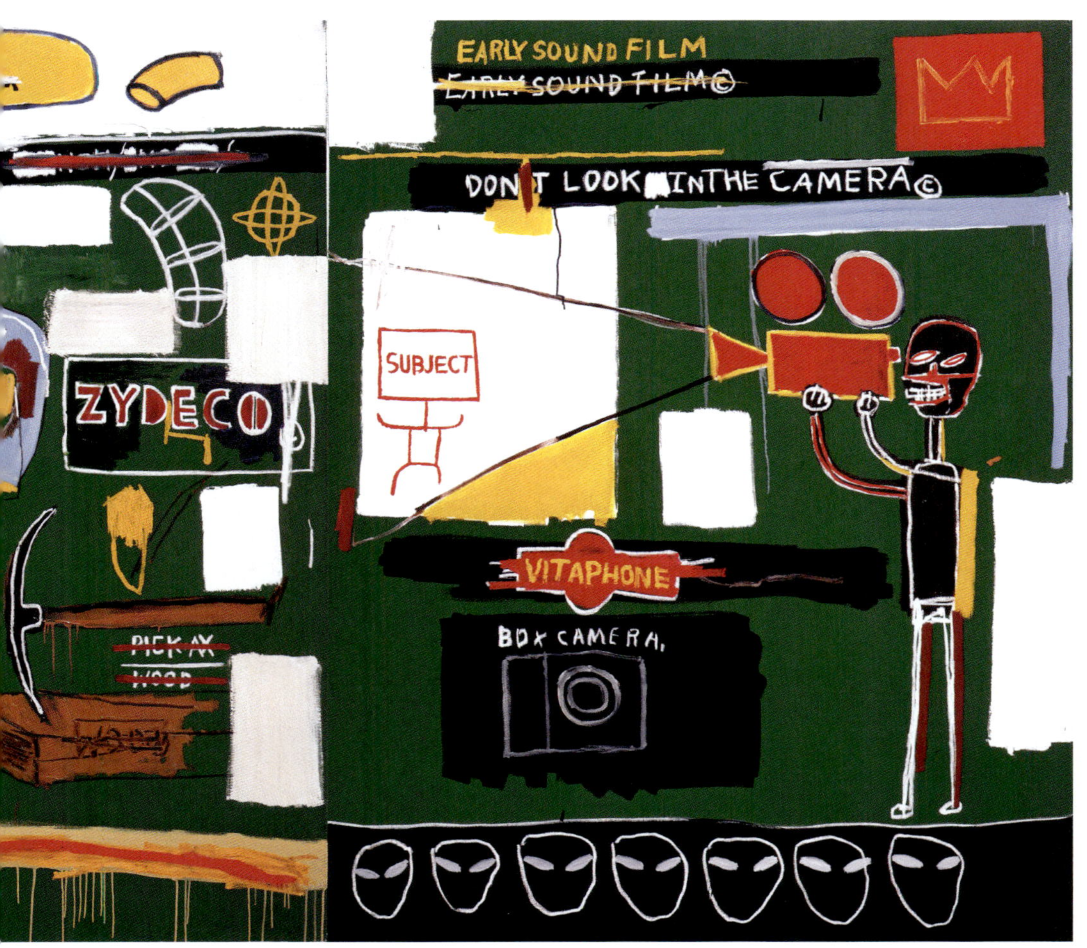
EARLY SOUND FILM
EARLY SOUND FILM ©
DON'T LOOK IN THE CAMERA ©
ZYDECO
SUBJECT
VITAPHONE
BOX CAMERA.
PICK AX
WOOD

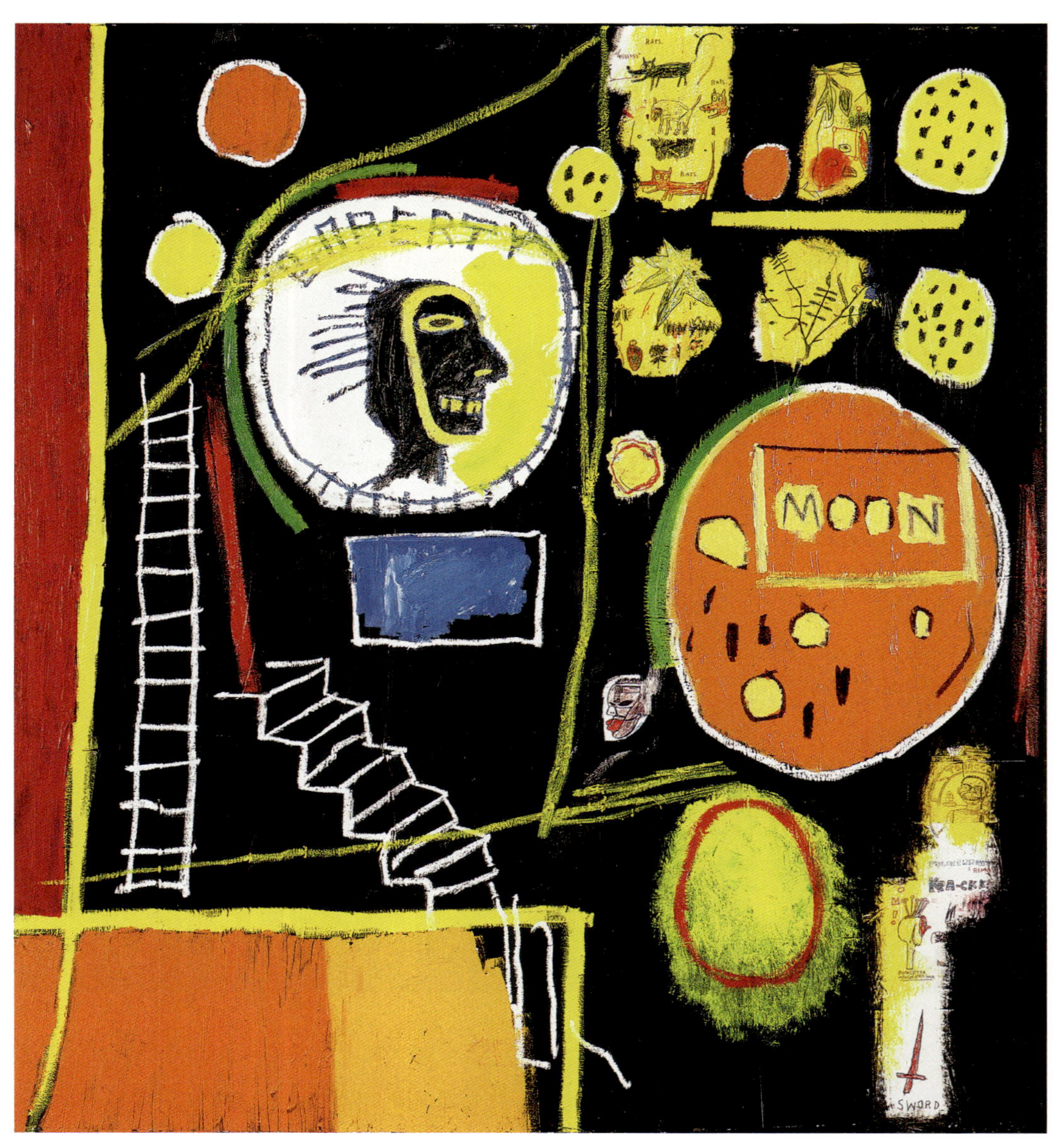

Moon View, 1984
Acrylic and oilstick on canvas,
167.5 x 152.5 cm / 66 x 60 inches

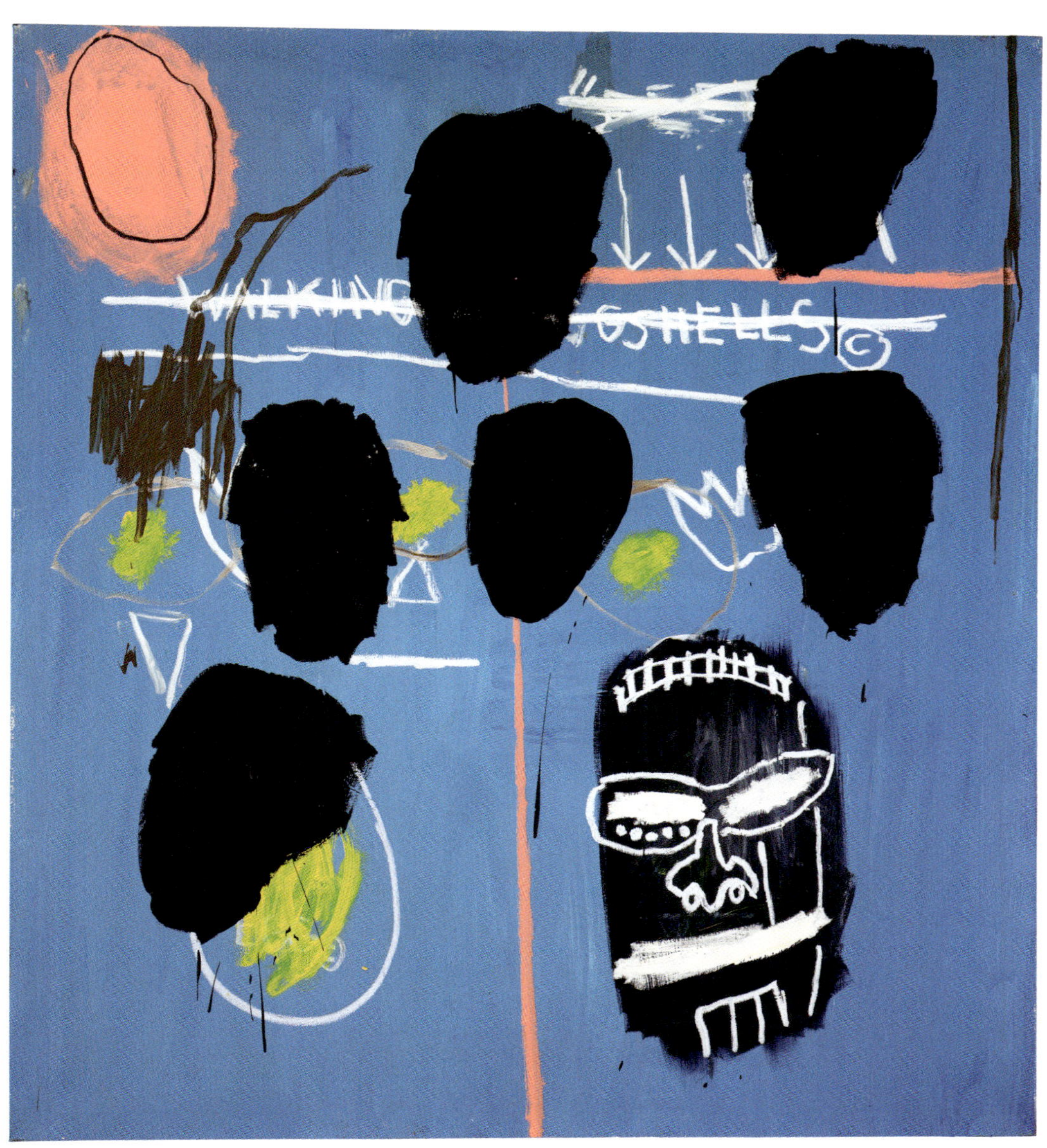

Untitled, 1984
Acrylic and oilstick on canvas,
167.5 x 152.5 cm / 66 x 60 inches

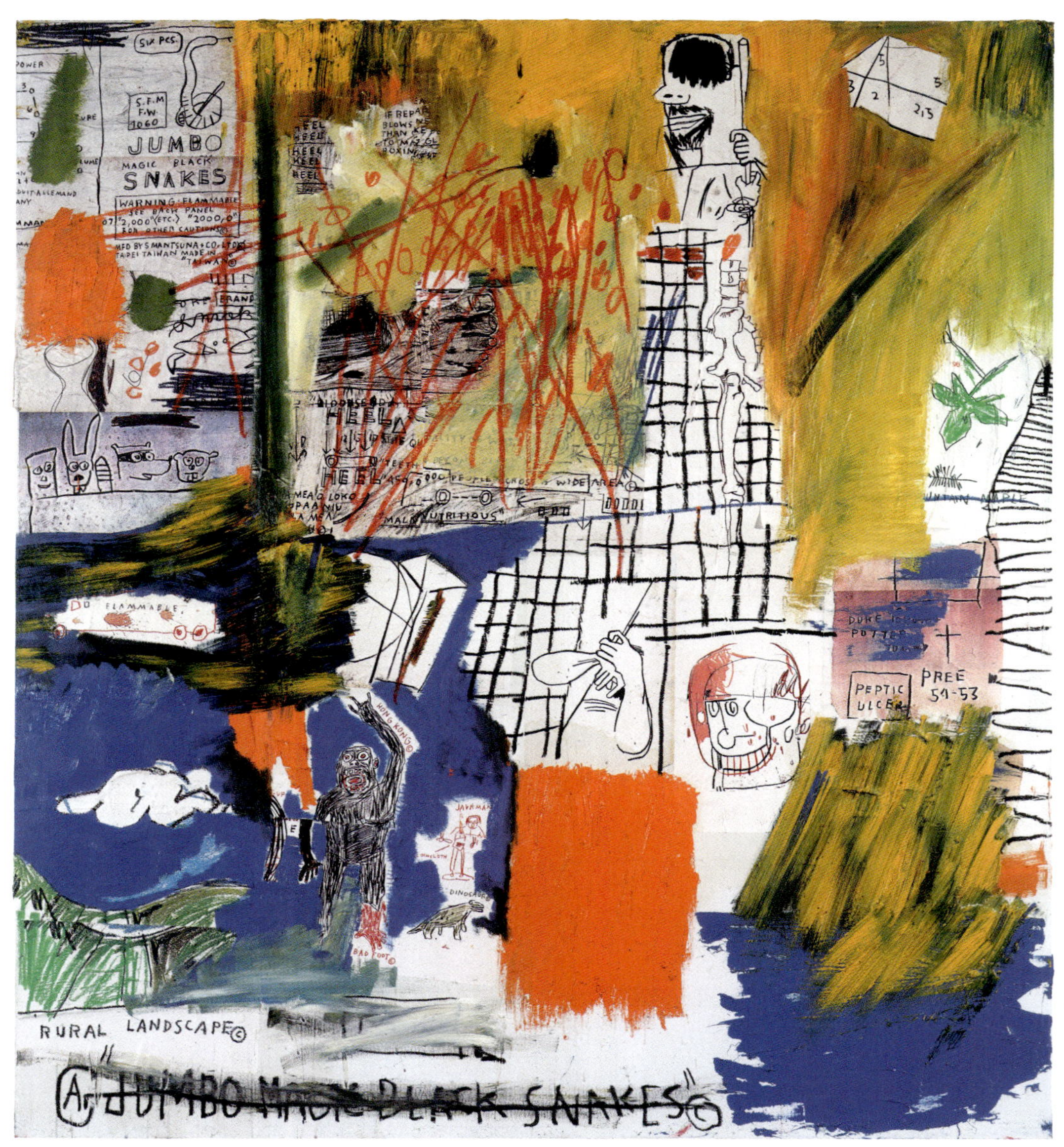

Untitled, 1984
Acrylic, oilstick, and photocopy collage
on canvas, 167.5 x 152.5 cm / 66 x 60 inches

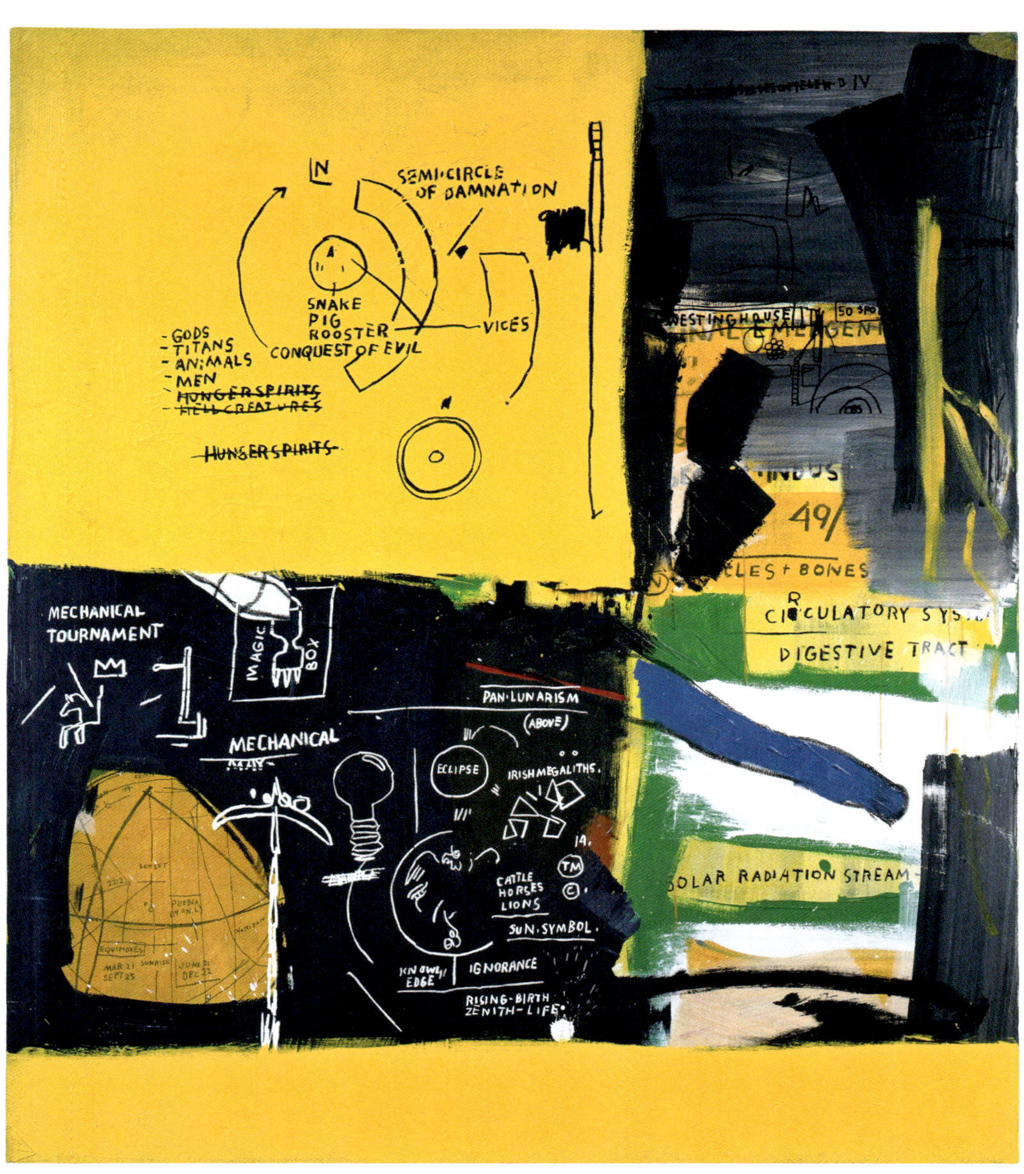

Untitled, 1984
Acrylic and silkscreen on canvas,
223.5 x 198 cm / 88 x 78 inches

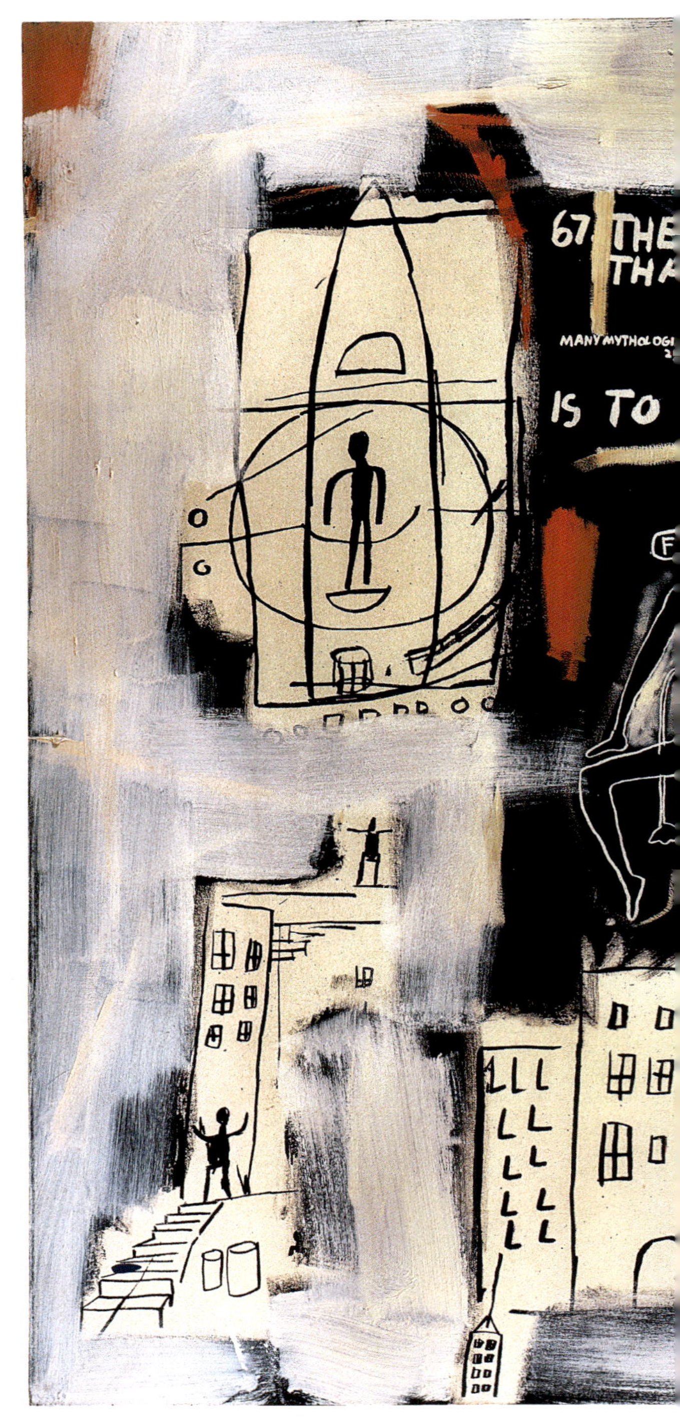

Prayer, 1984
Acrylic, oilstick, and silkscreen
on canvas, 172.5 x 218.5 cm /
68 x 86 inches

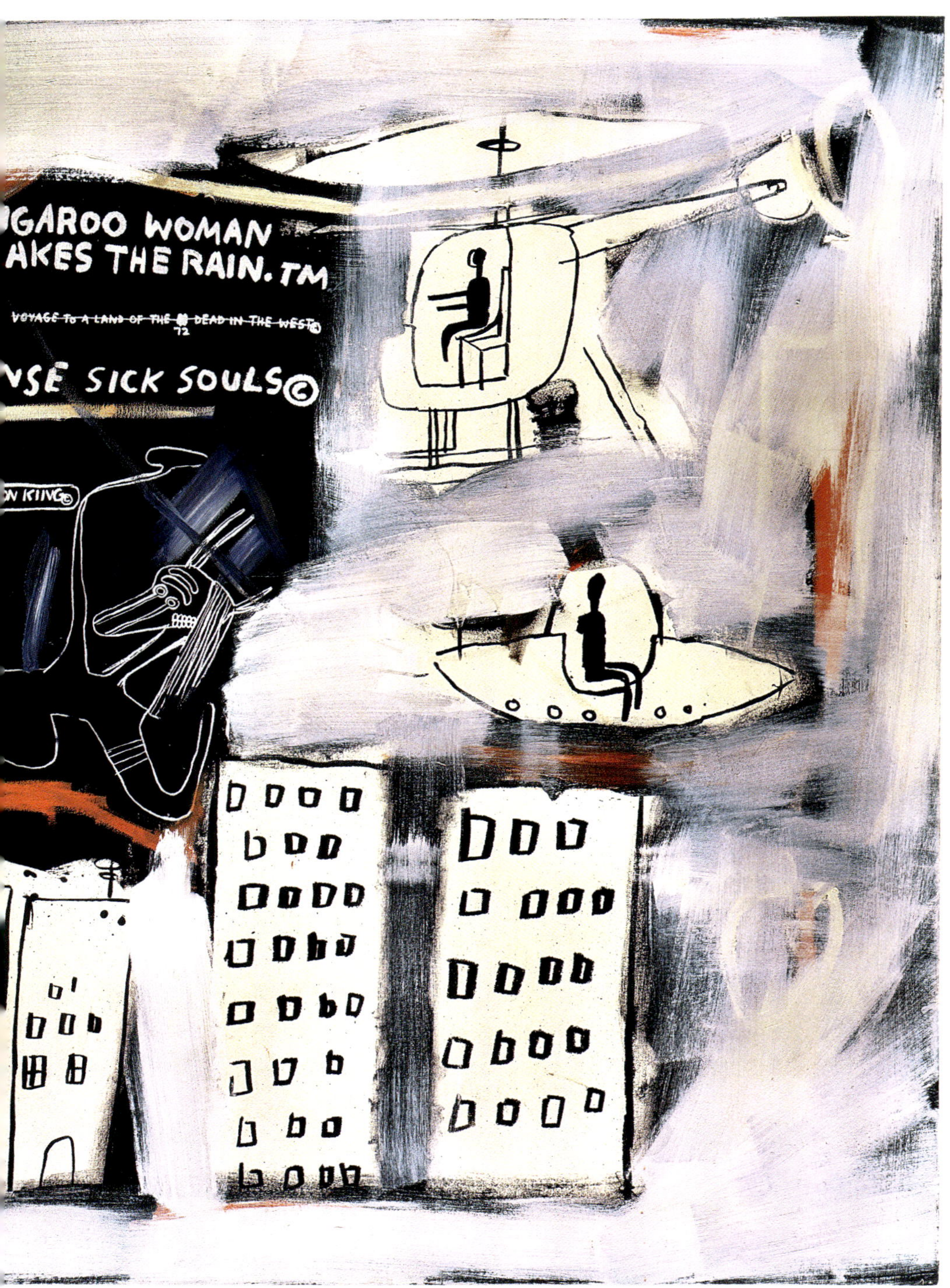
GAROO WOMAN
AKES THE RAIN. TM
VOYAGE TO A LAND OF THE DEAD IN THE WEST
72
SE SICK SOULS©
N KING©

Untitled, 1984
Acrylic, oilstick, and photocopy collage
on canvas, 76 x 50 cm / 30 x 19 $^1/_2$ inches

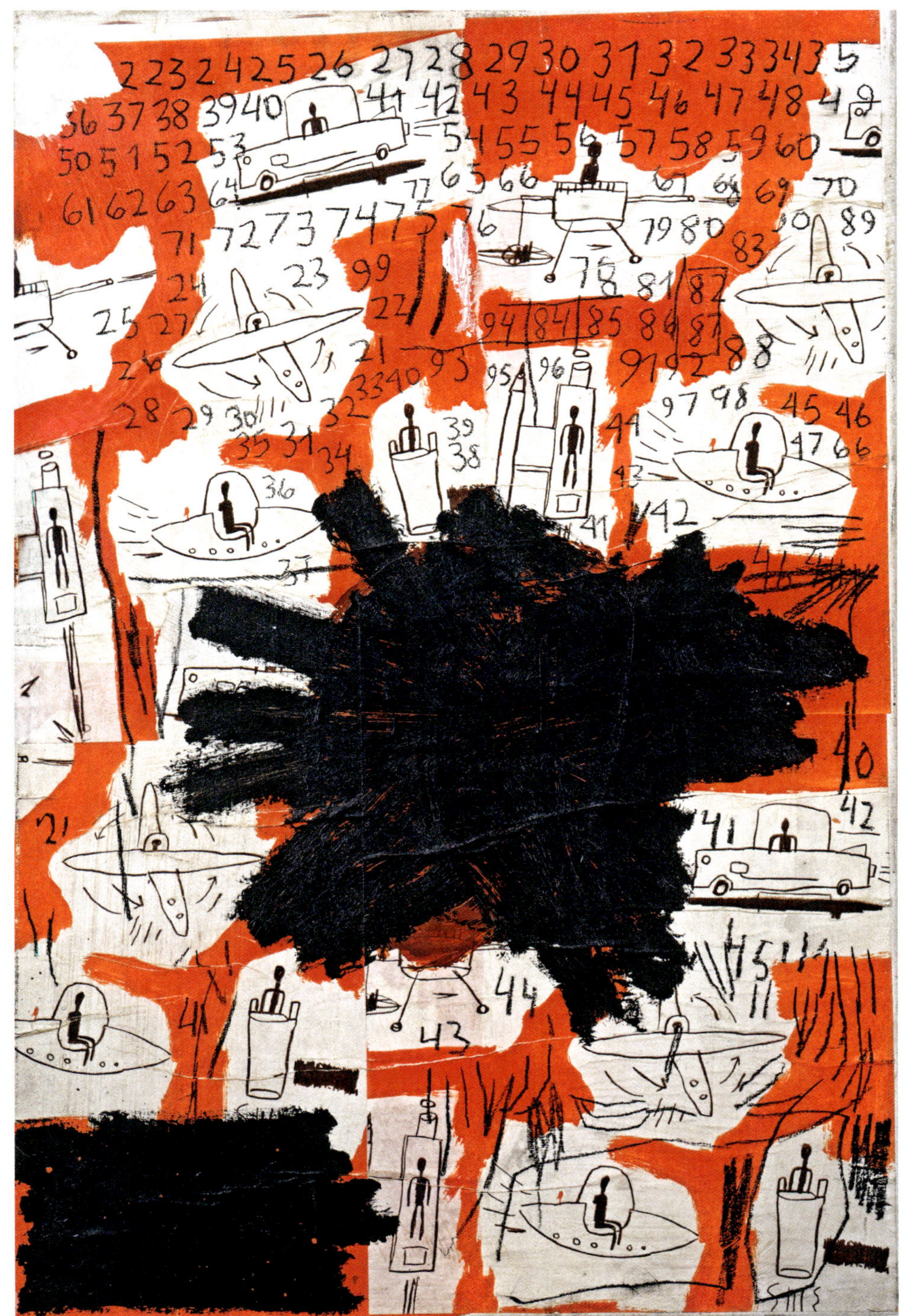

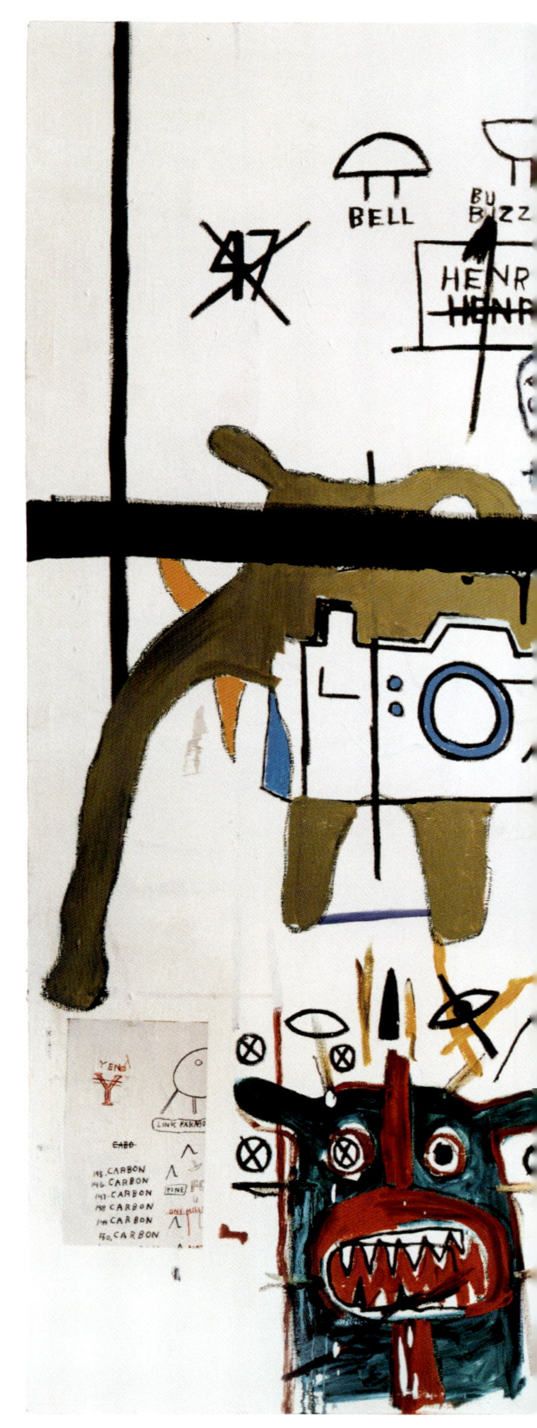

Wicker, 1984
Acrylic, oilstick, and photocopy collage
on canvas, 218.5 x 249 cm / 86 x 98 inches

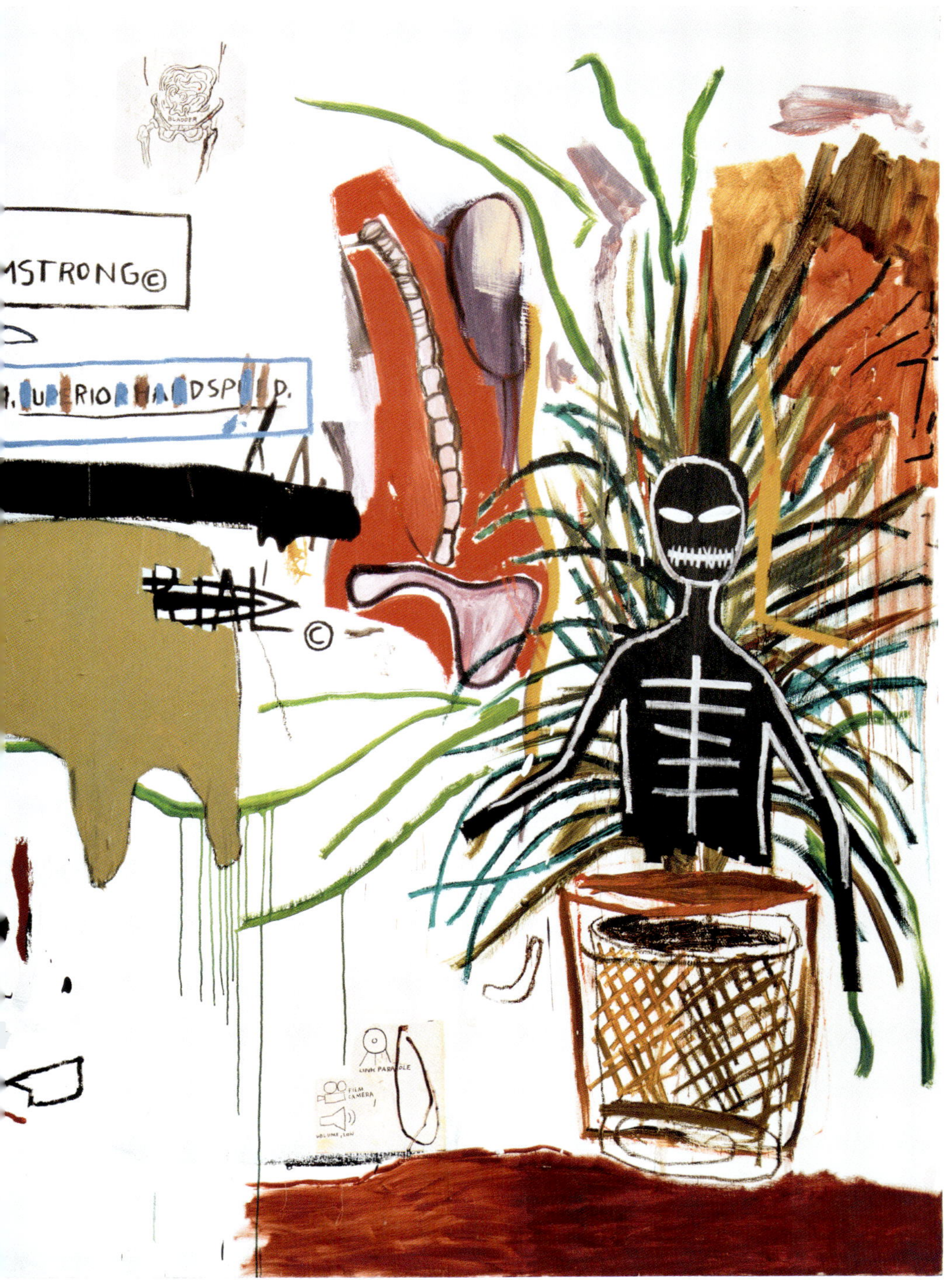
MSTRONG ©
SUPERIOR HANDSPEED.
BLADDER
©
LINK PARABLE
FILM CAMERA
VOLUME, LOW

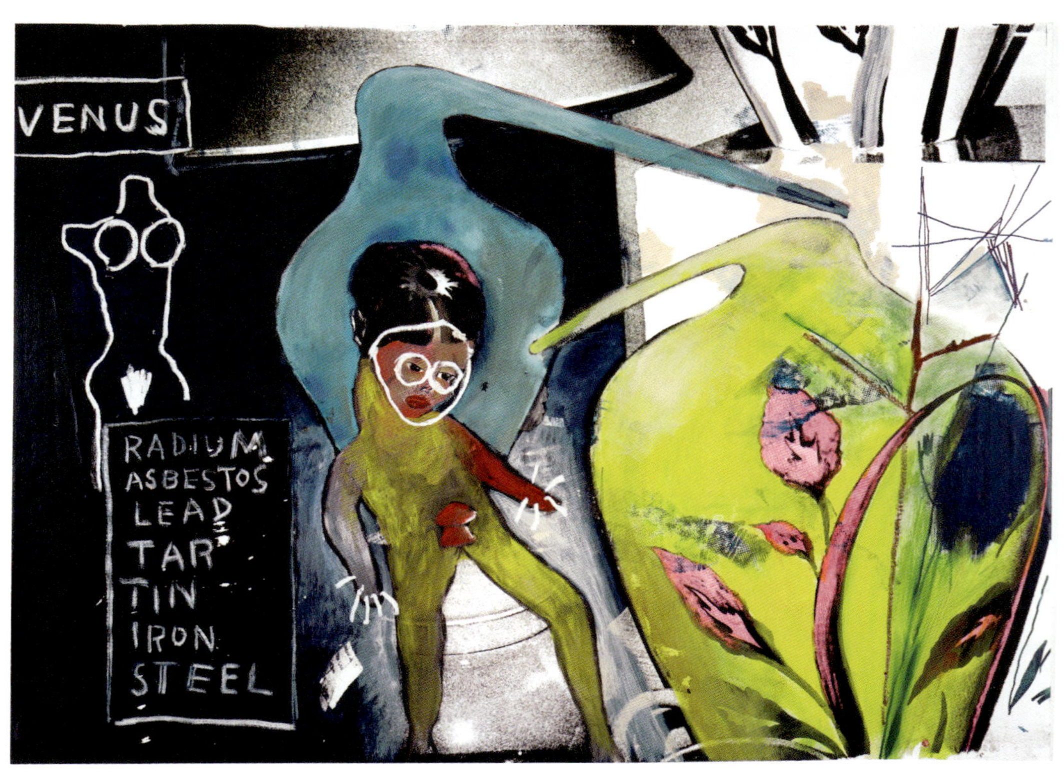

Ex-Ringeye (with Francesco Clemente
and Andy Warhol), 1984
Oil on canvas, 122 x 168 cm / 48 x 66 ¼ inches

GE (with Andy Warhol), 1984
Acrylic, oil, oilstick, and silkscreen on canvas,
218.5 x 172 cm / 86 x 68 inches

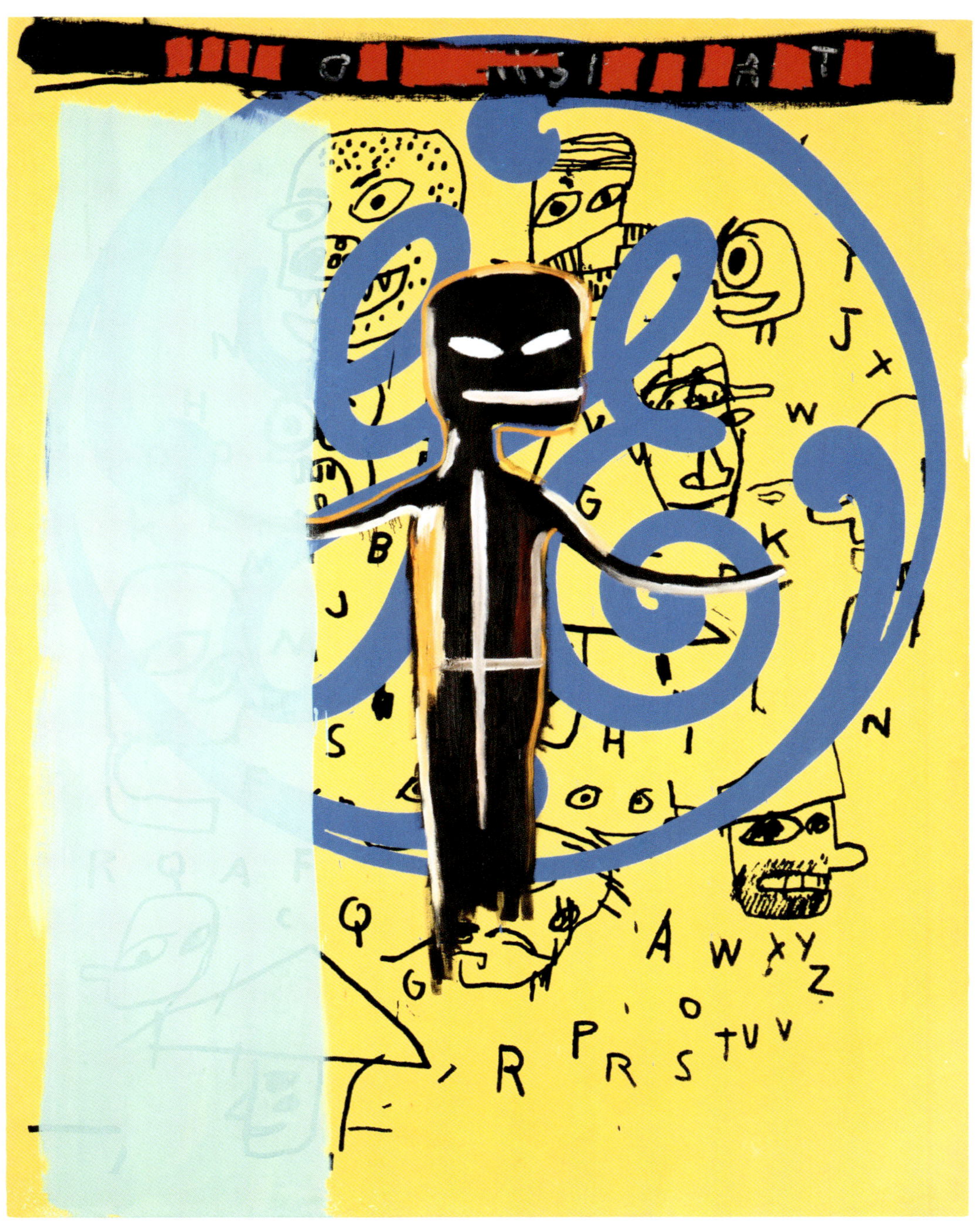

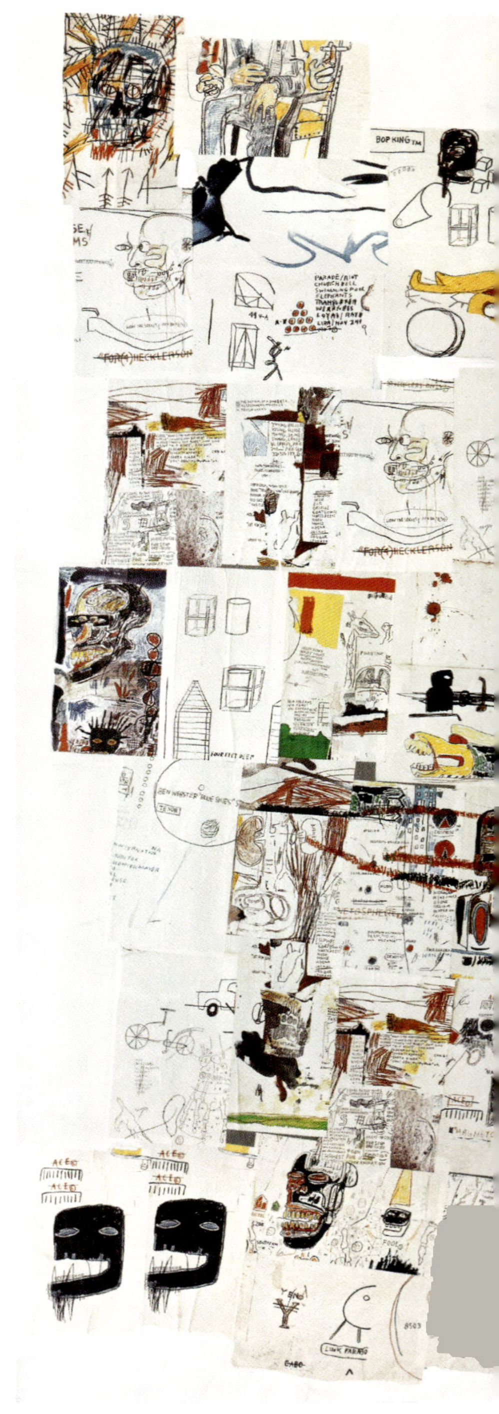

Glenn, 1984
Acrylic, oilstick, and photocopy collage
on canvas, 254 x 289.5 cm / 100 x 114 inches

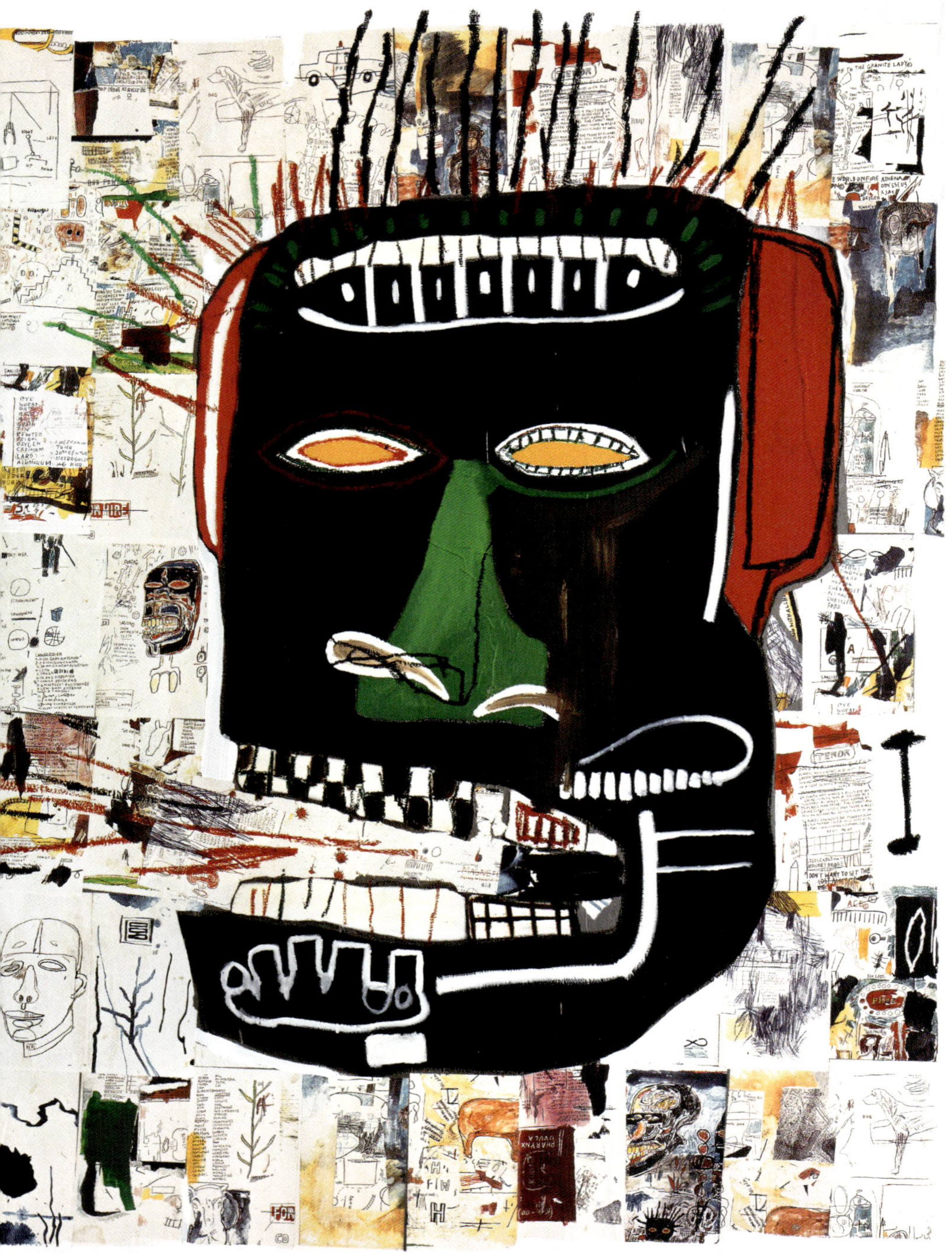

VI.

1985
New Art New Money

"The extent of Basquiat's success would no doubt be impossible for an artist of lesser gifts. Not only does he possess a bold sense of color and composition, but, in his best paintings, unlike many of his contemporaries, he maintains a fine balance between seemingly contradictory forces: control and spontaneity, menace and wit, urban imagery and primitivism. Still, the nature and rapidity of his climb is unimaginable in another era."

—CATHLEEN McGUIGAN, *NEW YORK TIMES MAGAZINE*, 1985[1]

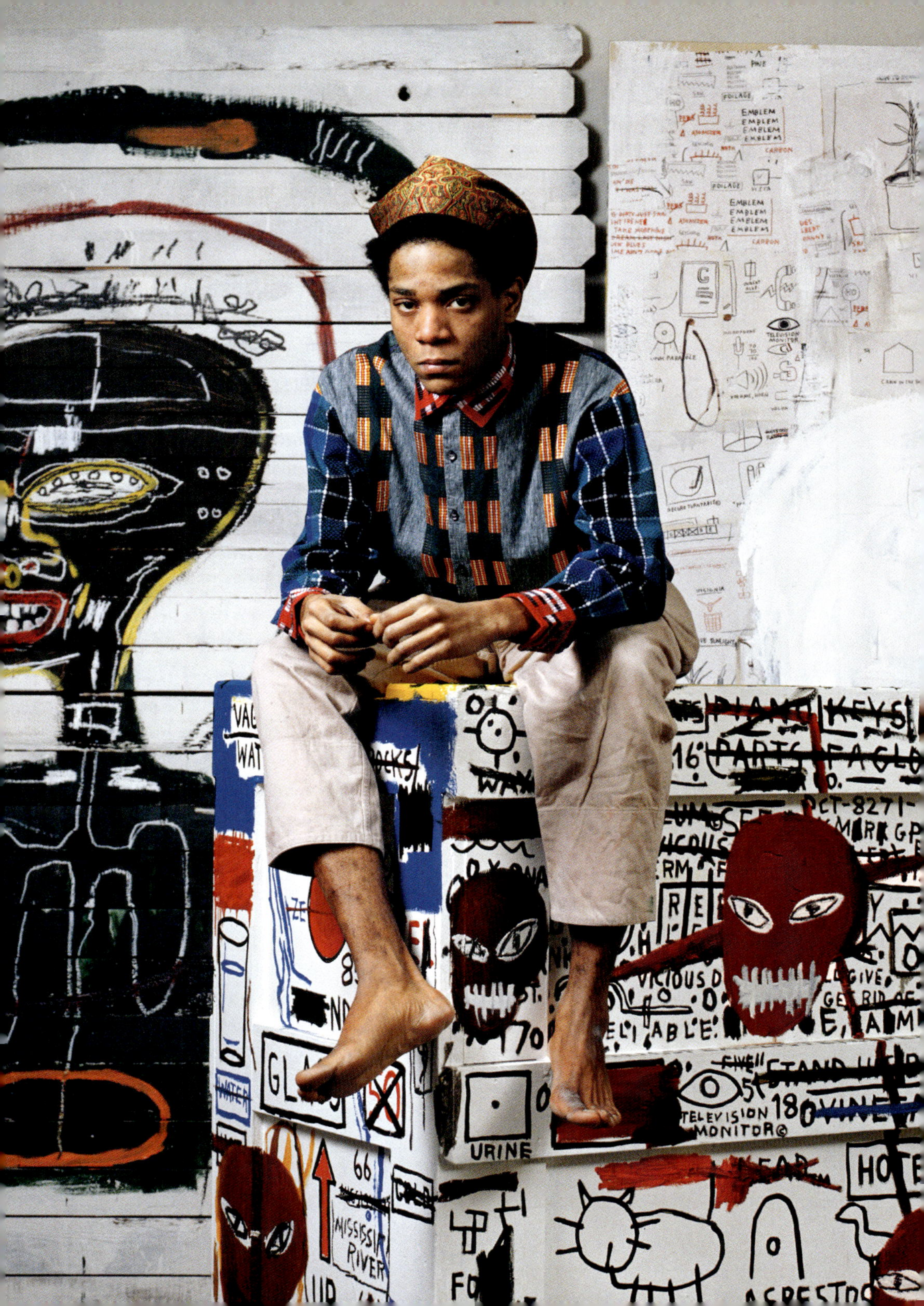

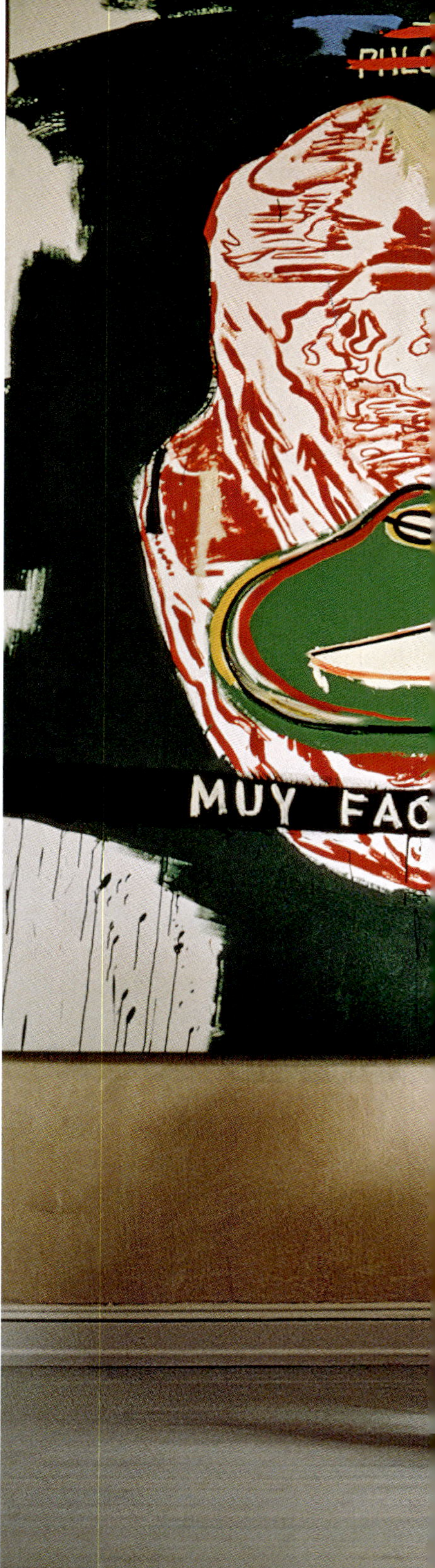

Andy Warhol and Jean-Michel Basquiat in front of
an untitled collaborative work, Tony Shafrazi Gallery,
New York 1985. Photo Tseng Kwong Chi

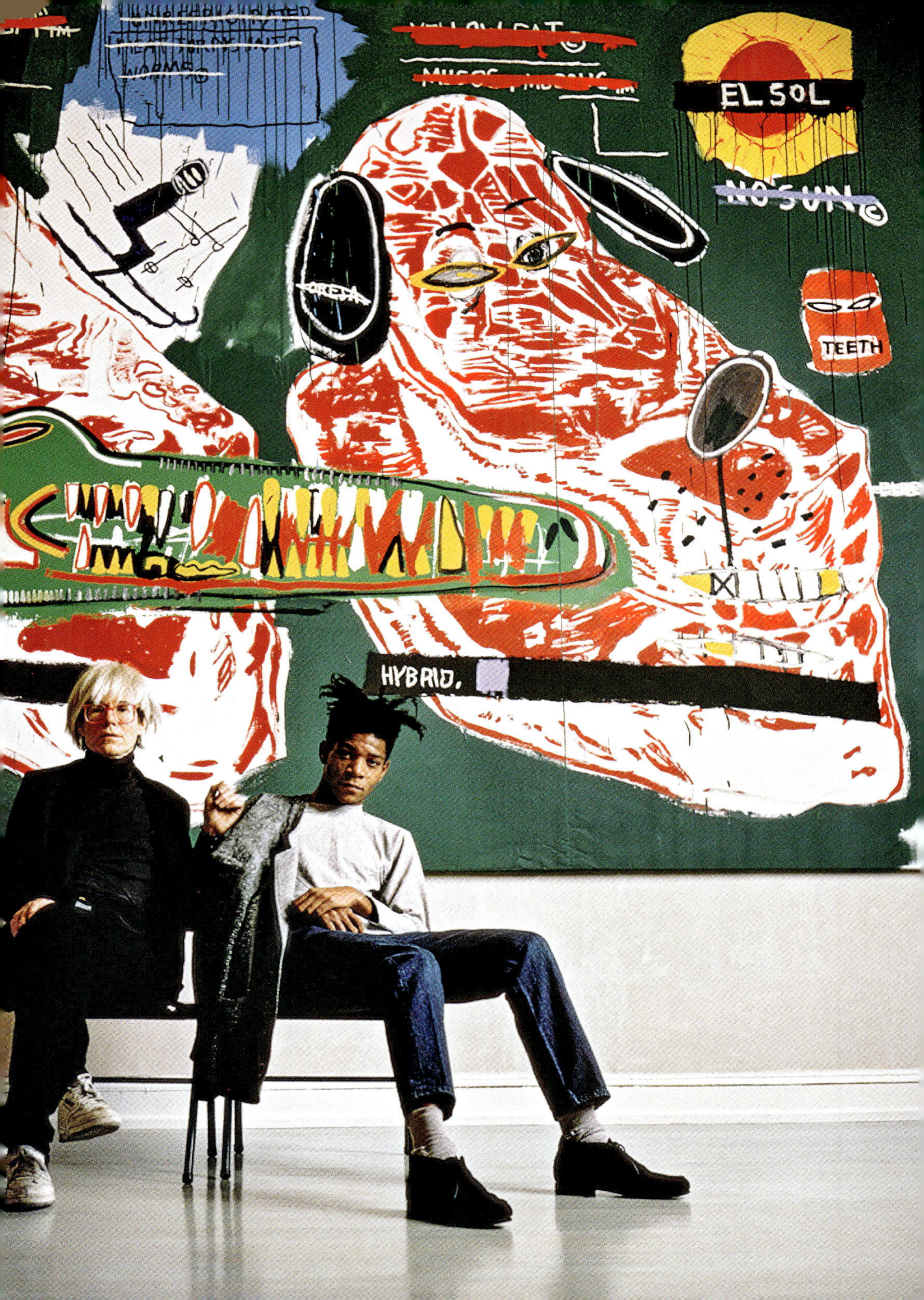

YELLOW RAT
MUSEO AMBROSIM
EL SOL
NO SUN
OREDA
TEETH
HYBRID,

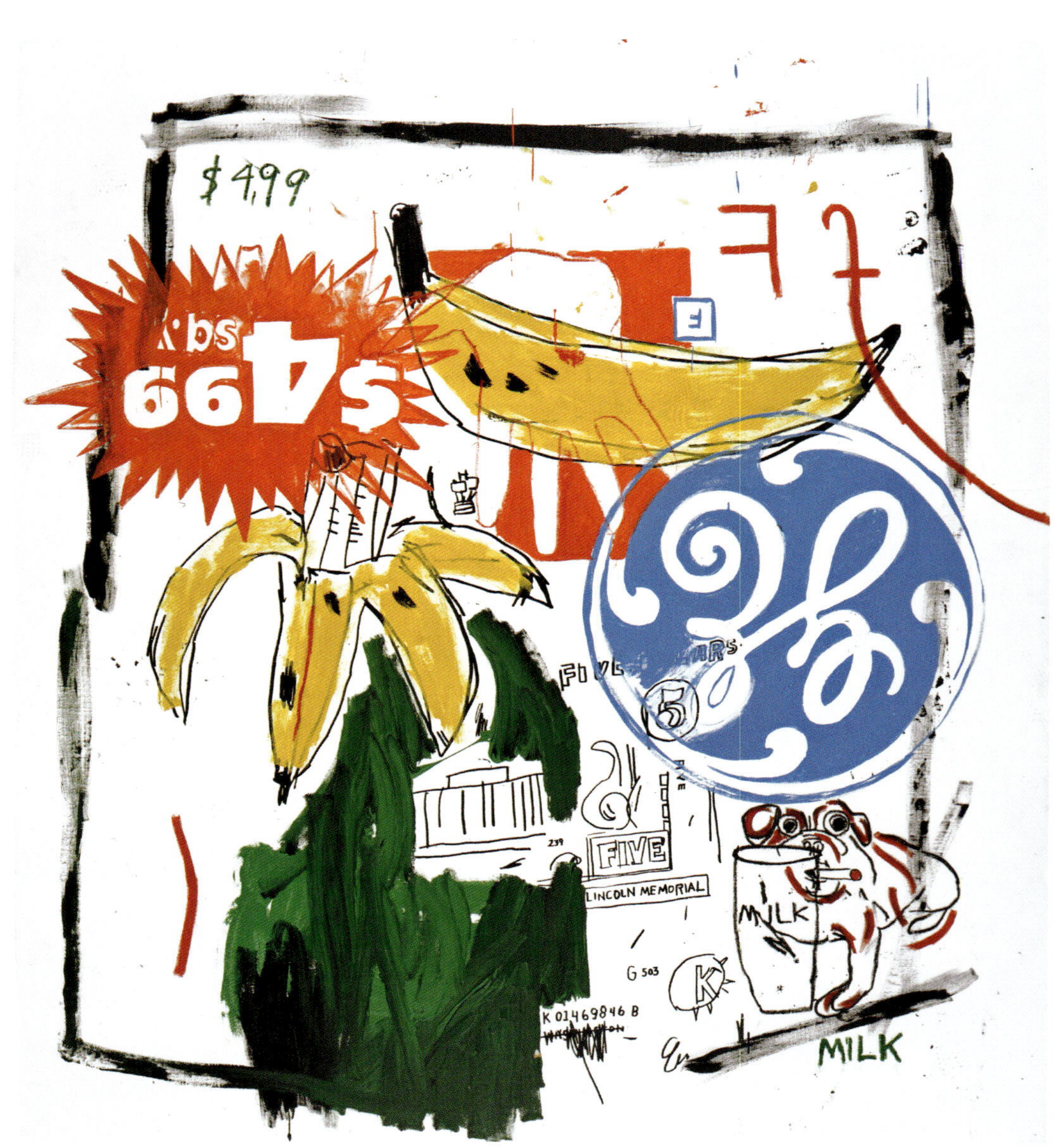

$4.99
$4.99
lbs
FIVE
LINCOLN MEMORIAL
239
FIVE
G 503
K 01469846 B
MILK
MILK
5

Basquiat paints a large mural for the new club Palladium (pp. 374/375), and continues his collaborative paintings with Warhol. In September, an exhibition of these opens at the Tony Shafrazi Gallery in New York. Reviews are generally bad, even mean-spirited. Vivien Raynor in the *New York Times*: "Last year, I wrote of Jean-Michel Basquiat that he had a chance of becoming a very good painter providing he didn't succumb to the forces that would make him an art world mascot. This year, it appears that those forces have prevailed for Basquiat is now onstage … doing a pas de deux with Andy Warhol, a mentor who assisted in his rise to fame. Actually, it's a version of the Oedipus story: Warhol, one of Pop's pops, paints, say, General Electric's logo, a *New York Post* headline or his own image of dentures; his 25-year-old protégé adds to or subtracts from it with his more or less expressionistic imagery. The 16 results—all *Untitleds*, of course—are large, bright, messy, full of private jokes and inconclusive."[5] Eleanor Heartney in *Flash Art* strikes a similar note: "Having presided over our era for considerably more than his requisite fifteen minutes, Andy Warhol keeps his star in ascendency by tacking it to the rising comets of the moment."[6] The personal nature of these reviews sours Basquiat's relationship to Warhol, and for a time he severs the ties.

During the exhibition, Basquiat is interviewed by the British Channel 4 and speaks freely about what his paintings have to say: "If I see a painting from the Middle Ages, I can see the life, I can see how people were … like seeing a sculpture from Africa, I can see the tribe, I can see the life around it … Even with things that aren't so obvious, like the abstract expressionist painters … you know it looks like New York in the 50s … they seem to be true historical documents, you know, that I can get more from them than reading or other things." What do you think you're saying about today? "Black people are never portrayed realistically in … not even portrayed in modern art enough, and I'm glad that I do that. I use the 'black' as the protagonist because I am black, and that's why I use it as the main character in all the paintings."[7]

[1–7] *See Endnotes on page 508.*

Bananas (with Andy Warhol), 1985
Acrylic and silkscreen on canvas,
224 x 206 cm / 88 ¼ x 81 inches

Pages 374/375: Palladium nightclub
with Jean-Michel Basquiat's *Nu-Nile*,
New York 1985. Photo Timothy Hursley

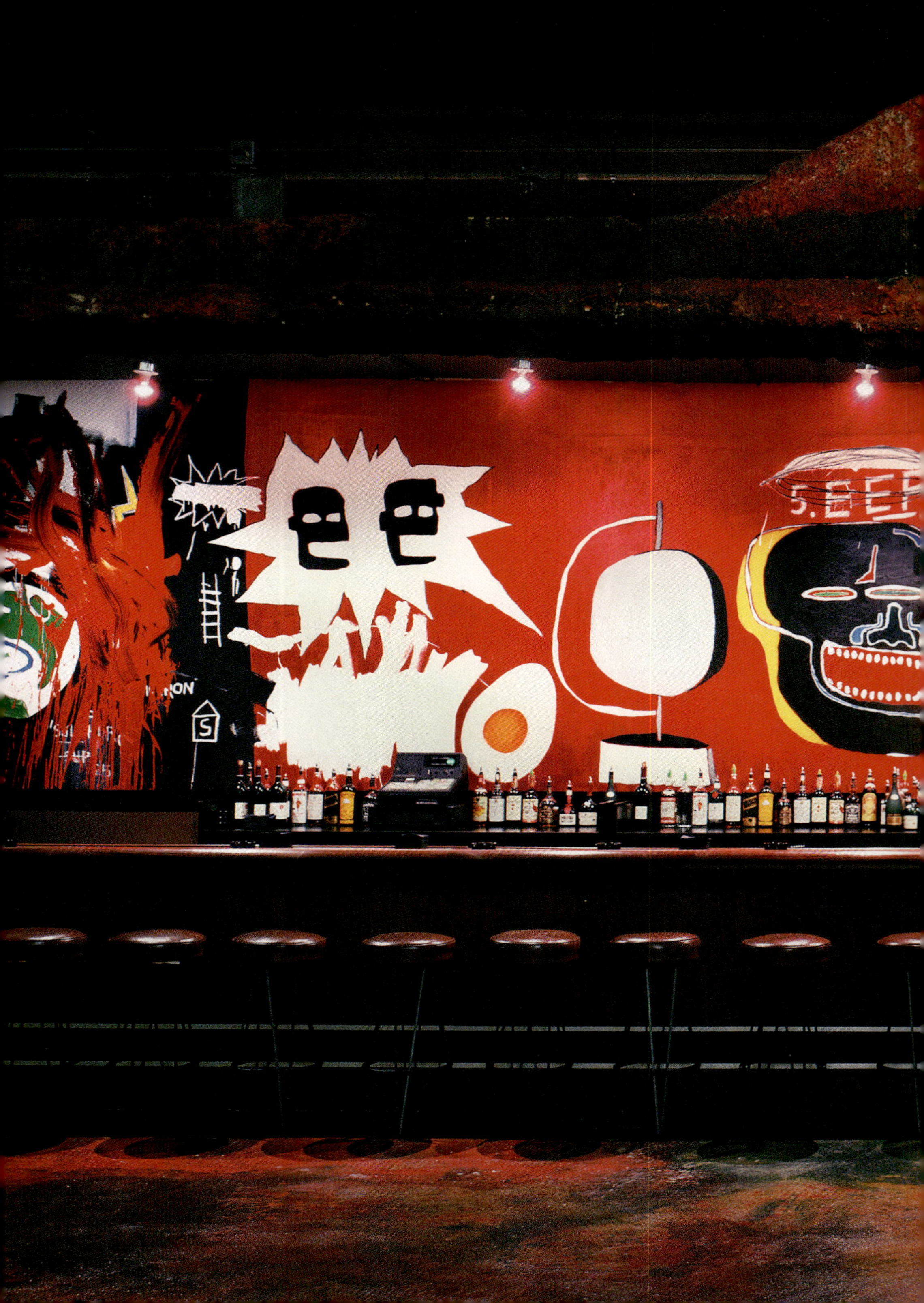

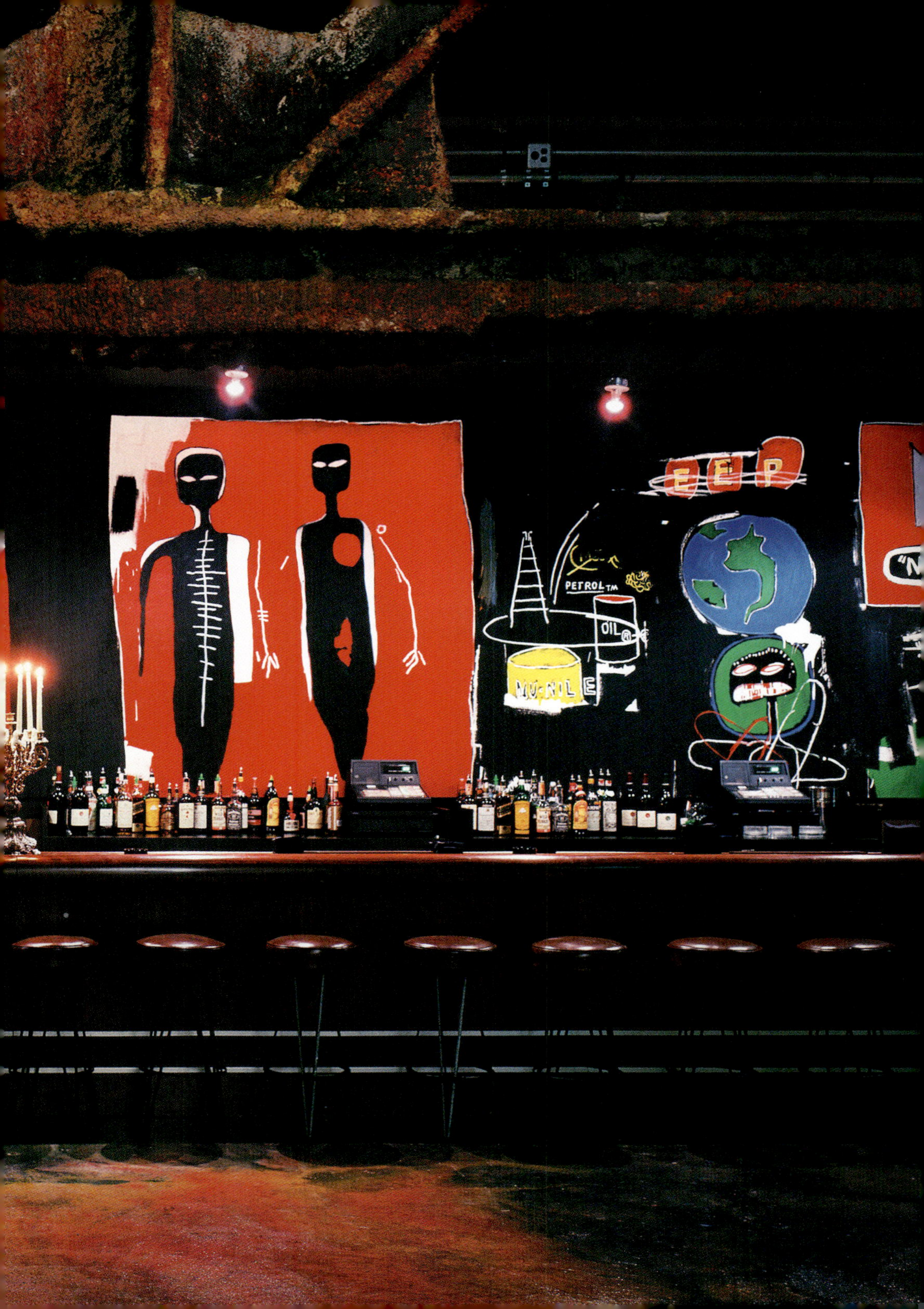

E P
PETROL TM
OIL
MU-RIL E

Untitled, 1985
Acrylic, oil, spray paint, oilstick, and
hardware on wooden construction,
163 x 131 x 31 cm / 64 ¹/₄ x 51 ¹/₂ x 12 ¹/₄ inches

Pages 378/379: **Untitled**, 1985
Graphite and colored pencil on paper,
76 x 106.5 cm / 30 x 42 inches

Pages 380/381: **Untitled (Armstrong)**, 1985
Acrylic, oilstick, and photocopy collage
on paper, 56 x 76 cm / 22 x 30 inches

Pages 382/383: **Untitled**, 1985
Acrylic, oilstick, and photocopy collage
on paper, 56 x 76 cm / 22 x 30 inches

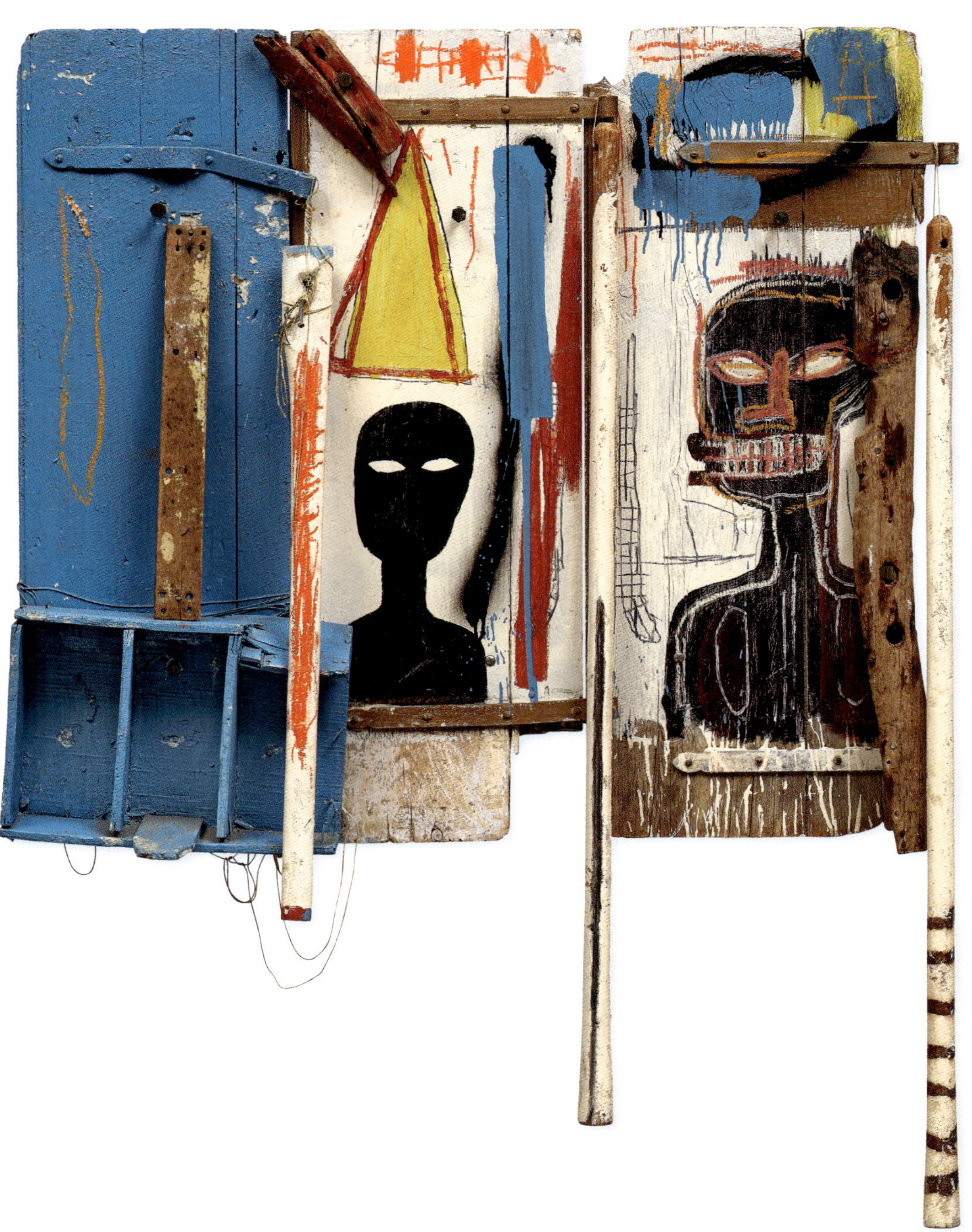

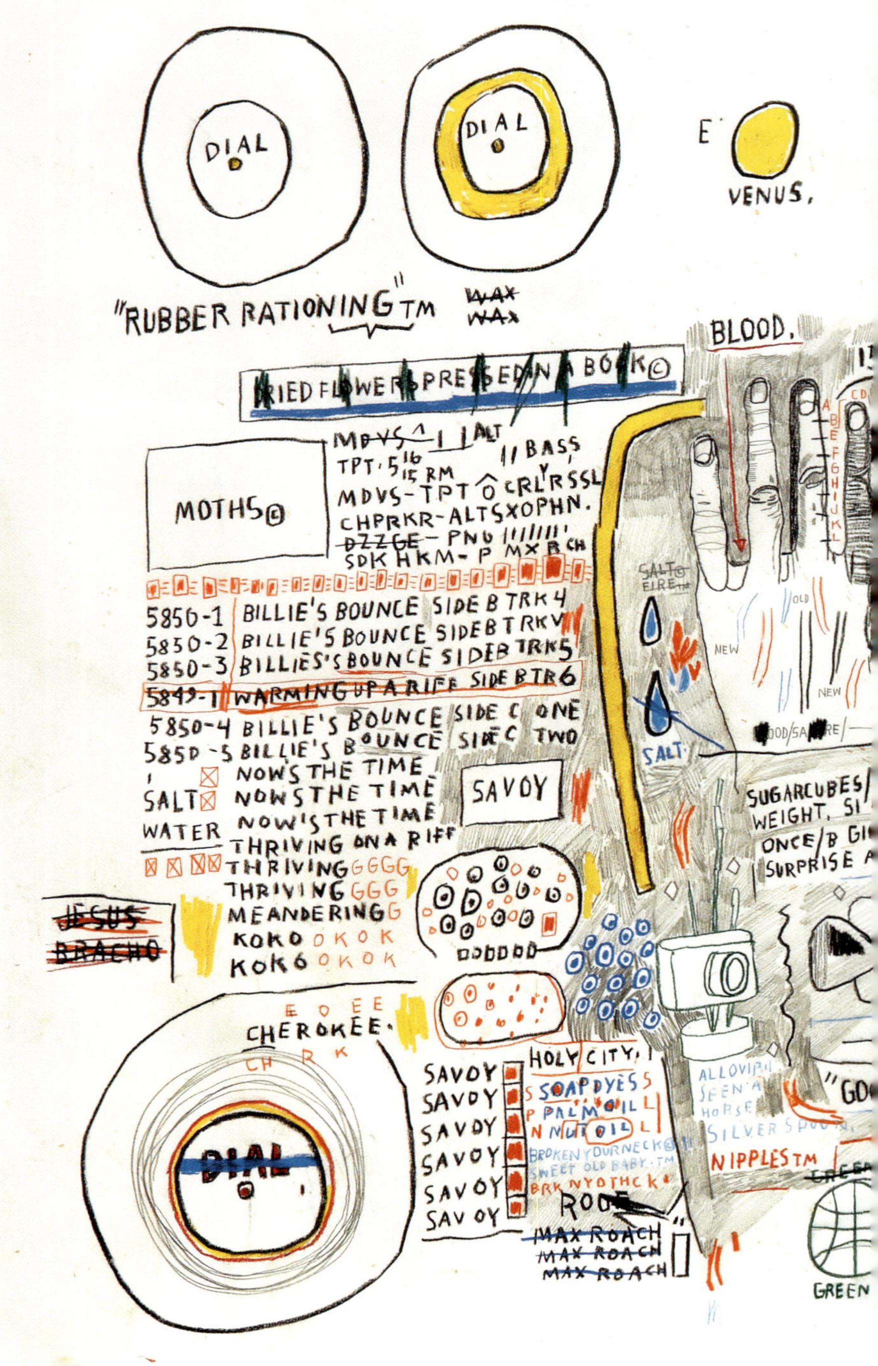

DIAL
DIAL
E VENUS,
"RUBBER RATIONING" TM
WAX WAX
BLOOD.
FRIED FLOWERS PRESSED IN A BOOK ©
MOTHS ©
MDVS I ALT
TPT 5 16 RM 15 BASS
MDVS - TPT CRL RSSL
CHPRKR - ALTSXOPHN.
DZZGE - PNU IIIIIII
SDK HKM - P MX R CH
SALT ©
FIRE TM
OLD
NEW
NEW
OOD/SA RE
SALT
5850-1 BILLIE'S BOUNCE SIDE B TRK 4
5850-2 BILLIE'S BOUNCE SIDE B TRK V
5850-3 BILLIES'S BOUNCE SIDE B TRK 5
5849-1 WARMING UP A RIFF SIDE B TR 6
5850-4 BILLIE'S BOUNCE SIDE C ONE
5850-5 BILLIE'S BOUNCE SIDE C TWO
I NOW'S THE TIME
SALT NOW'S THE TIME
WATER NOW'S THE TIME
THRIVING ON A RIFF
THRIVING GGGG
THRIVING GGG
MEANDERING G
KOKO OKOK
KOKO OKOK
SAVOY
SUGARCUBES/
WEIGHT, SI
ONCE/B GI
SURPRISE A
JESUS
ROACHO
E O EE
CHEROKEE.
CH R K
DIAL
HOLY CITY,
SAVOY
SAVOY S SOAP DYES S
SAVOY P PALM OIL L
SAVOY N NUT OIL L
SAVOY BROKEN YOUR NECK ©
SAVOY SWEET OLD BABY. TM
SAVOY BRK NYO THC k
ALLOVIR
SEEN A
HORSE
SILVER SPOON
NIPPLES TM
"GO
ROOF
MAX ROACH
MAX ROACH
MAX ROACH
GREEN

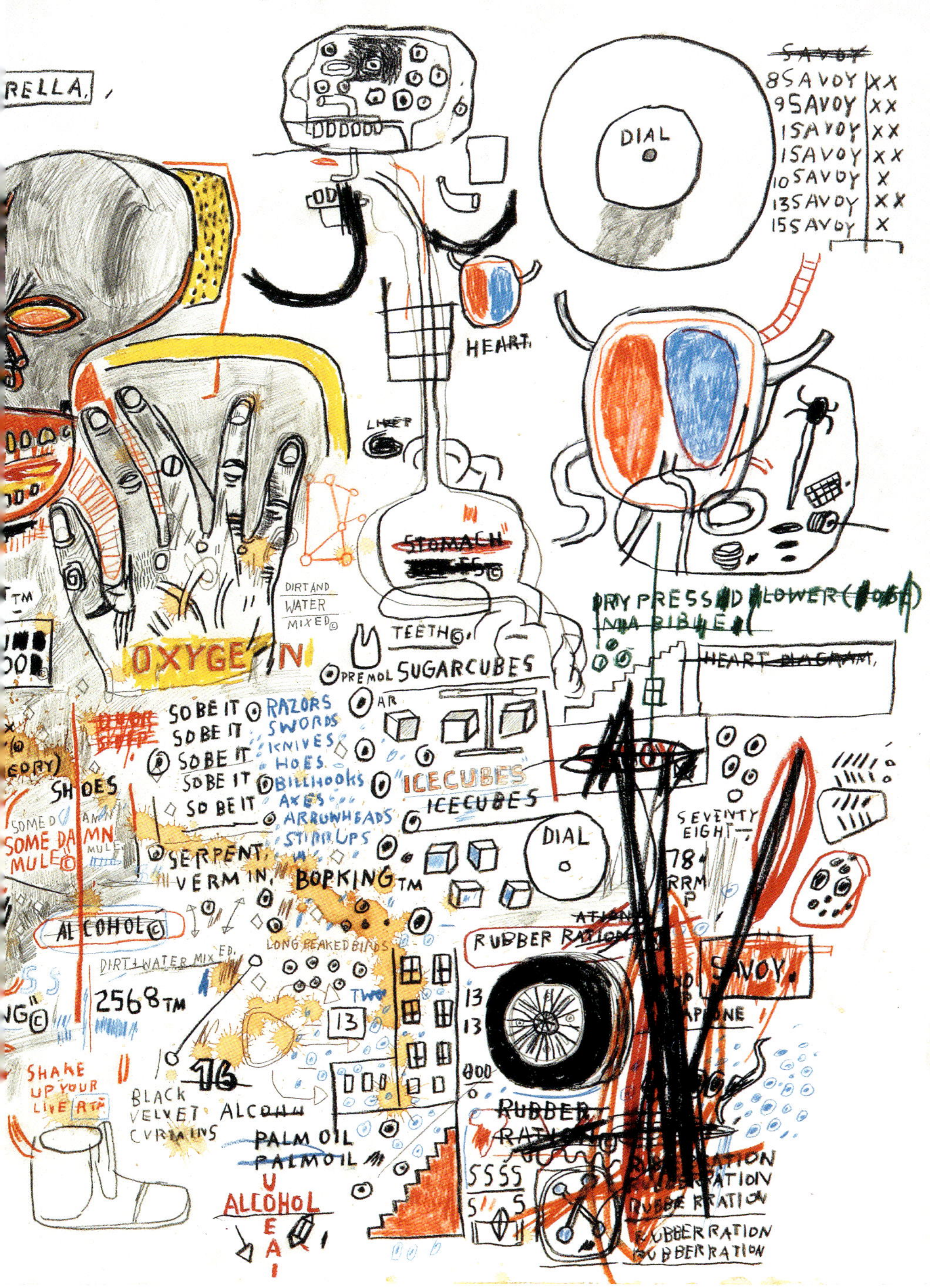
RELLA,
DIAL
SAVOY
8 SAVOY XX
9 SAVOY XX
1 SAVOY XX
1 SAVOY XX
10 SAVOY X
13 SAVOY XX
15 SAVOY X
HEART
L HEET
DIRT AND WATER MIXED ©
OXYGEN
STOMACH
TEETH ©
PREMOL SUGARCUBES
DRY PRESSED FLOWER (ROSE)
IN A BIBLE ©
HEART PLACARD,
SO BE IT
SO BE IT
SO BE IT
SO BE IT
SO BE IT
RAZORS
SWORDS
KNIVES
HOES
BILLHOOKS
AXES
ARROWHEADS
STIRRUPS
AR
ICECUBES
ICECUBES
SHOES
SOME D
SOME DAMN
MULE ©
AMN MULE
SERPENT
VERMIN
BOPKING TM
SEVENTY EIGHT
78
RRM
P
DIAL
ALCOHOL ©
ATION
RUBBER RATION
DIRT + WATER MIX ED.
LONG PEAKED BIRDS
2568 TM
TWO
13
13
13
SAVOY
PONE
SHAKE UP YOUR LIVER TM
16
BLACK VELVET ALCOHOL CURTAINS
PALM OIL
PALMOIL
ALCOHOL
U E A I
SSSS
S 5 5
RUBBER RATION
RUBBER RATION
RUBBER RATION
RUBBER RATION
RUBBER RATION
RUBBER RATION

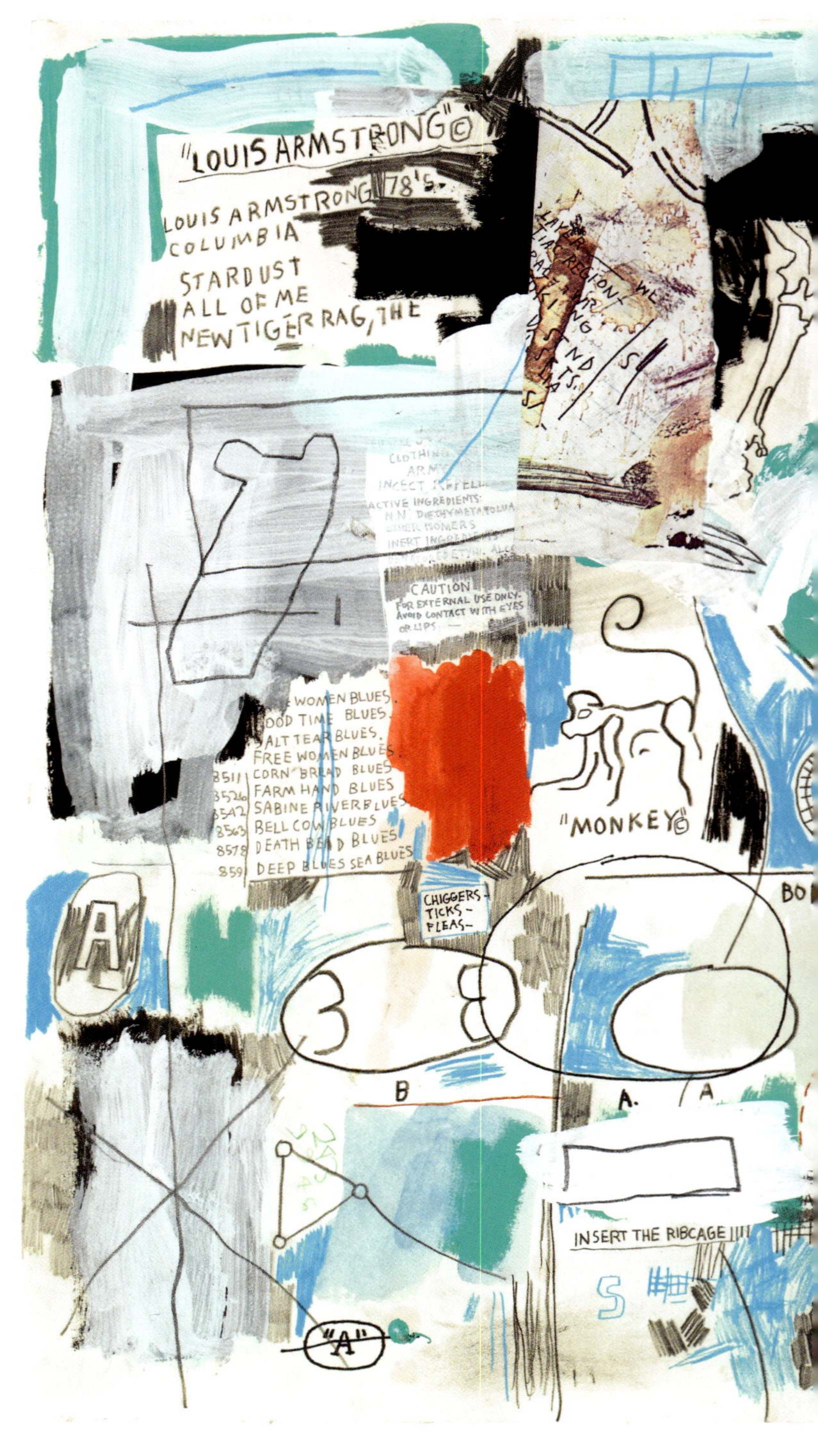

"LOUIS ARMSTRONG"©
LOUIS ARMSTRONG 78'S.
COLUMBIA
STARDUST
ALL OF ME
NEW TIGER RAG, THE
CLOTHING
ARMY
INSECT REPELL
ACTIVE INGREDIENTS:
N.N. DIETHYMETATOLUA
OTHER ISOMERS
INERT INGREDIENTS
CAUTION
FOR EXTERNAL USE ONLY.
AVOID CONTACT WITH EYES
OR LIPS
WOMEN BLUES
GOOD TIME BLUES
SALT TEAR BLUES
FREE WOMEN BLUES
CORN BREAD BLUES
FARM HAND BLUES
SABINE RIVER BLUES
BELL COW BLUES
DEATH BED BLUES
DEEP BLUES SEA BLUES
CHIGGERS -
TICKS -
FLEAS -
"MONKEY"©
B
A.
A
INSERT THE RIBCAGE
"A"

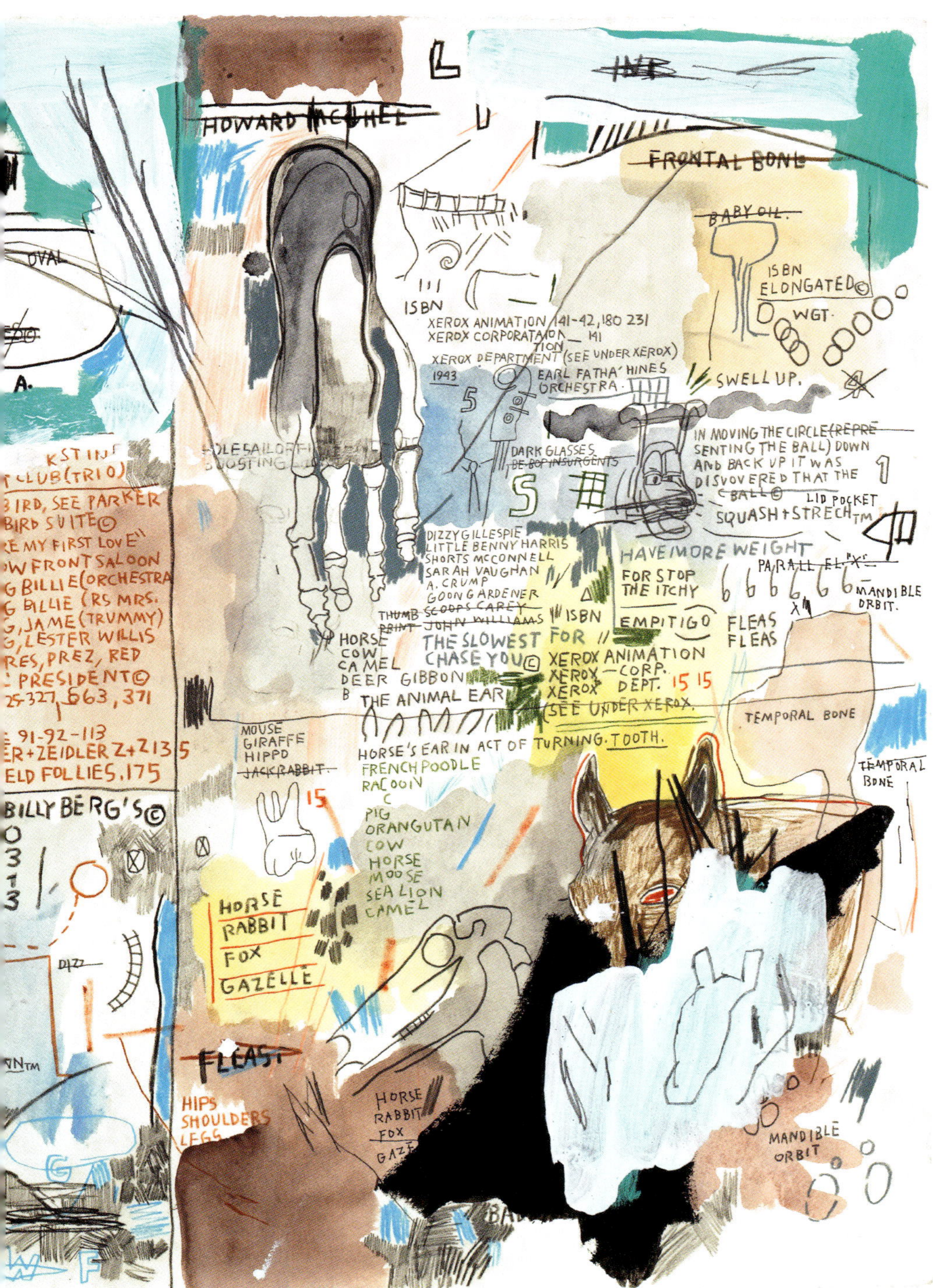

HOWARD McGHEE
FRONTAL BONE
BABY OIL.
ISBN ELONGATED©
WGT.
ISBN
OVAL
A.
XEROX ANIMATION 141-42,180 231
XEROX CORPORATION — 141
TION
XEROX DEPARTMENT (SEE UNDER XEROX)
1943
EARL FATHA' HINES ORCHESTRA
SWELL UP.
5
DARK GLASSES
BE-BOP INSURGENTS
S
IN MOVING THE CIRCLE (REPRE-
SENTING THE BALL) DOWN
AND BACK UP IT WAS
DISCOVERED THAT THE
BALL©
SQUASH + STRECH TM
LID POCKET
1
HOLE SAILOR
BOOSTING
KST IN
T CLUB (TRIO)
BIRD, SEE PARKER
BIRD SUITE©
RE MY FIRST LOVE"
W FRONT SALOON
G BILLIE (ORCHESTRA
G BILLIE (RS MRS.
G, JAME (TRUMMY)
G, LESTER WILLIS
RES, PREZ, RED
PRESIDENT©
25-327, 663, 371
91-92-113
ER + ZEIDLER Z + 213 5
ELD FOLLIES, 175
BILLY BERG'S©
0313
DIZZY GILLESPIE
LITTLE BENNY HARRIS
SHORTS McCONNELL
SARAH VAUGHAN
A. CRUMP
GOON GARDENER
SCOOPS CAREY
JOHN WILLIAMS
THUMB PRINT
ISBN
HAVE MORE WEIGHT
FOR STOP
THE ITCHY
PARALLEL X's
6 6 6 6 6 6
MANDIBLE ORBIT.
EMPITIGO
FLEAS FLEAS
THE SLOWEST FOR //
CHASE YOU©
XEROX ANIMATION
XEROX — CORP.
XEROX DEPT. 15 15
SEE UNDER XEROX.
HORSE
COW
CAMEL
DEER GIBBON
B THE ANIMAL EAR
MOUSE
GIRAFFE
HIPPO
JACK RABBIT
HORSE'S EAR IN ACT OF TURNING. TOOTH.
FRENCH POODLE
RACOON
C
PIG
ORANGUTAN
COW
HORSE
MOOSE
SEA LION
CAMEL
TEMPORAL BONE
TEMPORAL BONE
15
HORSE
RABBIT
FOX
GAZELLE
DIZZ
FLEAS
HIPS
SHOULDERS
LEGS
HORSE
RABBIT
FOX
GAZE
MANDIBLE
ORBIT
BA
G
F
N TM

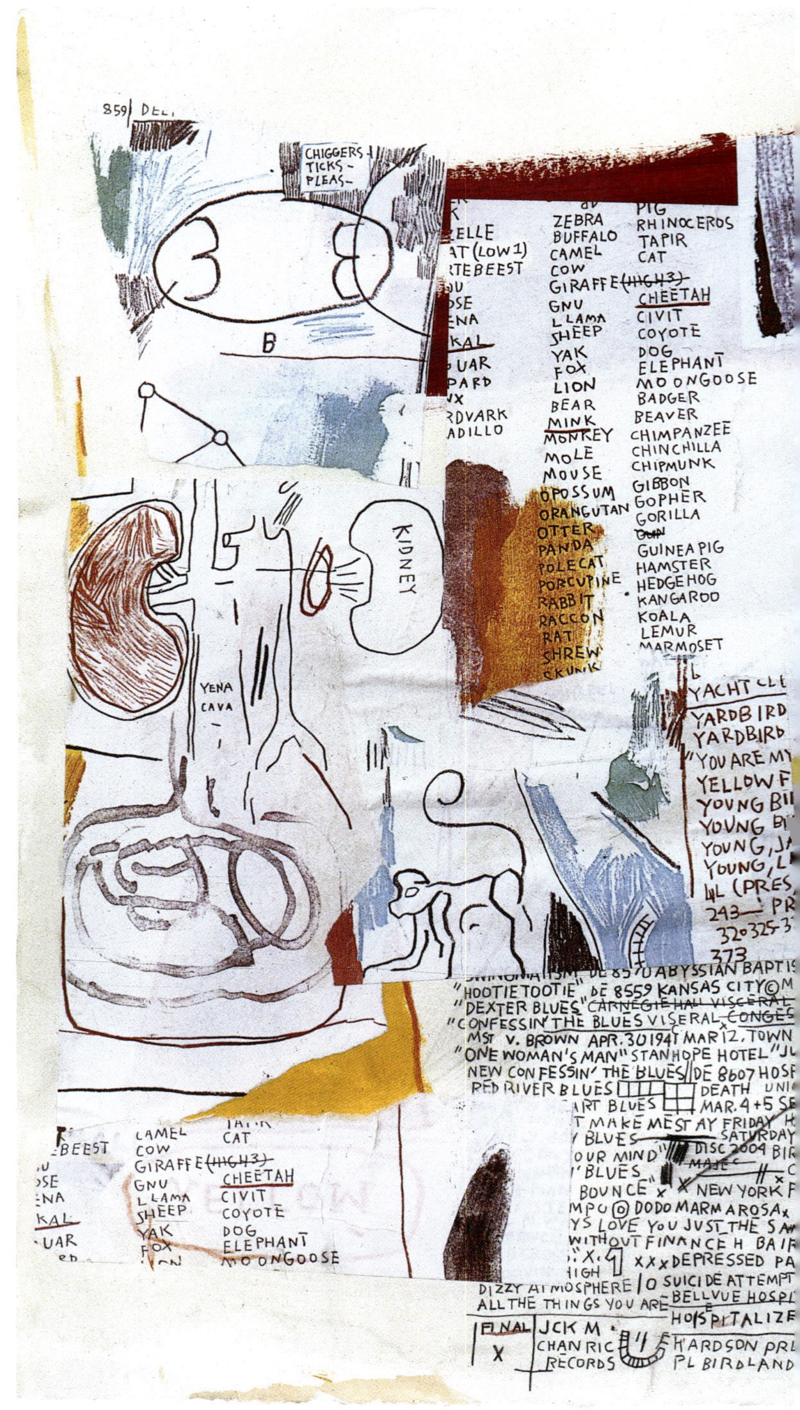
859 DEL
CHIGGERS
TICKS
PLEAS-
B
PIG
ELLE ZEBRA RHINOCEROS
AT (LOW 1) BUFFALO TAPIR
RTEBEEST CAMEL CAT
OU COW
OSE GIRAFFE (HIGH 3)
ENA GNU CHEETAH
KAL LLAMA CIVIT
UAR SHEEP COYOTE
PARD YAK DOG
X FOX ELEPHANT
RDVARK LION MOONGOOSE
ADILLO BEAR BADGER
MINK BEAVER
MONKEY CHIMPANZEE
MOLE CHINCHILLA
MOUSE CHIPMUNK
OPOSSUM GIBBON
ORANGUTAN GOPHER
OTTER GORILLA
PANDA GUINEA PIG
POLECAT HAMSTER
PORCUPINE HEDGEHOG
RABBIT KANGAROO
RACCON KOALA
RAT LEMUR
SHREW MARMOSET
SKUNK
KIDNEY
YENA
CAVA
L
YACHT CL
YARDBIRD
YARDBIRD
"YOU ARE MY
YELLOW F
YOUNG BI
YOUNG B
YOUNG, J
YOUNG, L
WL (PRES
243 PR
320 325-3
373
WINONA ISM DE 8570 ABYSSIAN BAPTIS
"HOOTIE TOOTIE" DE 8559 KANSAS CITY © M
"DEXTER BLUES" CARNEGIE HALL VISCERAL
"CONFESSIN' THE BLUES VISERAL CONGES
MST V. BROWN APR. 30 1941 MAR 12, TOWN
"ONE WOMAN'S MAN" STANHOPE HOTEL "JU
NEW CONFESSIN' THE BLUES DE 8607 HOSF
RED RIVER BLUES DEATH UNI
ART BLUES MAR. 4 +5 SE
T MAKE ME ST AY FRIDAY H
Y BLUES SATURDAY
OUR MIND DISC 2004 BIR
'BLUES MAJE
BOUNCE NEW YORK F
MPU © DODO MARMAROSA
YS LOVE YOU JUST THE SA
WITHOUT FINANCE H BAIF
X XXX DEPRESSED PA
HIGH
DIZZY ATMOSPHERE 10 SUICIDE ATTEMPT
ALL THE THINGS YOU ARE BELLVUE HOSPI
HOSPITALIZE
FINAL JCK M
X CHAN RIC HARDSON PR
RECORDS PL BIRDLAND
CAMEL TAPIR
EBEEST COW CAT
U GIRAFFE (HIGH 3)
OSE GNU CHEETAH
ENA LLAMA CIVIT
KAL SHEEP COYOTE
UAR YAK DOG
FOX ELEPHANT
ON MOONGOOSE

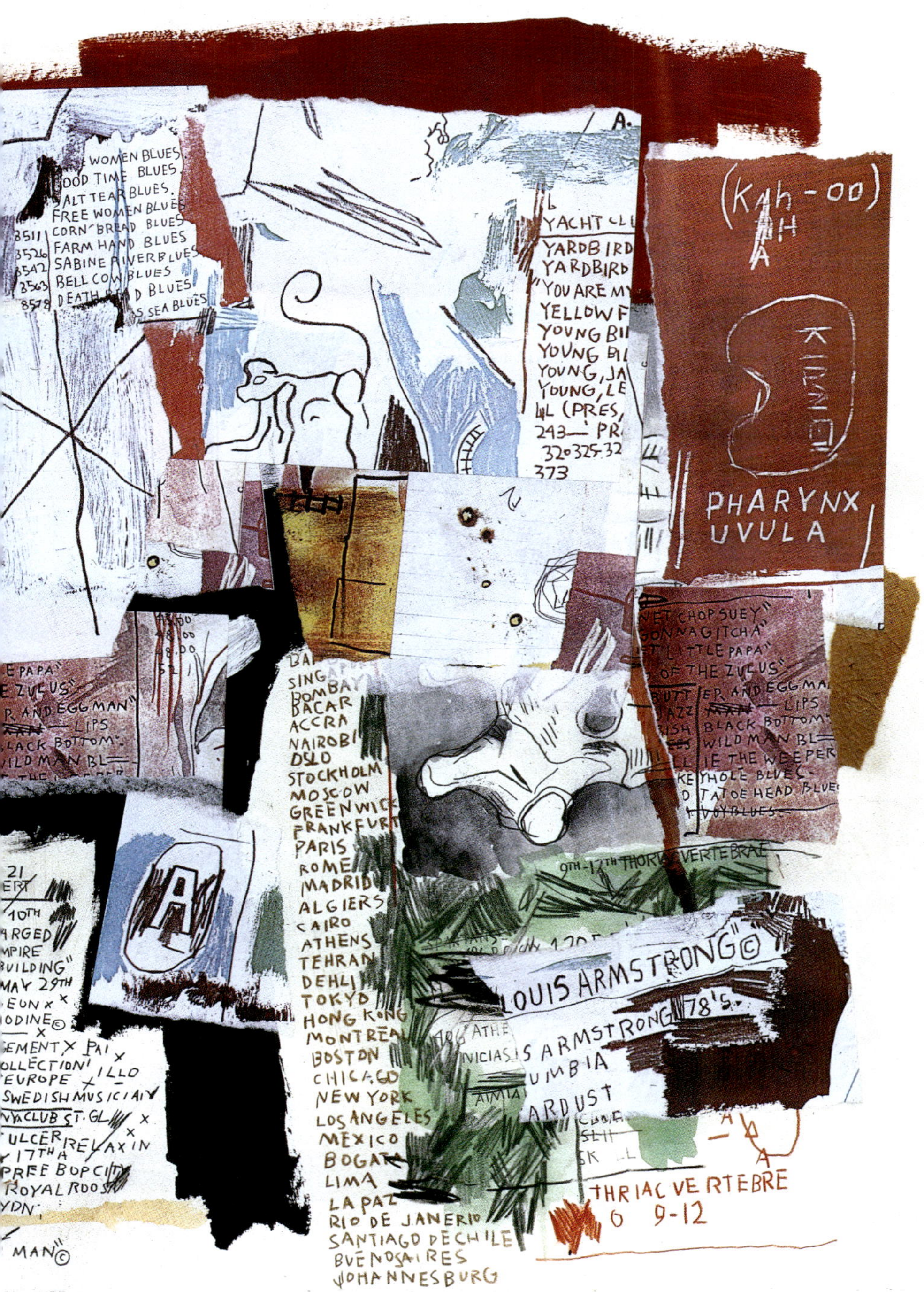
WOMEN BLUES
GOOD TIME BLUES
SALT TEAR BLUES
FREE WOMEN BLUES
CORN-BREAD BLUES
FARM HAND BLUES
SABINE RIVER BLUES
BELL COW BLUES
DEATH BED BLUES
S SEA BLUES
8511
8526
8542
8563
8578
A.
YACHT CLE
YARD BIRD
YARD BIRD
"YOU ARE MY
YELLOW F
YOUNG BI
YOUNG BI
YOUNG, JA
YOUNG, LE
L (PRES,
243 PR
32 325 32
373
(Kah - oo)
AH
A
KIDNEY
PHARYNX
UVULA
E PAPA'
ZULUS"
P AND EGGMAN"
LIPS
LACK BOTTOM'
ILD MAN BL
SINGAPORE
BOMBAY
DACAR
ACCRA
NAIROBI
OSLO
STOCKHOLM
MOSCOW
GREENWICH
FRANKFURT
PARIS
ROME
MADRID
ALGIERS
CAIRO
ATHENS
TEHRAN
DEHLI
TOKYO
HONG KONG
MONTREA
BOSTON
CHICAGO
NEW YORK
LOS ANGELES
MEXICO
BOGATA
LIMA
LA PAZ
RIO DE JANERIO
SANTIAGO DE CHILE
BUENOS AIRES
JOHANNESBURG
NET CHOP SUEY"
GONNA GITCHA
T LITTLE PAPA"
OF THE ZULUS"
UTTER AND EGGMA
LIPS
BLACK BOTTOM
WILD MAN BL
IE THE WEEPER
KE HOLE BLUES
TATOE HEAD BLUES
UY BLUES"
9TH-12TH THORL VERTEBRAE
LOUIS ARMSTRONG ©
S ARMSTRONG 78's.
UMBIA
ARDUST
THRIAC VERTEBRE
9-12
21
ERT
10TH
ARGED
MPIRE
BUILDING"
MAY 29TH
EUN
IODINE ©
EMENT PAI
OLLECTION ILLO
EUROPE ILLO
SWEDISH MUSICIAN
CLUB ST. GL
ULCER RELAXIN
17TH
REE BOP CITY
ROYAL ROOS
YDN
MAN ©

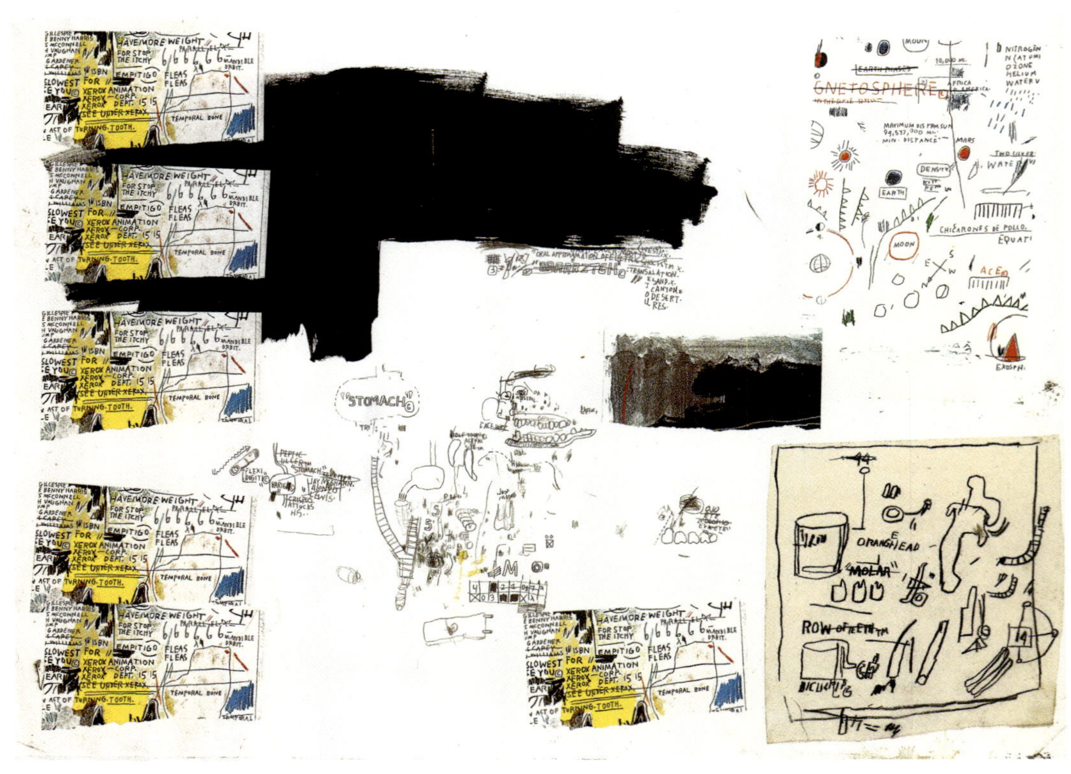

Untitled, 1985
Acrylic, oilstick, and photocopy collage
on paper, 76 x 105.5 cm / 30 x 41 $^1/_2$ inches

Ave Maria, 1985
Acrylic, oilstick, graphite, colored pencil, and paper
collage on paper, 103 x 76 cm / 40 $^1/_2$ x 30 inches

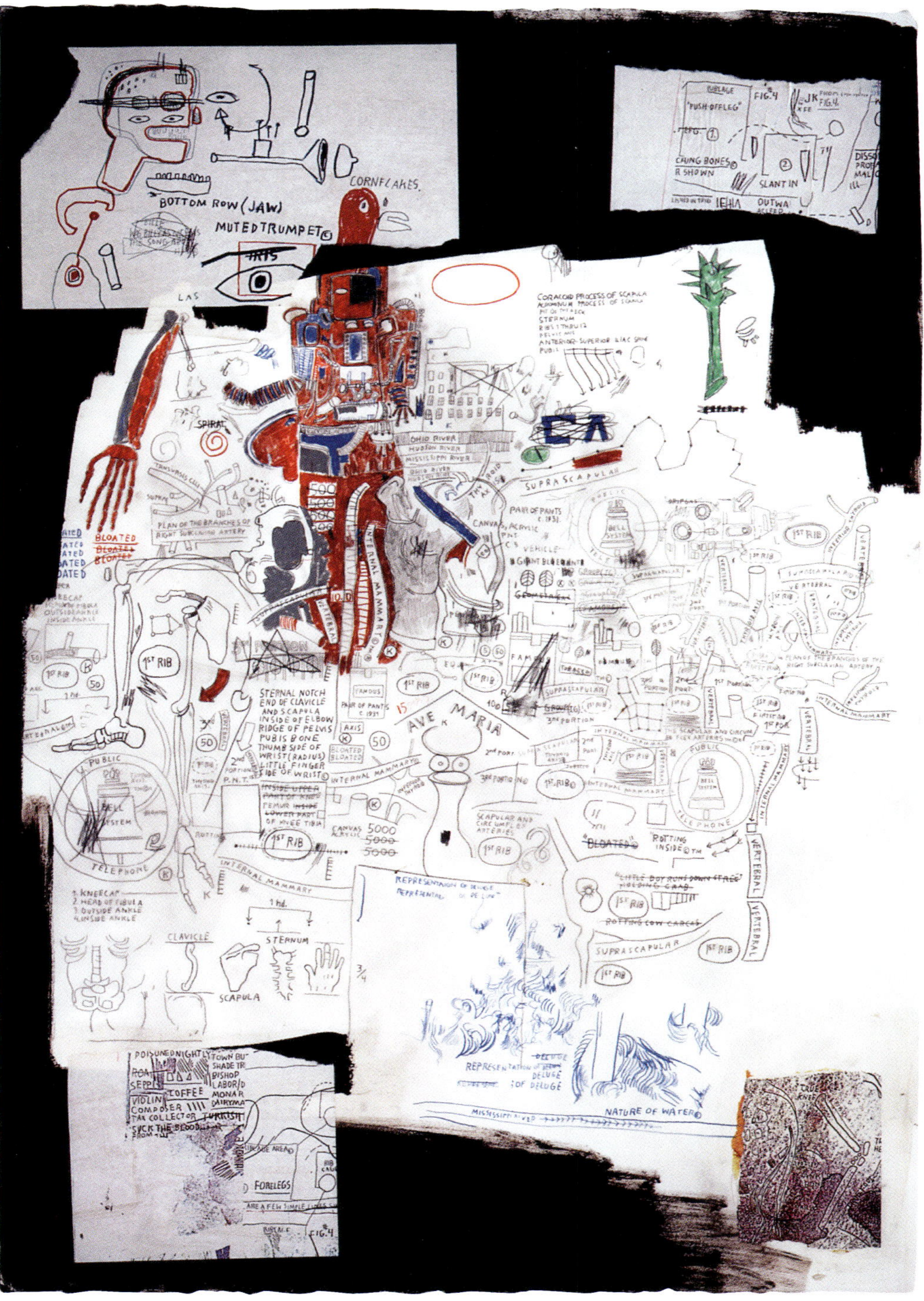

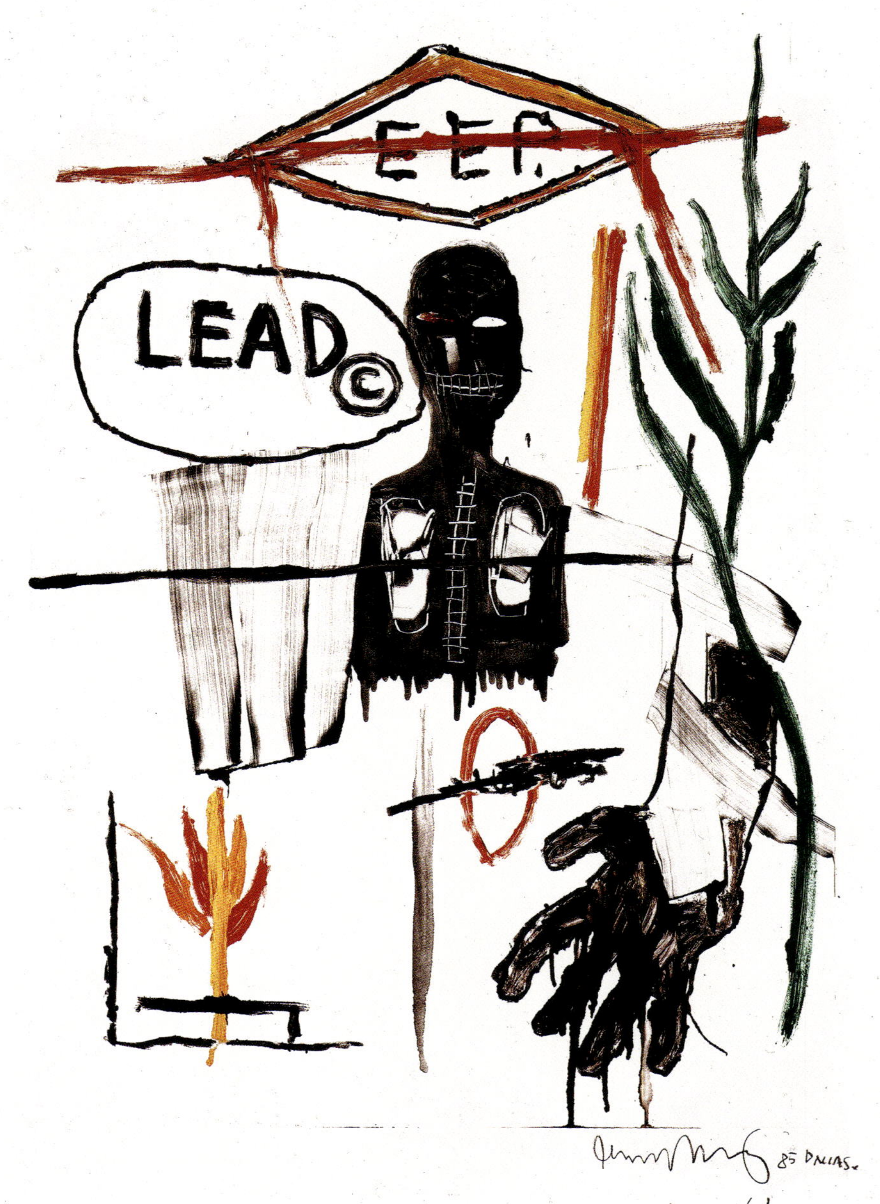

Untitled, 1985
Monotype: typographic ink on paper,
137 x 99 cm / 54 x 39 inches

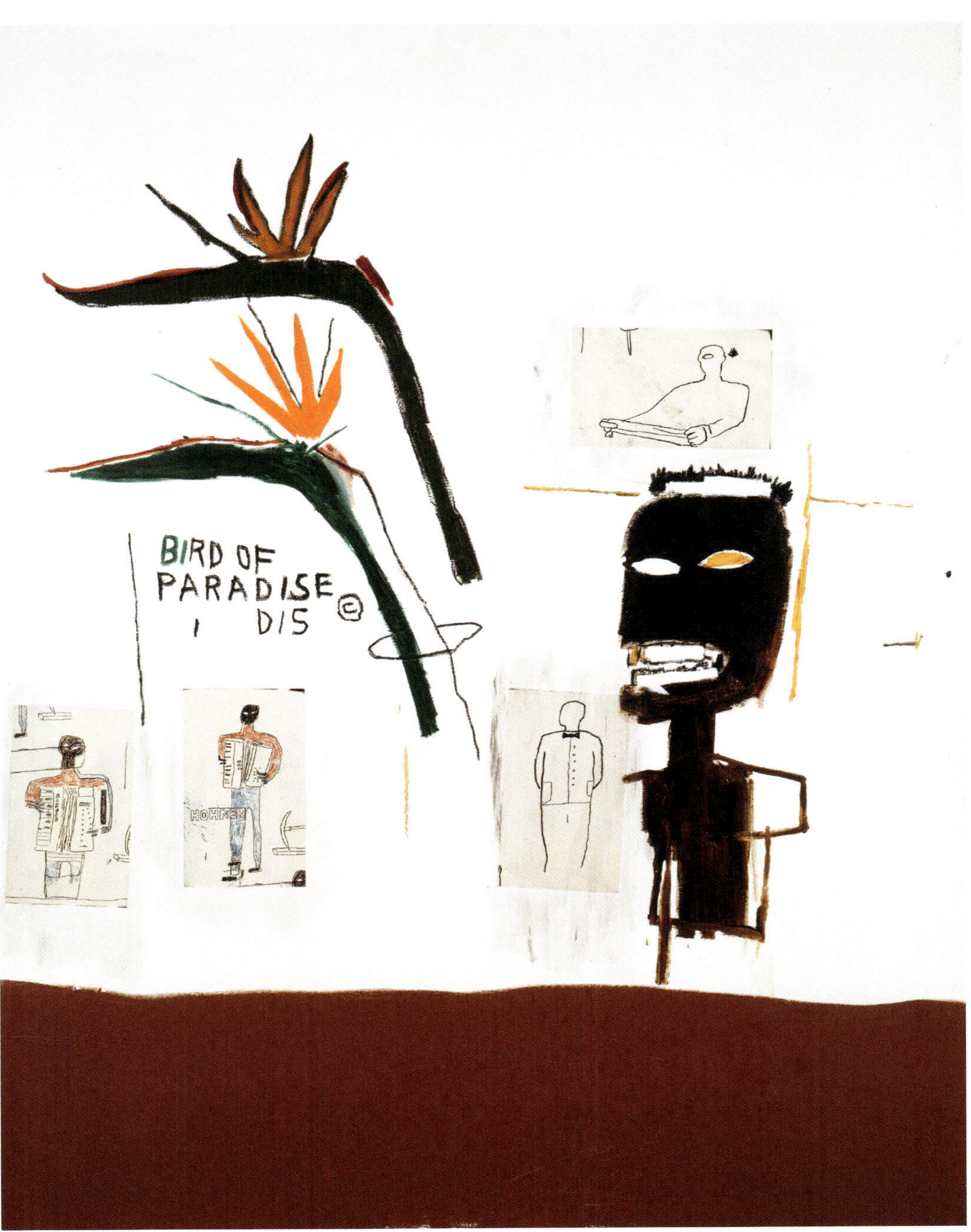

Bird of Paradise, 1985
Acrylic, oilstick, and photocopy collage on canvas,
218.5 x 172.5 cm / 86 x 68 inches

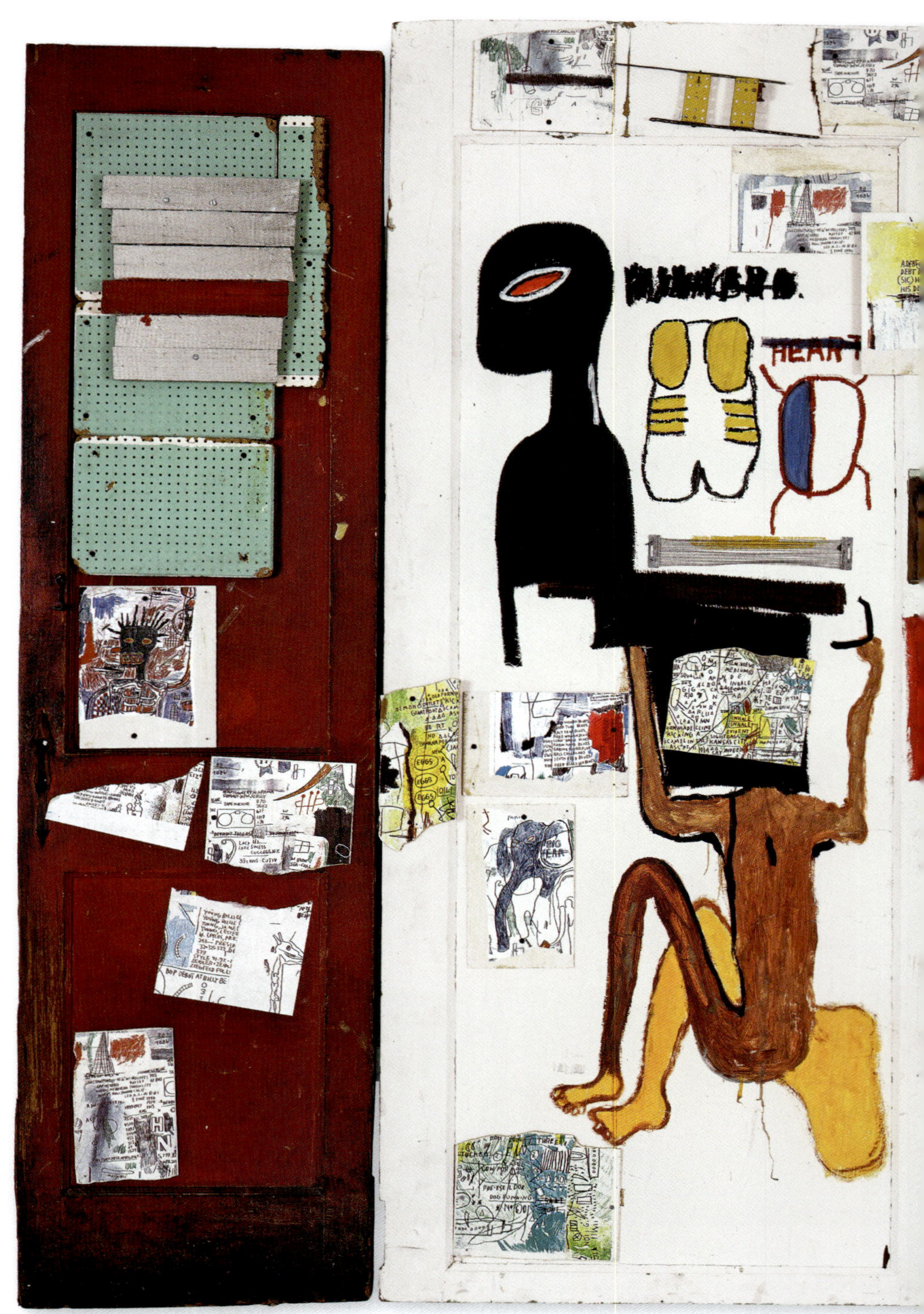

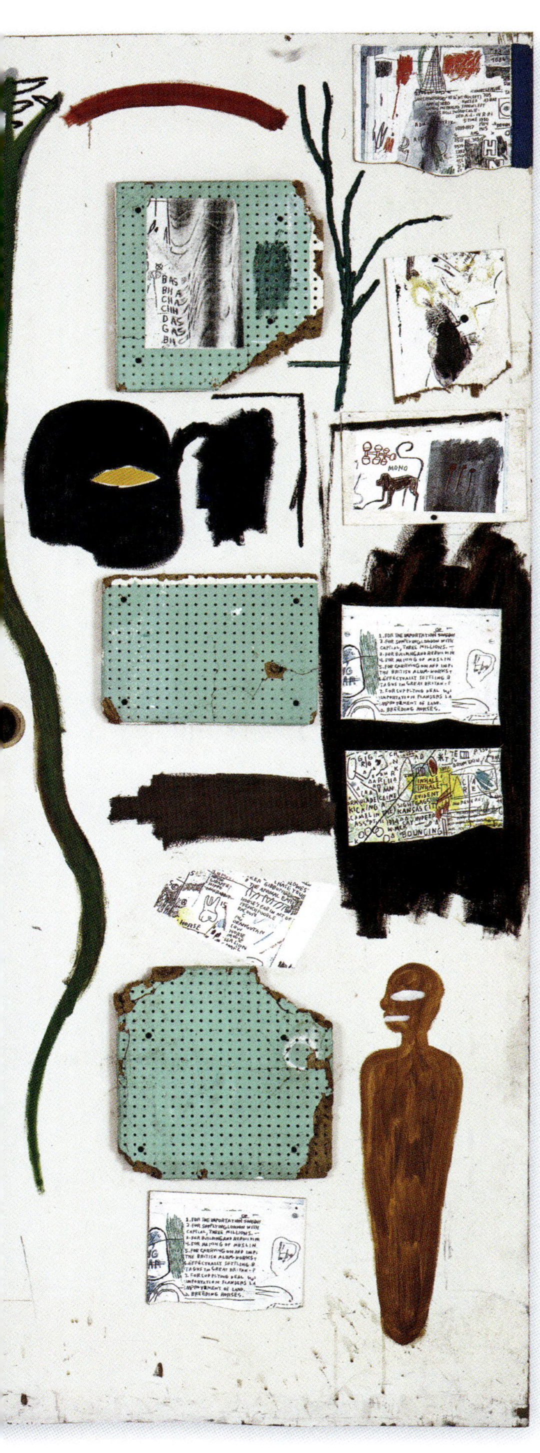

J'S Milagro, 1985
Acrylic, oil, oilstick, photocopy
collage, and metal on wood,
triptych: 203 x 228.5 cm /
80 x 90 inches

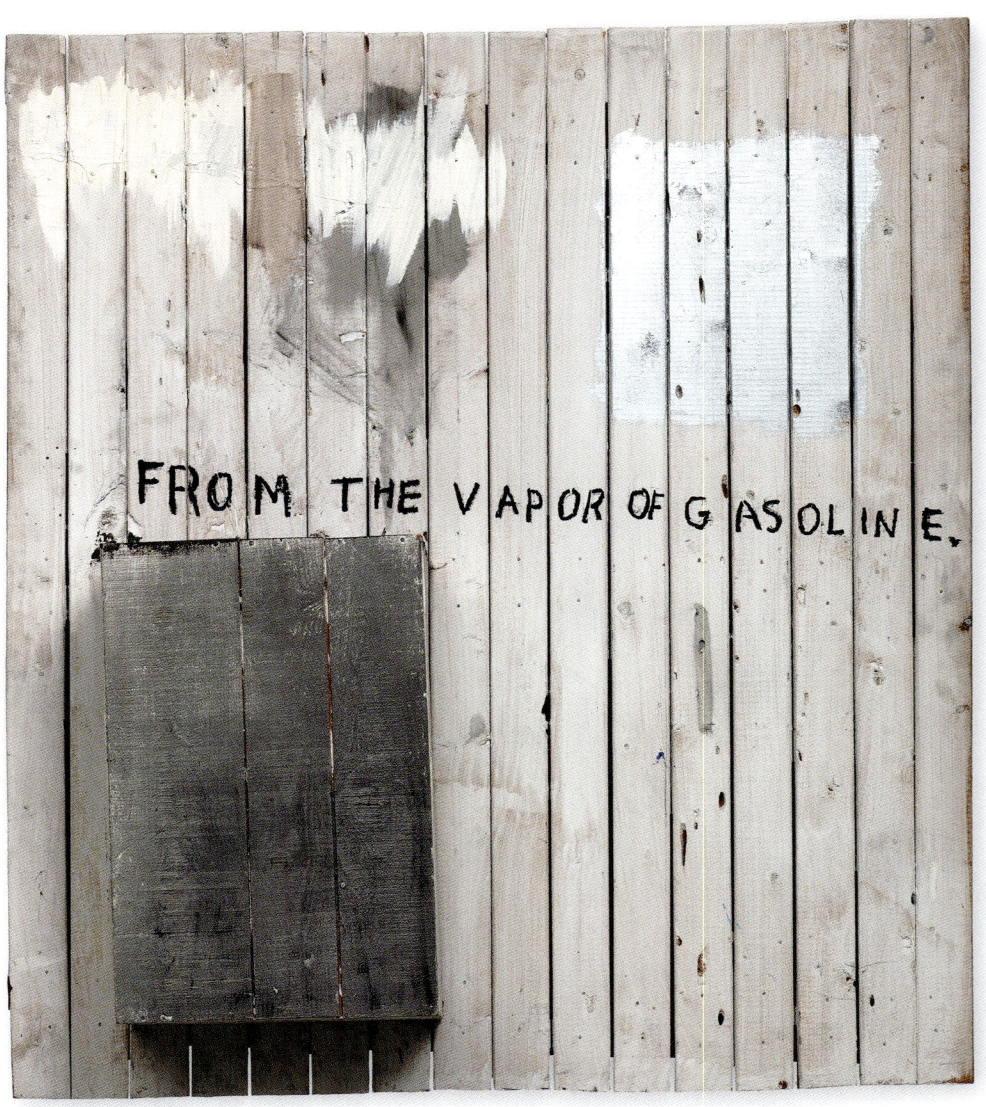

Peruvian Maid, 1985
Acrylic and oilstick on wood,
114.5 x 101.5 x 24 cm / 45 x 40 x 9 ¹/₂ inches

Anthony Clarke, 1985
Acrylic, oil, oilstick, and photocopy collage
on wood, 244 x 139 cm / 96 x 54 ³/₄ inches

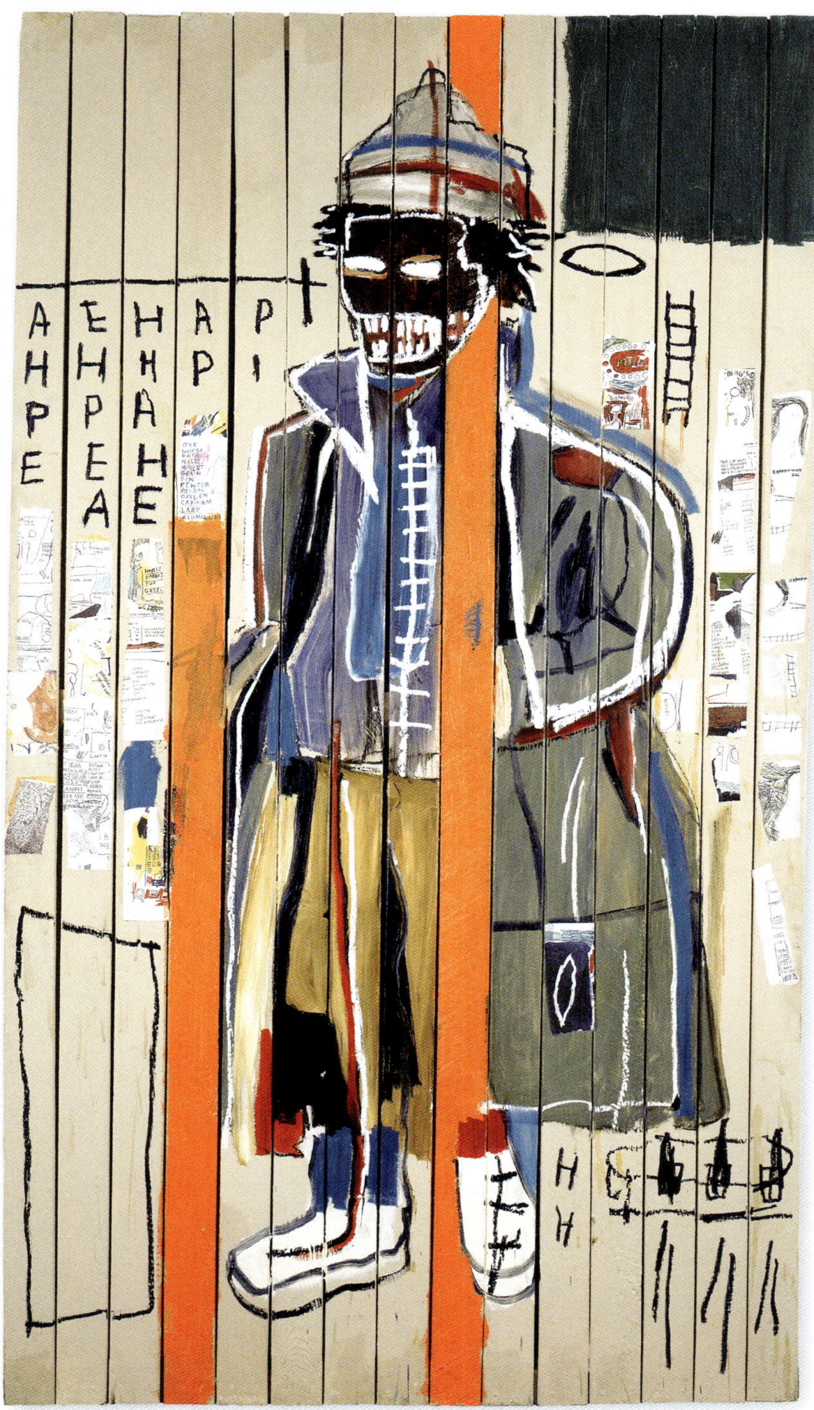

A H P E
A E H P E A
E H H A H E
H A P
A P I
P I

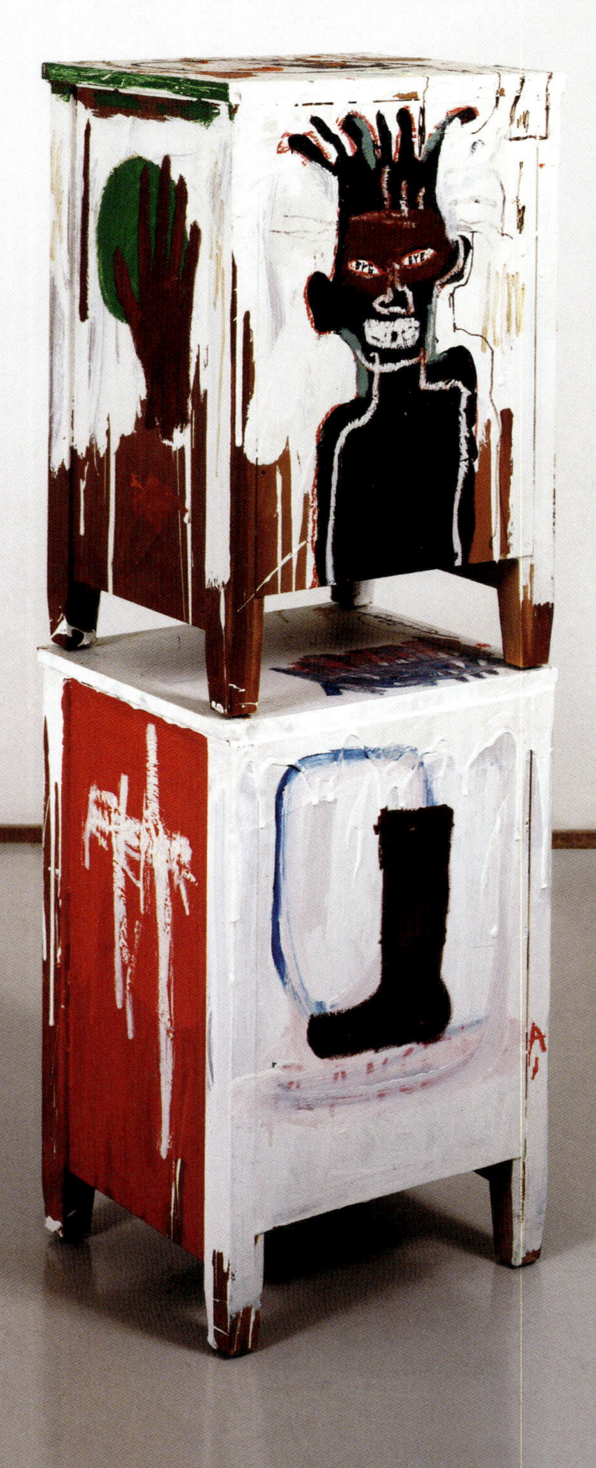

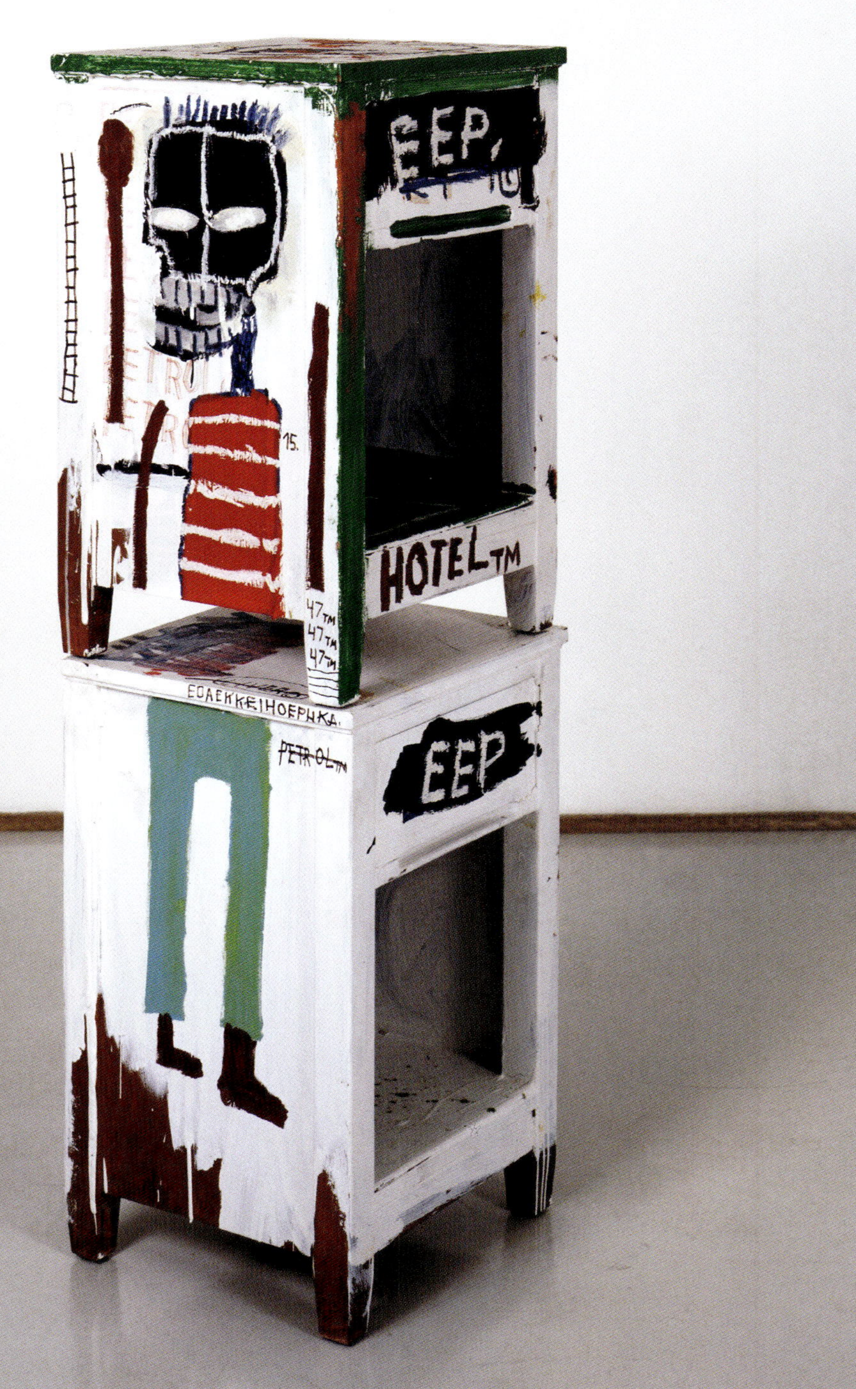

EEP,
HOTEL TM
47 TM
47 TM
47 TM
EOAEKKEIHOEPHKA.
PETROL TM
EEP

Pages 392/393: **Untitled** (recto and verso), 1985
Acrylic, oil, and oilstick on wood,
127 x 40.5 x 35.5 cm / 50 x 16 x 14 inches

Natchez, 1985
Acrylic, oil, photocopy collage, and wood
collage on panel, 216 x 154 x 10 cm /
85 x 60 ³/₄ x 4 inches

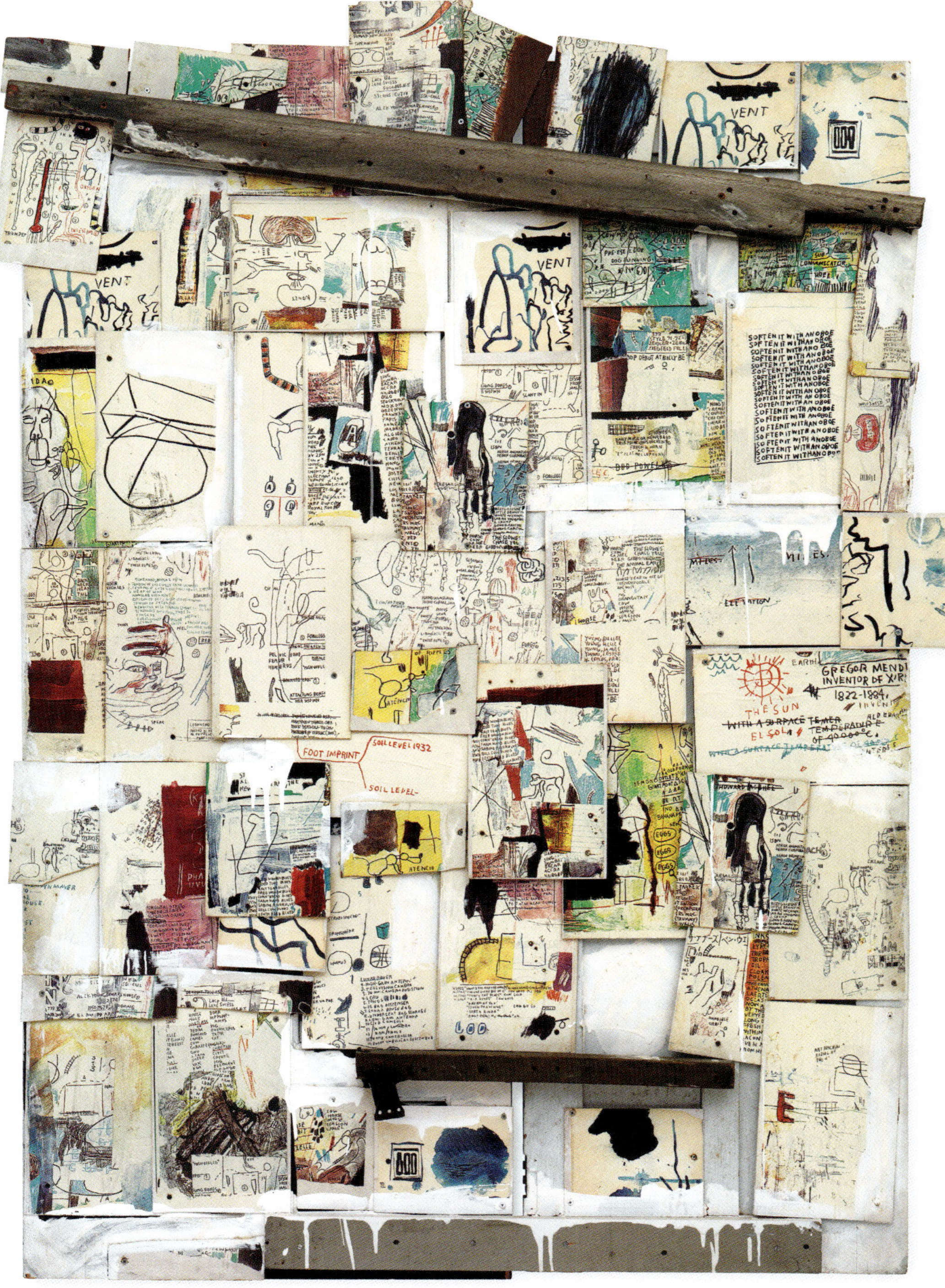

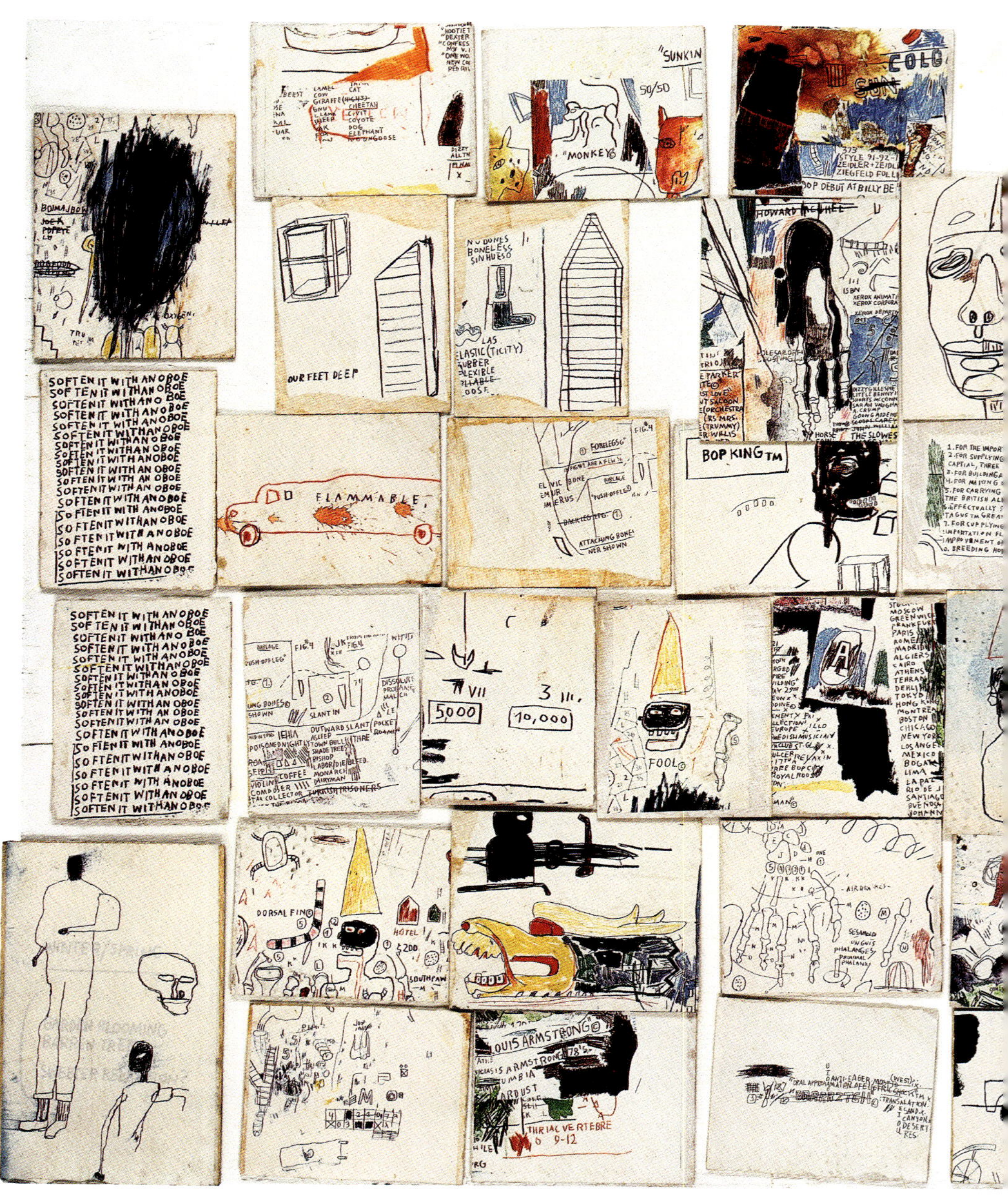

Untitled, 1985
Photocopy collage mounted on panels
on painted wood, 122 x 217 cm / 48 x 85 ½ inches

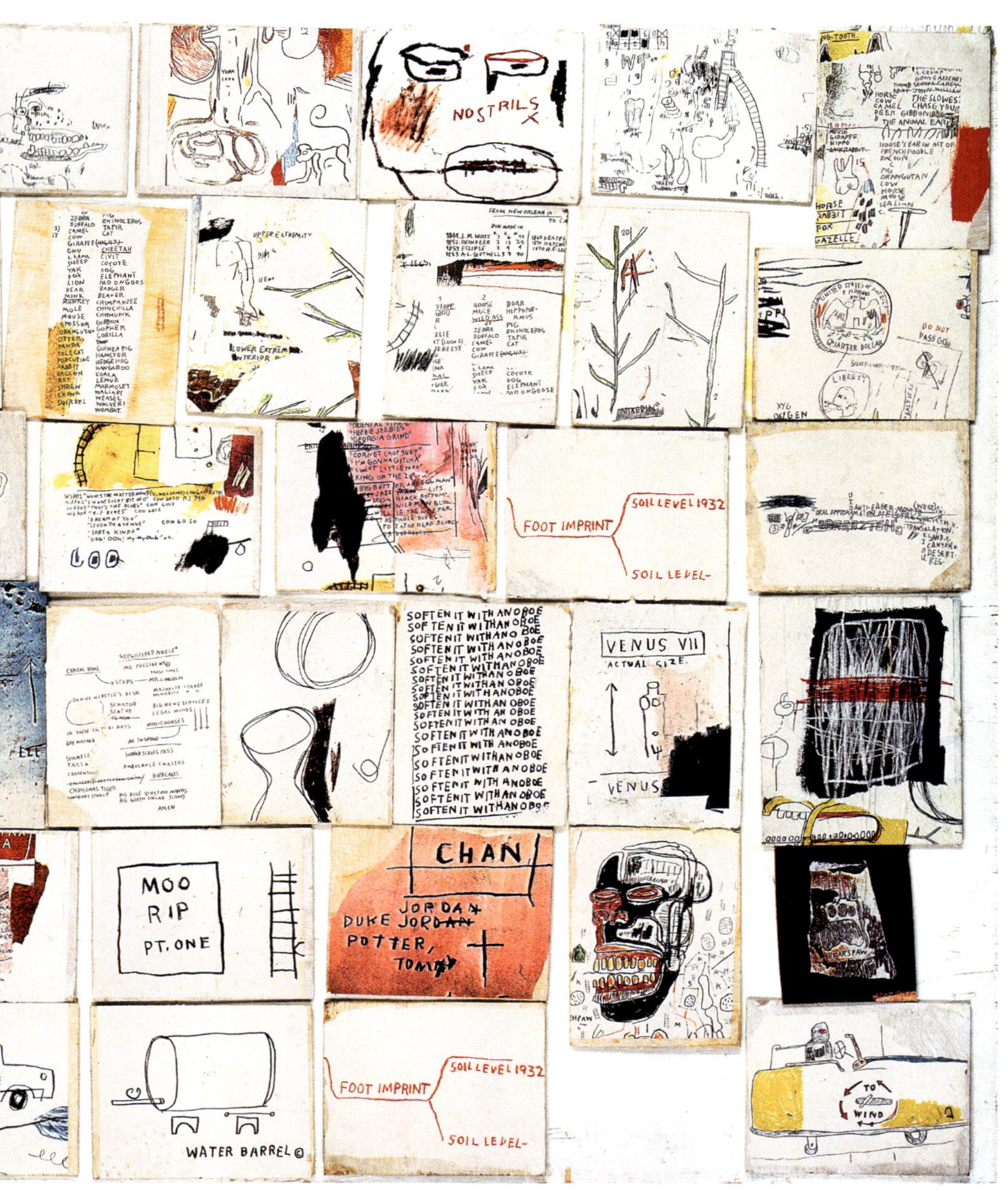

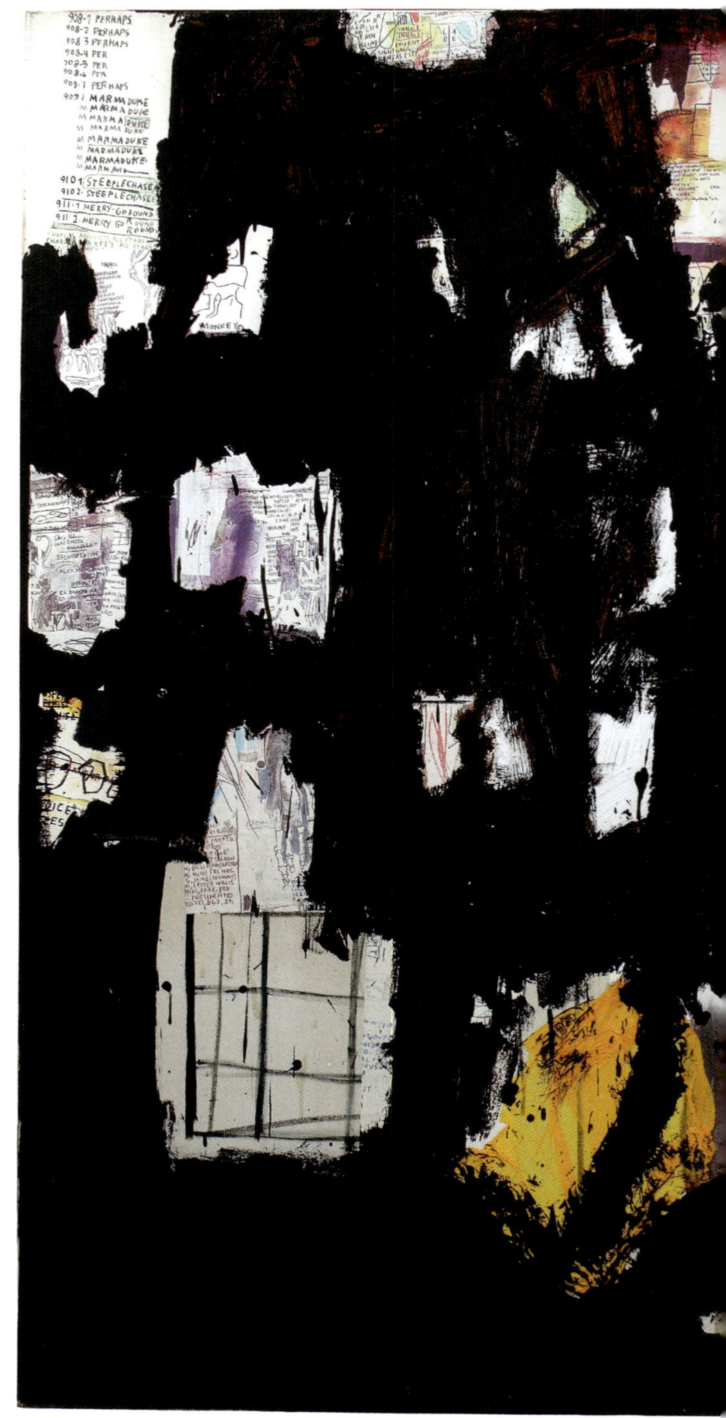

Marmaduke, 1985
Acrylic, oilstick, photocopy
collage, and paper collage
on wood, diptych:
203 x 259 cm / 80 x 102 inches

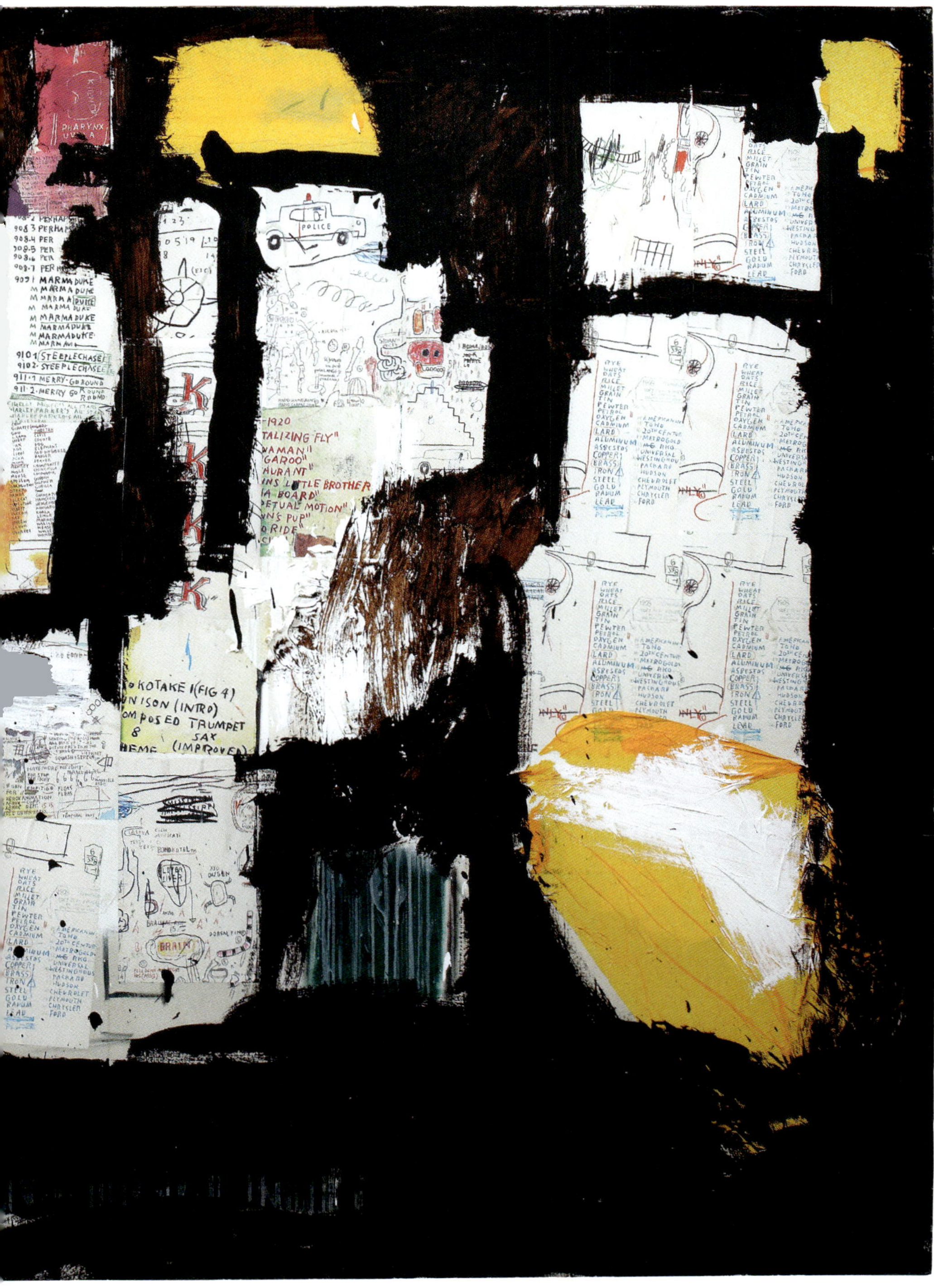

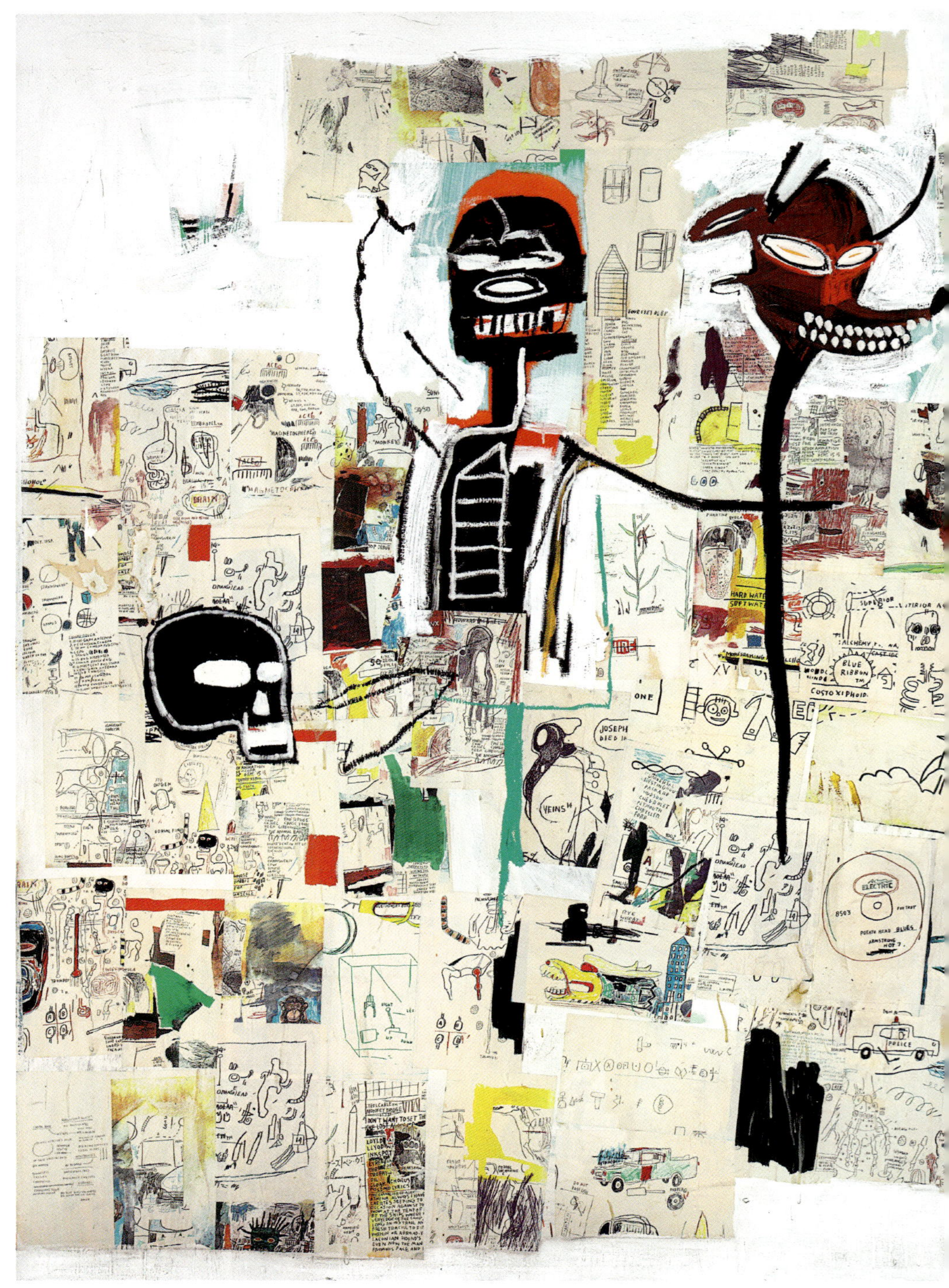

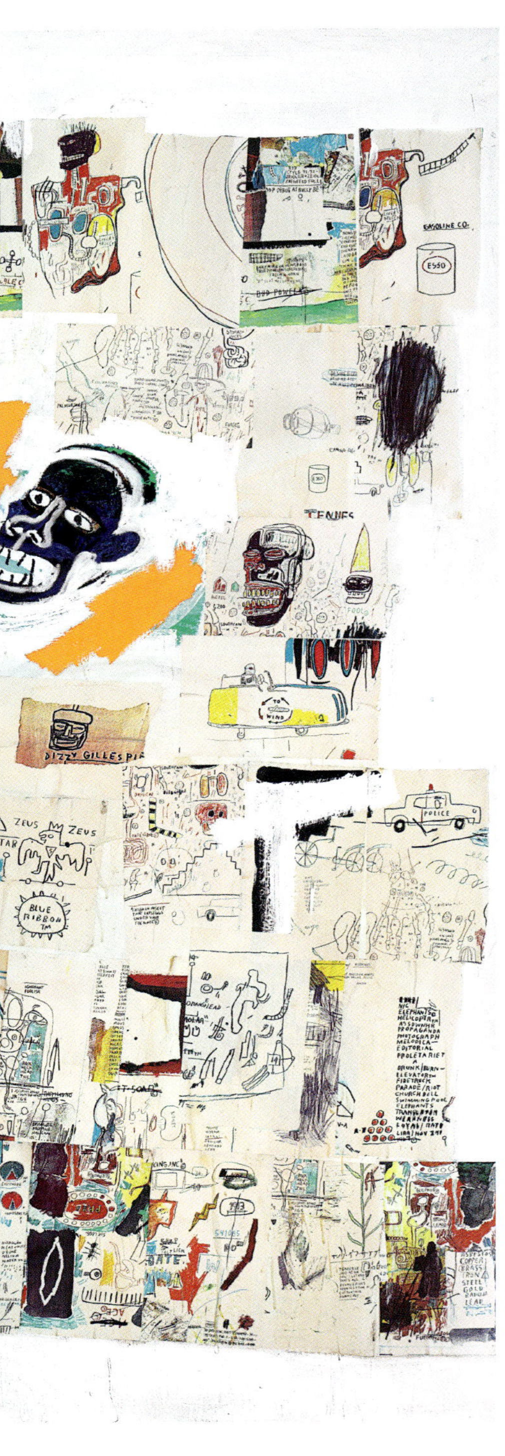

Peter and the Wolf, 1985
Acrylic, oilstick, and photocopy
collage on canvas, 254 x 289 cm /
100 x 113 ³/₄ inches

Pages 402/403: **Untitled (Tit)**, 1985
Acrylic, oilstick, and photocopy
collage on canvas, 203 x 259 cm /
80 x 102 inches

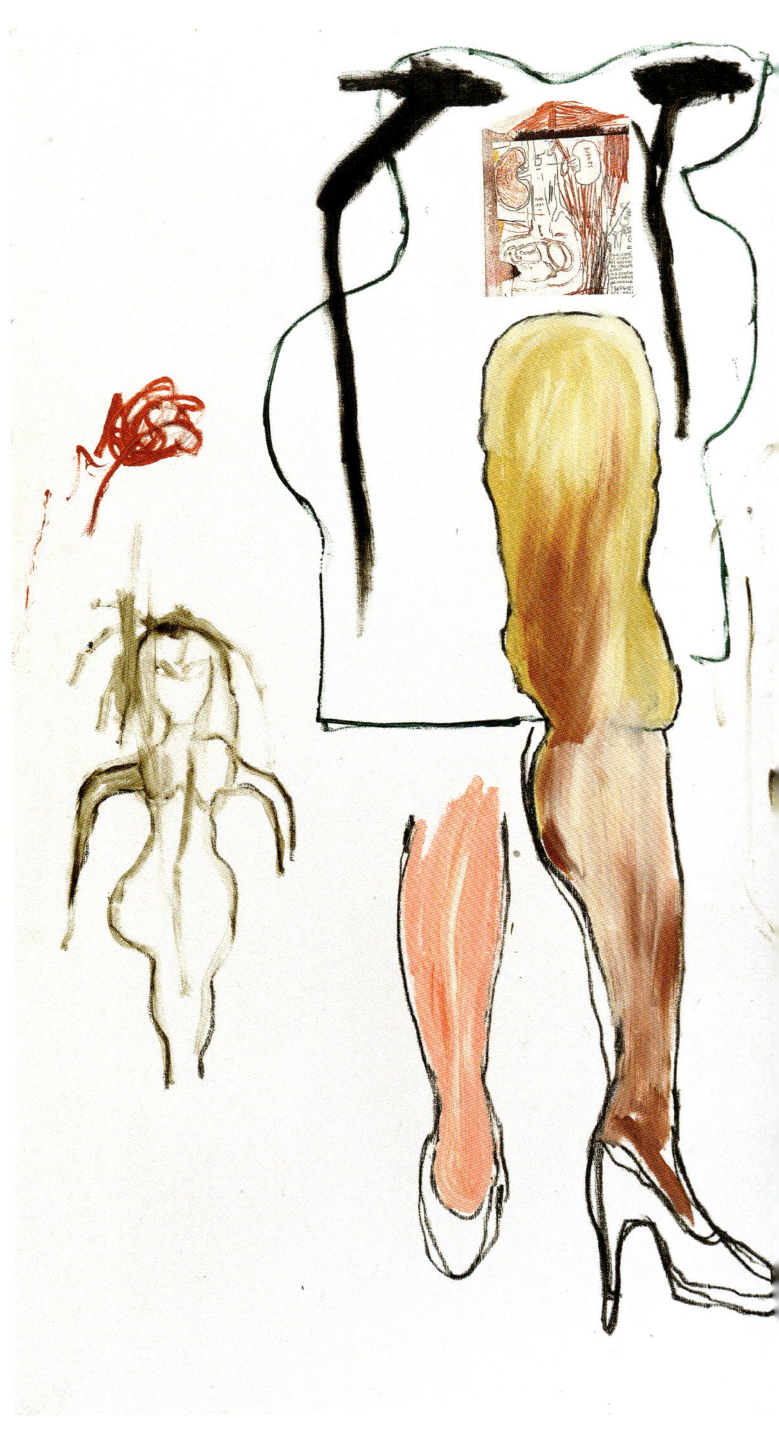

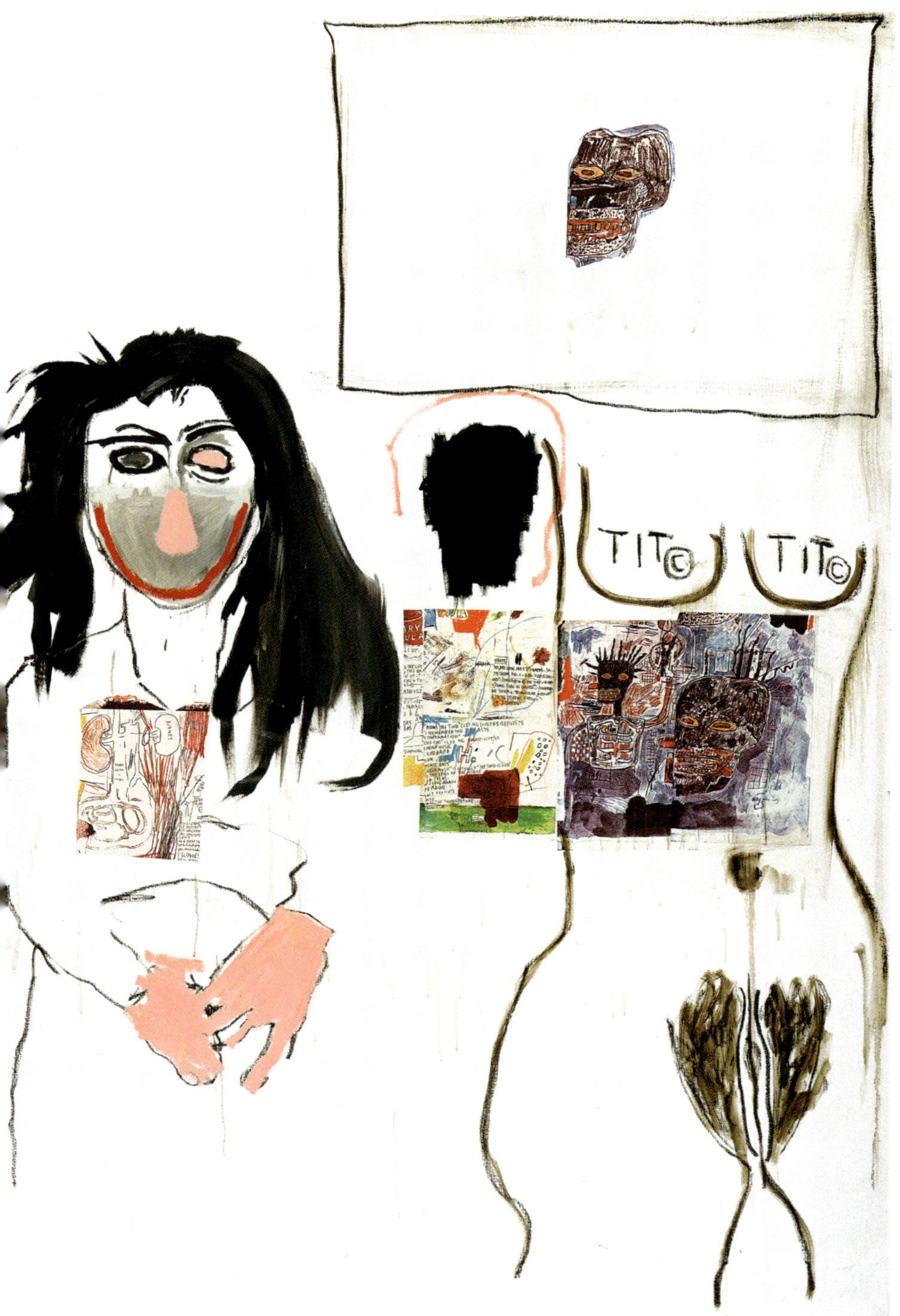

TIT©   TIT©

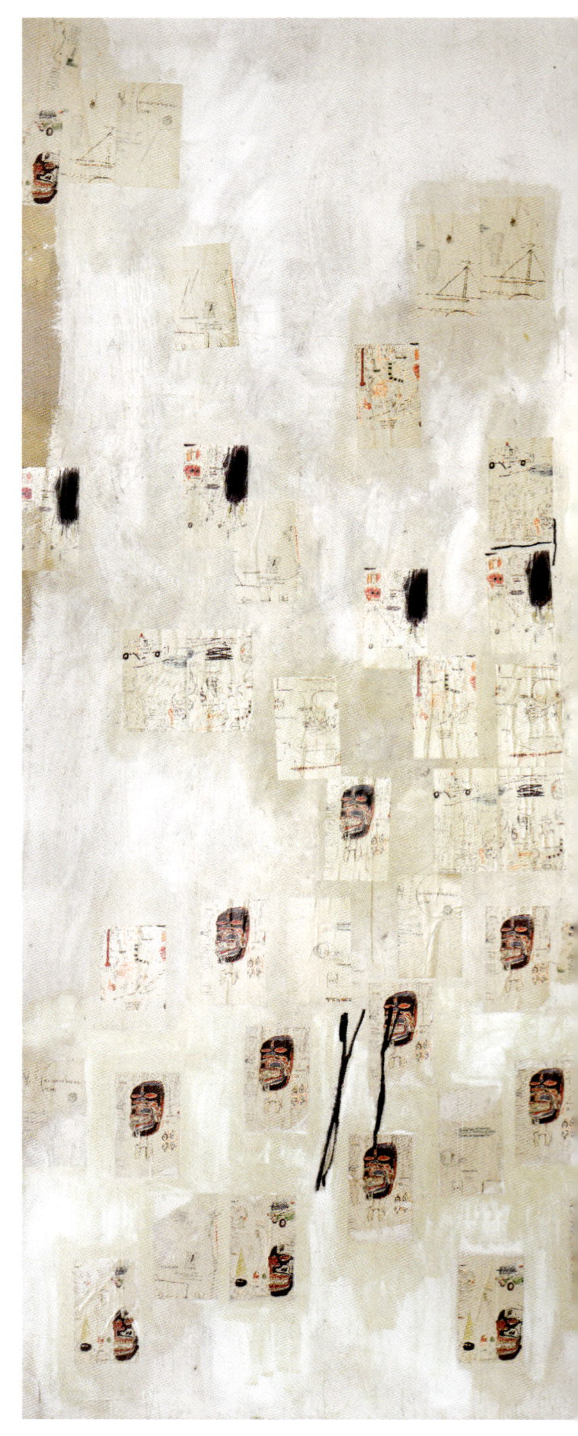

Untitled (Palladium Painting), 1985
Acrylic, ink, oilstick, and photocopy
collage on canvas, diptych:
480.5 x 564 cm / 189 ¹/₄ x 222 inches

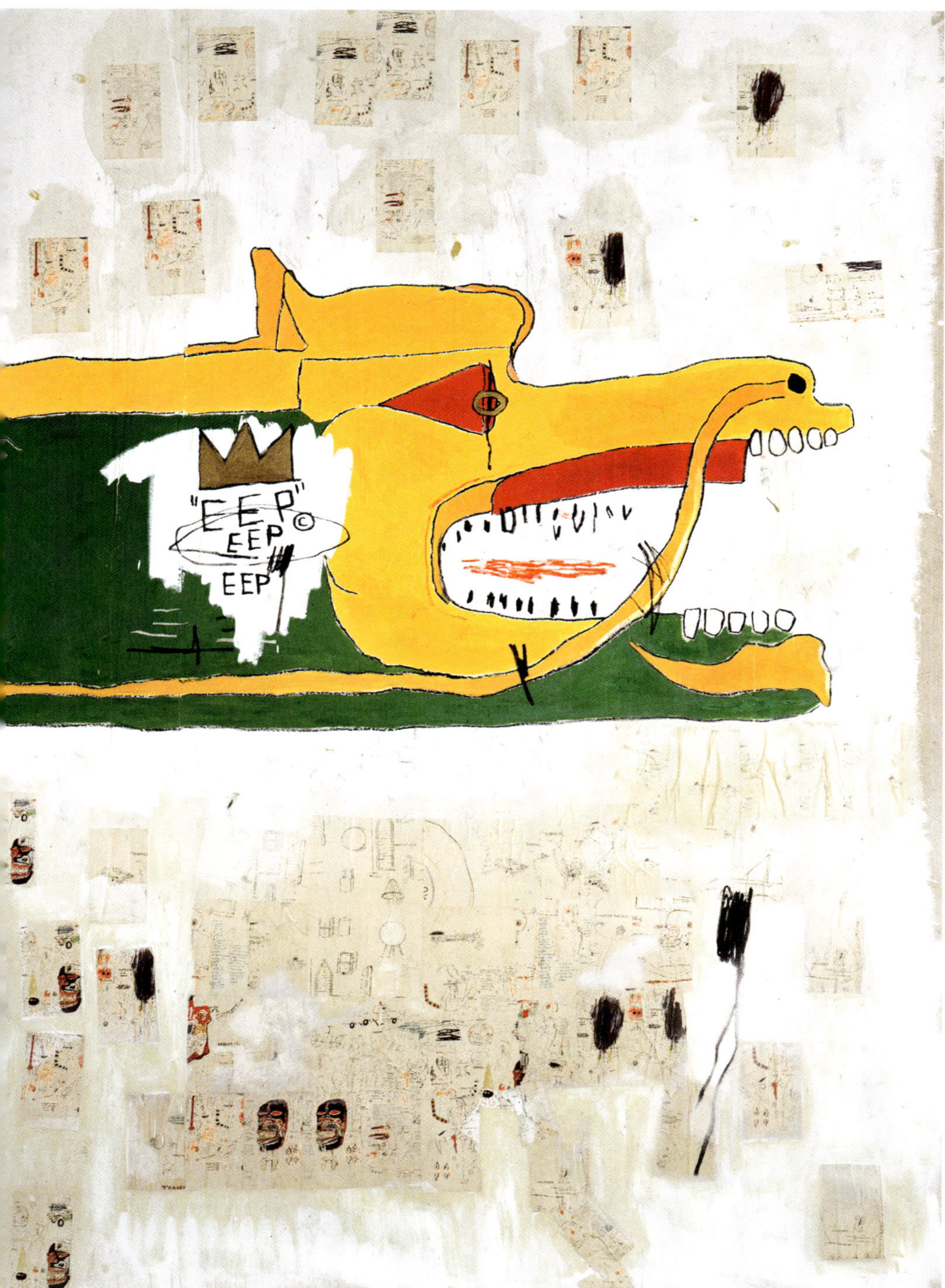
"EEP"©
EEP
EEP

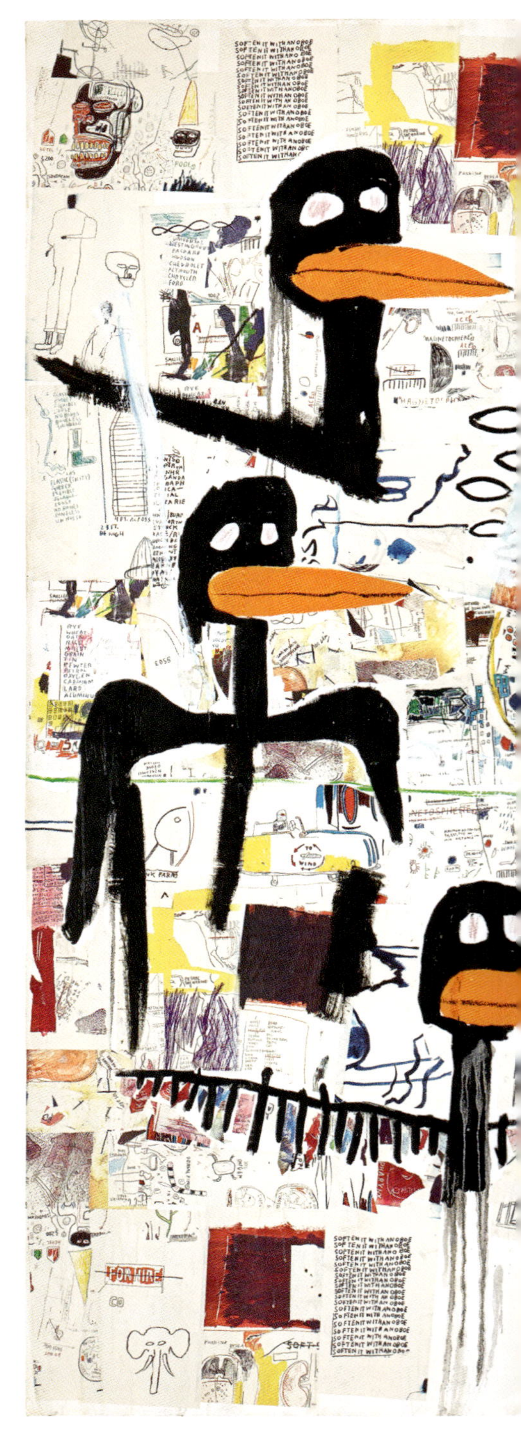

Tenor, 1985
Acrylic, oilstick, and photocopy collage
on canvas, 254 x 289.5 cm / 100 x 114 inches

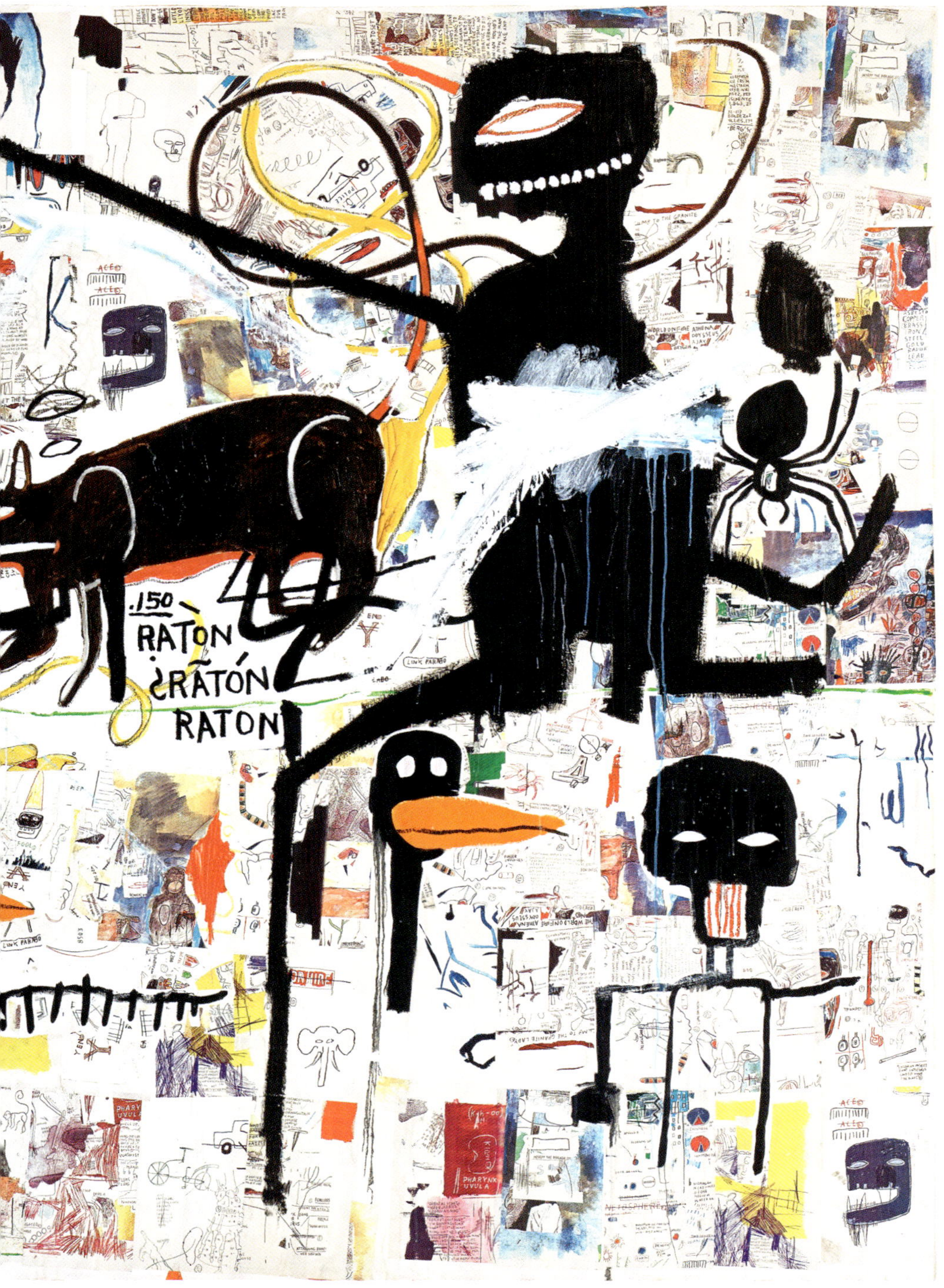

.150
RATON
¿RATÓN
RATON

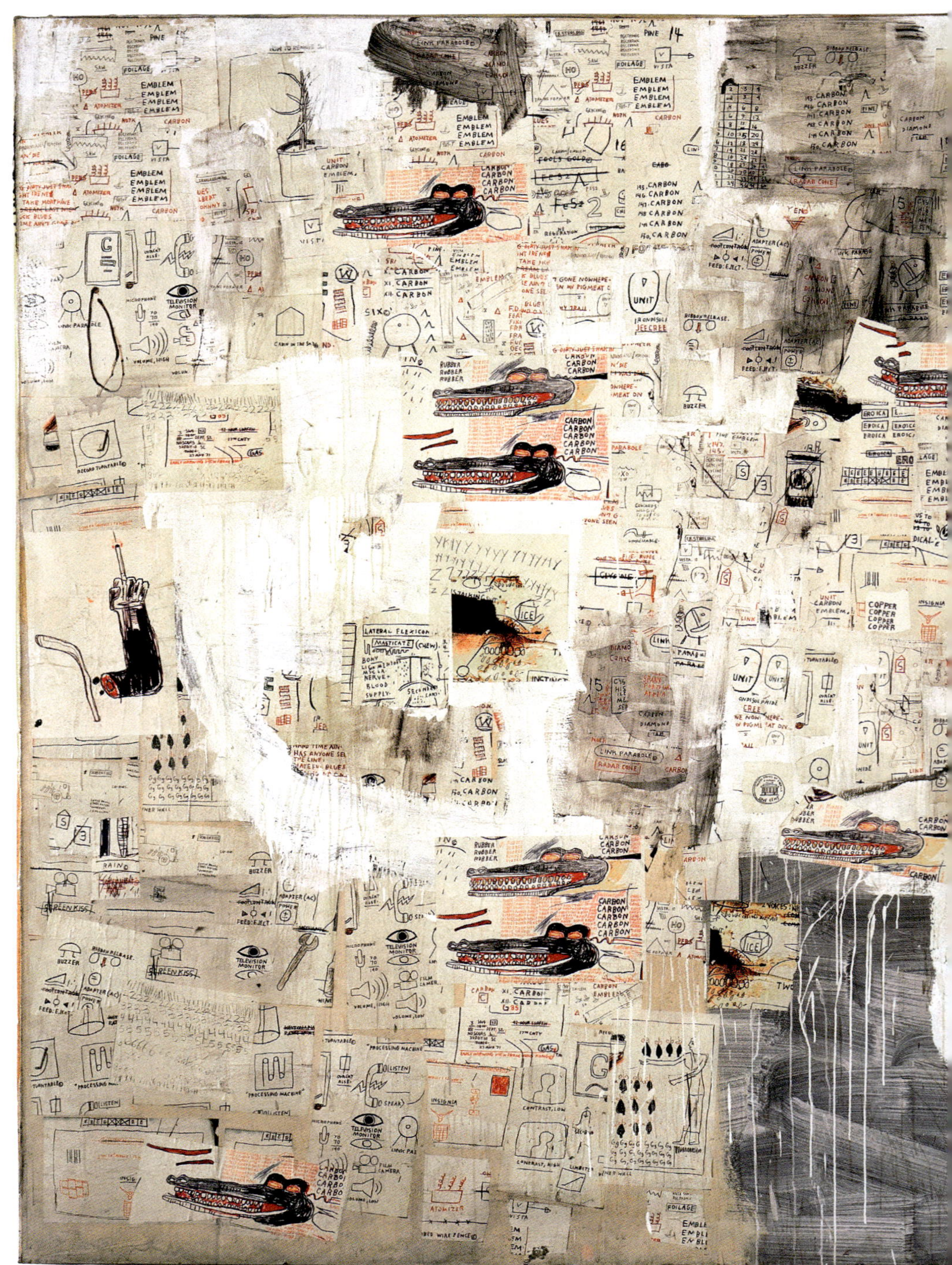

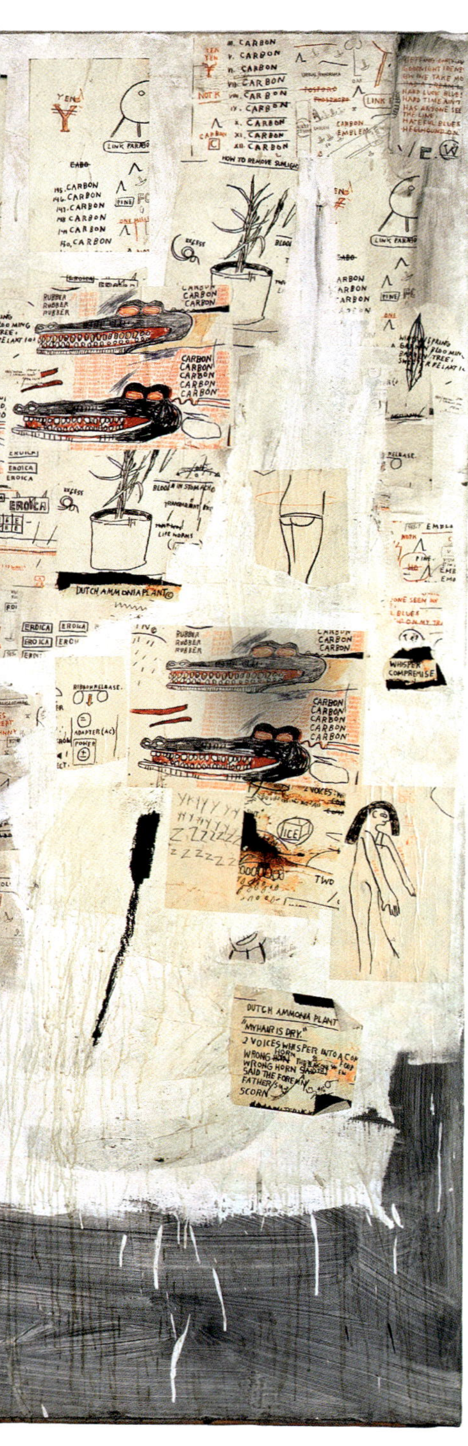

Untitled, 1985
Acrylic, oilstick, and photocopy
collage on canvas, 254 x 289.5 cm /
100 x 114 inches

1986
Roots

Becky Johnston: "Do you still see yourself as naive … in relation to this incredibly high pressure, competitive art world that you're part of? Do you maintain a distance from it so that you don't get cynical about it?" Jean-Michel Basquiat: "I don't see what—being cynical about it doesn't make sense. It's like being cynical about yourself, 'cause it's just you, really, it has nothing to do with them … I don't think there really is an art world. There's a few good artists and then everything else is extra."[1]

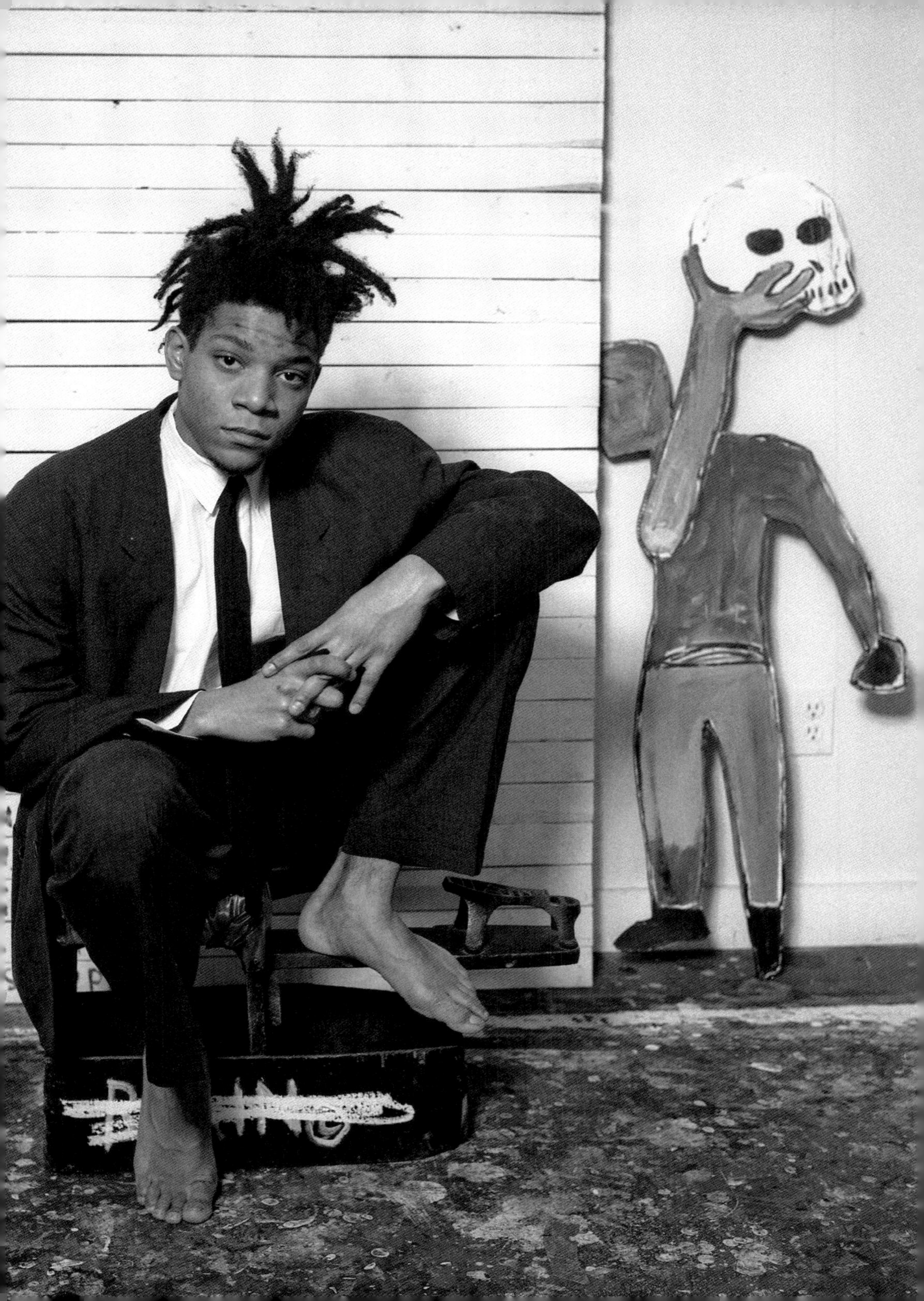

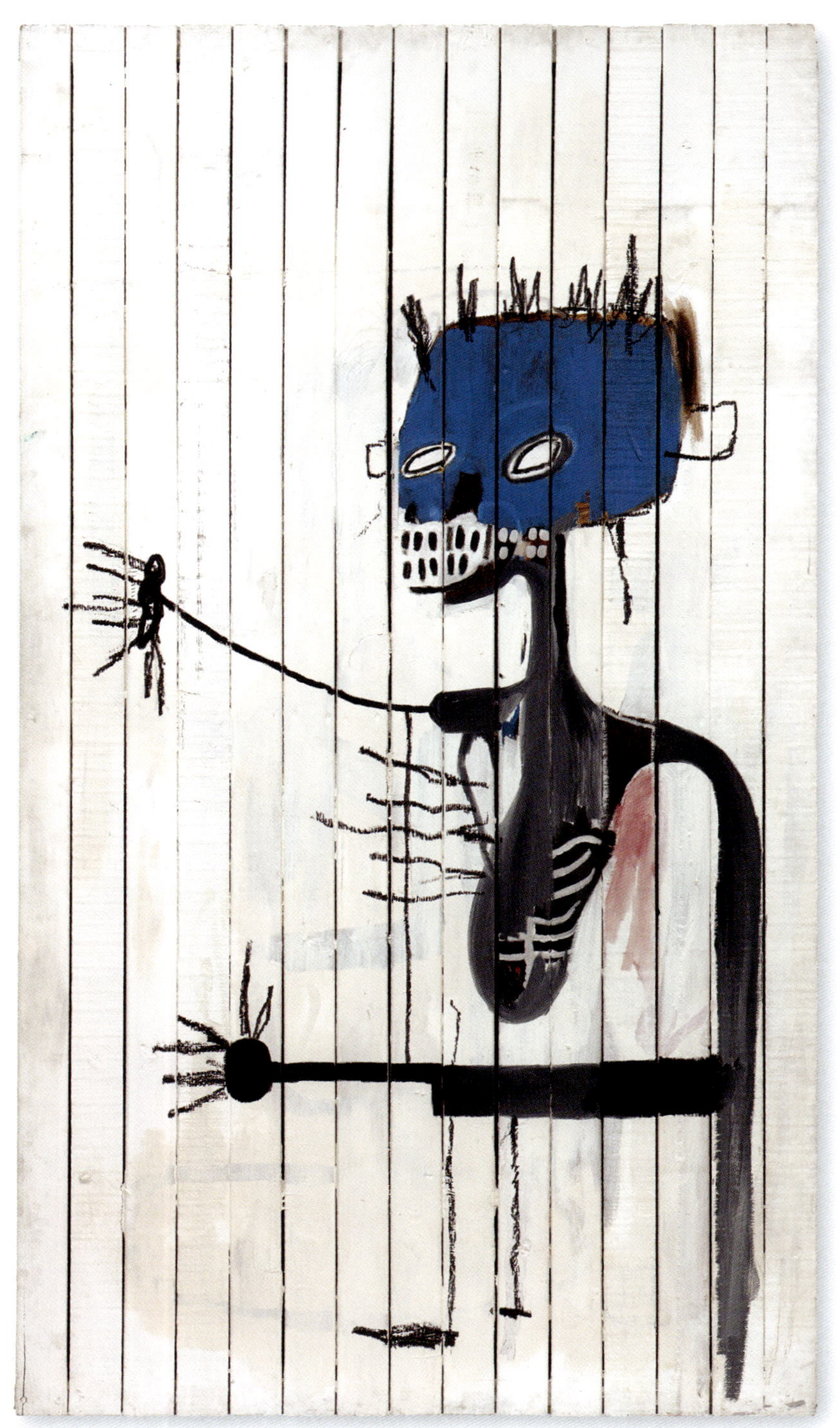

In January, Basquiat opens at Larry Gagosian in Los Angeles. Kristine McKenna reviews the show for the *L.A. Times*: "An exhibition of new work by New York artist Jean-Michel Basquiat looks as though it was pieced together out of debris scavenged at an abandoned elementary school. Weathered doors, the rusted remains of an erector set, banged-up little desks and hunks of pegboard are combined in whimsical assemblages that chronicle the aimless ramblings of a restless young mind … Pictures and words are sometimes painted directly onto the surface but often appear as though they were scribbled on ragged scraps of notebook paper, converted into color Xerox, then silk-screened onto a hunk of wood. This makes for pristine graffiti that's been drained of angry blood. But then Basquiat is far too stylish, hip, and cool to get mad, and the blasé mood of this show suggests that he's well aware that he needn't raise his voice to attract attention."[2]

Basquiat is interviewed by Becky Johnston and Tamra Davis in what remains his most lengthy and in-depth statement on film, discussing both biographical facts and his art process. BJ: "Do you have a specific method of working? Are there certain hours when you always work?" JMB: "I'm usually in front of the television. I have to have some source material around me to work off." BJ: "You don't mind having a lot of people around too while you're painting, do you?" JMB: "I've discovered that I think I rather work alone, more than anything. I used to have assistants, a lot, around me. And then on days when they wouldn't come, I would be a lot more productive … I think I have to learn more not to work around what's around me and just work with what I think, I guess. I shouldn't let what's around me affect my work at all."[3]

In this more intimate setting among friends, he also talks about his unwillingness to be his own interpreter: "I don't know how to describe my work, 'cause it's not always the same thing." BJ: "Do you feel that that's important to you, though, not to be able to describe it? That if you did, it would reify or objectify the work? And you'd feel like you were stuck with a definition you didn't want?" JMB: "It's like asking Miles, 'How does your horn sound?' I don't think he could really tell you why he played—you know, why he plays this at this point in the music. You know you're just, you're sort of on automatic … most of the time." Basquiat mentions Mark Twain and William Burroughs as his favorite writers, and in this year he strikes up a friendship with Burroughs. He also makes a sort of peace with Warhol, and they meet again intermittently.

Basquiat has long felt some interest in African art, as discussed with Demosthenes Davvetas, who asks him: "There are almost always totems, primitive signs, and fetishes in your images. Is that a search for your African roots?" JMB: "I've never been to Africa. I'm an artist who has been influenced by his New York environment. But I have a cultural memory. I don't need to look for it; it exists. It's over there, in Africa. That doesn't mean

Untitled (Lung), 1986
Acrylic on wood,
244 x 140 cm / 96 x 55 inches

Page 411: Jean-Michel Basquiat,
New York 1986.
Photo Dmitri Kasterine

that I have to go there. Our cultural memory follows us everywhere, wherever you live."[4] Then in August, Basquiat finally gets a chance to travel to Africa with Jennifer Goode and her brother, as Bruno Bischofberger has arranged a show at Abidjan in Ivory Coast. "It was Jean-Michel's first visit to Africa," Goode later remembers. "We had a wonderful time. Artists came and talked to him. I remember he was disappointed that they were doing copies of Western art. He thought it would be more like his work, but the only things that were anything like his were on the outside of houses. Or just signs."[5]

The collaborative paintings with Warhol continue to travel, to the Akira Ikeda Gallery in Tokyo and Galerie Bruno Bischofsberger in Zürich. In November, Basquiat has a solo show as the youngest artist ever at Kestner Gesellschaft in Hannover, but on short notice decides not to travel to the opening. An interview with Isabelle Graw, who had waited at the airport for him, accordingly turns out edgy: "How do you work?" JMB: "I start with a picture and then finish it. I don't think about art when I'm working. I try to think about life." IG: "All the art critics see a mixture of Afro-Caribbean elements and Cy Twombly in your work …" JMB: "I don't listen to anything that art critics say. I don't know anyone who needs a critic to find out what art is."[6] He does travel to Hamburg to collaborate on an amusement park organized by the Austrian artist and all-around showman André Heller, called Luna Luna, which will open to the public in the summer of the following year with works by Georg Baselitz, Joseph Beuys, Salvador Dalí, Keith Haring, David Hockney, Rebecca Horn, Roy Lichtenstein, and many others. Among smaller contributions, Basquiat paints a Ferris wheel.

Meanwhile, he has parted ways with gallerist Mary Boone and is again without a dealer in New York. Toward the end of the year, unable to cope with Basquiat's frantic lifestyle, Jennifer Goode breaks up with him.

[1–6] *See Endnotes on page 508f.*

The Thinker, 1986
Acrylic on canvas,
213 x 132 cm / 84 x 52 inches

Pages 416/417: Jean-Michel Basquiat,
exhibition view, Gagosian Gallery,
Los Angeles 1986

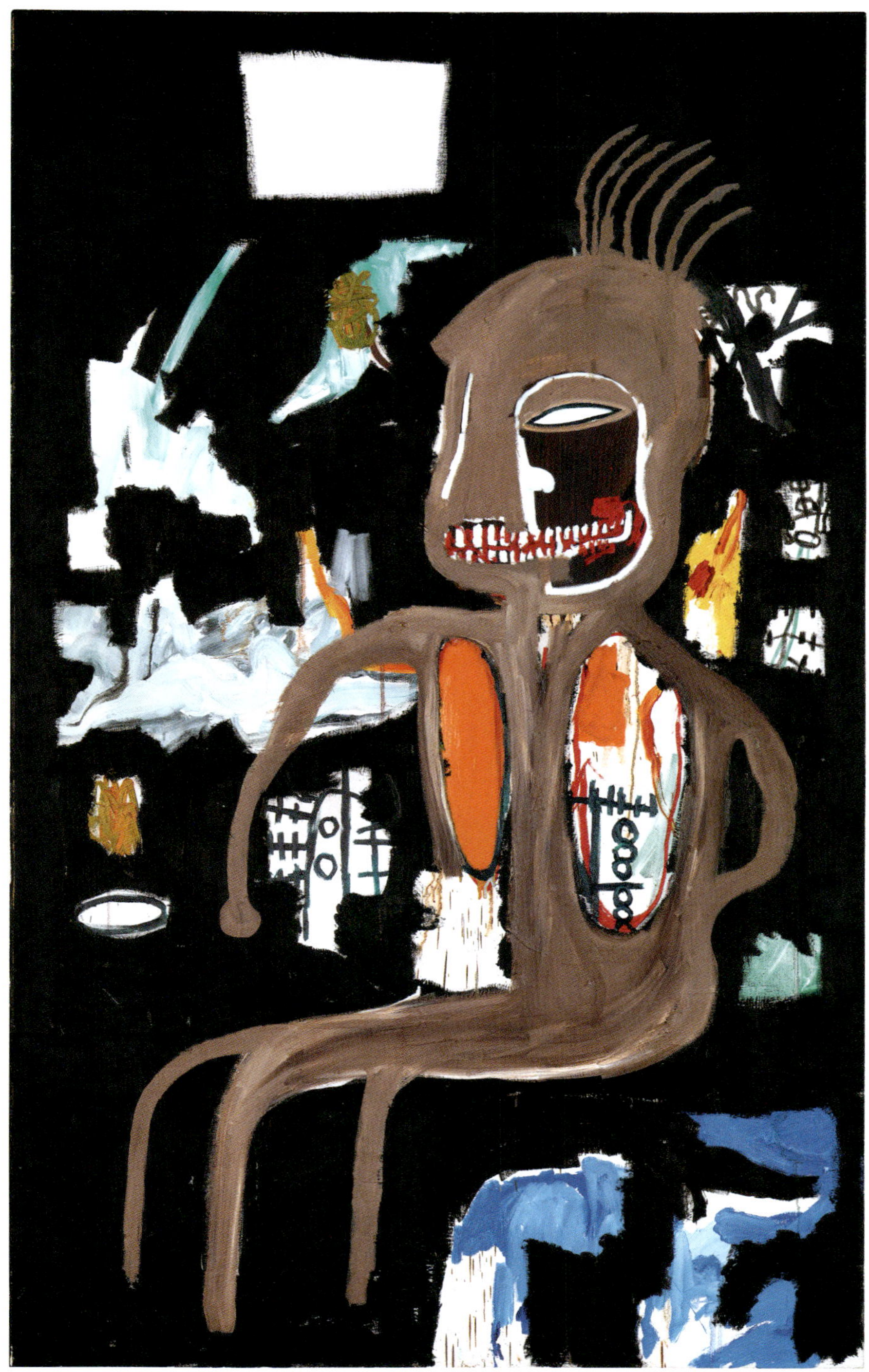

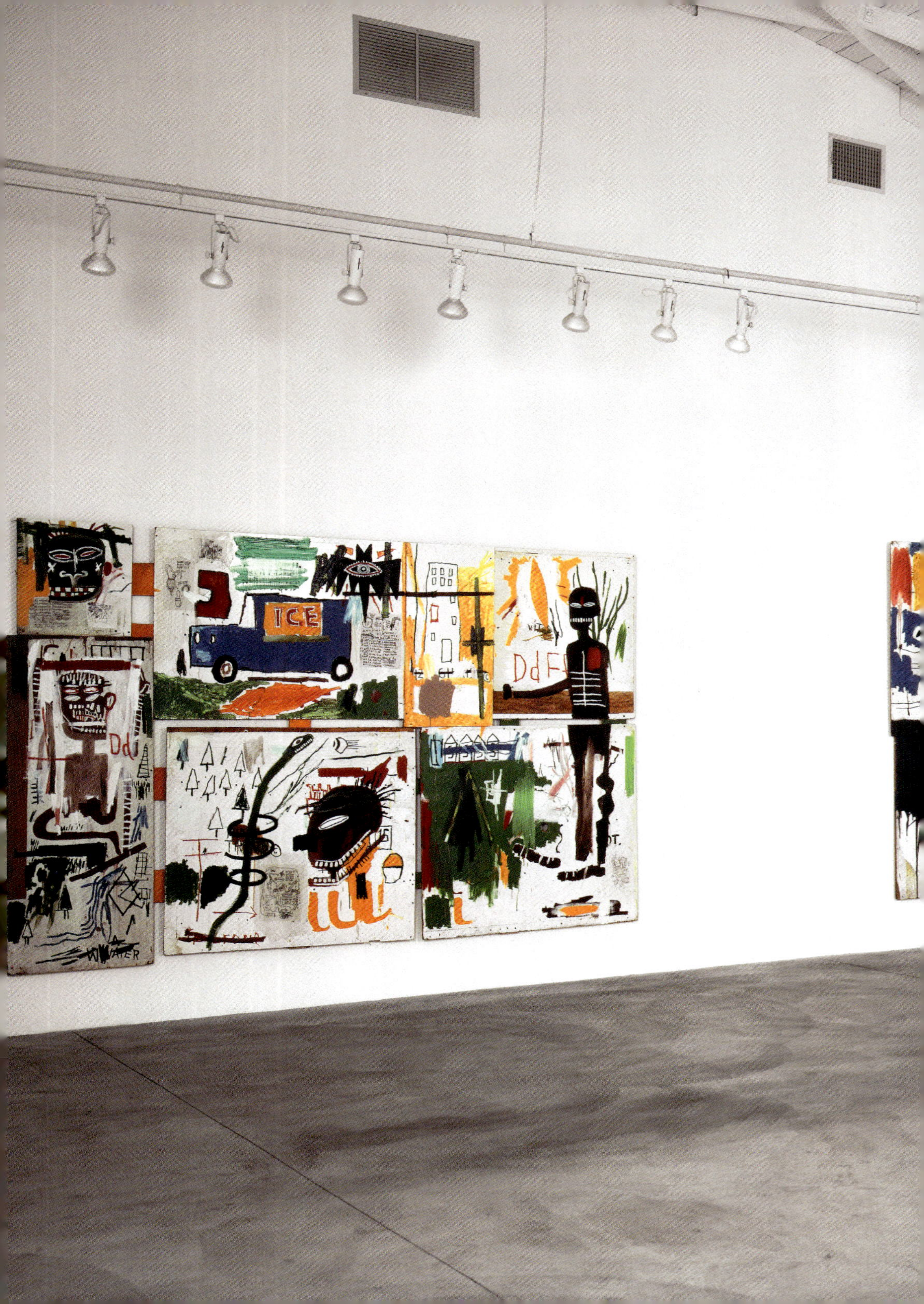

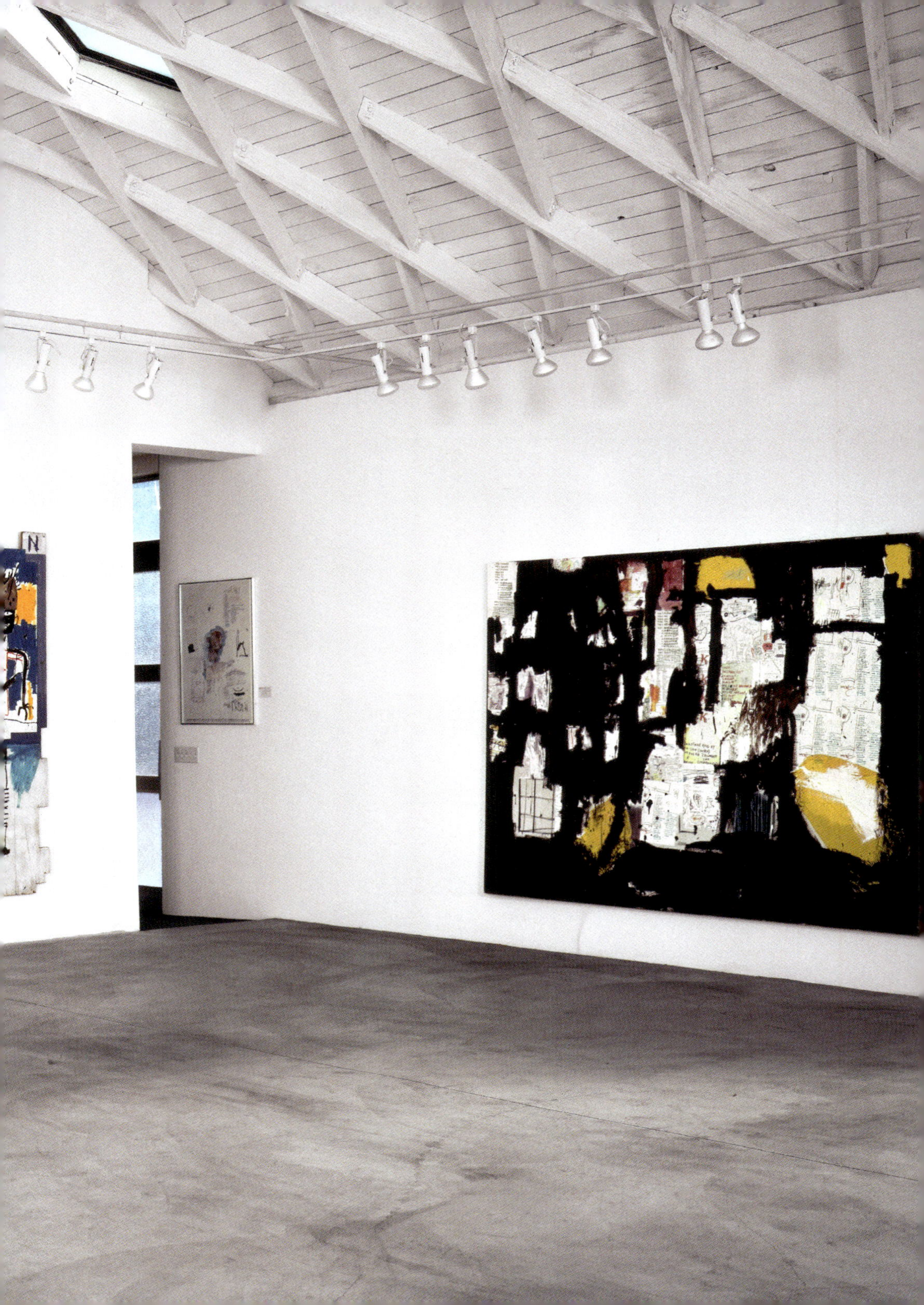

Untitled, 1986,
Monotype: typographic ink on paper,
119 x 83.5 cm / 46 ³/₄ x 32 ³/₄ inches

Page 420: **Untitled**, 1986
Acrylic, oilstick, and ink on paper,
76 x 56 cm / 30 x 22 inches

Page 421: **Odalisque**, 1986
Graphite, oilstick, and acrylic on paper,
105.5 x 76 cm / 41 ¹/₂ x 30 inches

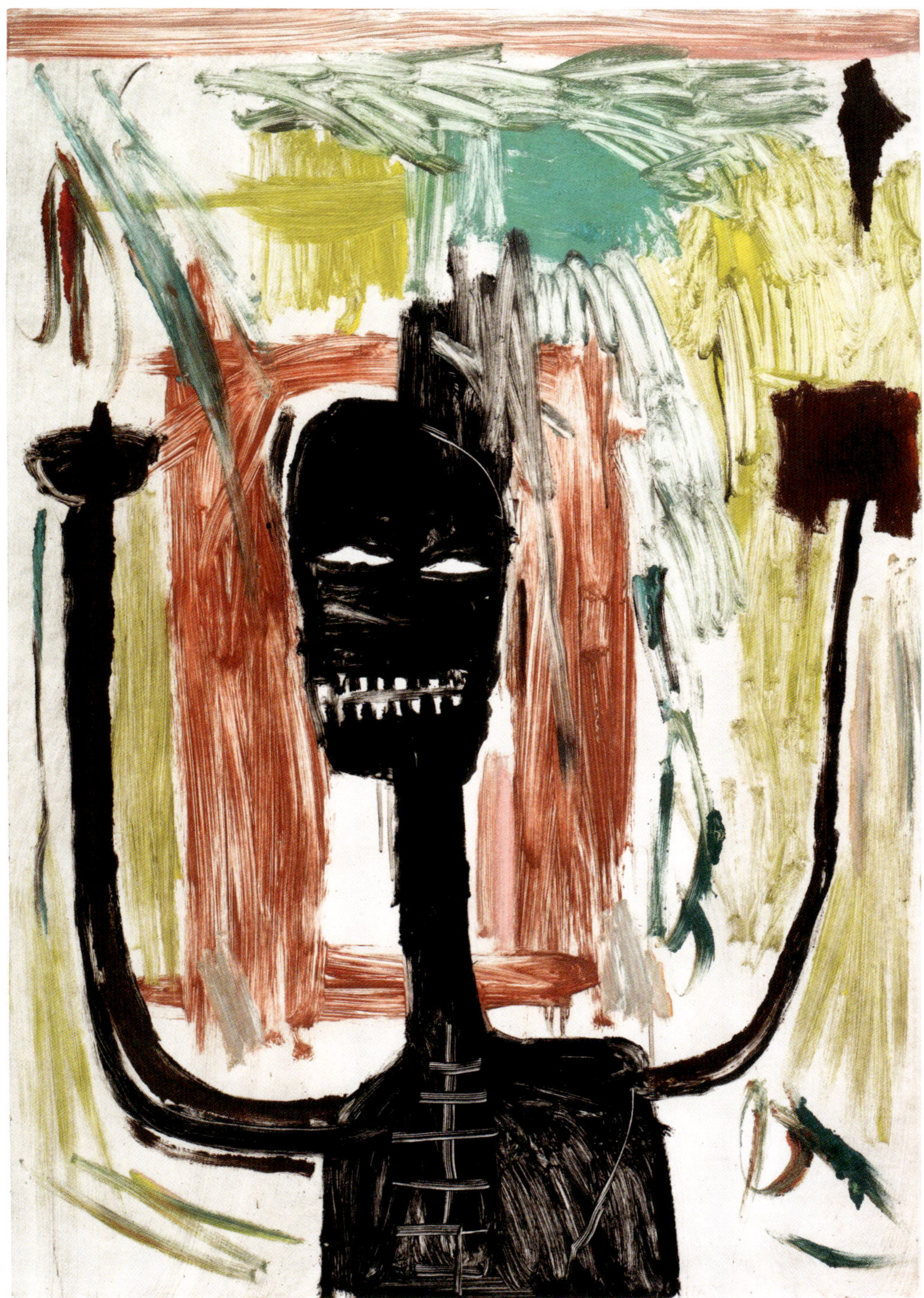

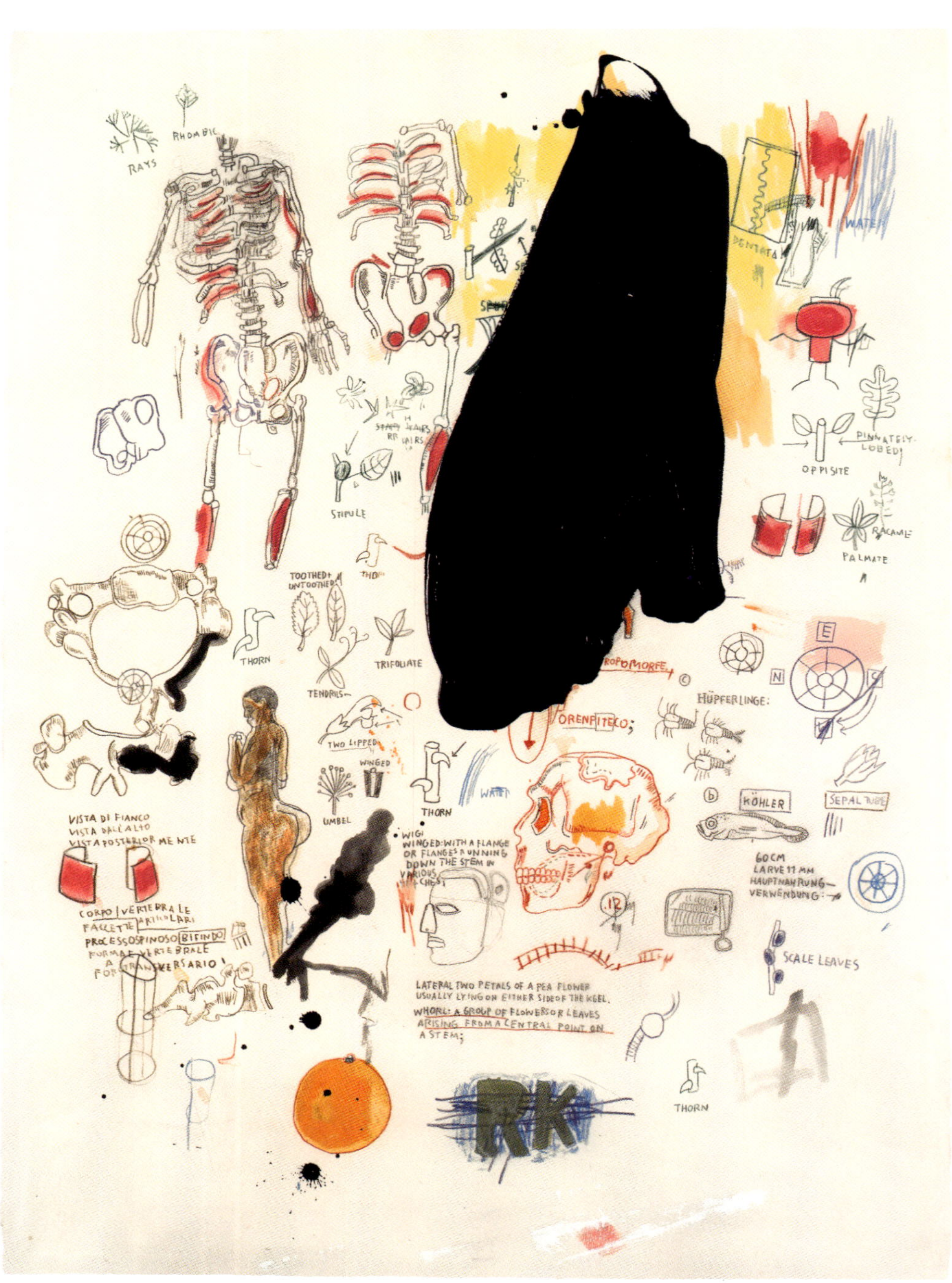

RAYS
RHOMBIC
WATER
DENTATA
PINNATELY LOBED
OPPISITE
RACAME
PALMATE
STIPULE
TOOTHED + UNTOOTHED
THORN
THORN
TRIFOLIATE
TENDRILS
TWO LIPPED
WINGED
UMBEL
HÜPFERLINGE:
KÖHLER
SEPAL TUBE
WATER
THORN
VISTA DI FIANCO
VISTA DALL'ALTO
VISTA POSTERIOR MENTE
CORPO VERTEBRALE
FACCETTE ARTICOLARI
PROCESSO SPINOSO BIFINDO
FORME VERTEBRALE
A TRANSVERSARIO
WIGI
WINGED: WITH A FLANGE
OR FLANGES RUNNING
DOWN THE STEM IN
VARIOUS CHEST
60 CM
LARVE 11 MM
HAUPTNAHRUNG
VERWENDUNG:
SCALE LEAVES
LATERAL TWO PETALS OF A PEA FLOWER
USUALLY LYING ON EITHER SIDE OF THE KEEL.
WHORL: A GROUP OF FLOWERS OR LEAVES
ARISING FROM A CENTRAL POINT ON
A STEM;
THORN
RK

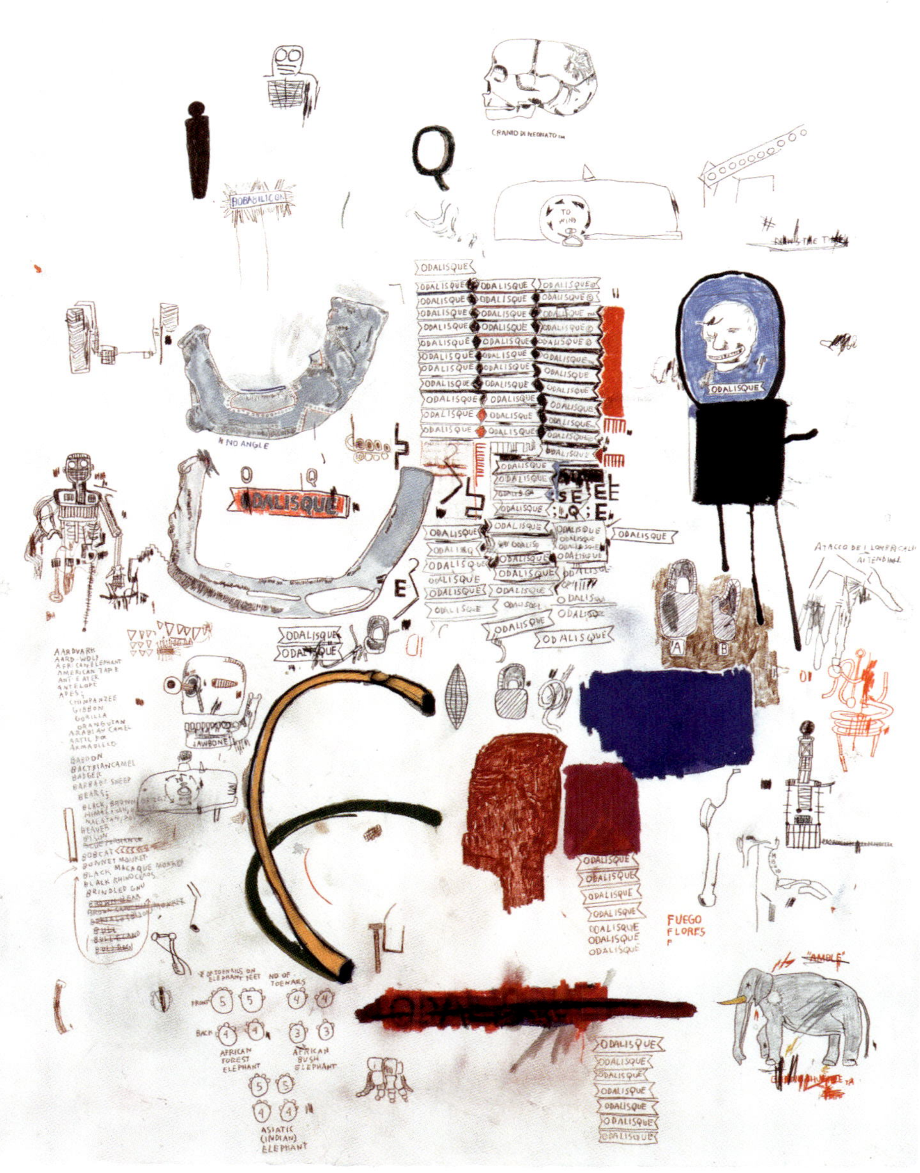

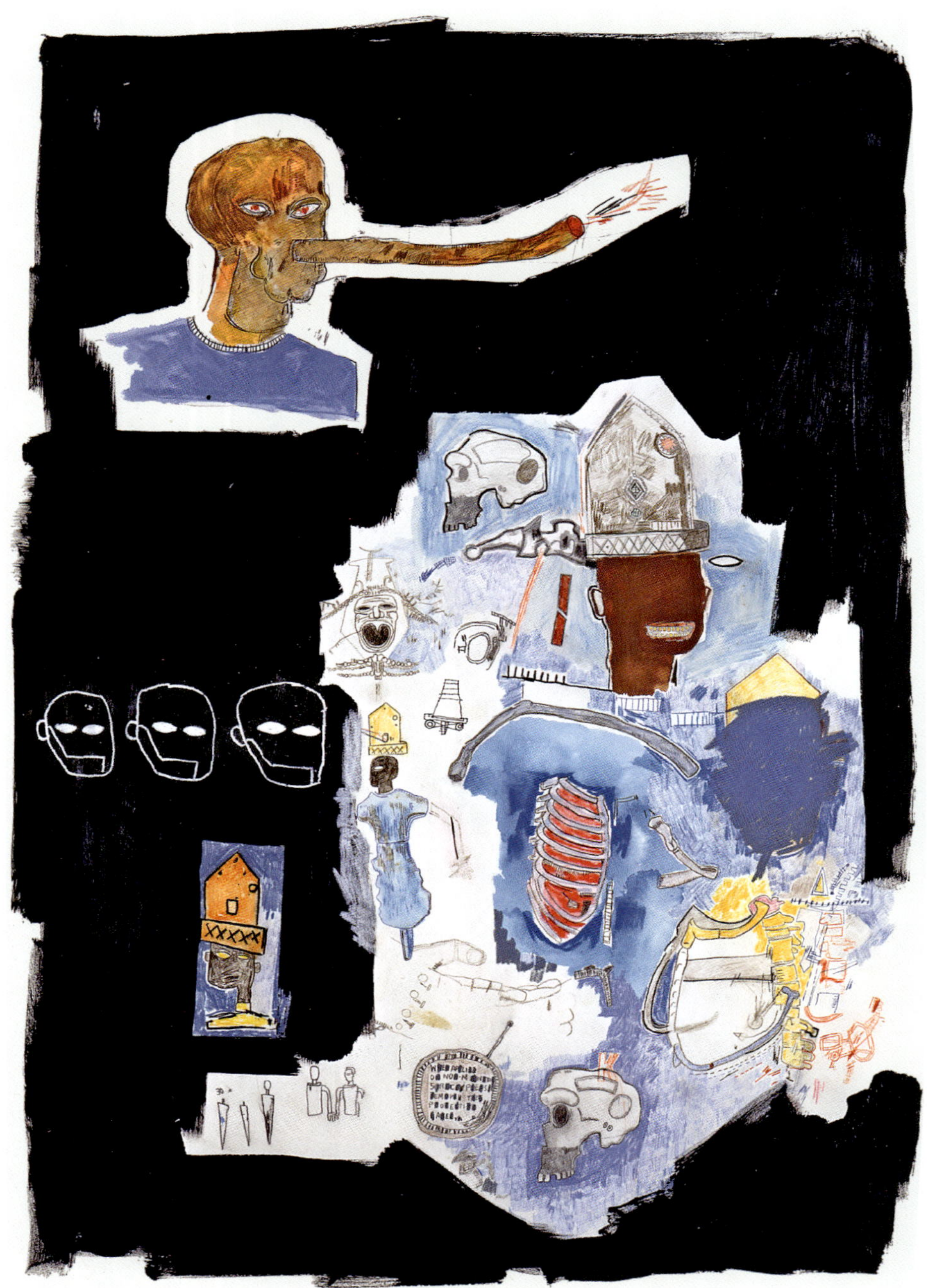

Black Pope, 1986
Acrylic, oilstick, colored pencil, and graphite
on paper, 105.5 x 76 cm / 41 $\frac{1}{2}$ x 30 inches

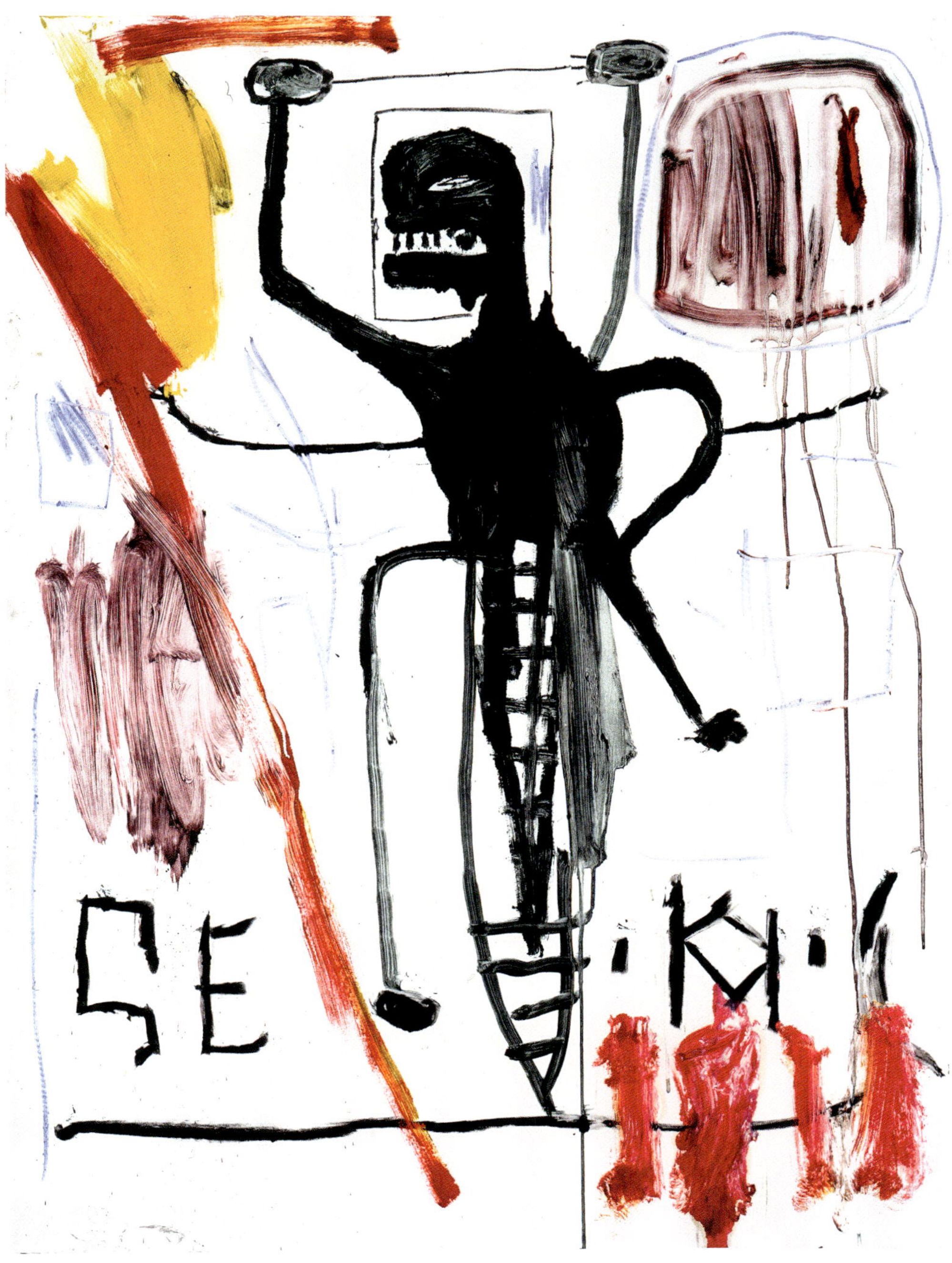

Untitled, 1986
Monotype: typographic ink on paper,
137 x 99 cm / 54 x 39 inches

Pages 424/425: **Untitled**, 1986
Acrylic, oilstick, graphite, and photocopy collage
on paper, 76 x 105.5 cm / 30 x 41 ¹/₂ inches

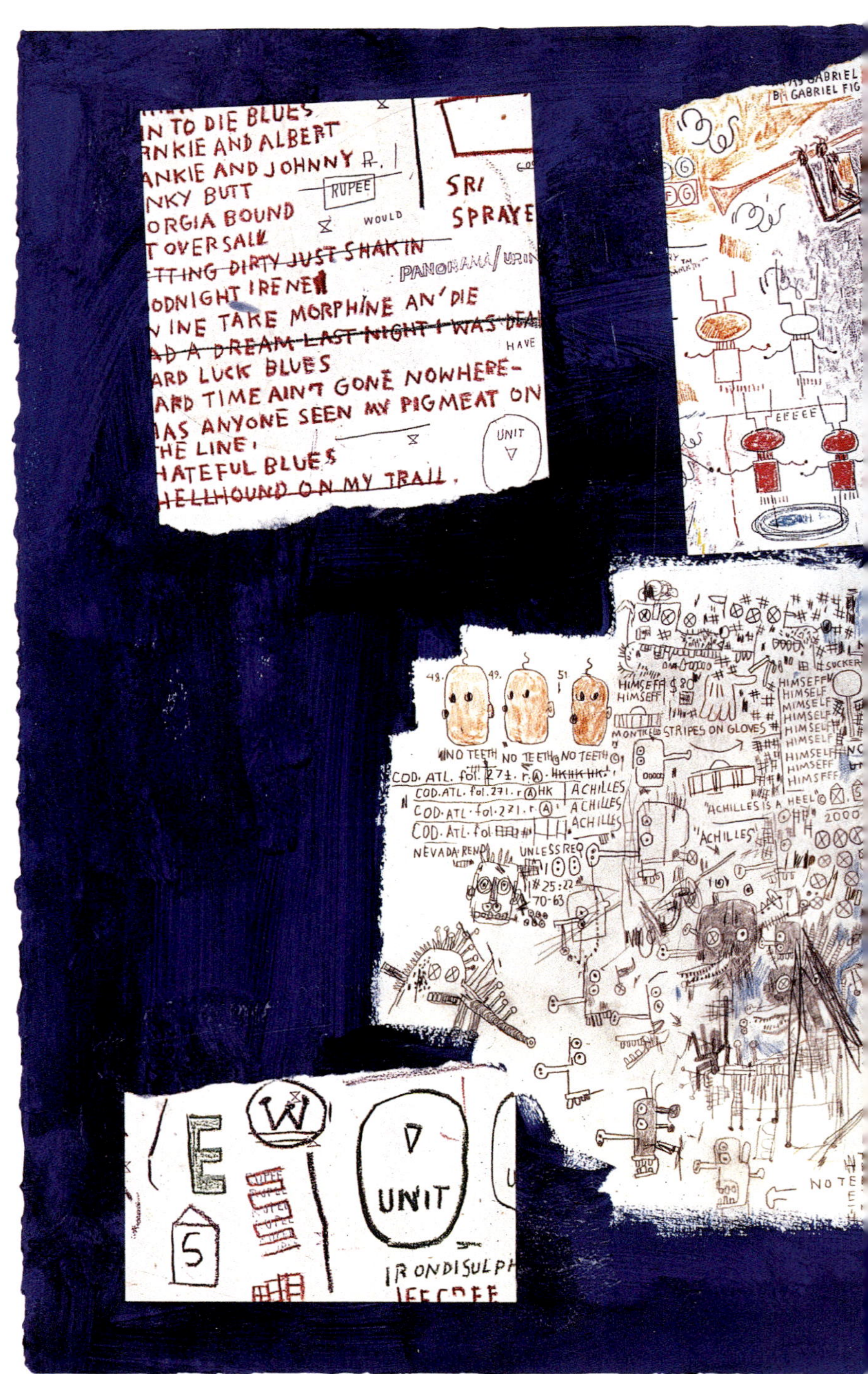
IN TO DIE BLUES
RNKIE AND ALBERT
ANKIE AND JOHNNY
NKY BUTT
ORGIA BOUND
T OVER SALT
TTING DIRTY JUST SHAKIN
ODNIGHT IRENE
N INE TAKE MORPHINE AN' DIE
AD A DREAM LAST NIGHT I WAS DEAD
ARD LUCK BLUES
ARD TIME AIN'T GONE NOWHERE —
AS ANYONE SEEN MY PIGMEAT ON
HE LINE
HATEFUL BLUES
HELLHOUND ON MY TRAIL
RUPEE
WOULD
SRI
SPRAYE
PANORAMA / URIN
HAVE
UNIT
NO TEETH NO TEETH NO TEETH
COD. ATL. fol. 271. r. A. HKHK HK
COD. ATL. fol. 271. r A HK ACHILLES
COD. ATL. fol. 271. r A ACHILLES
COD. ATL. fol A ACHILLES
NEVADA RENO UNLESS REQ
25:22
70-63
HIMSEFF $ 80
HIMSELF
MONTICLLO STRIPES ON GLOVES
SUCKER
HIMSEFF
HIMSELF
HIMSELF
HIMSELF
HIMSELF
HIMSELF
HIMSELFF
HIMSEFF
HIMSFFF
"ACHILLES IS A HEEL"
"ACHILLES"
2000
NOTE
E
W
5
UNIT
IRONDISULPH

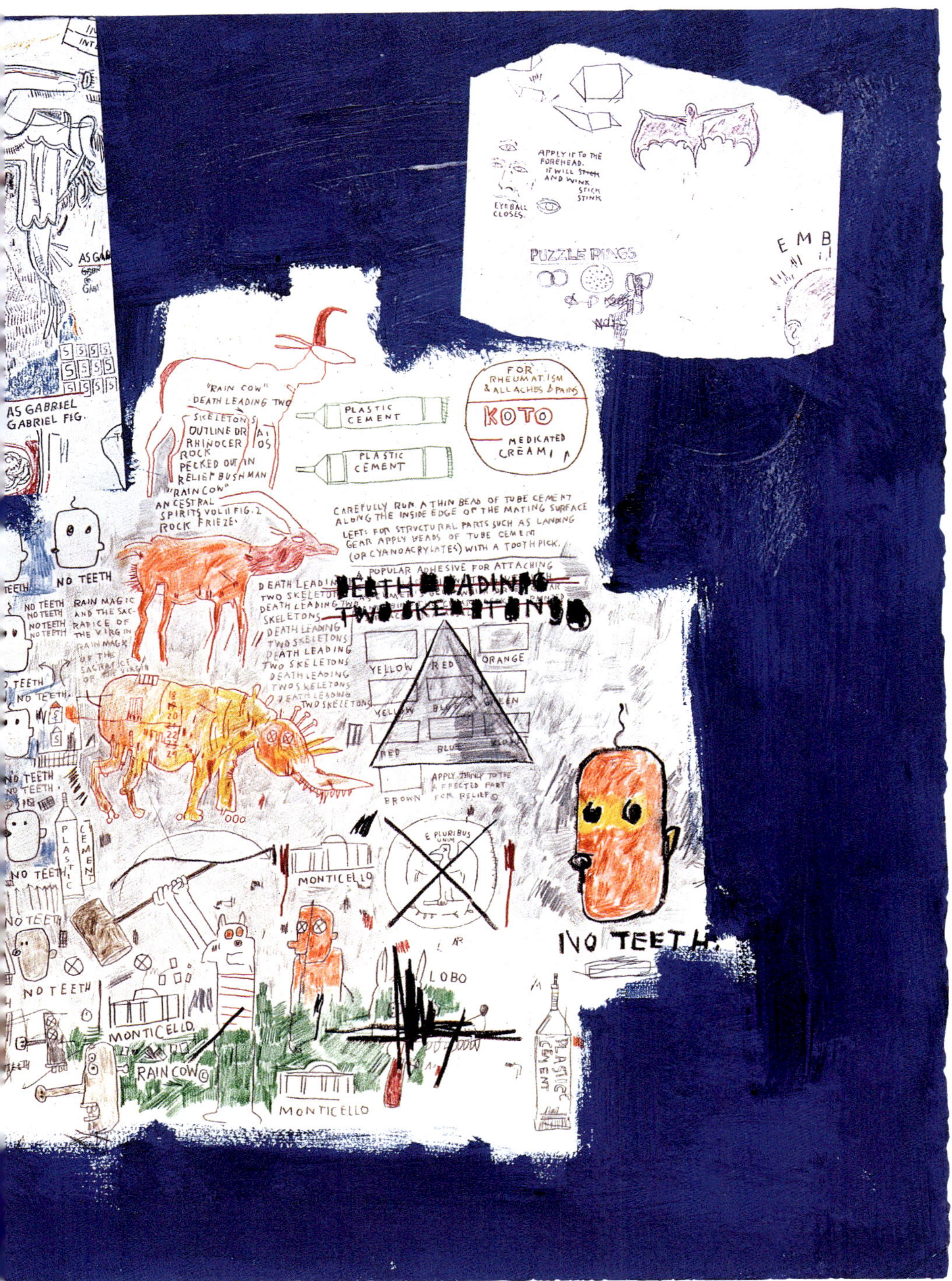
APPLY IT TO THE FOREHEAD.
IT WILL STICK
AND WINK
STICK
STINK
EYEBALL CLOSES.
PUZZLE RINGS
E M B
AS GABRIEL
GABRIEL FIG.
"RAIN COW"
DEATH LEADING TWO
SKELETONS
OUTLINE DR
RHINOCER
ROCK
PECKED OUT IN
RELIEF BUSHMAN
"RAIN COW"
ANCESTRAL
SPIRITS VOL.II FIG.2
ROCK FRIEZE
AI
OS
PLASTIC CEMENT
PLASTIC CEMENT
FOR
RHEUMATISM
& ALL ACHES & PAINS
KOTO
MEDICATED
CREAM
CAREFULLY RUN A THIN BEAD OF TUBE CEMENT
ALONG THE INSIDE EDGE OF THE MATING SURFACE
LEFT: FOR STRUCTURAL PARTS SUCH AS LANDING
GEAR APPLY BEADS OF TUBE CEMENT
(OR CYANOACRYLATES) WITH A TOOTH PICK.
A POPULAR ADHESIVE FOR ATTACHING
DEATH LEADING
TWO SKELETONS
DEATH LEADING TWO
SKELETONS
DEATH LEADING
TWO SKELETONS
DEATH LEADING
TWO SKELETONS
DEATH LEADING
TWO SKELETONS
DEATH LEADING
TWO SKELETONS
DEATH LEADING TWO SKELETONS
NO TEETH
NO TEETH
NO TEETH
RAIN MAGIC
AND THE SAC
RAFICE OF
THE VIRGIN
RAIN MAGIC
OF THE
SACRIFICE
OF VIRGIN
NO TEETH
NO TEETH
NO TEETH
YELLOW
RED
ORANGE
YELLOW
GREEN
RED
BLUE
BROWN
APPLY THINLY TO THE
AFFECTED PART FOR RELIEF
E PLURIBUS
UNUM
MONTICELLO
LOBO
NO TEETH
NO TEETH
PLASTIC CEMENT
NO TEETH
MONTICELLO
RAIN COW
MONTICELLO
PLASTIC CEMENT

To Repel Ghosts, 1986
Acrylic on wood, 112 x 83 x 10 cm /
44 x 32 ³/₄ x 4 inches

Pages 428/429: **Embittered**, 1986
Acrylic, graphite, photocopy collage, and
wood collage on panel, 125.5 x 184 x 30 cm /
49 ¹/₂ x 72 ¹/₂ x 11 ³/₄ inches

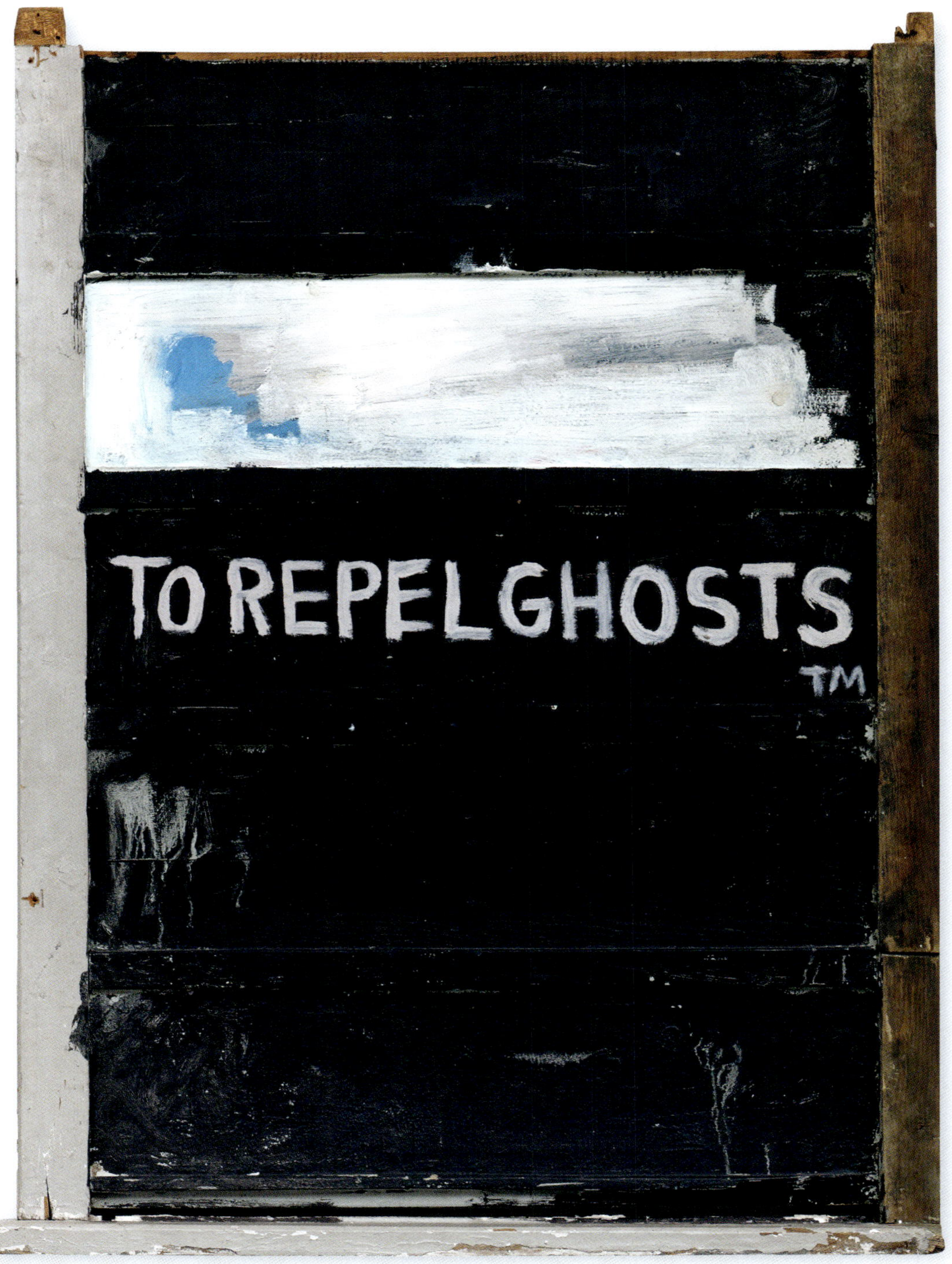
TO REPEL GHOSTS
TM

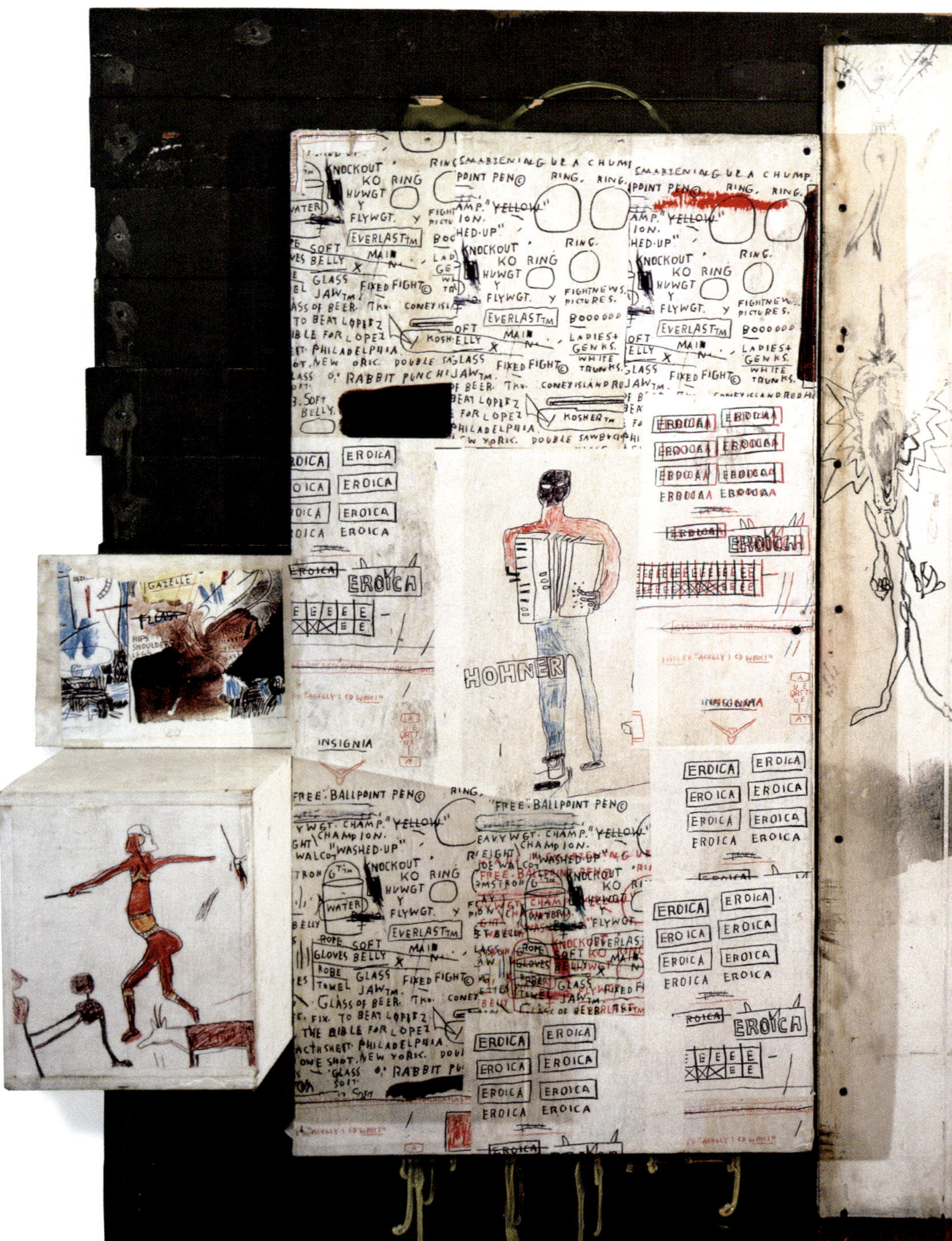

EROICA
HOHNER
INSIGNIA
GAZELLE
FREE BALLPOINT PEN
EVERLAST
KNOCKOUT
KO RING

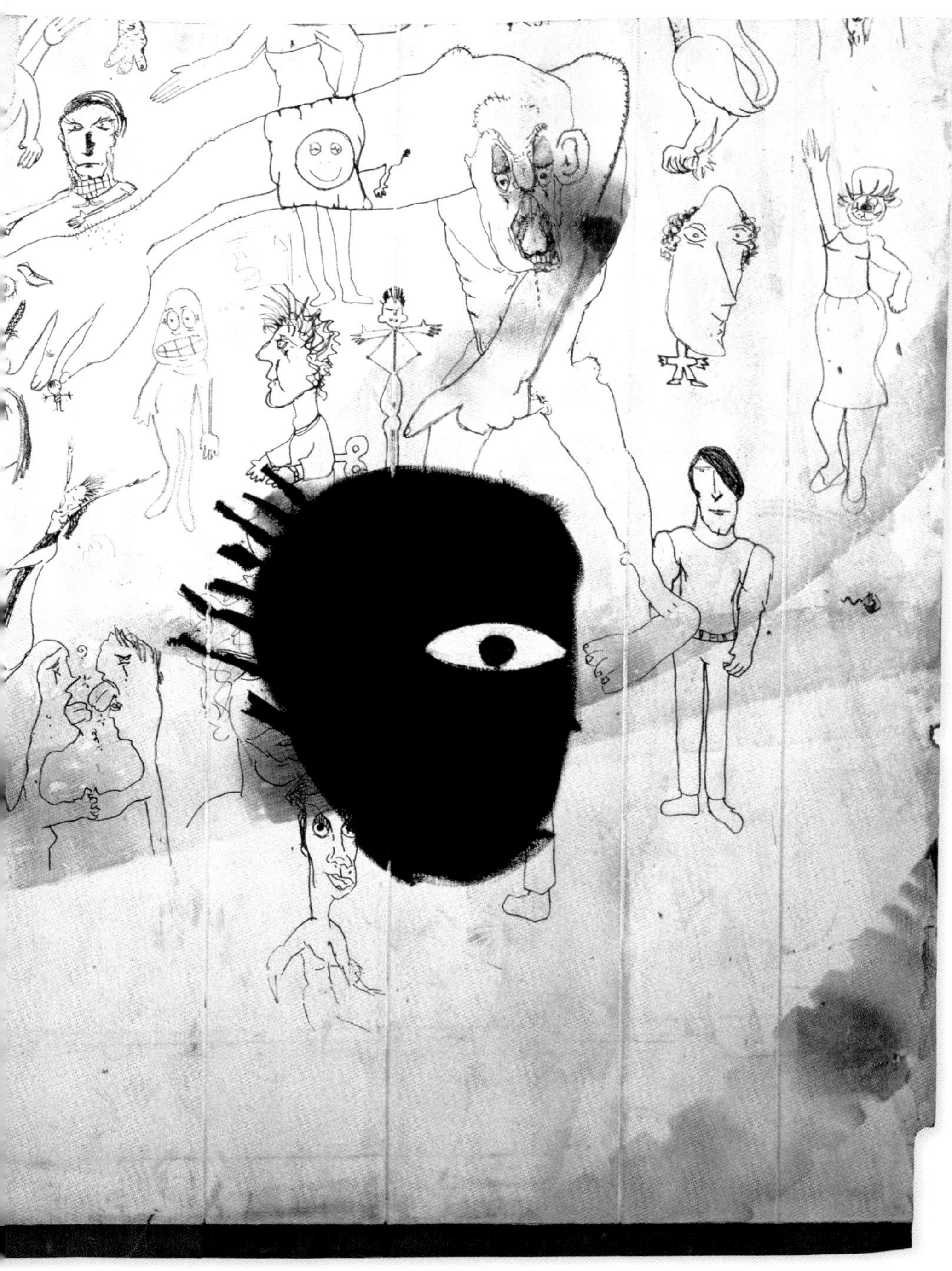

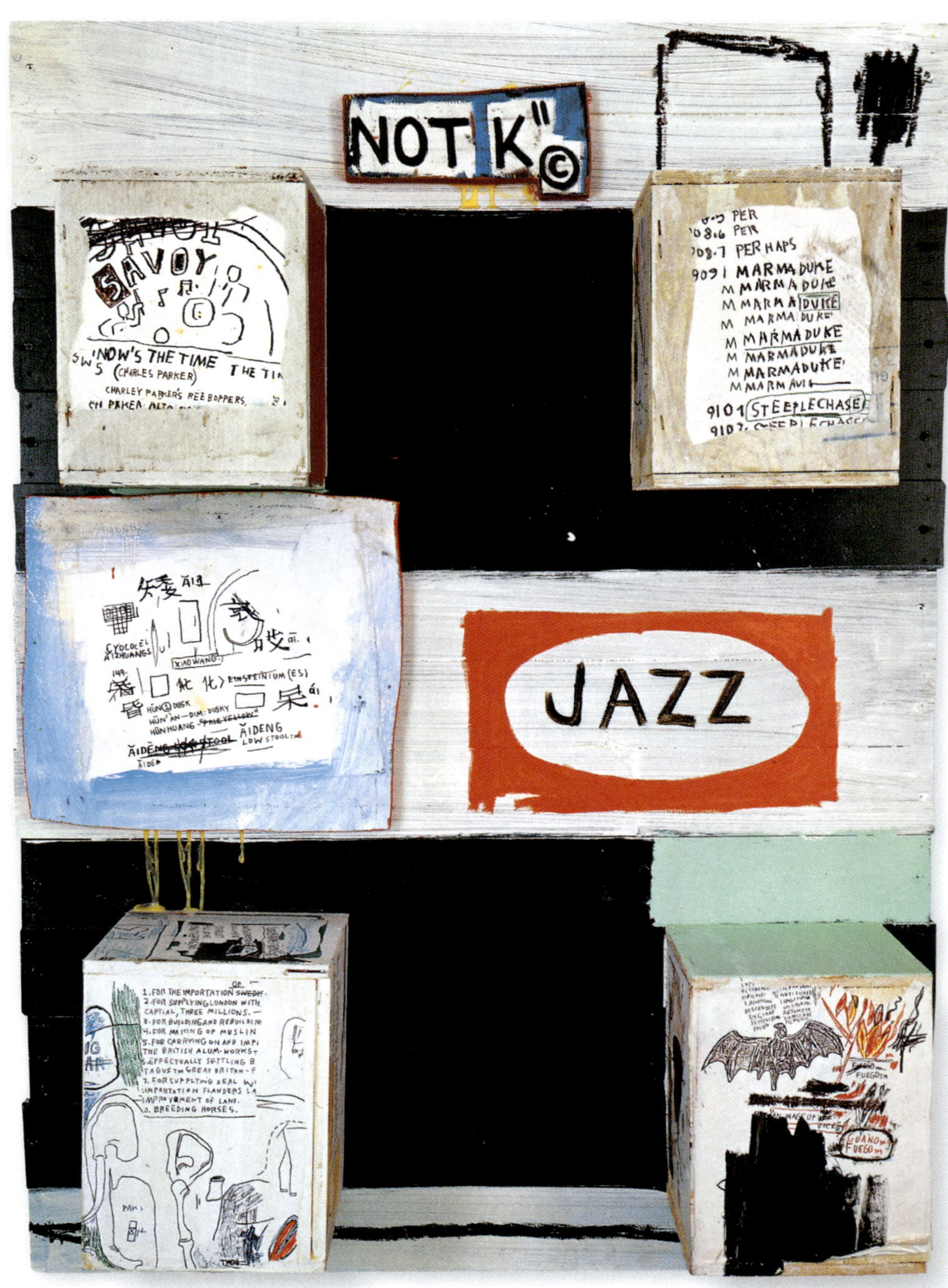

Jazz, 1986
Acrylic, oilstick, photocopy collage, and wood collage
on panel, 127 x 92 x 21.5 cm / 50 x 36 $\frac{1}{4}$ x 8 $\frac{1}{2}$ inches

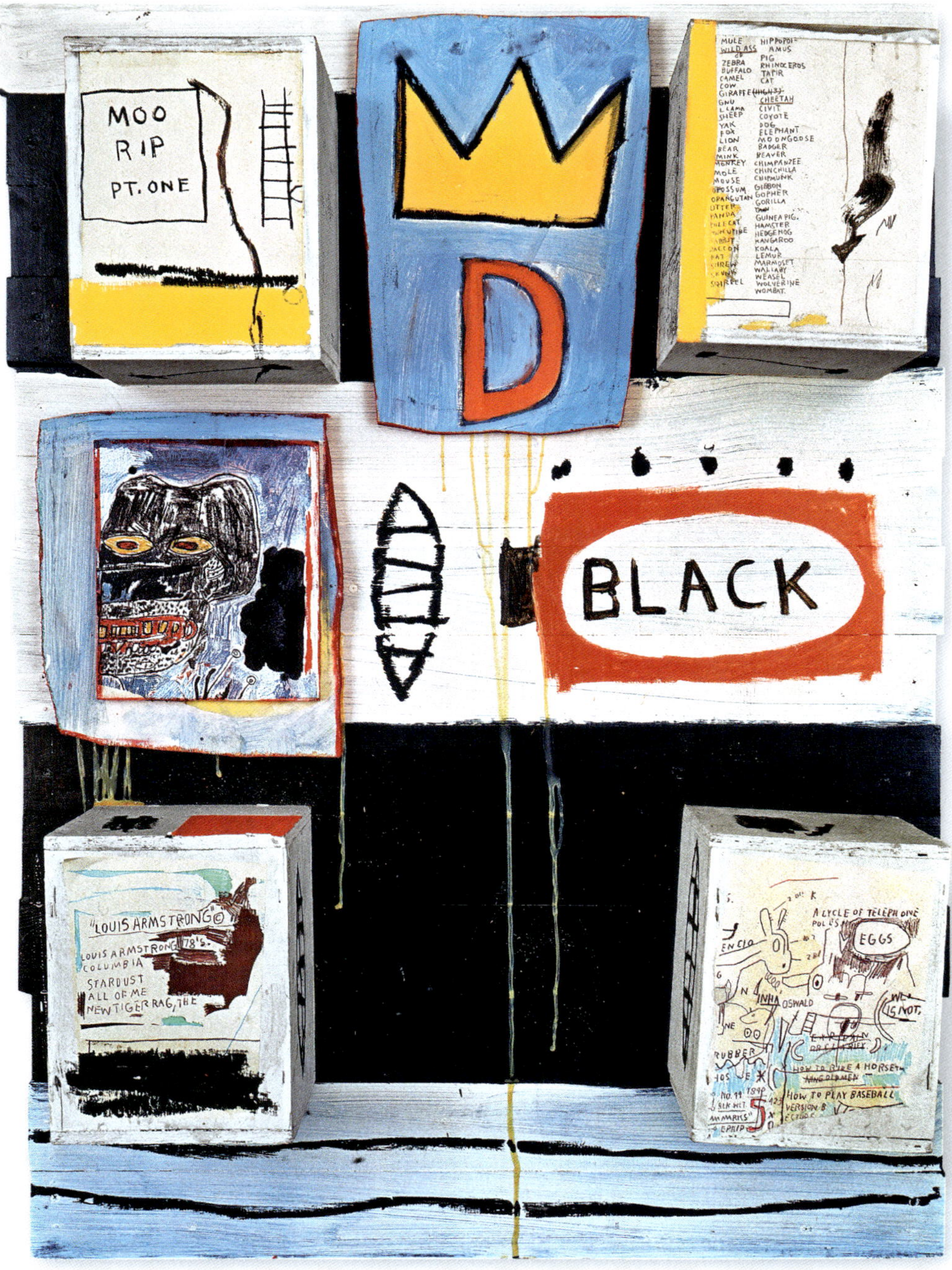

Black, 1986
Acrylic, oilstick, photocopy collage, and wood collage
on panel, 127 x 92 x 21.5 cm / 50 x 36 $\frac{1}{4}$ x 8 $\frac{1}{2}$ inches

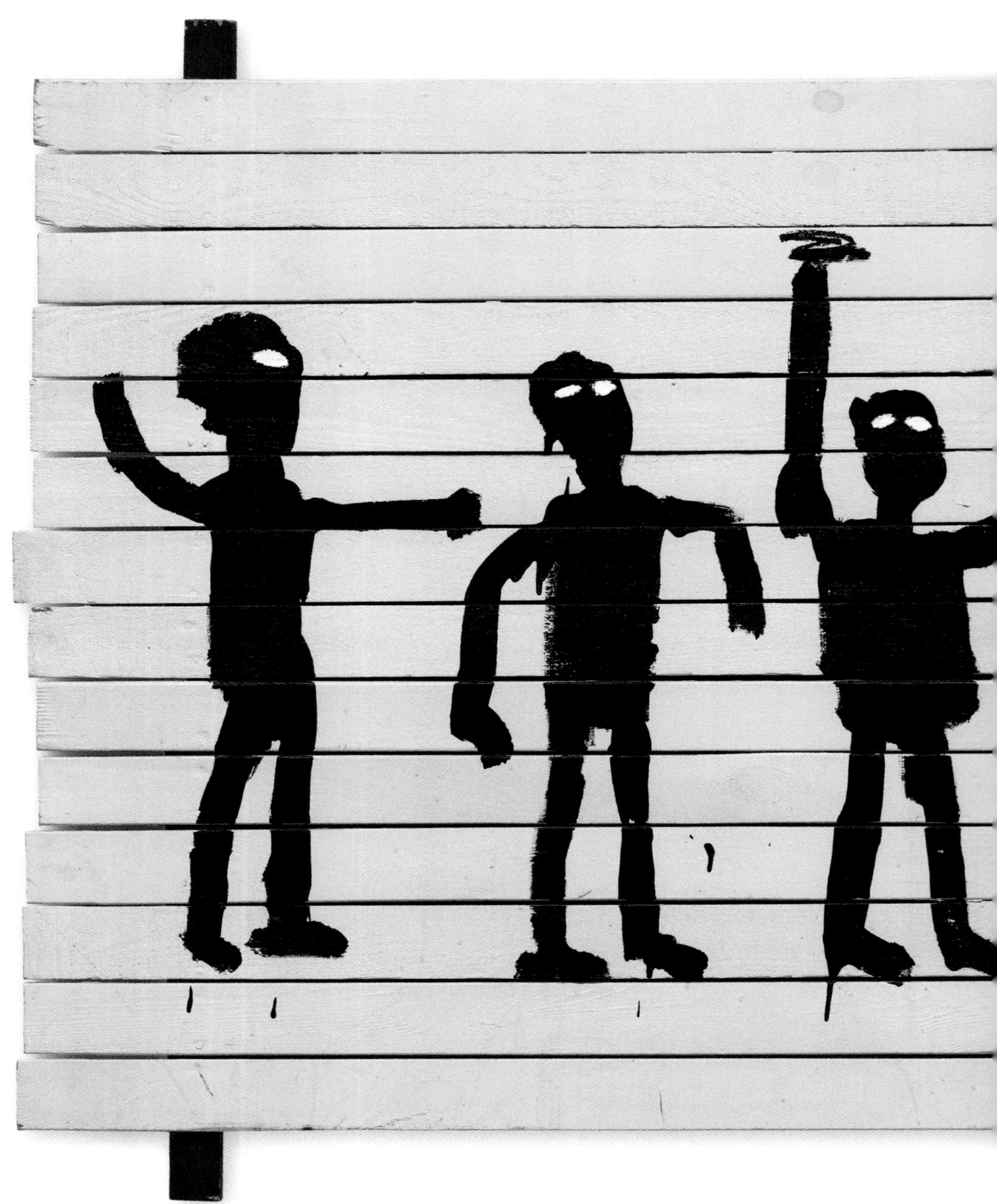

Procession, 1986
Acrylic and wood relief on wood,
162 x 244 cm / 63 ³/₄ x 96 inches

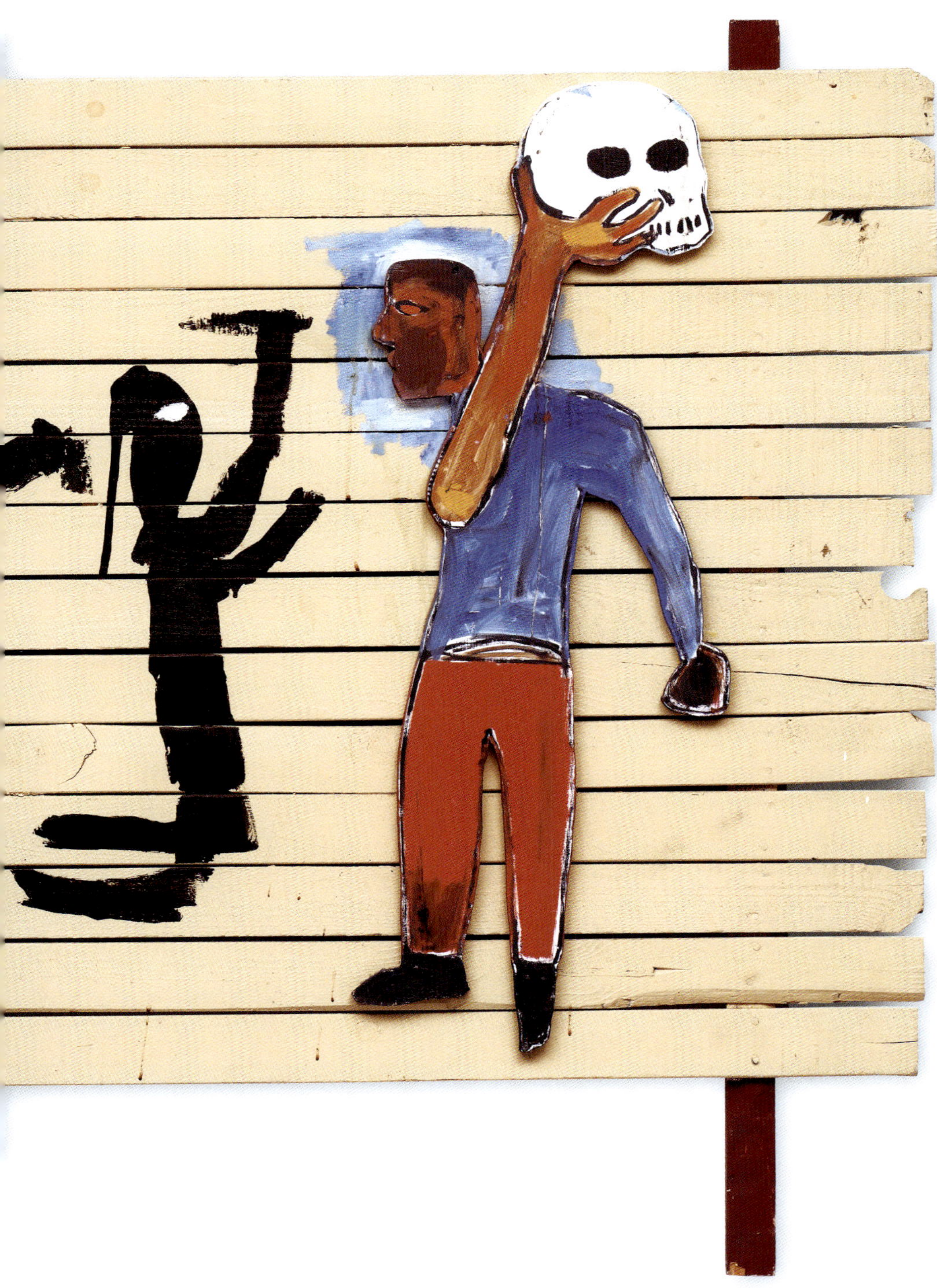

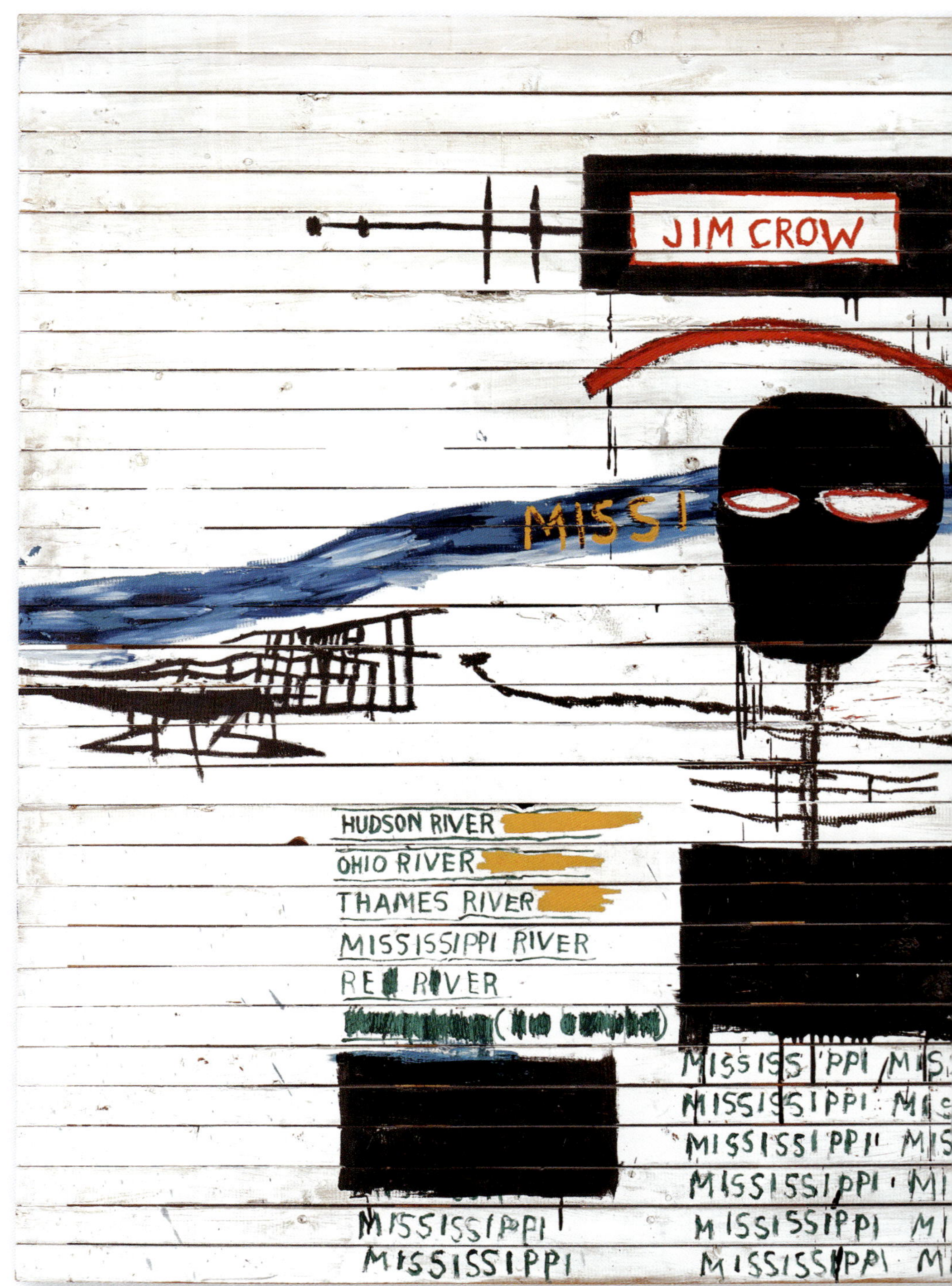
JIM CROW
MISSI
HUDSON RIVER
OHIO RIVER
THAMES RIVER
MISSISSIPPI RIVER
RED RIVER
MISSISSIPPI
MISSISSIPPI
MISSISSIPPI
MISSISSIPPI
MISSISSIPPI
MISSISSIPPI
MISSISSIPPI
MISSISSIPPI
MISSISSIPPI
MISSISSIPPI
MISSISSIPPI
MISSISSIPPI

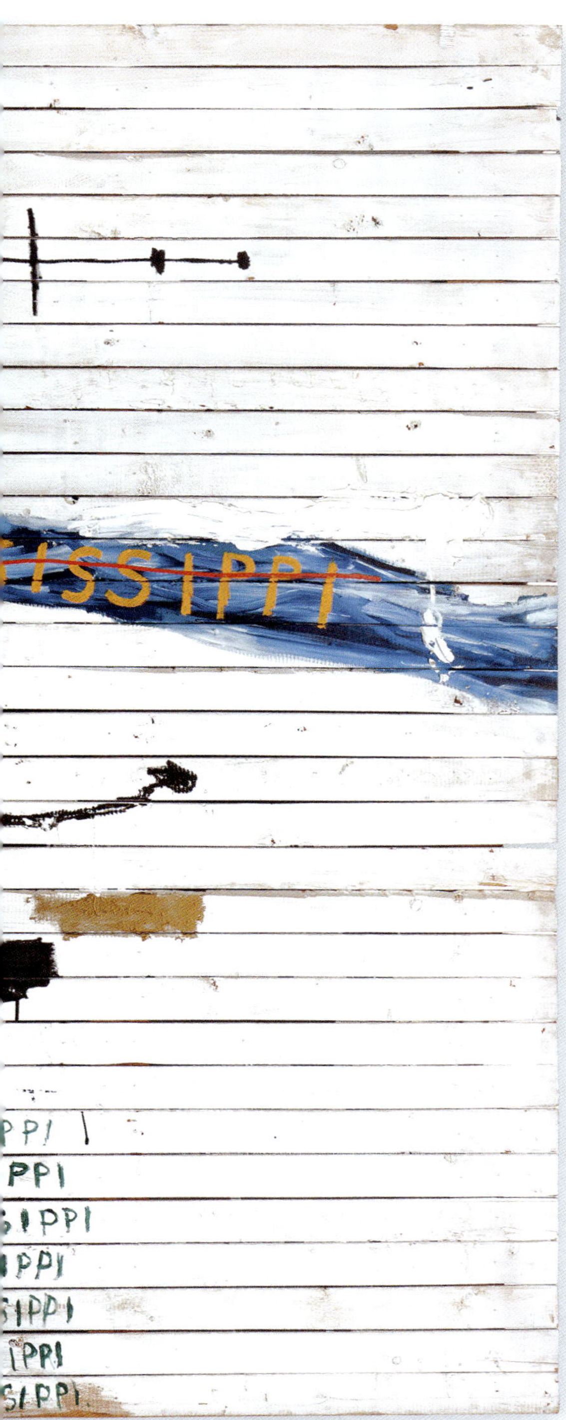

Jim Crow, 1986
Acrylic and oilstick on wood,
206 x 244 cm / 81 x 96 inches

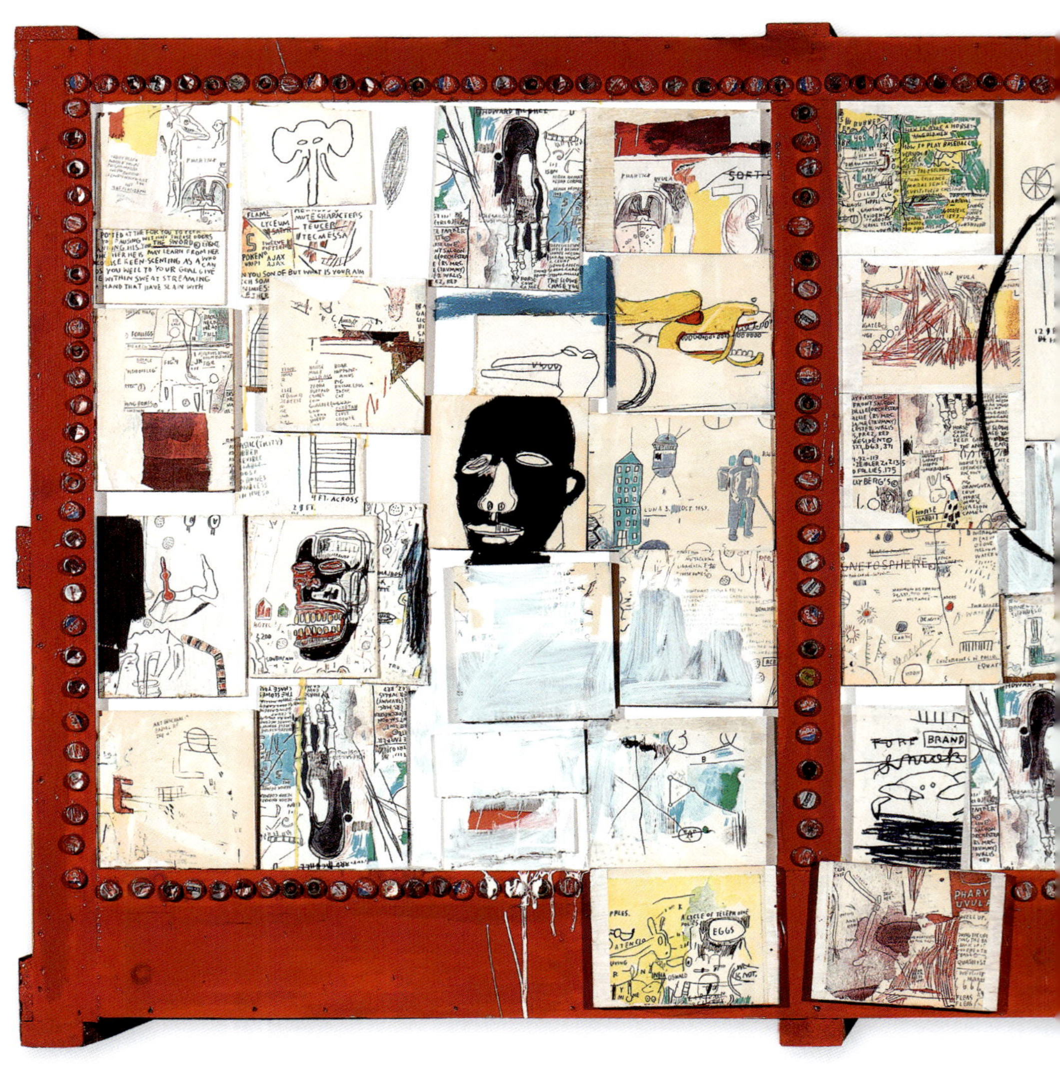

Negro Period, 1986
Acrylic, oil, photocopy collage,
and crown cork on wood, diptych:
144 x 306 x 16.5 cm / 56 ³/₄ x 120 ¹/₂ x 6 ¹/₄ inches

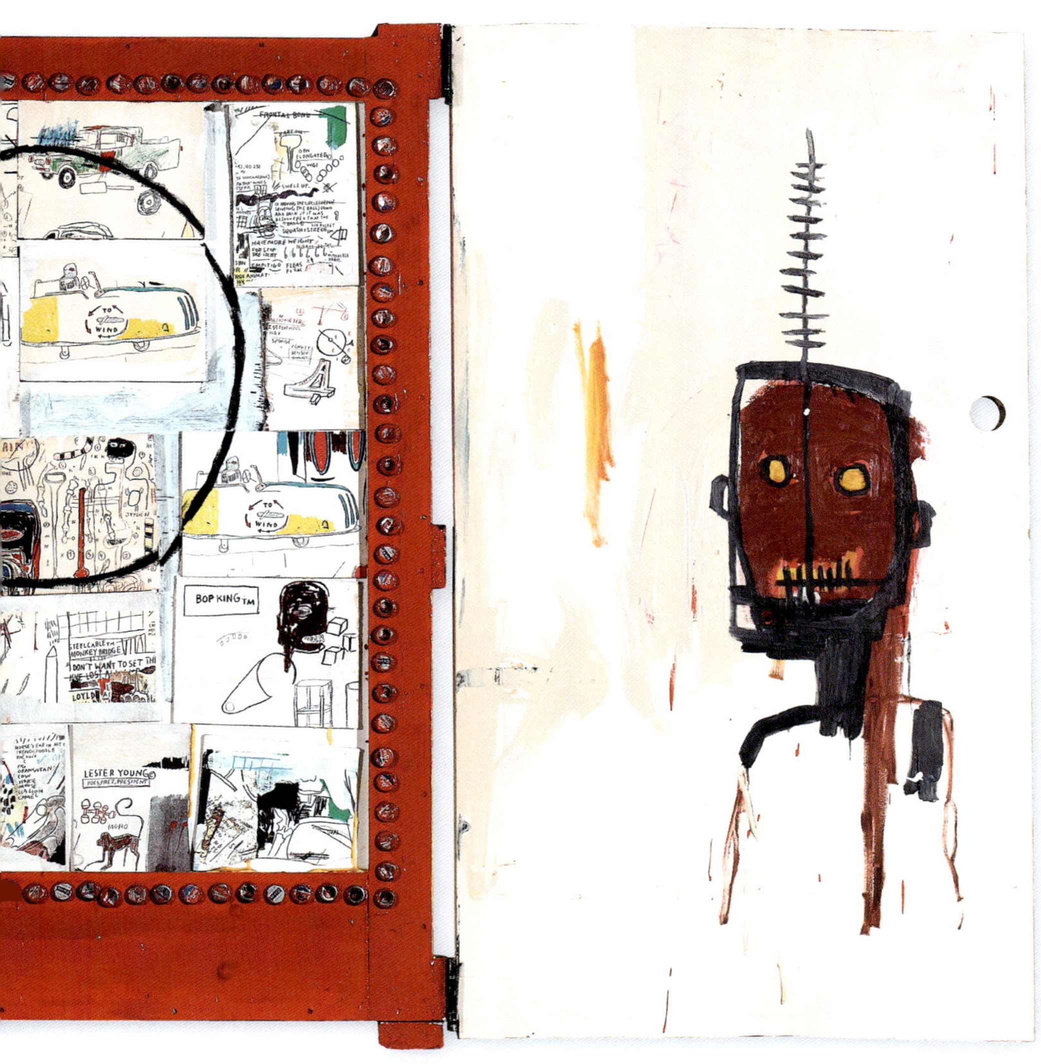

Pages 438/439: **Worthy Constituents**, 1986
Acrylic, oilstick, coffee, and photocopy collage
on canvas, 70 x 90 cm / 27 $^{1}/_{2}$ x 35 $^{1}/_{2}$ inches

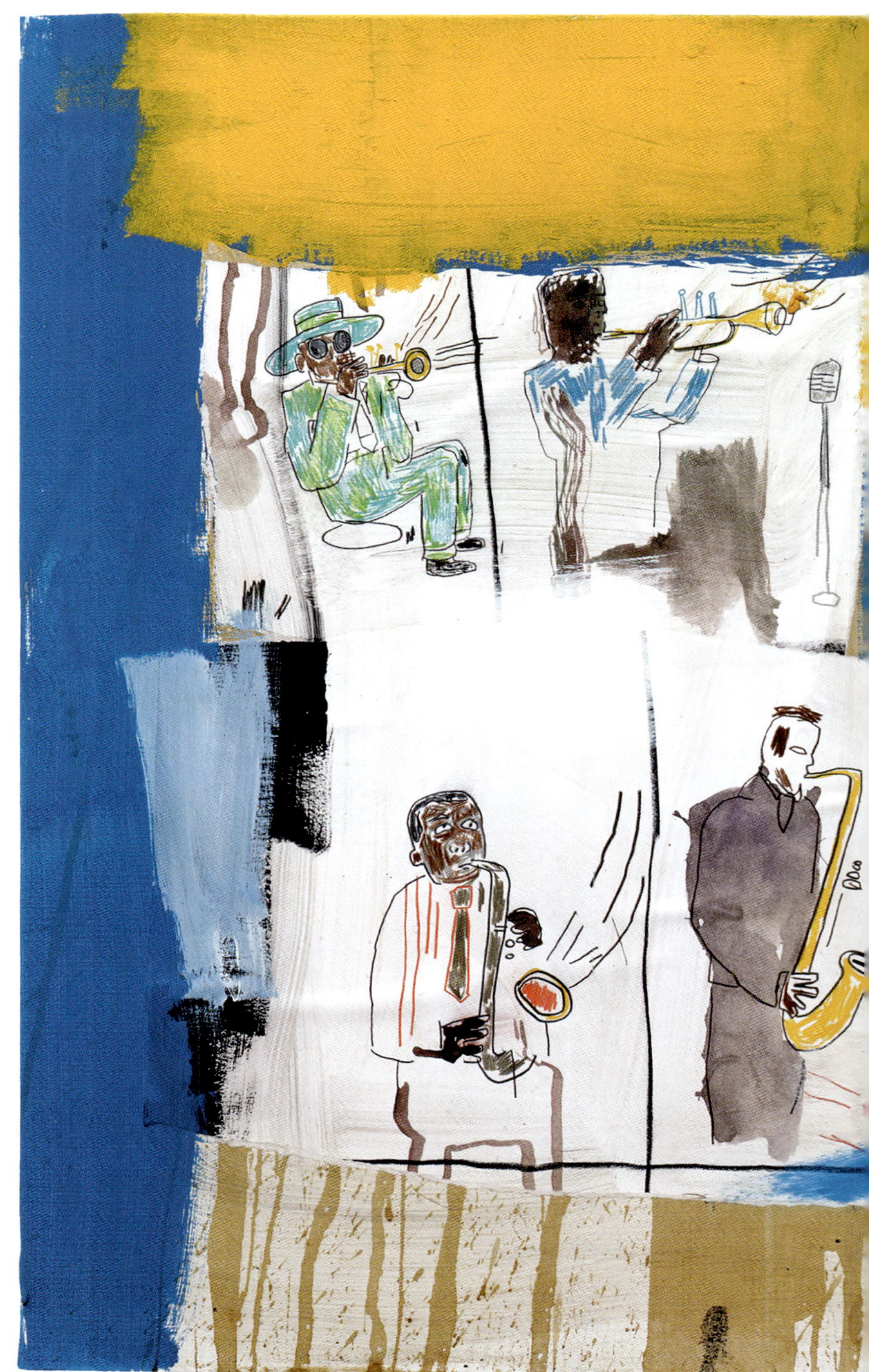

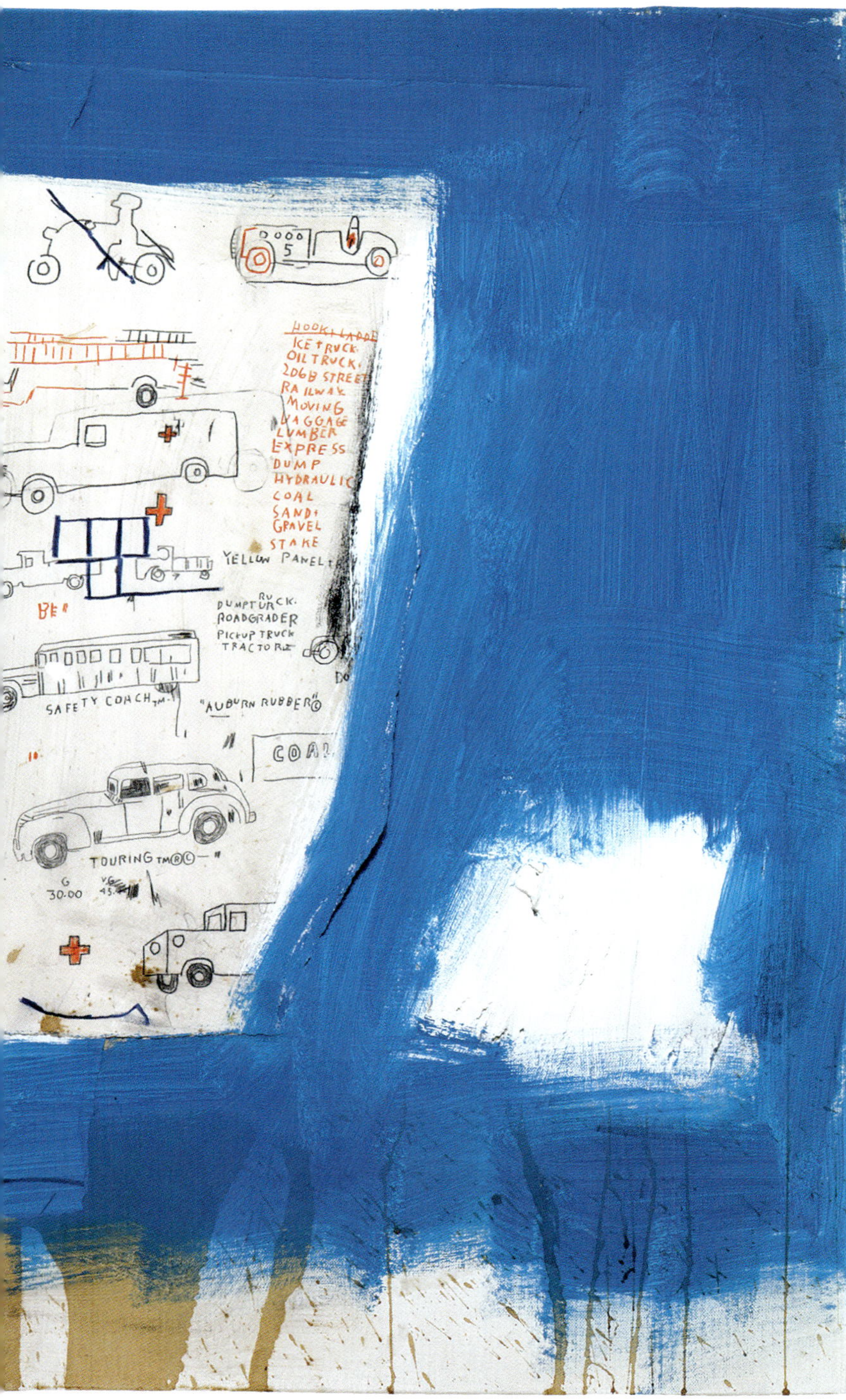
HOOK + LADDE
ICE TRUCK.
OIL TRUCK.
206B STREET
RAILWAY
MOVING
BAGGAGE
LUMBER
EXPRESS
DUMP
HYDRAULIC
COAL
SAND +
GRAVEL
STAKE
YELLOW PANEL +
RV
DUMP TRUCK.
ROADGRADER
PICKUP TRUCK
TRACTOR
SAFETY COACH, TM.
"AUBURN RUBBER"
COAL
TOURING TM R L
G
30.00
VG
45.
BE

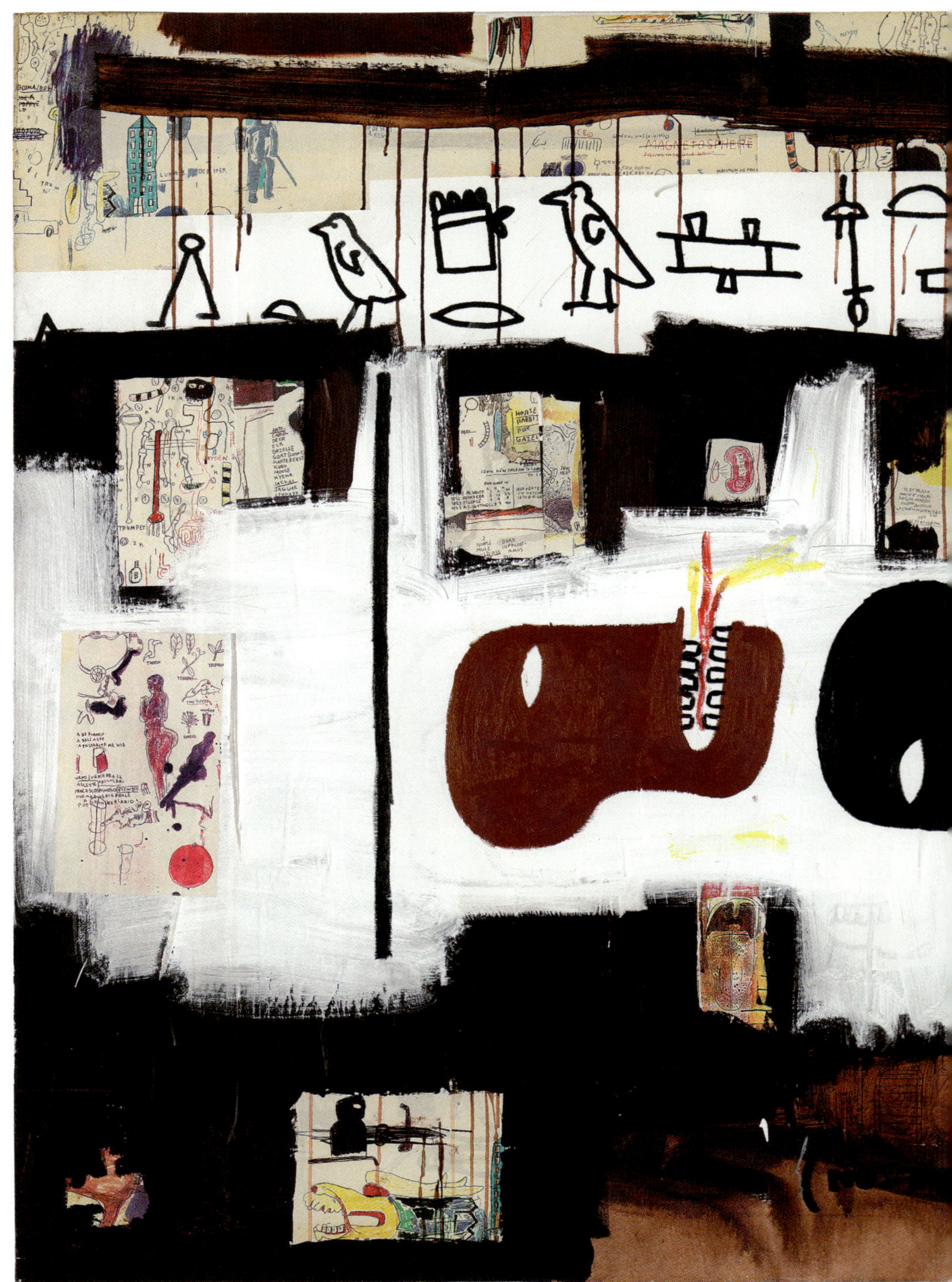

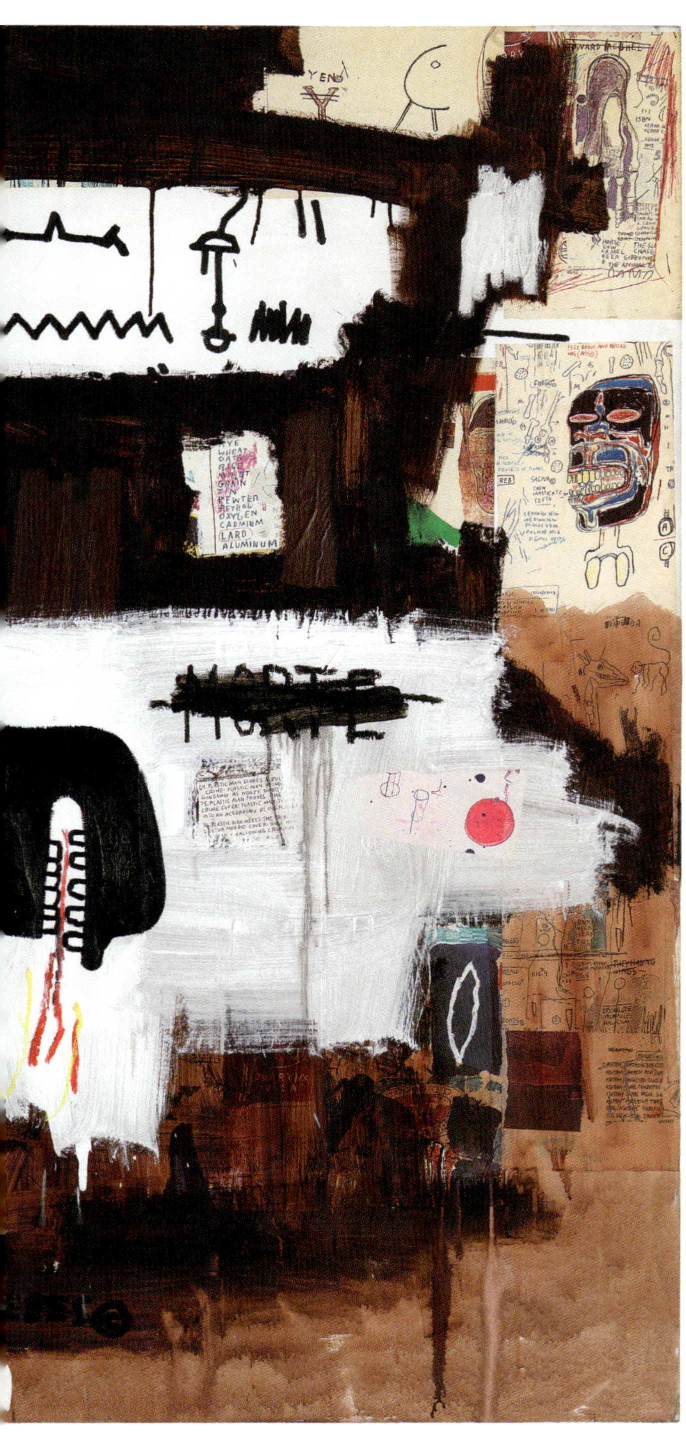

Dark Milk, 1986
Acrylic, oilstick, photocopy
collage, and paper collage on
canvas, 172.5 x 219.5 cm /
68 x 86 ¹/₂ inches

Pages 442/443: **Self-Portrait**, 1986
Acrylic on canvas,
178 x 251.5 cm / 70 x 99 inches

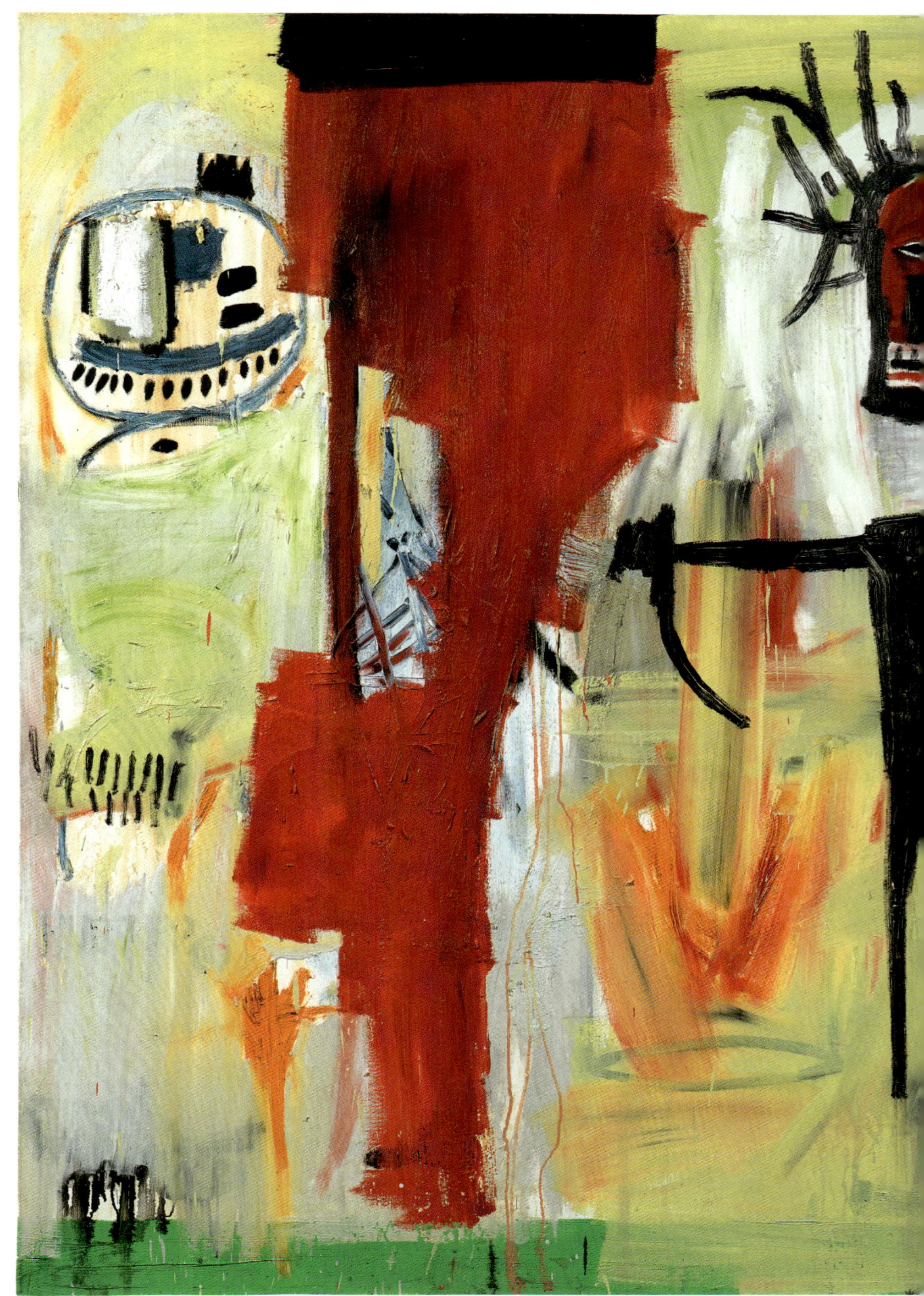

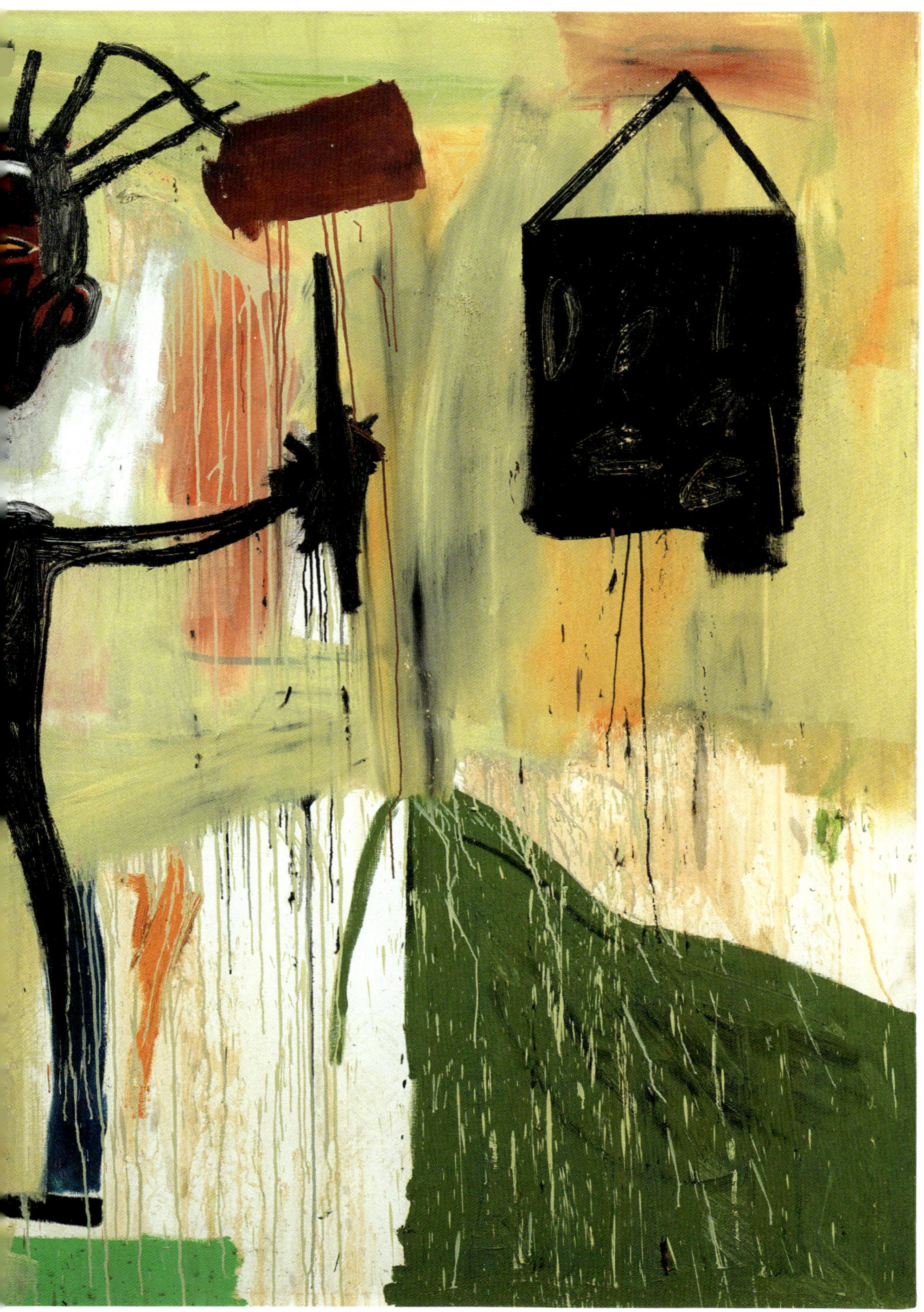

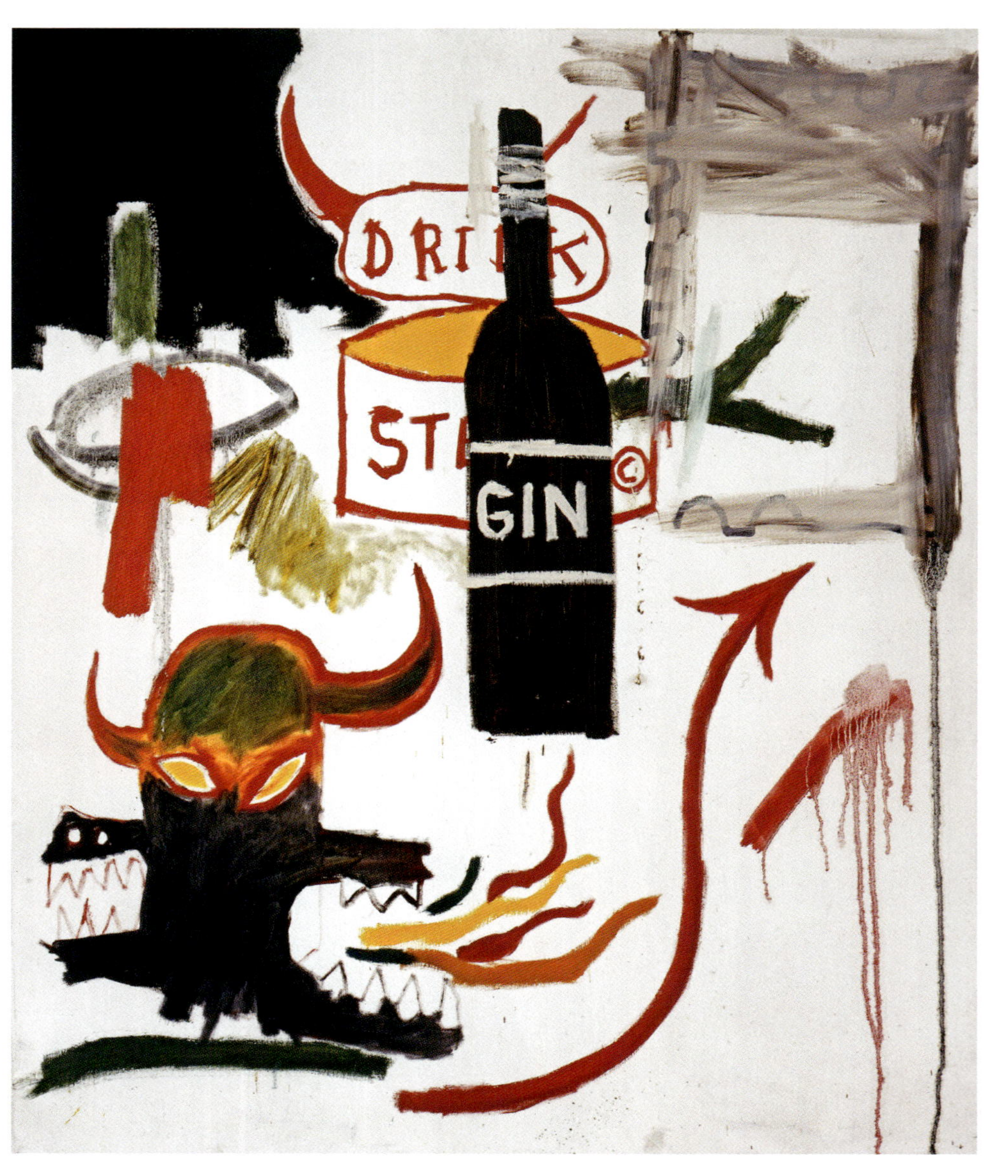

Sterno, 1986
Acrylic on canvas, 119 x 100.5 cm /
46 ³/₄ x 39 ¹/₂ inches

Because It Hurts the Lungs, 1986
Acrylic, oil, oilstick, and photocopy collage on wood,
183 x 107 x 22 cm / 72 x 42 ¹/₄ x 8 ³/₄ inches

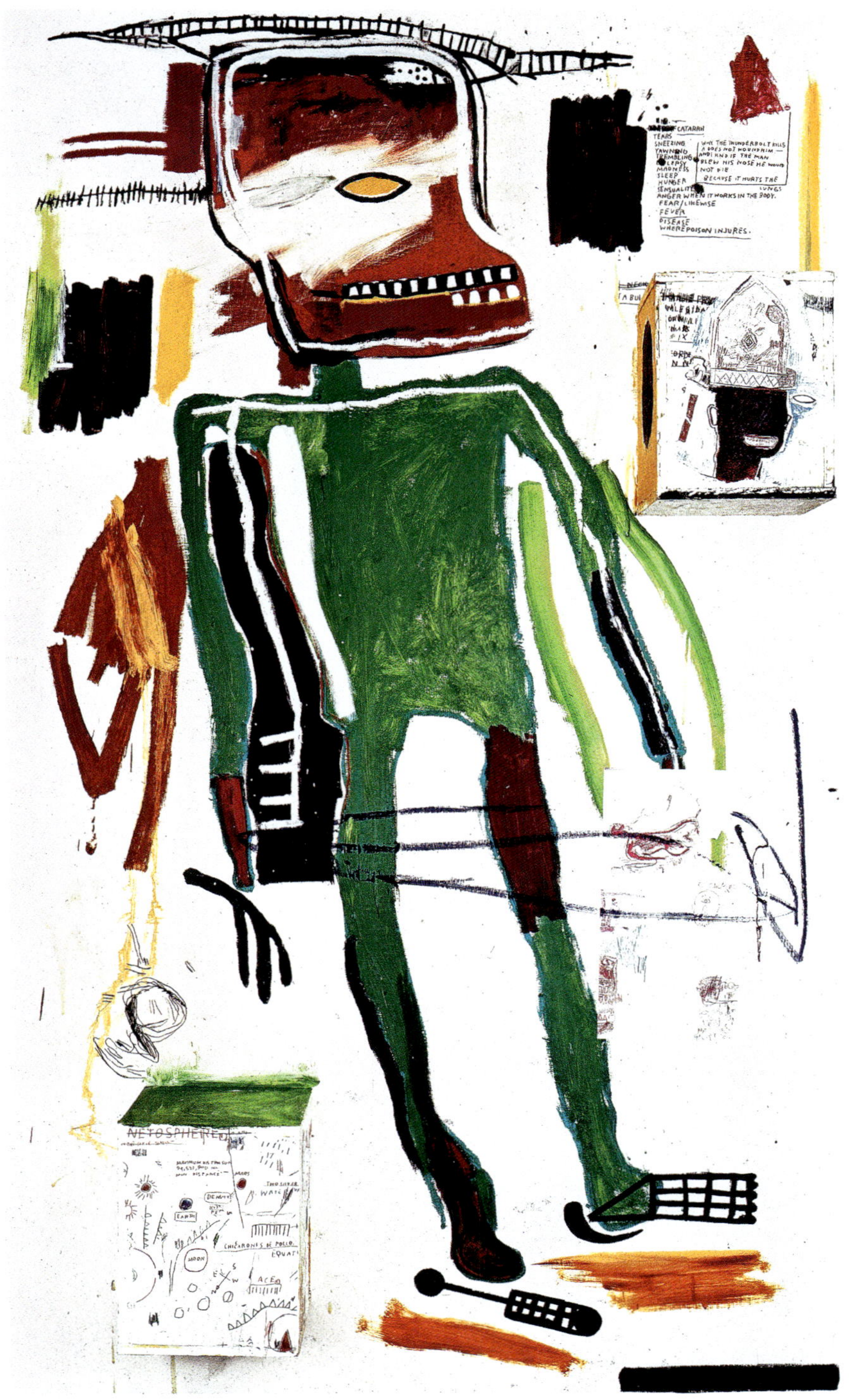

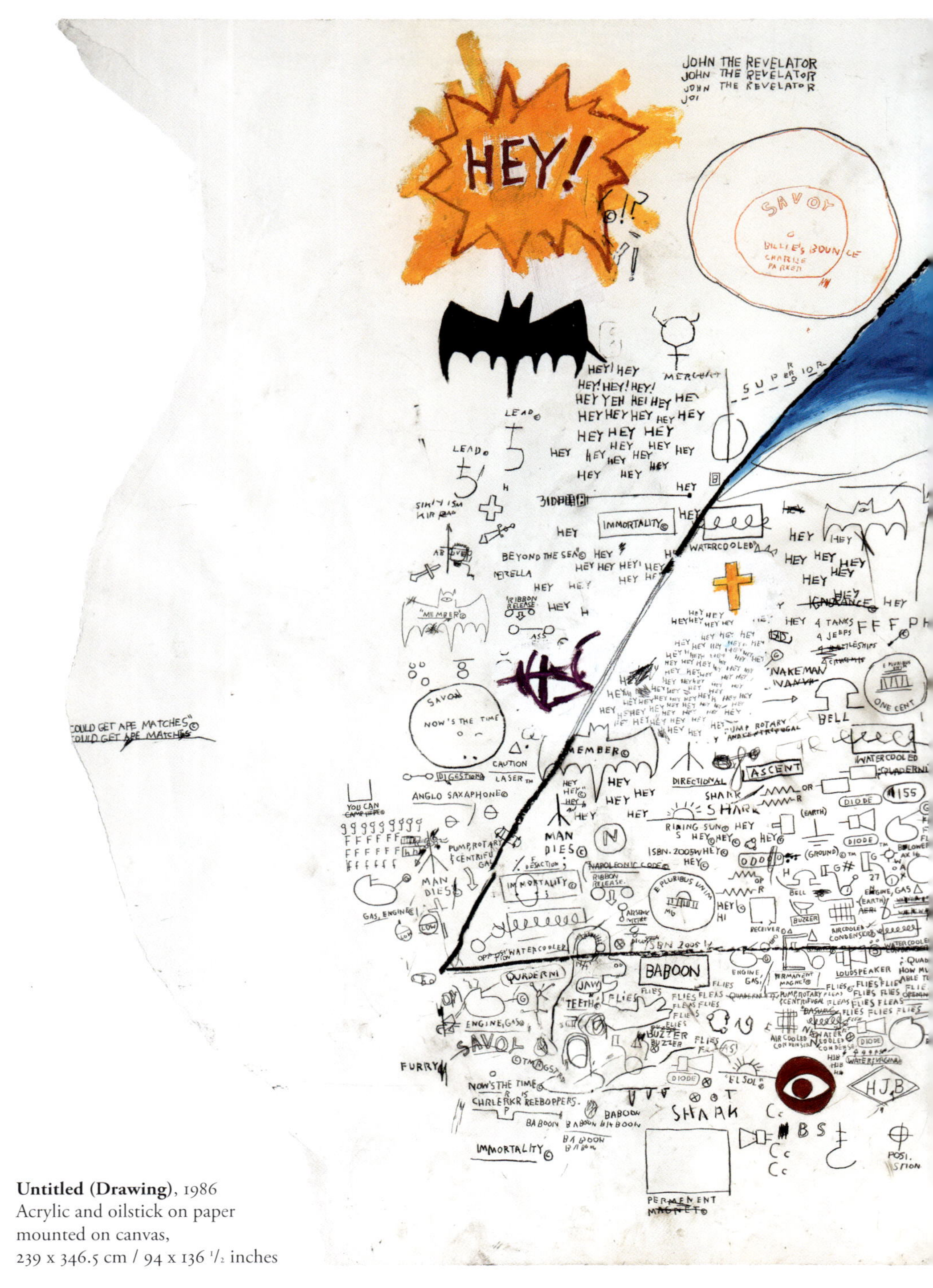

Untitled (Drawing), 1986
Acrylic and oilstick on paper
mounted on canvas,
239 x 346.5 cm / 94 x 136 ¹/₂ inches

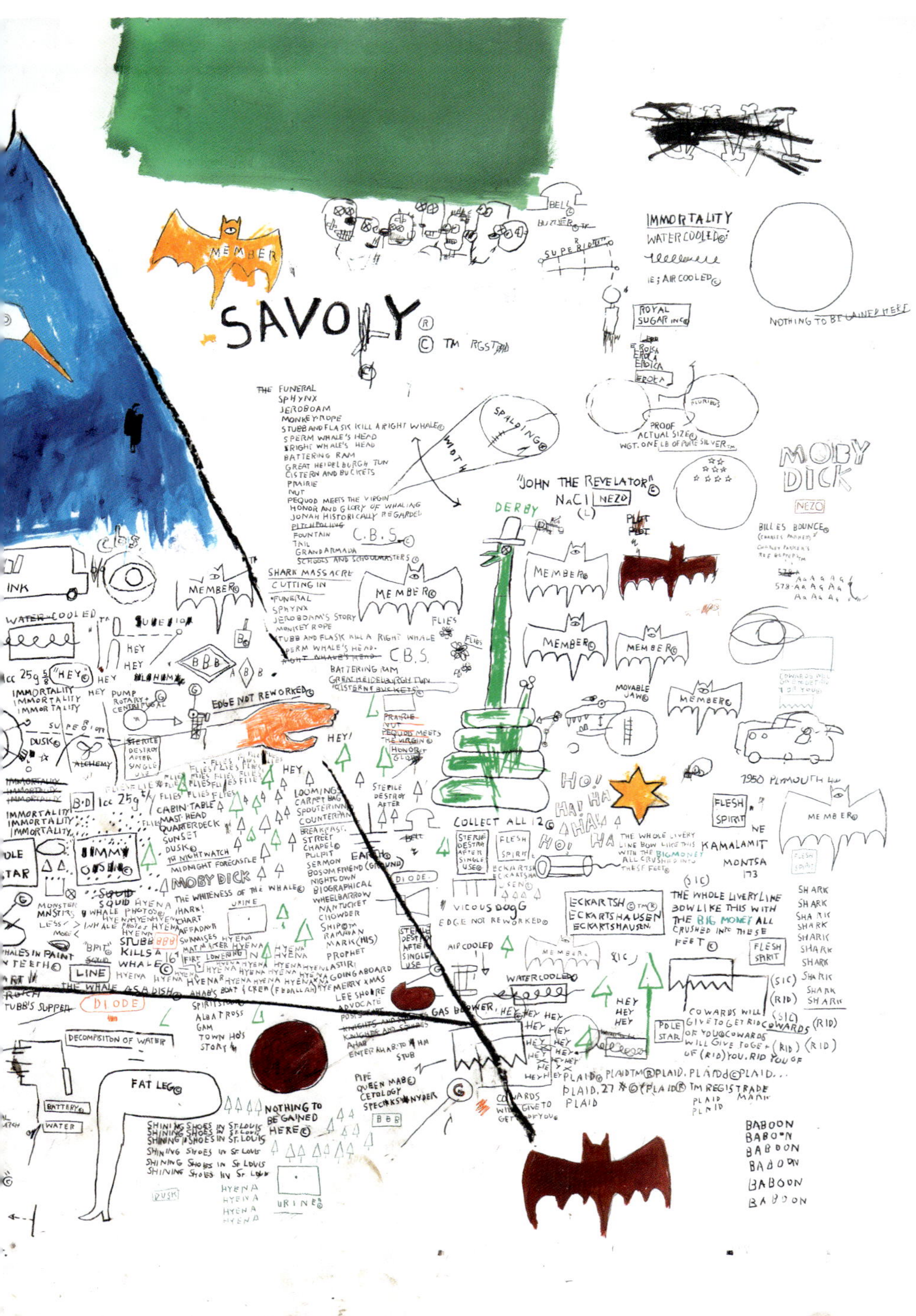

MEMBER
SAVOY ® © TM RGSTRD
IMMORTALITY
WATER COOLED ©
IE; AIR COOLED ©
NOTHING TO BE GAINED HERE
ROYAL SUGAR INC ©
MOBY DICK
NEZO
BILLIE'S BOUNCE ©
THE FUNERAL
SPHYNX
JEROBOAM
MONKEY ROPE
STUBB AND FLASK KILL A RIGHT WHALE ©
SPERM WHALE'S HEAD
RIGHT WHALE'S HEAD
BATTERING RAM
GREAT HEIDELBURGH TUN
CISTERN AND BUCKETS
PRAIRIE
NUT
PEQUOD MEETS THE VIRGIN
HONOR AND GLORY OF WHALING
JONAH HISTORICALLY REGARDED
PITCHPOLING
FOUNTAIN
TAIL
GRAND ARMADA
SCHOOLS AND SCHOOLMASTERS ©
"JOHN THE REVELATOR"
NaCl NEZO
DERBY
SPALDING
WIDTH
PROOF ACTUAL SIZE
WGT. ONE LB OF PURE SILVER TM
SHARK MASSACRE
CUTTING IN
FUNERAL
SPHYNX
JEROBOAM'S STORY
MONKEY ROPE
STUBB AND FLASK KILL A RIGHT WHALE
SPERM WHALE'S HEAD
RIGHT WHALE'S HEAD
C.B.S.
BATTERING RAM
GREAT HEIDELBURGH TUN
CISTERN BUCKETS ©
MEMBER ©
FLIES
INK
WATER-COOLED
SUPERIOR
HEY
IMMORTALITY
PUMP ROTARY + CENTRIFUGAL
EDGE NOT REWORKED ©
STERILE DESTROY AFTER SINGLE USE ©
ALCHEMY
DUSK ©
SUPERIOR
JIMMY OSEI
POLE STAR
SQUID
MONSTER MNSTRS
HYENA WHALE PHOTOS
STUBB KILLS A WHALE
FIRST LOWERING
HYENA
THE WHALE AS A DISH ©
TUBB'S SUPPER
DIODE
SPIRIT SPOUT
ALBATROSS
GAM
TOWN HO'S STORY
DECOMPISITON OF WATER
BATTERY
WATER
FAT LEG ©
SHINING SHOES IN ST. LOUIS
SHINING SHOES IN ST. LOUIS
SHINING SHOES IN ST. LOUIS
SHINING SHOES IN ST. LOUIS
SHINING SHOES IN ST. LOUIS
SHINING SHOES IN ST. LOUIS
HYENA
URINE ©
NOTHING TO BE GAINED HERE ©
QUEEN MABE
CETOLOGY
PIPE
MOBY DICK
THE WHITENESS OF THE WHALE ©
CABIN TABLE
MAST-HEAD
QUARTERDECK
SUNSET
DUSK ©
1ST NIGHTWATCH
MIDNIGHT FORECASTLE
LOOMING
CARPET BAG
SPOUTER INN
COUNTERPANE
BREAKFAST
STREET
CHAPEL
PULPIT
SERMON
BOSOM FRIEND
NIGHTGOWN
BIOGRAPHICAL
WHEELBARROW
NANTUCKET
CHOWDER
SHIP
RAMADAN
MARK (HIS)
PROPHET
GOING ABOARD
MERRY XMAS
LEE SHORE
ADVOCATE
KNIGHTS AND SQUIRES
AHAB
ENTER AHAB: TO HIM STUB
EARTH (GROUND)
BELL
DIODE
COLLECT ALL 12 ©
STERILE DESTROY AFTER SINGLE USE ©
FLESH SPIRIT
HO! HA! HA! HA! HO!
VICIOUS DOGG
EDGE NOT REWORKED ©
AIR COOLED ©
WATER COOLED ©
GAS BLOWER
HEY HEY HEY
ECKARTSHAUSEN
ECKARTSH © TM ©
ECKARTSHAUSEN
THE WHOLE LIVERY LINE BOW LIKE THIS WITH THE BIG MONEY ALL CRUSHED INTO THESE FEET ©
KAMALAMIT
MONTSA 173
1950 PLYMOUTH
FLESH SPIRIT
MEMBER ©
SHARK SHARK SHARK SHARK SHARK SHARK SHARK
(SIC) (SIC) (SIC)
(RID) (RID) (RID) (RID) (RID)
COWARDS WILL GIVE TO GET RID OF YOU
POLE STAR
HEY HEY HEY
PLAID PLAID TM ® PLAID. PLAID © PLAID...
PLAID, 27 & © PLAID ® TM REGISTRADE
BABOON
BABOON
BABOON
BABOON
BABOON
BABOON
MOVABLE JAW
MEMBER ©
FLESH SPIRIT

VIII

1987–1988
A Lifetime of Works

"Every aspect of his work seemed symbolic of his disdain for conformity, watching him paint, wielding his brush like a weapon, walking on piles of finished and unfinished drawings spread across the floor, the transformation of things found in the garbage into beautiful objets d'art, the 'almost' stretched canvases that he tied and nailed together. The supreme poet; every gesture symbolic, every action an event."

—KEITH HARING, *VOGUE*, 1988[1]

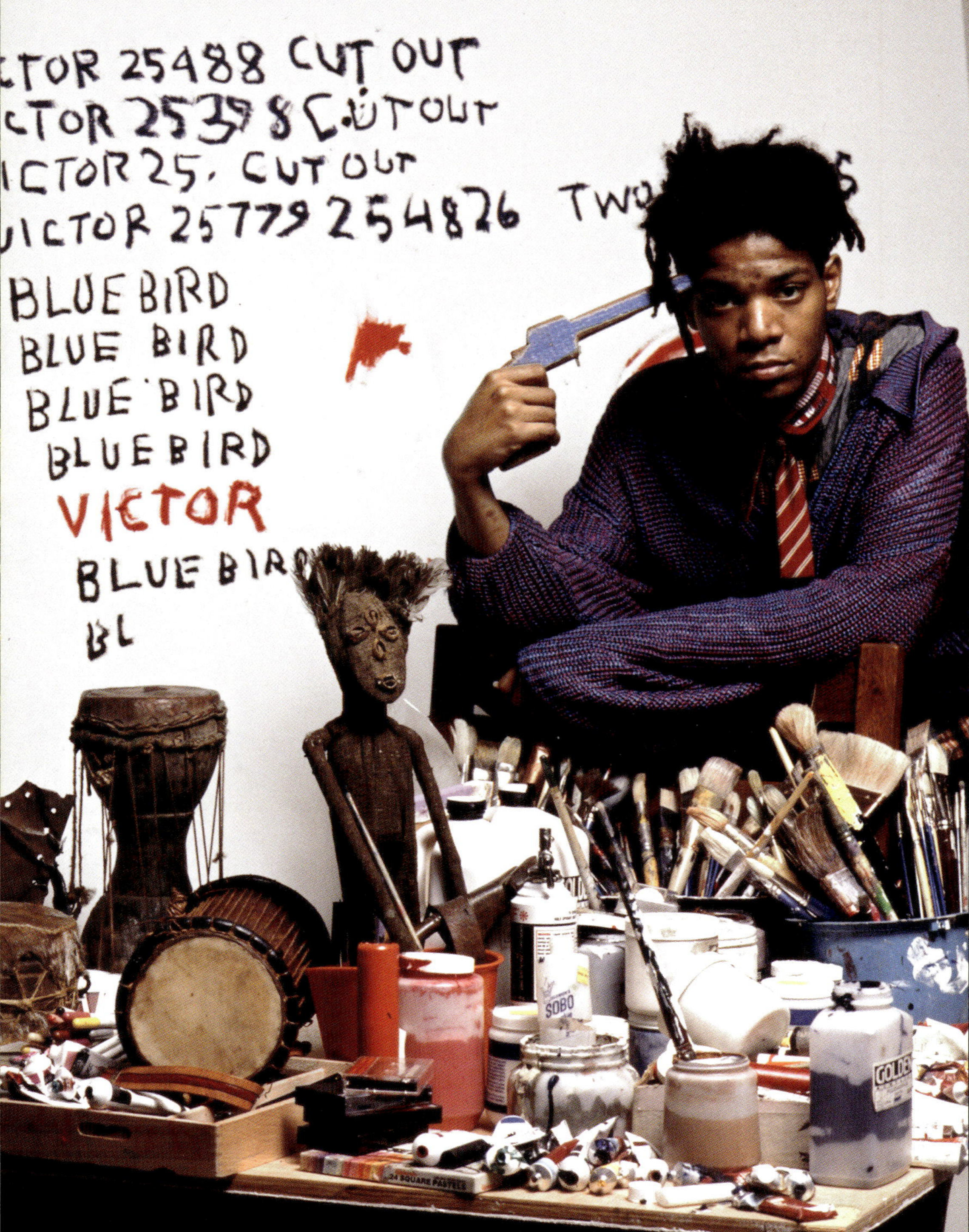
CTOR 25488 CUT OUT
ICTOR 25378 CUT OUT
ICTOR 25, CUT OUT
ICTOR 25779 254826 TWO
BLUE BIRD
BLUE BIRD
BLUE BIRD
BLUEBIRD
VICTOR
BLUE BIRD
BL

In January 1987, Basquiat exhibits at Galerie Daniel Templon in Paris. Then, in February, Andy Warhol unexpectedly dies from complications after a gallbladder operation. By all accounts, Basquiat is devastated, by the loss of both a friend and a stabilizing force for his own life.

While work is slow, and he has fewer exhibitions (which ties in with a general slowing of the boom in the New York's East Village art scene), recognition of Basquiat continues to grow internationally. In April, *Artforum* runs a big article by Demosthenes Davvetas, who discusses the artist's idiosyncratic style: "His line is the product of his mental process, the active proof of the passage from inner thought to articulation. It becomes a line that draws (perhaps his Samo crown), or that maps out fragments of a body (from the outside or from the inside); a line that records names, sometimes public ones (great musicians like Miles Davis and Charlie Parker), sometimes ambiguously historical and contemporary ones … Between the writing and the images is a complementary relationship: the writing becomes image and the image becomes word. Basquiat's line does not seem to me an expressionistic one, for it is a line with a characteristic distinguishable in these times: its attitude is not emotional but critical."[2]

In May, Basquiat shows three large works on paper at the Tony Shafrazi gallery. Shafrazi introduces the artist to his cousin Vrej Baghoomian, who starts buying some paintings, then becomes Basquiat's New York dealer, opening his own gallery in the process. In the artist Rick Prol, Basquiat finds a new studio assistant. He works on paintings for a string of exhibitions planned for the following year. He meets Kelle Inman, then a waitress at the nightclub Nell's, and the two start a relationship that will continue until his death.

The new paintings are presented for one night at Baghoomian's gallery in early 1988 before being sent to Europe. Their first stop is in Paris at Yvon Lambert, where Basquiat makes friends with a painter from Ivory Coast, Ouattara Watts, and they plan on joint projects. Other new works are presented at the gallery of Hans Mayer in Düsseldorf. They are described by Ursula Bode in the German weekly *Die Zeit* as having "a special, almost casual presence, a freshness that does not derive its stimulating qualities from clever graffiti gimmicks, but from the rhythm of the streets that has found its way into the paintings, the signs of the city, jazz, and advertising, and all the other codes from contemporary society that only seemingly are familiar to us all."[3]

In April, Basquiat holds his last solo exhibition at Vrej Baghoomian in New York. The work is impressive, if morose, with canvases bearing the stacked words and signs for "Man dies" in dense rows, and the picture *Riding with Death* (pp. 492/493) portraying a black figure sitting on a rudimentary skeleton composed of a few bones in a forward stride. While this exhibition at a hardly established gallery does not garner many reviews, it provokes a certain buzz and a general feeling that Basquiat is back again.

Soon after, he leaves New York for Hawaii, to recharge and to get clean again. His state of health appears precarious, but when Basquiat returns by the end of June he is optimistic

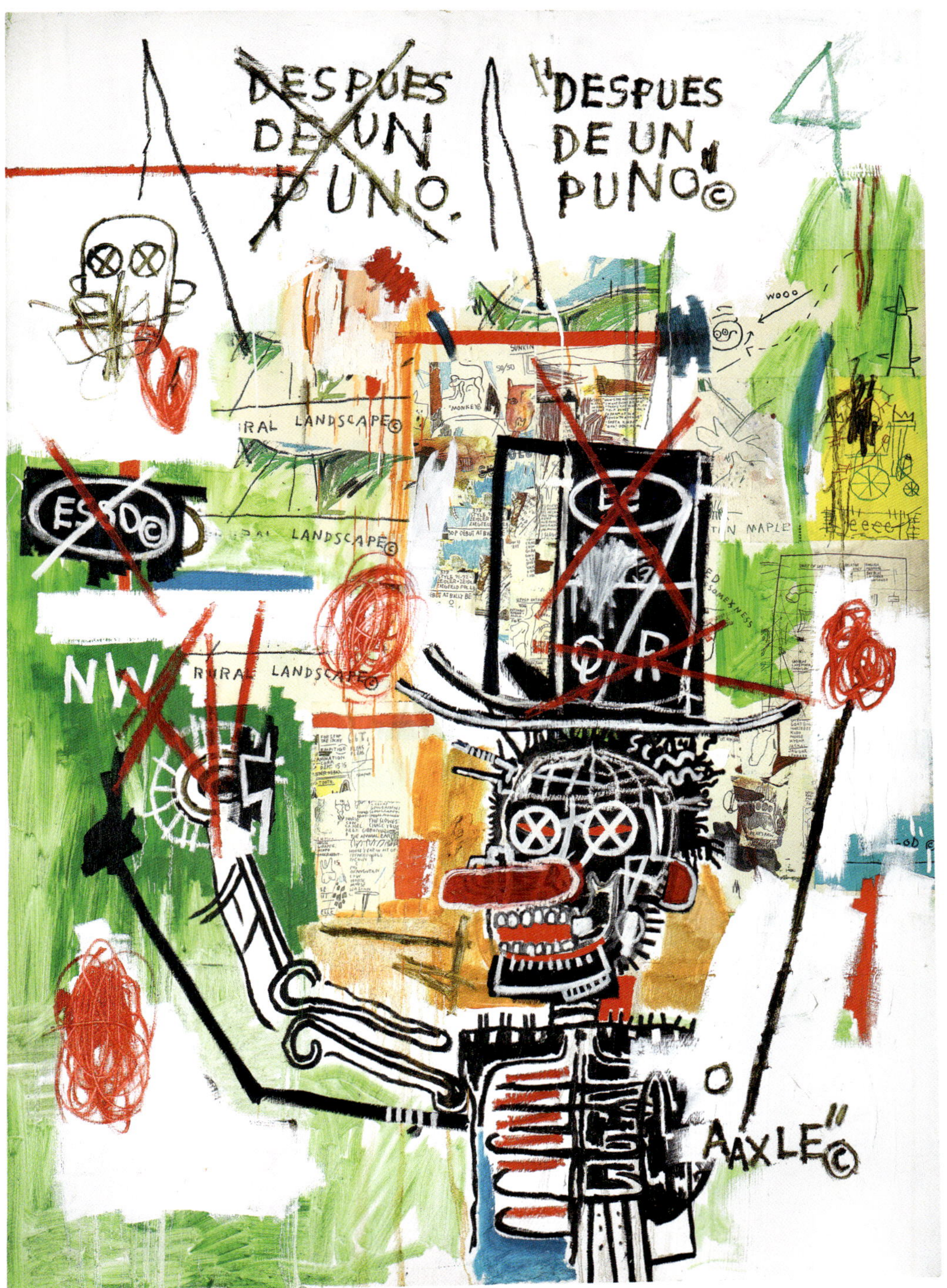
DESPUES
DE UN
PUNO.
DESPUES
DE UN
PUNO ©
4
WOOO
RURAL LANDSCAPE ©
SUNKIN
50/50
"MONKEY"
ESSO ©
RURAL LANDSCAPE ©
MAPLE
SOMENESS
NW
RURAL LANDSCAPE ©
AAXLE" ©

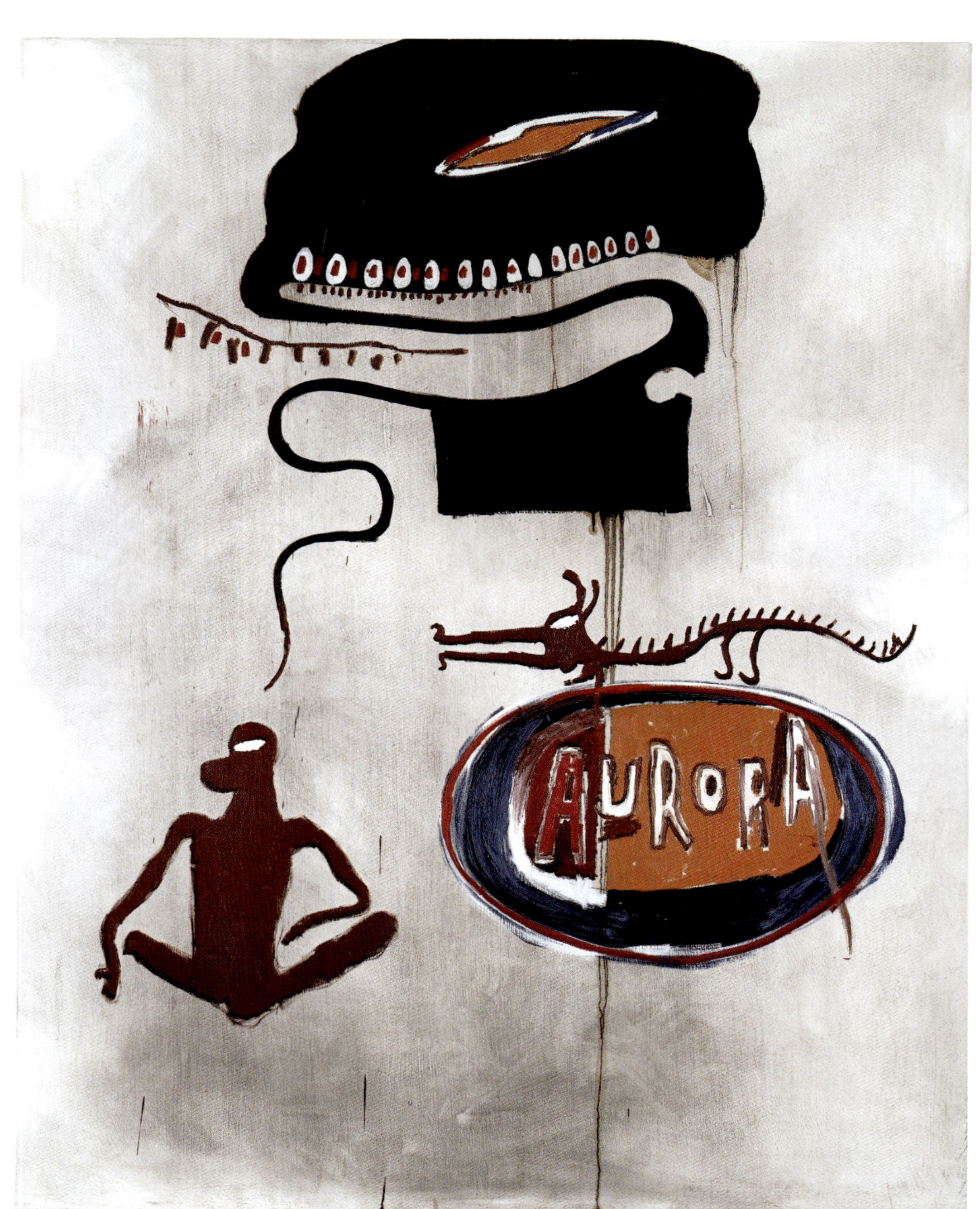
AURORA

and full of plans, which include maybe quitting the art scene and becoming a writer. "I saw him on the street," Keith Haring reports. "It was the first time I had seen him in a whole while. He was really up. He told me he had kicked. Which is the first time he had even acknowledged a habit at all. He seemed honestly excited."[4] But unfortunately there is a relapse, and on August 12, 1988, Basquiat dies at age 27 of an accidental overdose in his Great Jones Street loft. Five days later, a private funeral is held with close friends and family and Basquiat is buried at Brooklyn's Greenwood Cemetery. In November, a memorial gathering follows in St. Peter's Church in mid-Manhattan for 300 guests with poetry readings and reminiscences from his peers, his old band Gray as well as John Lurie contributing the music.

Anthony Haden-Guest, writing an article on the artist during his last days, catches the general feeling of loss: "Some, including Larry Gagosian, feel that Basquiat was facing 'a block.' Others feel his work was constantly getting stronger. It is now unknowable, as it cannot be known how seriously to take his plan of abandoning art, Rimbaud-like. 'The body of work is phenomenal,' says Tony Shafrazi. 'The guy produced maybe five to six hundred major canvases in about eight years. He was the epitome of the romantic artist— literally living the dark side of Van Gogh.'"[5] In his own memorial article, Haring adds: "He truly created a lifetime of works in ten years. Greedily, we wonder what else he might have created, what masterpieces we have been cheated out of by his death, but the fact is that he has created enough work to intrigue generations to come. Only now will people begin to understand the magnitude of his contribution."[6]

[1–6] *See Endnotes on page 509.*

Gris Gris, 1987
Acrylic and oilstick on canvas,
218 x 173 cm / 85 ³/₄ x 68 inches

Page 449: Jean-Michel Basquiat in his
Great Jones Street studio, New York 1987.
Photo Tseng Kwong Chi

Page 451: **Despues de un Puno**, 1987
Acrylic, olistick, and photocopy collage on
canvas, 215.5 x 153.5 cm / 84 ³/₄ x 60 ¹/₂ inches

Pages 454/455: Jean-Michel Basquiat: Neue Arbeiten,
exhibition view, Galerie Hans Mayer,
Düsseldorf 1988

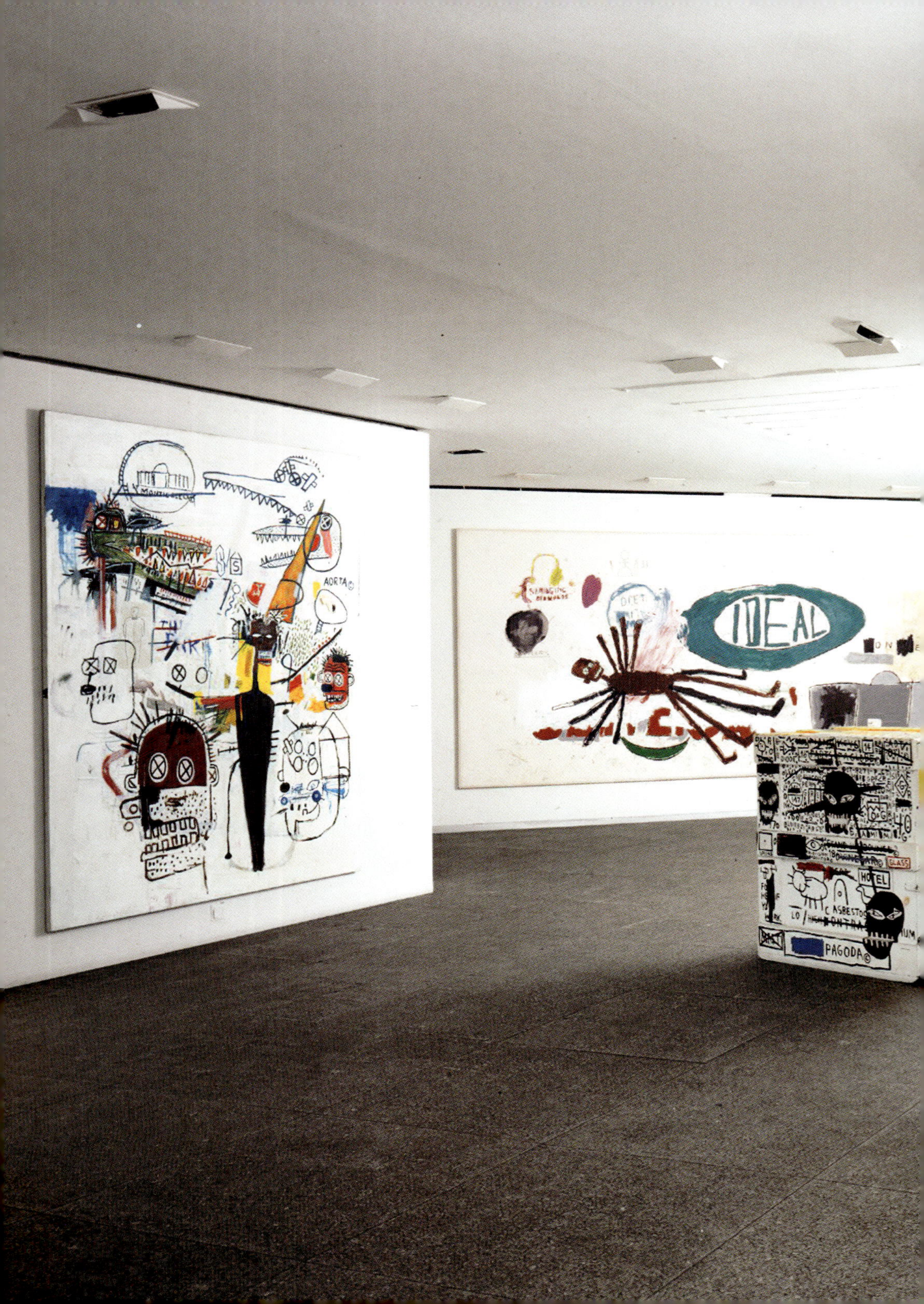

AORTA
THE
EARL
MANIC
IDEAL
DIET
GLASS
HOTEL
ASBESTOS
PAGODA

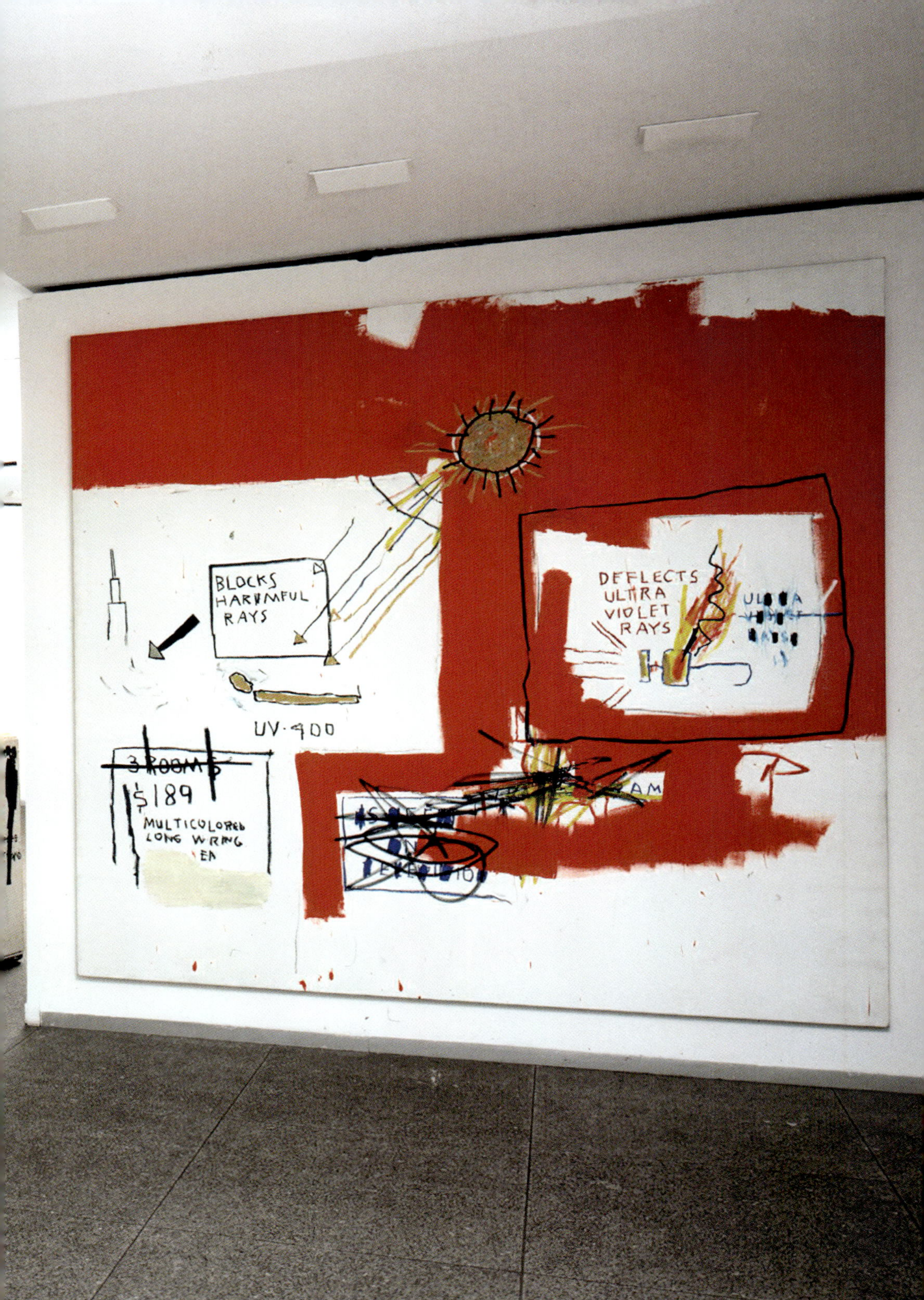

BLOCKS
HARMFUL
RAYS
UV·400
3 ROOMS
$189
MULTICOLORED
LONG WRING
EA
DEFLECTS
ULTRA
VIOLET
RAYS
ULTRA
VIOLET
RAYS

Untitled, 1987
Acrylic and oilstick on canvas,
247.5 x 178 cm / 97 ¹/₂ x 70 inches

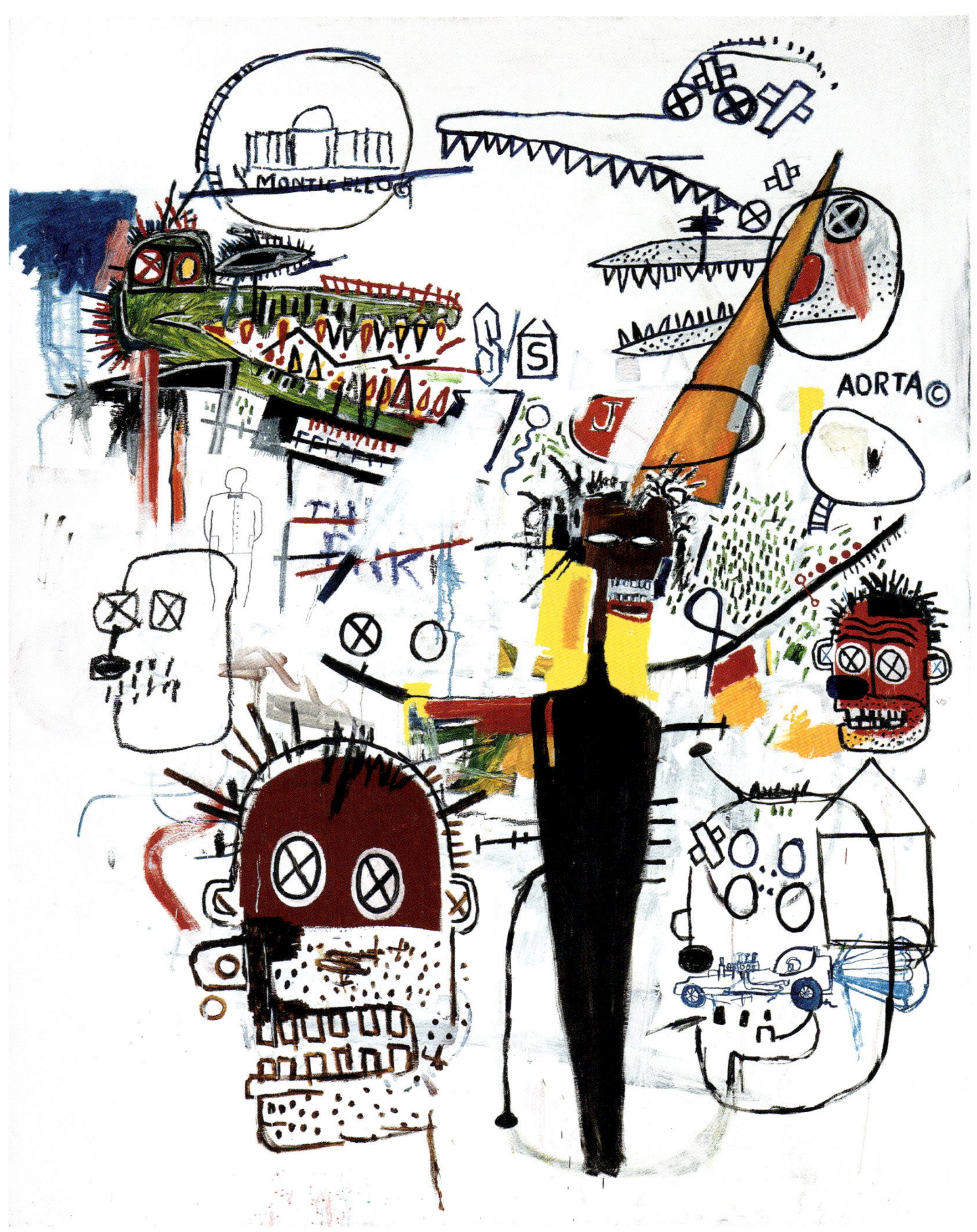

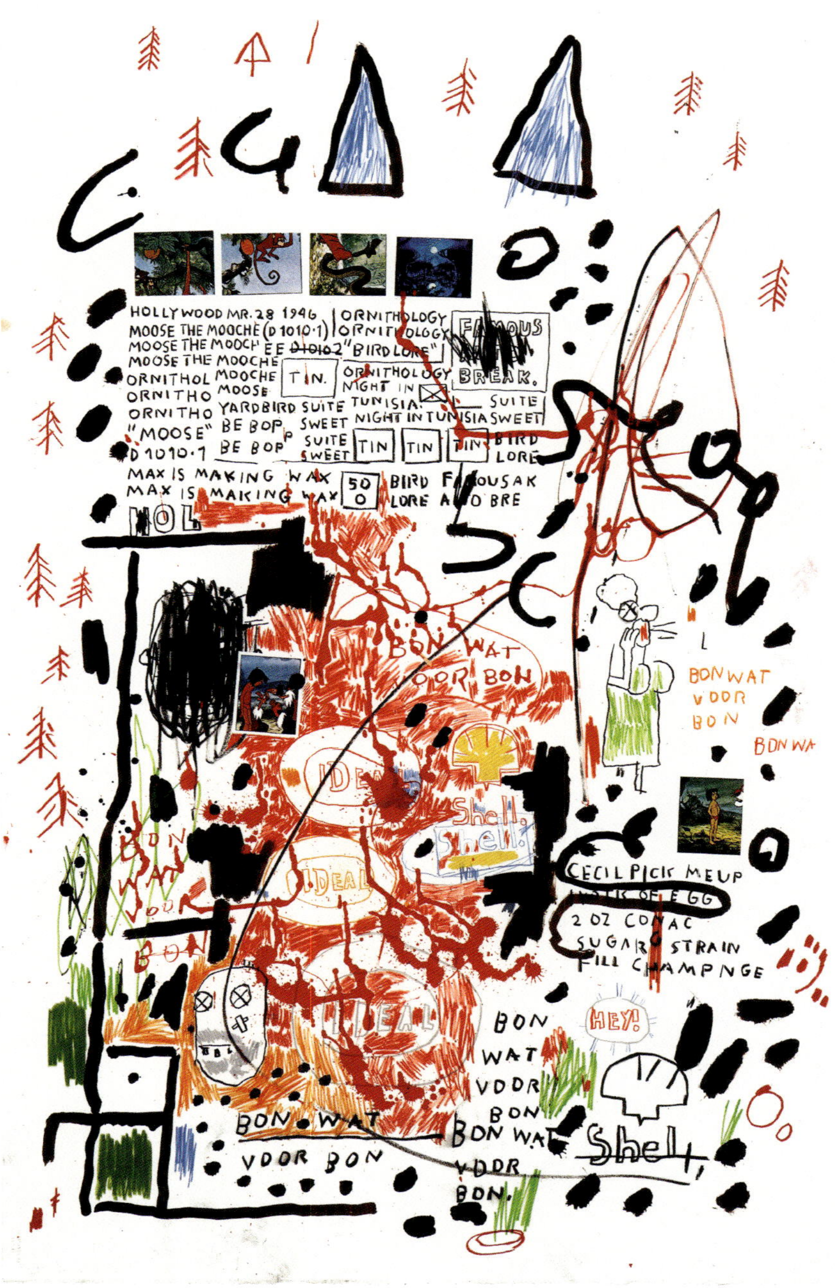

Untitled, 1988
Graphite, oilstick, acrylic, and sticker
on paper, 103.5 x 66 cm / 40 3/4 x 26 inches

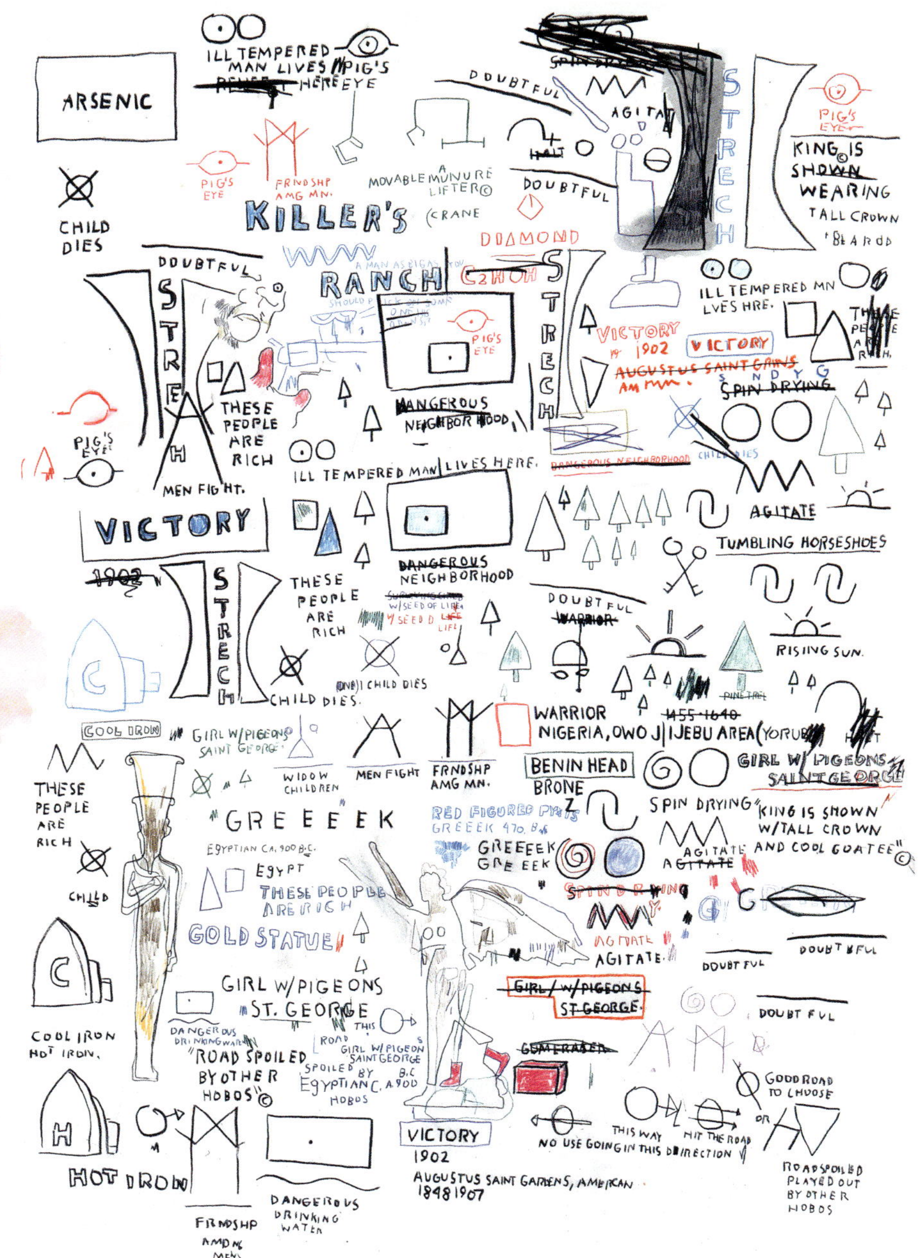

Untitled, 1987
Graphite, oilstick, and ink on paper,
105.5 x 76 cm / 41 ¹/₂ x 30 inches

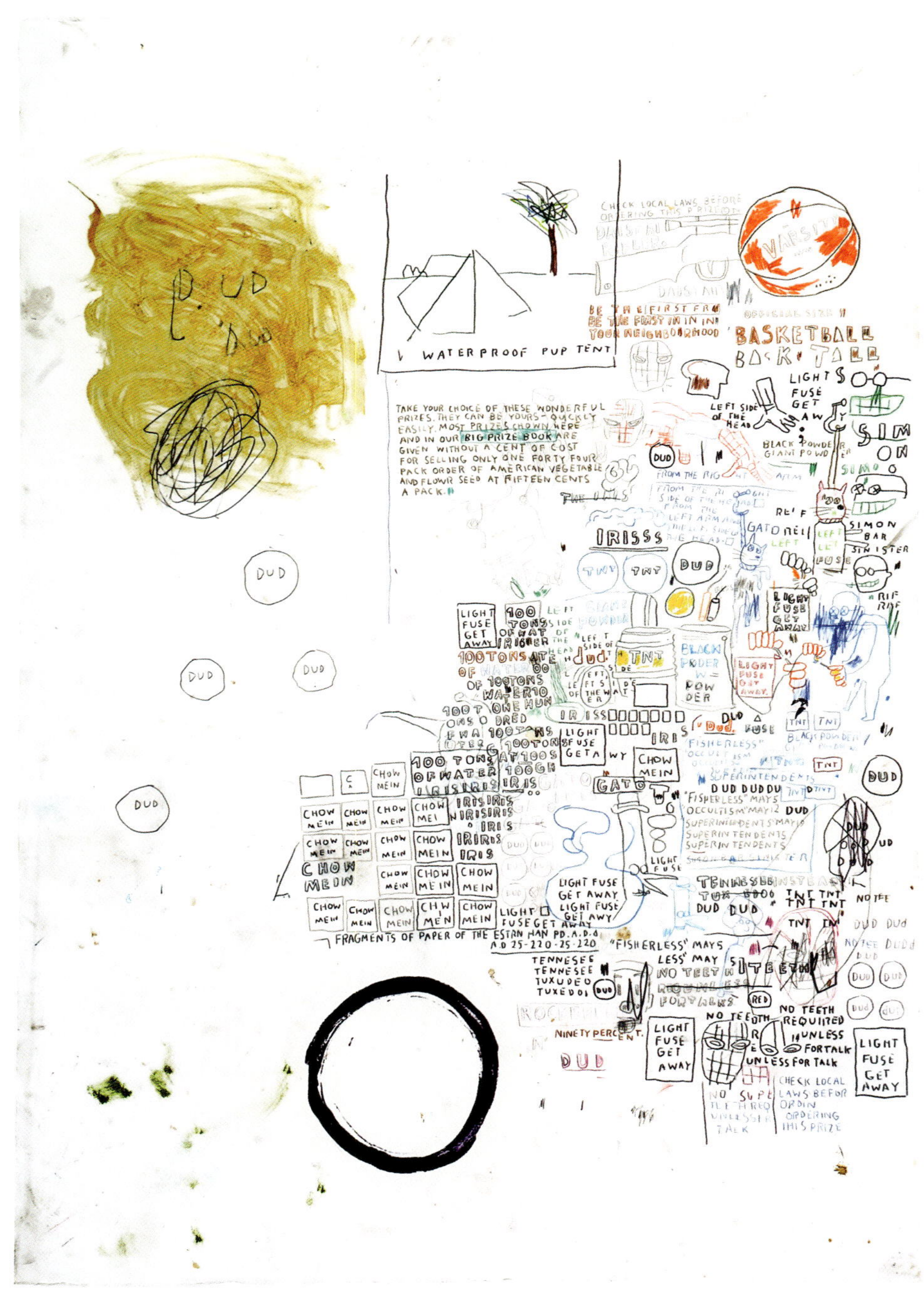

Untitled (N.Y.), 1988
Graphite, oilstick, and acrylic on paper,
105.5 x 75 cm / 41 ^{1}/$_2$ x 29 ^{1}/$_2$ inches

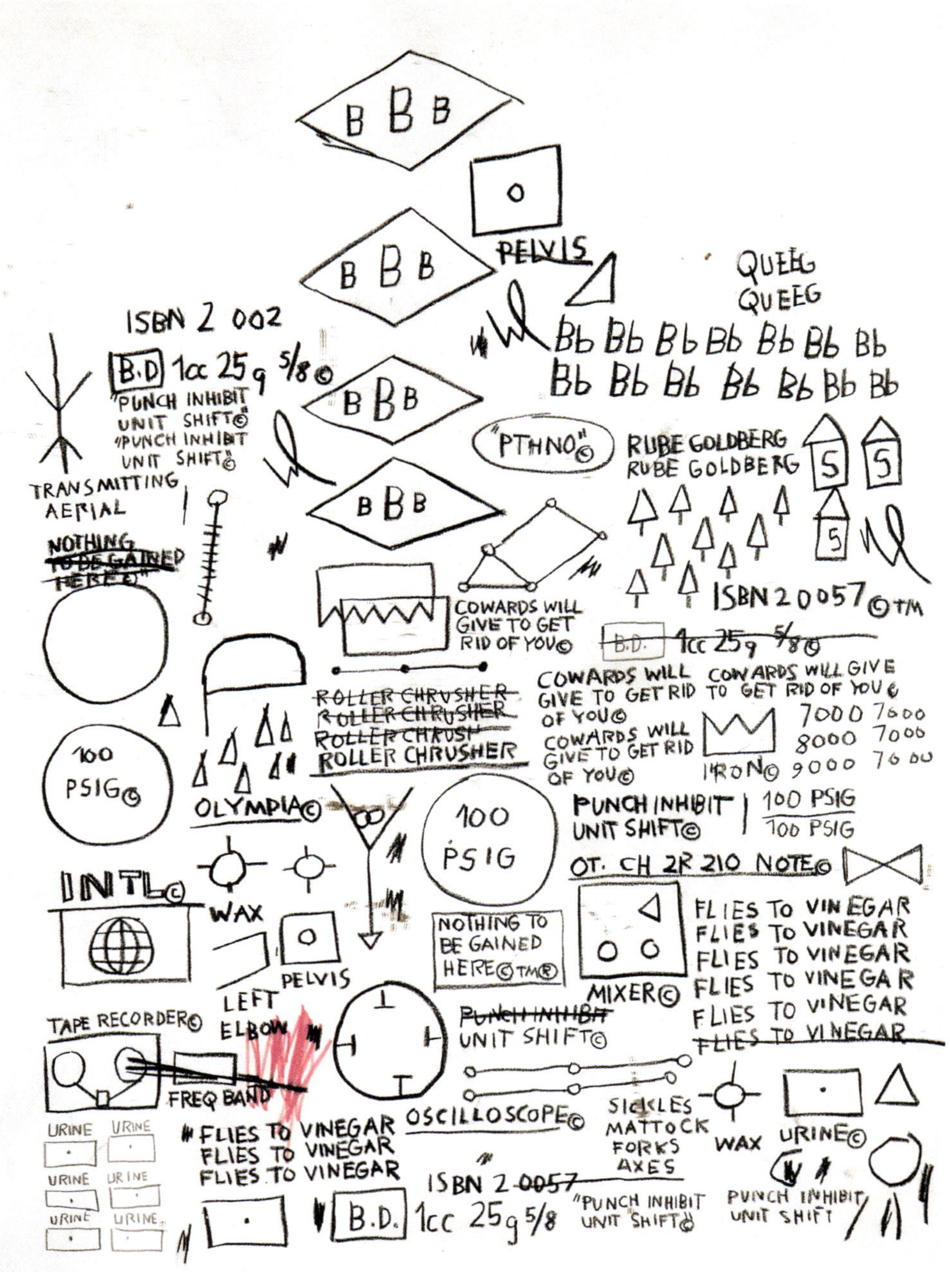

Untitled, 1987
Graphite and oilstick on paper,
76 x 56 cm / 30 x 22 inches

Pages 462/463: **Five Cents**, 1987
Acrylic, oilstick, and photocopy collage
on paper, 76 x 105.5 cm / 30 x 41 1/2 inches

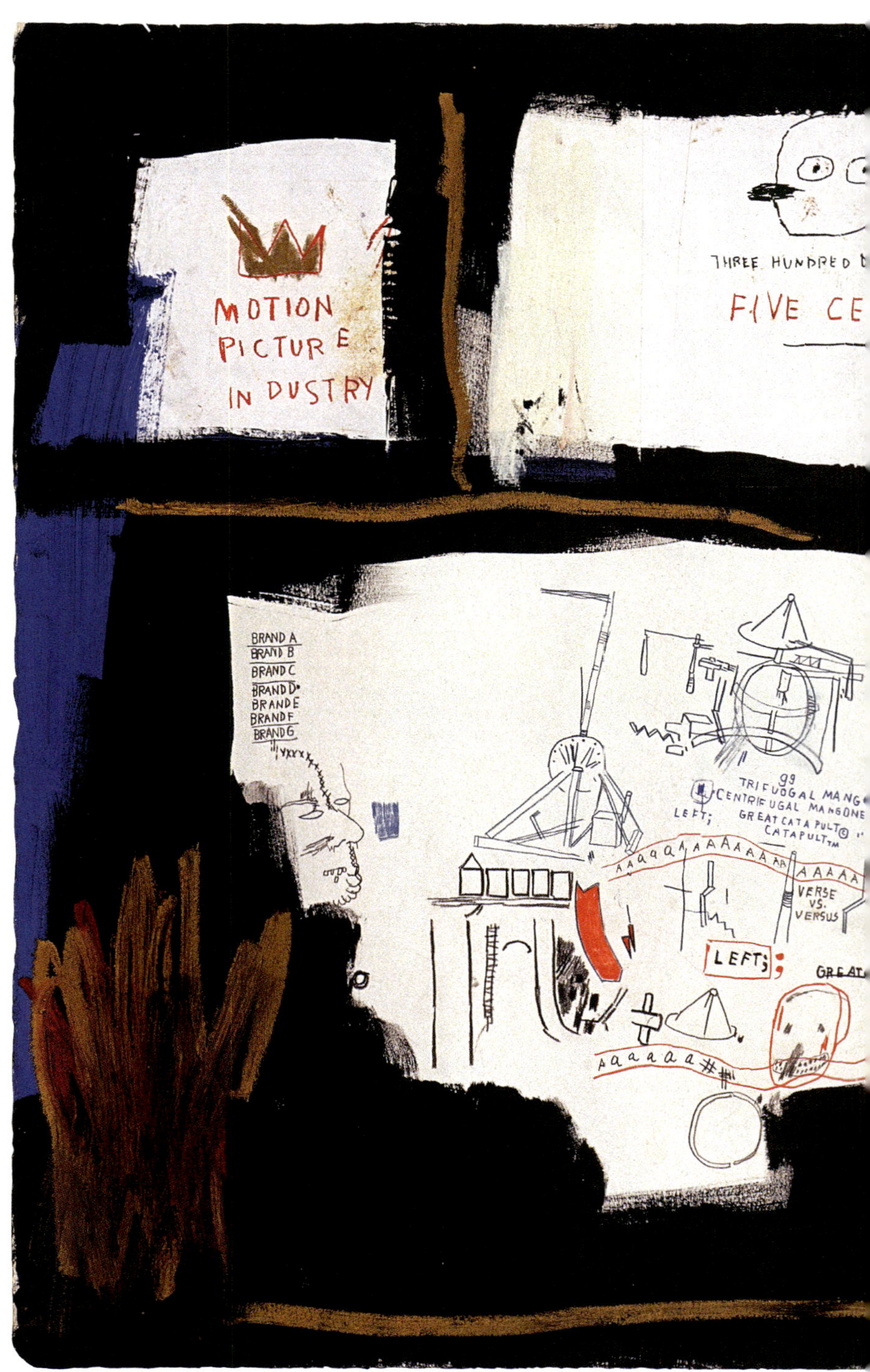

MOTION
PICTURE
INDUSTRY
THREE HUNDRED
FIVE CE
BRAND A
BRAND B
BRAND C
BRAND D
BRANDE
BRANDF
BRAND G
99
TRIFUGGAL MANG
CENTRIFUGAL MANGONE
LEFT;
GREAT CATAPULT©
CATAPULT™
VERSE
VS.
VERSUS
LEFT;
GREAT

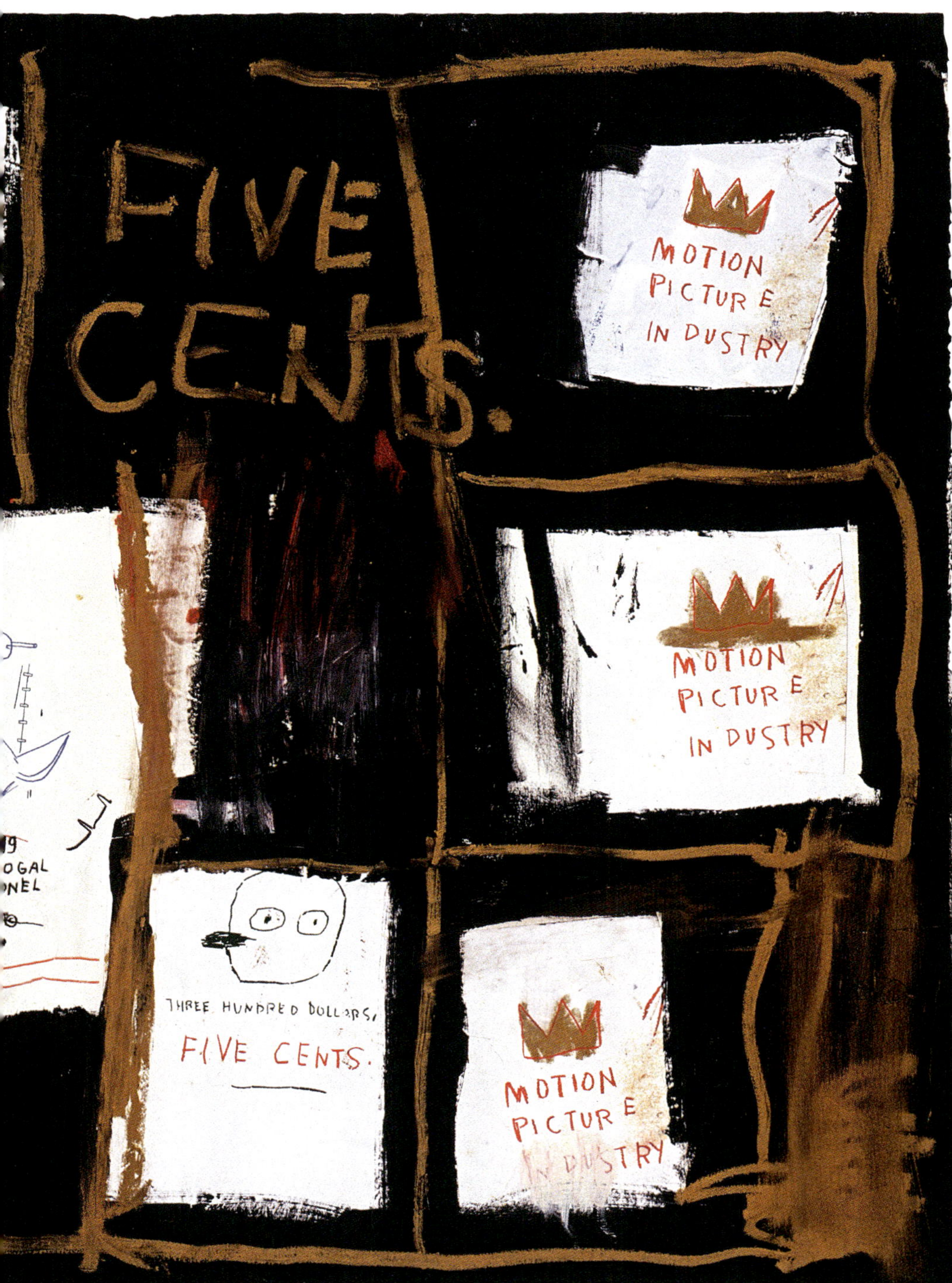

FIVE CENTS.
MOTION PICTURE INDUSTRY
MOTION PICTURE INDUSTRY
MOTION PICTURE INDUSTRY
THREE HUNDRED DOLLARS,
FIVE CENTS.
OGAL
NEL

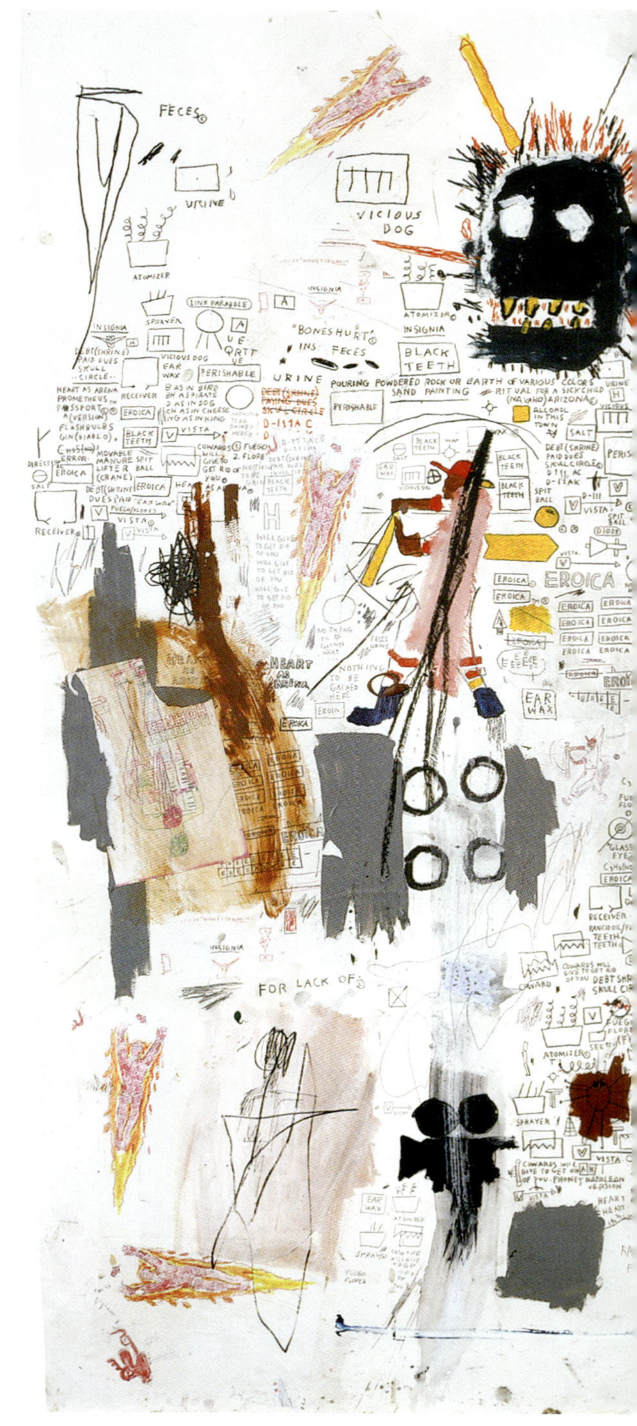

Untitled, 1987
Acrylic, oilstick, graphite, colored crayon,
and photocopy collage on paper mounted
on canvas, 228.5 x 272 cm / 90 x 107 inches

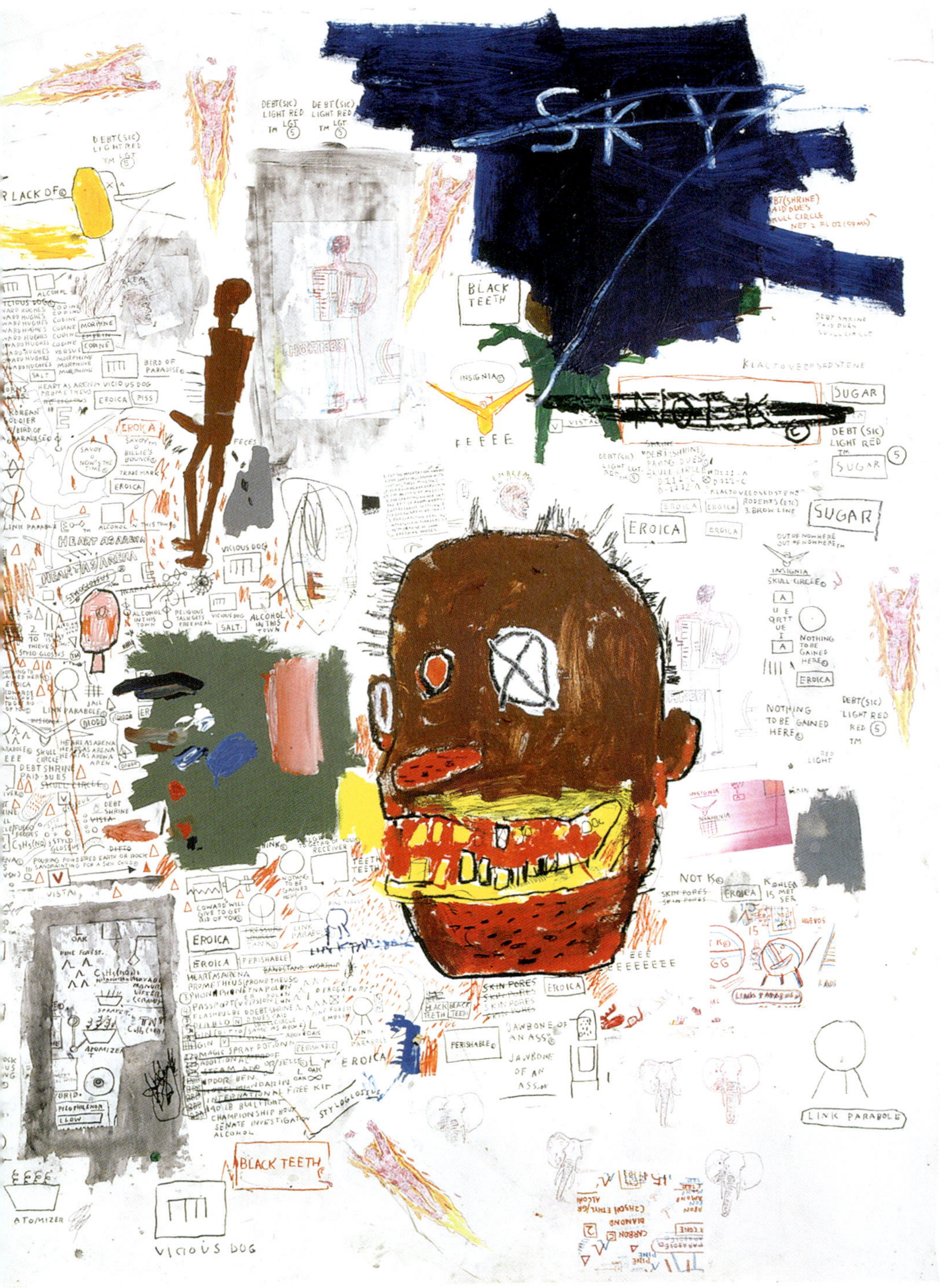

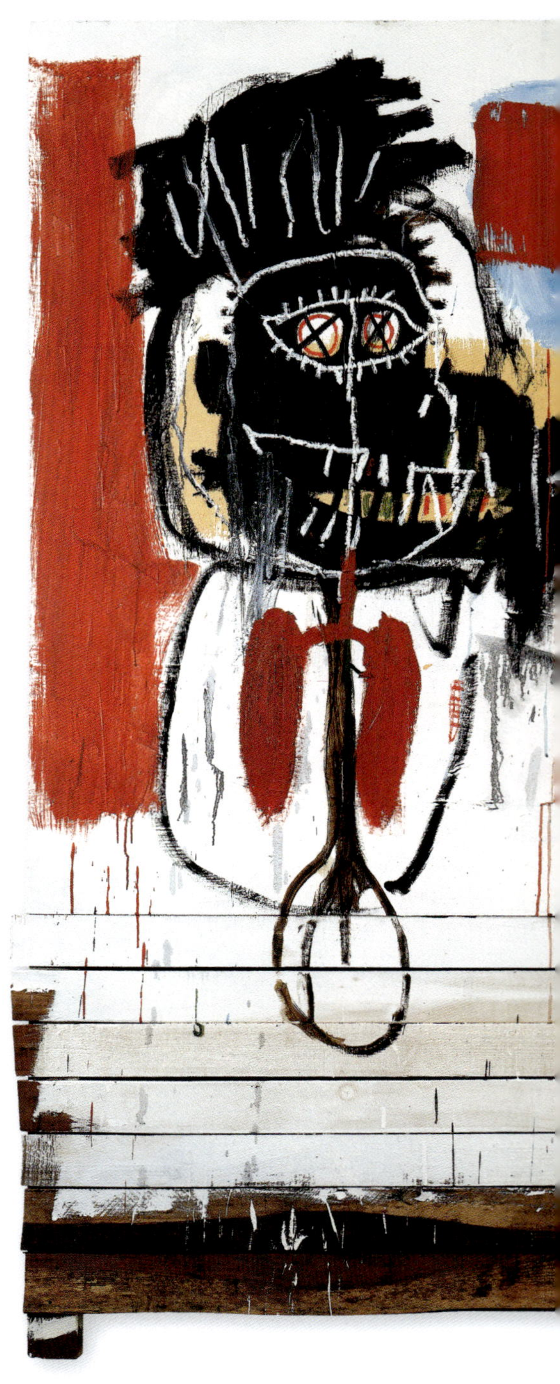

**She Installs Confidence and Picks
His Brain Like a Salad**, 1987
Acrylic and oilstick on wood,
232.5 x 292 x 5 cm / 91 $^5/_8$ x 115 x 2 inches

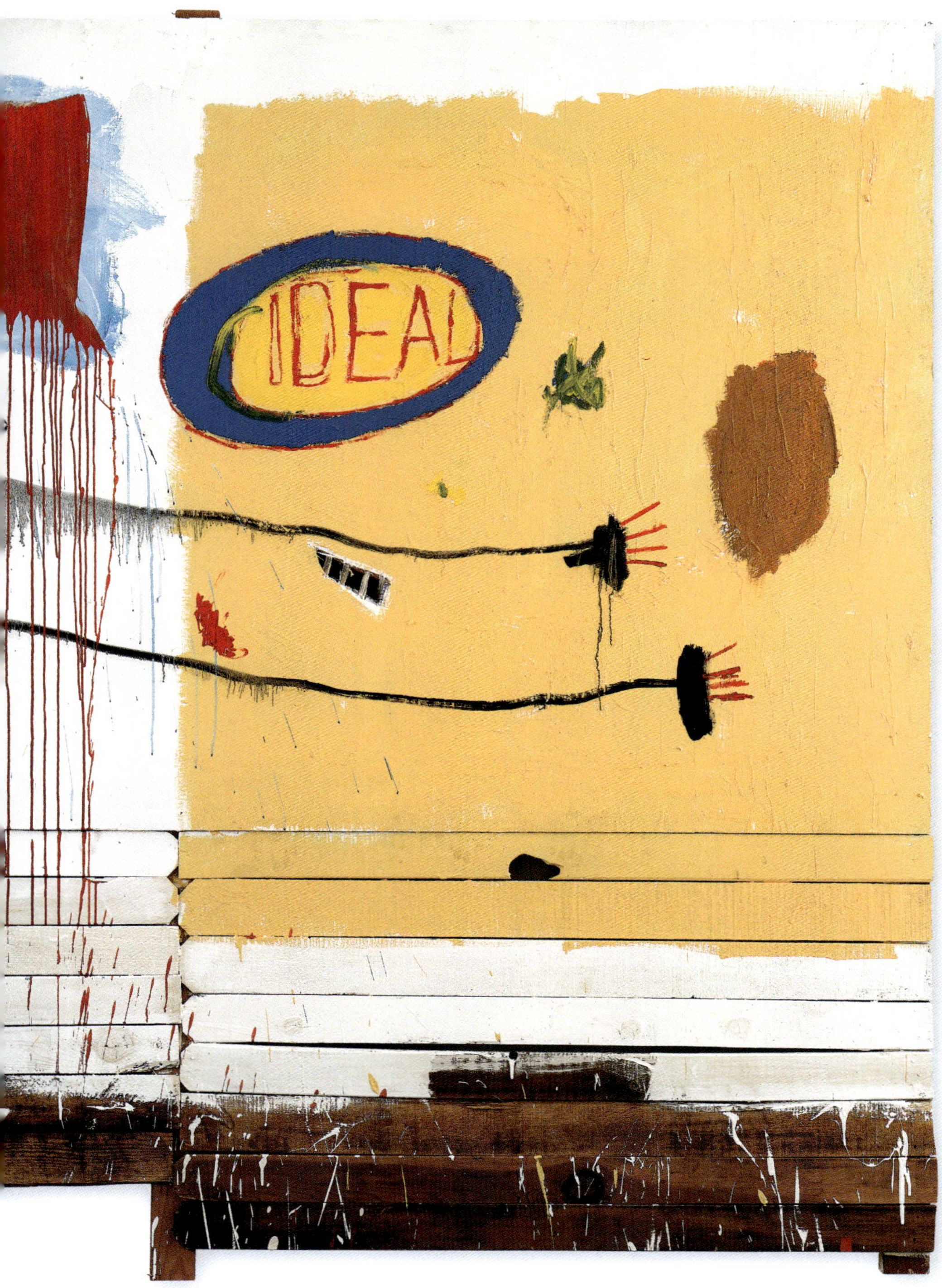
IDEAL

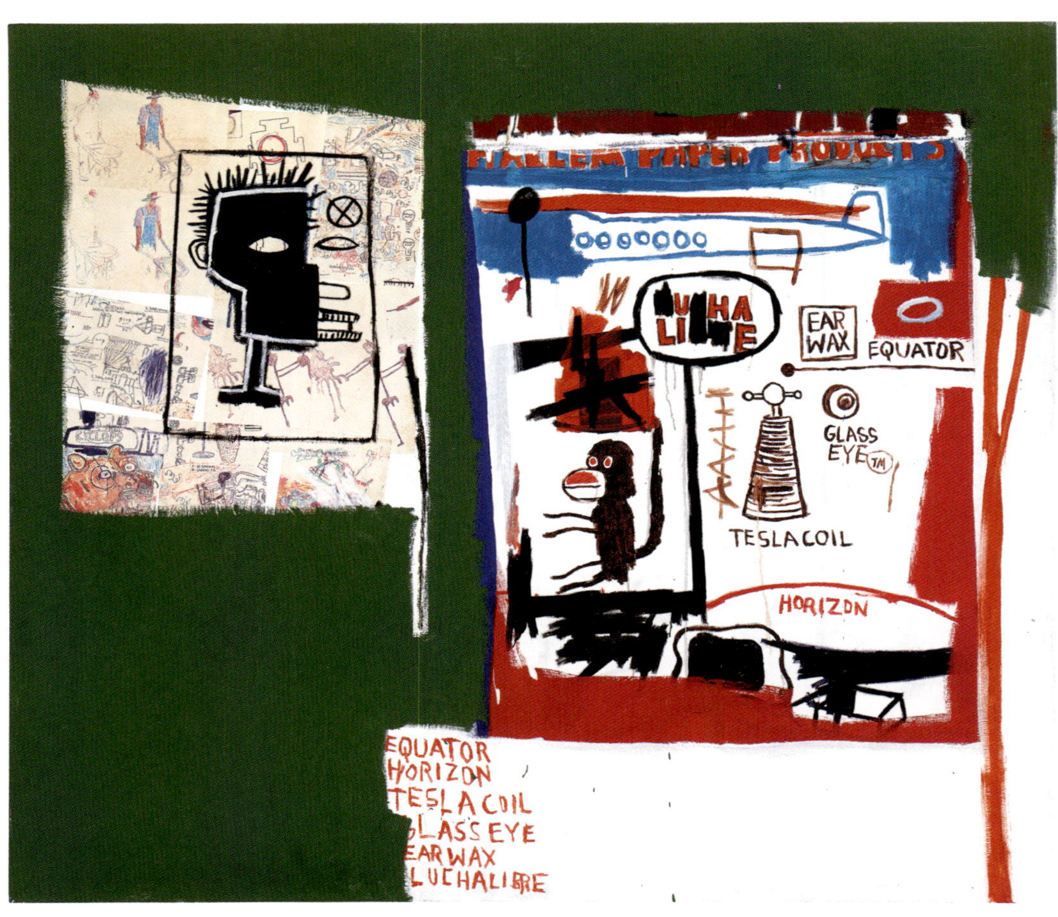

Harlem Paper Products, 1987
Acrylic, oilstick, and photocopy collage
on canvas, 188 x 213 cm / 74 x 83 ³/₄ inches

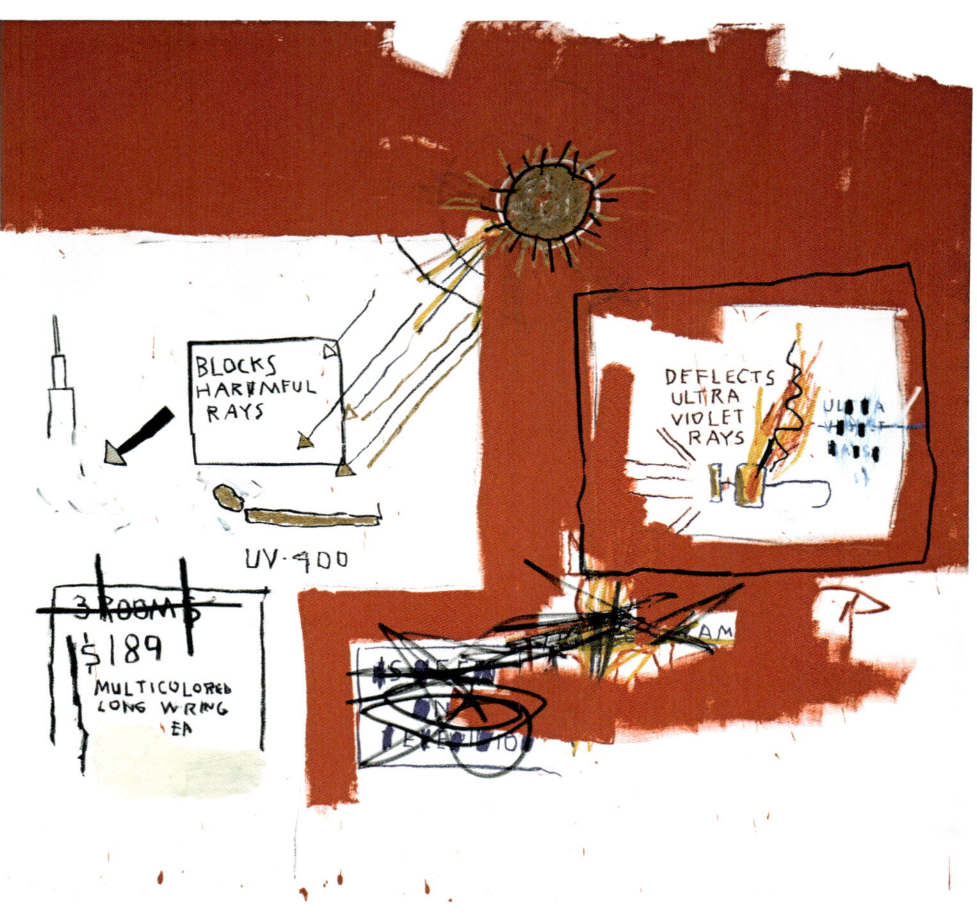

Amber Vision, 1988
Acrylic and oilstick on canvas,
264 x 289 cm / 104 x 113 ³/₄ inches

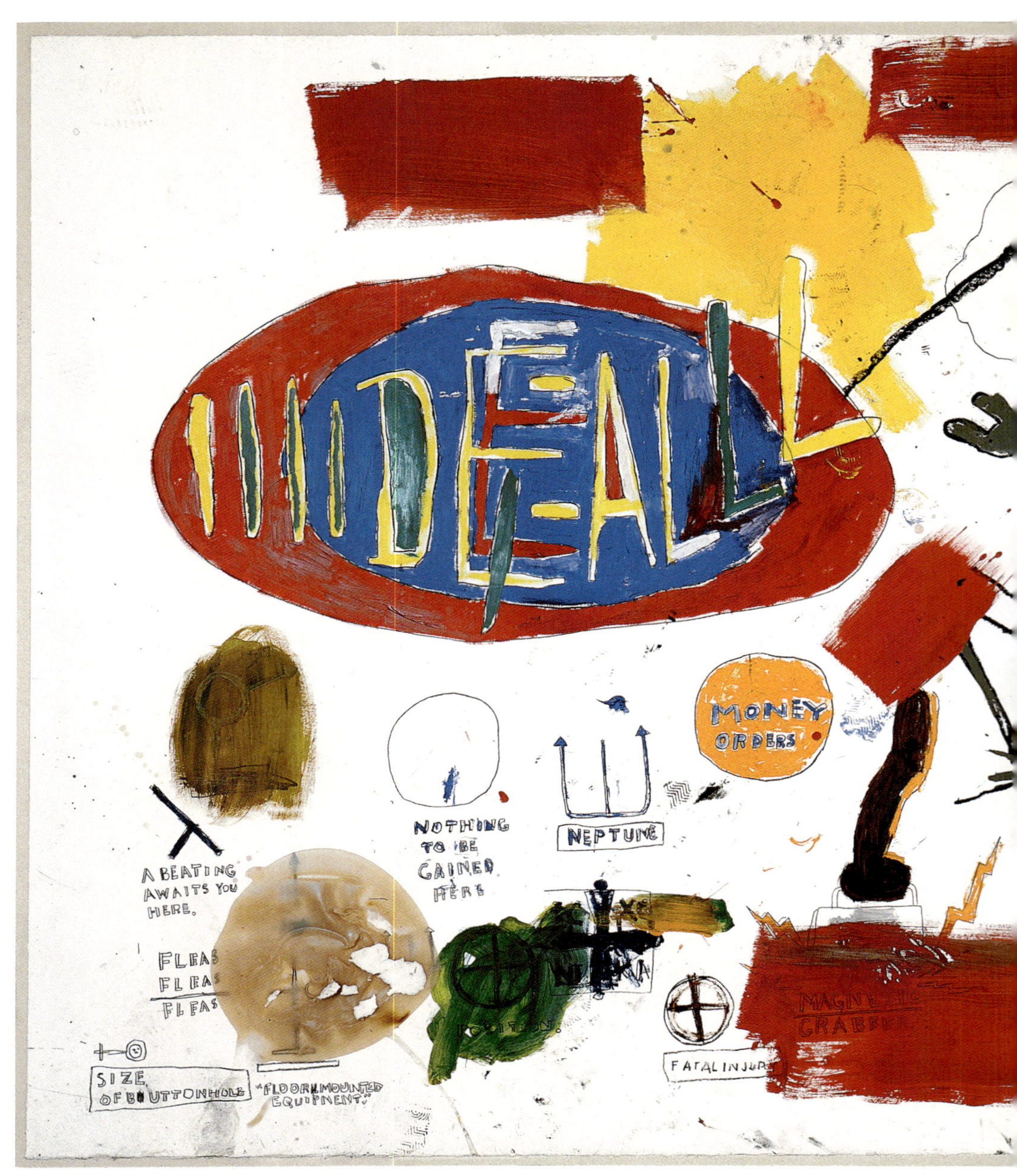

Victor 25448, 1987
Acrylic, oilstick, and graphite on paper mounted
on canvas, 185.5 x 338 cm / 73 x 133 inches

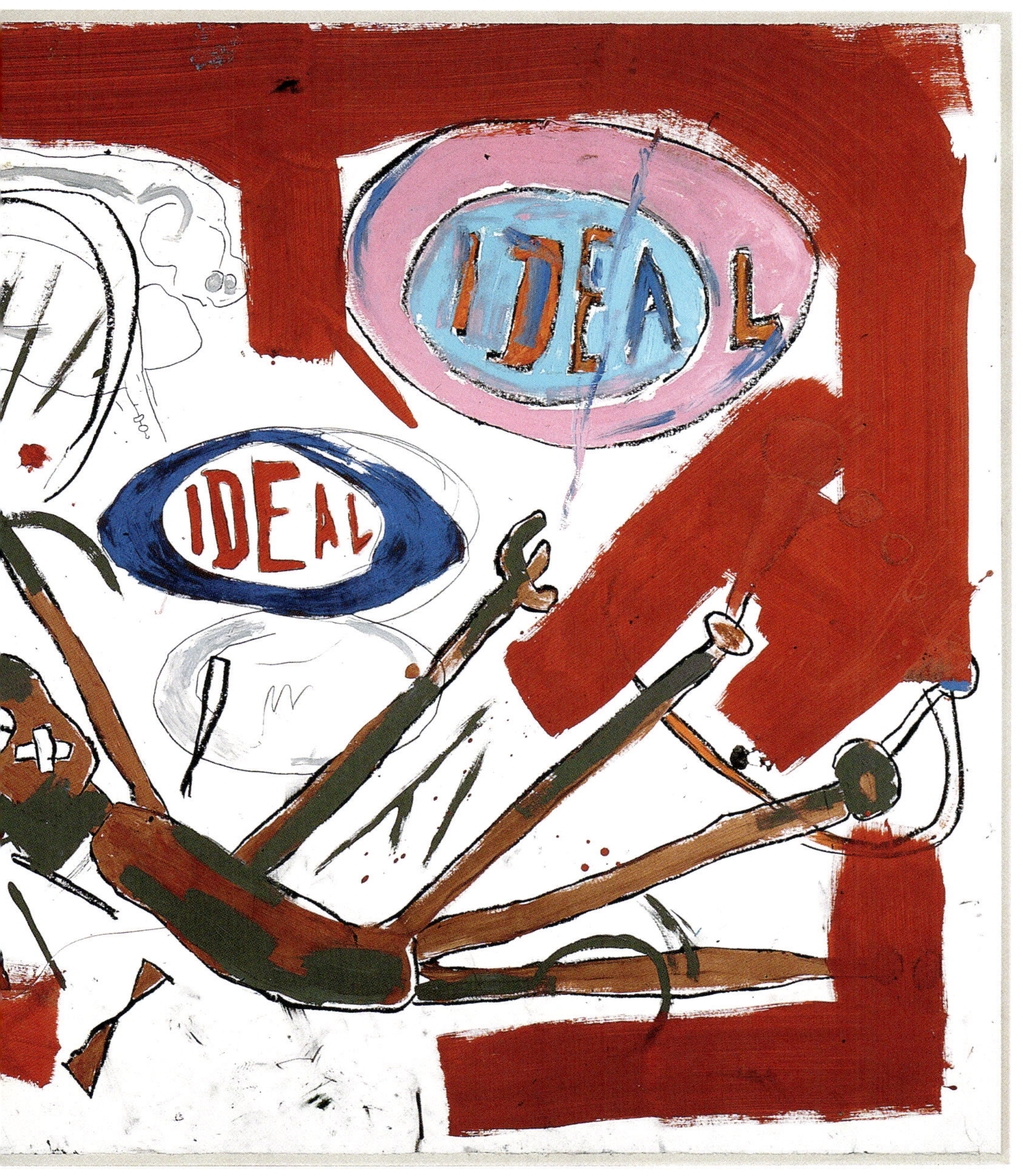
IDEAL
IDEAL

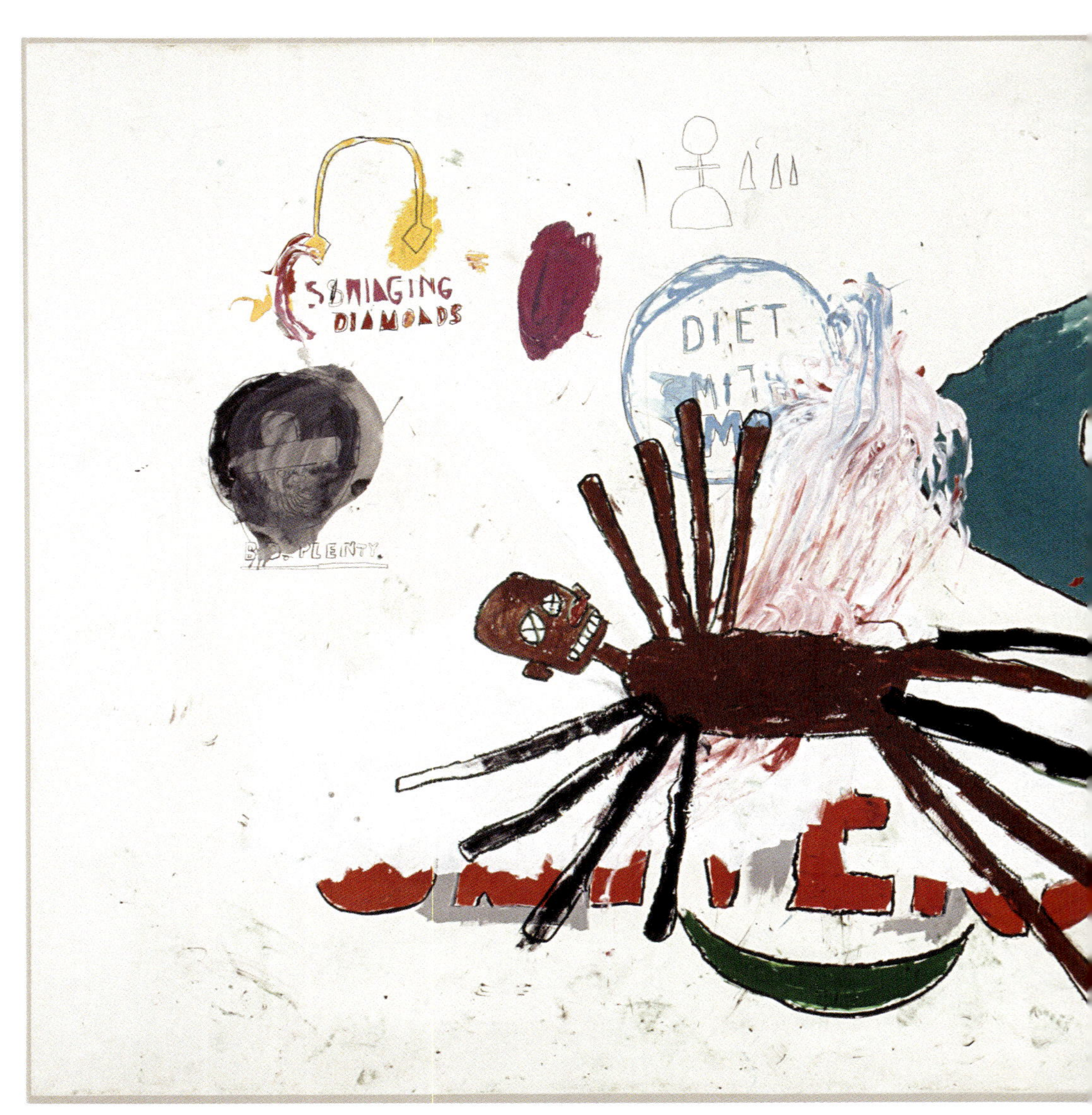

Levétation, 1987
Acrylic, marker, and oilstick on paper mounted
on canvas, 230 x 472 cm / 90 $^1/_2$ x 186 inches

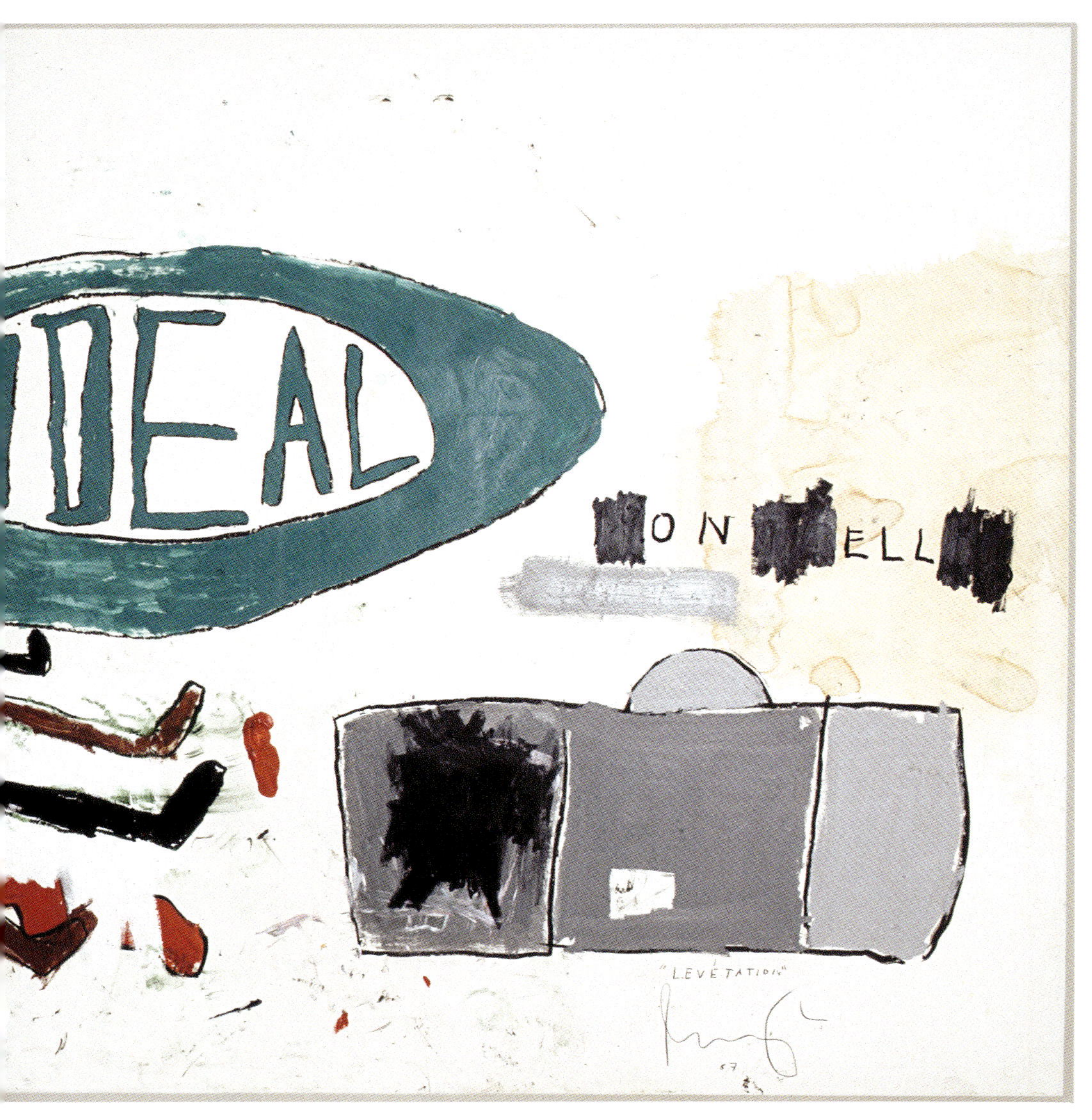
IDEAL
ON ELL
"LEVETATION"
57

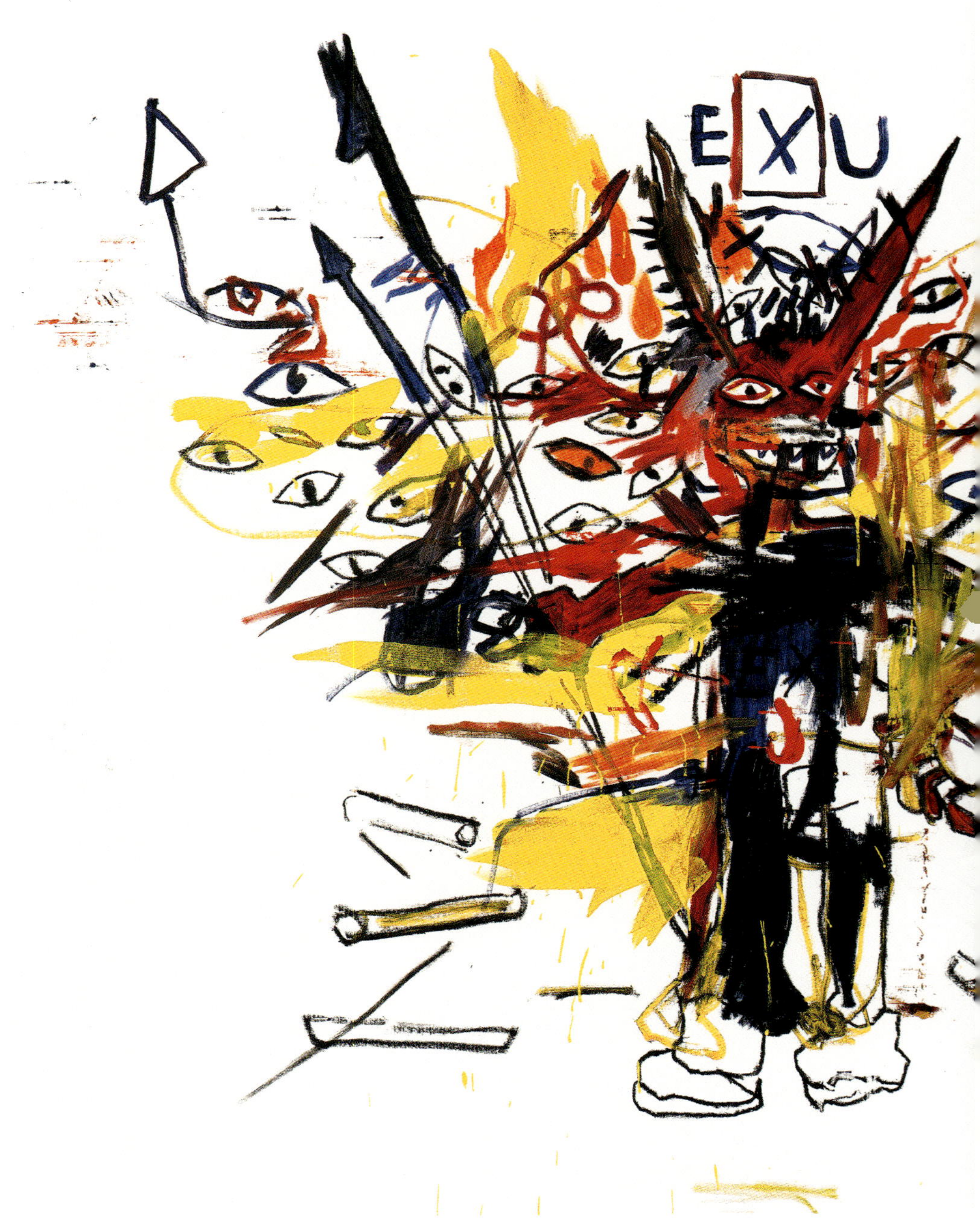

E X U

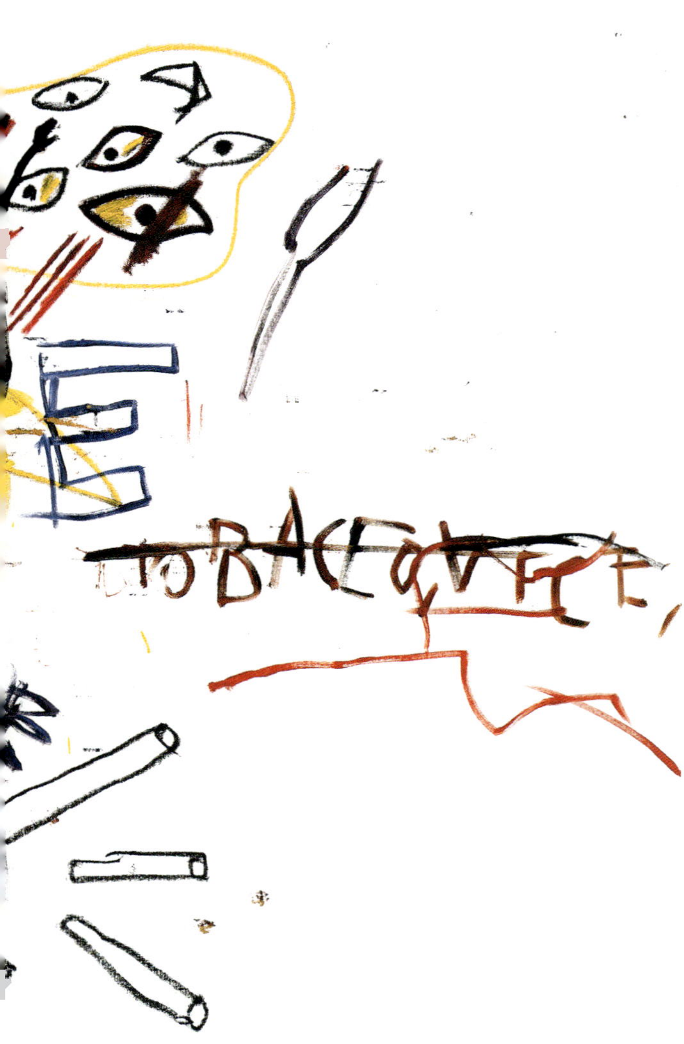

Exu, 1988
Acrylic and oilstick on
canvas, 199.5 x 254 cm /
78 ¹/₂ x 100 inches

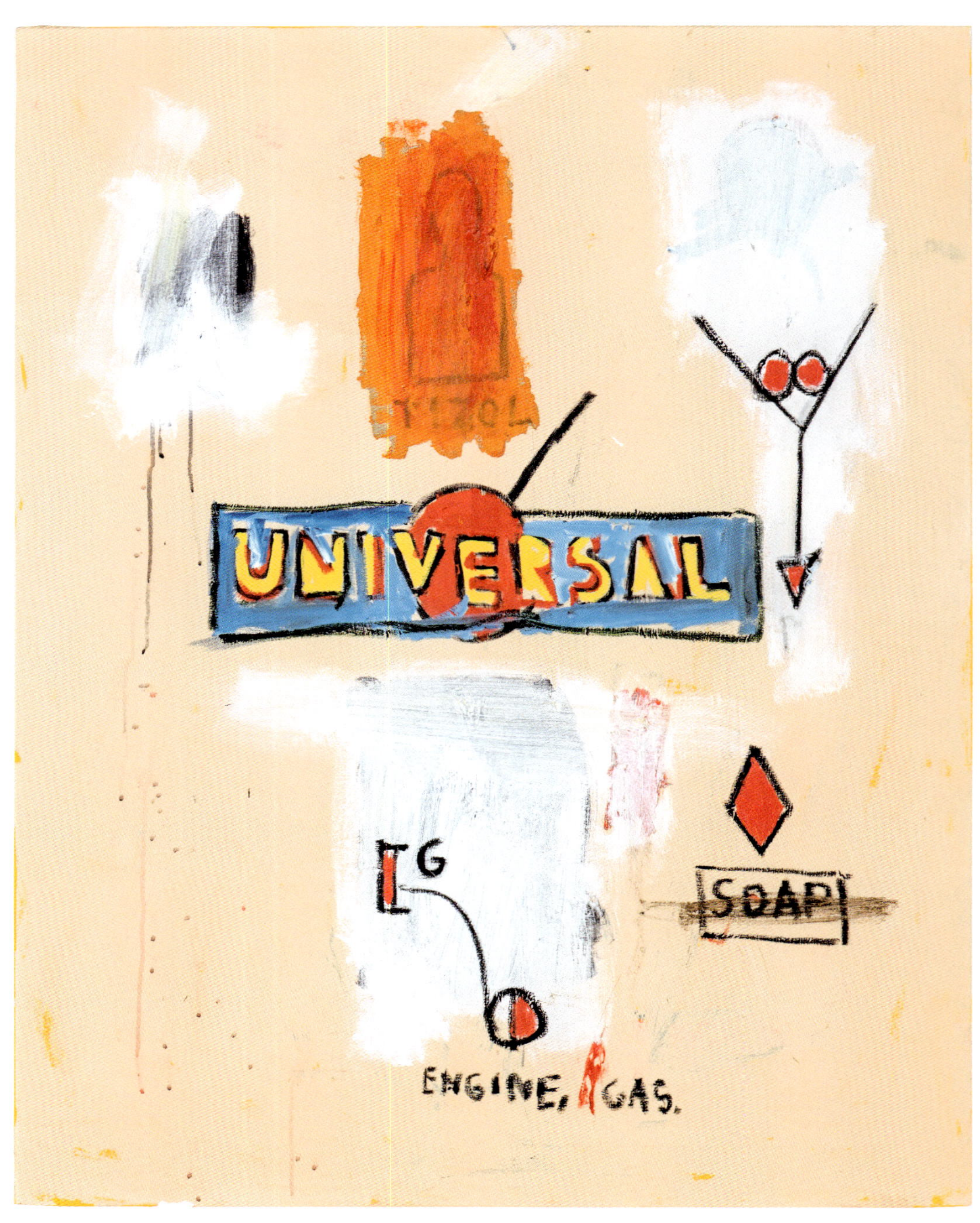

Universal, 1987
Acrylic and oilstick on canvas,
125.5 x 100.5 cm / 49 $^1/_2$ x 39 $^1/_2$ inches

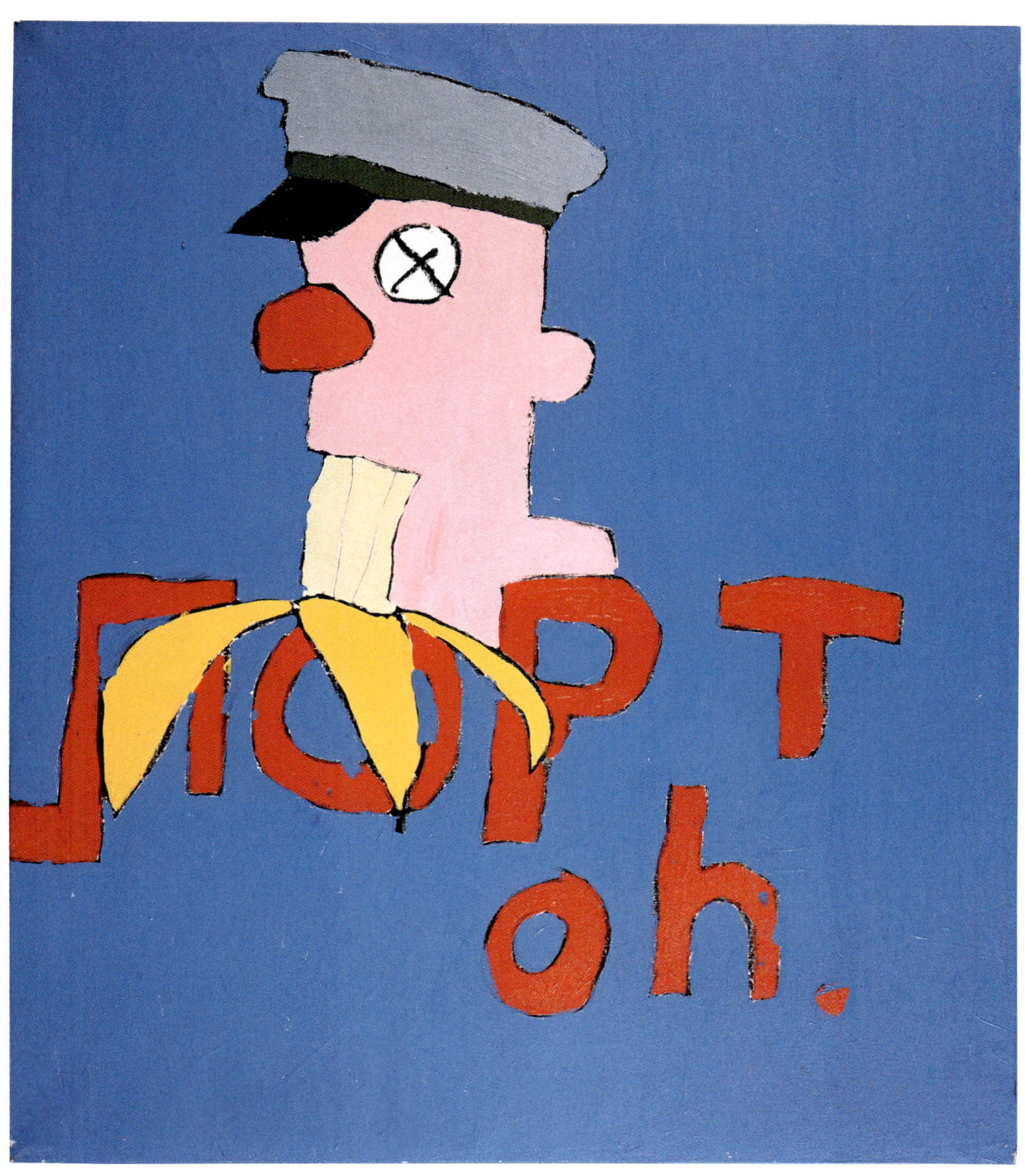

Glassnose, 1987
Acrylic on canvas,
168 x 145 cm / 66 ¼ x 57 inches

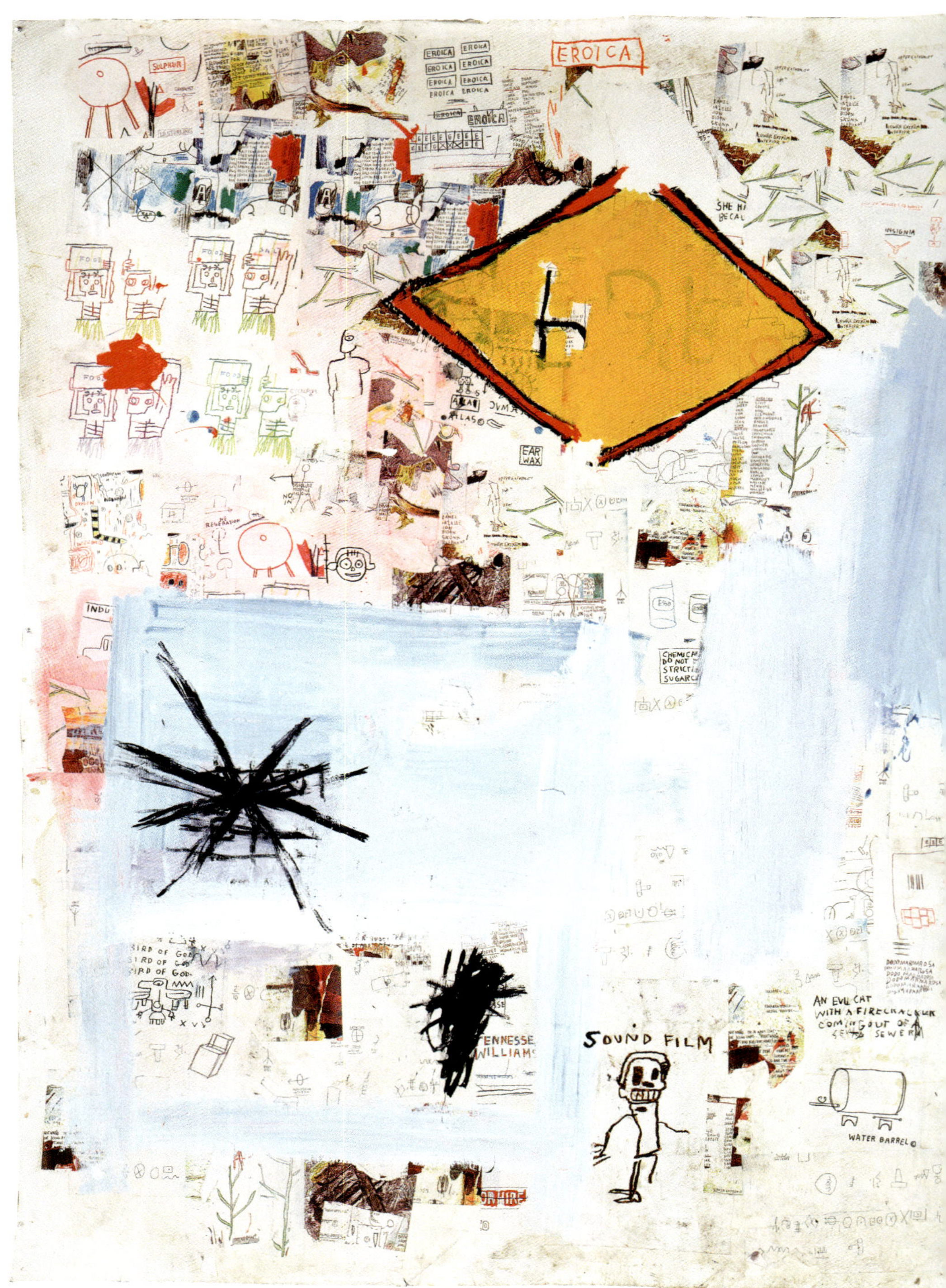

SULPHUR
EROICA
EROICA
SHE HI
BECAL
INSIGNIA
EAR
WAX
CHEMICAL
DO NOT
STRUCT
SUGARCA
BIRD OF GOD
BIRD OF GOD
BIRD OF GOD
XV
TENNESSE
WILLIAMS
SOUND FILM
AN EVIL CAT
WITH A FIRECRACKER
COMING OUT OF A
SEWER
WATER BARREL

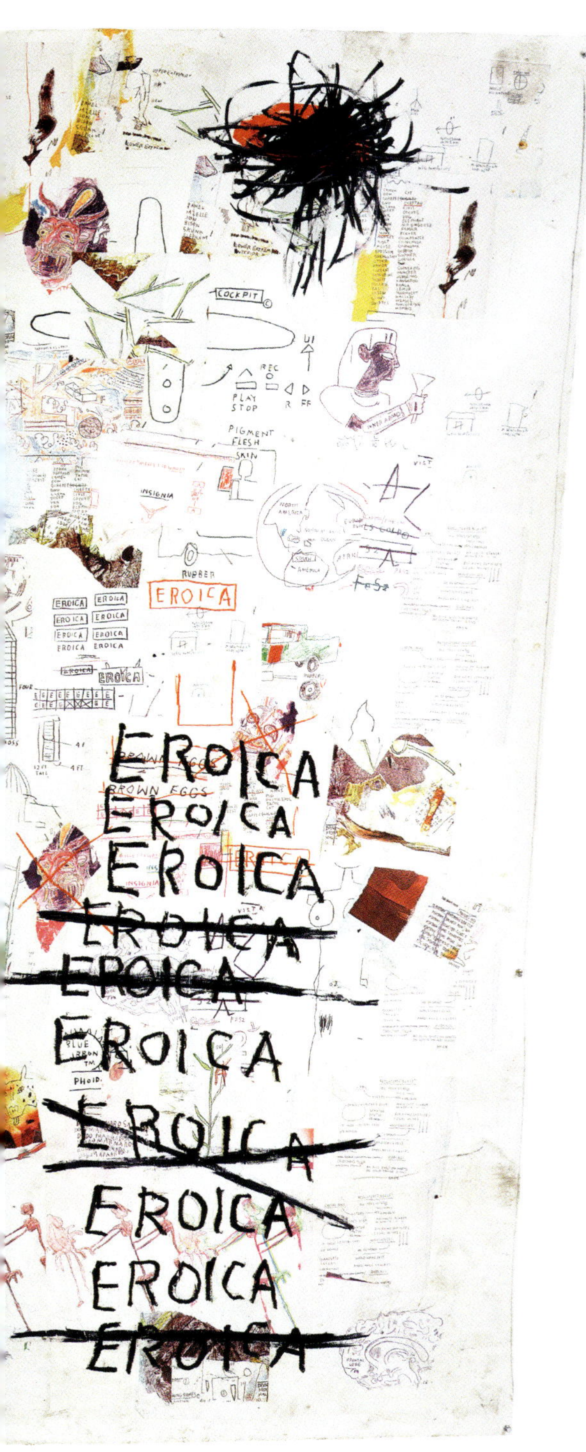

Eroica, 1987
Acrylic, oilstick, and photocopy
collage mounted on canvas,
228.5 x 271.5 cm / 90 x 107 inches

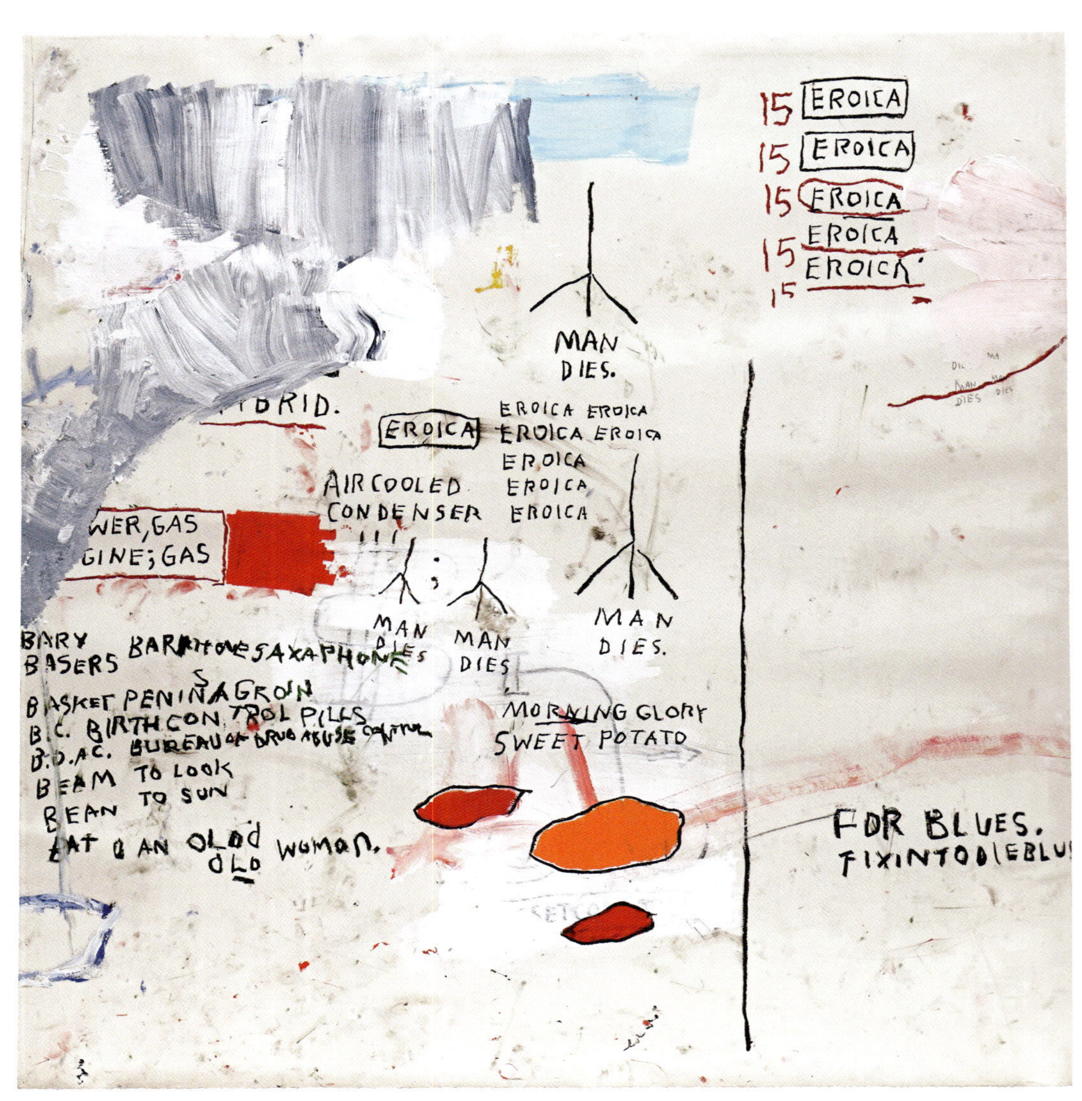

Eroica I, 1988
Acrylic and oilstick on paper mounted on canvas,
230 x 225.5 cm / 90 $^{1}/_{2}$ x 88 $^{3}/_{4}$ inches

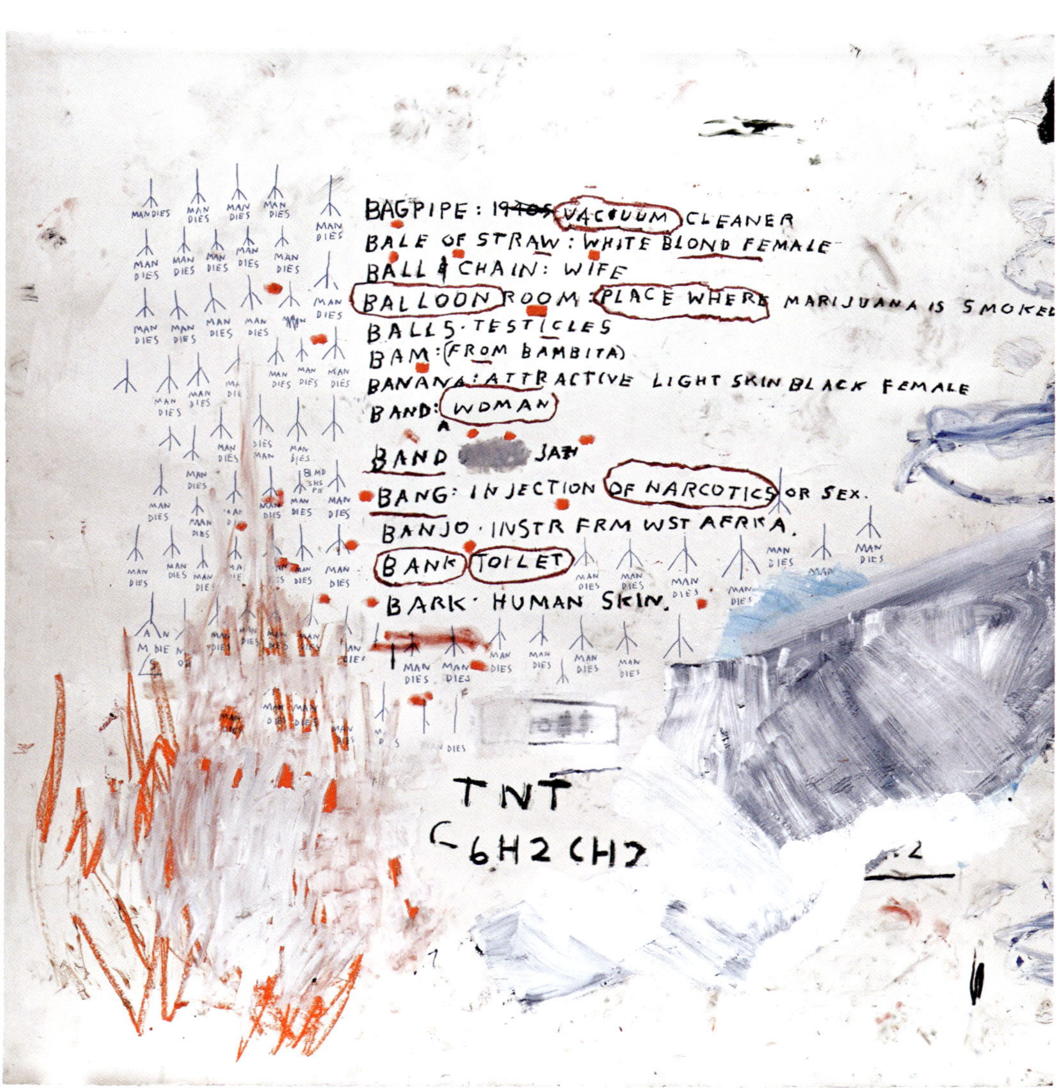

Eroica II, 1988
Acrylic and oilstick on paper mounted on canvas,
230 x 225.5 cm / 90 ¹/₂ x 88 ³/₄ inches

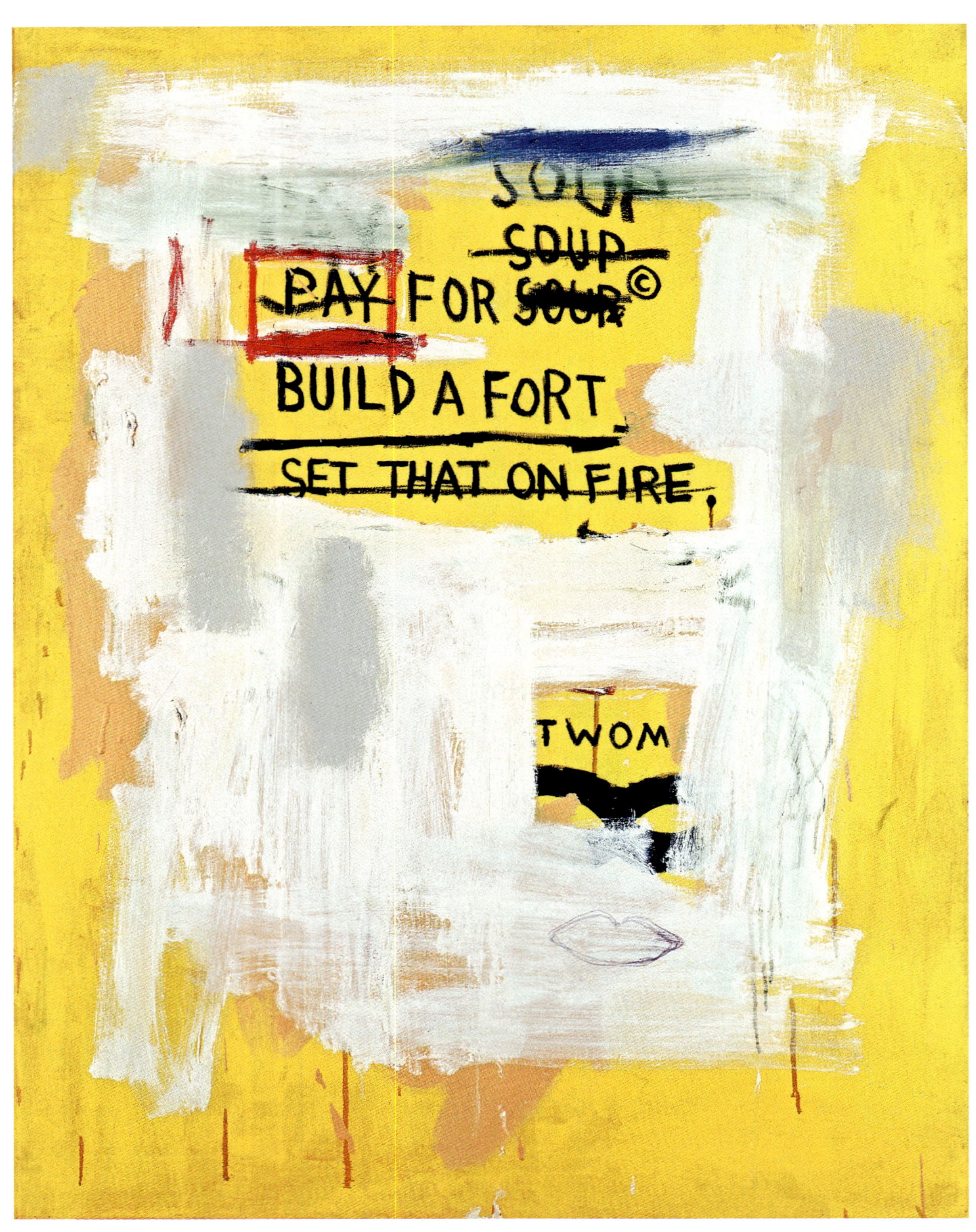

Pay for Soup, 1987
Acrylic and oilstick on canvas,
125.5 x 100.5 cm / 49 ¹/₂ x 39 ¹/₂ inches

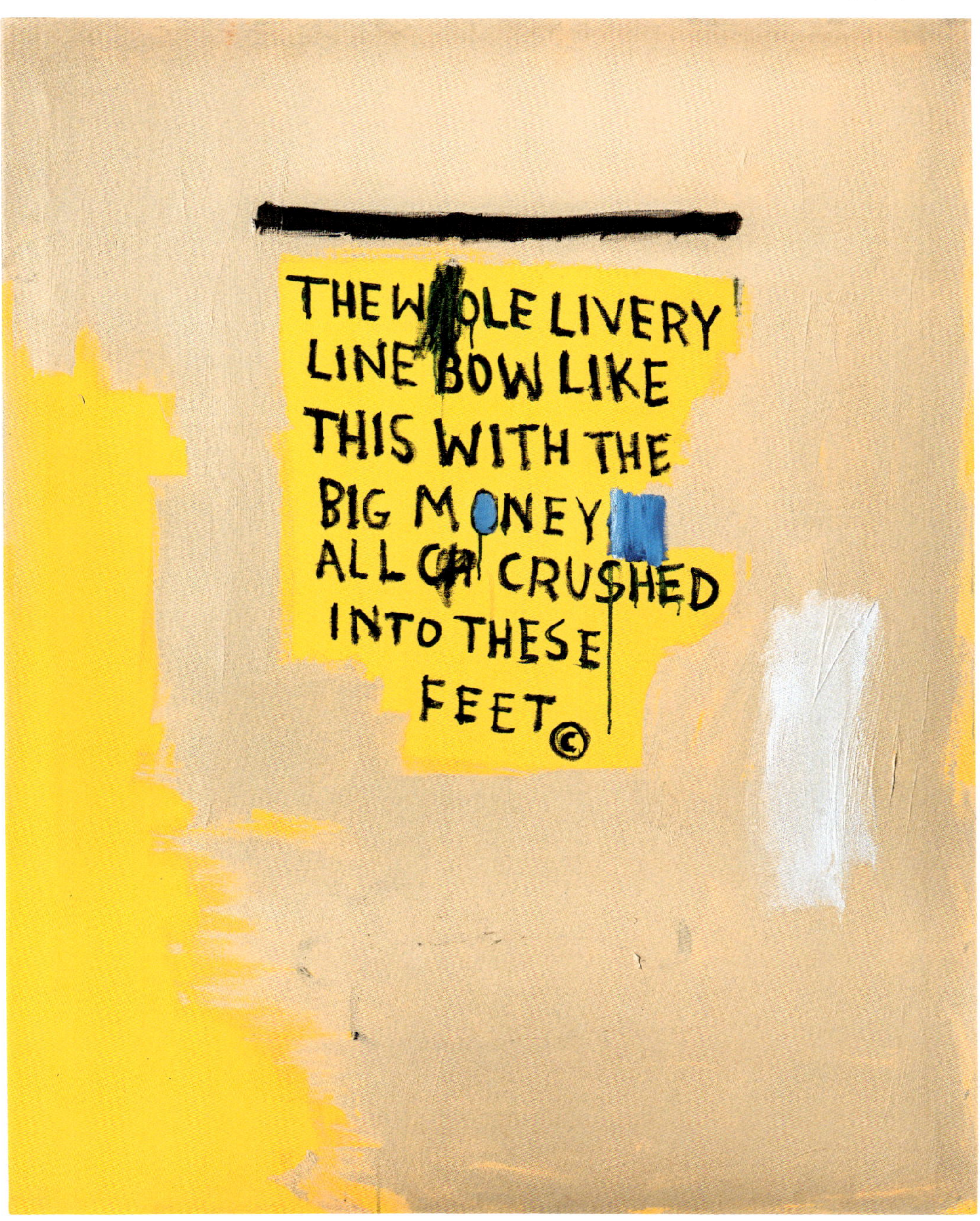

The Whole Livery Line, 1987
Acrylic and oilstick on canvas,
125.5 x 100.5 cm / 49 ¹/₂ x 39 ¹/₂ inches

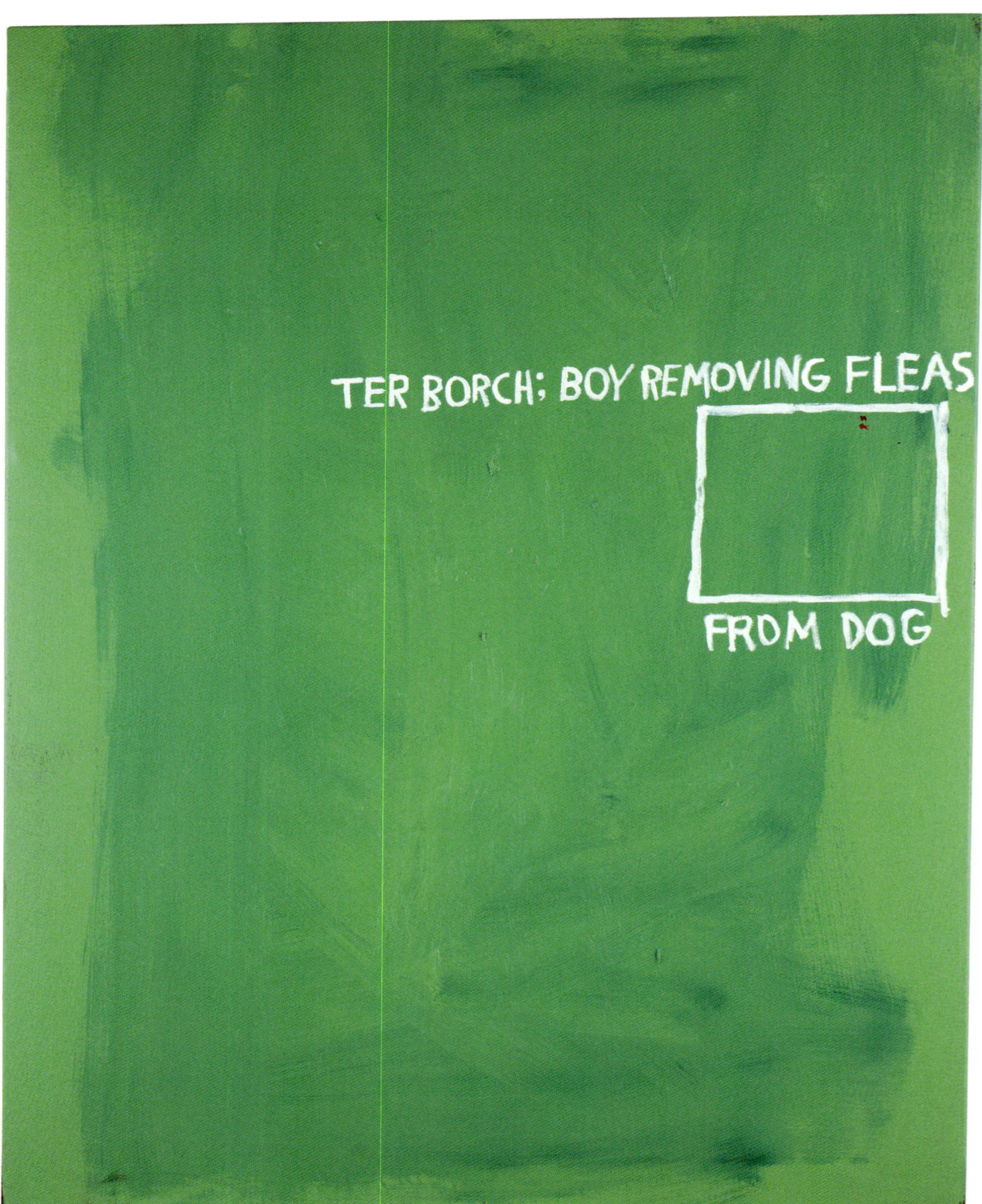

Untitled (Ter Borch: Boy Removing Fleas from Dog), 1984–1988
Acrylic and oilstick on canvas,
125.5 x 100.5 cm / 49 $^1/_2$ x 39 $^1/_2$ inches

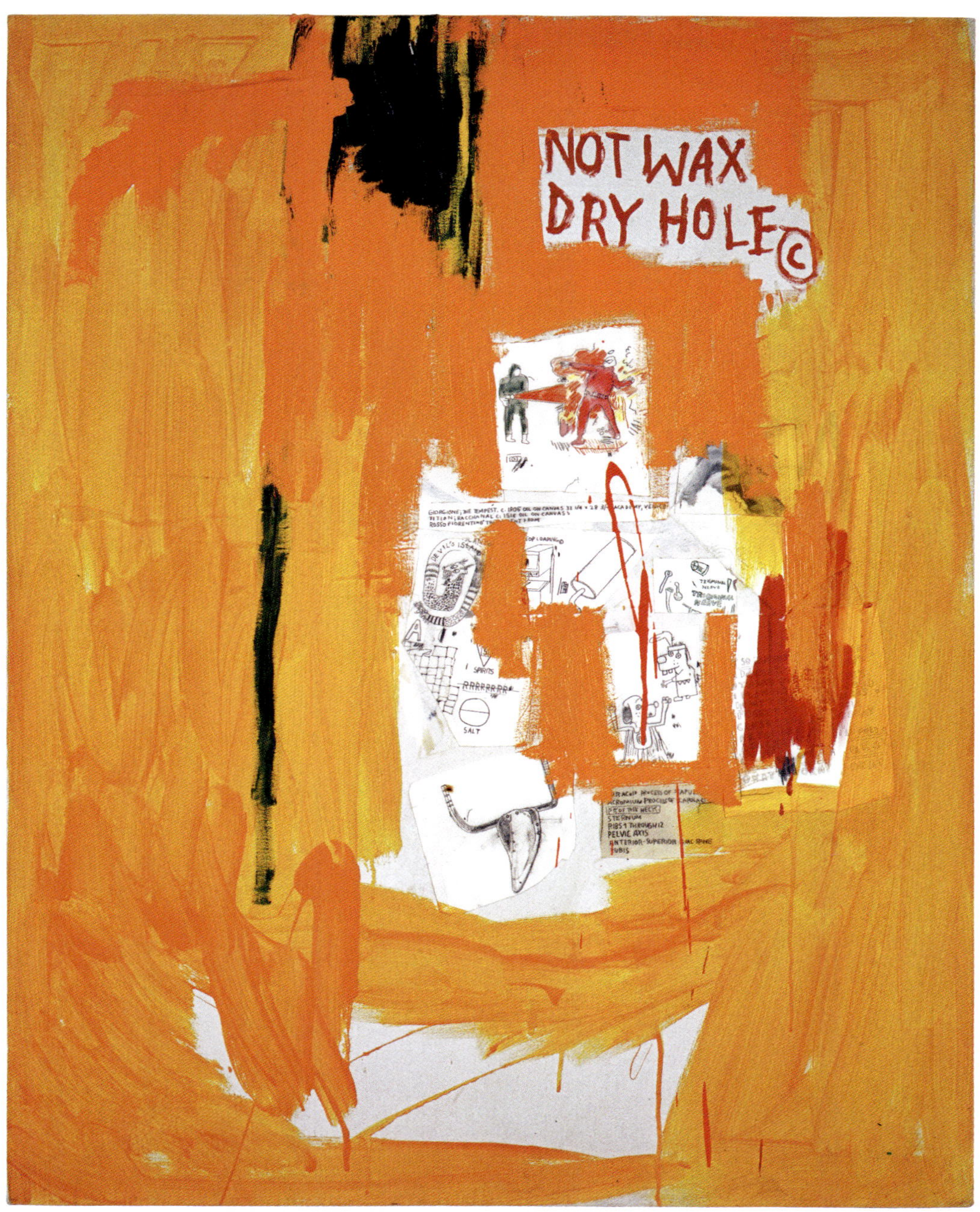

Orange, 1988
Acrylic and paper collage on canvas,
127 x 102 cm / 50 x 40 ¹/₄ inches

SCHWARZ
SCHWARZ
SCHWARZ
BLACK
SCHWARZ
BLACK
EROICA
YELLOW
NITROGEN
ROLLER CRUSHER
OAK
VISTA
BELL
WAX
RECEIVER
URINE
ATOMIZER
POLARIS
POLARIS
POLARIS
B AS IN BIRD
BH ASPIRATE
CH AS IN CHEESE
D AS IN DOG
NG AS IN KING
EASY MARK SUCKER
HEART AS ARENA
DIODE
SPIRITS
KIDNEY
NOTHING TO BE GAINED HERE
RECEIVER
BROKEN WING
BROKEN WING
BROKEN WING
BROKEN WING
PUNCH INHIBIT UNIT SHIFT
PEGASUS
ICARUS
PEGASUS
ZINC EARTH GROUND
PUNCH INHIBIT UNIT SHIFT
PUNCH INHIBIT UNIT SHIFT
PUNCH INHIBIT UNIT SHIFT
ICARUS > POLARIS
DA VINCI'S HELICOPTER
EROICA
PEGASUS
BS
BROKEN WING
BROKEN WING
BROKEN WING
BROKEN WING
BROKEN WING
HOT
ZINC
100 PSIG
STEAM HEAT
LEAD
AU EORTTUEA
AU EORTTUEA
AU EORTTUEA
POOR BEN
EROICA
OLEO
COWARDS WILL GIVE TO GET RID OF YOU
HEART AS ARENA
WATER COOLED CONDENSER
KOTO
VAPOR STEAM HEAT
DETAIL OF STONEHENGE
ANIMATED RAT
ANIMATED RAT
ANIMATED RAT
EROICA
EROICA
PLUTO
NAVAL
IRON
URINE
TAPE RECORDER
PEGASUS
PEGASUS
PLUTO
IVORY BLACK
NOIR S'VORE
STEP PYRAMID
FUNERAR DEPT.
SCHWARZ
SCHWARZ
AMPLIFIER
DIRECTIONAL
ATOMIZER
STEAM VAPOR
MONTICELLO
RECEIVER
RECEIVING STATION
ELVIC
ANDROMEDA
PEGASUS
PEGASUS
PEGASUS
PEGASUS
PEGASUS
GAS BLOWER
BELL
BUZZER
EROICA
UNIT SHIFT
EROICA
WAX
SCHWARZ
SCHWARZ
SCHWARZ
SPRAYER
EROICA
OLEO
HEART AS ARENA
HEART AS ARENA
HEART AS ARENA
HEART AS ARENA
HEART AS ARENA
HEART AS ARENA
HEART AS ARENA
PINE FOREST
GAS BLOWER
IL PUBLICO BRUTO
IL PUBLICO BRUTO
INTL
SCHWARZ
SCHWARZ
SCHWARZ
SCHWARZ
SCHWARZ
SCHWARZ
MONTICELLO
SO IT WAS'NT PETROL
SO IT WAS'NT PETROL
SO IT WAS'NT PETROL
SO IT WAS'NT PETROL
SO IT WAS'NT PETROL
SACHRINNE
SACHRINNE
IRON
EASY MARK SUCKER
OLEO
PRESSURE
NOTHING TO BE GAINED HERE
JET MIXER EJECTOR
WATER COOLED
EARTH (GROUND)
BELL
BUZZER
COWARDS WILL GIVE TO GET RID OF YOU
PEGASUS
GAS BLOWER
EROICA
EROICA
EROICA
EROICA
EROICA
EROICA
DIODE
PRESSURE
NUCLEAR REACTOR
FOOD
SALT
AU EORTTUEA
AU EORTTUEA
AU EORTTUEA
PUNCH INHIBIT UNIT SHIFT
JET MIXER EJECTOR
MERCURY
EROICA
RECEIVER
AMPLIFIER
LOANS
IRON
LINK PARABOLE
SPRAYER
VISTA
SALT
C3H5(NO3)3
OAK
MADE IN CHINA
MADE IN CHINA
MADE IN CHINA
MADE IN CHINA
PILOPHILENOR
YELLOW
PINE FOREST
VISTA
OAK
NITROGEN
ATOMIZER
C3H5(NO3)3
LOUDSPEAKER
KEY LAMP
WAX
SPIRITS
DIODE
PEGASUS
LOUDSPEAKER
KEY LAMP
FURNACE
ANIMATED RAT
PUMP, ROTARY + CENTRIFUGAL
WATER CONDENSED COOLER
GAS BLOWER
PUNCH INHIBIT UNIT SHIFT
INTL
ASPHALT
ASPHALT
UNIT SHIFT
EARTH (GROUND)
NAVEL
DIRECTIONAL
PRESSURE SOURCE
ZERVOS
PEGASUS
PEGASUS
PEGASUS
LOANS
RECEIVING STATION
PEGASUS
INSIGA
AUDIO FREQ
GRIFFITH OBSERVATORY (LOS ANGELES, CALIF)
SUPER EIGHT
PRESSURE
MONTICELLO
COWARDS WILL GIVE TO GET RID OF YOU
BS
JOE LOUIS VS. BILLY CONN
JACK DEMPSEY VS. GENE TUNNEY
JOE FRAIZER
JOE FRAIZER
COWARDS WILL GIVE TO GET RID OF YOU
URINE
PRESSURE
EROICA
AMPLIFIER
B AS IN BIRD
BH ASPIRATE
CH AS IN CHEESE
D AS IN DOG
NG AS IN KING
SALT
DETAIL OF STONEHENGE
IRON
LOANS
IL PUBLICO BRUTO
BULLSHIFTERS
PRESSURE
STEEL
FIRST COMMUNION
BARCELONA MIXER
OIL ON CANVAS
ANDROMEDA
VAPOR
STEAM
ROLLER CRUSHER
KEY LAMP
PABLO BEGINS TO DRAW AND PAINT
ATTENDS BULLFIGHT
COMPLETES EARLIEST WORK
THE FOOT
OUTSIDE OF FOOT
INSIDE OF FOOT
FRONT VIEW
BACK VIEW
TOP OF FOOT
BOTTOM FOOT
MUSCLES
WHAM
SALT
SHINBONE NIPPLES
VISTA DI FRANCO
VISTA DALL'ALTO
POSTERIOR MENTE (VISTA)
NOTHING TO BE GAINED HERE
NG AS IN KING
GRANITE CONCRETE GLASS
STEEL
SYRUP
HOT
VENUS
GRIFFITH OBSERVATORY (LOS ANGELES, CALIF)
MR UNIVERSE 1953
IRON
NG AS IN KING
ASPHALT
ASPHALT
ASPHALT
ASPHALT
ASPHALT
ASPHALT VAPOR
VULPECULA
ASPHALT
ASPHALT STEAM
MIXER
DETAIL OF STONEHENGE
PUNCH INHIBIT KEY LAMP
UNIT SHIFT
60 CM LARGE 11MM COAL
HAUPTNAHRUNGS
VERWENDUNG STEEL
WINGER WITH A FLANGE OF FE
ANDES RUNNING DOWN THE STEM
PLUTO
SUPER EIGHT
STEEL HOT
IRON
MIGHT MONEY MUSCLES
ASPHALT
ASPHALT
B AS IN BIRD
BH ASPIRATE
CH AS IN CHEESE
D AS IN DOG
BH CH CHH
ROLLER CRUSHER
KEY AUDIO FREQ
MERCURY
SUPER AUDIO FREQ
HEAT
GAS BLOWER
REVERSE
PLAY STOP
ENGINE GAS
TEMPERATURE EARTH (GROUND)
MONTICELLO
SELECTIVE BAND
COWARDS WILL GIVE TO GET RID OF YOU
PRESET
URINE
PEGASUS
AUTOCLAVE
ROLLER CRUSHER
SEMISOFT REGULAR SPREAD WITH SHORT POINTS
LOW BAND LONG POINT
SOFT WIDE SPREAD COLLAR
PUMP, ROTARY AND CENTRIFUGAL
B AS IN BIRD
BH ASPIRATE
CH AS IN CHEESE
STEAM VAPOR
MIXER
ROLLER CRUSHER
PRESSURE SOURCE TANK
RECEIVING STATION NUCLEAR REACTOR
TRANSMITTING AERIAL
HEAD
SALT
DISK AND DONUT COLUMN
PUNCH INHIBIT UNIT SHIFT
HEAT
AIR
DIODE
ASPHALT
SPIRITS
PRESSURE SOURCE TANK
CH AS IN CHEESE DOG
MONTICELLO
B AS IN BIRD
BH ASPIRATE
CH AS IN CHEESE
D AS IN DOG
NG AS IN KING
STEAM VAPOR
ROLLER CRUSHER
ASPHALT
ASPHALT
BELL
PLAY STOP
SPIRITS
TRANSMITTER
WAIST
FREQ
URINE TRANSMITTER FECES AMPLIFIER
DETAIL OF STONEHENGE
EASY MARK SUCKER
DETAIL OF STONEHENGE
COLD
WATER COOLED CONDENSER
RECEIVER
DIRECT CURRENT
ZENITH
ZENITH
ZENITH
ZENITH
JET MIXER EJECTOR
REVERSE
ARIES
REVERSE
AUTOCLAVE
MIXER
OSCILLOSCOPE
ASPHALT
ARIES
TAPE RECORDER
B AS IN BIRD
BH ASPIRATE
CH AS IN CHEESE
D AS IN DOG
PRESSURE SOURCE TANK
CH AS IN CHEESE DOG
ASPHALT
MONTICELLO
INTL STEAM VAPOR
AMPLIFIER
PUNCH INHIBIT UNIT SHIFT
ROLLER CRUSHER
DIODE
WATER COOLED CONDENSER
ROLLER CRUSHER DIODE
URINE FECES
ENGINE GAS
PEGASUS
DIRECT CURRENT
ROLLER CRUSHER
PEGASUS
PUMP ROTARY
DIODE
B AS IN BIRD
BH ASPIRATE
CH AS IN CHEESE
D AS IN DOG
NG AS IN KING
RECEIVER
AMPLIFIER
VULPECULA
AMPLIFIER RECEIVER
REVERSE
RECEIVING STATION
NOTHING TO BE GAINED HERE
PUMP, ROTARY AND CENTRIFUGAL
STEAM VAPOR
LINK PARABOLE
URINE
SPIRITS
SALT
WAX PRESSURE
PRESSURE SOURCE TANK
DIODE
ELECTRIC FAN
TAPE RECORDER
ROLLER CRUSHER
B AS IN BIRD
BH ASPIRATE
CH AS IN CHEESE
D AS IN DOG
NG AS IN KING
CHEST
PILOPHILE NOR
ZINC LEAD
IRON
DIRECT CURRENT
HIP
FURNACE
POOR BEN
PRESSURE
AMPLIFIER TEMPERATURE

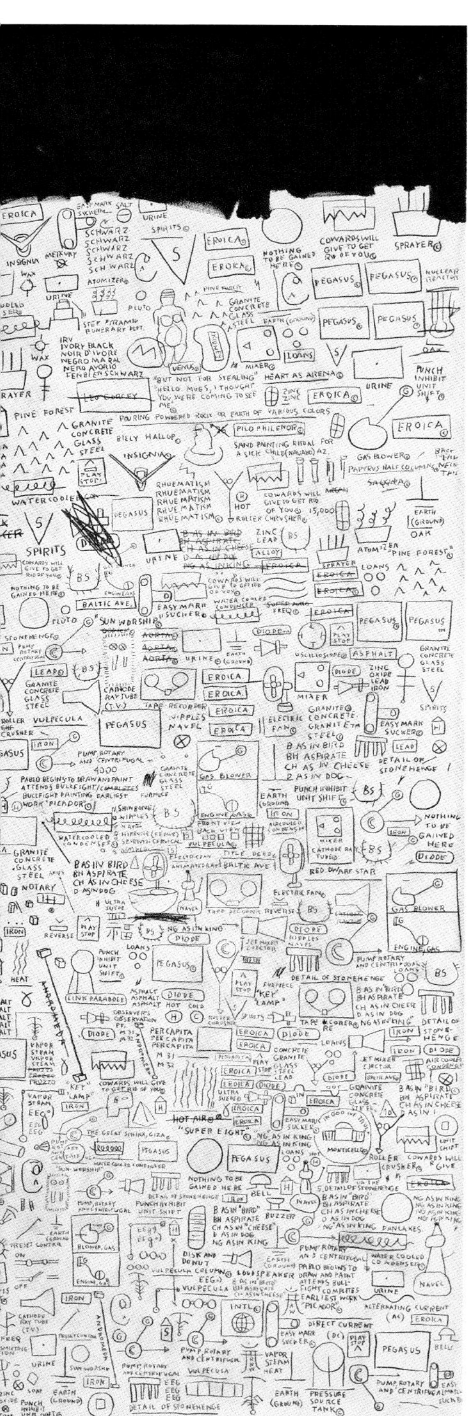

Pegasus, 1987
Acrylic, graphite, and colored pencil
on paper mounted on canvas,
223.5 x 228.5 cm / 88 x 90 inches

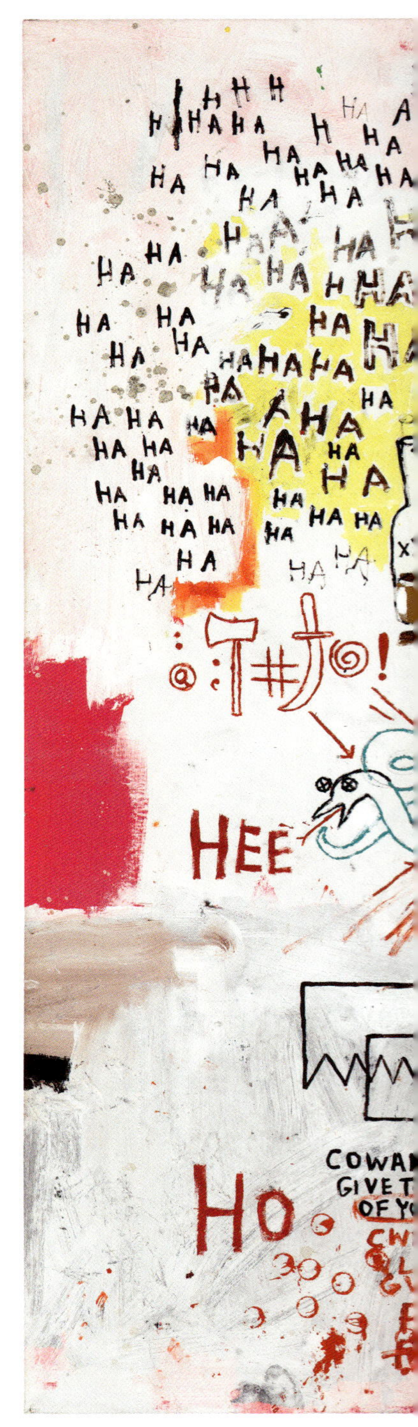

Riddle Me This Batman, 1987
Acrylic and oilstick on canvas,
297 x 290 cm / 117 x 114 $^1/_4$ inches

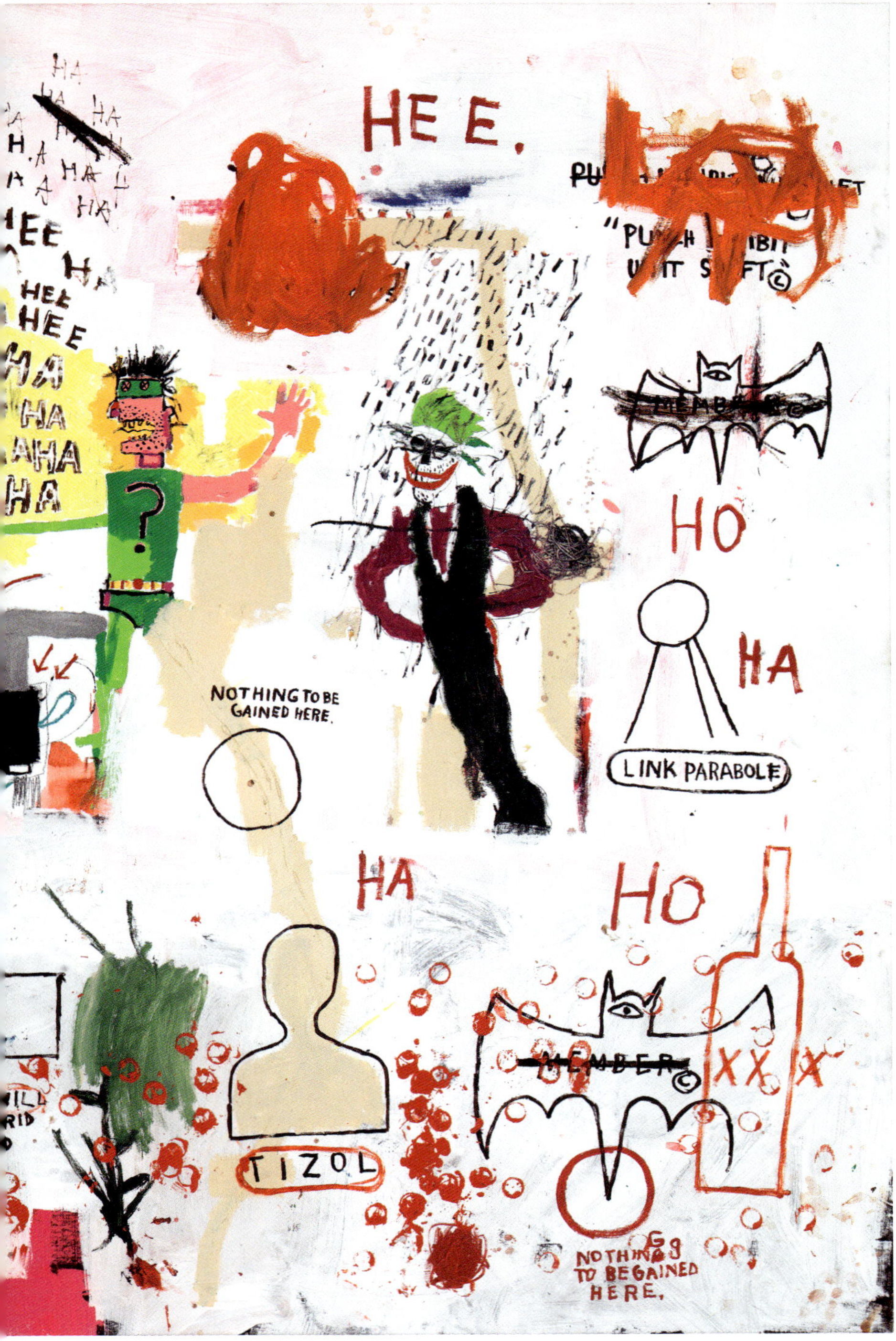
HA
HA HA
HA
HA
HA
HA HA
HA
HEE
HA
HEE
HEE
HA
HA
AHA
HA
HE E.
PUNCH EXHIBIT
"PUNCH EXHIBIT
UNIT SWIFT ©
HO
HA
LINK PARABOLE
NOTHING TO BE
GAINED HERE.
HA
HO
TIZOL
MEMBER © XX X
NOTHING
TO BE GAINED
HERE.

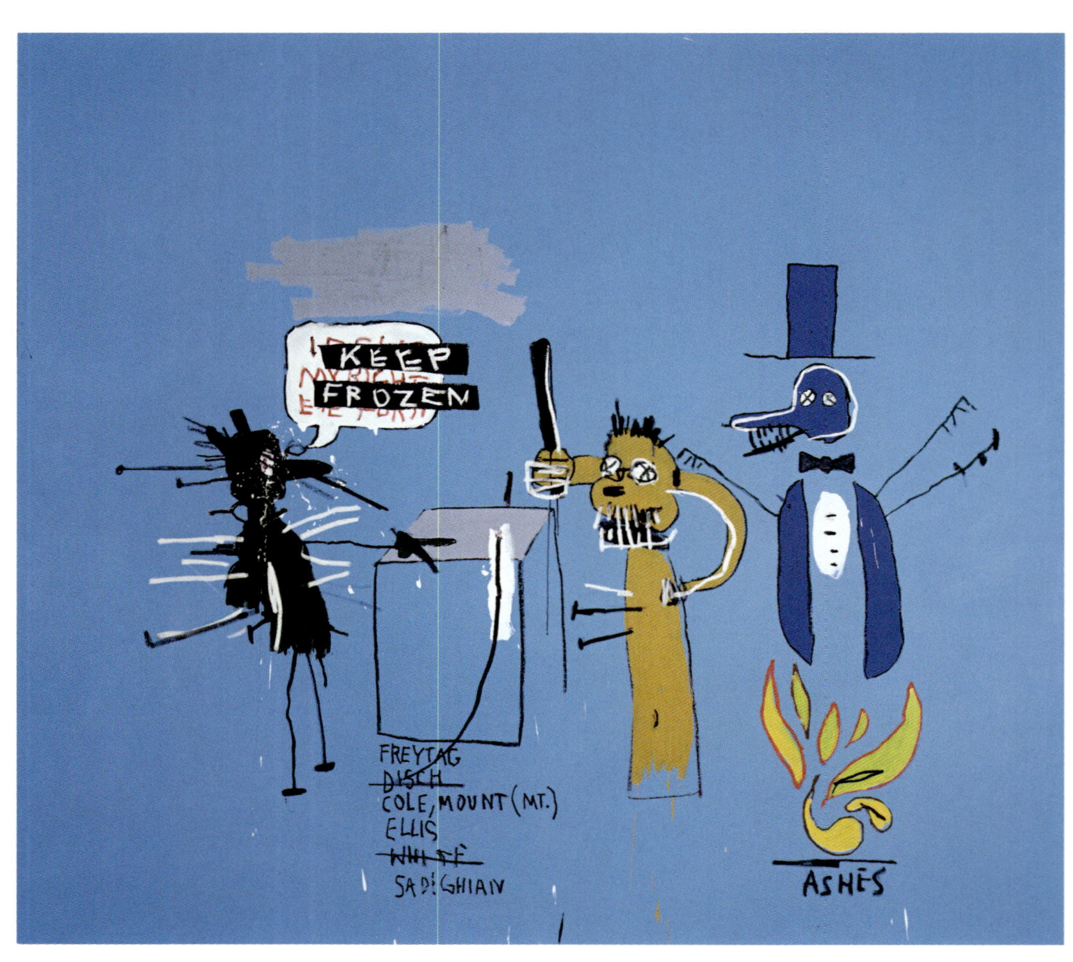

**The Dingoes That Park Their Brains
with Their Gum**, 1988
Acrylic and oilstick on linen,
254 x 289.5 cm / 100 x 114 inches

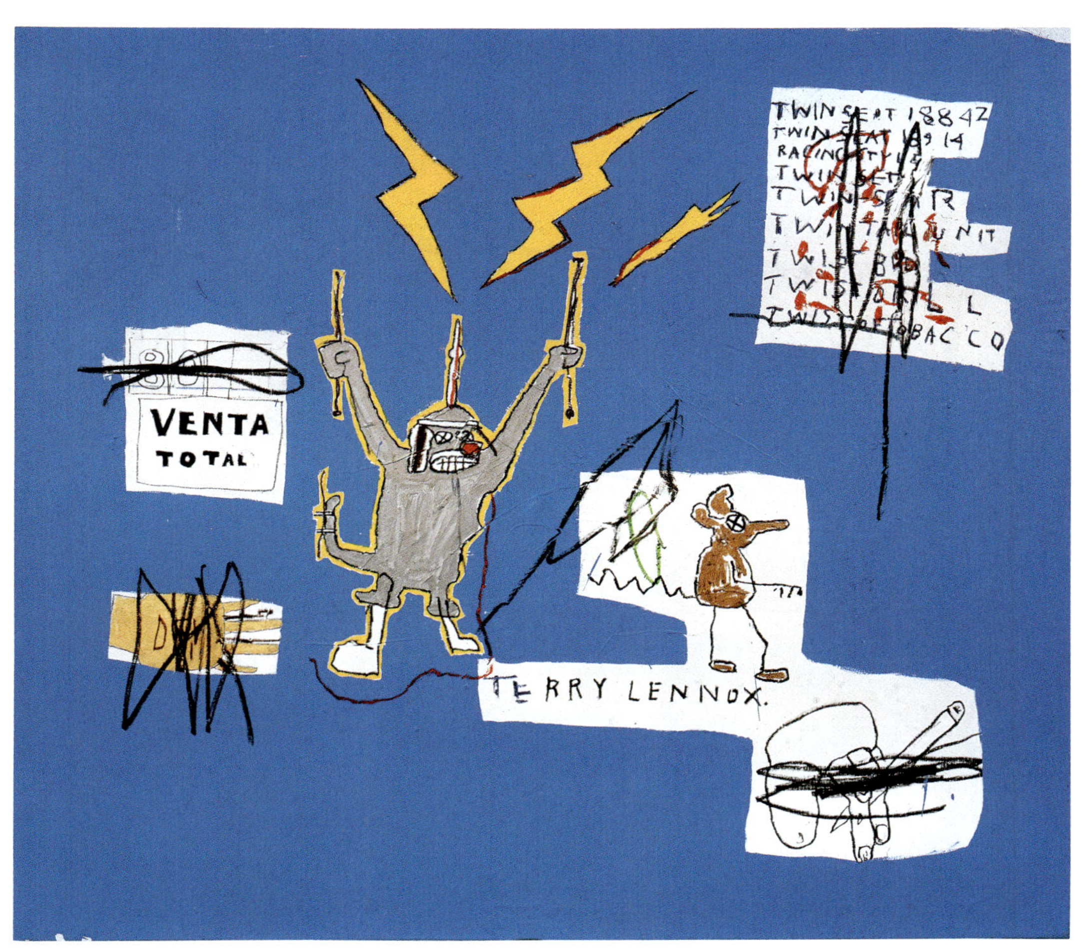

**The Mechanics That Always Have
a Gear Left Over**, 1988
Acrylic and oilstick on linen,
254 x 289.5 cm / 100 x 114 inches

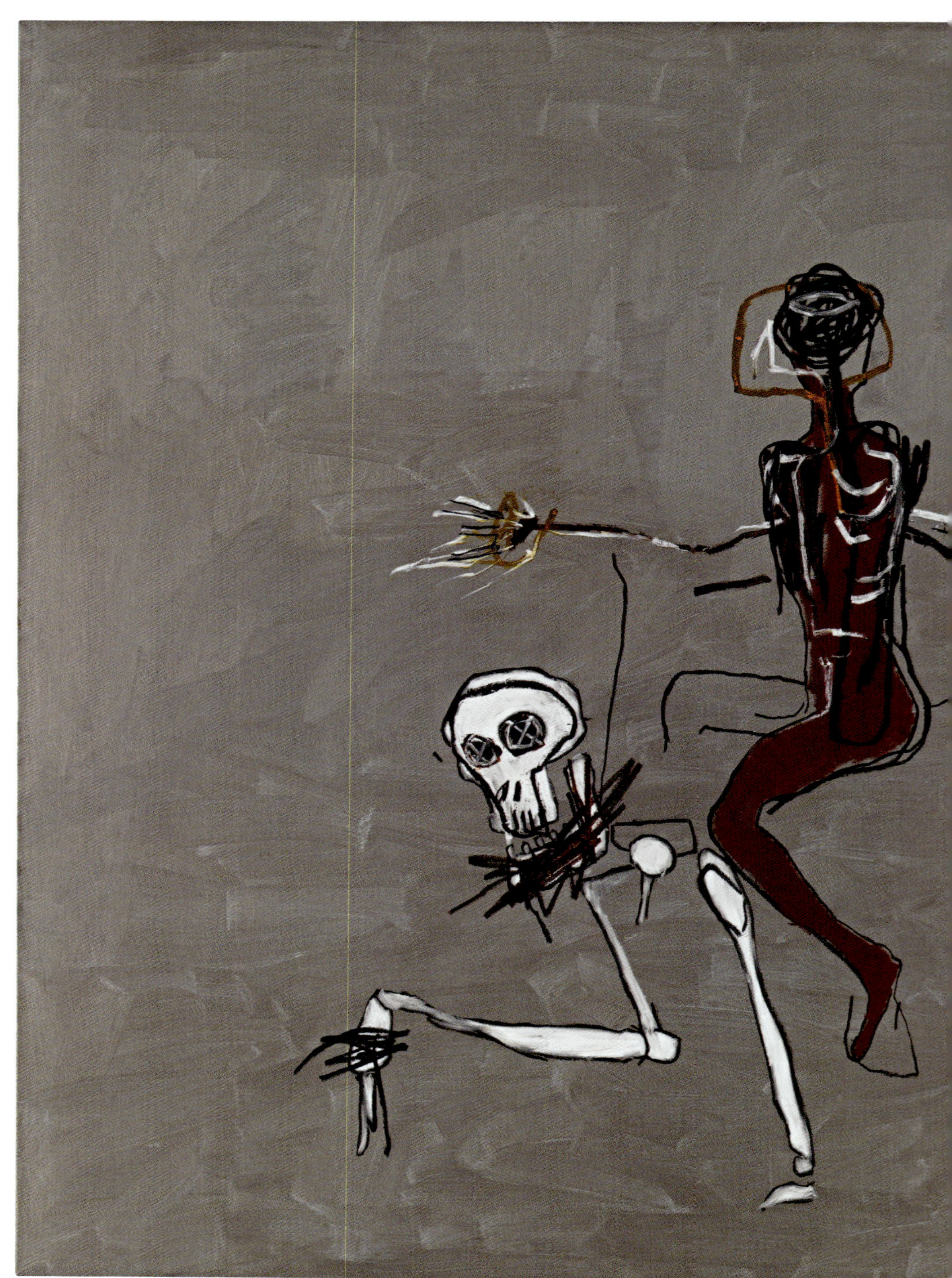

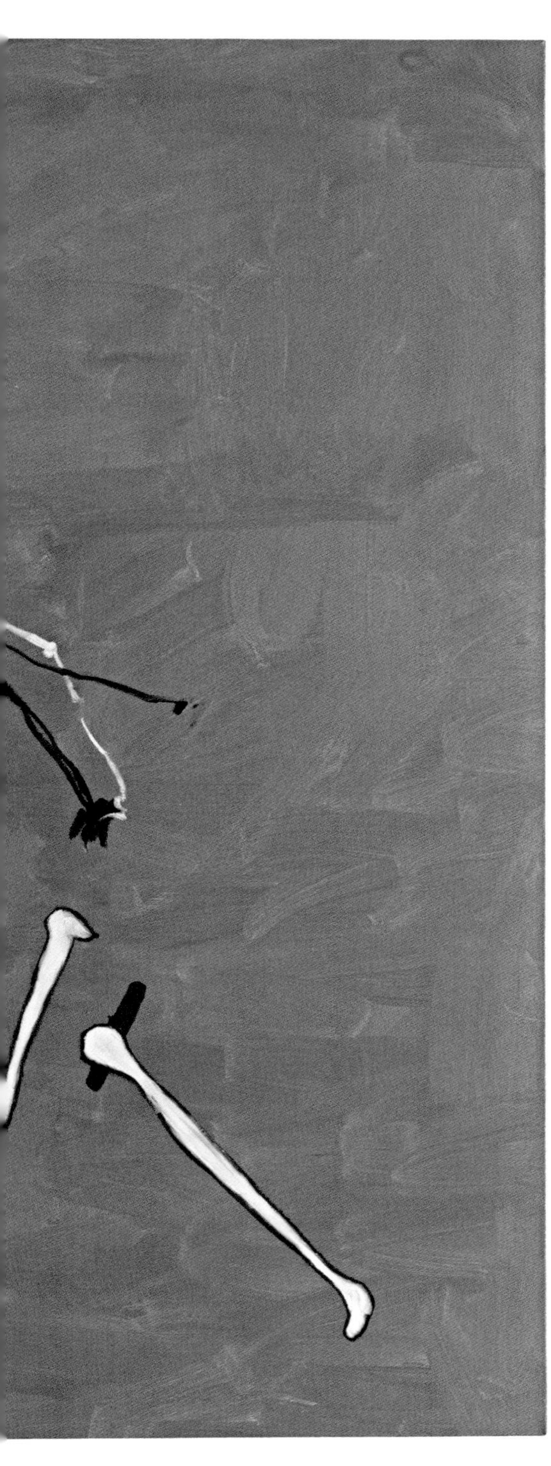

Riding with Death, 1988
Acrylic and oilstick on canvas,
249 x 289.5 cm / 98 x 114 inches

Pages 494/495: Jean-Michel Basquiat,
exhibition view, Vrej Baghoomian Gallery,
New York 1988

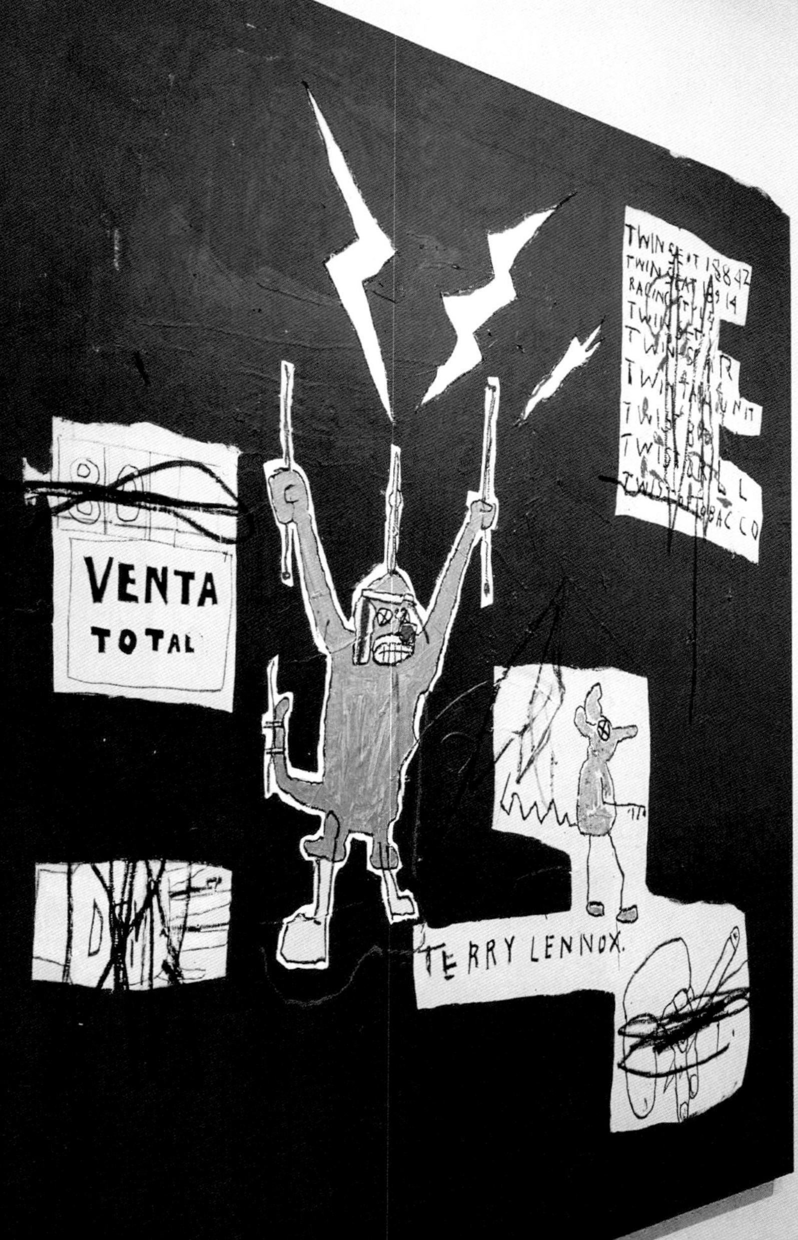
TWIN SEAT 1884 2
TWIN SEAT 1914
RACING
TWIN
TWIN SEAT
TWIN STAR
TWIN ACCOUNT
TWIST BAR
TWIST
TWIST TOBACCO
VENTA
TOTAL
TERRY LENNOX.

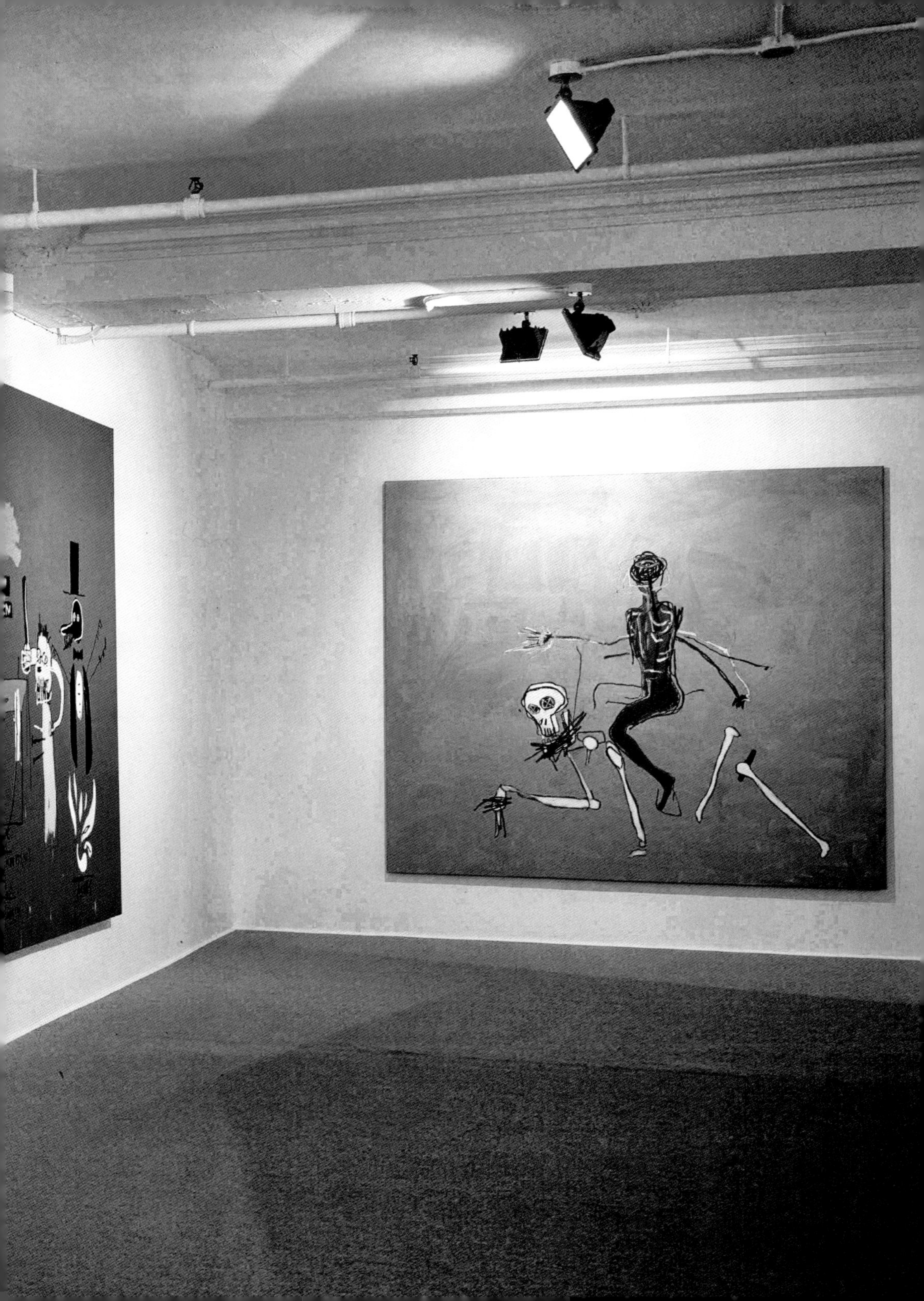

Jean-Michel Basquiat

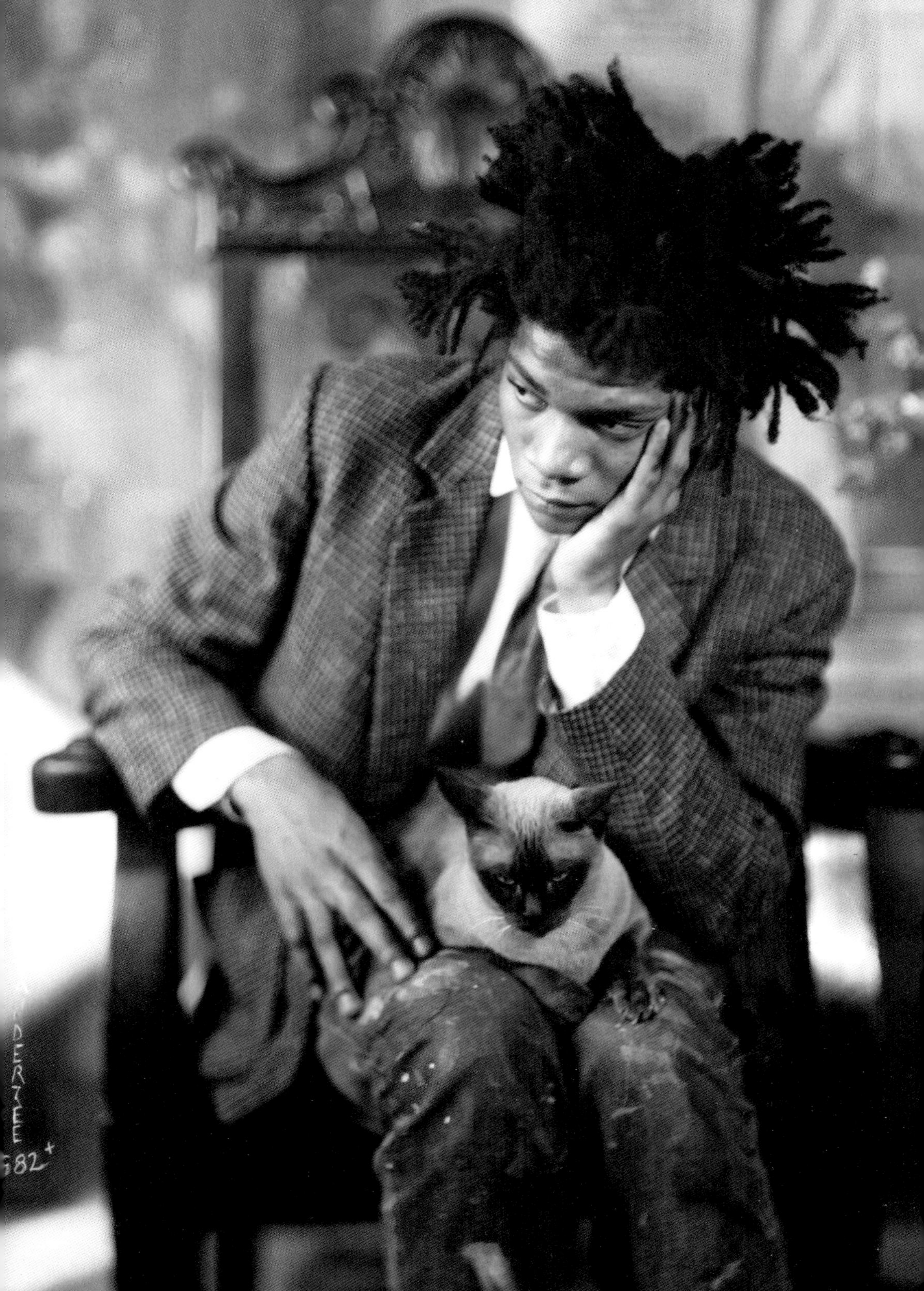
DERZEE
'82

Biography

Jean-Michel Basquiat

Born December 22, 1960, in Brooklyn, New York. Died August 12, 1988, in Manhattan, New York.

Solo Exhibitions during the Artist's Lifetime
(*catalog)

1981
Samo. Galleria d'Arte Emilio Mazzoli, Modena (May 23–Jun 20)

1982
Annina Nosei Gallery, New York (Mar 6–Apr 1)
Paintings. Gagosian Gallery, Los Angeles (Apr 8–May 8)
Galerie Bruno Bischofberger, Zürich (Sep 11–Oct 9)
*Galleria Mario Diacono, Rome (Oct 23–Nov 20)
Fun Gallery, New York (Nov 4–Dec 7)
*Galerie Delta, Rotterdam (Dec)
Blum Helman Gallery, New York
Marlborough Gallery, New York

1983
Annina Nosei Gallery, New York (Feb 12–Mar 3)
New Paintings. Gagosian Gallery, Los Angeles (Mar 8–Apr 2)
Paige Powell's apartment, New York (Apr)
West Beach Café, Venice, CA (May–Jun)
Neue Bilder. Galerie Bruno Bischofberger, Zürich (Sep 28–Oct 22)
Paintings. Akira Ikeda Gallery, Tokyo (Nov 14–Dec 10)

1984
*Mary Boone Gallery, New York (May 5–26)
Paintings 1981–1984. The Fruitmarket Gallery, Edinburgh (Aug 11–Sep 23); traveled to Institute of Contemporary Arts, London (Dec 15, 1984–Jan 27, 1985); Museum Boymans-van Beuningen, Rotterdam (Feb 9–Mar 31, 1985)

Collaborations: Basquiat, Clemente & Warhol. Galerie Bruno Bischofberger, Zürich (Sep 15–Oct 13)
New Paintings. Carpenter and Hochman Gallery, Dallas (Sep 20–Oct 20)

1985
Collaborations: Jean-Michel Basquiat, Francesco Clemente, Andy Warhol. Akira Ikeda Gallery, Tokyo (Jan 14–31)
Neue Werke. Galerie Bruno Bischofberger, Zürich (Jan 19–Feb 16)
*University of California Art Museum, Berkeley (Jan–Mar); traveled to La Jolla Museum of Contemporary Art, La Jolla (May 4–Jun 16)
Akira Ikeda Gallery, Nagoya (Feb 12–Mar 9)
*Mary Boone Gallery, New York (Mar 2–23)
Warhol and Basquiat: Paintings. Tony Shafrazi Gallery, New York (Sep 14–Oct 18)
Paintings. Akira Ikeda Gallery, Tokyo (Dec 2–25)
Paintings from 1982. Annina Nosei Gallery, New York (Dec 14, 1985–Jan 9, 1986)

1986
Gagosian Gallery, Los Angeles (Jan 7–Feb 8)
Drawings. Fay Gold Gallery, Atlanta (Feb 7–Mar 5)
Zeichnungen. Galerie Bruno Bischofberger, Zürich (Apr 26–Jun 30)
Bilder 1984–1986. Galerie Thaddaeus Ropac, Salzburg (Jul 27–Aug 31)
Collaborations: Jean-Michel Basquiat and Andy Warhol. Akira Ikeda Gallery, Tokyo (Sep 8–30)
Centre Culturel Français, Abidjan (Oct 10–Nov 7)
Galerie Delta, Rotterdam (Nov)
Drawings. Akira Ikeda Gallery, Nagoya (Nov 5–29)
Collaborations: Jean-Michel Basquiat and Andy Warhol. Galerie Bruno Bischof-berger, Zürich (Nov 14, 1986–Jan 17, 1987)

*Kestner Gesellschaft, Hanover (Nov 28, 1986–Jan 25, 1987)
Galerie Michael Werner, Cologne

1987
Galerie Daniel Templon, Paris (Jan 10–Feb 7)
New Works. Akira Ikeda Gallery, Tokyo (Feb 7–28)
Drawings. Tony Shafrazi Gallery, New York (May 23–Jun 13)
Drawings. Galerie Thaddaeus Ropac, Salzburg (Jun 6–31)
*PS Gallery, Tokyo (Oct 8–Dec 4)

1988
Galerie Yvon Lambert, Paris (Jan 9–Feb 10)
Peintures 1982–1987. Galerie Beaubourg, Paris (Jan 9–Feb 16)
Neue Arbeiten. Galerie Hans Mayer, Düsseldorf (Jan 12–Mar 15)
Galerie Michael Haas, Berlin (Feb 5–Mar 12)
Vrej Baghoomian Gallery, New York (Apr 29–Jun 11)
Paintings, Drawings. Galerie Thaddaeus Ropac, Salzburg (Jun 15–Jul 26)

Posthumous Solo Exhibitions (selection)

1988
Important Drawings. Fay Gold Gallery, Atlanta (Sep 6–Oct 4)
Collaborations: Andy Warhol, Jean-Michel Basquiat. Mayor Rowan Gallery, Mayor Gallery, and Grob Gallery, London (Nov 21, 1988–Jan 21, 1989)
Paintings. Gallery Schlesinger, New York (Nov)
Memorial Exhibition. Annina Nosei Gallery, New York (Dec 3, 1988–Jan 14, 1989)

1989
Das zeichnerische Werk. Kestner Gesellschaft, Hanover (Sep 15–Oct 22)
Warhol and Basquiat: Collabora-tions. Didier Imbert Fine Art, Paris (Sep 28–Nov 25)

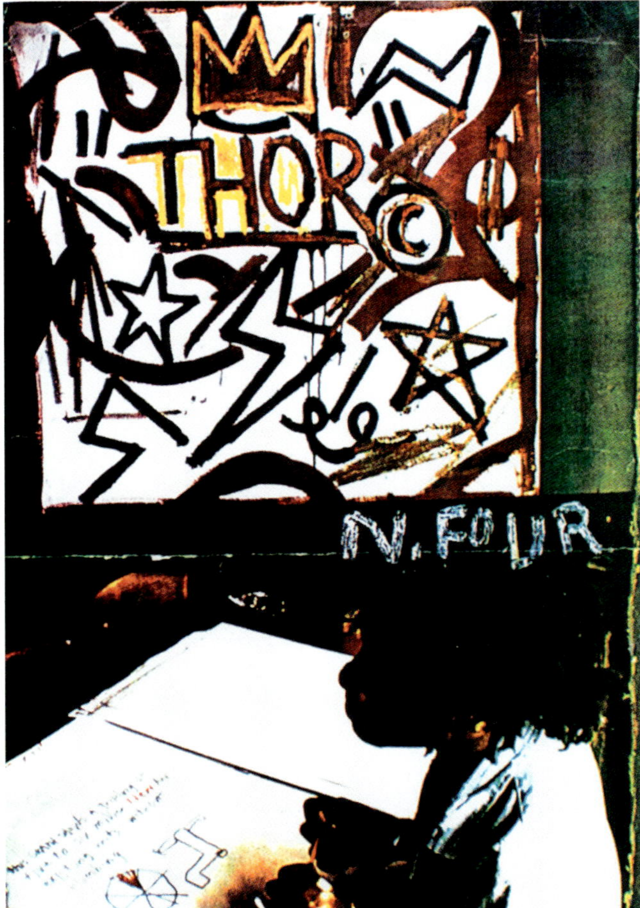

Invitation card, *Jean-Michel Basquiat,* Fun Gallery,
New York 1982

*Dau al Set, Galeria d'Art,
Barcelona (Oct–Nov)
*Vrej Baghoomian Gallery,
New York (Oct 21–Nov 25)
*Peintures, sculptures, œuvres sur
papier et dessins.* Galerie Enrico
Navarra, Paris (Nov 8–Dec 31)

1990
Œuvres sur papier. Galerie Le Gall
Peyroulet, Paris (Jan 23–Mar 3)
*Galerie Fabien Boulakia, Paris
(Sep 27–Nov 3)
*Jean-Michel Basquiat and Andy
Warhol.* Ho-Am Gallery, Seoul
(Oct 1–31)

Drawings. Robert Miller Gallery,
New York (Nov 3–Dec 1)
*Keith Haring, Jean-Michel Basquiat:
Paintings.* Tony Shafrazi Gallery,
New York (Dec 15, 1990–Jan 26, 1991)

1991
Oil Paintings, Drawings, etc.
PS Gallery, Tokyo (Mar 4–May 17)
*Andy Warhol and Jean-Michel
Basquiat.* Sonje Museum of Contem-
porary Art, Gyeongju (Sep 14–Oct 20);
traveled to The National Museum of
Contemporary Art, Seoul (Nov 1–30)
Œuvres sur papier. Galerie de Poche,
Paris (Dec 5–28)

1992
Vrej Baghoomian Gallery, New York
(Feb 8–Mar 7)
*Galerie Eric van de Weghe,
Brussels (Apr 9–May 23)
Une Rétrospective. Musée Cantini,
Marseille (Jul 4–Sep 20)
Installation of *Nu-Nile* and *Untitled
(Palladium Painting)* on loan from
the Estate of Jean-Michel Basquiat.
Metropolitan Museum of Art,
New York (Oct 19, 1992–Apr 22, 1993)
*Whitney Museum of American
Art, New York (Oct 23, 1992–Feb 14,
1993); traveled to Menil Collection,
Houston (Mar 11–May 9, 1993); Des
Moines Art Center, Des Moines
(May 22–Aug 15, 1993); Montgomery
Museum of Fine Arts, Montgomery
(Nov 18, 1993–Jan 9, 1994)

1993
*Alpha Cubic Gallery, Tokyo (Mar)
Paintings and Drawings. Gallery
Sho Contemporary Art, Tokyo
(May 11–Jun 6)
Galerie Bruno Bischofberger, Zürich
(Jun 10–Sep 11)
Newport Harbor Art Museum,
Newport Beach (Jul 10–Sep 12)
*FAE Musée d'Art Contemporain,
Pully-Lausanne (Jul 10–Nov 7)
Paintings. Tony Shafrazi Gallery,
New York (Nov 20, 1993–Jan 8, 1994)
Peinture, dessin, écriture.
Musée-Galerie de la Seita, Paris
(Dec 17, 1993–Feb 26, 1994)
Galerie Delta, Rotterdam

1994
Henry Art Gallery, University of
Washington, Seattle (Feb 18–Apr 28)
The Blue Ribbon Paintings. Mount
Holyoke College Art Museum, South
Hadley (Sep 8–Dec 22); traveled to
Wadsworth Atheneum, Hartford
(Jan–Mar 1995); The Andy Warhol
Museum, Pittsburgh (Apr 12–Sep 17,
1995); Museum of Contemporary Art,
Miami (Oct 15–Dec 8, 1996)
*Johnson County Community
College, Gallery of Art, Overland
Park (Sep 11–Oct 18)
Works in Black and White. Robert
Miller Gallery, New York (Nov 15,
1994–Jan 7, 1995)

1995
*Two Cents: Works on Paper by
Jean-Michel Basquiat and Poetry by*

Kevin Young. Centre Gallery, Miami-Dade Community College, Miami (Oct 20, 1995–Jan 14, 1996); traveled to Castellani Art Museum, Niagara University, Niagara Falls (Feb 11–Mar 31, 1996); The University of Memphis (Apr 19–Jun 22, 1996); University of South Florida Art Museum, Tampa (Jul–Aug 1996); Otis Gallery of Art and Design, Los Angeles (Sep 14–Oct 19, 1996); Austin Museum of Art, Austin (Nov 1996–Jan 1997)

1996

Collaborations: Warhol, Basquiat, Clemente. Museum Fridericianum, Kassel (Feb 4–May 5); traveled to Museum Villa Stuck, Munich (Jul 25–Sep 29)

Bodies and Heads. Robert Miller Gallery, New York (Feb 6–Mar 9)

*The Serpentine Gallery, London (Mar 6–Apr 21)

Peintures. Galerie Enrico Navarra, Paris (Apr 2–Jun 12)

**Œuvres sur papier.* Galerie Enrico Navarra and Galerie Lucien Durand, Paris (May 3–Jun 15)

*Junta de Andalucia, Palacio Episcopal, Málaga (May 16–Jul 7)

Obras sobre papeis. Galeria Luisa Strina, São Paulo (May–Jun)

*Galerie Bruno Bischofberger, Zürich (Jun 1–Aug 31)

The Bruce Museum, Greenwich, CT (Aug 4–Sep 8)

A Tribute: Important Paintings, Drawings and Objects. Tony Shafrazi Gallery, New York (Sep 21–Nov 23)

1980–1988. Quintana Gallery, Coral Gables (Dec 17, 1996–Feb 21, 1997)

1997

*Kaohsiung Museum of Fine Arts, Kaohsiung (Jan 26–Apr 27); traveled to Taichung Museum, Taichung (May 4–Jun 4)

Collaborations: Andy Warhol and Jean-Michel Basquiat. Gagosian Gallery, New York (Mar 15–Apr 26)

**Œuvres sur papier.* Fondation Dina Vierny-Musée Maillol, Paris (May 23–Sep 29)

*Gallery Hyundai, Seoul (Jul 15–Aug 17)

**King for a Decade.* Parco Gallery, Tokyo (Jul 22–Sep 17)

*Art Beatus Gallery, Vancouver (Sep 10–Oct 14)

Galerie Sho, Tokyo (Oct 1–Nov 15)

Big Step Inc. Osaka (Oct 16–21)

*Mitsukoshi Museum, Tokyo (Oct 28–Nov 24); traveled to Marugame Genichiro-Inokuma Museum of Contemporary Art, Marugame (Apr 18–May 31, 1998)

**Obras sobre papel.* Museo Nacional de Bellas Artes, Buenos Aires (Dec 8, 1997–Feb 13, 1998)

1998

**Paintings and Drawings 1980–1987.* Gagosian Gallery, Los Angeles (Feb 12–Mar 14)

**Obras sobre papeis.* Museu de Arte Moderna, Recife (Apr 1–May 31)

Tony Shafrazi Gallery, New York (Apr 25–May 30)

**Pinturas / Obras sobre papeis.* Pinacoteca do Estado, São Paulo (Jun 16–Aug 23)

**La Tête d'obsidienne.* Fort Napoléon, La Seyne-sur-Mer (Jun 26–Aug 14)

**Témoignage, 1977–1988.* Galerie Jerôme de Noirmont, Paris (Oct 2–Nov 27)

1980–1988. Galería Maeght, Barcelona (Oct 27–Nov 28)

Jean-Michel Basquiat with Jennifer Goode and her brother, Tiagba Island, Ivory Coast 1986. Photo Georges Courrèges

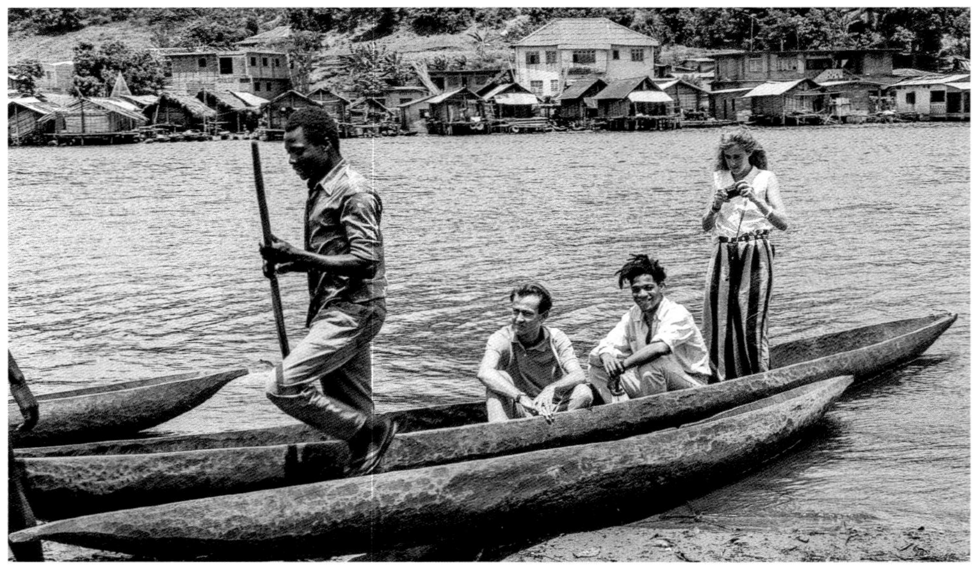

Collaborations: Jean-Michel Basquiat/Andy Warhol. Galerie Bruno Bischofberger, Zürich (Dec 10, 1998– Apr 27, 1999)

1999
*Kunsthaus Wien, Vienna (Feb 11–May 2)
*Centre Culturel L'Espal, Le Mans (Apr 29–Jun 15)
*Civico Museo Revoltela, Trieste (May 15–Sep 15)
Basquiat a Venezia. Fondazione Bevil-acqua La Masa, Venice (Jun 9–Oct 30)
**Werke auf Papier.* Stadtgalerie, Klagenfurt (Jun 18–Sep 26)
*Gallerìa Dante Vecchiato, Forte dei Marmi (Jul 10–Aug 5); traveled to Gallerìa Dante Vecchiato. Cortina d'Ampezzo (Aug 6–29)
Selected Paintings and Drawings. Tony Shafrazi Gallery, New York (Oct 1–Nov 13)
Fondazione Mudima, Milan (Oct 14–Nov 30)
Basquiat a Napoli. Museo Civico Castel Nuovo, Naples (Dec 19, 1999– Feb 27, 2000)

2000
Stephen Lacey Gallery, London (Feb 16–Mar 18)
Peintures. Galerie Enrico Navarra, Paris (Apr 27–Jul 8)
Dessins originaux. Galerie Frédéric Gollong, Saint-Paul-de-Vence (Jun 2–30)
Galerie Sho, Tokyo (Sep 1–Oct 14)
Basquiat en la Habana. Casa de las Américas, Fundación Havana Club, Havana (Nov 17, 2000– Jan 10, 2001)

2001
Hits on Paper. Galerie Pictureshow, Berlin (Jul 12–Sep 23)
**Gemälde und Arbeiten auf Papier / Paintings and Works on Paper: The Mugrabi Collection.* Museum Würth, Künzelsau (Sep 27, 2001–Jan 1, 2002)
**Jean-Michel Basquiat a Cuneo.* Il Prisma Galleria d'Arte, Cuneo (Oct 1–30)

2002
Dipinti. Chiostro del Bramante, Rome (Jan 20–May 17)
**Andy Warhol, Jean-Michel Basquiat, Francesco Clemente: Obras*

en colaboracíon. Museo National Centro de Arte Reina Sofía, Madrid (Feb 5–Apr 29)
Editions. Marcel Sitcoske Gallery, San Francisco (Feb 7–23)
War Paint. Spike Gallery, New York (Apr 13–Jun 15)
**Andy Warhol, Jean-Michel Basquiat: Collaboration Paintings.* Gagosian Gallery, Los Angeles (May 23–Jun 22)
Exhibition of Andy Warhol and Jean-Michel Basquiat: Rare Collections. Galerie Sho Contemporary Art, Tokyo (Oct 21–Dec 21)

2003
Works from the May Collection. Pollock Gallery, Meadows School of the Arts, Southern Methodist University, Dallas (Feb 24–Mar 29)
Basquiat by Edo. Galleria Barbara Mahler, Pura (May 21–Jul 20)
Histoire d'une œuvre. Fondation Dina Vierny-Musée Maillol, Paris (Jun 27–Oct 23)
Paintings. Jablonka Galerie, Cologne (Oct 29, 2003–Jan 31, 2004)

2004
An Intimate Portrait. Castellani Art Museum, Niagara University, Niagara Falls (Mar 5–May 31)
Crossing Currents: The Synergy of Jean-Michel Basquiat and Quattara Watts. Hood Museum of Art, Dartmouth College, Hanover, NH (Mar 30–Jun 6)
*Museo del Palacio de Bellas Artes, Mexico City (Oct 5–Dec 21)

2005
*Darga Gallery, Bali (Jan 15–Feb 23)
In Word Only. Cheim & Read, New York (Feb 17–Mar 26)
*Brooklyn Museum, New York (Mar 11–Jun 5); traveled to Museum of Contem-porary Art, Los Angeles (Jul 17–Oct 10); Museum of Fine Arts, Houston (Nov 18, 2005– Feb 12, 2006)
*Museo d'Arte Moderna, Lugano (Mar 20–Jun 19)
Galerie Bruno Bischofberger, Zürich (May 2–Sep 17)

2006
*Duolun Museum of Modern Art, Shanghai (Feb 24–Apr 10); traveled to Beijing Imperial City Art Museum, Beijing (May 12–Jun 9)

Heads. Van de Weghe Fine Art, New York (Mar 11–May 13)
Small Works. Westwood Gallery, New York (Apr 29–Jun 10)
1981: The Studio of the Street. Deitch Projects, New York (May 4–27)
The Jean-Michel Basquiat Show. Fondazione La Triennale di Milano, Milan (Sep 19, 2006–Jan 28, 2007)
*Kukje Gallery, Seoul (Oct 12– Nov 12)
Basquiat: Una antologia para Puerto Rico. Museo de Arte de Puerto Rico, San Juan (Oct 19, 2006– Jan 7, 2007)

2007
French Collections. Cultural Services of the French Embassy, New York (Mar 3–Apr 27)
Works on Paper. Van de Weghe Fine Art, New York (May 5–Jun 9)
Jean-Michel Basquiat in Cotonou. Fondation Zinsou, Cotonou (Sep 29– Nov 30)

2008
Ahuyentando fantasmas. Fundación Marcelino Botín, Santander (Jul 10– Sep 14)
Fantasmi da scacciare. Fondazione Memmo, Palazzo Ruspoli, Rome (Oct 2, 2008–Feb 1, 2009)
Paintings. Van de Weghe Fine Art, New York (Nov 8–Dec 20)

2009
Large Drawings. Stellan Holm Gallery, New York (Nov 3–Dec 5)

2010
Basquiat and Warhol. Bowdoin College Museum of Art, Brunswick, ME (Jan 19–Apr 4, 2010)
*Fondation Beyeler, Riehen (May 9–Sep 5); traveled to Musée d'art Moderne de la Ville de Paris (Oct 14, 2010–Jan 30, 2011)
Flash in Naples. Nevada Museum of Art, Reno (Jul 3–Nov 28)
*Galerie Pascal Lansberg, Paris (Oct 22–Dec 4)
Galerie Bruno Bischofberger, St. Moritz (Dec 18, 2010–Apr 11, 2011)

2011
Warhol and Basquiat. Arken Museum of Modern Art, Ishøj (Sep 3, 2011–Jan 11, 2012)

2012

Jean-Michel Basquiat and Andy Warhol: Olympic Rings. Gagosian Gallery, London (Jun 19–Aug 11, 2012)

2013

*Gagosian Gallery, New York (Feb 7–Apr 6)

*Kukje Gallery, Seoul (Feb 14–Mar 31)

Gagosian Gallery, Hong Kong (May 21–Aug 10)

Paintings and Drawings. Galerie Bruno Bischofberger, Zürich (Jun 3–Sep 13)

Warhol and Basquiat. Kunstforum, Vienna (Oct 16, 2013–Feb 2, 2014)

2014

Drawing: Work from the Schorr Family Collection. Acquavella Galleries, New York (May 1–Jun 13)

Basquiat and the Bayou. Ogden Museum of Southern Art, New Orleans (Oct 25, 2014–Jan 25, 2015)

2015

The Unknown Notebooks. Brooklyn Museum, New York (Apr 3–Aug 23); traveled to The High Museum of Art, Atlanta (Feb 28–May 29, 2016)

Now's the Time. Art Gallery of Ontario, Toronto (Feb 7–May 10); traveled to Guggenheim Bilbao (Jul 3–Nov 1)

2016

Words Are All We Have. Nahmad Contemporary, New York (May 2–Jun 18)

2017

Basquiat before Basquiat: East 12th Street, 1979–1980. MCA Denver (Feb 10–May 14); traveled to Cranbrook Art Museum, Bloomfield Hills (Nov 17, 2017–Mar 11, 2018)

Boom for Real. Barbican Art Gallery, London (Sep 21, 2017–Jan 28, 2018); traveled to Schirn Kunsthalle, Frankfurt am Main (Feb 16–May 27, 2018)

Group Exhibitions during the Artist's Lifetime (selection)

1980

New York/New Wave. P.S. 1, New York (Feb 15–Apr 5)

Lower Manhattan Drawing Show. Mudd Club, New York (Feb 22–Mar 15)

Beyond Words: Graffiti Based-Rooted-Inspired Works. Mudd Club, New York (Apr 9–24)

Times Square Show. 41st Street and Seventh Avenue, New York (Jul)

Public Address. Annina Nosei Gallery, New York (Oct 31–Nov 19)

Group Show. Annina Nosei Gallery, New York (Dec 19, 1981–Jan 24, 1982)

1982

Body Language: Current Issues in Figuration. University Art Gallery, San Diego State University, San Diego (Mar 13–Apr 10)

New New York. University Fine Arts Galleries, School of Visual Arts, Florida State University, Tallahassee (Mar 17–Apr 17); traveled to Metropolitan Museum and Art Centers, Coral Gables (Jul 9–Aug 30)

Transavanguardia: Italia/America. Galleria Civica del Comune di Modena (Mar 21–May 2)

Avanguardia Transavanguardia: 68 to 77. Mura Aureliane da Porta Metronia a Porta Latina, Rome (Apr–Jul)

New Work. Sidney Janis Gallery, New York (May 5–Jun 3)

The Pressure to Paint. Marlborough Gallery, New York (Jun 4–Jul 9)

Group Show. Annina Nosei Gallery, New York (Jun 5–30)

Fast. Alexander F. Milliken Gallery, New York (Jun 11–Jul 15)

documenta 7. Kassel (Jun 19–Sep 23)

Drawings. Blum Helman Gallery, New York (Jun 23–Jul 30)

The Expressionist Image: American Art from Pollock to Today. Sidney Janis Gallery, New York (Oct 9–30)

Still Modern after All These Years. The Chrysler Museum, Norfolk, VA (Oct 22–Dec 12)

New York Now. Kestner Gesellschaft, Hanover (Nov 26, 1982–Jan 23, 1983); traveled to Kunstverein, Munich (Feb 2–Mar 6, 1983); Musée Cantonal des Beaux-Arts, Lausanne (Mar 30–May 15, 1983); Kunstverein für die Rheinlande und Westfalen, Düsseldorf (Jul 22–Aug 28, 1983)

Group Show. Annina Nosei Gallery, New York (Dec 18, 1982–Jan 6, 1983)

1983

Champions. Tony Shafrazi Gallery, New York (Jan 15–Feb 19)

1983 Biennial Exhibition. Whitney Museum of American Art, New York (Mar 15–May 29)

Intoxication. Monique Knowlton Gallery, New York (Apr 9–May 7)

Back to the USA: Amerikanische Kunst der Siebziger und Achtziger. Kunstmuseum Luzern (May 29–Jul 31); traveled to Rheinisches Landesmuseum Bonn (Oct 27, 1983–Jan 15, 1984); Württembergischer Kunstverein, Stuttgart (May 3–Jun 17, 1984)

Group Show. Annina Nosei Gallery, New York (Jun 11–Jul 29)

Food for the Soup Kitchens. Fashion Moda, New York (Oct 1–15)

Mary Boone and Her Artists. Seibu Museum of Art, Tokyo (Oct 6–18)

From the Streets. Greenville County Museum of Art, Greenville, SC (Oct 25–Nov 20)

Expressive Malerei nach Picasso. Galerie Beyeler, Riehen (Oct–Dec)

Written Imagery Unleashed in the Twentieth Century. Fine Arts Museum of Long Island, Hempstead (Nov 6, 1983–Jan 22, 1984)

Post-Graffiti. Sidney Janis Gallery, New York (Dec 1–31)

Paintings. Mary Boone Gallery, New York (Dec 3–31)

Terminal New York. Brooklyn Navy Yard, New York

1984

Van Der Zee Memorial Show: James Van Der Zee, 1886–1983. New York City Department of Cultural Affairs, New York (Feb 1–Mar 2)

Modern Expressionists: German, Italian, and American Painters. Sidney Janis Gallery, New York (Mar 10–Apr 7)

Since the Harlem Renaissance: 50 Years of Afro-American Art, Center Gallery of Bucknell University, Lewisburg, PA (Apr 13–Jun 6); traveled to The Amelie A. Wallace Art Gallery, State University of New York, Old Westbury (Nov 1–Dec 9); Munson-Williams-Proctor Institute Museum of Art, Utica (Jan 11–Mar 3, 1985); The Art Gallery, University of Maryland, College Park (Mar 27–May 3, 1985); The Chrysler Museum, Norfolk, VA (Jul 19–Sep 1, 1985); Museum of Art, Pennsylvania State University, University Park (Sep 22–Nov 1, 1985)

Arte di Frontiera: N.Y. Graffiti. Gallería Comunale d'Arte Moderna di Bologna (Apr)

Painting and Sculpture Today. Indianapolis Museum of Art, Indianapolis (May 1–Jun 10)

An International Survey of Recent Painting and Sculpture. The Museum of Modern Art, New York (May 17–Aug 19)

American Neo-Expressionists. The Aldrich Museum of Contemporary Art, Ridgefield, CT (May 20–Sep 9)

Art. Area, New York (May)

Aspekte amerikanischer Kunst der Gegenwart. Neue Galerie-Sammlung Ludwig, Aachen (Jul 3–Aug 29)

Drawings by 11 Artists. Willard Gallery, New York (Sep 5–Oct 6)

Content: A Contemporary Focus, 1975–1984. Hirshhorn Museum and Sculpture Garden, Smithsonian Institution, Washington, D.C. (Oct 4, 1984–Jan 6, 1985)

Painting Now: The Restoration of Painterly Figuration. Kitakyushu Municipal Museum of Art, Kitakyushu (Oct 6–28)

The East Village Scene. Institute of Contemporary Art, University of Penn-sylvania, Philadelphia (Oct 12–Dec 2)

Figuration Libre France/USA. Musee d'Art Moderne de la Ville de Paris (Dec 21, 1984–Feb 17, 1985)

1985

*XIII Biennale de Paris, Grande Halle du Parc de la Villette, Paris (Mar 21–May 21)

The Door. Annina Nosei Gallery, New York (Jun 7–Jul 7)

Das Oberengadin in der Malerei. Segantini Museum, St. Moritz (Jun 20–Oct 20)

Drawing the Line: Painting. Annina Nosei Gallery, New York (Sep 21–Oct 17)

Vom Zeichnen: Aspekte der Zeichnung 1960–1985. Frankfurter Kunstverein, Frankfurt am Main (Nov 19, 1985–Jan 1, 1986); traveled to Kasseler Kunstverein, Kassel (Jan 15–Feb 23, 1986); Museum Moderner Kunst, Vienna (Mar 13–Apr 27, 1986)

Drawings. Knight Gallery, Spirit Square Arts Center, Charlotte, NC (Dec 20, 1985–Feb 7, 1986)

1986

Figure as Subject: The Last Decade. Whitney Museum of American Art at Equitable Center, New York (Feb 13–Jun 4)

75th American Exhibition. The Art Institute of Chicago (Mar 8–Apr 27)

Contemporary Issues III. Holman Hall Art Gallery, Trenton State College, Trenton, NJ (Apr 2–25)

Portrait of a Collector: Stephane Janssen. Louisiana Museum of Modern Art, Humlebaek (Apr 5–May 11); traveled to University Art Museum, California State University, Long Beach (Jan 27–Mar 8, 1987)

Heads. Mokotoff Gallery, New York (Apr–May)

Zeichen, Symbole, Graffiti in der aktuellen Kunst. Suermondt-Ludwig-Museum und Museumsverein Aachen (Jul 6–Aug 17)

Esprit de New York: Paintings and Drawings. Galerie Barbara Farber, Amsterdam (Jul 18–24)

Prospekt 86. Frankfurter Kunstverein, Frankfurt am Main (Sep 9–Nov 2)

Focus on the Image: Selections from the Rivendell Collection. Phoenix Art

Jean-Michel Basquiat, exhibition view, Mary Boone Gallery, New York 1984

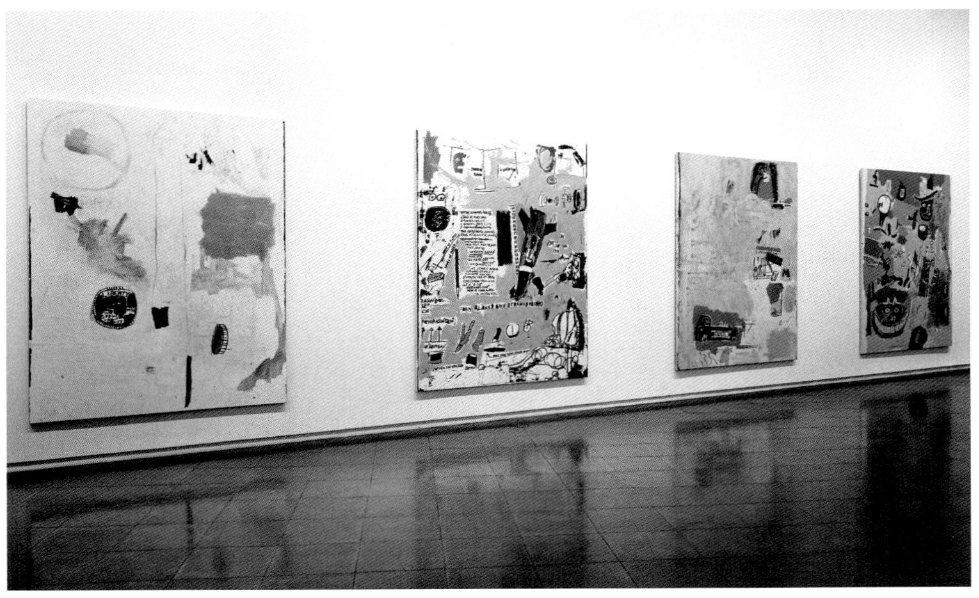

Museum, Phoenix (Oct 5, 1986–Feb 7, 1987); traveled to The University of Oklahoma Museum of Art, Norma (Apr 25–Aug 30, 1987); Munson-Williams-Proctor Institute Museum of Art, Utica (Sep 27, 1987–Mar 20, 1988); University of South Florida Art Galleries, Tampa (Apr 17–Sep 10, 1988); Lakeview Museum of Art and Sciences, Peoria (Oct 1, 1988–Jan 2, 1989); University Art Museum, California State University, Long Beach (Jan 30–May 28, 1989); Laguna Gloria Art Museum, Austin (Jun 25, 1989–Jan 2, 1990)

1976–1986: Ten Years of Collecting Contemporary American Art. Wellesley College Museum, Wellesley (Nov 13, 1986–Jan 18, 1987)

1987

Avant-Garde in the Eighties. Los Angeles County Museum of Art, Los Angeles (Apr 23–Jul 12)

The East Village Force de Frappe Comes to the South Bronx. Fashion Moda, New York (May 9–Jun 1)

16 @ 56: Summer Salon. 56 Bleecker Gallery, New York (Jul 28–Aug 28)

The Frederick R. Weisman Collection: An International Survey. San Antonio Art Institute, San Antonio (Sep 16–Oct 16)

Logos. Anne Plumb Gallery, New York (Dec 19, 1987–Jan 23, 1988)

1988

An Eclectic Eye: Selections from the Frederick R. Weisman Art Foundation. Bridge Center for Contemporary Art, El Paso, and New Mexico State University, Las Cruces (Jan 11–Dec 14); traveled to Cheney Cowles Art Museum, Spokane (Jan 6–Feb 12, 1989); Boise Art Museum, Boise (Apr 15– Jun 11, 1989); University of Wyoming Art Museum, Laramie (Jun 25–Oct 22, 1989); Virginia Beach Center for the Arts, Virginia Beach (Nov 13, 1989– Jan 28, 1990); Gibbes Art Gallery, Charleston (Mar 9–May 4, 1990)

1900 to Now: Modern Art from Rhode Island Collections. Museum of Art, Rhode Island School of Design, Provi-dence (Jan 22–May 1)

Figure as Subject: The Revival of Figura-tion Since 1975. Organized by the Whitney Museum of American Art, New York: Erwin A. Ulrich Museum of Art, Wichita State University, Wichita (Apr 6–Jun 12); traveled to The Arkansas Arts Center, Little Rock (Jun 24–Aug 21); Amarillo Art Center, Amarillo (Sep 10–Oct 22); Utah Museum of Fine Arts, University of Utah, Salt Lake City (Nov 13, 1988–Jan 15, 1989); Madison Art Center, Madison (Feb 4–Mar 26, 1989)

Rebop. Paula Allen Gallery, New York (Apr 26–May 27)

After Street Art. Boca Raton Museum of Art, Boca Raton, FL (Apr 29–May 29)

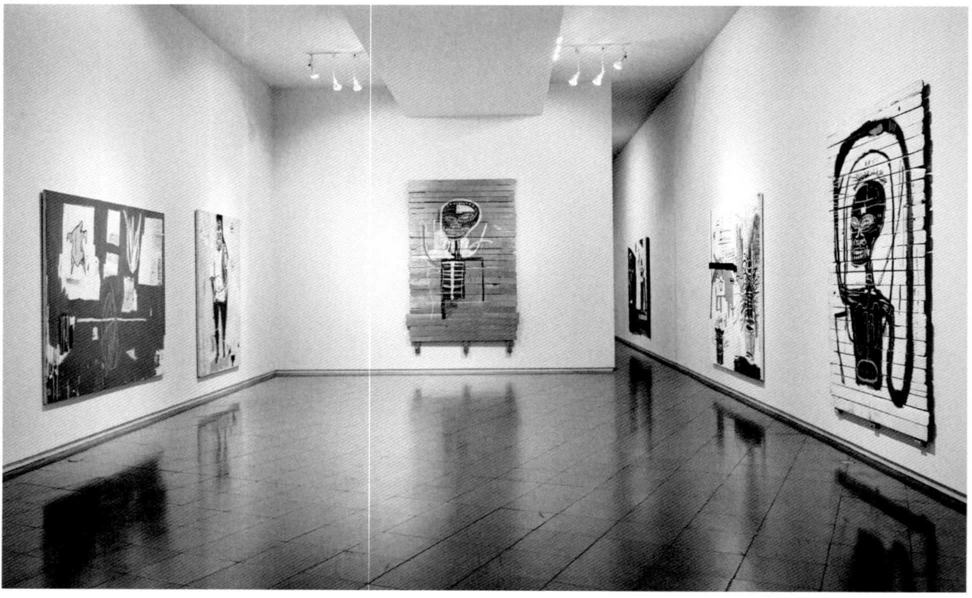

Jean-Michel Basquiat, exhibition view, Mary Boone Gallery, New York 1985

Selected Bibliography

1984

Jean-Michel Basquiat. New York: Mary Boone Gallery. Text A.R. Penck

Jean-Michel Basquiat: Paintings 1981–1984. Edinburgh: The Fruitmarket Gallery. Text Mark Francis

1985

Jean-Michel Basquiat. Berkeley: University of California Art Museum. Text Constance Lewallen

Jean-Michel Basquiat. New York: Mary Boone Gallery. Text Robert Farris Thompson

1986

Jean-Michel Basquiat. Hanover: Kestner Gesellschaft. Ed. Carl Haenlein

Jean-Michel Basquiat: Bilder 1984–1986. Salzburg: Galerie Thaddaeus Ropac. Text Thomas Zaunschirm

1989

Jean-Michel Basquiat. New York: Vrej Baghoomian Gallery. Texts Francesco Pellizzi and Glenn O'Brien

Jean-Michel Basquiat: Das zeichnerische Werk. Hanover: Kestner Gesellschaft. Texts Carsten Ahrens, Carl Haenlein, et al.

Jean-Michel Basquiat. Paris: Galerie Enrico Navarra. Text Démosthènes Davvetas, Annina Nosei, et al.

1990

Jean-Michel Basquiat: Drawings. New York: Robert Miller Gallery. Text Robert Storr

1992

Jean-Michel Basquiat. New York: Whitney Museum; Abrams. Text Dick Hebdige, Klaus Kertess, Richard D. Marshall, Rene Ricard, Greg Tate, Robert Farris Thompson

1993

Jean-Michel Basquiat: The Notebooks. New York: Art + Knowledge. Ed. Larry Warsh

1996

Collaborations: Warhol, Basquiat, Clemente. Ostfildern-Ruit: Cantz. Ed. Tilman Osterwold

Jean-Michel Basquiat. Paris: Galerie Enrico Navarra. Text Richard D. Marshall and Jean-Louis Prat

1999

Jean-Michel Basquiat. Trieste: Civico Museo Revoltella; Mailand: Charta. Text Démosthènes Davvetas, Henry Geldzahler, Isabelle Graw, Luca Marenzi, Lisa Licitra Ponti, et al.

2000

Jean-Michel Basquiat: Catalogue Raisonné. Paris: Galerie Enrico Navarra. Text Richard D. Marshall, Jean-Louis Prat, et al.

2003

Jean-Michel Basquiat, 1960–1988. Cologne: TASCHEN. Text Leonhard Emmerling

2005

Basquiat. New York: Brooklyn Museum. Text Fred Hoffman, Kellie Jones, Marc Mayer, Franklin Sirmans

Jean-Michel Basquiat. Lugano: Museo d'Arte Moderna; Milan: Skira. Text Achille Bonito Oliva et al.

2006

The Jean-Michel Basquiat Show. Milan: La Triennale Foundation; Skira. Ed. Gianni Mercurioi

2007

Jean-Michel Basquiat 1981: The Studio of the Street. New York: Deitch Projects; Milan: Charta. Ed. Diego Cortez and Glenn O'Brien

2010

Basquiat. Riehen: Fondation Beyeler; Ostfildern: Hatje Cantz. Text Dieter Buchhart, Glenn O'Brien, Franklin Sirmans, et al.

2014

Basquiat and the Bayou. New Orleans: Ogden Museum of Southern Art; New York: Prestel. Text Robert G. O'Meally, Franklin Sirmans, and Robert Farris Thompson

2015

Basquiat: The Unknown Notebooks. New York: Brooklyn Museum; Skira. Ed. Dieter Buchhart and Tricia Laughlin Bloom

Jean-Michel Basquiat. New York: Gagosian; Rizzoli. Text Rene Ricard, Robert Farris Thompson

Jean-Michel Basquiat: Now's the Time. Toronto: Art Gallery of Ontario; New York: Prestel. Ed. Dieter Buchhart

Jean-Michel Basquiat: The Notebooks. Princeton University Press. Ed. Larry Warsh

2016

Words Are All We Have: Paintings by Jean-Michel Basquiat. New York: Nahmad Contemporary; Ostfildern: Hatje Cantz. Text Dieter Buchhart

2017

Basquiat: Boom for Real. London: Barbican; Frankfurt am Main: Schirn; New York: Prestel. Ed. Dieter Buchhart and Eleanor Nairne

2018

Jean-Michel Basquiat. Cologne: TASCHEN. Ed. Hans Werner Holzwarth.

2019

Warhol on Basquiat. Cologne: TASCHEN. Texts Andy Warhol

Endnotes

Pages 8–31, "Introducing Jean-Michel Basquiat"

1 Basquiat in Isabelle Graw, "Warten auf Basquiat / Waiting for Basquiat," *Wolken-kratzer*, Jan–Feb 1987, pp. 44–51, 106–107.

2 Robert Farris Thompson, "Activating Heaven: The Incantatory Art of Jean-Michel Basquiat," in *Jean-Michel Basquiat*, New York: Mary Boone, 1985; reprinted in Thompson, *Aesthetic of the Cool*, Pittsburgh: Periscope, 2011, p. 41.

3 Richard D. Marshall, "Repelling Ghosts," in Marshall (ed.), *Jean-Michel Basquiat*, New York: Whitney Museum of American Art, 1992, p. 15.

4 Keith Haring, "Remembering Basquiat," *Vogue*, November 1988, p. 234.

5 "Jean-Michel Basquiat: From the Subways to SoHo," interview with Henry Geldzahler, *Interview* 13, January 1983, pp. 44–46/online.

6 "Interview between Jean-Michel Basquiat, Geoff Dunlop and Sandy Nairne," in Dieter Buchhart and Eleanor Nairne (eds.), *Basquiat: Boom for Real*, London: Barbican Art Gallery; Prestel, 2017, p. 266.

7 Geldzahler, "From the Subways to SoHo" (see note 5).

8 Graw, "Waiting for Basquiat" (see note 1).

9 Marshall, "Repelling Ghosts" (see note 3), p. 15.

10 Robert Farris Thompson, "Royalty, Heroism, and the Streets: The Art of Jean-Michel Basquiat," in Marshall, *Jean-Michel Basquiat* (see note 3), p. 32.

11 Ibid., p. 36.

12 Geldzahler, "From the Subways to SoHo" (see note 5).

13 Ibid.

14 Dunlop and Nairne, "Interview with Jean-Michel Basquiat" (see note 6), p. 265.

15 Démosthènes Davvetas, "Jean-Michel Basquiat," *New Art International*, Oct–Nov 1988, pp. 10–15. The interview used in this posthumous article is not dated, but must have taken place around 1985 or 1986, before the artist visited Africa.

16 Dunlop and Nairne, "Interview with Jean-Michel Basquiat" (see note 6), p. 264.

17 Davvetas, "Jean-Michel Basquiat" (see note 15).

18 *Jean-Michel Basquiat: An Interview* (no. 30A in the video series ART/new york), filmed interview with Marc H. Miller (1983), New York: Inner-Tube Video, 1989, VHS.

19 bell hooks, "Altars of Sacrifice: Re-Membering Basquiat," *Art in America*, June 1993, pp. 68–75/online.

20 Greg Tate, "Black Like B.," in Marshall, *Jean-Michel Basquiat* (see note 3), p. 56.

21 Robert Hughes, "Jean-Michel Basquiat: Requiem for a Featherweight," *The New Republic*, November 21, 1988, pp. 34–36/online.

22 Tate, "Black Like B." (see note 20), pp. 56f.

23 Dunlop and Nairne, "Interview with Jean-Michel Basquiat" (see note 6), p. 265.

24 This publication, p. 27.

25 Dunlop and Nairne, "Interview with Jean-Michel Basquiat" (see note 6), p. 266.

Pages 34–74, "The Art of Story Telling"

1 Rene Ricard, "The Radiant Child," *Artforum,* December 1981, p. 37.

2 While we cannot precisely date when the work was made, it must have been after Andy Warhol's death on February 22 and before it was exhibited at Tony Shafrazi Gallery on May 23.

3 This logo was used by Andy Warhol in his and Basquiat's collaborative painting *Amoco*, made in 1984.

4 The form of the work offers a visual allusion to Jean Dubuffet's landscapes, especially *Paysage* (1952) in the Joan and Lester Avnet Collection at the MoMA, New York.

5 Polaris was also the name of the 1960s US nuclear missile, offering another sky-bound reference.

6 See Cathleen McGuigan, "New Art, New Money: The Marketing of an American Artist," *The New York Times Magazine*, February 10, 1985, p. 26.

7 Vivien Raynor, "Art: Basquiat, Warhol," *The New York Times*, September 20, 1985, p. C22.

8 Although their friendship is often said to have ended abruptly following poor reviews of the *Collaborations* exhibition at Tony Shafrazi Gallery in September 1985, correspondence in the Warhol Museum, Pittsburgh, shows that they continued to have a relationship, even if with less intensity or intimacy, in the period after this.

9 Annina Nosei in Glenn O'Brien, Diego Cortez, et al., *Jean Michel Basquiat: The Studio of the Street*, New York: Deitch Projects, 2007, pp. 88f.

10 Ibid., p. 89.

11 These were developed during the Depression era as a means for migrant communities to be in touch with one another, by chalking simple marks onto fences or sidewalks. See Henry Dreyfuss, *Symbol Sourcebook: An Authoritative Guide to International Graphic Symbols*, New York: John Wiley & Sons, 1984, pp. 90f.

12 Ibid.

13 Leo Steinberg, "Reflections on the State of Criticism," *Artforum*, March 1972, p. 49.

14 Ricard, "The Radiant Child" (see note 1), p. 37.

15 Dorothy Seiberling, "SoHo: The Most Exciting Place to Live in the City," *New York Magazine*, May 20, 1974, cover, pp. 52–54.

16 "Ford to City: Drop Dead," *New York Daily News*, October 30, 1975, p. A30.

17 Kevin Baker, "'Welcome to Fear City': The Inside Story of New

York's Civil War, 40 Years On," *The Guardian*, May 18, 2015, online.

[18] Glenn O'Brien, "SAMO©'s New York," in Dieter Buchhart and Eleanor Nairne (eds.), *Basquiat: Boom for Real*, London: Barbican Art Gallery; Prestel, 2017, p. 103.

[19] Basquiat quoted in Philip Faflick, "SAMO© Graffiti: BOOSH-WAH or CIA?" *The Village Voice*, December 11, 1978, p. 41; reprinted in Buchhart and Nairne, *Boom for Real* (see note 18), p. 65.

[20] *Soho Weekly News*, September 21, 1978, reprinted ibid., p. 62.

[21] *Soho Weekly News*, September 28, 1978, reprinted ibid., p. 63.

[22] Faflick, "SAMO© Graffiti" (see note 19).

[23] Glenn O'Brien's *TV Party*, episode from April 24, 1979.

[24] Basquiat quoted in McGuigan, "New Art, New Money" (see note 6), p. 26.

[25] Stein was working as an apprentice to Stan Peskett, who had rented the loft to throw the Canal Zone Party.

[26] Interview between the author and Jennifer Von Holstein, August 20, 2015.

[27] Several close friends including Jennifer Von Holstein recalled the importance of this book.

[28] "Jean-Michel Basquiat: From the Subways to SoHo," interview with Henry Geldzahler, *Interview* 13, January 1983, pp. 44–46/online.

[29] Interview Von Holstein (see note 26).

[30] Entry "November 17, 1979" in Keith Haring, *Keith Haring Journals*, London: Penguin Modern Classics, 2010, ebook pp. 194f.

[31] Pat Hackett (ed.), *The Andy Warhol Diaries*, London: Penguin Modern Classics, 2010, p. 644.

[32] Jeffrey Deitch, "Report from Times Square," *Art in America*, September 1980, p. 61.

[33] *New York Beat* struggled with financial problems for years before being resurrected as *Downtown 81*, New York Beat Films LLC, 2000.

[34] Although Basquiat presented work at Patricia Field's boutique, there is insufficient information about the nature of this event to count it among his early exhibitions. Elsewhere in the *New York/New Wave* exhibition were a number of other works by Basquiat.

[35] In October 1985, Basquiat was interviewed by my father, Sandy Nairne, and director Geoff Dunlop, for a UK television series called *State of the Art*. The series was produced by John Wyver of Illuminations and broadcast on Channel 4 on January 11, 1987. A transcript of the interview is published in Buchhart and Nairne, *Boom for Real* (see note 18), pp. 262–267.

[36] Robert Rauschenberg quoted in Hal Foster, "At Tate Modern," *London Review of Books*, December 1, 2016, pp. 26f.

[37] "Enola Gay" was also an anti-war track by the British synthpop group Orchestral Manoeuvres in the Dark (OMD) released in September 1980.

[38] William Leggett, "A Tortured Road to 715," *Sports Illustrated*, May 28, 1973, pp. 28–35. Hank Aaron received the most amount of mail apart from politicians that year.

[39] "From the Subways to SoHo," interview with Geldzahler (see note 28).

[40] Peter Schjeldahl, "New Wave No Fun," *The Village Voice*, March 4, 1981, p. 69; reprinted in Buchhart and Nairne, *Boom for Real* (see note 18), p. 94.

[41] Ibid.

[42] Audio cassette of conversation between Diego Cortez and Bob Colacello, April 7, 1981, Series III A 19, MoMA PS1 Archives, The Museum of Modern Art, New York.

[43] Nosei in *The Studio of the Street* (see note 9), p. 86.

[44] Fab 5 Freddy quoted in Anthony Haden-Guest, "Burning Out," *Vanity Fair*, November 1988, pp. 180–198/online.

[45] *Jean-Michel Basquiat: An Interview* (no. 30A in the video series ART/new york), filmed interview with Marc H. Miller (1983), New York: Inner-Tube Video, 1989, VHS.

[46] Raymond Foye, "In Memoriam: Rene Ricard," *The Brooklyn Rail*, December 18, 2014, online.

[47] Ricard, "The Radiant Child" (see note 1), p. 37.

[48] Both ibid., p. 40.

[49] Jeffrey Deitch, "Jean-Michel Basquiat at Annina Nosei," *Flash Art International*, May 1982, p. 49.

[50] Rene Ricard, "World Crown: Bodhisattva with Clenched Mudra," in Richard D. Marshall (ed.), *Jean-Michel Basquiat*, New York: Whitney Museum of American Art, 1992, p. 47.

[51] Lisa Liebmann, "Jean-Michel Basquiat at Annina Nosei," *Art in America*, October 1982, p. 130.

[52] See the exhibition catalog *documenta 7*, Kassel: D + V Paul Dierichs, 1982.

[53] *Genesis* 3:14.

[54] See McGuigan, "New Art, New Money" (see note 6), p. 26.

[55] Letter from Bill Stelling to Richard D. Marshall, November 22, 1991, Richard D. Marshall's uncataloged papers, Whitney Museum of American Art Archives, New York.

[56] Jesse Owens quoted in Jacqueline Edmonson, *Jesse Owens: A Biography*, Westport: Greenwood Press, 2007, p. 57.

[57] Jennifer Clement, *Widow Basquiat: A Love Story*, Edinburgh: Payback Press, 2000; ebook: Random House, 2014, p. 119.

[58] Published on the Carnegie Hall blog, June 28, 2012, https://www.carnegiehall.org/BlogPost.aspx?id=4294987557, no longer available.

[59] *Jean-Michel Basquiat: An Interview*, interview Miller (see note 45).

[60] Harold Bayley, *The Lost Language of Symbolism: An Inquiry into the Origin of Certain Letters, Words, Names, Fairy-Tales, Folklore and Mythologies* (first published 1912), San Diego: The Book Tree, 2007, pp. 90f.

[61] *Judges* 15:16.

[62] Dunlop and Nairne, "Interview with Jean-Michel Basquiat" (see note 35), p. 263.

[63] Thompson went on to write a catalog essay for Basquiat's exhibition at Mary Boone Gallery in Spring 1985: Robert Farris Thompson, "Activating Heaven: The Incantatory Art of Jean-Michel Basquiat," in *Jean-Michel Basquiat*, New York: Mary Boone, 1985.

[64] Robert Farris Thompson, *Flash of the Spirit: African and Afro-American Art and Philosophy*, New York: Random House, 1983, p. 245.

[65] Ibid., p. 227.

[66] Ibid., p. 196.

[67] Dunlop and Nairne, "Interview with Jean-Michel Basquiat" (see note 35), p. 266.

⁶⁸ Kevin Bray worked at Time Shifts Video and gave Basquiat a much-used free membership. They became very close toward the end of Basquiat's life when he was not making work and exhibiting frequently. Interview between the author and Kevin Bray, October 26, 2016.

⁶⁹ Jean Michel Basquiat, "I Have to Have Some Source Material Around Me: Jean-Michel Basquiat Interviewed by Becky Johnston and Tamra Davis," in Dieter Buchhart and Sam Keller (eds.), *Basquiat*, Ostfildern: Hatje Cantz, 2010.

⁷⁰ Ibid.

⁷¹ Gerard Basquiat, "In His Own Words," *The Studio of the Street* (see note 18), p. 94.

Pages 82–86, "1978–1980"

¹ Philip Faflick, "SAMO© Graffiti: BOOSH-WAH or CIA?" *The Village Voice*, December 11, 1978, p. 41.

² Ibid.

³ Glenn O'Brien's *TV Party*, episode from April 24, 1979.

⁴ Jeffrey Deitch, "Report from Times Square," *Art in America*, September 1980, p. 61.

⁵ Anne Ominous [Lucy Lippard], "Sex and Death and Shock and Schlock: A Long Review of the Times Square Show," *Artforum*, October 1980, p. 52.

Pages 96–100, "1981"

¹ Peter Schjeldahl, "New Wave No Fun," *The Village Voice*, March 4, 1981, p. 69.

² Ibid.

³ Glenn O'Brien, "I Am New Wave (or Something Like That)," *Interview*, April 1981, p. 71.

⁴ Rene Ricard, "The Radiant Child," *Artforum*, December 1981, pp. 42f.

Pages 150–155, "1982"

¹ Lisa Liebmann, "Jean-Michel Basquiat at Annina Nosei," *Art in America*, October 1982, p. 130.

² Ibid.

³ Jeanne Silverthorne, "Reviews: Jean-Michel Basquiat," *Artforum*, Summer 1982, pp. 82f.

⁴ William Wilson, "N.Y. Subway Graffiti: All Aboard for L.A.," *Los Angeles Times*, April 16, 1982, p. 135/online.

⁵ Noel Frackman and Ruth Kaufmann, "documenta 7: The Dialogue and a Few Asides," *Arts Magazine*, October 1982, p. 97.

⁶ Entry "October 4, 1982" in Pat Hackett (ed.), *The Andy Warhol Diaries*, New York: Warner Books, 1989; ebook New York: Grand Central Publishing, 2009.

⁷ Nicolas A. Moufarrege, "East Village." *Flash Art*, March 1983, p. 38.

⁸ Susan Hapgood, "New York: Jean-Michel Basquiat. Fun Gallery," *Flash Art*, March 1983, pp. 58f.

Pages 236–243, "1983"

¹ "Jean-Michel Basquiat: From the Subways to SoHo," interview with Henry Geldzahler, *Interview* 13, January 1983, pp. 44–46/online.

² Ibid.

³ Suzanne Muchnic, "The Galleries: La Cienega Area," *Los Angeles Times*, March 11, 1983, p. 137/online.

⁴ Entry "September 5, 1983" in Pat Hackett (ed.), *The Andy Warhol Diaries*, New York: Warner Books, 1989; ebook New York: Grand Central Publishing, 2009.

⁵ Lisa Ponti, "The House of Jean-Michel," *Domus*, January 1984, p. 68.

⁶ Entry "December 20, 1983" in *The Andy Warhol Diaries* (see note 4).

Pages 316–321, "1984"

¹ Kate Linker, "Jean-Michel Basquiat," *Artforum*, October 1984, p. 91.

² Ibid.

³ Vivien Raynor, "Paintings by Jean-Michel Basquiat at Boone," *The New York Times*, May 11, 1984, p. C25.

⁴ Donald Kuspit quoted in Ellen Lubell, "New Kid on the (Auction) Block," *The Village Voice*, May 29, 1984, p. 45; taken from Franklin Sirmans, "Chronology," in Richard D. Marshall (ed.), *Jean-Michel Basquiat*, New York: Whitney Museum of American Art, 1992, p. 244.

⁵ Entry "May 22, 1984" in Pat Hackett (ed.), *The Andy Warhol Diaries*, New York: Warner Books, 1989; ebook New York: Grand Central Publishing, 2009.

⁶ Entry "July 2, 1984," ibid.

⁷ Max Wechsler, "Reviews: Collaborations," *Artforum*, February 1985, p. 99.

⁸ "Interview: Jean Michel Basquiat with Becky Johnston and Tamra Davis," transcript of the 1986 interview by the Barbican Gallery, https://www.barbican.org.uk/sites/default/files/documents/2017-12/Interview_Becky_Johnson_Tamra_Davis.pdf.

Pages 366–373, "1985"

¹ Cathleen McGuigan, "New Art, New Money: The Marketing of an American Artist," *The New York Times Magazine*, February 10, 1985, p. 26.

² Ibid.

³ Robert Farris Thompson, "Activating Heaven: The Incantatory Art of Jean-Michel Basquiat," in *Jean-Michel Basquiat*, New York: Mary Boone, 1985; reprinted in Thompson, *Aesthetic of the Cool*, Pittsburgh: Periscope, 2011, p. 38.

⁴ Ibid., p. 43

⁵ Vivien Raynor, "Art: Basquiat, Warhol," *The New York Times*, September 20, 1985, p. C22.

⁶ Eleanor Heartney, "Basquiat/Warhol: Tony Shafrazi," *Flash Art*, December 1985, p. 43.

⁷ "Interview between Jean-Michel Basquiat, Geoff Dunlop and Sandy Nairne," in Dieter Buchhart and Eleanor Nairne (eds.), *Basquiat: Boom for Real*, London: Barbican Art Gallery; Prestel, 2017, p. 265.

Pages 410–414, "1986"

¹ "Interview: Jean Michel Basquiat with Becky Johnston and Tamra Davis," transcript of the 1986 interview by the Barbican Gallery, https://www.barbican.org.uk/sites/default/files/documents/2017-12/Interview_Becky_Johnson_Tamra_Davis.pdf.

² Kristine McKenna, "The Art Galleries: La Cienega Area," *Los Angeles Times*, January 10, 1986, p. 112/online.

³ Interview Johnston and Davis (see note 1).

⁴ Démosthènes Davvetas, "Jean-Michel Basquiat," *New Art International*, Oct–Nov 1988, pp. 10–15.

The interview used in this posthumous article is not dated, but must have taken place around 1985 or 1986, before the artist visited Africa.

5 Jennifer Goode quoted in Anthony Haden-Guest, "Burning Out," *Vanity Fair*, November 1988, pp. 180–198/online.

6 Isabelle Graw, "Warten auf Basquiat / Waiting for Basquiat," *Wolkenkratzer*, Jan–Feb 1987, pp. 44–51, 106–107.

Pages 448–453, "1987–1988"

1 Keith Haring, "Remembering Basquiat," *Vogue*, November 1988, pp. 230f.

2 Démosthènes Davvetas, "Lines, Chapters, and Verses: The Art of Jean-Michel Basquiat," *Artforum*, April 1987, p. 120.

3 Ursula Bode, "Kunstkalender," *Die Zeit*, January 22, 1988, online.

4 Keith Haring quoted in Anthony Haden-Guest, "Burning Out," *Vanity Fair*, November 1988, pp. 180–198/online.

5 Ibid.

6 Keith Haring, "Remembering Basquiat" (see note 1).

Page 497: Jean-Michel Basquiat, New York 1982. Photo James Van Der Zee

Acknowledgments

The editor wishes to thank first of all Lisane Basquiat, Jeanine Heriveaux, and Nora Fitzpatrick, who take care of the artist's legacy at the Estate of Jean-Michel Basquiat, for their unwavering encouragement of this project. Thanks especially to David Stark and Artestar for patiently solving our requests and knowing the answers to our inquiries. Thanks for the many insights offered to us by those who knew Jean-Michel Basquiat during inspiring conversations that helped this book take shape. Thanks to the photographers who have caught the artist's personality and the vibe of his times for us. Thanks also to the many galleries, agencies, and collectors who went to considerable efforts to help us obtain the best images for these pages. A special thanks to Eleanor Nairne for her marvelous essay, delving deep into the artist's intricate storylines, and to Lutz Eitel for his concise chronological chapters. And, as always, a most heartfelt thanks to Benedikt Taschen for the ongoing dialog and another intense collaboration to create a rich, comprehensive monograph on this outstanding artist.

Photo credits

Art, New York: 123 // Private Collection/James Goodman Gallery, New York/Bridgeman Images: 205 // Courtesy of Rubell Family Collection, Miami: 148/149 // The Eli and Edythe L. Broad Collection: 147, 174/175 // Courtesy Sotheby's, Inc. © 2018: 54/55, 62, 159, 168, 177, 287–289, 347, 406/407, 430, 451 // Naoki Okamoto: 6/7 // © FOTOEARTE SA, courtesy Collection Pierino e Martine Ghisla: 167 // Courtesy Van de Weghe Fine Art, New York: 179, 203, 226, 490 // The Schorr Family Collection; on long-term loan to the Princeton University Art Museum. Photo Bruce M. White: 180/181, 294/295 // Courtesy Vedovi Gallery, Brussels: 186 // The Broad Art Foundation: 189, 212, 319, 349 // Courtesy Gagosian: 190/191, 331, 354, 416/417 // © Roland Hagenberg: 46/47, 237 // Daros Collection, Switzerland: 246–265 // Courtesy Acquavella Galleries: 268/269 // Private Collection, Courtesy Galerie Bruno Bischofberger, Männedorf-Zurich, Switzerland: 270, 298, 300/301, 320, 422 // Whitney Museum of American Art, New York; gift of Douglas S. Cramer/Digital Image © Whitney Museum, N.Y.: 277 // © 2018: Adagp Images, Paris/ Scala, Florence: 285 // Private Collection, courtesy Tony Shafrazi Gallery, New York: 293, 464/465 // Collection Ludwig Forum, Aachen. Photo Carl Brunn: 314/315 // Brian Williams: 317 // Courtesy Mary Boone Gallery, New York: 503, 504 // Zindman/ Fremont, courtesy Mary Boone Gallery, New York: 322/323 // Private Collection. Photo © Stephen White: 324/325 // Galerie Bruno Bischofberger, Männedorf-Zurich, Switzerland: 328 // Private Collection. Photo Kent Pell: 332, 333, 334/335 // The Broad Art Foundation. © 2018: Adagp Images, Paris/Scala, Florence: 352 // Private Collection, Switzerland, courtesy Tornabuoni Art: 355 // The Broad Art Foundation. Photo Douglas M. Parker Studio: 360/361 // Courtesy Galerie Bruno Bischofberger, Männedorf-Zurich, Switzerland; © Francesco Clemente: the artist; © 2018 The Andy Warhol Foundation for the Visual Arts, Inc. Licensed by Artists Rights Society (ARS), New York; © The Estate of Jean-Michel Basquiat. Licensed by

Artestar, New York: 362 // Courtesy Vedovi Gallery, Brussels; © 2018 The Andy Warhol Foundation for the Visual Arts, Inc. Licensed by Artists Rights Society (ARS), New York; © The Estate of Jean-Michel Basquiat. Licensed by Artestar, New York: 363 // Timothy Hursley: 374/375 // Courtesy Collection of Kyoko Tamura: 380/381 // Private Collection, courtesy Galerie Bruno Bischofberger, Männedorf-Zurich, Switzerland: 385, 421 // Private Collection, courtesy Nahmad Contemporary: 390, 427 // Akira Ikeda Gallery: 392/393 // Private Collection, courtesy Tajan SA: 398/399 // Collection of the Artist. © 2018: Adagp Images, Paris/Scala, Florence: 404/405 // Private Collection, courtesy Bischofberger Collection, Männedorf-Zurich, Switzerland; © 2018 The Andy Warhol Foundation for the Visual Arts, Inc. Licensed by Artists Rights Society (ARS), New York; © The Estate of Jean-Michel Basquiat. Licensed by Artestar, New York: 372 // Dmitri Kasterine: 411 // © Georges Courrèges: 500 // MACBA Collection. Government of Catalonia long-term loan. Formerly Salvador Riera Collection. Photo Gasull Fotografia: 442/443 // Museu d'Art Contemporani de Barcelona. Fons d'Art de la Generalitat de Catalunya. © 2018: Adagp Images, Paris/Scala, Florence: 444 // Courtesy Galerie Hans Mayer, Düsseldorf: 454/455 // Courtesy Kunsthalle Weishaupt: 457, 469 // Collection Lambert: 458 // Centre national des arts plastiques. Photo Collection Lambert: 460, 466/467 // Staatliche Kunstsammlungen Dresden, Schenkung Sammlung Hoffmann: 472/473 // Private Collection. © The Estate of Jean-Michel Basquiat. Licensed by Artestar, New York: 476, 483 // Private Collection, courtesy Galerie Thaddaeus Ropac, London/Paris/ Salzburg: 485 // Kravis Collection: 486/487 // James Van Der Zee. © Donna Mussenden Van Der Zee. All rights reserved: 497 // Douglas M. Parker Studio, courtesy Gagosian: 244/245 // Michael Holman: endpapers spread.

If not otherwise indicated, the copyright is held by the artists and photographers, or their assignees. Despite intensive research, it has not always been possible to establish copyright ownership. Where this is the case we would appreciate notification.

Imprint

**EACH AND EVERY TASCHEN BOOK
PLANTS A SEED!**
TASCHEN is a carbon neutral publisher. Each year,
we offset our annual carbon emissions with carbon
credits at the Instituto Terra, a reforestation program in
Minas Gerais, Brazil, founded by Lélia and Sebastião
Salgado. To find out more about this ecological partner-
ship, please check: www.taschen.com/zerocarbon
Inspiration: unlimited. Carbon footprint: zero.

To stay informed about TASCHEN and our
upcoming titles, please subscribe to our free magazine at www.taschen.com/magazine, follow us on
Instagram and Facebook, or e-mail your questions
to contact@taschen.com.

Cover: **Grillo**, 1984
Acrylic, oil, photocopy collage, oilstick, and nails
on wood, polyptych: 244 x 537 x 45.5 cm /
96 x 211 ¹/₂ x 18 inches

Endpapers spread: Jean-Michel Basquiat in
Michael Holman's film *Pesceador©*, New York 1982

Front and back endpaper / pages 1–3: SAMO© graffiti,
New York 1979. Photo Henry Flynt

Page 5: **Warrior**, 1982
Acrylic and oilstick on wood panel,
183 x 122 cm / 72 x 48 in.

Jean-Michel Basquiat
Edited by Hans Werner Holzwarth
With an essay by Eleanor Nairne
Chronology by Lutz Eitel

© 2021 TASCHEN GmbH
Hohenzollernring 53, D–50672 Köln
www.taschen.com

Original edition: © 2018 TASCHEN GmbH

Printed in Bosnia-Herzegovina
ISBN 978–3–8365–8092–2